Clergy of the Church of England 1835

Part Three: P to Z

Map showing the Dioceses of England (and Wales) in 1835

CLERGY OF THE CHURCH OF ENGLAND

1835

A Biographical Directory

Part Three: P to Z

Compiled by Peter Bell

Published 2021 by Peter Bell

68 West Port, Edinburgh EH1 2LD

Scotland, UK

portsburghpress@gmail.com

0131-556-2198

ISBN (Part One): 978-1-871538-13-7

ISBN (Part Two): 978-1-871538-14-4

ISBN (Part Three): 978-1-871538-15-1

The right of Peter Bell to be identified as the compiler of this work has been asserted by him in accordance with the Copyrights, Designs & Patents Act 1988

Book production assistance by
Pixel Tweaks Publications
SELF PUBLISHING MADE SIMPLE
www.pixeltweakspublications.com

Cover: Depiction of English antiquarian James Raine, circa 1852
Public Domain image licensed under CC-PD-Mark

FOREWORD

Ten years ago I purchased a copy of the massive Report of the Ecclesiastical Revenues Commission, published in May 1835, with its detailed statistical information of every parish in England and Wales for the three years ending 1833. Among that information was a column listing the holder of every benefice in England and Wales, albeit abbreviated (e.g. T. Jones). Having made a list of these names, I decided that a biographical directory could be made from it, one in which both the professional and the personal lives of each cleric could be combined to their mutual benefit, along the lines of Venn's Alumni Cantabrigienses. If I had known what I was letting myself in for, I would probably never have begun!

The resulting Directory has been made possible only because of the existence of the Clergy of the Church of England Database, 1540-1835, a vast online database (abbreviated here as CCEd, or C followed by each cleric's unique identifying number). Compiled locally by record offices throughout England and Wales (but only England here), and not yet complete, the resulting information varies depending on what records survive. Details usually include university degrees, exact dates of ordination, and exact dates of the curacies, benefices and other appointments held by each man until c.1835; although the great problem of what Wikipedia calls disambiguation - the mixing of two or more men of exactly the same name - remains unresolved in too many cases.

For further information it is necessary to turn to existing sources, both printed and electronic, some printed and familiar (such as the registers for Oxford and Cambridge Universities, at a time when eighty percent of the clergy were graduates of those two places), but also to a number of less familiar titles as listed here under Existing Published Sources with Biographical Material, in which some biographical work has already been done by others, usually in a specific diocese.

Regarding the online resources, especially Ancestry.co.uk, all of these must be used with great caution. If used last of all they can often provide additional or expanded personal information, especially (it would seem) of wives and children. Few men warrant a Wikipedia entry, although each man has been checked online for any relevant information whatsoever. Contradictions occur frequently, and these have been noted only if currently unresolvable. New online information appears regularly (and some, especially online links, disappear), reminding us that biographical information is always in a state of change and incompleteness. This is why this is essentially a work in progress, and a first draft which I hope people will feel free to correct and add to where necessary (using the email link below).

A very specific source which must be noted is in the University of Durham's Special Collections Library in Palace Green, namely the Hudleston Index, consisting of thousands of hand-written index cards covering the Northern Province only. I now realise that so much of the information here about the Northern clergy (recorded ten years ago) comes from that source alone.

Special mention must also be made of the two volumes of York Clergy Ordinations for 1750-1799 and 1800-1849 respectively, which include ordination details of every man ordained in the (large) Archdiocese of York between 1750 and 1849. This is a model which should be adopted by every diocese, and would enable the missing dates, places of birth, and parentage to be filled in.

Writing this book on and off over a decade has, rather strangely, involved only a few people, but each of them important. Professor Arthur Burns, the director of the CCEd project responsible for this period of the long Eighteenth Century, allowed me at an early stage to access unpublished CCEd material, for which I am most grateful. With Emeritus Professor Ted Royle of York University I learnt enormous amounts about the workings of the Church of England in this period, for which I am again extremely grateful. My sister Judith has rescued me from computer problems and losses, and has proofed the whole work. Finally, my dear MaryCatherine Burgess has endured ten years of clerical trivia and monologue (which probably makes her a not inconsiderable authority on the men here).

Peter Bell

EDITORIAL METHOD & METHODOLOGY

The following model entry, accompanied by an interpretation, is rarely followed completely, as some vital information is invariably missing for most clergy. Many are anonymous, even after 200 years, and only persistent work (especially by a descendant) can produce fuller results.

> **HADEN** (Alexander Bunn) Bapt. Wednesbury, Staffs. 25/3/1783, | s. Rev. Alexander Bunn Haden, sen., and Mary Rotten. | St Edmund Hall, Oxford 1806, BA1810, dn10 (C&L), p11 (C&L), MA1813. | PC. Woore, Shropshire 1811-19 (res.), V. Brewood, Staffs. 1830 to death 16/8/1863, | leaving £1,000 | [C11358] | Married (1) Chetton, Shropshire 7/2/1826 Marianne Heptinstall (d.1850, 1st q.) (2) London 27/4/1859 Mary Ward (w). |
>
> **HADEN** (Alexander Bunn) Baptised Wednesbury, Staffordshire 25/3/1783, son of Reverend Alexander Bunn Haden, senior, and Mary Rotten. St. Edmund Hall, Oxford University 1806, Bachelor of Arts 1810, deacon 1810 (Coventry & Lichfield Diocese), priest 1811 (Coventry & Lichfield Diocese), Master of Arts 1813. Priest-in-Charge of Woore, Shropshire 1811-19 (resigned), Vicar of Brewood, Staffordshire 1830 to death 16/8/1863, leaving under £1,000 [Clergy of the Church of England Database 11358] Married (1) at Chetton, Shropshire 7/2/1826 Marianne Heptinstall (died 1850, 1st quarter) (2) in London 27/4/1859 Mary Ward (his widow). |

Names. In this example the father and son are identically named, an immediate cause of confusion. The father here was married twice, and this is his first wife. Mothers' names are often elusive, and often appear by their first name only, usually in the Census returns. The very many changes of surname are not normally noted here, although some doubled-barrelled names, and the many aristocratic titles, are usually cross-referenced. Future corrections should include a son's order in the male line (i.e. 2nd son). People with common surnames (not only Smith and Jones, but also Dixon, Carter, Wilkinson, &c.) when combined with identical forenames are a nightmare, and sometimes cannot be differentiated after 200 years.

Birth and Baptism. Not always differentiated in many original records, although attempted here. Baptism dates are recorded in the original ordination papers, and are given preference here if noted in CCEd. Saying that someone was, say, 60 at death in 1860, does not automatically make him born 1800, as birth and baptism dates could vary. Also the place of birth and/or baptism may not automatically be the parents' place of residence. Place names have been modernised wherever possible, though the original Report has some wild spellings and some joining of parishes which are not helpful in identifying them today.

Schools are not noted – something which should be rectified at a later date. Suffice it to say that the numbers at the 'Great Public Schools', especially Eton and Westminster, were high, especially among the clerical elite.

University. At this date, the vast majority of clergy were graduates of Oxford and (especially) Cambridge, as recorded in Foster and Venn respectively. Note that Foster gives the date of matriculation to the University; while Venn gives dates of admission to a particular college; matriculation at Cambridge was separate and is not noted here, but does account for children of 12 or 13 entering the university. Degrees did not have to be formally taken to make a man a university graduate, only matriculation. 'Ten Year Men' at Cambridge were extra-mural men, matriculating annually for 10 years, after which they could claim to be MA (Cantab.). Note that Foster described Doctors of Divinity as 'doctors', who are not Doctors of Medicine (who were MDs - as some were). Note also the number of men with legal degrees, or who were law students or actual lawyers of some sort before ordination. Non-graduates, known as literates (or 'literate persons'), were ordained at the discretion of the ordaining bishop.

Ordination. Deacons could only be ordained at the age of 23; priests at 24; and the vast proportion of men seem to have been ordained at this age, straight out of university. Bishops had to be 30 or more (and only George Murray, q.v., had a problem with this!).

Careers. Here I have followed a combination of CCEd and existing printed sources to ascertain the parishes in which a man was rector, vicar, or perpetual curate. (The Report also includes a number of 'miscellaneous' men who by rights should not really be there). Assistant or Stipendiary curacies are not noted (but are in CCEd), and information after 1835 (the cut-off date for CCEd) must be pieced together from all available sources, including early editions of The Clergy List (from 1840) and Crockford's (first useable edition 1860). The whereabouts of a man ordained and dying between 1835 to 1860 is the most difficult of all to track down.

Date of death. This is usually available, often from FreeBMD (Free Births, Marriages and Deaths) online; or alternatively that of burial, which is differentiated. Age at death is quoted when specifically given, and is not estimated from date of birth.

Wealth at death. This is available after January 1868 from the photographed printed records on Ancestry, and, as a printed legal document, is the most reliable of all documents. It gives all sums left at death as 'under' - which can be assumed here whenever a round figure is given. Many men did not leave a will at all; bishops can be found under their title, e.g. Samuel Winchester for Samuel Wilberforce, Bishop of Winchester.

Marriage. Marriages are included where known, and the absence of a wife here does not mean that a person was never married. Wives who had previously been married are designated Mrs., with their birth surname in brackets, whereas (w) – widow – indicates that a wife outlived her husband. Numbers of children vary with the original sources, which may or may not include those dying in infancy. Numbers of surviving children tend to be more reliable.

References. These are in square brackets. The CCEd is the unique reference number given to each individual in the Clergy of the Church of England Database 1540-1835, which is free to search. It can be assumed that Foster and Venn have been checked for every graduate clergyman - but the result, especially for a 'literate person', can be disappointing, or, in a few cases, almost non-existent.

Notes. Any miscellaneous information is included here, much of it trivial, but it may help to enliven what are often repetitive entries.

LIST OF ABBREVIATIONS

Abp.	Archbishop
b.	born
BA	Bachelor of Arts
BCL	Bachelor of Civil Law
BD	Bachelor of Divinity
Bapt.	baptised
Bp.	Bishop
C.	Curate
Cam.	Cambridge
CCEd/C	Clergy of the Church of England Database 1540-1835
Chap.	Chaplain
d.	died
dau.	daughter
DCL	Doctor of Civil Law
DD	Doctor of Divinity
D.L.	Deputy Lieutenant [of a county]
Dom. Chap.	Domestic Chaplain
Don. Chap.	Donative Chaplain [of a church outside the jurisdiction of the diocesan bishop]
dn.	deacon
d.s.p.	died without issue (*decessit sine prole*)
ERC	Ecclesiastical Revenues Commission [Report, 1835]
FreeBMD	Free Births Marriages and Deaths [online resource]
G/S	Grammar School
HEIC	[Honourable] East India Company
H/M	headmaster
Hon.	The Honourable/honorary
J.P.	Justice of the Peace
Lect.	lecturer
LLD	Doctor of Laws
LNCP	Library of Nineteenth Century Photographs [Online resource with many clergy]
MA	Master of Arts
Min.	Minister
M.P.	Member of Parliament
non-res.	non-resident [only when specified]
NPC	National Probate Calendar [from Jan. 1858]
ODNB	Oxford Dictionary of National Biography
Ox.	Oxford
p.	priest
PC.	Perpetual Curate
pop.	population
Preb.	Prebendary
Prof.	professor
q.	quarter [of the year; from FreeBMD]
R.	Rector
(res.)	resigned (only when specified)
R.N.	Royal Navy
s.	son (of)
Sec.	Secretary
S/M	schoolmaster
s.p.	without issue (*sine prole*)
Univ.	university
V.	Vicar
(w)	widow, indicating that she outlived her husband (whereas Mrs. indicates that she was previously married).

Entries will be found in Foster or Venn for all men at Oxford or Cambridge respectively unless otherwise specified.

**OXFORD UNIVERSITY
COLLEGES & HALLS**

All Souls'
Balliol
Brasenose
Christ Church
Corpus Christi
Jesus
Lincoln
Magdalen College
Magdalen Hall
Merton
New College
New Inn Hall
Oriel
Pembroke
Queen's [The Queen's]
St Catherine's
St Edmund Hall
St John's
St Mary Hall
Trinity
University
Wadham
Worcester

**CAMBRIDGE UNIVERSITY
COLLEGES & HALLS**

Christ's
Clare
Corpus Christi
Downing
Emmanuel
Gonville & Caius
Jesus
King's
Magdalene
Pembroke
Peterhouse
Queens'
Selwyn
Sidney Sussex
St Catharine's
St John's
Trinity College
Trinity Hall

BISHOPS OF THE CHURCH OF ENGLAND 1835

(appear in the text under their surname)

Bath and Wells (B&W)	George Henry Law
Bristol (Bristol)	Robert Gray [as Bristol and Gloucester after 1836]
Canterbury (Cant.)	William Howley
Carlisle (Car.)	Hon. Hugh Percy
Chester (Chester)	John Bird Sumner
Chichester (Chich.)	Edward Maltby
Coventry & Lichfield (C&L)	Hon. Henry Ryder [as Lichfield after 1836]
Durham (Dur.)	William Van Mildert
Ely (Ely)	Bowyer Edward Sparke
Exeter (Ex.)	Henry Phillpotts
Gloucester (Glos.)	James Henry Monk [as Gloucester and Bristol after 1836]
Hereford (Heref.)	George Isaac Huntingford (to 1832) [Hon. Edward Gray from 1832, not included here]
Lincoln (Lin.)	John Kaye
London (London)	Charles James Blomfield
Norwich (Nor.)	Henry Bathurst
Oxford (Ox.)	Richard Bagot
Peterborough (Peterb.)	Herbert Marsh
Rochester (Roch.)	George Murray
Salisbury (Salis.)	Thomas Burgess
Sodor and Man (S&M)	William Ward
Winchester (Win.)	Charles Richard Sumner
Worcester (Wor.)	Robert James Carr
York (York)	Hon. Edward Venables-Vernon (then Harcourt)

The four Welsh bishoprics (excluded from this survey) were:

Bangor (Bangor)	Christopher Bethell
Llandaff (Llandaff)	Edward Copleston
St Asaph (St Asaph)	William Carey
St David's (St David's)	John Banks Jenkinson

EXISTING PUBLISHED SOURCES WITH BIOGRAPHICAL MATERIAL

Al.Dub.	Alumni Dublinenses: a register of students, graduates … in the University of Dublin. Edited by G.D. Burtchaell and T.U. Sadleir. (1924).
ATV	Archbishop Thomson's Visitation Returns for the Diocese of York, 1865. Edited Edward Royle & Ruth M. Larsen. (York: Borthwick Institute for Archives, 2006).
Austin	The Church in Derbyshire in 1823-4: the parochial visitation of the Rev. Samuel Butler, Archdeacon of Derby, in the Diocese of Lichfield and Coventry. Edited M.R. Austin. (Derbyshire Archaeological Society, 1972).
Austin2	'A time of unhappy commotion': the Church of England and the people of central Nottinghamshire 1820-1870. (Chesterfield: Merton, 2010).
BBV	Bishop Bickersteth's Visitation Returns for the Archdeaconry of Craven, Diocese of Ripon, 1858. Edited Edward Royle. (York: Borthwick Institute for Archives, 2009).
Bennett1	Lincolnshire parish clergy c.1214-1968: a biographical register. Part I: The Deaneries of Aslacoe and Aveland. Compiled by Nicholas Bennett (Lincoln Record Society, 2013).
Bennett2	Lincolnshire parish clergy c.1214-1968: a biographical register. Part II: The Deaniers of Beltisloe and Bolingbroke. Compiled by Nicholas Bennett (Lincoln Record Society, 2016) And many more volumes to come!
Bertie	Scottish Episcopal Clergy 1689-2000. By David M. Bertie. (Edinburgh: T & T Clark, 2000). New edition in preparation.
Boase	Modern English Biography … of persons who have died between the years 1851-1900 … Compiled by Frederic Boase. (1908. Reprinted London: Cass, 1965). 6 volumes.
DEB	The Blackwell Dictionary of Evangelical Biography 1730-1860. Edited Donald M. Lewis. (Oxford, 1995). 2 volumes.
Fasti	Fasti Ecclesiae Anglicanae 1541-1857. By Joyce M. Horn [and others]. London, 1969-2014. 13 volumes. [Excludes the Welsh Dioceses]
Foster	Alumni Oxonienses: the Members of the University of Oxford, 1715-1886. Compiled by Joseph Foster. (1888-92. Reprinted Bristol: Thoemmes, 2000). 4 volumes.
Gelling	A history of the Manx Church (1698-1911). By John Gelling (Douglas, IoM: The Manx Heritage Foundation, 1998).
Hodson	Visitations of the Archdeaconry of Stafford 1829-1841. Edited David Robinson (HMSO for Historic Manuscripts Commission, 1980).
Kaye	Lincolnshire parish correspondence of John Kaye, Bishop of Lincoln, 1827-53. Edited R.W. Ambler. (Lincoln Record Society, 2006).
LFBI	Landed Families of Britain and Ireland. [The very beginnings of an extraordinary project by Ben Kingsley to link country houses and their owners – obviously including many clergy here. Only on letter 'B' at time of writing – unfortunately.] landedfamilies.blogspot.com/
McClatchey	Oxfordshire clergy, 1777-1869 … By Diana McClatchey (Oxford, 1960).

Platt	The Diocese of Carlisle, 1814-1855: Chancellor Walter Fletcher's Diocesan Book, with additional material from Bishop Percy's notebooks … Edited by Jane Platt (Surtees Society, 2015).
Romilly	Romilly's Cambridge diary 1832-42. Edited J.P.T. Bury. (Cambridge, 1967).
Romilly2	Romilly's Cambridge diary 1842-1847. Edited M.E. Bury & J.D. Pickles. (Cambridgeshire Records Society, 1994).
Romilly3	Romilly's Cambridge diary 1848-1864. Edited M.E. Bury & J.D. Pickles. (Cambridgeshire Records Society, 2000).
Smart	Biographical Register of the University of St. Andrews 1747-1897. By Robert N. Smart. (St. Andrews University Library, 2004).
Snell	The Snell Exhibitions. From the University of Glasgow to Balliol College, Oxford. By W. Innes Addison. (Glasgow: James Maclehose, 1901).
Venn	Alumni Cantabrigienses … Part 2 from 1752 to 1900. Compiled by J.A. Venn (1922-54. Reprinted Bristol: Thoemmes, 2001). 6 volumes.
Wilberforce	The Diocese Books of Samuel Wilberforce, Bishop of Oxford 1845-1869. Edited Ronald and Margaret Pugh. (Oxfordshire and Berkshire Record Societies, 2008).
Wilberforce2	The letter-books of Samuel Wilberforce, 1843-68. Transcribed and edited by R.K. Pugh. (Buckingham Record Society & Oxfordshire Record Society, 1970).
Wilberforce3	Bishop Wilberforce's Visitation Returns for the Archdeaconry of Oxford in the year 1854 … Edited E.P. Baker. (Oxfordshire Record Society, 1954).
YCO	York Clergy Ordinations 1750-1799. Compiled by Debbie Usher (York: Borthwick Institute, 2002) [and] York Clergy Ordinations 1800-1849. Compiled by Sara Slinn (York: Borthwick Institute, 2001). [The latter has a most important Introduction.]

Clergy of the Church of England 1835

Part Three: P to Z

Parishes underlined (thus) are the ones held in
plurality by one clergyman in the early 1830's

PACE (William) Bapt. Battersea, London 15/2/1762, s. Rev. William Pace, sen. and Susannah Hughes. Trinity, Cambridge 1781, BA1785, dn85 (Lin. for London), p86 (Glos. for London), MA1819. R. Rampisham w. Wraxall, Dorset 1794 to death (Bath) 22/3/1845 aged 82 [C53469] Married Holborn, London 3/12/1820 Mrs Charlotte Sinfeild [who signed the wedding certificate with a cross], and had issue.

PACKARD (Harrison) Bapt. Middleton, Suffolk 15/11/1783, s. Rev. Daniel Packard and Anne Crowe. Caius, Cambridge 1800, BA1805, dn07 (Nor.), p08 (Nor.), MA1808. V. Blythburgh w. Walberswick, Suffolk 1809-16, PC. Peasenhall, Suffolk 1809-60, V. Bruisyard, Suffolk 1814, PC. Butley, Suffolk 1814-25, R. (and patron) of Fordley w. Westleton, Suffolk 1820 to death (Darsham, Suffolk) 29/12/1860, leaving £3,000 [C114307] Married Sibton, Suffolk 12/12/1809 Esther Leggett (a clergy dau.).

PACKE (Augustus) Born Hanthorpe House, Norton, Lincs. 8/10/1805, s. Lt.-Col. Charles James Packe (Prestwold Hall, Leics.) and Penelope Dugdale. Christ's, Cambridge 1823, BA1827, dn29 (Lin.), MA 1830, p31 (Lin.). Chap. of the Donative of Prestwold cum Hotton, Leics. 1826-8, R. Claythorpe, Leics. 1844-6, R. Walton-on-the-Wolds, Leics. 1847 to death (St Leonards on Sea, Sussex) 1/2/1861, leaving £25,000 [C71983] Married 1/11/1843 Frances Henrietta Campion (w) (Danny Park, Sussex).

PACKE (Christopher) From Edinburgh, s. Herbert Packe, *M.D.*, and Elizabeth North Worcester, Oxford 1810 (aged 18), BA1814, dn14 (Cant.), p15 (Cant.), MA1825. 3rd Minor Canon of St Paul's Cathedral, London 1817-23 (10th 1821-7, 12th 1825-33, 3rd 1833-78), Minor Canon of Windsor 1821-67, PC. St Michael Bassishaw, City of London 1821-34 (res.), V. Ruislip, Middx. 1834 to death. Priest in Ordinary in Chapel Royal 1821. Died 4/6/1878, leaving £8,000 [C120815. Boase] Married 1821 Mary Halsnod Wood, with issue.

PACKER (Richard Waldegrave) Born Stepney, London 15/9/1789, s. Richard Packer and Mary Waldegrave. Stockbroker. St Catharine's, Cambridge 1825, BA1829, dn29 (Chich.), p30 (Chich.), MA1832. R. Woodton, Suffolk 1832-74, V. Witcham, Cambs. 1846 [to death] 12/1874, leaving £6,000 [C64754] Married Stepney, London 12/6/1817 Esther Bone, with clerical son of father's name.

PACKMAN (Robert Collier) Bapt. Faversham, Kent 9/1/1792, s. Isaac and Sarah Packman. Peterhouse, Cambridge 1816, BA 1820, dn20 (London), p21 (London). R. Langdon Hills, Essex 1825-75, 9th Minor Canon (and Librarian) of St Paul's Cathedral, London 1829. Priest in Ordinary in Chapel Royal 1825. Died 27/1/1875 aged 83, leaving £600 [C120816] Married Marylebone, London 21/7/1832 Catherine Eells, with issue.

PADDON (Thomas) Born Bungay, Suffolk 5/5/1784, s. Rev. Thomas Paddon, sen. (R. South Elmham, Suffolk). Caius, Cambridge 1801, BA1806, Fellow 1806-23, dn07 (Ely for Nor.), p08 (Nor.), MA1809, incorporated at Trinity, Oxford 1831. V. (and Sinecure R.) Mattishall Burgh w. Patteley, Norfolk 1821 to death 24/8/1861, leaving £7,000. Dom. Chap. to Duke of Leeds [C100145] Married Norwich 8/10/1833 Elizabeth Anne Smith (w) (a clergy dau., of Bawdsley, Suffolk).

PADWICK (Nicholas) Bapt. Gosport, Hants. 12/11/1794, s. Nicholas and Elizabeth Padwick. Queens', Cambridge 1820, dn23 (Lin.), BA 1824, p24 (Lin.), MA1828. PC. Linthwaite, Huddersfield, Yorks. 1828-37, PC. Milnthorpe, Westmorland 1837 (w. Chap. to Milnthorpe Workhouse) to death (Petersfield, Hants.) 30/11/1860 aged 66, leaving £3,000 [C71988. DEB] Married Syston, Leics. 30/6/1829 Mary Ann Dalley (w).

PAGE (John) Born Frodsham, Cheshire 15/4/1781, s. Rev. William Emmanuel Page and Jane Davis. BNC, Oxford 1798, BA 1802, MA1804, dn95 (Ox.) p06 (Ox.), BD 1815, Fellow to 1823, DD1825. V. Gillingham, Kent 1822 (and Governor of St John Hawkins Hospital [almshouses], Chatham, Kent 1831) to death 31/3/1867, leaving £3,000 [C21089] Married (1) Oxford 16/5/1822 Mary Yalden (d.1849), w. issue (2) Croydon, Surrey 9/8/1853 Mary Anne Rowles (in 1861 he was 79, she 31).

PAGE (Robert Leman) Born Ipswich, Suffolk 31/3/1767, s. Benjamin Page and Anne Leman. Emmanuel, Cambridge 1785, BA1789, dn89 (Nor.), p91 (Nor.). R. Kettlebaston, Suffolk 1800, R. Panfield, Essex 1809 to death 29/1/1852 [C114332] Married 13/4/1792 Mary Tibenham Cuffley, with issue.

PAIGE (William Michael Tucker) Bapt. Slapton, Devon 20/5/1808, s. William Paige and Betsy Tucker. Trinity, Cambridge 1824, BA 1829, dn30 (Ex.), p31 (Ex.). PC. Slapton 1832, V. Ilsington, Devon 1835-68. Died 20/7/1873 aged 66, leaving £1,500 [C146038] Married Kidlington, Oxon. 25/2/1834 Laura Thomasine Chave, with issue.

PAIN (Richard) Bapt. Banbury, Oxon. 20/8/1774, s. John Pain and Mrs Sarah (?Osborne) Lucas. Pembroke, Oxford 1793, BA1796, BCL 1820. R. Radbourne, Warwicks. 1801 (and Sinecure R. 1802) [blank in ERC], V. Lindsell, Essex 1801, R. Little Wigborough, Essex 1820 to death (Aspley Guise, Beds.) 21/3/1854 [C18758/ 71992] Married Bodmin 18/6/1800 Elizabeth Fisher, 10 ch. (including clerical s. Edmund)

PAINE (John) Bapt. Charlbury, Oxon. 17/7/1795, s. Jonathan Paine (miller) and Sally Eden Walton. Literate: dn26 (York), p27 (York). PC. Dewsbury St John, Dewsbury Moore, Yorks. 1827 to death 2/3/1858, leaving £300 [C135672. YCO] Married (1) Kidlington, Oxon. 25/5/1817 Maria Pentycross (d.1855) (2) Almondbury, Yorks. 31/7/1856 Mrs Martha (Nowell) Lees (w).

PALEY (Edmund) Bapt. Carlisle 11/11/1782, s. Ven. William Paley (Archdeacon of Carlisle, the famous Christian apologist) and Jane Hewitt. Jesus, Cambridge 1800, then Queen's, Oxford 1801, BA1805, dn08 (York), p08 (York), MA 1808. V. Cawthorne, Yorks. 1809-22, V. Easingwold, Yorks. 1812-37, R. Gretford w. Wilsthorpe, Lincs. 1838 to death Erpingham, Norfolk) 1850 (3rd q.) [C109601. YCO] Married Cambridge 14/10/1812 Sarah Jane Apthorp, with clerical s. Francis Henry, and academic issue. Brother James, below.

PALEY (George Barber) Born Bowling, Bradford. Yorks. 28/10/1799, s. John Green Paley, J.P., and Anne Barber. Trinity, Cambridge 1816, then Peterhouse, Fellow 1820, BA 1822, MA1825, dn25 (Ely), p26 (Ely), BD 1833. PC. Cambridge St Mary the Less (or Little St Mary) 1832-3, V. Cherry Hinton, Cambs. 1833-5, R. and V. Frecken-ham, Suffolk (and RD) 1835 to death (London) 10/2/1880 aged 98, leaving £300,000 [C6719. Boase - not Barker] Married 18/5/1837 Catherine Anne Robertson (dau. of a Bath doctor), with issue. Succ. to the Langcliffe estates, North Yorks. 1860.

PALEY (James) Bapt. Carlisle 1/1/1784, s. Ven. William Paley (Archdeacon of Carlisle, the famous Christian apologist) and Jane Hewitt. Queen's, Oxford 1807, then Magdalen 1811, dn12 (Salis.), p12 (Salis.), BA1813. V. Lacock, Wilts. 1814 to death (Burton Grange, Yorks.) 9/12/1863 aged 80, leaving £4,000 [C88997] Married Bury, Lancs. 10/7/1810 Ann Hutchinson, with clerical son John Paley. Brother Edmund, above.

PALEY (Joshua) Born Preston, Lancs. 3/7/1804, s. John Paley and Mary Townsend. St John's, Cambridge 1823, BA1828, dn30 (C&L), p31 (C&L), MA 1832. (first) PC. Pemberton, Wigan, Lancs. 1832 to death (at his father's house in Preston) 5/12/1849 aged 45 [C18736]

PALK (Wilmot Henry) Born Devon 24/10/1796, s. Sir Lawrence Palk, 2nd Bart. and Lady Dorothy Vaughan (dau. of 1st Earl of Lisburne). Trinity, Cambridge 1814, BA1819, dn19 (London), p20 (Lin. for London). R. Ashcombe, Devon 1820-85 and V. Chudleigh, Devon 1841 to death (unmarried) 28/7/1885 aged 88, leaving £29,647-14s-0d. [C72027]

PALLING (Edward) Born Serampore, Calcutta 21/3/1801 (bapt. 15/7/1804), s. John and Mary Palling. St John's Cambridge 1818, then Christ's 1820, BA1823, dn25 (York), p25 (York). PC. Tithby w. Cropwell Butler, Notts. 1827-8, V. Norton Cuckney, Notts. 1828 to death 1843 (1st q.) [C135673. YCO] Confusion in Foster with an Oxford man.

PALMER (Charles) Bapt. Ladbrooke, Warwicks. 23/11/1782, s. Charles Palmer. Christ Church, Oxford 1801, BA1805, dn06 (C&L), p07 (C&L), MA1808. R. Ladbrooke 1807-34, R. Kimcote, Leics. 1811-34, R. Lighthorne, Worcs. 1834 and R. Chesterton, Worcs. 1843 to death. Dom. Chap. to 2nd Baron Walsingham 1811. Died 13/2/1871 aged 88. Will not traced [C18761] Married Harrow, Middx. 22/1/1823 Charlotte Finch [*not* Lady Charlotte Finch].

PALMER (Daniel) Probably born Dublin, s. George Palmer. TCD 1785 (aged 16), dn91 (Ossory), p92 (Cork & Ross), BA, MA. V. West Hythe, Kent 1820-[40]. Died? [C64769]

PALMER (Edmund Richard Hopper Griffith) Bapt. Thurnscoe, Yorks. 12/10/1795, s. Charles Palmer. Queen's, Oxford 1814, BA

1818, dn19 (Lin.), p20 (Lin.), MA1869. PC. Mareham on the Hill, Lincs. 1830, PC. High (or Upper) Toynton, Lincs. 1830, R. Greetham, Rutland 1843-9, V. North Somercotes, Lincs. 1849-64, R. South Somercotes, Lincs. 1864 to death 24/10/1886, leaving £3,543-15s-6d. [C72029] Married Horncastle, Lincs. 1/11/1836 Elizabeth Charlotte Pike, with issue.

PALMER (Edward) Born Moseley, Birmingham, s. Rev. Edward Palmer, sen. and Mary Freeth. Queens', Cambridge 1826 (a Ten Year Man). PC. Deritend St John, Birmingham 1828. Died (Great Malvern, Worcs.) 31/1/1846 aged 53 [C18764] Married Birmingham 15/1/1838 Mary Mason, w. issue. Brother William, below.

PALMER (Francis) Bapt. Kilmington, Som. 22/4/1776, s. Rev. William Palmer and Mary Bartlett. Magdalen Hall, Oxford 1799, BA1801, dn01 (Ex.), SCL 1803, p03 (Ex.), LLB1807, BD 1810. R. Wambrook, Dorset 1803-5, R. Combe Pyne, Devon 1805-7, R. Alcester, Warwicks. 1807 to death 1/12/1842 [C47447]

PALMER (George) Bapt. Itchingfield, Sussex 30/10/1781, s. Ann Palmer [*sic*]. Jesus, Cambridge 1800, BA1804, dn05 (Chich.), p05 (Chich.), MA1808, Fellow 1809-23. R. Harlton, Cambs. 1822, V. Lyminster, Sussex 1823, R. Sullington, Sussex 1824 and R. Parham, Sussex 1825 to death. Dom. Chap. to Charlotte, Baronesss King 1824. Died 6/2/1859 aged 77, leaving £1,500 [C64771] Married Chelsea, London 18/6/1828 Charlotte Elizabeth Bonnor, with clerical son Henry Palmer.

PALMER (Henry) Bapt. Newington, Oxon. 1/11/1796, s. Rev. William and Elizabeth Palmer. Worcester, Oxford 1813, BA1820, p20 (B&W). PC. Broadway, Som. 1811, R. Cricket Malherbie, Som. 1842 to death 24/2/1855 [C40184]

PALMER (Henry) Born Dorney Court, Bucks., s. Sir Charles Harcourt Palmer, 6th [and last] Bart. and Caroline Bonin (from Antigua, West Indies - probably illegitimate, 'no marriage recognised'). Christ Church, Oxford 1814 (aged 16), BA1817, MA1820, dn23 (London), p23 (London). V. Little Laver, Essex 1824, V. (and patron) Dorney 1832-56. Died (Dorney Court - inherited 1853) 20/11/1865, leaving £10,000 [C120886] Married City of London 2/11/1827 Sarah Gerrard, with issue.

PALMER (John) Born Bath 13/9/1773, s. John Palmer. Trinity, Cambridge 1791, BA1795, dn96 (London), MA1798, p01 (Salis.). Prebend of Leicester St Margaret in Lincoln Cathedral 1807-27, V. South Benfleet, Essex 1811-27, R. Peldon, Essex 1817 to death 17/5/1851 (CCEd has wrong death date here) [C66829] Was married.

PALMER (Philip Hall) Bapt. East Bridg-ford, Notts. 12/1/1802, s. Philip Palmer and Sophia Boulton. Jesus, Cambridge 1820, BA1824, dn25 (Heref.), p26 (Heref.), MA1828. V. Kneeton, Notts. 1831-6, V. Granby, Notts. 1836-44, V. Hose, Leics. 1837-44, R. Woolsthorpe, Grantham, Lincs. 1844 to death 1/9/1878 aged 76, leaving £10,000 [C136847. Kaye] Married Edge Hill, Liverpool 9/4/1831 Beatrice Aspinall, with issue.

PALMER (Richard) Born Hurst, Berks. 28/12/1795, s. Richard Palmer and Jane Oldfield Bowles. Christ Church, Oxford 1813 (aged 17), Student [Fellow] 1813-25, BA1816, MA1819 [adm. Lincoln's Inn 1819] dn22 (Ox.), p23 (Ox.). R. Blaby, Leics. 1824-45, R. Purley, Berks. 1844 to death (Holme Park, Sonning, Berks.) 25/10/1874, leaving £300,000 [C21094] Clerical son Hugh.

PALMER (William) Bapt. Chardstock, Dorset 15/8/1770, s. Rev. William Palmer, sen. and Mary Bradstock.Worcester, Oxford 1788, then Balliol, BA1791, MA1793, dn95 (Salis.), p95 (Bristol for Cant.), BD and DD1812. V. Ilton, Som. 1798 to death, V. Yarcombe, Devon 1800 to death. Dom. Chap. to Sophia Charlotte, 2nd Baroness Howe 1807. Died 19/11/1853 [C40201]

PALMER (William) Born London, s. William Palmer. Trinity, Cambridge 1798 (aged 18), BA1802, dn03 (Lin.), p095 (Lin.), MA1805. V. Eynesbury, Hunts. 1808-51, Prebend of Welton Paynshall in Lincoln Cathedral 1819 to burial 1/12/1851 [C72041]

PALMER (William) Born Moseley, Birmingham, s. Rev. Edward Palmer. Queens', Cambridge 1808, BA1813, dn15 (B&W), MA1816, p17 (Glos.). PC. Lea Marston, Warwicks. 1817 and V. Poles-worth, Warwicks. 1824 to death 23/1/1841 [C18769] Brother Edward, above.

PALMER (William Jocelyn) Born Mixbury, Oxon. 5/2/1778, s. William Palmer (West

Indian slaver and merchant) and Mary Jane Horsley. BNC, Oxford 1796, BA1799, MA1802, BD1811. R. Mixbury 1802-53, R. Beachampton, Bucks. 1811-15, R. Finmere, Oxon. 1815 to death 28/9/1853 [C2045. Boase. LBSO] Married York 10/9/1810 Dorothea Richardson Roundell (a clergy dau., Gledstone Hall, Yorks.) with issue (including Roundell Palmer, 1st Earl of Selborne [*q.v.* ODNB] www.shelswellparishes.info/.../palmer/william_jocelyn_palmer.htm has a port.

PANNELL (John) Born Fulham, London, s. John Edward Pannell (of Bosham, Sussex). St John's, Oxford 1804 (aged 18), then St Mary Hall, BA1809, dn11 (Win.), MA1811. V. West Wittering, Sussex 1816-24, R. Burton w. Coates, Sussex 1819, R. Ludgershall, Wilts. 1824 to death. Dom. Chap. to Eleanor, Baroness de Blaquière 1820. Died (Pimlico, London) 12/5/1872, leaving £6,000 [C64776] Wife Lucy Wilder, and issue.

PANTIN (Thomas Pindar) Born London 2/4/1792, s. Thomas Pantin and Elizabeth Lidgould. Queen's, Oxford 1817, BA1821, dn24 (Lin.), p25 (Lin.), MA1827. R. (and patron) of Westcote, Glos. 1828 to death 2/9/1866. Will not traced [C72046. ODNB. Boase - not Pinden] Married Bloomsbury, London 25/1/1822 Hannah Godfrey, with issue.

PAPILLON (John) Bapt. Acrise, Kent 26/2/1807, s. Thomas Papillon and Ann Cressett Pelham. University, Oxford 1825, BA 1828, dn30 (London), p31 (London), MA1858. R. Bonnington, Kent 1831-5, R. Knowlton, Kent 1835-41, R. Lexden, Essex 1841 to death 19/10/1889, leaving £1,854-14s-3d. [C120889] Married Frances Ann Prudentia Leslie (dau. of a Bishop of Dromore) before 1841, with clerical son Thomas Leslie Papillon.

PAPILLON (John Rawstorne) Born Acrise, Kent., s. David Papillon and Bridget Turner. Queens', Cambridge 1781, BA1786, dn86 (Roch.), p88 (Roch.), Fellow 1788, MA1789. V. Tonbridge, Kent 1791-1804, R. Chawton, Hants. 1802 to death (Lexdon Manor, Essex) 4/4/1837 [C407] Jane Austen and her mother and sister were living at Chawton at this time, and there are numerous references to P. in her letters (a 'fidgety' bachelor). Brother below. www.janeaustensoci.freeuk.com/pages/branches/cambridge_connections.htm

PAPILLON (William) Born Acrise, Kent, s. David Papillon and Bridget Turner. University, Oxford 1779 (aged 18), BA1783, dn83 (Ox.), p85 (Roch. for Cant.), MA1786. PC. Norwich St George Tombland 1787-8 (res.), V. Wymondham, Norfolk 1788 to death. Dom. Chap. to 3rd Earl of Rosebery 1786. Died 26/9/1836 [C2048] Brother John above.

PARDOE (George Dansey) Born Nash Court, Burford, Shropshire, s. George Pardoe and Ellen Dansey. Balliol, Oxford 1804 (aged 18), BA1808, p12 (Heref.). R. Hopton Castle, Shropshire 1812 to death 28/5/1856; living at Fishmore Hall, Shrop-shire [C173051 as George] Was married, with clerical son Arthur Pardoe.

PARE (Frederick Harry) Bapt. Exeter, Devon 12/7/1798, s. John and Marianne Pare. Christ Church, Oxford 1817, BA1821, MA1825, p28 (Win.). PC. St Helens, IoW 1829, R. Cranborne, Dorset 1830-[42]. Lived in Southampton and died Ryde, IoW 15/5/1877, leaving £25,000 [C53470] Married London 25/11/1830 Geraldine FitzGerald DeRos, with issue.

PARFITT (Peter Lewis) Born Wells, Som. 24/5/1778, s. Edward Parfitt and Anne Brunt. Balliol, Oxford 1795, BA1799, dn00 (Ex. for B&W), MA1802, p02 (B&W). Vicar-Choral in Wells Cathedral 1801-13, R. (and patron) of (Chapel) Allerton, Som. 1814 to death 17/12/1857, leaving £14,000 [C40185] Married Bristol 3/1/1809 Eliza Griffiths (w), with issue. Brother, below.

PARFITT (Thomas) Born 'Liberty of St Andrews, Wells' 20/5/1776, s. Edward Parfitt and Anne Brunt. Balliol, Oxford 1794 (aged 18), BA1798, dn98 (B&W), p00 (Salis.), MA1801, BD and DD 1833. PC. Glastonbury St Benedict, Som. 1812 (w. West Pennard 1823) to death 13/1/1865, leaving £2,000 [C40186] Widower 1861. Brother, above.

PARHAM (John Dolbeare) Born Stoke Damerel, Devon 11/4/1796, s. Benjamin Parham and Susanna Dolbeare. St John, Cambridge 1816, BA1820, dn20 (Chester), p21 (Salis. for Ex.), MA1823. V. Holne, Devon 1829 to death 29/8/1858 aged 62 [C89001] Married Elizabeth Lane by 1828.

PARK (George) Born Hawkshead, Lancs. 19/10/1803, s. John Park (a saddler) and Mary

Brunskill (*or* James Park, a landowner?). St Bees adm. 1825, dn27 (Chester), p28 (Chester). (first) PC. Over Darwen Holy Trinity, Lancs. 1829-34, R. Hawkshead 1830-4 (and RD 1845) to death (Boroughbridge, Yorks.) 19/9/1866 aged 62, leaving £6,000 [C170159 has wrong ordination date and date of death which belong to another cleric of this name] Married (1) Hawkshead 18/1/1830 Marianne Bowman (d.1850), with issue (2) Ulverston, Lancs. 2/12/1851 Harriet Huish. Founded the Park Bread Charity at Hawkshead. Surrogate 1831.

PARK (James Allan) Born Barnes, Surrey 12/8/1800, s. Sir James Allan Park (Judge of Common Pleas) and Lucy Atherton. Balliol, Oxford 1818, BA1821, dn23 (Glos. for London), p24 (London), MA1825. R. Elwick Hall, Castle Eden, Durham 1828 (and Hon. Canon Durham Cathedral 1848) to death (Newbus Grange, Durham) 8/11/1871 aged 71, leaving £14,000 [C120890] Married Cherington, Warwicks. 8/1/1823 Mary Dickins, with clerical son of his name.

PARKE (Benjamin) Bapt. Kirkham, Lancs. 3/8/1759, s. William (a skinner) and Ellen Parke. Pembroke, Cambridge 1777, BA1782, Fellow 1783, dn84 (Lin.), MA1785, p85 (Peterb.), etc. V. Tilney, Norfolk 1805 and Canon of 4th Prebend in Ely Cathedral 1831 to death 16/1/1835 (CCEd says 6/3/1835) [C18240] Married Walgrave, Northants. 17/9/1807 Katherine Stockdale.

PARKE (Thomas) Bapt. Tunstall, Lancs. 10/2/1754, s. Rowland Parke and Emma Hodgson. Christ's, Cambridge 1771, BA 1775, dn76 (Peterb.), then Peterhouse 1777, MA1778, p79 (Ely), Fellow 1779-86. V. Staunton All Saints, Glos. 1779, R. Stathern, Leics. 1783 to death 18/8/1839 aged 85 [C72055]

PARKER (Charles Frederick) Born Churcham, Glos. 31/8/1787, s. Rev. Thomas Parker and Susanna Frances Wintle. Pembroke, Oxford 1792, BA1806, MA1809, dn10, p12 (B&W), Fellow to 1819. R. Ringshall, Suffolk 1819-64-, R. Little Finborough, Norfolk 1832. Died Newtown, Montgomery 30/4/1870, leaving £1,500 [C47459] Married Tooting Graveney, Surrey 20/7/1820 Elizabeth Eyre, with clerical son Frederick William Parker.

PARKER (Charles Hubert) Bapt. Tamworth, Staffs. 15/8/1800 (Presbyterian congregation), s. William and Mary Parker. Lincoln, Oxford 1818, BA 1822, dn23, p24, MA 1825. R. (and patron) of Great Comber--ton w. Little Comberton, Worcs. 1826 to death 26/11/1883, leaving £11,742-4s-5d. [C121969] Married Alcester, Staffs. 29/11/1831 Jane Elizabeth Handy, with clerical son Charles William Parker.

PARKER (Francis) Bapt. Sheffield, Yorks. 14/9/1762, s. Kenyon Parker (attorney) and Hannah Shirecliffe. Trinity, Cambridge 1781, BA1785, dn85 (York), p88 (York), MA1789. R. Hawksworth, Notts. 1788, PC. Dore, Derbys. 1807 to death 10/10/1840 [C18800. YCO] Married 9/1793 Catharine Hare (Dronfield, Derbys.).

PARKER (Henry John) Born London 6/7/1772, s. Henry Parker and Alice Combs. St Edmund Hall, Oxford 1790, BA1794, dn95 (Salis. for Chich.), MA1797 (both as Parkes), Professor of Divinity at Gresham College, London 1800 (*q.v.* Wikipedia). PC. Maidstone Holy Trinity, Kent 1828, R. High Halden, Kent 1837 to death (Canterbury) 19/10/1867, leaving £3,000 [C89002] Married Wansted, Essex 11/2/1808 Eliza Knowles, with clerical sons William Russell Parker, and Henry Parker. Photo. online.

PARKER (John Fleming) Born Browsholme Hall, Waddington, Yorks. 17/4/1782, s. John Parker, *M.P.*, and Beatrix Lister. BNC, Oxford 1801, BA1804, dn05 (Glos.), p06 (Ex.), MA 1807. V. Acton, Middx. 1808-11, Prebend of Llangwm 1809, then of Warthacwm 1813 in Llandaff Cathedral, PC. Waddington 1818-51-, V. Almondbury, Yorks. 1822-3, R. Bentham, Yorks. 1825 to death. Chap. to HRH Duke of Clarence 1825; Dom. Chap. to Anne Maria, Lady Grey de Ruthyn 1827. Died Browsholme Hall 26/11/1862, leaving £12,000 [C4394 is confused with William, below] Married 1817 Hon. Catherine Lister, dau. of Baron Ribblesdale, and widow of James Skurr Day ('and thereby relieved [her] from a most cruel state') (w), with issue. Brother William, below.

PARKER (John Thomas) Born Newbold on Avon, Warwicks. 10/3/1787, s. Rev. John Parker and Catherine Caldecott. Christ Church, Oxford 1805, BA1809, dn10 (Salis. for C&L), p11 (C&L), MA1812. R. Bilton, Warwicks. 1813 and V. Newbold on Avon 1817 to death 26/10/1852 [C18802] Married Alveston,

Warwicks. 21/12/1824 Anne Skipwith, with issue.

PARKER (Pelley) Bapt. Hawton, Notts. 25/12/1789, s. Rev. Robert Parker and Lucy Henrietta Bird. Christ Church, Oxford 1807, BA1811, dn13 (C&L), p14 (C&L), MA1823. R. West Hallam, Derbys. 1828-49, R. Hawton 1849 to death (St Leonard's on Sea, Sussex) 18/11/1865, leaving £30,000 [C18803] Married Malpas, Cheshire 4/9/1823 Frances Rosamond Dod (w), with issue.

PARKER (Thomas) Born Astle, Cheshire, s. Rev. John Parker. Christ Church, Oxford 1784 (aged 18), BA1789, dn94 (Chester), p95 (Chester). PC. Rainow, Cheshire 1795-1835 and PC. Saltersford, Cheshire 1798 to death 31/12/1835 (CCEd thus) [C170169]

PARKER (William) Son of John Parker, 'formerly of Jamaica'. Christ's, Cambridge 1795, BA1800, dn01 (Ely), p02 (Ely), MA 1803. R. St Ethelburga's, City of London 1807 (and Oxgate Prebend in St Paul's Cathedral, London) 1833 to death (Islington, London) 15/1/1843 aged 65. Secretary to the S.P.C.K. for 32 years [C100149] Married 1807 Ann Gaskin (w) (a clergy dau.), with issue.

PARKER (William) Born Browsholme Hall, Waddington, Yorks. 1/1/1785, s. John Parker, *M.P.*, and Beatrice Lister. [some say BA but NiVoF]. V. Waddington to 1818, V. Skipwith, Yorks. 1818 to death (Browsholme Hall) 24/9/1848, *s.p.* [C136845 says Packer] *J.P.* and *D.L.* East Riding. Brother John Fleming, above.

PARKES (Richard) Bapt. Birmingham 9/2/1762, s. Pryn and Jenny Parkes. All Souls, Oxford 1778, dn84 (Heref.), BA1786, p86 (Heref.). V. Kingsbury, Warwicks. 1794-1800, V. Loppington, Shropshire 1799-1832, PC. Newtown Chapel, Wem, Shropshire 1799 [vacant in ERC], V. Hanmer, Flint 1807-8. Will proved 6/3/1833 [C19083] Married Hanmer, Flint 1803 a Miss Edwards, with issue.

PARKHURST (Fleetwood) Bapt. St Pancras, London 27/4/1773, s. Fleetwood Parkhurst (High Sheriff of Worcester 1792) and Ann Danforth. Trinity, Oxford 1794, BA1797, MA 1801, p04 (Win.). V. Epsom, Surrey 1804 to death 29/10/1844, living at Ripple Hall, Worcs. [C40187] Left a son.

PARKIN (Charles) Born Dacre, Cumber-land 15/10/1799, s. Hugh and Sarah Margaret Parkin. BNC, Oxford 1818, BA 0.1821, dn23 (York), MA1824, p25 (York). V. Lenham, Kent 1827-64-. Lived Sidmouth Devon; died Bromley, Kent 1/2/1884, leaving £79,291-14s-1d. [C135675. YCO] Married Otterden, Kent 25/1/1831 Harriet Ann Goodyar, with clerical son Charles Inglewood Parkin.

PARKIN (James) Bapt. Oakford, Devon 15/5/1789, s. Rev. James Parkin, sen. and Grace Scamp. Pembroke, Oxford 106, BA1810, dn12 (Ox.), p13 (Salis. for Ex.), MA 1813. R. Skilgate, Som. 1813-17 (res.), R. Oakford (a family living) 1813 to death. Dom. Chap. to 15th Lord Somerville 1813. Died 5/5/1871 aged 81, leaving £30,000 [C21102]

PARKINS (Samuel) Bapt. Chesham, Bucks. 19/2/1773, s. Rev. Thomas Parkins. St John's, Cambridge 1791 (as Thomas), BA1795, MA by 1802, dn02 (London), p03 (Lin.). V. Preston Deanery, Northants. 1821-55, PC. Horton w. Piddington, Northants. to 1826. Died 21/10/1855 [C72070]

PARKINSON (John) Born Ravendale, Lincs. 7/3/1754, s. Robert and Mary Parkinson. Corpus Christi, Oxford 1770, then Magdalen 1772-6, BA1774, Fellow 1775-98, MA1777, dn77 (Ox.), p78 (Ox.), DD1797, etc. R. Brocklesby, Lincs. 1785-40, R. Fittleton, Wilts. 1797-40, V. East Raven-dale, Lincs. 1803. Died 29/8/1840 [C28812. ERC links them].

PARKINSON (John) Born Healing, Lincs. 20/6/1758, s. Rev. John Parkinson, sen. and Frances Green. Balliol, Oxford 1777, BA 1780, dn81 (Ox.), p82 (Ox.), MA1787. V. Immimg-ham, Lincs. 1782, R. Healing 1793 to death 11/1/1837 [C28815] Married Stallingborough, Lincs. 17/8/1798 Frances Grantham, and had issue.

PARKINSON (Richard) Born Admarsh, Lancaster 17/9/1797, s. John Parkinson (a yeoman farmer) and Margaret Blackburne. St John's, Cambridge 1815, BA1820 [S/M Preston 1820-1; and editor of the *Preston Sentinel* 1821] dn22 (Chester), p23 (Chester), MA1824, BD 1838, DD1852. Theological Lecturer St Bees College, Cumberland 1826-46, PC. Whitworth, Rochdale, Lancs. 1830-41 (non-res.), Principal and V. St Bees 1846-58, Fellow (then Canon 1847) Manchester Collegiate Church 1833 to death (St Bees) 28/1/1858, leaving £18,000 [C170173. ODNB. Boase. T. Park, *St Bees College* (2nd edn. St Bees, 2007; with port.)] Married Egremont, Cumberland 18/7/1831 Catherine Hartley, with issue. Antiquarian; co-founder of the Chetham Society; the remains of his now lost but interesting diary are transcribed in part at: www.stbees.org.uk/history/theo_college/parkinson_diary.html

PARKINSON (Thomas) Literate: p13 (Chester). PC. Radcliffe St Thomas, Lancs. 1820 to death 1838 (1st q.) [C170176] Married Kirkby Lonsdale, Westmorland 5/6/1811 Sarah Robinson. Ran a school. Another man of this name was Chancellor of Chester Diocese.

PAROISSIEN (Challis) Bapt. Hackney, London 31/7/1794, s. Rev. George Paroissien [of Huguenot extraction] and Jane Elizabeth Issanchon [*sic*]. Clare, Cambridge 1815, BA 1817, dn17 (London), Fellow 1817, p18 (London), MA1820. V. Everton w. Tetworth, Beds. 1832-6 [vacant in ERC], R. Hardingham, Norfolk 1839 to death 14/12/1873, leaving £6,000 [C412. CR65 as Charles] Married 30/8/1864 Julia Jane Hovell.

PARR (John Owen) Bapt. Bloomsbury, London 15/11/1798, s. John Owen Parr and Elizabeth Mary Patrick. BNC, Oxford 1815, BA1818, dn21 (Salis.), p23 (Ely), MA1830. V. Durnford, Wilts. 1824, V. Preston St John the Divine, Lancs. 1840-77 (and RD), Hon. Canon of Manchester Cathedral 1853 to death 12/2/1877, leaving £800 [C89031. In A. Hewitson, *Visits to some Preston & district churches & chapels* (Blackpool, 2010) is revealing] Married (1) St Pancras, London 24/4/1821 Mary Elizabeth Wright (d.1841), w. clerical son of his name (2) St George's Hanover Square, London 1846 (3rd q.) Jane Proctor, with further issue (3) St James's, Westminster, London 21/6/1858 Alice Stewardson (d.1861).

PARR (Thomas) Born Lythwood Hall, Shrewsbury, Shropshire 5/3/1805, s. Thomas Parr and Katharine Walter. St John's, Cambridge 1823, BA1828, dn28 (Heref.), p29 (Heref.). R. Westbury (in Dextra Parte), Heref. 1829 to death Sept. 1852 aged 57 [C173063] Married Westbury, Shropshire 28/4/1831 Anne Penelope Toffs. *J.P.* Shropshire.

PARR (Thomas Gnosall) Bapt. Mavesyn Ridway, Staffs. 1/3/1775, s. Thomas Gnosall Parr and Ann Bramall. St John's, Cambridge, 1818, BA1822, dn22 (Chester), p23 (Chester), MA1825. Priest Vicar of the United Prebends of Brewood and Adbaston in Lichfield Cathedral 1829 and PC. Lichfield St Michael 1831 to death 23/12/1867, leaving £12,000. Dom. Chap. to Earl of Lichfield [C18743] Married Lichfield 5/11/1798 Ann Bramall, w. issue.

PARRY (Frederick) St Bees adm. 1817, dn18 (Chester), p19 (Chester) St John's, Cambridge 1820 (a Ten Year Man, BD 1830). PC. Eastham, Cheshire 1818, PC. Threapwood, Cheshire 1823-9, (first) PC. Chester St Paul, Boughton 1830-41, PC. St Clement, Liverpool 1843-60. Died Litchurch, Derbys. 9/5/1865 aged 69, leaving £5,000 [C170178] Married 1822 Jane Ward (w) (dau. of a Bishop of Chester's secretary), with clerical issue.

PARRY (John) Bapt. Liverpool 31/3/1804, s. Henry Parry and Ellen Parker. BNC, Oxford 1822, BA1825, Fellow 1826-35, MA1828, dn28 (Ox.), p29 (Peterb.). Curate Bethnal Green St John, London 1831, R. Wapping, Essex 1833 to death 13/8/1852 [C21103]

PARRY (Joseph Markham) Born Shrewsbury, Shropshire 21/11/1795, s. Henry Parry (a draper) and Ann Daw. St John's, Cambridge 1816, BA1820, dn21 (Bristol for Heref.), p21 (Heref.), MA1823. R. North Muskham w. Holme, Notts. 1825 to death 19/8/1853 [C53473] Married Holt, Norfolk 26/10/1837 Elizabeth Barwick (b. St Petersburrg). Brother below.

PARRY (William Henry) Born Shrewsbury, Shropshire 3/2/1785, s. Henry Parry (a draper) and Ann Daw. St John's, Cambridge 1803, BA 1808, dn08 (Salis. for Ely), p08 (Ex. for Ely), MA1811, Fellow 1811-29, BD1818. Tutor to the sons of the Duke of Portland; R. North Muskham w. Holme, Notts. to 1825 (res.), R. Holt, Norfolk 1828-37, R. Bothal, Northumberland 1837 to death. Dom. Chap. to 4th Duke of Portland 1814. Died 11/5/1845 [C89035] Married Cambridge 10/10/1829 Elizabeth Cory (dau. of a Master of Emmanuel College there), and had issue. 'Few persons have died more regretted as a pastor and as a friend'. Brother above.

PARSABLE (William) Bapt. Great Broughton, Cumberland 16/1/1760, s. John Parsable and Sarah Grisedale. Literate: dn83 or 84 (Car. has 2 ordination dates in CCEd), p85 (Car.). S/M Crosthwaite G/S, Cumber-land 1802; PC. Borrowdale, Cumberland 1806-37, PC. Newlands, Crosthwaite 1826, V. Gilcrux, Cumberland 1826 to death 3/12/1837 aged 78 [C5716. Platt] Married Crosthwaite 12/8/1817 Mary Cocking. Known as 'Peppery Bill', 'he was arraigned for the assault of a pupil's uncle' (Platt).

PARSON (Joseph) Born Rushall Hall, Staffs. 3/12/1780, s. Joseph Parson and Ann Kent. Clare, Cambridge 1797, BA1802, Fellow 1804-10, MA1805, dn05 (Peterb.), p05 (Lin.). *H.E.I.C.* Chap. at Berhampore, Bengal 1805; R. (and patron) of Ashwicken (and Leziat), Norfolk 1826 and R. Campsea Ashe, Suffolk 1829 to death (London) 23/12/1835 [C72105] Married Kampur, Uttar Pradesh 30/1/1810 Sophia Hardwicke, w. issue. Port online.

PARSON (William Woodley) Born Little Parson, Essex, s. Edward Parson and Frances Webbe. Christ's, Cambridge 1792, BA1796, dn96 (Nor.), p96 (Nor.). R. Brandon w. Wangford, Norfolk (and Preacher throughout the Diocese of Norwich) 1796-1838, R. East Wretham, Norfolk 1797-1803 (res.). Died 18/9/1838 ('after a long and excessive illness') [C114349. LBSO].

PARSONS (George Stickler) Born Petersfield, Hants. 31/10/1795, s. John Parsons and Mary Parr. Literate: dn20 (S&M), p21 (S&M). S/M Castletown G/S, IoM 1823-27; Chaplain Malew St Mary, Castletown, IoM 1827 to death. 'Government Chaplain' 1849. Died 11/4/1855 [C7312. Gelling] Married Castletown 25/6/1827 Ann Evans (d. at childbirth 1837).

PARSONS (Henry) Born Bridgwater, Som., s. Rev. Francis Crane Parsons and Jane Evered. Exeter, Oxford 1781 (aged 16), BA1785, then Oriel, Fellow 1787, MA1788, dn88 (B&W), p89 (London for B&W). R. Goathurst, Som. 1789 to death, V. Wembdon, Som. 1791, Prebend of East Harptree in Wells Cathedral 1791-1845, 'Min. of Bridgwater Town' 1819. Dom. Chap. to 4th Earl Poulett 1791. Died 9/1/1845 [C40203. Boase] Married Bath 3/1/1797 Susanna Poole, many ch. Brother John, below.

PARSONS (Henry James) Born Ashford, Kent 1/8/1787, s. Joseph and Elizabeth Parsons. Christ Church, Oxford 1804, then Magdalen 1806-9, BA1808, Fellow 1809-20, MA1811, dn12 (Ox.), p13 (Heref.), BD1818. R. Saunderton, Bucks. 1819-28 and V. Arundel, Sussex 1828 to death 3/8/1844 [C21108] Married Arundel 27/5/1820 Mary Gibbs Puddick (a minor), w. clerical s. Henry George Joseph..

PARSONS (James) Born Cirencester, Glos. 30/3/1762, s. Rev. James Parsons. Wadham, Oxford 1777, BA1781, dn84 (Ox.), p88 (Ox.), MA1796, then St Alban Hall, BD1815, etc. PC. Newnham w. Littledean, Glos. 1800 to death 6/4/1847 [C28834] Married Stafford 30/11/1793 Sophia Maria Packer, with issue.

PARSONS (John) Bapt. Lincoln 25/10/1758, s. John and Sarah Parsons. BNC, Oxford 1776, BA1780, Fellow, dn81 (Lin.), MA1782, p83 (Ox.), BD and DD 1800. R. Skegness, Lincs. 1785, R. Wapping, Middx. 1800 to death 24/2/1834 (CCEd thus) [C28838]

PARSONS (John) Bapt. Yeovil, Somerset 14/12/1779, s. Rev. Francis Crane Parsons and Jane Evered. Worcester, Oxford 1798, BA1802, dn02 (B&W), p03 (B&W), MA 1804, Fellow until 1814. V. East Harptree, Som. 1806-31, V. Oborne w. Castleton, Dorset 1811-54, V. Sherborne, Dorset 1830 to death 1/7/1854 [C40204] Married Mary Smith, with issue. Brother Henry, above.

PARSONS (John) Born Barbados, West Indies 5/8/1782, s. Daniel Parsons (physician) and Rebecca Port Webb. University, Oxford 1800, BA1805, then Oriel, Fellow 1807-12, MA1807, dn08 (Ox.), p10 (Ox.). R. Marden, Wilts. 1816 to death (Bath) 31/7/1844; living at Begbrooke House, Bristol [C21115] Married 11/1/1801 Margaret Phillips, with clerical son Daniel Parsons.

PARTINGTON (Henry) Bapt. Hamsey, Sussex 2/5/1808, s. Thomas Partington and Penelope Ann Trollope. Christ Church, Oxford 1826, BA1830, dn31 (Ox.), MA 1832, p32 (Ox.), Student [Fellow] 1826-34. V. Wath upon Dearne w. Ardwick upon Dearne, Yorks. 1833-91. Died there 21/3/1897 aged 88, leaving £5,770-11s-7d. [C136848. CCEd as Patrington] Wife Sarah, and issue.

PARTRIDGE (John Anthony) Born Holborn, London 3/6/1794, s. Henry Partridge and Katherine Reynardson. BNC, Oxford 1817, dn17 (Nor.), p18 (Nor.), MA1820. R. Cranwich, Norfolk 1818-33, R. Town Barningham (o/w Barningham Winter), Norfolk 1819-32 (res.), R. East Wretham and West Wretham, Norfolk 1831-33, R. Malpas (Lower Moiety), Cheshire 1833, R. Baconsthorpe, Norfolk 1840 to death 27/2/1861, leaving £16,000 [C114350] Married St George's Hanover Square, London 18/5/1826 Louisa Isabella Tyrwhitt Drake, with issue.

PASCOE (James) Born St Keverne, Cornwall 8/6/1792, s. Rev. James Pascoe. St John's, Cambridge 1811, BA1815, dn16 (Ex.), p17 (Ex.). V. St Keverne 1817 to death 4/3/1839 aged 47 [C146047] Married Looe, Cornwall 30/12/1818 Anne Bennett (a clergy dau., of Newlyn, Cornwall).

PASCOE (Thomas) Bapt. Penzance, Cornwall 21/4/1789, s. of James Pascoe (a solicitor) and Catherine Edwards. Jesus, Cambridge 1806, BA1810, dn11 (Ex.), p12 (Ex.). V. St Hilary, Marazion, Cornwall 1814 to death 29/3/1870 aged 81, leaving £7,000 [C146048] Married Mawgan-in-Pydar, Cornwall 31/10/ 1815 Charlotte Champion Willyams.

PASHLEY (William) Bapt. Tinsley, Sheffield 9/5/1762, s. Robert and Jane Pashley. Literate: dn87 (York), p88 (York). PC. Holmesfield, Derbys. 1795 to death 27/6/1850 aged 89 [C19099. Possibly in YCO]

PASKE (Edward) Bapt. Needham Market, Suffolk 9/11/1792, s. George Paske and Anne Mudd. Clare, Cambridge 1810, BA 1814, dn15 (Nor.), MA1817, p17 (Nor.) R. (and patron) of Creeting St Peter, Suffolk 1818-85, V. Norton, Herts. 1819-26, V. (and patron) of Battisford, Suffolk 1821 to death 15/1/1885 aged 92, leaving £329-16s-0d. [C114354] Married Barking, Suffolk 9/1/1827 Helen Amelia Gourlay, with clerical s. Theophilus John Paske. Brother below. Detailed online entry.

PASKE ([George] Alexander) Born Madras 16/12/1801 (bapt. 27/8/1803), s. George Paske and Anne Mudd. Clare, Cambridge 1819, BA 1825, dn25 (Nor.), p26 (Nor.), MA1828. PC. Needham Market, Barking, Suffolk 1828 and PC. Willisham, Suffolk 1837 to death. Buried 8/12/1882 aged 80. Will not traced [C114355]

Married Shimpling, Suffolk 10/5/1830 Mary Isabella Fiske (a clergy dau.), 4 ch. Brother above. Detailed online entry.

PASSAND (Henry John) From Oxford, s. Henry Passand. Queen's, Oxford 1820 (aged 18), then St Alban Hall, BA1824, dn26 (Ox.), p26 (Ox.), MA1827. R. Shipton on Cherwell, Oxon. 1831 to death (Brighton) 16/10/1867, leaving £14,000 [C21117] Married Woodstock, Oxon. 1848 Catharine Turner (w). 'Wants gravity and sense - companies with lower class of farmers, &c - sporting - is he mad or drinks?' (Wilberforce).

PATERSON (Charles John) Born Marylebone, London 11/3/1800, s. William and Harriet Paterson. Caius, Cambridge 1818, BA1822, dn24 (Chester), p24 (Chich.). V. West Hoathly, Sussex 1827 to death 22/1/1837 [C64799] Married East Grinstead, Sussex 10/11/1836 Cordelia Cranston.

PATTENSON (John) Bapt. Gosforth, Cumberland 20/5/1791, s. John Pattenson. Literate: dn14 (Chester), p16 (Chester). PC. Dendron, Ulverston, Lancs. 1818 to death 20/11/1865, leaving under £300 [C170185] Widow Mary, and issue.

PATTESON (William) Bapt. Quatford, Shropshire 24/6/1787, s. Rev. Edward and Sarah Patteson. Balliol, Oxford 1808, BA 1811, dn11 (Win.), p12 (Win.), MA1817. R. Shaftesbury Holy Trinity, Dorset 1825-33, R. Sutton Waldron, Dorset 1826-33, R. Shaftesbury St James 1833 to death. Dom. Chap. to 2nd Earl of Clancarty 1826. Died 17/3/1859, leaving £1,000 [C53481] Married Eleanor Raebone, with issue.

PATTESON (William Frederick) Born Norwich 21/3/1800, s. John Patteson. Trinity, Cambridge 1820, dn23 (Nor.), p24 (Nor.), BA 1825, MA1860. PC. and V. Norwich St Helen 1824 (and RD) and Hon. Canon of Norwich Cathedral 1860 to death 14/11/1881 aged 81, leaving £23,457-1s-0d. [C114359] Married Hockliffe, Beds. 14/6/1840 Eleanor Robinson.

PATTINSON (John) Born Wigton, Cumberland, s. John Pattinson and Mary Dand. [NiVoF] PC. Repton, Derbys. 1804 to death 17/5/1843 aged 78 [C19166] Married Repton 8/7/1807 Elizabeth Orchard, with issue.

PATTINSON (Thomas) Schoolmaster to 1771. Literate: dn72 (Car.), p77 (Car.). R. Kirklinton, Cumberland 1777-1831, R. Stapleton, Cumberland 1796-1834, PC. Grinsdale, Cumberland 1804-29 (res.), PC. Dendron, Lancs. to 1818. Died 28/4/1834 aged 88 [C5725. Platt. J.F. Chance, *The Pattinsons of Kirklinton* (1899), port.] Married Kirkandrews-on-Esk, Cumberland 15/12/1778 Mary Story, with issue. 'Employed three curates at the same time' (Platt).

PATTISON (Edward) Born Ipswich, Suffolk 17/8/1797, s. Lilly [*sic*] Pattison and Sarah Collins. St Catharine's, Cambridge 1821, then Queens' 1822, BA1826, dn26 (B&W for Ely), p27 (Nor.). R. Gedding, Suffolk 1831 to death (Bradfield St George, Suffolk) 29/6/1871, leaving £1,500 [C40208] Married Letheringham, Suffolk 13/12/1831 Mary Taylor (w), with issue.

PATTISON (Mark James) Born Plymouth, Devon 8/12/1788, s. Capt. Mark Smith Pattison, *Royal Artillery* and Eleanor Miller. BNC, Oxford 1805, BA1809, dn11 (Ex.), p12 (Ex.), MA1812. R. Hawkswell (o/w Hauxwell), Richmond, Yorks. 1825 to death 30/12/1865 aged 77, leaving £14,000 1825 (but intermittently insane: 1834 in Acomb House Asylum, York). Chap. to 6th Duke of Leeds 1816 [C146052. DEB. John Sparrow, *Mark Patttison and the idea of a university* (Cambridge, 1967) pp33-36 for this 'raging domestic tyrant'] Married Richmond 16/4/1812 Jane Winn (then aged 19 - 'a pale and pious shadow'), 10 dau., 2s. (including Mark Pattison, Rector of Lincoln College, and author of the psychologically revealing *Memoirs*).

PAUL (Charles) Bapt. Marylebone, London 16/1/1803, s. Robert Paul (President of the Council of the Island of St Vincent, West Indies) and Elizabeth Warner. Adm. Lincoln's Inn 1820. Caius, Cambridge 1822, BA1826, dn26 (B&W), p27 (B&W), MA1829. V. Knowle St Giles, Som. 1828-39, V. Wellow, Som. 1839-45, R. Lickmolassy, Co. Galway 1855 to death (Portumna, Galway) on or about 11/4/1861 aged 58 ('effects in England *nil*') [C40209] Married (1) Bath 22/5/1827 Frances Kegan Horne (d.1848), with issue (inc. Charles Kegan Paul, the publisher) (2) Marylebone, London 4/3/1851 Gertrude Cossins (w).

PAUL (Samuel Woodfield) Bapt. Hackney, London 22/4/1778, s. Nathaniel Paul and Sarah Woodfield. Literate: dn06 (Peterb.), p07 (Peterb.). V. (and patron) of Finedon (o/w Thingdon), Northants. 1810. Buried 7/8/1847 [C110685] Married Finedon 11/9/1806 Charlotte (dau. of Sir John English Dolben, 4th Bart.), with clerical son George Woodfield Paul.

PAULET (Charles, Lord) Born 13/8/1802, s. Charles Paulet, 13th Marquess of Winchester and Anne Andrews. Clare, Cambridge 1822, BA 1822, MA 1824, dn26 (Lin.), p30 (Win.). R. Walton D'Eivile, Warwicks. 1830-41, V. Wellesbourne, Warwicks. 1830 and Prebend of Coombe and Harnham in Salisbury Cathedral 1833 to death (Brighton) 23/7/1870 aged 67, leaving £45,000 [C72119] Married (1) Marylebone, London 18/8/1831 Caroline Margaret Ramsden (dau. of a baronet, she d.1847), w. issue (2) Wellesbourne 10/8/1850 Joan Frederica Mathewana Granville (of Wellesbourne Hall), with further issue.

PAVER (Richard) Bapt. Ledsham, Yorks. 8/11/1793, s. Richard Paver. Literate: dn16 (York), p17 (York). V. Brayton w. Barlow, Selby, Yorks. 1819 to death 19/9/1870 aged 77, leaving £800 [C135678. YCO] Married Great Ouseburn, Yorks. 5/5/1835 Mary Howe, with issue.

PAWSEY, *later* PASSY (Frederick) Bapt. Westminster, London 15/3/1784, s. Joseph Pawsey and Ann Nancy Walton. St John's, Cambridge 1802, BA1806, dn07 (Nor.), p10 (Nor.). V. Wilshamstead, Beds. 1816 to death 23/1/1843 [C72125] Changed name 1842. Brother below.

PAWSEY (Joseph Wilton) Born Silsoe, Beds. 30/4/1777, s. Joseph Pawsey and Ann Nancy Walton. St John's, Cambridge 1795, BA1799, dn99 (Nor.), p01 (Nor.), MA1802. V. Leire, Leics. 1808 and R. Clowne (o/w Heath), Derbys. 1822 to death. Chap. to HRH Duke of York 1806. Died 29/3/1833 (CCEd says 26/7/1833), aged 55 [C19167] Married Hackney, London 15/5/1805 Sophia Read (of Silsoe). Brother above.

PAWSON (George) From Essex, s. Rev. George Pawson. Peterhouse, Cambridge 1788 (aged 18), BA1792, dn93 (London), p94 (London). V. Mettingham, Suffolk 1805-24 (res.), R. Little Tey, Essex 1805 to death 3/12/1853 aged 83 [C114363]

PAYLER (Anthony Charles) Born Ashford, Kent, s. Thomas Payler. Merton, Oxford 1806 (aged 17), BA1810, dn11 (Cant.), p12 (Salis. for Cant.), MA1818. V. Headcorn, Kent 1822-36, R. Chiddingstone St Mary, Kent 1836 to death 28/1/1852 [C89054]

PAYN (Philip/Philippe) Born St Lawrence, Jersey 31/12/1797, s. Philippe Payn and Mary Guillaume. Literate: dn21 (Win.), p22 (Win.). R. Jersey St Ouen, Channel Islands 1826 to death 25/3/1860, leaving under £50 [C82554] Married St Saviour, Jersey 27/10/1829 Jane Le Geyt (w), and had issue,

PAYNE (Coventry, Sir, 5thBart.) Born Tempsford, Beds. 31/8/1794, s. Sir John Payne, 4th Bart. and Mary Monoux (dau. of a baronet). Trinity Hall, Cambridge 1812, dn19 (Salis. for Win.), LLB1820, p20 (Chester for Glos.). V. Hatfield Peverell, Essex 1823 and V. Munden, Essex 1830 to death. Dom. Chap. to 3rd Baron Ongley 1830. Died 28/11/1849 [C82556] Married Marylebone, London 27/5/1820 Henrietta Wright (of Hatfield Priory, Essex), and had s. of same name. Succ. to title 1841 (although *Gentleman's Magazine* said his claims to the baronetcy were spurious).

PAYNE (Edward René) Born Knighton House, Chichester 25/3/1778, s. Edward Payne and Mary Baker. Queens', Cambridge 1797, then King's 1797, Fellow 1800-19, dn01 (Lin.), BA 1802, p02 (Nor.), MA1805, etc. R. Hepworth, Norfolk 1819 to death 21/12/1850 [C72132] Married Ixworth, Suffolk 2/1/1802 Frances Boldero, with clerical son Charles Richard Payne.

PAYNTER (Charles Henry) Born St Columb Minor, Cornwall 20/1/1790, s. Francis Paynter and Margaret Pender. Jesus, Cambridge 1808, BA1812, dn13 (Ex.), p15 (Ex.). PC. St Columb Minor (including Newquay) 1817-38 and PC. Crantock, Cornwall 1817. Died Jersey 31/12/1838 [C146039] Married St Columb 19/9/1818 Fanny Peter, and had issue.

PAYNTER (Samuel) Born Camberwell, London 12/4/1801, s. Francis Paynter and Sarah Whitbourne. St John's, Cambridge 1819, then Trinity 1821 [adm. Lincoln's Inn 1823] BA1823, dn24 (Lin. for Glos.), p26 (Glos.), MA 1827. R. Hatford, Berks. 1825-32, R. Stoke next Guildford, Surrey 1831-58. Resident in Nice 1884; and in London at death. Died 23/1/1893 aged 91, leaving £110,227-14s-7d. [C74364] Married Richmond, Surrey 18/10/1826 his cousin Eliza Paynter, w. clerical son Francis Paynter.

PEACH (Henry) Bapt. Derby 25/5/1754, s. Henry (of Langley Hall, Derbys.) and Dorothy Peach. St John's, Oxford 1772, BA1776, dn77 (Ox.), p79 (C&L). PC. Boulton, Derbys. 1809 to death 9/2/1833 aged 78 [C19170]

PEACH (William) Bapt. Derby 6/1/1796, s. Rev. Henry (PC. Langley, Derbys.) and Mary Peach. St John's, Cambridge 1814, BA1818, Fellow 1820-3, dn20 (Ely), p21 (Ely), MA1821. PC. Brampton, Derbys. 1826 (and RD of Brampton 1836) to death 31/1/1867 aged 71, leaving £7,000 [C19171. Boase] Married Morcott, Rutland 21/12/1822 Mary Ann Pochin (a clergy dau.), w. issue.

PEACHEY (John) From Kirdford, Sussex, s. William Peachey and Ann Alcock. Peter-house, Cambridge 1812, BA1816, dn17 (London for Chich.). R. Alford, Surrey 1817-49, unbeneficed, living at Kirdford to death 14/1/1860 aged 76, leaving £4,000 [C64809] Married Godalming, Surrey 25/4/1816 Ann Hall Burnett, with issue.

PEACHEY (John William, Hon.) Born Middx. 10/12/1788, s. 2nd Baron Selsey and Hester Elizabeth Jennings. Emmanuel, Cambridge 1808, MA1811, dn12 (London). R. Barkway w. Reed >< Herts. 1813 and R. Treyford w. Didling, Sussex 1815 to death (unm.) 6/7/1837. Dom. Chap. to his father 1812 [C64810]

PEACOCK, *later* CUST (Daniel Mitford) Born Northallerton, Yorks. 8/5/1768, s. Rev. William Peacock (R. Danby Wiske, Yorks.) and Elizabeth Mitford. Trinity, Cambridge 1786 [adm. Inner Temple 1789] BA1791 [Senior Wrangler], dn91 (Chester), Fellow 1792, p92 (Nor. for Chester), MA1794. V. Sedbergh, Yorks. 1798-1840 and R. Stainton le Street (or Great Stainton), Durham 1812 to death. Dom. Chap. to 1st Baron Redesdale 1812. Died 10/7/1840 aged 72 [C114368] Married King's Lynn, Norfolk 13/8/1798 Catharine Edwards, with clerical son Mitford Peacock. J.P. Brother William, below.

PEACOCK (Edward) Born South Kyme, Lincs. 5/1/1787, s. Anthony Peacock and Mary Wilkinson. Trinity, Cambridge 1803, BA1808,

Fellow 1810, MA1811. V. Fifehead Magdalen, Dorset 1819 (and RD of Shaftes-bury) 1835 to death 14/2/1848 [C53532] Married (1) 9/9/1819 Anne Mansel (dau. of a Bishop of Bristol and Master of Trinity College, she d.1832), w. clerical s. Edward Peacock (2) Windsor, Berks. 23/11/1837 Maria Slingsby.

PEACOCK (George) Born Thornton Hall, Denton, Darlington, Yorks. 9/4/1791, s. Rev. Thomas Peacock and Jane Thompson. Trinity, Cambridge 1809, BA1813, Fellow 1814, MA 1816, dn19 (Bristol), p22 (Nor.), Tutor 1823-39, incorporated at Oxford 1830, DD1839, Lowndean Professor of Astronomy and Geometry, Cambridge 1837-58. V. Wymeswold, Leics. 1826-35 (res.), Dean of Ely (where he restored the Cathedral fabric, and improved the health of the city) 1838 to death (London) 8/11/1858, leaving £10,000 [C53533. ODNB. Boase] Married Richmond, Surrey 20/10/1847 Frances Elizabeth Selwyn, s.p. F.R.S. (1818), F.R.A.S. (1820); member of the University Commission and of the Statutory Commissioners; a founder of the Analytical Society, and of the Cambridge Philosophical Society.

PEACOCK (Thomas) Born Murrah, Cumberland 6/1/1756, s. John Peacock and Margaret Railton. Literate: dn79 (Nor. for Chester), p80 (Lin. for Chester). PC. Denton, Gainford, Durham 1780-1835 (where he also kept a school), R. North Tuddenham, Norfolk 1846 to death 27/9/1851 aged 95 [C72365] Married (1) Denton 9/11/1781 Ann Hodgson, w. issue (2) Denton 2/5/1789 Jane Thompson, with further issue.

PEACOCK, *later* CUST (William) Bapt. Anderby Steeple, Northallerton, Yorks. 21/10/1763, s. Rev. William Peacock, sen. (R. Danby Wiske, Yorks.) and Elizabeth Mitford. St Catherine's, Cambridge 1783, BA1787, p88 (York for Chester), MA1790. PC. (succeeded his father as) R. (and patron) of Danby Wiske, 1811 to death (Danby Hall) 22/2/1840 aged 76 [C134772 and Venn and YCO under Peacock] J.P.; changed name 1817. Brother Daniel Mitford, above.

PEARCE (Henry) Bapt. Hereford 4/1/1795, s. John and Catherine Pearce. Christ Church, Oxford 1814, BA1817, p19 (Glos.), MA1820. Vicar-Choral, etc. in Hereford Cathedral 1818, V. Norton Canon, Heref. 1820, V. Yarkhill, Heref. 1822 to death 1/5/1849 [C159811]

PEARCE (Robert) Bapt. Hereford 24/5/1770, s. Thomas and Margaret Pearce. Christ Church, Oxford 1789, then St Alban Hall 1792, dn92 (Heref.), p94 (Heref.), MA1795. Vicar Choral in Hereford Cathedral 1792 (Custos 1840), V. Putley, Heref. 1795-6 (res.), R. Thruxton, Heref. 1796, V. Kington w. Huntington, Heref./Radnor 1796-1835 [ERC disagrees], V. Norton Canon, Heref. 1796-8, V. Marden w. Amberley, Heref. 1798-9, V. Allensore (w. Cleongher), Heref. 1799-1822, V. Stanford Bishop, Heref. 1808-50, V. Holmer w. Huntington, Heref. 1819 to death 16/2/1850 [C173133] Wife Mary.

PEARCE (Thomas) Born Lambeth, Surrey, s. Thomas Pearce. Corpus Christi, Oxford 1801 (aged 18), BA1805, dn05 (London for Cant.), then Exeter, MA1807, p07 (Cant.). V. Rickling, Essex 1808-10, V. Hartlip, Kent 1810-18, R. Hawkinge, Kent 1818-54, V. Folkestone, Kent 1818, R. Mareston, Kent 1818 to death. Dom. Chap. to 2nd Duke of St Albans 1819. Died (a widower) 5/9/1855 [C1444]

PEARCE (Thomas) Bapt. Holsworthy, Devon 21/18/1783, s. Thomas and Mary Pearce. Exeter, Oxford 1802, BA1807, dn07 (Ex.), p08 (Ex.). PC. St Sampson, Cornwall 1815-22, PC. Tywardreath, Cornwall 1820-[42], R. Roche, Cornwall 1841. Died Exeter 9/4/1874, leaving £1,000 [C146060 as Pearse]

PEARCE see also under **PEARSE**

PEARS (James) Born Oxford 23/10/1778, s. James Pears and Elizabeth Beale. New, Oxford 1795, then St Mary Hall, dn01 (Ox.), p02 (Ox.), BCL1810. R. Charlecombe, Som. 1823 (and S/M Bath G/S) to death 21/1/1853 [C21125] Married Lambeth, Surrey 1/11/1797 Mary Radcliffe, with titled military son.

PEARSE (George) Born Carlton Colville, Suffolk 23/5/1798, s. Charles Pearse (a farmer) and Mary Wiseman. Caius, Cambridge 1815, BA1820, dn21 (Nor.), p22 (Nor.), MA1831. Minor Canon of Norwich Cathedral 1830, V. Henley, Suffolk 1831, PC. Norwich St Saviour 1831, PC. Norwich St Martin at Oak 1831-50, V. Martham, Norfolk 1834-76. Died (Haberg-ham Eaves, Burnley, Lancs.) 5/9/1882 aged 84, leaving £4,951-18s-0d. [C1100] Married Hingham, Norfolk 30/6/1823 Laura Elizabeth Buck Matthews, with issue.

PEARSE (Samuel Winter) Born Cadleigh, Devon 11/12/1782, s. Samuel Winter Pearse and Grace Edwards. Exeter, Oxford 1800, BA 1804, dn06 (Ex.), p08 (Ex.). PC. Sampford Spiney w. Shaugh (Prior) >< Devon 1808 to death (Cadleigh) 3/8/1866 aged 83, leaving £4,000 [C146058] Married West Alvington, Devon 19/11/1819 Elizabeth Hele Ford, with issue.

PEARSE (Thomas) Born Bedford 6/12/1797, s. Rev. Theed Pearse and Susannah Rebecca Dickens. St John's, Cambridge 1815, BA1819, dn20 (Lin.), p22 (Lin.), MA1822. V. Westoning, Beds. 1823-91, V. Harlington, Beds. 1826-54. Dom. Chap. to Harriet, Viscountess Hampton 1826. Died 14/6/1891 aged 93, leaving £4,856-0s-2d. [C72378. Boase] Clerical sons John Thomas, and Arthur Henry Pearse.

PEARSE (William) Bapt. Offord D'arcy, Hunts. 12/12/1785, s. William and Elizabeth Pearse. Corpus Christi, Cambridge 1803, BA 1808, dn09 (Salis. for London), p10 (London), MA1811. PC. Stuston, Norfolk 1813 and R. Hanwell, Oxon. 1816 to death (Goodman-chester, Hunts.) 29/8/1861 aged 75 [C19174] Married Watton, Norfolk 1/8/1815 Sarah Shelford, w. clerical s. Vincent Pearse. 'Respectable - humdrum - no energy' (Wilberforce).

PEARSE see also **PEARCE**

PEARSON (Arthur) Bapt. London 2/9/1803, s. John Pearson (Bognor, Sussex) and Anne Broadhurst. Trinity, Cambridge, BA1827, dn27 (London), p27 (London), MA1832. R. Springfield Richards w. Boswell, Essex 1827 (w. RD of Chelmsford, Essex 1877) to death 24/9/1886, leaving £1,989-8s-10d. [C120975] Married (1) Chelmsford 11/2/1836 Sophia Jane Jepp (d.1843), with issue (2) Aylesbury, Bucks. 1846 (1st q.) Mary Isabella Tindal, with further issue. Brother John, below.

PEARSON (Charles Buchanan) Bapt. Elmdon, Warwicks. 15/7/1807, s. Rev. Hugh Nicholas Pearson (later Dean of Salisbury, below) and Sarah Maria Elliott. Oriel, Oxford 1825, BA1828, dn30 (Win.), p31 (Win.), MA 1831. R. Chiddingfold, Surrey (w. Master of St John the Baptist Hospital [almshouses], Wilton, Wilts.) 1831, Prebend of Fordington w. Wrightlington in Salisbury Cathedral 1832-81, R. Knebworth, Herts. 1838-74. Died Bath 7/1/1881 aged 70, leaving £14,000 [C82577. ODNB under his father. Boase] Married Salisbury Cathedral 30/4/1833 Harriet Elizabeth Pinkerton (w), with issue.

PEARSON (George) Born Lichfield 18/9/1791, s. Rev. John Batteridge Pearson and Elizabeth Falconer. Emmanuel, Cam-bridge 1809, BA1814, then St John's, dn14 (Chester), Fellow 1814-24, p15 (Chester), MA1817, BD1824, incorporated at Durham 1839. PC. Chester St Olave 1819-22, Minor Canon of Chester Cathedral 1822-5, R. Castle Camps, Cambs. 1825 (and RD of Camps) to death (Saffron Walden, Essex) 13/5/1860, leaving £25,000 [C109367. Boase] Married Chester 16/9/1825 Catherine Maria Humberston, with clerical son John Batteridge Pearson. Fine photo. online.

PEARSON (Henry) Born 2/1/1769, s. Henry Pearson (a Nottingham brass-founder) and Ann Hollingsworth. Jesus, Cambridge 1786, dn91 (Lin.), LLB1793, p93 (Lin.). V. (and patron) of Norton, Derbys. 1812-43, V. Prestbury, Cheshire 1854 to death 21/6/1858, leaving £1,500 [C19176] Married (1) Leicester 9/12/1794 Jane Arnold (d.1795) (2) 29/8/1798 Harriet Wilson, with clerical sons Henry Hollings-worth Pearson, and William Pearson.

PEARSON (Hugh Nicholas) Born Lymington, Hants. 2/12/1776, s. Hugh Pearson. St John's, Oxford 1796, BA1800, p02 (Win.), MA 1804, BD and DD1821. R. Sandford, Oxon. 1812-17, Chap. Brighton St James [Proprietary Chapel] 1817-22, V. Abingdon St Helen w. St Nicholas, Berks. 1822-3 (res.), Dean of Salisbury (w. Prebend of Heytesbury annexed) and Canon Residentiary 1823-46 (res.), R. Chiddingford, Surrey 1826-31 (res.), R. Guildford St Nicholas, Surrey 1832-7. Chap. to Prince of Wales when in Brighton. Died Sonning, Berks. 17/11/1856 [C64813. ODNB. Boase. DEB] Married Brighton 13/9/1803 Sarah Maria Elliott, w. clerical sons Henry Pearson, Charles Buchanan Pearson (above), and William Henley Pearson-Jervis. Surrogate 1825.

PEARSON (John) Bapt. Farndon, Notts. 26/10/1783, s. Samuel and Mary Pearson. Literate: dn13 (York), p18 (Lin.). V. Osbournby, Lincs. 1826 to death 7/7/1863, leaving £3,000 [C72381. YCO. Bennett1] Wife Elizabeth, w. issue.

PEARSON (John) Born London, s. John Pearson (Bognor, Sussex) and Anne Broadhurst. Trinity, Cambridge 1823 (aged 18) [adm. Lincoln's Inn 1827] BA1827, dn29 (Chich.), p30 (Chich.), MA1832. R. (and patron) of East Horndon, Essex 1831-73, R. (and patron) of Little Warley, Essex 1837 (and RD of Billericay 1845). Died Eastbourne, Sussex 27/8/1882 aged 76, leaving £515-6s-8d. [C64815] Married South Bersted, Sussex 21/2/1832 Frances Harriet Brown, with issue. Brother Arthur, above.

PEARSON (Joseph) Born Whitbeck, Cumberland, s. William Pearson (a farmer 'of good, old yeoman family') and Hannah Ponsonby. Literate: dn96 (Car.), p97 (Car.), MA in *Gentleman's Magazine*. PC. Camerton, Cumberland 1797 to death ('whilst engagaged in the Communion Service') 6/6/1841, leaving £450 (probate granted 30/5/1860) [C3469. Platt] Married Workington, Cumberland 25/12/1799 Nancy Osborne, with issue.

PEARSON (Robert) Born Torpenhow, Cumberland, s. Robert Pearson. Queen's, Oxford 1814 (aged 18), BA1819, dn20 (Car.), p22 (Car.). V. Newton Reigny, Cumberland 1832-43, R. Great Orton, Cumberland 1845 to death 20/8/1857 [C5732. Platt] Married Rufford, Lancs. 22/11/1813 Margaret Abram, w. issue (all b. Rufford, where he was curate *c*.1825 - Platt).

PEARSON (Thomas) Bapt. Bampton, Westmorland 16/9/1758, s. John and Mary Pearson. Literate: dn82 (Car.), p83 (Car.). V. Bampton 1802 to death 10/12/1833 (CCEd says 13/4/1834) aged 75 [C5734. Platt] Widow Frances (married before 1784), with issue.

PEARSON (Thomas) Bapt. Kirkby Stephen, Westmorland 5/10/1760, s. John Pearson [*pleb*.]. Queen's, Oxford 1780, BA 1784, dn87 (Ox.), Fellow 1788, MA1788, p88 (Ox.), BD1797. V. Sparsholt, Berks. 1803-41. Died 17/2/1841 [C28860] Clerical son Thomas (not here).

PEARSON (Thomas) [NiVoF] R. Stockton (on Terne), Worcs. 1808, V. Great Witley, Worcs. 1828-57. Probate granted 14/4/1857. Chap. to Dowager Queen Adelaide (then living at Witley Court) [ERC links. C110689 has university and ordination dates mixed with another of the same name. Foster is similarly confused].

PEARSON (William) Bapt. Muncaster, Cumberland 25/8/1763, s. William Pearson. Literate: dn88 (Chester), p89 (Chester). PC. Broughton in Furness (or Broughton West Chapel in Kirkby Ireleth), Lancs. 1794-1835. Died there 23/5/1843 aged 79 [C170195] Married Sarah Brockbank, with issue.

PEARSON (William) Born Whitbeck, Cumberland 23/4/1767, s. William Pearson (a farmer 'of good, old yeoman family') and Hannah Ponsonby. Clare, Cambridge 1793 (did not reside), no degree, Hon. LLD Glasgow 1819. PC. Killington, Westmorland 1799-1801, R. Perivale, Middx. 1810-12. Owner of a large private school at Temple Grove, East Sheen, Surrey in 1812-21(where he established an observatory). R. (South) Kilworth, Leics. 1817 to death there 6/9/1847 [C72383. ODNB. S. J. Gurman and S. R. Harratt, 'Revd Dr William Pearson (1767-1847): a founder of the Royal Astronomical Society', *Quarterly J. of the Royal Astronomical Society*, 35 (1994), 271-292] Married (1) East Retford, Notts. 22/2/1796 Frances Low (d.1831), 1 dau. (2) *c*.1833 Mrs Eliza Sarah ?Hunter. Brother Joseph (above). An important astronomer and constructor of astronomical instruments; F.R.S. (1819); a founder of the Royal Astronomical Society (1820); J.P. adsabs.harvard.edu/full/1994QJRAS..35..271G

PEASE (George) Born Hull 30/6/1796 (into a Presbyterian Congregation), s. Joseph Robinson Pease (a banker who had assumed the surname of Pease in 1773) and Anne Twigge. St John's, Cambridge 1814, BA 1819, dn21 (York), MA 1822, p23 (York). V. Darrington, Yorks. 1831 to death (Bridlington Quay, Yorks.) 23/10/1876 aged 80, leaving £7,000 [C19185. YCO] Married Leamington, Warwicks. 14/4/1831 Jane Swinfen, with issue.

PEAT (Robert, Sir) Bapt. Darlington, Co. Durham 2/11/1770, s. John Peat (a watchmaker and silversmith) and Anne Heron. Literate: dn93 (Lin. for York), p94 (Lin.), then Trinity, Cambridge 1795 (as Patt), a Ten Year Man, DD1799 Glasgow. PC. Buxton, Derbys. 1797-1808, PC. Chelmorton, Derbys. 1798-1815, R. Ashley and Sylverley w. Kirtling, Cambs. 1803-5 (res.), PC. New Brentford, Middx. 1808 to death. Chap. in Ordinary to George 1V. Died 20/4/1837 aged 65 [C21462. YCO] Married Houghton-le-Spring, Co. Durham 6/11/1815 Jane Smith, 'an elderly (and Catholic) maiden lady of large property in

Durham', but from whom he lived apart. His masonic library sold June 1837. The Order of St Stanislaus conferred on him (then a layman) by the King of Poland 1790, *q.v.* the intriguing article about this extraordinary man at: https://en.wikipedia.org/wiki/Robert_Peat

PECHELL (Horace Robert) Born Marylebone, London 12/5/1792, s. Augustus Pechell ('Receiver General of the Customs') and Sarah Drake. Christ Church, Oxford 1810, BA1814, then All Souls, Fellow 1814-26, dn15 (Ox.), p17 (Ox.), MA 1817. R. Nettleden, Oxon. 1820-22, R. Bix (o/w Bixband), Oxon. 1822-72, Chancellor and Canon of Llanbister in Brecon Collegiate Church 1829 to death (Moorlands Bitterne, Southampton) 22/2/1882 aged 89, leaving £115,372-15s-6d. [C21129. Boase] Married 29/7/1826 Caroline Mary (dau. Vice-Adm. Lord Mark Robert Kerr), with naval issue.

PECK (Edward Martin) Born 1/9/1779 (bapt. Hemingford Abbots, Hunts.), s. Walter and Ann Peck. St John's, Cambridge 1798, BA1802, dn02 (Lin.), p04 (Ely), MA1805. R. Coveney, Cambs. 1804 and R. Houghton w. Wyton, Hunts. (and Preacher throughout the Diocese of Lincoln) 1811 to death. Dom. Chap. to 3rd Baron Rokeby 1811. Died 9/8/1847 aged 67 [C72388] Married 27/9/1813 Margaret Ansley (London), w. clerical son Edward Ansley Peck.

PEDDER (James) Born Garstang, Lancs. 13/7/1796, s. Rev. John Pedder (below) and Isabella Fletcher. Christ's, Cambridge 1815, BA1819, dn19 (Chester), p21 (Chester), MA 1829. PC. Garstang All Saints 1822-35, (succ. his father as) V. Garstang St Hilda 1835 to death 13/12/1855 (but there are alternative death dates) [C170196] Married Garstang 8/1/1828 Elizabeth Greenhalgh, Myerscough Hall, Garstang.

PEDDER (John) Born Garstang, Lancs. 12/12/1767, s. Rev. James Pedder. Trinity, Cambridge 1787, BA1791, dn91 (Roch. for Ely), p92 (Ely), MA1794. V. Garstang St Hilda 1794 to death 6/5/1834 (CCEd says 27/7/1835). Dom. Chap. to 3rd Earl of Harrington 1815 [C2053] Married (1) Lancaster 23/4/1795 Isabella Fletcher, with clerical son (above) (2) Ulverston, Lancs. 8/4/1801 Elizabeth Taylor (of Stott Park, Finsthwaite, Lancs.), with further issue.

PEDDER (William Newland) Bapt. Andover, Hants. 21/3/1796, s. Rev. William Pedder and Sophia Newland. Worcester, Oxford 1814, BA 1818, Fellow 1818-31, dn18 (Heref. for Win.) p20 (London for Win.), MA1821. V. Clevedon, Som. 1830 to death 15/6/1871, leaving £1,500 [C40211] Married Kingsclere, Hants. 14/4/1831 Caroline Elizabeth Cotes (w), with issue.

PEDDLE (John) Born Yeovil, Som., s. Henry Peddle. St Mary Hall, Oxford 1771 (aged 19), dn73 (London), p77 (Salis.), BCL1778. Chap. *R.N.*; V. Charlton Horethorne, Som. 1784 to death 1842 (2nd q.) 'at an advanced age' [C47657] Eccentric - lived totally alone - amassed considerable wealth, etc.

PEEL (Frederic) Born Ardwick, Manchester 24/11/1780 (bapt. 6/1/1790), s. Lawrence Peel and Alice Haworth. Trinity, Cambridge 1806, BA1811, dn12 (York), MA1814, p14 (York). R. Willingham by Stowe, Lincs. 1827-54, V. Coates, Lincs. 1832-48, Prebend of Lincoln Cathedral 1855 to death (Escrick, Yorks.) 21/8/1860 aged 70, leaving £25,000 [C72396. YCO. Kaye] Married Bury, Lancs. 29/12/1812 Susannah Howarth, with issue.

PEEL (Giles Haworth) Bapt. Accrington, Lancs. 20/8/1778, s. Jonathan Peel ('an extensive manufacturer') and Ann Haworth. Pembroke, Oxford 1801, no degree, dn03 (Chester), p04 (Chester). PC. Ince, Cheshire 1820-[52]. Died Wycombe, Bucks. 23/12/1854 [C170198] Married Oxford 18/12/1804 Maria Halse, with issue.

PEEL (John) Born Bury, Lancs. 22/8/1798, s. Sir Robert Peel, 1st Bart. (and thus brother of the Prime Minister of the same surname) and Ellen Yates. Christ Church, Oxford 1817, BA 1822, dn22 (Llandaff), p25 Llandaff), MA 1828, BD and DD1845. V. Stone, Worcs. 1828, Canon of 7th Prebend in Canterbury Cathedral 1828-45, Dean of Worcester 1845-74 [total income in CR65 £2,010]. Died Waresley, Worcs. 20/2/1875, leaving £180,000 [C4406. Boase] Married Weeford, Staffs. 6/5/1824 Augusta Swinfen (of Swinfen House), w. clerical son Herbert Richard Peel.

PEERS (John) From Morden, Surrey, s. Rev. John Witherington Peers. Magdalene, Cambridge 1789 (aged 17), BA1793, dn84 (Salis.), MA1796. PC. Lane End, Bucks. 1832 to death 23/2/1855; living at Shenley, Herts. [C82589]

Married (2?) Wife Lucy in 1841, w. clerical sons Charles, and John Witherington Peers (not below, but doubtless related).

PEERS (John Witherington) Born Bromley, Kent 23/9/1745, s. Charles Peers and Katherine Knapp. Merton, Oxford 1766, BA1767, dn68 (Ox.), p69 (Ox.), MA 1770, DCL1778. Chap. of the Donative of Chiselhampton, Oxon. 1769, R. Ickleford cum Pirton, Herts. 1773-1835, R. Morden, Surrey 1778-1835, Chap. Stadhampton (o/w Stodham), Oxon. 1790? to death 29/4/1835 (CCEd says 13/5/1835) [C21133] Married Horsleydown, London 9/2/1767 Ann Bird, with clerical son of father's name. Family group port. online.

PEGLAR (John) Bapt. King's Norton, Worcs. 20/7/1783, s. John and Nancy Peglar. Worcester, Oxford 1802, BA1805, dn06 (C&L), p07 (C&L), MA1808. PC. Bishopston, Warwicks. 1822, PC. Shareshill, Staffs. 1822-[25], V. Alveston, Warwicks. 1846 to death (Stratford on Avon, Warwicks.) 23/4/1856 [C19190] Married Stratford on Avon 7/10/1824 Mary Davenport, with issue.

PEILE (Thomas Williamson) Born Whitehaven, Cumberland 10/11/1806, s. John Peile, J.P., and Betsy Williamson. Trinity, Cambridge 1823, BA1828 [S/M Shrewsbury School 1828-9] Fellow 1829-31, dn29 (Chester), p30 (Chester), MA1831, Tutor Durham Univ. 1834-41, DD 1843. Min. 1831 then PC. Liverpool St Catherine's 1834 (res.) (with H/M Liverpool Collegiate School 1829-33), PC. Croxdale, Durham 1836-41, H/M Repton School 1841-54, V. Luton, Beds. 1857-60, V. St Paul, St John's Wood, London 1860-73 (res.). Chap. to Lord Westmoreland 1831. Died St John's Wood 29/11/1882 aged 76, leaving £29,546-17s-6d. [C170201. ODNB. Boase] Married Whitehaven 26/1/1831 Mary Braithwaite, with clerical s. Arthur Lewis Babington Peile.

PELLEW (Edward, Hon.) Born 3/11/1799, s. Edward Pellew, 1st Viscount Exmouth and Susannah Frowde. Oriel, Oxford 1818, BA1823, dn24 (Bristol), MA 1824, p24 (Bristol). V. Nazeing, Essex 1820, PC. (Great) Yarmouth St Nicholas, Norfolk 1831, PC. Bury St Edmunds St James, Suffolk 1845-65. Died (Mansfield, Notts.) 29/8/1869 aged 69, leaving £35,000 [C1101] Married 10/4/1826 Marianne Winthrop, with clerical son George Israel Pellew. Brother below.

PELLEW (George, Hon.) Born Flushing, Cornwall 3/4/1793, s. Edward Pellew, 1st Viscount Exmouth and Susannah Frowde. Corpus Christi, Oxford 1812, BA1815, dn16 (Salis.), MA1818, BD and DD1828. V. Nazeing, Essex 1819-20, V. Sutton on the Forest (o/w Sutton Galtries), Yorks. 1820-4 (res.), Canon of 7th Prebend in Canterbury Cathedral 1822-8 (res.), Prebend of Osbald-wick in York Minster 1824-8, R. Canterbury St George the Martyr w. St Mary Magdalen 1826-8, Prebend of Wistow in York Minster 1828-52 (res.), R. St Dionis Backchurch, City of London 1828-52, Dean of Norwich 1828 (w. R. Great Chart, Kent 1852) to death 13/10/1866 aged 73, leaving £30,000 [C1102. Boase] Married 20/6/1820 Hon. Frances Addington (dau. 1st Viscount Sidmouth) (w). Brother above.

PELLY (Francis) Born Upton, Essex 24/12/1780. s. Henry Hinde Pelly and Sally Hitchin Blake. Christ Church, Oxford 1799, BA1802, dn04 (Lin.), p05 (Lin.), MA1810. R. Syston, Glos. 1806-44, R. Weston-sub-Edge, Glos. 1810-15. Died (Keynsham, Som.) 3/7/1844 [C72403] Married (1) Birmingham 30/10/1806 Mary Nutt (d.1810) (2) Birmingham 16/2/1813 Mary Ann Richards.

PEMBERTON (Jeremy) Bapt. Belchamp St Paul, Essex 25/11/1785, s. Rev. Jeremy Pemberton, sen. and Ursula Ewer. Peterhouse, Cammidge 1802, dn08 (Salis. for Ely), BA1808, dn08 (Ely), p09 (Ely), MA1811. R. Foxearth 1810-45. In 1851 an 'unemployed clergyman'. Died London 1/12/1864, leaving £25,000 [C89073] Married Bedford 9 or 27/10/1827 Margaretta Cave Raymond (a clergy dau.).

PEMBERTON (Robert Norgrave) Born Shrewsbury, Shropshire 7/8/1791, s. Robert Pemberton and Sarah Lloyd. Christ Church, Oxford 1809, BA1814, MA1816, p16 (Heref.). PC. Ford, Shropshire 1817-19, R. Church Stretton w. All Stretton and Little Stretton, Shropshire 1818 and Canon of Hereford Cathedral to death (at his seat Millichope Park in the parish) 11/10/1848 [C173153] Married Marylebone, London 11/11/1820 Caroline Pechell.

PENFOLD (George Saxby) Bapt. Epsom, Surrey 27/11/1769, s. Hugh Penfold and

Susannah Saxby. Merton, Oxford 1788, BA 1792, dn92 (C&L for Salis.), p96 (Salis.), MA 1814, BD and DD 1825. R. Pulham, Dorset 1797-1832, V. Goring-by-Sea, Sussex 1815-32 (res.), (first) R. Marylebone Christ Church, London 1825, R. Marylebone Holy Trinity, London 1828, R. Kingswinford, Shropshire 1831 to death (Marylebone) 13/10/1846 [C19192] Married Westminster 12/9/1792 Sarah Fleming.

PENFOLD (John) Born Steyning, Sussex 1/7/1764, s. Richard Penfold and Charity Marchant. St Alban Hall, Oxford 1788, dn91 (London), p92 (London), BA and MA1798. V. Steyning 1792 and V. Pyecombe, Sussex 1808 to death. Chap. to HRH Duke of Sussex 1808. Died 30/4/1840 [C64838] Married Steyning 4/10/1792 Charlotte Jane Brooks, with issue. Port. online.

PENNANT (Thomas) Born Downing Hall, Whitford, Flint. 30/8/1780, s. Thomas Pennant (the naturalist and traveller, *q.v.* ODNB) and Ann Mostyn. Christ Church, Oxford 1797, BA 1801, MA1804, then All Souls, Fellow 1805-18, p09 (Ox.), BD1814. V. New Romney, Kent 1811-17, R. Weston Turville, Bucks. 1817 and R. Leckhamstead, Bucks. 1831 to death 4/12/1845, *s.p.* [C21134] Married (1) Hawarden, Flint 5/1/1819 Caroline Griffith (2) St George's Hanover Square, London 4/5/1837 Emma Clarke.

PENNINGTON (George) Born South Morton, Berks. 5/12/1758, s. Rev. William and Mary Pennington. St Alban Hall, Oxford 1776, dn81 (Lin.). V. Bassingbourn, Cambs. 1801 to death 21/12/1832 (CCEd says 9/3/1833) [C72421]

PENNINGTON (John) Possibly bapt. Finsthwaite, Lancs. 1/2/1770, s. William and Agnes Pennington. Literate: dn92 (Chester), p94 (Chester). (first) PC. Lowton, Winwick, Lancs. 1806 to burial (a widower) 19/1/1853 aged 83 [C170204] Wife Sarah, and issue.

PENNINGTON (Montague) Bapt. Great Mongeham, Kent 3/1/1764, s. Rev. Thomas Pennington and Margaret Carter (a clergy dau., and sister of Elizabeth Carter, the famous bluestocking, after whose friend, the equally famous Mrs Elizabeth Montague, he was named). Trinity, Oxford 1777, BA1781, MA 1784, dn85 (Cant.), p86 (Lin. for Cant.). PC. Sutton by Dover, Kent 1789-1835, V. Westwell, Kent 1803-6, V. Northbourne, Kent 1806, PC. (Lower) Deal St George, Kent 1814 to death 15/4/1849. Dom. Chap. to 3rd Earl of Hopetoun 1786; to 4th Earl of Hopetoun 1816 [C72424. ODNB as editor & biographer] Married Deal, Kent 23/1/1804 Mrs Mary Watts (d.1830), *s.p.* Brother below.

PENNINGTON (Thomas) Born Deal, Kent 16/2/1761, s. Rev. Thomas Penning-ton, sen. and Margaret Carter (a clergy dau. and sister of the famous bluestocking Elizabeth Carter). Trinity, Cambridge 1775, BA1780, then Clare, Fellow, MA1783, dn83 (Ely), p85 (Cant.). (succ. his father as) R. (and patron) of Kingsdown, Kent 1786 [C107368] and R. Thorley, Herts. 1798 [C72425] to death. Dom. Chap. to 4th Earl Waldegrave 1785; to the Countess of Bath; and to Lord Chief Justice Ellenborough. Died Pimlico, London 21/12/1853 aged 91 [C108368] Married 13/2/1789 Mary Sarah Sale, with one surviving dau. Excellent online entry followed here rather than CCEd]. The 'much travelled' Mr Penning-ton (author of a European travelogue) is described by Elizabeth Grant in her *Memoirs of a Highland Lady* (1806) 'as tall and thin and clever in an odd sort of way. They lived, this dreamy old clergyman, his managing wife, and spoilt child, in a parsonage standing in one of the shady lanes leading up to the church. The line of the front wall of the house was the line of the hedge that stretched on either side. The entrance was into the parlour without any passage or hall. The house was like a curiosity shop with a microscope that good Mr Penning-ton was ever ready to let us peep into'. Brother above.

PENNY (Benjamin) Born Liverpool 11/6/1775, s. James Penny and Ann Cooper. BNC, Oxford 1798, dn03 (Chester), BCL and DCL1834. R. Heswall, Cheshire 1807-39, then 'no cure of souls.' Died Chester 28/11/1857 [C170206] Married 1809 Jane Margarita Williams, of Cardigan. *J.P.* Chershire.

PENRICE (Charles) Bapt. Great Yarmouth, Norfolk 24/9/1791, s. Thomas Penrice (surgeon) and Harriet Waite. St John's, Cambridge 1809, BA1813, dn14 (Nor.), p15 (Nor.), MA1816. R. Hampnett w. Stowell, Glos. 1815-18 (res.), R. Small-burgh, Norfolk 1818-53, R. (and patron) of Little Plumstead w. Witton, Norfolk 1821 and V. Neatishead, Norfolk 1848 to death 7/11/1853 aged 63 [C114380]

PENROSE (John) Born Cardinham, Cornwall 15/12/1778, s. Rev. John Penrose, sen. (R. Bracebridge, Lincs.) and Jane Trevenen. Exeter, Oxford 1795, then Corpus Christi 1795, BA 1799, dn01 (Ex.), MA1802, p02 (Lin.).V. Langton by Wragby, Lincs. 1802-59, V. Poundstock, Cornwall 1804-9, V. Bracebridge, Lincs. 1809-38, PC. North Hykeham, Lincs. 1837 to death. Dom. Chap. to 2nd Earl Manvers 1809. Died 9/8/1859, leaving £6,000 [C72430. Boase] Married 6/5/1814 Elizabeth Cartwright (children's writer *aka* 'Mrs Markham', a clergy dau.), with clerical son Charles Thomas Penrose. Brother Thomas Trevenen, below.

PENROSE (Thomas) Born Newbury, Berks., s. Rev. Thomas Penrose, sen. New, Oxford 1788 (aged 18), Fellow 1788-1815, dn92 (Salis.), p94 (Ox.), BCL1803, DCL 1818. R. Hampstead Marshall, Berks. 1809-11, R. Writtle cum Roxwell, Essex 1814 to death. Chap. in Ordinary 1815; Chap. and Secretary to the British Embassy at Florence. Died 8/2/1851, living at Shaw Place (now House), Berks. [C28909. Boase]

PENROSE (Thomas Trevenen) Born Constantine, Cornwall 6/5/1793, s. Rev. John Penrose (R. Bracebridge, Lincs.) and Jane Trevenen. Corpus Christi, Oxford 1811, BA 1815, then Exeter, Fellow 1815-24, dn17 (Ox.), p19 (Ox.), MA1819. V. Radcliffe upon Trent, Notts. 1827-30, V. Coleby, Lincs. 1828-62, R. Fledborough, Notts. 1830-34, Prebend of Bedford Minor in Lincoln Cathedral 1834 and R. Weston, Notts. 1834 to death (Coleby) 5/7/1862, leaving £9,000 [C21135. Boase] Married East Retford, Notts. 7/9/1824 Susanna Mary Brooke, w. issue. Brother John, above.

PENSON (John) Born Oxford, s. John Penson. Christ Church, Oxford 1787 (aged 17), BA1791, Chap. Christ Church 1793-1806, p93 (Ox.), MA1795. R. Oxford St Peter le Bailey 1800-56, V. Brize Norton, Oxon. 1805 to death 10/7/1858, leaving £2,000 [C21136] Widow Elizabeth, and issue.

PENSON (Peter) Born Oxford, s. of Robert Penson (a gardener: *pleb*). New, Oxford 1804 (aged 16), then Magdalen 1807-12, BA1808, MA 1811, dn11 (Salis.), p12 (Ox.), Chap. New 1812-15, and of Christ Church 1812-16. Minor Canon (and Precentor) of Durham Cathedral 1815-31-. V. Durham St Oswald 1819-48. Died Cambridge 18/3/1870 aged 82, leaving £2,000 [C21138] Married Barnes, Surrey 1822 Louisa Elizabeth Barley, with issue. In 1848 he was tried in York for 'irreverent and immoral conduct by committing a lewd and indecent assault upon the person of William Oliver in the parish church of St Oswald.'

PENTON (Thomas) Bapt. Bath Abbey 4/3/1775, s. Rev. Thomas Penton and Dorothy Gulston. Pembroke, Oxford 1820 (aged 17), BA1825. V. (East and West) Wellow, Som. 1802, V. Nether (Lower) Wallop, Hants. 1806, Chap. of Donative of North Baddesley, Hants. 1824. Died 6/7/1834 (CCEd thus) [C82582 is confused with son of same name] Married South Stoneham, Hants. 4/3/1799 Margaret Delicia Stewart, with clerical son, also Thomas, in Wellow.

PEPPER (John) Bapt. Nottingham 11/7/1769, s. John and Ann Pepper. Jesus, Cambridge 1787, BA1792, dn92 (Car. for York), p93 (Car. for York). V. Alfreton, Derbys. 1817 to death 9/12/1850 aged 81 [C123956. YCO]

PEPYS (Henry, *later* Bishop of Sodor & Man, *then of* Worcester) Born 18/4/1783, s. Sir William Weller Pepys, 1st Bart. and Elizabeth Dowdeswell (dau. of a Chancellor of the Exchequer). Trinity, Cambridge 1800, BA1804, then St John's, Fellow 1806-23, MA1807, dn07 (Lin. for Ely), p08 (Ely), BD1814, DD 1840. R. Aspenden, Herts. 1818-27, R. Moreton, Essex 1822-40, Prebend of Barton St. David in Wells Cathedral 1826-40, R. Westmill, Herts. 1827-40, Bishop of Sodor and Man 1840-1, a popular Bishop of Worcester 1841 to death (Hartlebury Castle, Stourport, Worcs.) 13/11/1860, leaving £50,000 [as Henry Worcester] [C40214. ODNB. Boase. Gelling] Married Marylebone, London 27/1/1824 Maria (dau. of Rt. Hon. John Sullivan), w. issue, incl. a dau. Emily who left *The journal of Emily Pepys* (1984), the introd. by Gillian Avery suggests he was 'rather a secular bishop, who in these days would probably not have entered the church at all'. Younger brother of 1st Earl of Cottonham. Fine port. online.

PERCEVAL (Arthur Philip, Hon.) Born 22/11/1799, s. Charles George Perceval, 2nd Baron Arden and Margaretta Elizabeth Wilson (dau. of a baronet). Oriel, Oxford 1817, BA 1820, All Souls, Fellow 1821-5, dn22 (Ox.), p23 (Ox.), BCL1824. R. East Horsley, Surrey 1824 to death. Chap. in Ordinary 1826-53. Died 11/6/1853 ('after taking laudanum: verdict temporary insanity' - implying *suicide*?). [C21140. ODNB. Boase] Married 15/12/1825 Charlotte Anne Legge (dau. of a titled clergyman), with issue. Key figure in the Oxford Movement. Brother below.

PERCEVAL (Charles George, Hon.) Born 25/12/1796, s. Charles George Perceval, 2nd Baron Arden and Margaretta Elizabeth Wilson. Christ Church, Oxford 1815, no degree, dn20 (Lin.), p20 (Lin.). R. Calverton, Bucks. 1820 to death 26/7/1858 aged 61, leaving £35,000 [C72435] Married (1) Shenley, Bucks. 21/4/1829 Mary Knapp (a clergy dau., d.1832), w. issue (2) Welling-ton, Somerset 13/9/1842 Frances Agnes Trevelyan (a clergy dau.), with son the 7th Earl of Egmont. Brother above.

PERCEVAL (Henry) Born Hampstead, London 2/8/1799, s. Spencer Perceval (the assassinated Prime Minister) and Jane Wilson. BNC, Oxford 1817, BA1820, dn22 (Heref.), p23, MA1823. R. Charlton next Woolwich, Kent 1825-6, V. West Hoathley, Sussex 1825-7, R. Washington, Durham 1826-37, R. Elmley Lovett, Worcs. 1837-83. Dom. Chap. to Bishop of Chester 1825. Died Salwarpe, Worcs. 1/4/1885 aged 85, leaving £63,324-16s-3d. [C7011] Married Westminster, London 27/3/1826 Catherine Isabella Drummond (of the Drummond's Bank family), with issue.

PERCIVAL (Thomas Cozens) Born Manchester 18/3/1797, s. Rev. Thomas Basnet Percival and Henrietta Cozens. Christ Church, Oxford 1815, BA1819, MA 1821, dn21 (Ox.), p23 (Ox.). R. Horseheath, Cambs. 1825, Prebend of Dunham in Southwell Minster 1829, R. Little Gransden, Cambs. 1829-31 (res.), R. Bamborough, Yorks. 1848 to death (Leeds, a bachelor) 19/7/1863, leaving £7,000 [C21141]

PERCY (Hugh, Bishop of Rochester, *then* of Carlisle) Born London 29/1/1784 (a twin), s. Algernon Percy, 1st Earl of Beverley and Isabella Susannah Burrel. St John's, Cambridge 1802, MA1805, dn07 (Cant.), p08 (Cant.), DD 1825, admitted Oxford 1834. Chap. to Archbishop of Canterbury 1808, V. Bishops-bourne, Kent (1808-9) and Ivychurch, Kent 1809-22, Chancellor and Prebendand Canon Residentiary of Exeter 1810-16, Chancellor of Salisbury w. Brixworth Prebend 1811, Canon of 2nd Prebend in Canterbury 1816-25, Finsbury Prebend in St Paul's Cathedral 1816 to death (total income here £6,000), Archdeacon of Canterbury 1822-5, Dean of Canterbury 1825-7. Bishop of Rochester June to Sept. 1827, then Bishop of Carlisle 1827 to death. Master of St Nicholas Hospital [almshouses] Horbledown 1822 and of St John's Hospital [almshouses], Kent 1822-5. Died Rose Castle, Carlisle (on which he spent £40,000) 5/2/1856 [C1446. ODNB. Boase] Married (1) Lambeth, Surrey 19/5/1806 Mary (dau. of Charles Manner-Sutton, Archbishop of Canterbury, she d.1831), 3s., 8 dau. (1) London 3/2/1840 Mary Hope-Johnstone (dau. of a baronet).

PERIGAL (Charles) Bapt. St Bartholomew's, Bishopsgate, London 1777, s. of Jean Perigal (a silkman) and Susanne Bouyer (a clergy dau.). Peterhouse, Cambridge 1796, BA 1800, dn00 (Lin.), p01 (Lin.), MA 1803. V. Ellingham, Northumberland 1803 to death 7/12/1854 aged 79 [C72439. F. Perigal, *Some account of the Perigal family* (1887)].

PERING (John) Bapt. Harberton, Devon 16/7/1765, s. Richard Pering. Christ Church, Oxford 1784, BA1788, dn89 (Ox.), p90 (Ex.), MA1791. V. Skipton w. Kildwick, Yorks. 1806 to death. Dom. Chap. to 9th Duke of Hamilton 1806. Died (unmarried) 30/4/1843 [C28913]

PERKINS (Benjamin Robert) Bapt. Westminster, London 22/11/1797, s. Robert and Sara Perkins. Lincoln, Oxford 1820, BA1824, dn24 (Ox.), then Chap. Christ Church 1825-31, p26 (Ox.), BCL 1831. PC. Linslade, Bucks. 1826, V. Wotton under Edge, Glos. 1829-82 (and S/M 1840). Died 7/2/1886, leaving £3,330-16s-6d. [C21142] Married City of London 5/1/1830 Sarah Clode (w), with clerical son Charles Mathew Perkins.

PERKINS (Frederick David) Born Heavitree, Exeter 10/8/1792, s. Rev. John David Perkins (below) and Bridget Maria Jane Northcote. BNC, Oxford 1810, BA 1814, dn15 (Ex.), p16 (Ex.), MA1825. V. Ham, Kent 1816-27, V. Stoke w. Sowe (o/w Walgrave), Warwicks. 1817, R. Swayfield, Lincs. 1820 (non-res.), V. Down Hatherley, Glos. 1827 to death. Chap. in Ordinary 1823; Dom. Chap. to 13th Marquess of Winchester 1816. Died 19/4/1856 [C19197. Bennett2]

PERKINS (John) From Oxford, s. John Perkins. Chorister at Magdalen, Oxford 1811-20; matr. Christ Church 1820 (aged 17), BA 1824, dn26 (London), MA1827, p27 (London).

V. Lower (o/w Nether) Swell, Glos. 1832 [vacant in ERC] to death. Probate granted 25/7/1850 [C120995] Millais painted his port. (online).

PERKINS (John David) Born Staines, Middx., s. John Perkins and Elizabeth Reynolds Phillips. Magdalen, Oxford 1784 (aged 20), then St Mary Hall, dn88 (London for Lin.), BA1789, p90 (Lin.), MA1792, BD and DD1808. R. (West) Deeping, Lincs. 1801-06, V. Dawlish, Devon 1807-9, R. Mamhead, Devon 1809, R. Exeter St Lawrence 1809, PC. East Teignmouth, Devon 1816-23. Chap. in Ordinary 1816. Died 30/9/1845 [C72485] Married (1) Bath 23/3/1790 Bridget Maria Jane Northcote (d.1835), with son Frederick David, above (2) Heavitree, Exeter 4/1/1837 Anne Gilbert Roberts.

PERKINS (Samuel Wootton) Born/bapt. Leek Wootton, Warwicks. 26/2/1795, s. James Perkins and Catherine Wootten. Wadham, Oxford 1811, BA1815, MA1818, dn18 (C&L), p20 (Chester for C&L). R. Stockton, Warwicks. 1822-35 (depr.), there-after without cure. Died 1867 (2nd q. as Samuel only) aged 75 [C19198] Married Childwall, Liverpool 28/10/1824 or 1828 Mary Anne Swan. Bankrupt 1830 in his capacity as a broker!

PERRING (Peter) Bapt. Modbury, Devon 18/10/1771, s. Philip Perring and Susannah Legassick. Exeter, Oxford 1792, then St Mary Hall, BA1796, dn96 (Chich. for Ex.), p96 (Win. for Ex.), then Emmanuel, Cam-bridge 1800, MA1800. R. North Huish, Devon [blank in ERC] 1796 to death 11/6/1851 [C146067]

PERRY (Thomas Corbett) Born Wolver-hampton, Staffs. 14/9/1808, s. John Perry and Catharine Corbett. Lincoln, Oxford 1828, BA 1832. Stipendiary Curate Netherton Chapel, Staffs. 1832. Died (unm.) *in the union workhouse*, Wolver-hampton 11/3/1872, leaving under £300 [C121986] Described as 'Clerk and a manufacturer's clerk', the implication being that he could find no clerical employment? A tragic, if unique case.

PESHALL (Samuel) Born Guildford, Surrey 28/12/1761, s. John Peshall and Rebecca Ryde Hall. Pembroke, Oxford 1779, dn84 (Heref.), p86 (Glos. for London), BA and MA1787. R. Oldberrow, Worcs. 1799-1835, R. Morton Bagott, Worcs. 1800-20. Died 4/8/1835 [C121001. Foster corrected] Married Charlotte Crawford, with clerical son, below.

PESHALL (Samuel Doyly, *or* D'Oyly) Bapt. Morton Bagot, Worcs. 18/6/1792, s. Rev. Samuel Peshall (above) and Charlotte Crawford. Worcester, Oxford 1809, BA 1813, MA1815. (succ. has father as) R. Morton Bagott 1820-59 (and as) R. Old-berrow, Worcs. 1835 to death 3/1/1859, leaving £900, having been confined in Sandywell Park, Glos. (a private lunatic asylum) 1857 [C121987] Married Keynsham, Som. 1841 (3rd q.) Elizabeth James (w), with clerical son Samuel (born in Normandy).

PETER (John) Born/bapt. Mawnan, Cornwall 27/8/1779, s. Rev. Robert Peter and Martha Franklin. Balliol, Oxford 1799, dn02 (B&W), BA1802, p03 (Ex.). R. Grade, Cornwall 1817 to death 12/11/1852 aged 73 [C47711] Married St Ives, Cornwall 21/3/1816 Mary Morgan, with clerical son.

PETERBOROUGH (Bishop of) see under **MARSH (Herbert)**

PETERS (John William) Born West-minster, London 13/3/1791, s. (the Irish) Rev. William Peters (Prebend of Lincoln). Sidney, Cambridge 1809, BA1814, dn14 (Lin.), p15 (Nor.), MA 1817. V. Womersley, Yorks. 1815-17, R. Queningon, Glos. 1822-34, PC. Ampney St Mary, Glos. 1824-33 (w. PC. Ampney St Peter 1833), V. Langford, Oxon. 1825-34. Seceded from the CoE 1834 and lived in Clifton, Bristol. Died Ryde, IoW 11/9/1861 ('a fundowner'), leaving £6,000 [C21145. Confusion in Venn] Married (1) Grantham, Lincs. 18/4/1816 Catherine Colclough (d.1846), w. issue (2) Cirencester, Glos. 13/4/1852 Mary Bowly (hymn-writer, *q.v.* ODNB).

PETO (James) Born Ewhurst, Surrey 4/4/1789, s. James Peto and Mary Tugwell. St John's, Cambridge 1808, then Trinity Hall 1809, LLB 1814, dn14 (Ely), p15 (Ely). R. Charlton by Dover, Kent 1829-36, PC. Guston and West Langdon, Kent 1830-6, V. Preston next Faversham, Kent 1837 to death 17/3/1878 aged 89, leaving £40,000 [C82590] Married Shalford, Surrey 9/6/1829 Ann Jones, with issue.

PETTAT (Thomas) Born Stonehouse, Glos. 26/2/1772, s. John Pettat and Martha Hicks. University, Oxford 1790, BA1794, dn95 (Glos.), MA1797, p97 (Glos.). R. Quenington, Glos.

1797-8, R. Hatherop, Glos. 1797, V. Stonehouse 1798-1803, R. Beverston, Glos. 1803 to death. Dom. Chap. to 3rd Earl Bathurst 1798-1803. Died 10/3/1839 [C159055]

PETTINGAL (Charles Thomas) Born Leighton Buzzard, Beds. 26/5/1782, s. John and Mary Pettingal. Christ Church, Oxford 1800, BA1804, dn05 (Ox.), p07 (Win.), MA 1819. R. Ore (Oare), Sussex 1810, R. Little Braxted, Essex 1810 to death (The Castle Hotel, Richmond, Surrey, where he appeared to live) 28/8/1858, leaving £450 [C21147] 1 ch..

PETTIWARD (Daniel) Bapt. Putney, Surrey 30/9/1752, s. Rev. Roger Pettiward (born Mortlock) and Douglass Sandward. Trinity, Cambridge 1785, BA1789, dn89 (Nor.), MA 1792, p92 (Nor.). R. Onehouse, Suffolk 1797 and R. Great Finborough, Suffolk 1798 to death ('at The Angel Inn, Bury St Edmunds, on his way to London') 14/11/1833 (CCEd says 15/1/1834) aged 68 [C100161]

PEYTON (Algernon) Born Emneth, Norfolk 19/8/1786, s. Sir Henry Dashwood Peyton, 1st Bart., M.P., and Frances, dau. of Sir John Rous. Emmanuel, Cambridge 1805, BA1810, dn10 (Ely), p11 (London for Ely), MA1813. R. Doddington, Cambs. [net income £7,306 - 'the richest preferment in England'] 1811 to death 1/11/1868, leaving £16,000 [C100162. Boase] Married 22/6/1811 Isabella Anne Hussey (of Galtrim, Ireland), with issue.

PHAYRE (Richard) Born London 22/11/1807, s. Richard Phayre and Maria Ridgeway. TCD1824, BA1830, dn31 (C&L), p32 (C&L), MA1862. PC. Norwich St Mary Coslany 1832, R. East and West Raynham, Norfolk 1832 to death 1/1/1886, leaving £8,903-6s-2d. [C19238. Al.Dub.] Married Brighton, Sussex 5/1/1847 Charlotte Laura Wodehouse.

PHEAR (John) Born Bratton Clovelly, Devon 4/6/1794, s. John Phear (a farmer). Pembroke, Cambridge 1811, BA1815, Fellow 1815, dn17 (Ex.), p18 (Ex.), MA 1819, Tutor. PC. Earl Stonham, Suffolk 1823 to death 5/10/1869, leaving £3,000 [C114404. ODNB. Boase] Married North Tawton, Devon 22/6/1834 Catherine Wreford Budd (dau. of a physician), with clerical son Samuel George Phear.

PHELIPS (Charles) Bapt. Montacute, Som. 25/12/1765, s. Edward Phelips and Maria Wright. University, Oxford 1784, BA1788, MA 1821. R. St Margaret Pattens and St Gabriel Fenchurch, City of London 1792 to death 27/10/1834 (CCEd says 26/12/1834) [C121008] Married 6/2/1792 Mary Blackmore (Briggin Park, Herts.), with issue.

PHELIPS (Richard Colston) Born Montacute, Som. 22/8/1802, s. Rev. William Phelips and Anna Aletheia Elizabetha Paget (a clergy dau.). Trinity, Oxford 1819, BA 1822, MA1825. V. Montacute 1826, R. Stoke-sub-Hamden, Hants. 1833, V. Cucklington w. Stoke Trister, Som. 1833 to death 15/3/1862, leaving £1,000 [C40217] Married Melcombe Regis, Dorset 1/2/1836 Caroline Ann Hoskyns (w), with clerical s. Henry Benett Phelips. Brothers below.

PHELIPS (Robert) Bapt. Cucklington, Som. 22/1/1791. s. Rev. William Phelips and Anna Aletheia Elizabetha Paget (a clergy dau.). Christ Church, Oxford 1810, BA1814, dn15 (B&W), MA1817. V. Yeovil w. Preston Plucknett, Som. 1815, R. Lufton, Som. 1827 to death. Dom. Chap. to 10th Earl of Leven and Melville 1827. Died 24/2/1855 [C40218] Married Yeovil 13/3/1818 Maria Harbin, one dau. Brothers above and below.

PHELIPS (William) Bapt. Cucklington, Som. 6/11/1788, s. Rev. William Phelips and Anna Aletheia Elizabetha Paget (a clergy dau.). Trinity, Oxford 1807, BA1811, dn11 (B&W), p12 (B&W), MA1817. R. Cucklington w. Stoke Trister 1812 to death 4/3/1833 [C47739] Married Woolwich, Kent 2/11/1822 Mary Messiter, with issue. Brothers above.

PHELP (William Awbery) From Reading, Berks., s. Philip Phelp. Trinity, Oxford 1784 (aged 17), BA1787, MA1790. V. Hanwell, Essex 1792. Dom. Chap. to 2nd Baron Dorchester 1814. Died 13/6/1853 [C82592] Married Stanwell, Richmond 19/3/1798 Jane Patey.

PHELPS (Henry Dampier) From Sherborne, Dorset, s. Rev. Thomas Phelps and Elizabeth Dampier. Hertford, Oxford 1795 (aged 18), BA1799, dn99 (Lin.), p01 (Lin.), MA1801. R. Snodland, Kent 1804 to death (unmarried) 30/7/1865, leaving £6,000 [C425] Nephew Thomas Prankerd, here. The following is revealing: www.snodlandhistory.org.uk/localhis/phelps.htm

PHELPS (John) Born St Mary Wilton, Wilts. 7/12/1803, s. Rev. John Phelps, sen. and Jane Whitmarsh. Queen's, Oxford 1820, BA 1824, dn29 (Salis.), p29 (Salis.), MA 1830. PC. Burcombe, Wilts. 1829, R. Little Langford, Wilts. 1845, V. Hatherleigh, Devon 1862 to death 18/2/1878 leaving £4,000 [Not yet in CCEd] Married Abingdon, Berks. 12/3/1831 Catharine Latham, w. clerical sons Philip Ashby, John, and Arthur Whitmarsh Phelps.

PHELPS (Thomas Prankerd) Born Shepton Mallet, Som., s. Rev. Thomas Phelps. Hertford, Oxford 1799 (aged 17), BA1803, dn04 (Roch.), MA1806, p08 (Lin.). R. Crowell, Oxford 1820-30 (res.), V. Tarrington, Heref. 1832 to death 28/4/1854 [C1519. For his son see: Gerald van Loo, *A Victorian parson: the life and times of Thomas Prankerd Phelps, Ridley, Kent, rector, 1840-1893* (Upton-upon-Severn, 1989)]. Married Thame, Oxon. 10/7/1809 Jane Theodosia Lupton, w. issue.

PHELPS (Thomas Spencer) Born East Pennard, Som. 12/12/1774, s. William Phelps and Catherine Phelps [*thus*]. Balliol, Oxford 1793, BA1797, dn97 (Bristol), p99 (Bristol), incorporated at Emmanuel, Cambridge, MA 1836. R. Maperton, Som. 1802 [not 1820] and R. Weston Bampfylde, Som. 1836 to death 6/12/1856 [C40223] Married Sturminster Newton, Dorset 9/4/1804 Catharine Bird, w. clerical s. Edward Spencer Phelps.

PHELPS (William) From Flax Bourton, Som., s. Rev. John Phelps. Balliol, Oxford 1793 (aged 17), then St Alban Hall, BA1797, p00 (Salis.). V. Bicknoller, Som. 1811-51, V. Meare, Som. 1824-51, R. Oxcombe. Lincs. 1851 to death 17/8/1856 [C40224. ODNB as topographer. Boase] Author of the major Somerset history; botanist.

PHILIPS (George Washington Edwards) Born South Carolina 5/3/1781, s. Charles Philips (godson of General George Washington) and Elizabeth Spence. Pembroke, Oxford 1811, no degree, dn12 (Salis.), p13 (Salis.). V. Wendy w. Shingay, Cambs. 1827 to death (at the Pier Hotel, Brighton) 24/10/1865, leaving £12,000 [C109371] Married 13/2/1836 Mrs Charlotte Elizabeth (Jesson) Jones 13/2/1836, w. military issue.

PHILLIMORE (George) Born St Pancras, London 2/2/1808, s. William Phillimore and Almeria Thornton. Christ Church, Oxford 1825, Student [Fellow] 1825-33, BA1829, MA1831, dn31 (Ox.), p32 (Lin.). V. Willen, Bucks. 1832-51, R. Radnage, Bucks. 1851. Died Maidstone, Kent 14/10/1889, leaving £15,188-0s-6d. [C21153] Married (1) Elstree, Herts. 7/5/1832 Emily Haworth (d.1837) (2) St George's Hanover Square, London 13/7/1841 Harriette Maria Prescott, w. clerical son Arthur Phillimore.

PHILLIMORE (Robert) Bapt. St Pancras, London 17/11/1783, s. Rev. Joseph Phillimore and Mary Machin. Christ Church, Oxford 1802, Student [Fellow] 1802-12, BA 1806, MA 1808 [Student of Lincoln's Inn 1808], dn10 (Durham), p11 (Ox.). PC. Hawkhurst, Kent/ Sussex 1812-14, V. Shipton under Wychwood, Oxon. 1814 and V. Slapton, Bucks. 1815 to death. Dom. Chap. to 4th Earl of Dartmouth 1815. Died (unm.) 28/9/1852 [C21155]

PHILLIPPS (Edward Thomas March) Born Crakemarsh, Staffs. 21/6/1784, s. Thomas Phillipps (formerly March, of Garendon Park, Leics.) and Susan Lisle. Sidney, Cambridge 1800, BA1804, MA1807, dn07 (London for Roch.), p08 (Lin.). R. Hathern, Leics. 1810-59, Min. Dishley w. Thorpe Acre, Leics. 1816-43. Chancellor of the Diocese of Gloucester 1820-59. Dom. Chap. to Bishop of Gloucester / C&L 1815. Died 12/7/1859, leaving £4,000 [C2070. Boase. [L.F. Phillipps], *Records of the ministry of Edward Thomas March Phillipps, MA, for fifty years Rector of Hathern in the County of Leicester* (1862)] Married Liverpool 20/4/1812 Elizabeth Hayes.

PHILLIPPS (John Weston) Born Spalding, Lincs. 13/12/1765, s. George and Sarah Phillipps. [NiVoF] dn96 (Heref.), p96 (Heref.), p97 (Heref.). PC. Brockhampton, Heref. 1817, R. Llandinabo, Heref. 1827. Died 5/11/1838 (*Gentleman's Magazine* as Philipps) [C173211. In ERC as T.W.] Married Birmingham 13/7/1798 Elizabeth Spenser, w. issue.

PHILLIPPS, *later* PHILLIPPS FLAMANK (William) Born Lanivet, Cornwall 13/12/1786, s. Rev. Nicholas Phillipps and Denise Flamank. Queen's, Oxford 1805, then Jesus, Cambridge 1810, BA1811, dn11 (Ex.), p12 (Ex.). R. (and patron) Lanivet 1817 to death 6/12/1861, leaving £1,000 [C146082 as Phillips)] Alderman 1817 and Mayor 1821 of Bodmin, Cornwall.

PHILLIPS (Edward, *not* Edmund) Born St Martin's, Shropshire. [NiVoF] Chap. of the Donative of East Tytherley, Hants. 1802 to death 1851[C82594] Wife Thomasin, and issue.

PHILLIPS (Henry George) Bapt. Bury St Edmunds 2/10/1791, s. John Phillips (surgeon to the Royal Household) and Frances Crew. Emmanuel, Cambridge 1810, BA1814, dn15 (London for Ely), p15 (Ely), MA1817. R. Great Whelnetham, Suffolk 1816 and V. Mildenhall, Suffolk 1818 to death. Dom. Chap. to Elizabeth, Duchess of Grafton 1816. Died 29/7/1873, leaving £4,000 [C109372] Wife Frances, and son Benezra Phillips.

PHILLIPS (Herbert) Bapt. Berkeley, Glos. 8/11/1789, s. Joseph Phillips. St Catherine's, Cambridge 1809, BA1813, dn14 (Nor. for Win.), MA1816, p17 (London). (Sinecure R. 1817 then) V. Folkton, Yorks. 1820 to death 23/4/1856 [C121012] Was married, with issue.

PHILLIPS (Hugo Moreton) Bapt. Shifnal, Shropshire 10/1/1796, s. Revell Phillips and Hannah Hall. Christ Church, Oxford 1814, then Worcester, BA1818, dn19 (Ely for C&L), p20 (Chester for C&L), MA1822. PC. Dawley, Shropshire 1823-31, R. Stirchley, Shropshire 1827 to death 12/10/1877, leaving £4,000 [C19213. Foster as Hugh] Married (1) Wem, Shropshire 13/7/1822 Maria Hassall (d.1843), with issue (2) Stirchley 25/10/1846 Helen Garbett, with further issue.

PHILLIPPS (James Evans, Sir, 11th Bart.) Bapt. King's Lynn, Norfolk 16/11/1793, s. William Hollingworth Phillipps and Harriet Fonblanque. Queen's, Oxford 1813, BA 1817, dn17 (Glos.), p18 (Salis.), MA1820. V. Osmington, Dorset 1832 to death 13/2/1873, leaving £4,000 [C53557. Boase] Married Bristol 4/7/1822 Mary Ann Bickley (d.1833), with son Rev. Sir James Erasmus Phillips. Succ. 1857. Port. online.

PHILLIPS (John) [MA but NiVoF?]. R. Ninfield, Sussex 1832-53. Probate granted 16/1/1854 [C64859] Note the Rev. John Phillips [educational] Charity and the Mary Phillips Charity in the village.

PHILLIPS (John Michael) Bapt. Louth, Lincs. 1/7/1786, s. Thomas Phillips (Town Clerk) and Ann Bentley. St John's, Cam-bridge 1807, then St Catharine's 1809, BA 1811, dn13 (Lin.), MA1814, p15 (Lin.). V. Skidbrooke cum Saltfleetby Haven 1815 to death 28/6/1862, leaving £2,000 [C72633]

PHILLIPS (Samuel) Bapt. Brecon 26/5/1794, s. Thomas Phillips and Margaret Church. Literate: dn17 (St David's), p18 (St David's). R. Llandewi, Glamorgan 1821 (w. RD of Gower West 1833), R. Puddington, Devon 1826-[36], R. Pickwell, Leics. 1850 (non-res.). Died 15/12/1855 [C132654] Married (1) Little Hallingbury, Essex 5/8/1830 Ann Shaftesbury Horsley (dau. of a Bishop of St Asaph, she d.1833) (2) Pitminster, Som. 20/6/1834 Juliana Hicks Noel, with issue.

PHILLIPS (William Joseph George) Born Westminster, London 7/3/1779, s. William Phillips and Frances Slade. Trinity, Oxford 1797, BA1801 (as William Phillips), dn02 (Nor. for Salis.), p02 (Win.), then Caius, Cambridge, MA1806. V. Eling, Herts. 1803 and R. Millbrook, Hants. 1812 to death. Chap. to Prince of Wales 1812. Died 2/10/1855 [C82604. Foster as William George Thomas] Married (1) St George's Hanover Square, London 25/7/1802 Susannah Ramsden White (d.1845), w. clerical sons William Parr (below), and Francis Robert Phillips (2) St James, Piccadilly, London 31/8/1851 Jane Petty.

PHILLIPS (William Parr) Bapt. Great Canfield, Essex 19/11/1812, s. Rev. William Joseph George Phillips (above) and Susannah Ramsden White. Trinity, Oxford 1826, BA1831, dn31 (Win.), p32 (Win.). R. Woodford, Essex 1832 to death 20/3/1875, leaving £4,000 [C82605] Married Binfield, Berks. 25/8/1835 Caroline Phillips Wilder, with issue.

PHILLIPS (William Spencer) Bapt. Great Bardfield, Essex 24/1/1775, s. Rev. William Phillips. Trinity, Oxford 1810, BA1815, MA 1817, Fellow 1822-9, p24 (Ox.), Tutor 1824, BD1828, Philosophy Lecturer 1828. V. Newchurch w. Ryde, IoW 1839-1863, Curate Cheltenham St John, Glos. 1828-63, V. Defynnog w. Ystradfellte, Brecon 1832. Died London 13/5/1863, leaving £6,000 [C21157] Married Charlton Kings, Glos. 18/5/1829 Penelope Boughton (w), with issue.

PHILLOTT (Charles) Bapt. Bath, 5/10/1774, s. Ven. James Phillott (Archdeacon of Bath) and Mary Farr. Christ Church, Oxford 1792, BA 1796, dn97 (Ox.), MA1798, p98 (Ox.). PC.

Badsey w. Aldington, Worcs. 1808, PC. Wickhamford, Worcs. 1808-51, R. Kingston Deverill, Wilts. 1808-13, PC. Frome Selwood (the 'New Church in the Woodlands'), Som. 1813 to death 26/11/1851 [C28953] Married Calne, Wilts. 6/4/1809 Frances Dudley Pender, with issue. Brothers below.

PHILLOTT (James) Bapt. Bath, Som. 30/9/1778, s. Ven. James Phillott, sen. (Archdeacon of Bath) and Mary Farr. Corpus Christi, Oxford 1795, BA1798, MA1802, dn02 (Ox.), p03 (Ox.). V. Stanton Drew w. R. Pensford and Stanton Prior >< Som. 1815 (and Master of the Hospital [almshouses] of St John the Baptist, Bath 1816) to death. Dom. Chap. to 1st Earl of Charleville 1816. Died 30/12/1865, leaving £12,000 [C21152] Married Esher, Surrey 18/10/1804 Caroline Harris, with issue. Brothers below, and above.

PHILLOTT (John Stevens) Born Bath, Som. 14/7/1776, s. Ven. James Phillott (Archdeacon of Bath) and Mary Farr. Balliol, Oxford 1793, BA1797, p99 (Salis.), MA1800. V. Wookey, Som. 1801 and R. Farmborough, Som. 1823 to death. Dom. Chap. to 3rd Earl of Howth 1823. Died 30/8/1837 [C477658] Brothers above.

PHILLPOTTS (Henry, Bishop of Exeter) Born Bridgwater, Som. 6/5/1778, one of 23 ch. of John Phillpott ('brick factor, afterwards landlord of the Bell Inn, Gloucester') and Sibella Glover. Christ Church, Oxford 1791, BA1795, then Magdalen, Fellow 1795-1804, MA1798, dn02 (Ox.), p04 (Chester), BD and DD 1821. V. Kilmarsdon, Som. 1804-6 (non-res.), V. (Bishop) Middleham, Durham 1805-8, V. Stainton le Street, Durham 1805, R. Gateshead, Durham 1808, 9th Prebend of Durham Cathedral 1809-16 (2nd Prebend 1815-20, 6th Prebend 1831-69), R. Stanhope, Durham 1820-31 (and Preacher throughout the Diocese of Durham), Dean of Chester 1828-30, Bishop of Exeter 1830 (w. R. Shobrooke, Devon 1830, and Treasurer 1831, Prebend 1831 and Canon Residentiary in Exeter Cathedral 1831) to death 18/9/1869 aged 91, leaving £60,000. Chap. to Bishop of Durham 1806-26 [C28960. ODNB. Boase. R.N. Shutte, *The life, times and writings of the Right Rev. Dr Henry Phillpotts Lord Bishop of Exeter* (1861. Vol. 1 all published); C.B.C. Davies, *Henry Phillpotts, Bishop of Exeter* (1954) The *Wikipedia* entry is good] Married North Cerney, Glos. .22/9/1804 Deborah Surtees, 18 ch. (some clerical, incl. the man below)

PHILLPOTTS (William John) Born Bishop Middleham, Durham 27/1/1807, s. Rt. Rev. Henry Phillpotts (Bishop of Exeter, above) and Deborah Surtees. Oriel, Oxford 1825, BA 1830, dn31 (B&W), MA1832. V. Lezant, Cornwall 1831-2, V. Grimley, Worcs. 1832-45, R. Holdgate (2nd Portion), Shropshire 1832, Prebend of Exeter Cathedral 1840 (Chancellor 1860-88, Precentor 1870-2), V. St Gluvias, Cornwall 1845 and Archdeacon of Cornwall 1845 to death (Falmouth) 10/7/1888, leaving £18,634-0s-8d.[C40231. Boase] Married Crediton, Devon 6/11/1832 Louisa Buller, with clerical sons Henry John, and Septimus Buller Phillpotts.

PHILPOT (Benjamin) Born Laxfield, Suffolk 9/1/1791, s. Benjamin Philpot and Lydia Gooden (but adopted by his uncle William). Christ's, Cambridge 1808, BA 1812, Fellow 1814, MA1815, dn15 (Nor.), p17 (Nor.). PC. Walpole St Mary, Suffolk 1817-32 (non-res.), Chap. St George, Douglas, IoM 1827-32, Vicar General of the IoM and Archdeacon of Man (w. R. Andreas annexed) 1832-9 (res.) [turned down the Bishopric], R. Great Cressingham w. Bodney, Norfolk 1839-59, V. Lydney, Glos. 1859-71, R. Dennington, Suffolk 1871-8. Lived at Putney, and died Surbiton, Surrey 28/5/1889 (just under his 100th year), leaving £5,165-1s-5d. [C7946. Gelling is illuminating. Boase. DEB. A.G. Bradley, *Our centenarian grandfather, 1790-1890: from the MS autobiography of the Rev. B. Philpot* ([1922] with port. at age 94)] Married (1) Richmond, Surrey 24/7/1816 his cousin Letitia Mary Philpot 1816 (d.1819 'after an illness of only half an hour'), 1 dau. lived (2) Aldeburgh, Suffolk 4/6/1822 Charlotte Vachall (a clergy dau.); 14 ch. Photo. online at: www.clement-jones.com/ps22/ps22_279.htm

PHILPOT (William) Born Esher, Surrey, s. Thomas Philpot. Pembroke, Oxford 1785 (aged 18), BA1789, p91 (Nor. for Win.), MA 1792. R. Everdon, Northants. 1809 to burial 30/9/1834. (CCEd says died 31/10/1834) [C114411]

PHILPOTT (Thomas) Bapt. Clent, Staffs. 20/5/1761, s. Rev. Other [*sic*] Philpott and Margaret Lowe. St Mary Hall, Oxford 1779, BA1782, dn84 (C&L), MA1785, p85 (C&L). R. Pedmore, Worcs. 1791 and PC. Newland, Worcs. 1831 to death 10/9/1855 [C19216. CL as two different men] Married Stafford 2/4/1793 Mary Jeffreys, with issue.

PHIPPS (Barré) Born Minorca, Spain 4/4/1771 (bapt. Wells 15/6/1771), s. (of the Irish) Capt. Isaac Phipps and Rebecca Dodd. St John's, Cambridge 1793, BA1797, dn98 (Chich.), p99 (Chich.), MA1800, incorporated at Oxford 1845. Selsey Prebend in Chichester Cathedral 1802-4 (then Mardon Prebend 1804, then Canon Residentiary 1848-63), V. East Marden, Sussex 1802-5, R. Nuthurst, Sussex 1805-17, R. East Wittering, Sussex 1813-17, R. & V. Selsey, Sussex 1817 to death 3/1/1863 aged 87, leaving £1,500 [C64863] Married Marylebone, London 33/1/1817 Anne Maria Goddard (a clergy dau., East Woodhay, Hants.).

PHIPPS (Edward James) Born Leighton House, Westbury, Wilts. 21/2/1806, s. Thomas Henry Phipps and Mary Leckonby. Exeter, Oxford 1823, BA1828, dn29 (B&W), p30 (B&W). PC. Stoke St Michael (o/w Stoke Lane), Som. 1830, R. Devizes, Wilts. 1833 and R. Stansfield, Suffolk 1853 to death 22/5/1884, leaving £2,967-6s-5d. Married Clonfert, Co. Galway 27/8/1844 Susanne Henrietta Anna Butson (w) (a clergy dau.), with issue [C40232]

PICART (Samuel) Born Carmarthen, s. Rev. Samuel Picart, sen. BNC, Oxford 1792 (aged 17), BA1796, MA1803, BD1810. H/M Hereford School (and Vicar Choral) 1803-7 (res.); Prebend of Moreton Parva in Hereford Cathedral 1805-35, R. Putley, Heref. 1805-14 (res.), V. Bridstow, Heref. 1807-8, R. Little Marcle, Heref. 1808-35, R. Newington, Surrey 1810-12 (res.), R. Rush-bury, Shropshire 1814-18, R. Holdgate (2nd Portion), Shropshire 1816-21 (res.), R. Hartlebury, Worcs. 1817 to death 28/9/1835 aged 60 (CCEd says 7/10/1835) [C148983]

PICCOP(E) (John) Born Manchester 26/3/1788, s. George and Ann Piccop. Lincoln, Oxford 1813, dn16 (Chester), BA1817, p17 (Chester), MA1820. PC. Manchester St Paul 1822-44 (res.), PC. Farndon, Cheshire 1844 to death 10/9/1854 [C710213] Married Manchester 18/5/1814 Elizabeth Rachel Bayley, with clerical son (with whom he collected the Piccope Manuscripts, now in Chetham's Library, Manchester). 'Dressed more like a dissenting minister'.

PICKARD (George, sen.) Born Bloxworth, Dorset 13/12/1756, s. Jocelyn Pickard and Henrietta Trenchard. Merton, Oxford 1774, SCL, dn80 (Ox. for Bristol), p80 (Chester for Bristol), BCL1781. R. Bloxworth 1781 and V. Warmwell w. Poxwell, Dorset 1781 to death 24/7/1840 [C29018] Married Ealing, Middx. 13/10 1783 Frances Payne, w. clerical son (below).

PICKARD, *later* PICKARD CAMBRIDGE (George, jun.) Born Warmwell, Dorset 17/1/1790, s. Rev. George Pickard (above) and Frances Payne. Merton, Oxford 1808, BA1812, MA1815. V. Staunton on Arrow, Heref. 1820, R. Winter-borne Tomson, Dorset 1822, R. Bloxworth, Dorset 1850 to death. Dom. Chap. to 1st Baron de Dunstanville 1820. Died 13/1/1868, leaving £5,000 [C105859. Foster under Cambridge] Married Marylebone, London 17/11/1820 Frances Amelia Whish, with clerical son Edward. Name changed on inheriting money.

PICKARD (William Leonard) Born York 8/12/1783, s. Leonard Pickard and Ann Robinson. Trinity Hall, Cambridge 1805, BA1810, dn10 (York), p11 (York), MA1813. V. Bishopthorpe, York 1814, R. York All Saints, North Street 1818 and V. Rufforth, Ainsty of York 1821 to death (York) 10/5/1854 [C109483. YCO] Married Wakefield, Yorks. 22/4/1815 Eliza Foljambe, and child.

PICKERING (George) Bapt. Lostwithiel, Cornwall 22/12/1777, s. Rev. John Pickering (V. Brewood, Staffs.) and Catherine Bowler. Jesus, Cambridge 1795, BA1800, dn00 (C&L), p02 (C&L). V. Mackworth, Derbys. 1802-58 (PC. Allestree Chapel 1806, V. Arksey, Yorks. 1831-40. Died Mackworth 11/6/1858, leaving £7,000[C136849] Married Mackworth 18/6/1823 Elizabeth Smart. 3 generations held Mackworth for 125 years.

PICKFORD (Francis) Born Frenchay, Bristol 10/6/1801, s. Capt. Charles Pickford and Mary Emilia MacKinnon. Queens', Cambridge 1820, BA1824, dn25 (Lin.), p26 (Lin.), MA1827. R. Muckton, Lincs. 1832-41, R. Hagworthingham, Lincs. 1839 to death 10/11/1883 aged 72, leaving £18,377-13s-9d. [C72638. Kaye] Married 1/12/1831 Sophia Bancroft Lister (w), with issue.

PICKFORD (Joseph) Bapt. Astbury, Cheshire 27/7/1772, s. Joseph Pickford (of Derby, 'one of the leading provincial architects in the reign of George 111') and Mary Wilkins. Oriel, Oxford 1790, BA1794, MA1796, dn99 (Chester for Ox.), p01 (Salis.). R. (West) Cholderton, Wilts. 1801, and PC. Little Eaton, Derbys. 1802 to death. ?Buried Stockport 20/11/1844 aged 72 [C19241]

PICKTHALL (Thomas) Bapt. Millom, Cumberland 10/9/1781, s. John and Joyce Pickthall. Literate: dn04 (York), p05 (York), MA1832 Lambeth. V. Broxbourne, Herts. 1821-53, Chap. Hoddeson Chapel, Broxbourne 1823, R. Wormley, Herts. 1832 to death 1853 (1st q.) [C103008. YCO] Married Lewisham, Kent 22/7/1814 Sophia Mary Reeves, w. clerical son Charles Grayson Pickthall. Surrogate.

PICTON (James *or* Jacob) Born Newton, Lancs. St Catherine's, Cambridge 1824, then Queens' 1825, BA1828, dn28 (Chester), p29 (Chester), MA1831. PC. Norbury, Stockport, Cheshire 1829-31, PC. Liverpool St Stephen 1831-41. Died Liverpool 1851 (3rd q.) [C170215] Married Liverpool 20/6/1838 Agnes Woodward, with clerical son John Owen Picton. Not to be confused with a RC Liverpool contemporary Father James Picton.

PIDCOCK (Benjamin) Bapt. Ashbourne, Derbys. 1/1/1770, s. John Pidcock and Martha Spencer. Wadham, Oxford 1787, BA1791, dn91 (C&L), MA1793, p96 (C&L). V. Youlgreave w. Middleton, Derbys. 1802 and PC. Elton, Derbys. 1811 to death 28/8/1835 (CCEd says 18/12/1835) [C19244] Married Kirk Ireton, Yorks. 4/5/1795 Ann Burton, with clerical son below.

PIDCOCK (Richard Burton) Born Alstonfield, Staffs., s. Rev. Benjamin Pidcock (above) and Ann Burton. St John's, Cambridge 1818, BA1822, dn22 (Chester for C&L), p23 (Chester for C&L). PC. Elkstone, Staffs. 1828 and PC. Warslow, Staffs. 1828-50. A man of this name emigrated and founded Pidcock, Texas, dying there 24/6/1851 [C109036] Married Darley Dale, Derbys. 22/7/1828 Harriet Millicent Gisborne (Horwick House, Derbys.), and had issue.

PIDDOCKE (John) Bapt. Ashby-de-la-Zouche, Leics. 24/12/1764, s. John Piddocke. Christ Church, Oxford 1781, BA1785, dn89 (Lin.), p91 (Lin.), MA1808. PC. Shuttington Warwicks. 1792, V. Clifton upon Dunsmore, Warwicks. 1795-1831 (res.), PC. Willesley, Derbys. 1830. Probate granted 11/11/1841 [C19246] His wife died 1798. *J.P.* Leics.

PIDSLEY (Sydenham) Bapt. Crediton, Devon 13/9/1808, s. Rev. Simon Pidsley and Mary Thomas. Worcester, Oxford 1826, BA1829, dn31 (B&W). R. (and patron) of Uplowman, Devon 1832 to death 25/8/1857 [C40235] Married Awliscombe, Devon 15/8/1832 Mary Ann Elizabeth Lott, and had issue.

PIERCE (William Matthews) Bapt. Weld Chapel, Southgate, London 26/1/1798, s. James Henry Pierce and Ann Rose. St John's, Cambridge 1817, BA1821, dn21 (Lin.), p22 (Lin.), MA1825. V. Goulceby w. Burwell 1823-7, PC. West Ashby, Lincs. 1826, R. Fulletby, Leics. 1826. Died West Ashby 2/4/1864, leaving £5,000 [C72639] Married Edmonton, Middx. 25/12/1827 Elizabeth Field, with issue.

PIERCY (George Henry) Born Shrawley, Worcs. 3/10/1768, s. Rev. Daniel Piercy and Jane Vernon Brazier. Worcester, Oxford 1786, BA1790, dn91 (Heref.), p92 (Heref.), MA1794. PC. Liverpool St Stephen 1796-1806 (res.), V. Chaddesley Corbet, Worcs., 1805 to death 8/5/1855 [C121999] Married 17/6/1794 Marianne Hopkins.

PIERS (Octavius [Samuel]) Born Co. Westmeath 20/8/1792, s. Sir Pigott William Piers, 5th Bart. and Elizabeth Smythe. TCD1805, BA 1809, incorporated Magdalen Hall, Oxford 1812, p14 (Heref.). V. Preston, Weymouth, Dorset 1815 to death there 23/2/1848 [C105860] Married Gloucester 21/12/1813 Jane Tristram (a clergy dau.), with issue.

PIGOT (Thomas) Born Blymhill, Staffs. 14/1/1778, s. Thomas Pigot and Charlotte Tayleur. Christ Church, Oxford 1795, BA 1799, dn00 (C&L), MA1802, p02 (C&L). PC. St Helens, Lancs. 1815-36, R. Blymhill 1836 to death 25/1/1840 aged 62 [C19248] Married Deane, Lancs. 23/10/1816 Mary Ann Kearsley, with clerical sons Edward, John Tayleur, Henry Septimus, and Octavius Frederick Pigot.

PIGOTT (James Noel) Bapt. Colton, Staffs. 27/4/1784, s. William Pigott and Sophia Wolseley. Worcester, Oxford 1810, BA1806, MA1812, Fellow to 1812. R. Grendon Underwood, Bucks. 1808 to death. Dom. Chap. to 1st Duke of Bucking-ham and Chandos 1815. Died 9/4/1855 [C72647] Brother below.

PIGOTT (John Dryden) Born Chetwynd, Shropshire 1/6/1778, s. Rev. William Pigott and

Sophia Wolseley. Christ Church, Oxford 1795, BA1800, dn00 (C&L), MA 1802, p02 (C&L). R. Habberley, Shropshire 1802, R. (and patron) of Edgmond, Shropshire [net income £2,600] 1811 to death (Newport, Shropshire) 17/4/1845 [C19249] Married Shrewsbury 3/2/1806 Frances Bevan, with clerical s. of same name (also R. Edgmond, who changed his name to Corbet in 1865). Brother above.

PIGOTT (John Robert) Born Doddershall Park, Bucks. 21/9/1799, s. Col. William Pigott and Anne King (a clergy dau.). Emmanuel, Cambridge 1819, BA1823, dn23 (Lin.), p24 (Lin.). PC. North Marston, Bucks. 1826 (w. Hughenden 1837-51), R. Ashwelthorpe w. Wremingham, Norfolk 1851 to death (Rainthorpe, Norfolk) 10/12/1852 [C72648] Married Sheringham, Norfolk 30/1/1835 Emma Upcher, with issue.

PIGOTT (Solomon) Born Haddenham, Bucks. 20/11/1779, s. John Pigott [*pleb.*] and Mary Bodington. St Edmund Hall, Oxford 1797, BA1800, dn02 (York), MA1803, p03 (Lin. for York). PC. Latchford St James, Lancs. 1809-25, R. Dunstable, Bucks. 1824 to death. Dom. Chap. to 5th Viscount Galway 1812; and to 1st Viscount Carleton 1815. Died 27/4/1845 [C73547. YCO] Married High Wycombe, Bucks. 11/1/1802 Jane Rotton, w. clerical sons Samuel Rotton Piggott, and John David Piggott.

PILKINGTON (Charles) Born Chichester 25/2/1802, s. Prebendary Charles Pilkington, sen. and Harriet Elizabeth Williams. New, Oxford 1820, Fellow 1822-35, dn25 (Heref.), p26 (Heref.), BCL1827, MA1861. S/M Winchester College 1826-36; R. Winchester St Lawrence 1831-40, Windham Prebend in Chichester Cathedral 1834-70, Canon Residentiary 1850-70, Chancellor 1854-70, R. Stockton, Warwicks. 1835 (and RD Dassett Magna 1838) to death 10/9/1870, leaving £12,000 [C19253. Boase] Married Winchester Cathedral 23/8/1836 Maria Garnier (w), with issue.

PILKINGTON (Matthew) Born Bridgnorth, Shropshire 1771, s. Capt. Thomas Pilkington. Pembroke, Oxford 1789 (aged 18), BA1793, dn94 (C&L), p96 (C&L), MA1797. R. Hopesay, Shropshire 1797 to 1804 (res.), PC. Alveley, Shropshire 1804 to death 15/10/1847 [C19257]

PINE-COFFIN, *born* COFFIN (Charles Pine) Bapt. East Down, Devon 3/11/1771, s. Rev. John Pine-Coffin and Grace Rowe. Trinity, Cambridge 1790, BA 1794, dn95 (Ex.), p96 (Ex.), MA1806. R. East Down 1800 and Chap. of the Donative of North Tamerton, Devon 1813 to death 26/1/1850 aged 78 [C146089] Married 7/8/1806 Charlotte Knight (Milton Hall, 'the largest private house in Cambs'.), 1s., 8 dau.

PITMAN (John) Born Tiverton, Devon 1784 (bapt. 18/7/1787), s. Rev. John, sen. and Elizabeth Pitman. Balliol, Oxford 1802, then Trinity Hall, Cambridge 1805, dn06 (Ex.), LLB 1808. PC. Broadhempston, Devon 1807-56 and R. Washfield, Devon 1816 to death (widower) 5/6/1856 (at the Angel Hotel, Tiverton) [C146093]

PITMAN (John Rogers) Bapt. Soho, London 22/8/1782, s. Thomas and Ann Pitman. Pembroke, Cambridge 1800, BA1804, dn08 (London for Win.), p09 (London for Ex.), MA1815. S/M Christ's Hospital School, London 1817-20; PC. Berden w. Ugley >< Essex 1818-46, PC. St Barnabas, Kensington, London 1833-50. Dom. Chap. to HRH Duchess of Kent at Bath 1851-61. Died Bath 27/8/1861, leaving £12,000 [C82712. ODNB. Boase] Married Merriott, Som. 13/1/1823 Elizabeth Lawrence (w), and had issue.

PITMAN (Thomas) Born St Pancras, London 31/12/1801, s. Thomas Dix Pitman (solicitor) and Anna Simmonds. Wadham, Oxford 1820, BA1826, dn26 (Cashel for Bp of Ox. - at Oxford), MA1827, p28 (Ox.). V. Eastbourne, Sussex 1828 and Wisborough Prebend in Chichester Cathedral 1841 to death (a widower) 13/5/1890, leaving £6,470-17s-10d. [C21172. Boase] Married Tooting, Surrey 27/3/1827 Frances Jane Bird, with clerical s., also Thomas. Surrogate.

PITT (Charles) Born Cirencester, Glos. (bapt. 4/8/1803), s. Joseph Pitt and Mary Robbins. Christ Church, Oxford 1818, BA1822, dn24 (Lin. for Salis.), p24 (Salis.). MA1825. V. Malmesbury, Wilts. 1828-74, R. Easton Gray, Wilts. 1829-34 (res.), V. Ashton Keynes w. Leigh, Wilts. 1834-66. Dom. Chap. to 16th Earl of Suffolk 1829. Died 18/10/1874, leaving £5,000 [C72667] Married Brinkworth, Wilts. 1/2/1842 Theresa Elizabeth Brock, with issue. Brother Cornelius, below.

PITT (Charles Whitworth) Bapt. British Embassy, St Petersburg 15/10/1802, s. Rev. London [*sic*] King Pitt and Frances Percy Brompton. BNC, Oxford 1821, BA1824, dn25 (London), p26 (London), MA1829. Curate Epping St John the Baptist, Essex 1831, R. Stapleford Abbotts, Essex 1841 to death 23/1/1867, leaving £2,000 [C121075] Married Snailwell, Cambs. 29/8/1829 Emma Hill (w), with issue.

PITT (Cornelius) Born Cirencester, Glos. 25/5/1787, s. Joseph Pitt and Mary Robbins. Oriel, Oxford 1803, BCL 1810 [barrister Lincoln's Inn 1813] dn17 (London), p18 (Glos.), BD by 1831. R. Haselton (w. Yarnworth), Glos. 1825 and R. Redcombe, Glos. 1831 to death 26/2/1840 [C121076] Married Gloucester 5/5/1818 Ann Elizabeth Horrocks, and had issue. Brother Charles, above.

PITT (George) Bapt. Marylebone, London 2/4/1796, s. Thomas and Anna Maria Pitt. Christ Church, Oxford 1814, then Trinity, Cambridge 1817, BA1822, dn22 (Nor.), p23 (Nor.), MA1825. PC. Over Peover (Peover Superior), Rostherne, Cheshire 1825-41, V. Audlem, Cheshire 1836 to death (Cricket Malherbie Court, Som.) 28/4/1865 aged 69, leaving £10,000 [C114442] Married Over Peover 21/2/1832 Charlotte Augusta (dau. Sir Henry Mainwaring, 1st Bart., Peover Hall), with issue.

PIXELL (Charles) Born Edgbaston, Birmingham 1/12/1763, s. Rev. John Pryn Parkes Pixell (V. Dalton le Dale, Durham). St John's, Cambridge 1781, BA1786, dn86 (C&L), MA1791, p92 (C&L). V. Edgbaston 1795 to death 12/5/1848 [C19040] Married 5/4/1792 Mary Jane Conquest, with issue.

PLACE (Henry Jordan) Bapt. Marnhull, Dorset 27/9/1802, s. Rev. John Conyers Place and Elizabeth Harvey. Clare, Cambridge 1821, BA1825, dn25 (Salis.), p28 (Llandaff for Bristol). (succ. his uncle as) R. Marnhull 1828 to death. By 1841 in Great Fosters House lunatic asylum, Wigham, Surrey. Died there 8/10/1842 aged 39. [C4428] Married Balsham, Cambs. 7/9/1825 Charlotte Anne Langden (a clergy sister!), 3 ch.

PLACE (Matthew Wasse) Bapt. Canford Magna, Dorset 30/11/1777, s. John Place and Penelope Warland. Wadham, Oxford 1796, BA1800, dn00 (Bristol), p03 (Win.). Chap. Wareham Holy Trinity, Dorset 1800, R. Hempreston, Dorset 1806 to death 15/3/1834 (CCEd says 16/6/1834) [C53579] Married Lytchett Minster, Dorset 26/4/1808 Frances Growden Jeffery (dau. of an *M.P.*), w. issue

PLATER (Charles Eaton) From Kent. Emmanuel, Cambridge 1786, BA1790, dn90 (Cant.), p91 (Cant.), MA1835. PC. Whitstable, Kent 1803-43, V. Seasalter, Kent 1810-43, V. River, Kent 1810-36. Died 5/5/1843 aged 76 [C159129] Married Westminster, London 27/2/1797 Sarah Hayward, with clerical son of father's name.

PLEES (William Gordon) Possibly bapt. Stepney, London 15/1/1781, s. William and Jane Plees. Literate: dn09 (Win.), p10 (Salis. for Win.). V. Cressing, Essex 1814, V. Ashbocking, Suffolk 1833 to death 1849 (3rd q.) [C82715] Married Putney, London 16/5/1803 Elizabeth Bunyon, with clerical son, also William Gordon, and also Robert George Plees.

PLIMLEY (Henry) Born Brewood, Staffs. 3/12/1764, s. Thomas Plimley and Catherine Stubbs. Hertford, Oxford 1781, dn87 (Lin.), p88 (London), BA1789, MA 1791. V. Shoreditch St Leonard, London 1801, V. New Windsor, Berks. 1804-17, Waltam Prebend 1814-17, then Prebend of Hova Ecclesia in Chichester Cathedral 1817, V. Cuckfield, Sussex 1817-41, Chancellor / Vicar General of the Diocese 1822 to death. Dom. Chap. to 1st Baron St Helens 1814-17; to Bishop of Chichester 1817. Died 10/3/1841 [C64885] Married (1) Thomasin Porter (d.1811) (2) Clewer, Berks. 12/11/1813 Mary Buckner.

PLUMER (Charles John) Born St Pancras, London 3/5/1800, s. Rev. Thomas and Mary Anne Plumer. Balliol, Oxford 1816, BA1820, then Oriel, Fellow 1821-30, MA1823, dn23 (Ox.), p26 (Ox.). V. Norton, Durham 1828-49, R. Elstree, Herts. 1849-68, V. Ilford, Sussex 1868-82. Died Brighton, Sussex 22/3/1887 aged 86, leaving £8,522-5s-2d. [C21175] Married (1) St James, Westminster, London 12/5/1831 Sarah Thompson (of Stockton on Tees, d.1861) (2) Broadwater, Sussex 23/1/1869 Mary Elizabeth Iford (40 years younger).

PLUMPTRE (Charles Thomas) Bapt. Nonington, Kent 13/12/1799, s. John Plumptre and Charlotte Pemberton. University, Oxford 1817, BA1821, dn23 (Lin.), p23 (Lin.), MA1825. R. Claypole (North Moiety), Lincs. 1823, R.

Wickhambreux, Kent 1842 to death (Hastings, Sussex) 3/1/1862 aged 62, leaving £9,000 [C72678] Married (1) Ancaster, Lincs. 25/5/1825 Caroline Calcraft (d.1833), with issue (2) Lenton, Notts. 9/4/1835 Elizabeth Wright, with further issue. Brother Henry Western, below.

PLUMPTRE (Henry) Bapt. 17/2/1762, s. Polydore Plumptre (barrister) and Elizabeth Eyre. Queens', Cambridge 1779 [adm. Lincoln's Inn 1783] re-adm. 1792, dn93 (Lin.), p93 (Bristol for Lin.), LLB1796. R. Claypole South Moiety, Lincs. 1793-1847 (w. North Moiety 1820-23-, res.), PC. Hinxton, Cambs. 1795-7 (res.). Died Canterbury 17/12/1847 [C53581] Married Dorothy Pemberton (d.1796), with issue.

PLUMPTRE (Henry Western) Bapt. Nonington, Kent 12/7/1803, s. John Plumptre and Charlotte Pemberton. University, Oxford 1821, BA1825, dn26 (London), p27 (London for Cant.), MA 1842. R. Eastwood, Notts. 1827 and R. Claypole, Lincs. (North Mediety) 1842 to death (Clifton, Bristol) 23/4/1863, leaving £1,000 [C113777] Married Goodnestone, Kent 10/4/1828 Eleanor (dau. Sir Brooke William Bridges, 4th Bart.), with clerical son of father's name. Brother Charles Thomas, above.

PLUMPTRE (Robert Bathurst) Born Worcester 27/9/1792, s. Very Rev. John Plumptre (Dean of Gloucester, q.v. ODNB) and Diana Plumptre [sic]. Pembroke, Cambridge 1810, BA 1814, dn16 (Glos.), MA 1817, p19 (Glos.). R. North Coates, Lincs. 1819-69, PC. Forthampton, Glos. 1819-56. Lived latterly and died Hyde Park, London 3/4/1883, leaving £25,723-5s-10d. [C72681] Married 7/4/1825 Susannah Nicholl (a clergy dau.), and had issue.

PLUNKET (Robert, Hon.) Born Dublin 11/3/1802, s. William Conyngham Plunket, 1st Baron Plunket (Lord Chancellor of Ireland) and Catherine McCausland (sister of the Bishop of Tuam). TCD 1815, BA 1822, MA1831, dn28. R. Barningham, Yorks. 1829-[40] (non-res.), R. Headford, Co. Galway 1840-67, Archdeacon of Killala 1847-50, Dean of Tuam 1850-62. Died (Monkstown, Dublin) 12/5/1867 aged 65. Will not traced in England [C170224. Al.Dub. Boase. D.W.T. Crooks, (ed.) *Clergy of Tuam, Killala and Achonry: biographical succession lists …* (Belfast, 2008)] Married 27/3/1830 Mary, dau. Sir Robert Lynch-Blosse, 8th Bart., many ch.

PLYMOUTH (Andrews Windsor, 7th Earl of) see under **WINDSOR, Andrews**

POCKLINGTON (Henry Sharpe) Born Gloucester 29/12/1802, s. Henry Sharpe (of Chelsworth, Suffolk) and Anne Harvey. Christ's, Cambridge 1819, BA1823, dn26 (Nor.), MA 1827, p27 (Nor.). PC. Overton, Lancs. 1827-32, V. Stebbing, Essex 1831 to death 23/7/1842 [C113778] Married 8/8/1827 Amelia Georgina, dau. of Gen. George Stracey Smyth (Lt.-Governor of New Brunswick).

POCKLINGTON (Roger) Born Winthorpe, Notts. 15/11/1802, s. Roger Pocklington and Jane Campbell. Exeter, Oxford 1821, BA1825, dn29 (York), MA 1829, p30 (York). R. West Bridgford, Notts. 1831-4, V. Walesby, Notts. 1833 and R. Skegness, Lincs. 1834 to death (Walesby, Notts.) 30/5/1880 aged 77, leaving £3,000 [C72683. YCO] Married (1) 17/11/1831 Mary Hutton (d.1864), with issue (2) Newton Abbot, Devon 1866 (1st q.) Anne Amelia Campbell, of Lanark (w).

PODMORE (Robert Beresford) From Condover, Shropshire, s. Rev. Richard Podmore. Trinity, Cambridge 1779 (aged 17), BA1783, dn85 (Peterb. for London), p86 (Chester for C&L), MA1791. V. Monks Kirby, Warwicks. 1785-1842, V. Withybrook, Warwicks. 1791-1842, R. Willey, Warwicks. 1802 to death. Dom. Chap. to 7th Earl of Denbigh 1802; and to Lord Chief Justice Denman. Died (Pailton House, Warwicks.) 4/9/1842 aged 81 [C19044] J.P. Warwicks. 'A man of extraordinary mental capacity', and an authority on church endowments and tithes.

POINTER (Robert) Born Southoe, Hunts. 14/2/1760, s. Rev. James Pointer. Sidney, Cambridge 1779, BA1783, dn83 (Lin.), p84 (Lin.), MA1787. R. Broughton, Hunts. 1784-97, R. Caldecote, Hunts. 1790-1, R. Boxworth, Cambs. 1791-1838, R. Southoe w. Hail Weston, Lincs. 1797-1838, Prebend of Walton Westhall in Lincoln Cathedral 1803 to death. Dom. Chap. to 5th Duke of Bedford 1790-7. Died 5/7/1838 aged 78 [C72687]

POLE ([Alexander] Edward) Bapt. Stoke Damerel, Devon 17/4/1758, s. Reginald Pole and Anne Buller. University, Oxford 1775, BA 1779, dn81 (Ox.), p82 (Ox.), then All Souls, Fellow, MA1783, BD1796, DD 1800. R. Lanreath, Cornwall 1785 (?), R. Dibden, Hants.

1796, V. New Romney, Kent 1797-8, R. Elmley, Kent 1798-1801, R. Barford St Martin, Wilts. 1801 to death. Dom. Chap. to 3rd Viscount Falmouth 1783. Died 28/12/1837 [C29031] Married Hackney, London 27/7/1801 Mrs Jane (Robinson) Carew, with clerical son, also Edward..

POLE (Henry Reginald Chandos) Born Radbourne, Derbys. 12/3/1797, s. Sacheverell Pole and Mary Ware. Trinity, Oxford 1815, then St Mary Hall, BA1821, dn22 (Chester), MA1822, p23 (Chester). R. Radbourne 1824 and R. Mugginton, Derbys. 1832 (and RD 1837) to death. Chap. to 7th Baron Byron 1827; Proctor in Convocation for the Diocese of Lichfield. Died (a bachelor) 19/6/1866, leaving £12,000 [C19270]

POLE (Reginald) Born Barford, Wilts. 27/10/1801, s. Rev. Edward Pole and Jane Robinson. Exeter, Oxford 1819, BA1822, dn24 (Salis.), p24 (Ex.), MA1826. R. Sheviock, Cornwall 1825-39 and R. Mary Tavy, Devon 1826-39, R. Yeovilton, Som. 1839 (and RD of Ilchester) to death. Dom. Chap. to Anne, Dowager Baroness Somers 1827. Died 7/9/1888 aged 86, leaving £643-11s-5d. [C136990] Married Baverstock, Wilts. 26/9/1835 Jane Powell (w), and issue.

POLE (Watson Buller [Van Notten]) Born Tooting, Surrey 20/7/1803, s. Charles Van Notten Pole and Felizarda Matilda Buller. Balliol, Oxford 1821, BA1825, dn26 (Glos.), p27 (Glos.). R. Upper Swell, Glos. 1828 and R. Condicote, Glos. 1840-81. Died Maidenhead, Berks. 26/9/1900 aged 97, leaving £70,022-6s-6d. [C161296. CR65 as V.N.W.B Pole] Married Marylebone, London 11/8/1846 Matilda Pole (dau. of a baronet).

POLLARD (Edward) Bapt. City of London 16/5/1802, s. Edward Pollard [*pleb.*]. St Edmund Hall, Oxford 1823, BA 1827, dn27 (Lin.), p28 (Lin.). PC. Swineshead, Lincs. 1828, R. Evedon, Lincs. 1837-74, V. Ewerby, Lincs. 1837-[72]. Died Great Malvern, Worcs. 5/9/1874, leaving £14,000 [C72688] Married (1) Donington, Lincs. 10/1/1828 Jane Moses (d.1839), with issue (2) Highworth, Wilts. 1852 (3rd q.) Mary Ann Hedges.

POLLARD (John) Born City of London 16/11/1782, s. William and Grace Pollard. BNC, Oxford 1801, BA1805, MA1808, dn08 (Roch.), p09 (Win.). R. Benington. Herts. 1813 to death 23/9/1851 [C2081]

POLLARD (Richard) Bapt. Poulton le Fylde, Lancs. 23/9/1763, s. Richard Pollard. St John's, Cambridge 1781, BA1785, dn85 (Ely), p86 (Ely), MA1788. PC. Parson Drove Chapel, Leveringham, Cambs. 1793 to death (Bath) 25/12/1843 [C100164] Married Leyland, Lancs. 7/5/1805 Dorothy Pollard [*thus*].

POLLEN, *born* BOILEAU (George Pollen Boileau) Born Alcester, Warwicks. 14/8/1798, s. John Peter Boileau (Tacolneston Hall, Norfolk) and Henrietta Pollen (a clergy dau.). Christ Church, Oxford 1818, BA1822, dn22 (Win.), p23 (Win.), MA1835, incorporated at Cambridge 1838. R. Little Bookham, Surrey 1823 to death 7/11/1847 [C82731] Married 13/2/1834 Elizabeth, dau. Sir James Hall, 4th Bart. Assumed additional name of Pollen 1821 on inheriting the Little Bookham estate.

POLWHELE (Richard) Born Truro, Cornwall 6/1/1760, s. Thomas Polwhele and Mary Thomas. Christ Church, Oxford 1778, no degree, dn82 (Ex.), p84 (Ex.). V. Manaccan, Cornwall 1794, V. St Anthony in Menage, Cornwall 1809-28, R. Newlyn, Cornwall 1821 to death 12/3/1838 aged 79 [C146102. ODNB and port.] Married (1) Breage, Cornwall 18/2/1784 Loveday Warren (d.1793), 3 ch. (2) Kenton, Devon 29/11/1793 Mary Tyrrell, with clerical son, below. Cornish antiquary, historian and poet:
https://en.wikisource.org/wiki/Polwhele,_Richard_(DNB00)

POLWHELE (William) Bapt. Manaccan, Cornwall 14/6/1803, s. Rev. Richard Polwhele (above) and Mary Tyrrell. Exeter, Oxford 1821, BA1825, dn26 (C&L). (succ. his father as) V. St Anthony in Menage, Cornwall 1828 to death 24/7/1858 aged 55, leaving £1,000, but a 'lunatic' from 1846 [C19191] Married St Anthony in Meneage, Cornwall 15/11/1831 Georgiana Quash Roskruge [*sic*] (w), with issue.

POMERY (John) Bapt. St Kew, Cornwall 9/7/1781, s. Rev. Joseph Pomery (below) and Mellony Scobell. Exeter, Oxford 1800, BA1804, dn04 (Ex.), p06 (Ex.). R. St Erme (o/w Hermes), Cornwall 1831 to death (a widower) 2/2/1867 aged 86, leaving £450 [Not yet in CCEd] Married Okehampton, Devon

29/4/1820 Margaret Connor Moriarty, with issue (inc. Phillipa Tingcombe Pomery).

POMERY (Joseph) Bapt. Liskeard, Cornwall 28/11/1749, s. John Pomery and Grace Truscott. Exeter, Oxford 1768, BA 1771, dn72 (Ex.), p74 (Ex.), MA1774. V. St Kew (o/w Lanow), Cornwall 1777 to death 7/2/1837 aged 87 [C146107] Married Madron, Cornwall 31/12/1778 Mellony Scobell, with clerical son (above). The senior magistrate of the County.

PONSONBY (John) Bapt. Barnby (upon) Don, Yorks. 12/6/1777, s. Rev. William Ponsonby and Bridget Barker. St Catherine's, Cambridge 1796, BA1800, Fellow 1800, dn00 (York), p01 (York), MA1803. V. Pickering, Yorks. 1814 to death (York) 6/1/1858, leaving under £1,000 [C123975. YCO] Wife Elizabeth, and issue.

PONSONBY (William) Born Ennerdale, Cumberland 25/9/1779, s. Thomas and Mary Ponsonby. Literate: dn03 (Chester), p04 (Chester). PC. Rampside, Lancs. 1804-7 (res.), V. Urswick, Lancs. 1805 (and S/M) to death 8/7/1841 aged 62 [C170227] Married Carlisle 13/4/1819 Agnes Ashburner (d.1820), with issue.

POOL (John) Schoolmaster. Literate: dn89 (Car.), p90 (Car.). R. Cliburn, Westmorland 1802 and PC. Plumpton Wall, Lazonby, Cumberland 1803 to death 2/3/1833 aged 68 (CCEd says 25/9/1833) [C5739. Platt] J.P. Westmorland.

POOLE (Charles) Born Bridgwater, Som. 6/11/1774, s. Thomas Poole and Ann Evered. Balliol, Oxford 1792, BA1798, p99 (B&W). PC. Williton, Som. 1800-[40]. Died 2/11/1848 aged 74 [C47813]

POOLE (Henry) Born Nether (o/w Over) Stowey, Som. c.1775, s. Thomas Poole (a wealthy tanner and farmer). Jesus, Cambridge 1791, BA1795, dn95 (Bristol), p96 (Bristol), MA1799. V. Watchet, Som. 1798-1835, V. Cannington, Som. 1798-1804 (res.). Dom. Chap. to 3rd Earl of Egremont 1798. Died 1835 [C40243 and Venn notes major confusion with the (distantly related?) man below].

POOLE (Henry) Bapt. Bristol 7/9/1784, s. William and Mary Poole. An architect in Bristol before ordination. Literate: dn11 (York), p18 (Glos.). PC. Bream, Glos. 1819-51-, PC. Coleford, Glos. 1819-34, PC. Dean Forest St Paul, Glos. 1822 to death 22/12/1857 [C135687. YCO]. Note above.

POOLE (John) From Nether (o/w Over) Stowey, Som., s. John Poole. Balliol, Oxford 1788 (aged 17), BA1792, then Oriel, Fellow to 1812, MA 1794, dn95 (Ox.), p96 (Ox.). R. Enmore, Som. 1796 and R. Swainswick, Som. 1811 to death. Dom. Chap. to 3rd Earl of Egremont 1813. Died (a widower) 16/5/1857 [C29033] Wife Elizabeth.

POOLE (Robert) Bapt. Cartmel, Lancs. 10/11/1762, s. John Poole and Jane Satterthwaite. Literate: dn87 (Chester for York), p87 (York). PC. Hook Chapel, Snaith, Yorks. 1792, PC. Barmby (on the) Marsh Chapel, Howden, Yorks. 1793, PC. Laxton, Howden, Yorks. 1793, Priest-Vicar of Ripon Collegiate Church 1811-23, PC. Monckton Bishop >< Yorks. 1814 and PC. Bishop Thornton, Yorks. 1836 to death 4/7/1843 [C123977. YCO] Married Airmyn, Yorks. 21/2/1792 Mary Elizabeth Godmond, with clerical son of same name.

POOLEY (Thomas Burrow) Bapt. Thornton in Lonsdale, Yorks. 7/11/1797, s. Rev. Thomas Pooley and Betty Burrow. Christ's, Cambridge 1816, BA1820, dn21 (Chester), p22 (Chester), MA1823. PC. Burton in Lonsdale Chapel, Yorks. 1823-6, V. Thornton in Lonsdale 1826 to death (Ingleton, Yorks.) 1/11/1847 aged 51 [C170231]

POORE (John) From Redbridge, Hants., s. Robert Poore. BNC, Oxford 1793 (aged 15), BA1797, MA1800, dn00, p02 (Win.), BD andDD1826. R. Murston, Kent 1814-66, R. Bicknor, Kent 1816-26 (res.), V. Rainham, Kent 1826 (and RD1833) to death 5/4/1866, leaving £50,000. Chap. to Bishop of Carlisle [C82738. Boase] Married Reading, Berks. 27/1/1803 Elizabeth Stroud. J.P. Kent 1816-59.

POORE (Philip [Henry]) From Andover, Hants., s. Philip Henry Poore (physician) and Mary Harrison. Queen's, Oxford 1822 (aged 18), BA1828, dn28 (Salis.). R. Fyfield, Hants. 1829 to death 28/7/1837 aged 33 [C82739]

POPE (Benjamin) From Worcester, s. Thomas Pope [*pleb.*]. Christ Church, Oxford 1801 (aged 18), BA1804, dn05 (Heref.), p06 (Ox.), Chap. 1806, MA1807. Minor Canon of Windsor Chapel 1817 (then Hon. Canon), V.

Caversham, Oxon. 1809, V. Nether (o/w Over) Stowey, Som. 1824 and V. Ogbourne St George, Wilts. 1826 to death 22/11/1871, leaving £8,000 [C21188] Married Wheatfield, Oxon. 25/4/1809 Caroline Viret.

POPE (Simeon Lloyd) Born City of London 22/12/1801, s. Simeon Pope and Anna Maria Lloyd. Trinity, Oxford 1820, BA1823, dn25 (Ely), p25 (B&W), MA 1829. V. Whittlesey St Mary, Cambs. 1829 to death 14/10/1855 [C40245] Married Mortlake, Surrey 19/1/1837 Sophia Edmunds, with issue.

POPE (Stephen) From Wraby, Lincs., s. John Pope. Trinity, Cambridge 1814 (aged 17), then Emmanuel 1814, BA1818, Fellow 1820, MA 1821, dn25 (Ely), p25 (Nor. for Ely). Curate Lambeth St Mary the Less Chapel, Surrey 1832 to death (Cheltenham) 24/10/1834 aged 37 (CCEd says 16/1/1834) [C82740]

POPPLE (Miles) From Hull, s. Edmund Popple. Trinity, Cambridge 1773 (aged 17), BA1778, dn79 (Ely), Fellow 1780, MA1781, p81 (Peterb.). V. Brading, IoW 1790 to death 25/7/1846 aged 90, living at Welton, Hull. Master of the Charterhouse, Hull [C82741] Married (1) Shoreditch, London 20/1/1794 Josephia L'Oste (a clergy dau., Cockington, Lincs., she d.1838), with issue (2) Nottingham 1841 (3rd q.) Anne Clegworth.

PORT (Bernard) Bapt. Ilam, Staffs. 17/3/1776, s. John Port (born Sparrow, of Ilam Hall) and Mary Pauline D'Ewes. BNC, Oxford 1794, BA1797, MA1800, dn01 (C&L), p01 (C&L). V. Ilam 1801 and R. Honiley, Warwicks. 1814 to death. Dom. Chap. to 9th Earl of Lindsey 1810. Died 30/1/1854 [C19364]

PORTER (George) Bapt. Carlisle 22/8/1790, s. William Porter and Mary Morgan. Queen's, Oxford 1805, BA1809, MA1812, p15 (London), Fellow 1815-30, Tutor 1819. V. Monk Sherbourne, Hants. 1830 to death 8/4/1848 [C21191]

PORTER (Jackson) Bapt. Corney, Cumberland 1/1/1797. Corpus Christi, Cambridge 1815, BA1819, dn20 (Glos.), p21 (Chester), MA1826. PC. Blackburn St John, Lancs. 1826-41, PC. Newcastle under Lyme, Staffs. 1844-7, PC. Burton Pidsey, Yorks. 1848, R. Oddingley, Droitwich, Worcs. 1852-72 (but living at Loughton, Essex in 1871). Died there 12/3/1879 aged 82, leaving under £100 [C135955] Married (1) Blackburn 28/1/1828 Jane Livesey, with issue (2) Blackburn 1/7/1841 Jane Neville.

PORTER (Joseph) From St Bees, Cumberland, s. John Porter. Magdalen Hall, Oxford 1795 (aged 19), dn11 (B&W), BA 1813, p13 (B&W), MA1814. R. Bristol St John the Baptist w. St Lawrence 1826 to death 2/11/1833 (CCEd says 7/1/1834) [C47846] Married 1816 Anne Coxwell.

PORTER (Robert) From Wigan, Lancs., s. William Porter. BNC, Oxford 1792 (aged 18), BA1796, MA1798, p98 (Ex. for Chester). R. Draycot-le-Moors, Staffs. 1806 to death 25/3/1838 [C19365]

PORTER (William) Bapt. Gosforth, Cumberland 31/12/1760, s. Philip Porter and Esther Bateman. Literate: dn85 (York), p86 (Lin. for London). V. Wethersfield, Essex 1786-[1814], PC. Bacup, Lancs. 1797-1837. Died there 4/5/1839 aged 78 [C73214. YCO]

PORTER (William James) Born Canter-bury 2/2/1775, s. Samuel Porter (organist of Canterbury Cathedral) and Sarah Hods. Corpus Christi, Cambridge 1792, BA1797, dn98 (Nor.), p99 (Nor.), MA1800. H/M King's School, Worcester 1813-20; Minor Canon of Peterborough Cathedral 1807-14 (res.), V. Himbleton, Worcs. 1815 to death. Dom. Chap. to 7th Viscount Fitzwilliam 1814. Died Hereford 24/2/1865, leaving £5,000 [C2138] Hymn writer.

PORTINGTON (Henry) Bapt. Bourne, Lincs. 10/3/1756, s. John Portington and Judith Green. Lincoln, Oxford 1773, BA1779, Fellow, MA1780. R. Winterbourne Abbas w. Winterbourne Steepleton, Dorset 1785-95 (res.), R. Wappenham, Northants. 1795 to death 7/12/1832 [C53687] Married (1) Kingsthorpe, Northants. 14/12/1790 Gertrude Joanna Fremaux (d.1803) (2) Shoreditch, London 8/1/1824 Mary Barrows, w. issue.

PORTIS (John) Bapt. St Pancras, London 1/3/1769, s. James and Mary Portis. University, Oxford 1786, BA1790, MA1793, dn93 (Lin. for Win.), p94 (Salis. for Win.). R. Little Leighs, Essex 1795 to death (London) 3/6/1841 [C73215]

POSTLE (Edward) Born Colney, Norfolk, s. Jehosophat Postle and Sarah Rigby. Trinity, Cambridge 1816 (aged 19), BA1821, p22 (Nor.) p23 (Nor.). R. Colney 1823 and R. Yelverton, Norfolk 1837 to death (Yelverton) 26/1/1865, leaving £4,000 [C114456]

POTCHET(T) (William) Bapt. Keying-ham, Yorks. 19/5/1776, s. Rev. William Potchet. St John's, Cambridge 1794, BA 1798, dn98 (York), Fellow 1798-1807, p00 (London), MA1801. R. Fairstead, Essex 1806-17, V. Grantham (North and South) united w. Londonthorpe, Braceby and Gunnerby, Lincs. [net income £1,006] (and Preacher throughout the Diocese of Lincoln) 1817-56, Prebend of Grantham Borealis in Salisbury Cathedral 1825-59, R. Great Ponton, Lincs. 1825-6 (res.), R. Denton, Lincs. 1826-40. Died Grantham 13/11/1859 aged 84. Dom. Chap. to 2nd Earl of Wilton 1826 [C73218. YCO] Married 20/7/1807 Margaret Bowles, with clerical sons Brownlow, Charles, George Thomas, and William Potchet.

POTENGER (Richard) From Guernsey, Channel Islands, s. Thomas Potenger. University, Oxford 1810 (aged 18), then Pembroke 1812-16, BA1814, dn16 (London), p17 (London), MA1819. R. Guernsey St Martin 1832 to death 5/2/1860, leaving £5,000 in England [C83666] Had issue.

POTT (Francis) Bapt. Rotherhithe, Kent 27/12/1792, s. James [*pleb.*] and Elizabeth Pott. St John, Oxford 1810, BA1813, dn16 (London), MA1818. V. Churchstowe w. Kingsbridge, Devon 1829. Died 1842 (4th q.) [C121085]

POTT (Joseph Holden) Bapt. London 221/11/1758, s. Sir Percivall Pott (surgeon, *q.v.* ODNB) and Sarah Elizabeth Cruttenden. St John's, Cambridge 1776, BA1780, dn81 (Peterb.), p82 (Lin.), MA1783. R. Beesby-le-Marsh, Lincs. 1783-90, R. Bratoft, Lincs. 1784-7, Prebend of Welton Brinkhall in Lincoln Cathedral 1785-1814 (res.), V. St Olave Old Jewry w. St Martin Pomeroy, City of London 1787-97, Archdeacon of St Albans 1789-1813, R. Little Burstead, Essex 1797-1806, V. North-olt, Middx. 1806-22 (res.), V. St Martin in the Fields, London 1812-24, Archdeacon of London 1813-42 (res.), Mora Prebend in St Paul's Cathedral 1822-47, V. Kensington St Mary Abbots, London [net income £1,242] 1824-42, Prebend, Chancellor and Canon Resident-iary Exeter Cathedral 1826 to death. Dom. Chap. to 1st Baron Thurlow 1784; to 1st Marquess of Camden 1812. Died (unm.) 16/2/1847 [C73221. ODNB]. https://en.wikipedia.org/wiki/Joseph_Pott

POTTS (James) Born Newcastle upon Tyne 20/12/1794, s. of James Potts (a merchant). Trinity, Cambridge 1815, then Caius 1816, BA 1819, dn22 (Lin. for Durham), p23 (Durham). PC. Whorlton, Durham 1827 to death Sept. 1849 aged 53 [C73255] Married 1831 Mrs Ruth Soulby.

POULDEN (James Bedford) Bapt. Portsea, Hants. 29/8/1800, s. Admiral Richard Poulden and Harriet Bedford. St John's, Cambridge 1818, dn23 (Heref.), BA1824, p24 (Salis.). R. Filton, Bristol 1832 to death 9/10/1876, leaving £1,000 [C53688] Married (1) Harriet (d.1835), with clerical son of father's name (2) Clifton, Bristol 16/8/1837 Emma Day (w), with further issue.

POUNTNEY (Humphrey) Bapt. Birmingham 30/12/1803, s. Humphrey Pountney and Mary Reynolds. Queen's, Oxford 1821 (aged 18), BA1825, dn26 (Lin. for Wor.), p27 (C&L), MA 1828. PC. Wolverhampton St John, 1831 to death (Munich, Bavaria) 31/12/1857, leaving £2,000 [C19369] Wife Emily Cooke, and issue.

POVAH (Richard) Bapt. Manchester 17/12/1763, s. Robert and Mary Povah. A Methodist preacher. Corpus Christi, Cam-bridge 1792, dn96 (York), re-adm. 1798, LLB1800, p10 (S&M), LLD1811. Chap. of the Donative of St. James' Duke Place, City of London 1823 to death (Stoke Newington, London) 18/11/1842 [C7943] Married Bristol 4/5/1796 Mary Worgan, w. clerical s. John Vigden Povah.

POWELL (Benjamin) Born Shropshire 11/1/1792, s. Benjamin Powell. St John, Cam-bridge 1813, no degree, dn15 (Chester), p15 (Chester). PC. Wigan St George, Lancs. 1821 to death (Bowden, Cheshire) 13/6/1861, leaving £4,000 [C170238. DEB] Married Bury, Lancs. 28/7/1824 Ann Wade (a clergy dau., Tottington, Lancs.), with clerical son. J.P. for Lancs.

POWELL (Daniel Philip) Bapt. Gladestry, Radnor 28/2/1765, s. Rev. Roger Powell. Jesus, Oxford 1786, BA1790, p90 (Wor.). R. Sarnes-field, Heref. 1799 to death 27/9/1851 [C119690]

POWELL (Henry Townsend) Born Walthamstow, Essex 11/1/1800, s. David Powell and Mary Townsend. Oriel, Oxford 1817, BA1821, p24 (Peterb.), MA1824. V. Stretton upon Dunsmore w. Princethorpe, Warwicks. 1830 to death (Brighton) 13/6/1854 [C19373. Foster as Henry. Boase] Married 30/9/1834 Harriet Eliza Grimes, w. issue.

POWELL (Howell Wooster) Bapt. High Wycombe, Bucks. 26/2/1775, s. Rev. Howell O. Powell and Elizabeth Saunders. Literate: dn98 (Chester), p99 (York). V. Nidd, Yorks. 1818, R. Heapham, Lincs. 1822, R. Ripley, Yorks. 1843 [C73259] to death 14/3/1848 [C123994. YCO - not Henry] Married Ripley 2/6/1823 Hannah Githings, with issue.

POWELL (James) Bapt. Hendon, Middx., s. James Powell and Elizabeth Longcroft. Clare, Cambridge 1782 [adm. Inner Temple 1785] BA 1787, dn89 (Chich.), MA1790. V. Bitteswell, Leics. 1789 to death (Colchester) 21/4/1844 [C73261] Married Mary Twining, with issue. *J.P.* for Leics.

POWELL (James) From Maesmynis, Brecon, s. Rev. Samuel Powell. Jesus, Oxford 1805 (aged 17), BA1809, dn11 (Heref.), p12 (Heref.), MA 1813. S/M Eardisland G/S. Heref. 1821; V. Long Staunton >< Shropshire 1822 to death (Dilwyn, Heref.) 26/2/1866, leaving £5,000 [C173320] Brother Samuel, below.

POWELL (John) From Hanwell, Middx., s. Robert Powell. Trinity, Cambridge 1799 (aged 19), BA1804, dn05 (London), Fellow 1806, MA1807, p13 (Bristol). R. Little Coates, Lincs. 1816 to death by June 1843 [C53690]

POWELL (John Giles) Possibly bapt. Dover, Kent 12/7/1800, s. Giles and Mary Powell. Peterhouse, Cambridge 1821, dn25 (Peterb.), BA1826, p26 (Peterb.). V. Hillmorton, Warwicks. 1827 to death (Paddington, London) 13/2/1864 aged 64, leaving under £100 [C19370] Had issue. Wrote about his visit to Australia.

POWELL (Joseph) Bapt. Solihull, Warwicks. 23/5/1805, s. John and Sarah Powell. TCD 1830, BA1831, dn31 (York), p31 (York). R. Normanton on Soar, Loughborough, Notts. 1831 [entry blank in ERC] to death 20/9/1868 aged 63, leaving £450 [C136854. Al.Dub. YCO] Widow Elizabeth.

POWELL (Richard) Bapt. Munslow, Shropshire 25/5/1780, s. Rev. Richard Powell, sen. and Elizabeth Crump. Christ Church, Oxford 1797, BA1802, dn03 (Heref.), p04 (Heref.), MA1805. R. Munslow 1806 to death 8/12/1845 [C173343] Married 1803 Maria Pardoe, w. son and successor Thomas Crump Powell.

POWELL (Richard Thomas) Literate: dn20 (Nor.), p20 (Nor.). V. Wiggenhall St Peter, Norfolk 1827 and Wiggenhall St Mary the Virgin, Norfolk 1835 to death 1852 (4th q.) [C114463]

POWELL (Roger) Born Weobley, Hereford, s. Rev. Roger Powell, sen. Worcester, Oxford 1781 (aged 17), BA1784, dn86 (Ox.), p87 (Ox.), MA1787. PC. Wibsey, Bradford, Yorks. 1804 to death 1833 [C29114]

POWELL (Samuel) From Maesmynis, Brecon, s. Rev. Samuel Powell, sen. Pembroke, Oxford 1807 (aged 16), BA1812, dn15 (Heref.), p15 ([Heref.]), MA1815. R. Willersley, Heref. 1825, R. Letton, Heref. 1835, R. Stretford, Heref. 1836 to death (Dilwyn, Heref.) 23/9/1869, leaving £16,000 [C173353] Brother James, above.

POWELL (Thomas) Jesus, Oxford [not indentifiable in Foster], dn78 (Ox.), p79 (Heref. for Wor.). V. Old Radnor w. Kinnerton, Heref./Radnor 1809 to death 26/4/1834 (CCEd thus) aged 71 [C29117]

POWELL (Thomas Baden) Born Hackney, London 14/10/1786, s. James Powell and Ann Cornthwaite. Oriel, Oxford 1804, BA1808, Fellow 1808-12, dn10 (Cant.), MA1810, p11 (Cant.). R. Newick, Sussex 1818 and Hon. Prebend of Sidlesham in Chichester Cathedral 1849 to death 25/4/1868, leaving £60,000 [C61118] Married Hackney 22/5/1811 Sarah Louisa Cottin, with clerical son William.

POWELL (Walter Posthumous) Born Bromsgrove, Worcs. 8/6/1806, s. Rev. Walter (presumably deceased) and Prudence Powell. Worcester, Oxford 1824, BA1828, dn29 (Heref.), p30 (Ox. for Bristol), MA 1831, BCL and DCL1836. S/M Bampton Free G/S. Oxon. 1831; S/M Clitheroe G/S, Lancs. 1835-41-; PC. Great and Little Hampton, Worcs. 1832, PC. Clitheroe St James 1839-1841. Died when Chaplain at Fort St George, Madras 8/6/1853 [C21200] Married Stroud, Glos. 29/6/1830 Matilda Perla Jones, with issue.

POWELL (William) From Dedham, Essex 26/11/1834. St John's, Cambridge 1787 (matr. 1790), BA1791, dn92 (Nor.), p92 (Nor.), MA 1794. R. Shelley, Suffolk 1813-44. Died 8/1/1844 aged 80 [C114464] Married w. issue.

POWLETT (Charles) Born Winchester 17/6/1764, s. Percy Powlett, *R.N.* Trinity, Cambridge 1781, no degree, dn87 (Win.), p89 (Lin.). R. Winslade, Hants. 1789, R. St Martin by Looe, Cornwall 1790-1807, R. Blackford Chapel, Wedmore, Som. 1794-6, V. Kingsclere , Hants. 1796, R. Itchen Stoke and Abbotstone, Hants. 1796-1817, R. Winslade, Hants. 1796-1811, PC. Swingfield, Kent 1817-27, R. High Roding, Essex 1817 to death. Chap. in Ordinary. Died 31/5/1834 (CCEd thus) aged 68, residing 'outside Boulogne' (debt?) [C47873] Married 29/11/1796 Anne, dau. Rev. William Johnson Temple (St Gluvias, Cornwall, the correspondent of James Boswell).

POWLEY (John) Bapt. Bridlington, Yorks. 6/2/1799, s. Robert Powley. Literate: dn22 (Lin.), p23 (Lin.). PC. (and patron of) Legbourne, Lincs. 1825. Died (unm.) 1860 (1st q.) [C73267]

POWLEY (Robert) Bapt. Bampton, Westmorland 24/11/1768, s. of John (a farmer) and Elisabeth Powley. Literate: dn95 (York). PC. Eskdale, Cumberland 1814. Died 1843 (4th q.) [C136661. YCO] Married 4/4/1820 Margaret Porter, w. clerical s. of same name here (1789-1873) - but major confusion here.

POWLEY (William) Bapt. Thornton Watlass, Yorks. 1/2/1800, s. Rev. William Powley. sen. Jesus, Cambridge 1821, BA1826, dn26 (Salis.), p27 (Salis.), MA1829. Curate Starcross, Devon 1832 to death 17/6/1865, leaving £3,000 [C146134] Wife Mary Anna, and clerical son.

POWNALL (George) Born Warmingham, Cheshire. Literate: dn78 (Chester), p79 (Chester). PC. Wincle, Prestbury, Cheshire 1815-32, PC. Bosley, Prestbury, Cheshire 1819 to death. Buried 13/1/1833 [C170244] Married Macclesfield, Cheshire 2/2/1809 Martha Twemlow.

POWYS (Edward) Born Shrewsbury, Shropshire 21/1/1786, s. Rev. Edward Powys, sen. (R. Stapleton, Shropshire) and Mary Hodges. St John's, Cambridge 1803, dn13 (C&L for Ely), BA1814, p14 (Chester). R. Cheddleton, Staffs. 1816 and R. Bucknall and Bagnall, Staffs. 1818 to death (Moreton Hall, Cheshire) 1851 (1st q.) [C19050]

POWYS (Frederick, Hon.) Born London 13/3/1782, s. Thomas Powys, 1st Baron Lilford and Eleanor Mary Mann. Trinity, Cambridge 1799, MA1802, dn06 (Peterb.), p06 (Peterb.). R. Pilton, Northants. 1806-26 (res.), R. Aldwinckle St Peter, Northants. 1806 and R. Thorpe Achurch w. Lilford, Northants. 1806 to death (Chelsea, London) 21/12/1860 [C110724] Married 15/10/1807 Mary Gould (dau. of the High Sheriff of Notts., and sister of the 19th Lord Grey de Ruthin), with issue. Brother Littleton, below.

POWYS (Littleton, Hon.) Born 23/1/1781, s. Thomas Powys, 1st Baron Lilford and Eleanor Mary Mann. Trinity, Cambridge 1799, MA 1802, dn03 (Peterb.). R. Titchmarsh, Northants. 1805-42 and R. Pilton Northants. 1826-36 (res.). Died 22/1/1842 [C110726] Married Godstone, Surrey 24/7/1809 Penelope Hatsell (Morden Park, Surrey), with issue. Brother Frederick, above.

POWYS (Thomas Arthur) Bapt. Remenham, Berks. 10/1/1802, s. Rev. Thomas Powys and Elizabeth Palgrave. St John, Cambridge 1819, Fellow 1819-31, BA1826, dn26 (Ox.), p26 (Cashel for Bishop of Ox. - in Oxford), MA 1829. R. Sawtrey St Andrew, Hunts. 1831 to death (Medmenham, Bucks.) 3/9/1871, leaving £4,000 [C21202] Married Ann Young, w. issue.

POYNDER (Henry) Born City of London 1/3/1785, s. Thomas Poynder and Mary Wix. Christ's, Cambridge 1805, BA1811, dn11 (London), p12 (London), MA1818. R. Horne, Surrey 1818 to death (Upminster, Essex, a bachelor) 17/3/1858, leaving £10,000 [C84905]

PRAT, PRATT (Richard) Bapt. Glaston-bury, Som., 6/12/1764, s. Rev. Richard Prat. Wadham, Oxford 1783, BA1787, dn92 (C&L for Ex.). V. Littleham cum Exmouth, Devon 1813 to death 6/6/1840 [C19382] Brother Joseph, below.

PRATT (Charles) Born Howden, Yorks. 14/2/1792 or 93, s. Rev. Joseph Stephen Pratt (below) and Frances Cecilia Cowper. Magdalene, Cambridge 1811, BA1815, dn16 (Chester for York), MA1816, p17 (Peterb.). V. Packington, Leics. 1823-53, Chap. 'of the Donative Peculiar' of Stanstead St Margaret, Herts. 1853 [value £6] to death 19/1/1889 aged 96, leaving £13,287-8s-8d. [C73854. YCO] Married Gedling, Notts. 24/6/1817 Harriet Smelt (a clergy dau.), w. issue. Brother Joseph, below.

PRATT (John) Bapt. Orpington, Kent 23/4/1773, s. Rev. Henry Pratt and Mary Pomeroy Roope. University, Oxford 1790, BA 1794, dn96 (Bristol for Cant.), MA1797, p97 (Cant.). V. Cudham, Kent 1796-1803, R. Sedlescombe, Sussex 1803 to death 6/8/1861, leaving £90,000 [C2914] Married St Mary Cray, Kent 4/3/1804 Maria Ann Berens, with clerical son John Joseph Pratt.

PRATT (Joseph) Born Whitkirk, Yorks. 29/7/1784, s. Rev. Joseph Stephen Pratt (below) and Frances Cecilia Cowper. Queens', Cambridge 1803, BA1807, dn08 (B&W), p09 (B&W), MA1813. R. Paston, Northants. 1811 to death 1/12/1876, leaving £16,000. Dom. Chap. to 6th Earl Waldegrave 1818 [C47875. ODNB] Married Brockley, Som. 19/8/1811 Mary Boak (a clergy dau.), with clerical son. Brother Charles above.

PRATT (Joseph Stephen) Bapt. Maryle-bone, London 17/6/1761, s. Jonathan Pratt and Mary Moule. Emmanuel, Cambridge 1778, then Magdalene 1790, dn02 (Peterb.), p03 (Peterb.), then Trinity Hall 1804, LLB 1805. V. Peterborough St John the Baptist, 1806-33, R. South Collingham, Notts. 1807-22, 4th Canonry of Peterborough Cathedral 1808-38, V. Maxey, Northants. 1817-31, Chap. of Stanstead St Margaret, Herts. 1832 to death 3/4/1838 [C110427] Married St George's Hanover Square, London 23/8/1782 Frances Cecilia Cowper ('a minor', Park House, Herts.), with clerical sons Charles, and Joseph, above. Port. online.

PRATT (Josiah) Born Birmingham 21/12/1768, s. Josiah Pratt (manufacturer) and Elizabeth Richardson. St Edmund Hall, Oxford 1789, dn93 (Heref.), BA1793, p93 (Heref.), MA 1796, BD1808. PC. Sir George Wheler's [Proprietary] Chapel, Spitalfields, London 1810, V. St Stephen Coleman Street, City of London 1826 to death 10/10/1844. Secretary of the C.M.S. 1802-24 [C121099. ODNB. DEB]. Josiah Pratt [jun], *Memoir of the Rev. Josiah Pratt, DD, late Vicar of St Stephen Coleman Street, and for 21 years Secretary of the Church Missionary Society* (1849)] Married Newington 7/9/1797 Elizabeth Jowett, with clerical sons Josiah, and John

Henry Pratt. Helped to form the British and Foreign Bible Society: https://en.wikipedia.org/wiki/Josiah_Pratt

PRATT (William) Bapt. Riston Hall, Norfolk 5/11/1804, s. Edward Roger Pratt and Pleasance Browne. Trinity, Cambridge 1823, dn29 (Ely), BA1828, p29 (Ely). R. Great Bircham, Norfolk 1832 and R. Harpley, Norfolk 1832 [total income in CR65 £1,242] to death 11/11/1874, leaving £35,000 [C109383] Married 1835 Louisa Coxhead Marsh (w) (Gaynes Park, Essex), with issue.

PREEDY (Benjamin) Born Evesham, Worcs. 12/6/1773, s. William Preedy and Alice Biddle. Merton, Oxford 1790, BA 1794, dn96 (Wor.), p97 (Nor.), MA1799. R. Hinton on the Green, Glos. 1813 and R. Willersey, Glos. 1814 to death. Dom. Chap. to 3rd Earl Harcourt 1814. Died 1/5/1849 [C114470] Married Ealing, Middx. 28/12/1813 Mary Allbone, with issue.

PREEDY (James) From Harding, Herts., s. Rev. Benjamin Preedy and Mary Osman. Queen's, Oxford 1771 (aged 18), BA1775, dn75 (London), p78 (Chester for Peterb.), then Clare, Cambridge, MA1796. R. Welton, Northants. 1783-5, R. Haselton w. Yanworth, Glos. 1785-93 (res.), V. Winslow, Bucks.1793, V. Brington, Northants. 1796-9 (res.), Preacher throughout the Diocese of Peterborough 1796, R. Hinton-in-the-Hedges cum Steane, Northants. 1809 to death. Dom. Chap. to Georgiana, Countess Spencer 1783; to 5th Duke of Marlborough 1817. Died (at his house in Regent's Park, London) 3/10/1836 aged 74 [C110728] Married Brington, Northants. 6/5/1783 Mary Stirling, with issue.

PRESCOT (Charles Kenrick) Born Stockport, Cheshire 29/12/1786, s. Rev. Charles Prescot and Jane Dyson. BNC, Oxford 1804, BA1808, MA1810, dn11 (London), p12 (London), incorporated at Cambridge MA1846. PC. Aughton, Lons-dale, Lancs. 1812-15, PC. Marple, Cheshire 1814-20, PC. Chadkirk, Cheshire 1815-20, (succ. his father as) R. Stockport St Mary 1820 [income in CR65 £2,200], RD of Warrington to death there 4/5/1875 aged 88, leaving £25,000 [C121103] Married Taxal, Cheshire 22/2/1821 Emma Octavia Warre, with clerical issue.

PRESCOTT (Clarke) Born Southwell, Notts. 1/6/1758, s. John Prescott and Maria Clarke.

Literate: dn84 (Dur.), p85 (Dur.), then St John's, Cambridge 1786 (a Ten Year Man). V. Burrington, Heref. 1786 and V. Downton (on the Rock), Heref. 1786 to death (Chetham Hill, Manchester) 12/4/1838 [C131533] Married Leint-wardine, Heref. 26/12/1793 Frances Gibbons, with issue. Brother below.

PRESCOTT (John) Probably born Halifax, Yorks. 22/7/1773, s. John Prescott and Maria Clarke. St John's, Cambridge 1791, then St Catharine's 1792, BA1795, dn95 (Lin. for Peterb.), MA1798. V. Dunston, Lincs. 1813, R. Benington, Lincs. 1815-17, V. North Somercotes, Lincs. 1817 to death. Dom. Chap. to 4th Earl of Buckinghamshire 1813-14; to Eleanor, Baroness Auckland 1814. Died (Louth, Lincs.) 11/6/1849 [C19384. Kaye] Married 1823 Maria Eliza Philips. Brother Clarke, above.

PRESTON (George, sen.) Bapt. Beeston St Laurence, Norfolk 27/7/1760, s. Isaac Preston and Esther Pettingal. University, Oxford 1777, BA1783, MA1784, dn85 (Heref.), p86 (Nor.). R. Beeston St Laurence 1785-37, PC. (and patron) of Tasburgh, Norfolk 1832 to death 23/10/1837 [C114474] Son, 2 below.

PRESTON (George) Bapt. Ulverston, Lancs. 13/4/1771, s. George Preston (a merchant) and Isabel Sandys. Trinity, Cam-bridge 1787, BA 1792, dn93 (Ely), MA1795, p96 (Nor.). V. (and patron) of Briston, Norfolk 1803-40, PC. Cartmel, Lancs. 1804-33, R. Lexden, Essex 1804 to death there 29/9/1840 [C100166]

PRESTON (George, jun.) Born Beeston St Laurence, Norfolk, s. Rev. George Preston, sen. (above). Trinity, Cambridge 1809, BA1813, dn13 (Nor.), p14 (Nor.), MA1821. Usher at Westminster School 1818-26, then Under-Master 1826; V. Christ Church Newgate Street w. St Leonard Foster Lane, City of London 1829 to death. Chap. to the Foundling Hospital, London 1820. Died 6/9/1851 aged 50 [C114475] Married 19/8/1822 Emma Van Heythuysen (dau. of a London solicitor), with issue.

PRESTON (Matthew Morris) Bapt. Sheffield, Yorks. 19/10/1781, s. Rev. Matthew Preston and Jane Morris. Trinity, Cambridge 1799, BA 1804, dn05 (Lin.), Fellow 1805, MA1807, p09 (Bristol). Kept a school at Shelford, Cambs. 1808-13; then at Aspenden Hall, Herts., 1813-25 (where Lord Macaulay and other eminent men were his pupils); V. Cheshunt, Herts. 1826 to death 18/4/1858, leaving £30,000 [C53696. Boase] Married Clapham, Surrey 7/7/1818 Eliza Garratt, with clerical sons Theodore, John William, and Alfred Matthew Preston.

PRESTON (William) Bapt. Bulmer, Yorks. 7/10/1781, s. Rev. Charles Preston and Elizabeth Mather. Peterhouse, Cambridge 1794, BA1799, dn05 (York), p06 (York), MA 1812 (Lambeth, so a Ten Year Man). V. Bulmer 1806 and V. Whenby, Yorks. 1806-66, R. Ergham, Yorks. 1812-22, Prebend of Bilton in York Minster 1812-67, V. Sculcoates, Hull 1815-66. Died Bulmer 4/7/1867 aged 86, leaving £1,500 [C124011. YCO. Platt] Married 26/4/1810 Frances Plumer (aged 18), with issue.

PRESTON (William Michael Stephen-son) Bapt. Warcop, Westmorland 22/11/1785, s. William Michael Stephenson Preston (of Warcop Hall) and Sarah Todd. Queen's, Oxford 1803, BA1807, dn09 (Ex.), p10 (Ex.), MA1811, Fellow 1815-21. V. Acklam with Middlesbrough, Yorks. 1816-23, V. Startforth, Yorks. 1816-23 (res.), R. Bowness, Cumberland 1823-8, V. (and patron) of Warcop 1828 (living at Warcop Hall) to death (Falkland, Fife - 'where he was travelling for the benefit of his health') 21/9/1842 aged 56 [C5747] Married Edinburgh 1820 Margaret Moyes (of Fife), with clerical issue. J.P. Westmorland.

PRETYMAN (George Thomas) Born London 5/4/1790, s. Rt. Rev. George Pretyman, Bishop of Lincoln (later Rt. Rev. Sir George Pretyman-Tomline, 5th Bart.) and Elizabeth Maltby. Trinity, Cambridge 1808, dn13 (Lin.), LLB1814, p14 (Lin.). R. Walgrave w. Hannington, Northants. 1814-17, Prebends of Biggleswade and of Stoke 1814-59, Chancellor of Lincoln Cathedral (w. PC. Nettleham annexed, and Preacher throughout the Dioceses of Lincoln and of Peterborough 1814-59), R. Wheathampstead w. Harpenden, Herts. [net income £1,356] 1814-59, R. Chalfont St Giles, Bucks. 1814-59, R. Walgrave cum Hannington, Northants. 1814-17 (then Walgrave only), Canon Residentiary of 2nd Prebend in Winchester Cathedral 1825 to death (Batts Hotel, Piccadilly, London) 23/6/1859, leaving £140,000. 'His income from ecclesiastical sources seems to have been upwards of £6,250' [C73870. Boase. Kaye] Married St Margaret's, Westminster, London 25/5/1814 Amelia Tower (Weald Hall, Essex), w. clerical son Frederick.

Retained the name Pretyman, but abandoned claims to the baronetcy. Brother Richard, below.

PRETYMAN (John) Born Sudbury, Suffolk 15/11/1785, s. Rev. John Pretyman, sen. (later Rt. Rev. Sir George Pretyman-Tomline, 5th Bart.) and Anne Keddington. St John's, Cambridge 1802, BA1807, dn08 (Lin.), p09 (Lin.), MA1811. V. Chiswick, London 1809-11, Prebend of Aylesbury in Lincoln Cathedral 1810-42, R. Winwick, Northants. 1810-42, R. Sherington, Bucks. 1811-42, 'official' of the Archdeacon of Lincoln 1836 to death. Dom. Chap. to Bishop of Norwich 1811. Died 22/11/1842 [C73871] Married Chiswick, London 14/6/1814 Dorothy Jane Sidebottom (Sutton Court, Chiswick), with issue.

PRETYMAN (Richard) Born 21/3/1793, s. Rt. Rev. George Pretyman, Bishop of Lincoln, then of Winchester (later Rt. Rev. Sir George Pretyman-Tomline, 5th Bart.) and Elizabeth Maltby. Trinity, Oxford 1809 [adm. Lincoln's Inn 1812] BA1814, dn16 (Lin.), p17 (Lin.), MA1817, incorporated at Oxford 1834. V. Hambleton, Rutland 1817-19, Prebend of Langford Ecclesia (and Precentor) of Lincoln Cathedral 1817-66, R. Walgrave, Northants. 1817 (w. Hannington 1817-66 [blank in ERC], R. Middleton Stoney, Oxon. 1819-66 [blank in ERC], (Sinecure R. Wroughton, Wilts. 1825) to death. Dom. Chap. to his father 1814. Master Northampton Hospital [almshouses] of St John the Baptist and St John the Evangelist 1814; Master St John's Hospital [almshouses], Mere, Lincs. 1817. Dom. Chap. to his father 1817. Died 25/3/1866 [total income £2,204], leaving £50,000 [C21203. Boase] Married (1) Southwark, London 31/8/1820 Sarah Alicia Porter (d.1820), with clerical son Richard (2) Market Harborough, Leics. 1849 (2nd q.) Harriet Thorpe (a clergy dau.), (w), with further issue. Brother George Thomas, above.

PRICE (Andrew) From Leigh, Essex, s. Rev. Roger Price. Chorister Magdalen, Oxford 1767-72; matr. 1771 (aged 17), usher Magdalen College School 1772-88, BA1775, dn76 (Salis.), MA1778, p78 (Ox.), Chap. Christ Church 1788-1800. R. Britwell Salome, Oxon. 1782 and R. Down Ampney, Glos. 1788 to death 7/6/1851. Chap. Bishop Warner's College, Bromley, Kent 1795 [C2146]

PRICE (Aubrey Charles) Bapt. Broadwindsor, Dorset 11/12/1787, s. Rev. Aubrey Charles Price, sen. and Mary Slade. New, Oxford 1806, Fellow 1806-27, BA 1810, dn11 (Salis.), p12 (Salis.), MA1815. V. Colerne, Wilts 1816-27, V. Chesterton, Oxon. 1826 to death 29/9/1848 [C21204] Married 1827 Theodora Ann Hewitt, with issue. Once in gaol for debt (Wilberforce).

PRICE (Charles) [NiVoF] R. Ashford Carbonell, Shropshire w. R. Little Hereford, Heref. 1814 to death 9/1/1835 ('at an advanced age') [C73916 as Pryce fits these dates, except he death date is s obviously wrong].]

PRICE (Charles Parker) Bapt. Beechley, Glos. (in an Independent chapel) 4/11/1800, s. Walter and Catherine Price. Pembroke, Oxford 1820, BA1824, dn26 (Cashel for Ox. - in Oxford), MA 1827, p27 (Ox.). V. Uxbridge, Hillingdon, Middx. 1827 to death. Chap. to Uxbridge Union 1836. Died 4/5/1872, leaving £600 [C21205] Married Plymouth 2/10/1827 Mary Barzey Curgenven (w), with issue.

PRICE (Evan) Literate: dn22 (Llandaff), p23 (Llandaff). PC. Dunston, Penkridge, Staffs. 1824 and PC. Coppenhall, Penkridge 1850 to death 14/5/1875, leaving £7,000 [C19389] Widow Ann, and issue.

PRICE (George) Bapt. Lyminge, Kent 29/6/1780, s. Rev. Ralph Price and Albinia Woodward. Wadham, Oxford 1798, Fellow to 1827, BA1802, dn03 (Ox.), p04 (Ox.), MA1808. R. Fryerning, Essex 1826 and V. Eastwood, Essex 1826 to death. Dom. Chap. to Louisa, Marchioness Cornwallis 1826. Died 9/5/1861, leaving £12,000 [C21206] Brother Ralph, below.

PRICE (George) Born Farnham, Surrey 26/6/1801, s. Col. Barrington Price and Lady Mary Jane Bowes (dau. 9th Earl of Strathmore & Kinghorne, she d.1806). Trinity, Oxford 1819, then St Alban Hall BA1824, dn25, p25 (Chich.). R. Romaldkirk, Yorks. 1828-41. Died Cheltenham, Glos. 6/9/1877 aged 76, leaving £1,000 [C170257] Married (1) Clapham, Surrey 6/10/1830 Georgina Pelly (d.1835), with issue (2) Wargrave, Beds. 8/6/1838 Elizabeth Harbie Oddy (or Wayment?). But note another man of this name.

PRICE (Hugh) From Worcs. St John's, Cambridge 1794, then Queens' 1798, BA 1799, dn00 (Lin.), p01 (Lin.), MA1802, Fellow 1802. S/M Bromsgrove GS 1804-10; R. Newton

Tony, Wilts. 1809 to death 4/5/1853 aged 76 [C73879] Married 1825 Charlotte Emly, with issue.

PRICE (Humphrey) From Kidderminster, s. of a weaver. Literate: dn97 (Heref.), p00 (C&L). PC. Needwood (Forest) Staffs. 1809 to death 1853 (2nd q.) [C19052. E. Groth Lyon, *Politicians in the pulpit* (Aldershot, 1999), pp 101-5] Gaoled 1829-30 for slandering the carpet manufacturers of Kidderminster; a Chartist and anti-Establishment figure.

PRICE (James) From High Wycombe, Bucks., s. Rev. James Price, sen. Merton, Oxford 1781 (aged 18), BA1785, dn86 (Lin.), p87 (Lin.), MA 1788. V. High Wycombe 1788 and R. Great Munden, Herts. 1817 to death. Dom. Chap. to 1st Earl of Verulam 1817. Died 16/6/1846 [C73881]

PRICE (John) Born Breconshire, s. David Price and Joan Gwynne. Literate. H/M Standish G/S, Lancs. 1817; PC. Burton, Cheshire 1814, PC. Douglas Chapel, Chorley, Lancs. 1829-51. Died Standish 3/1/1860, leaving £7,000 [C170265] Married Madley, Heref. 25/1/1814 Margaret Smith, with clerical son William.

PRICE (John) Literate: dn30 (Chester), p30 (Chester). (first) PC. Blackburn St Paul, Lancs. 1799 [the church building and Price himself were in Lady Huntingdon's Connection until 1829] 1830 to death 1841 [C170260] Was presented with a silver tea service for 33 [*sic*] years' service.

PRICE (Ralph) Bapt. Lyminge, Kent 9/4/1778, s. Rev. Ralph Price, sen. and Albinia Woodward. Trinity, Oxford 1796, BA1800, dn00 (Cant.), MA1803, p04 (Roch. for Cant.). V. (and patron and Sinecure R.) Lyminge w. Sanford and Paddlesworth 1811 to death (Milsted, Kent) 9/7/1863. Lived at Penshurst, Kent, leaving £1,500 [C2147] Married Milsted 10/8/1813 Maria Isabella Tylden. Brother George, above.

PRICE (Robert) Born London, s. James Price (merchant). Pembroke, Cambridge 1792 (aged 18), BA1796, dn96 (London), p02 (London). 3rd Prebend 1794-1804 then 5th Prebend of Durham Cathedral 1804-23, V. Shoreham, Kent 1816 to death 21/12/1842 aged 68 [C2148. Fasti says d. 7/4/1823]

PRICE (Thomas) From Soho, London, s. Rees Price. St Edmund Hall, Oxford 1812 (aged 23), BA1815, dn15 (C&L for Salis.), p15 (B&W), MA1818. V. Llanrothal, Heref. 1826 and R. Shelsley Beauchamp, Worcs. 1832 [C122012] to death 17/9/1848 [C19393]

PRICE (Thomas) [NiVoF] V. Foston, Leics. 1830 to death 30/4/1834 (CCEd thus) [C73886]

PRICE (Thomas) From Lichfield, s. Rev Thomas Price. Christ Church, Oxford 1792 (aged 17), BA1796, MA1799, p99 (C&L). R. Maxstoke, Worcs. 1811-14 (res.), R. Bredicot, Worcs. 1821 and R. Enville, Worcs. 1824 to death 4/1/1837 [C19391]

PRICE (William) Born Wantage, Berks. 1/2/1784, s. William Henry and Ann Price. Pembroke, Oxford 1799, BA1803, Fellow, MA1806, dn07 (Ex.), p08 (Ex.). Chap. Coln St Denis, Glos. 1809 and R. Farnborough, Berks. 1815 to death. Dom. Chap. to Anne, Countess of Albemarle 1815. Died 13/4/1860, leaving £8,000 [C146136] Clerical sons William Henry, and Bartholomew Price. J.P. and Tax Commissioner for Gloucester County; Chairman of Board of Guardians.

PRICE see also **PRYCE**

PRICHARD (Robert) From Llangaffo, Angelsey, s. Robert Prichard. Jesus, Oxford 1784 (aged 18), BA1787, dn89 (Ox.), p90 (Ox.), Fellow, MA1790, BD1798. R. Llansantffraid, Denbigh 1798-1800, R. Llanfihangel-Glyn-Myfyr, Denbigh 1800 and of R. Rotherfield Peppard, Oxon. 1808 to death 30/3/1848 [C114121]

PRICHARD see also **PRITCHARD**

PRICKITT, PRICKETT (Giles) Bapt. Albury, Oxon. 4/3/1771, s. Giles Prickitt and Mary Crewes (Tiddington, Glos.). New, Oxford 1786, BA1790, dn93 (Lin.), MA 1794, p95 (Ox.). R. Newbold Vernon, Leics. 1803-16, R. Ravenstone, Leics. 1809 to death 8/2/1855 [C19394] Wife Elizabeth (though there is a possible earlier wife), with issue.

PRIDEAUX (Gostwycke) Born North Tawton, Devon 25/1/1797, s. Thomas Prideaux. Sidney, Cambridge 1816, dn20 (Peterb. for Cant.), BA1821, p21 (Cant.). PC. Boyton, Wilts. 1822-6, PC. Iwade, Kent 1826-

37, V. Elmsted, Kent 1833 and R. Hastingleigh, Kent 1833 to death 24/3/1880, leaving £1,000 [C111854] Married Sittingbourne, Kent 16/10/1833 Lucretia Castle, with issue.

PRINCE (John) From London, s. John Prince [*pleb*.]. Oriel, Oxford 1772 (aged 18), BA1775, dn75 (Oxon.), p77 (*sede vacante*). V Grays Thurrock, Ex. 1785-93 (res.), V. Enford, Wilts. 1793 to death. Chap. to Magdalen Asylum, Lambeth 'for 40 years'. Died 13/11/1834 aged 80 [C37338] Clerical son Thomas.

PRITCHARD (William) *'known and passing by the name of'* **William Pritchard Gee**. Born 1788, natural s. William Gee and Jane Pritchard. St John's, Cambridge 1805 (re-adm. 1807), BA 1800, dn10 (Win.), p11 (Win.), MA1814. R. Walton-on-the-Hill, Surrey 1815-22, R. Great Yeldham, Essex 1822-31 (res.), V. Great Wakering, Essex 1822-38. Dom. Chap. to HRH Duke of Sussex 1822. Died 1/11/1838 [C108610] Married Lewes, Sussex Sarah Wilds 15/10/1810, w. clerical s. William Amon Gee Pritchard. Chronic debtor, often living in France.

PRITCHARD see also **PRICHARD**

PRITCHETT (Delabere) Born Cambridge 12/1/1775, s. Rev. Charles Piggot Pritchett and Ann Rogers. Trinity, Cambridge 1792, dn98 (Glos.), BA1799, MA1799, p00 (Glos.). PC. St David's, Pembroke 1802 (only), Prebend of St Nicholas Penyfos in St David's Cathedral 1813-38, R. Cheadle, Staffs. 1814 to death (Edinburgh) 23/12/1838. H/M of the 'highly respectable' Whitchurch English Grammar School 1804 [C19401 where death date is obviously wrong] Married Kempsey, Worcs. 18/5/1815 Harriet Warren.

PRITCHETT (George) Born Brimfield, Heref. 4/11/1800, s. Delabere (pleb., not above) and Martha Pritchett. Jesus, Oxford 1768, BA 1772, dn72 (Heref.), p74 (Heref.). V. Mathon, Worcs. 1794 to death 1835 aged 84 [C173464]

PROBY (Charles) Born Thornhaugh, Northants. 23/1/1771, s. Very Rev. Baptist Proby (Dean of Lichfield) and Mary Russel (a clergy dau.). St John's, Cambridge 1788, BA 1792, dn93 (C&L), MA1795, p95 (Peterb.). R. of Waddesdon, Bucks. (3rd Portion) 1800-23, V. Bishops Tachbrook, Warwicks. 1803-59, Canon of Windsor 1814 and V. Twickenham, Middx.

1818 to death there. Chap. to his cousin Earl of Carysford 1802 when Ambassador in Berlin; to Duke of Marlborough 1803; to Mary, Baroness Seaforth 1817. Died 2/2/1859, leaving £10,000 [C19055] Married Canwick, Lincs. 30/6/1814 Frances Sharrer (a clergy dau.), w. issue.

PROBYN (Edmund) Bapt. Abinghall, Glos. 8/9/1788, s. Rev. John Probyn and Anne Raynor Jones. University, Oxford 1806, BA 1810, dn10 (Glos.), MA1814, p11 (Glos.). (succ. his father as) V. Longhope, Glos. 1827 and R. Abenhall (o/w Abinghall) 1827 to death 8/3/1837, having been certified insane in 1835 [C161148. DEB. T.C.F. Stunt, 'The case of a Gloucestershire clergyman'. *Journal of Ecclesiastical History* 39 (1988) 95-105] Married Witley, Surrey 3/7/1821 Julianna Webb, w. clerical son Edmund Thomas Webb.

PROCTER, PROCTOR (Joseph) Bapt. Ferry Fryston, Yorks. 25/3/1791, s. Rev. Francis Procter. St Catharine's, Cambridge 1779, BA 1783, Fellow 1783-99, dn84 (Lin. for York), p85 (York), MA1786, BD1799, DD1801, Master of St Catharine's College, Cambridge 1799-1845 [when there was 'a partial revival in the fortunes of the College during his mastership' - Venn]. Vice- Chan-cellor of Cambridge 1801-2, 1825-6. Canon of 4th Prebend in Norwich Cathedral 1799-1845, R. Steeple Gidding, Hunts. 1807-34, R. Walgrave cum Haddington, Northants. 1810-14 (res.), R. Conington, Hunts. 1824 to death 10/11/1845 [C117183. YCO]

PROCTER (Richard) Bapt. Long Preston, Yorks. 5/6/1774, s. John and Elizabeth Procter. Christ's, Cambridge 1794, 1795, BA1799, dn04 (Chester for York), MA1804, p05 (York). S/M Tuxford Free School. Notts. 1806; V. Laxton (o/w Lexington), Notts. 1826 to death 12/1/1858 aged 72, leaving £25,000 [C117186. YCO] Widow Ann.

PROCTOR (George) Bapt. Clewer, Bucks. 29/4/1795, s. George and Elizabeth Proctor. St Edmund Hall, Oxford 1813, BA1817, then Worcester, MA1820, BD 1828, DD1829. R. Lewes St Michael, Sussex 1826, Chap. of Donative of Monk Hadley, Middx. 1846-60. Chap. to Fishmongers" Almshouses, Maidenhead, Kent 1860-80. Died London 7/8/1881, leaving £3,570-12s-2d. [C65021]

PROCTOR (Robert) Bapt. Long Preston, Yorks. 4/5/1760, s. Robert Proctor and Mary

Hamerton. Literate: dn84 (York for Chester), p86 (Chester). V. Tunstall, Lancs. 1790-1800 (res.), PC. Euxton, Leyland, Lancs. 1799, PC. Hornby, Melling, Lancs. 1800 to death (Tunstall) 3/8/1840 aged 80 [C117187. YCO] Married Tunstall 20/1/1791 Jane Tatham; had 'a large family and many pupils'.

PROCTOR, PROCTER (William) Born Long Preston, Yorks. 21/10/1762, s. George and Isabel Proctor. S/M. Literate: dn91 (Chester, p92 (Chester), MA1812 Lambeth. PC. Alnwick, Northumberland (with S/M Alnwick G/S 1794) 1799, R. Longhoughton, Northumberland 1811 and V. Lesbury, Northumberland 1812 to death. Dom. Chap. to 3rd Duke of Northumber-land 1812. Died Alnwick 19/3/1839 aged 77 [C134604. Reference in Venn under son of same name] Married 1784 Mary Aislabie, with clerical son of same name.

PROCTOR see also **PROCTER**

PRODGERS (Edwin) Born Worcester 1787, s. Rev. Edwin Prodgers. Trinity, Oxford 1803 (aged 17), BA1807, dn10 (Win.), MA1810, p11 (Win.), DD1827. Chap. of the Donative of Brixton St Matthew, Surrey 1824, R. Ayot St Peter, Herts. 1842 to death (London) 5/12/1861, leaving £60,000 [C108619] Married Brixton 21/10/1828 Caroline Blades (w), with issue.

PROSSER (Henry) Born Presteigne, Radnor 1794. Literate: p19 (Ox. for Peterb.). PC. Garway, Heref. 1821-82 and PC. Welch (o/w Welsh) Newton, Heref. 1821, PC. Dulas, Heref. 1827-64-, Chap. of the Donative of Orcop, Ross, Heref. before 1859 [income £31]. Died Hereford 22/9/1882 aged 88, leaving £5,368-13s-8d. [C110733]

PROSSER (Thomas) Born Dorstone, Heref., s. Rev. Thomas, sen. and Hannah Prosser. BNC, Oxford 1789 (aged 19), BA 1793, d94 (Heref.). (succ. his father as) V. Dorstone 1794 to death 2/3/1843 [C173541]

PROSSER (William) [NiVoF] S/M Tewkesbury G/S, Worcs. 1802; PC. Walton Cardiff, Glos. 1814 [C161595], PC. Bushley, Glos. Worcs. 1815, PC. Chaceley, Worcs. 1819. Died Tewksbury 1847 aged 87 [C122020]

PROUT (John) Literate: dn13 (Heref. for Llandaff), p14 (Heref.), then St John's, Cambridge 1817 (a Ten Year Man). V. Goulceby w. Burwell, Lincs. 1827-36, R. Trusthorpe, Lincs. 1840-52, R. Sutton in the Marsh, Lincs. 1852 to death 15/12/1858, leaving £3,000 [C73912. Kaye] Married Rainham, Kent Harriet Towle (w).

PROWDE (Richard) Bapt. Hovingham, Yorks. 9/5/1787, s. Robert and Alice Prowde. Trinity, Cambridge 1806, BA1811, dn11 (York), p12 (York), MA1814. PC. Hinderwell w. Roxby, Yorks. 1823-30, PC. Hovingham, Yorks. 1832 to death 27/2/1842 [C135692. YCO]

PROWER (John Mervin) Born Purton, Wilts. 14/1/1784, s. Rev. John Prower and Anne Lipyeatt. Wadham, Oxford 1802, BA 1806, dn24 (Salis.), p27 (Salis.), MA1835. V. Purton, Wilts. 1828 (and Hon. Canon of Bristol Cathedral) to death 2/4/1869, leaving £3,000 [Not yet in CCEd] Married Purton 20/9/1809 Susannah Coles, with issue.

PROWETT (Charles) Bapt. Addenbury, Oxon. 26/9/1780, s. Robert Prowett and Elizabeth Bathurst. Literate: dn12 (Nor.), p12 (Nor.). R. Happisburgh, Norfolk 1814-30, R. Stapleford, Herts. 1820 to death 8/2/1851 [C114515] Married Cecilia Wolseley, with issue. Doubtless related to the man below.

PROWETT (John) From Addenbury, Oxon., s. Willam Prowett. New, Oxford 1792 (aged 18), dn97 (Ox.), Fellow, BA 1796, p98 (Ox.), MA 1801 R. Bealugh, Norfolk 1807-10, R. Edburton, Sussex 1810-33, R. Heigham, Norfolk 1829-33, R. Catfield, Norfolk (1st then both Moieties) 1833 and (Sinecure R. Great Tey, Essex 1845) to death 20/3/1851 [C37347] Clerical son John Henry. Doubtless related to the man above.

PRUEN (Henry) Bapt. Cheltenham, Glos. 3/1/1803, s. Richard (Ashmead) Pruen and Sarah Lesingham. Oriel, Oxford 1821, BA 1825, dn26 (Bangor), p26 (Glos.), MA1833. V. Child's Wickham, Glos. 1828, R. Ashchurch, Glos. 1838, PC. Hucclecote, Glos. 1856. Chap. to the General Hospital, Cheltenham. Died Charlton Kings, Chelten-ham 12/4/1867 aged 64, leaving £5,000 [C161598] Married Cropthorne, Worcs. 4/11/1829 his first cousin Mary Pruen, with issue.

PRUEN (Thomas) Born Churchdown, Glos. 4/1/1797, s. Richard Pruen and Ann Roberts.

'A literate person': dn12 (Salis.), p12 (Salis.), then St John's, Cambridge 1819, re-adm. 1820 (a Ten Year Man), BA1823, p23 (Glos.). PC. Mountsorrel Chapel (part), Barrow upon Soar, Leics. 1832 to death 8/7/1855 [C73914]

PRUST (Joseph Prust) Born Woolfardisworthy, Devon 3/11/1780, s. Rev. Joseph Prust, sen. (formerly Hamlyn) and Susann Silke. Exeter, Oxford 1799, BA1803, dn03 (B&W), p04 (Ex.), Fellow 1805-23, MA 1806, BD1817. R. West Worlington, Devon 1804-22, R. Virginstow, Devon 1811 and R. Langtree, Devon 1822 to death 13/5/1839 [C47936]

PRYCE (Thomas) From Birmingham, s. Rev. Richard Pryce. Wadham, Oxford 1786 (aged 18), BA1790, dn90 (Heref.), p91 (Heref.). PC. Leinthall Starkes, Heref. 1821and R. Aston, Heref. 1828 to death 1841 (4th q.) [C173448]

PRYCE (William) Literate: p93 (Lin.). PC. Loudwater (Ludwater), Bucks. 1801 to death 3/3/1833 (CCEd thus) [C73917]

PRYCE see also under **PRICE**

PUCKLE (Benjamin) Born Clapham, Surret 28/12/1790, s. Thomas Puckle and Catherine Driffield. Queens', Cambridge 1810, BA1814, dn14 (Lin.), p15 (Lin.), MA 1818. Sequestrator of Ellington, Hunts. 1814, R. Grafham, Hunts. 1825 to death (Bagnères de Bigorre, Hautes Pyrénées, France) 28/9/1853 aged 62 [C73919. Kaye] Married Kensington, London 2/3/1819 Elizabeth Hale (dau. of a general, from Guisborough, Yorks.), with clerical son Benjamin Hale Puckle.

PUDDICOMBE (Stephen) Bapt. Talland, Cornwall 15/12/1773. Corpus Christi, Cambridge 1791, BA1796, dn97 (Ex.), p97 (Ex.), MA1799. V. Morval, Cornwall 1803-43, R. Lanreath, Cornwall (and Preacher through out the Diocese of Exeter) 1827-9. Died ('suddenly') Morval 2/1/1843 aged 69 [C146147] Married London 27/7/1797 Elizabeth Brett.

PUGH (Charles) From Sible Headingham, Essex, s. Rev. James Baldwyn Pugh and Mary Steare. Christ's, Cambridge 1798 [adm. Lincoln's Inn 1798] BA1803, dn04 (C&L), MA1806, p15 (Ely). V. Foxton, Leics. 1817-34, V. Goadby Marwood, Leics. 1824-5 (res.), V. Barton, Cambs. 1828 to death (Upwey, Weymouth, Dorset) 15/12/1834 aged 55 [C19058] Married Wilbaston, Northants. 9/8/1814 Sarah Essam.

PULLEN (William) Bapt. City of London 24/8/1802, s. John Pullen and Eliza Taverner. Clare, Cambridge 1823, then Queens' 1824, BA 1827, MA1837. R. Little Gidding, Hunts. 1831-43, PC. Redhill St John, Surrey 1843-6. Moved to Babbacombe, Devon because of ill-health. Died Banstead, Surrey 28/8/1870 aged 67. No will traced [C73932] Married Hampsteed, London 14/1/1834 Amelia Wright, w. clerical sons Henry William (political satirist), and Joseph Pullen.

PULLEY (William) From Bedford, s. Anthony Pulley. Trinity, Cambridge 1793 (aged 19), BA 1798, dn98 (Ely), p00 (Lin.), MA1801. H/M Holt Free G/S, Norfolk 1805-57; V. Clapham, Beds. 1803 and V. Haynes, Beds. 1815 to death. Dom. Chap. to Frances, Baroness Ongley 1815. Died 16/4/1843 aged 68 [C73934] Clerical son Anthony Pulley.

PULLEYNE or PULLEN (Benjamin) Bapt. Scarborough, Yorks. 30/9/1785, s. Benjamin Pullen and Elizabeth Tate. Clare, Cambridge 1804, BA1808, dn08 (Bristol), Fellow 1808-9, p10 (Nor.), MA1811. H/M Gresham's School, Holt, Norfolk 1809-57; V. (Upper) Shering-ham, Norfolk 1825 and V. Weybourne, Norfolk 1845 to death (Sheringham) 20/10/1861 aged 76, leaving under £200 (as Pulleyne) [C8180. C. Linnell, *Some East Anglian clergy* (1961), Chapter 9] Married (1) Cambridge 9/11/1809 Rebecca Gee (d.1853), with issue (2) Blofield, Norfolk 1853 (2nd q.) Mary Dinah Partridge (w). Surrogate.

PULSFORD (Charles [Henry]) Born Bradninch, Devon, s. Rev. Luke Pulsford and Jane Gould. Merton, Oxford 1799 (aged 17), then Jesus, Cambridge 1806, dn06 (London), p06 (B&W), BA1807, MA1827. V. Barton St David, Som. 1810-30, Prebend of Combe the Eighth in Wells Cathedral 1815 (then Canon Residentiary 1826-41), R. Kingweston, Som. 1819-27, V. Burnham on Sea, Som. 1827 to death (Wells) 15/3/1841 aged 58 [C40255] Married Wells 1841 (1st q.) Letitia Sarah Napier (of East Pennard. Som.), with issue.

PURRIER (Henry) Born City of London 17/7/1771, s. Henry Purrier and Elizabeth Guest. St John's, Cambridge 1788, BA1793, dn94 (Glos.), p03 (C&L), MA1812. R. Deptford St Paul, Kent 1809-11 (res.), R. Hinton Parva (o/w Little Hinton), Wilts. 1811 to death 14/8/1838 aged 67 [C2150] Married Bristol 29/10/1801 Ann Wasbrough, w. clerical s., also Henry.

PURVIS (Bartholomew George) Born Beccles, Suffolk 13/4/1782, s. Robert Purvis (surgeon). Caius, Cambridge 1800, BA1805, dn06 (Nor.), p07 (Nor.). V. Whitchurch, Hants. 1818-44. Died? [C108623. Not in FreeBMD]

PURVIS (Robert Fortescue) Born Wickham, Hants. 4/1/1789, s. Admiral John Child Purvis and Catherine Sowers. [Officer in the *H.E.I.C.*'s navy 1803-20]. Jesus, Cambridge 1819, dn20 (Win.), p21 (Nor.), LLB 1825. V. Whitsbury, Hants. 1824 to death. Dom. Chap. to Earl of Limerick 1846. Died 27/5/1868. Will not traced [C108624. Iain Gordon, *Soldier of the Raj ...* (Bradford, 2001)] Married 10/1/1824 Elizabeth Ellen/Helen Baker, with issue.

PUTT (Thomas) Born Plymouth, Devon, s. Raymundo Putt. Corpus Christi, Oxford 1775 (aged 17), BA1779, MA1782, Fellow, dn88 (Chester for Ox.), p88 (London for Ex.), BD1792. R. (and patron) of Farway, Devon 1791 and R. Trent, Som. 1802 to death. Probate granted 21/2/1833 [C37366]

PYE (Henry Anthony) Bapt. Holborn, London 29/11/1766, s. Anthony Pye and Anne Bathurst. Merton, Oxford 1782, BA1786, Fellow, MA1789, dn89 (Roch.), p90 (Ox.). PC. Wolvercott, Oxon. 1790-1802, V. Wolford, Warwicks. 1793-1821, R. Lapworth, Warwicks. 1793-1810, PC. Cirencester, Glos. 1806-39, Canon of 4th Prebend of Worcester Cathedral 1818-39, R. Harvington, Worcs. 1818, R. Gamlingay, Cambs. 1835 (1st Moiety). Dom. Chap. to 12th Baron Zouche 1818. Died Cirencester 25/3/1839 [C37369] Married Marylebone, London 4/1/1794 Frances Ursula Wilkinson, with issue. Brother William, below.

PYE (James) Born Skelmersdale, Lancs. St Catharine's, Cambridge 1785, dn87 (Chester), BA1789, p89 (Lin.), MA1792. V. Dean, Beds. 1815 to death Kimbolton, Cambs. 26/2/1845 aged 80 [C73941] Had issue.

PYE (William) Bapt. St Austell, Cornwall 26/3/1756, s. Rev. Charles Pye. Exeter, Oxford 1774, BA1778, dn78 (Ex.), p80 (Ex.). R. (and patron) of Blisland, Cornwall 1780 to burial there 6/2/1834 aged 78 [C146152]

PYE (William) Born Lapworth, Warwicks., s. Rev. Henry Anthony Pye and Anne Bathurst. Christ Church, Oxford 1823 (aged 18), Fellow 1823-31, BA1827, dn28 (Ox.), MA 1830. PC. Baunton, Glos. 1829-33 (res.), R. Sapperton, Glos. 1833-83, R. Stratton, Glos. 1833. Dom. Chap. to 22nd Baron de Ros 1833. Bankrupt 1883. Possibly died Cleveland, Som. 17/10/1891: no will traced [C21232] Brother Henry Anthony, above.

PYKE (John) From Pewsey, Wilts., s. Henry Pyke. Merton, Oxford 1801 (aged 17). BA1805, dn06 (Salis.), p07 (Salis.). R. Upaven, Wilts. 1827. Died 21/1/1870 - but will of the man below attached! [C89134]

PYKE (John) Bapt. Barnstaple, Devon 29/12/1798, s. John Pyke and Ann Hogg Salmon. Exeter, Oxford 1818, BA1821, dn22 (Ex.), p23 (Ex.), MA1825. R. Parracombe, Devon 1826 to death 25/1/1868 aged 69, leaving £300 (unadministered) [C146153] Married Swimbridge, Devon 14/3/1838 Elizabeth Nott, with issue.

PYM (Robert) Bapt. Hazells Hall, Sandy, Beds. 13/8/1793, s. Francis Pym and Ann Jane Palmer. Christ Church, Oxford 1819, no degree, dn20 (Nor.), p20 (Nor.). R. Elmley (o/w Emley), Yorks. 1830 [135963] to death 22/8/1862 aged 69, leaving £2,000 [C73948?] Brother below.

PYM (William Wollaston) Born Hazells Hall, Sandy, Beds. (bapt. 9/4/1792), s. Francis Pym and Jane Palmer. St John's, Cambridge 1809, BA1813, dn15 (Lin.), MA1816, p16 (Lin.). R. Willian, Herts. 1816 to death 4/9/1852 [C73949. Boase] Married (1) Marylebone, London 30/5/1822 Sophia Rose Gambier (dau. of an admiral, she d.1841), with issue (2) Jersey 25/7/1843 Mrs Edith Elizabeth (Noble) Nicoll, with further issue. Brother above, and doubtless related to the man below. Romilly calls him 'The Jews' Man' because of his presidency of The Society for the Promotion of Christianity among the Jews.

PYM (Wollaston) Born Hazells Hall, Sandy, Beds. 18/8/1759, s. William Pym and Elizabeth Kingsley. Christ's, Cambridge 1775 (aged 16), BA1779, MA1782, dn85 (Lin.), p86 (Lin.). R.

Radwell, Herts. 1786-1834, R. Willian, Herts. 1792-1803 (res.), V. Willen, Bucks. 1803. Died 15/2/1846 aged 86 [C73950] Married St George's Hanover Square, London 1796 Mary Cartwright. Doubtless related to the two men above.

PYNE (William) Bapt. Charlton Mackrell, Som. 25/9/1800, s. Rev. Anthony and Catherine Pyne. Pembroke, Oxford 1818 [but not in F.], BA 1822, dn23 (Glos.), p24 B&W), MA1825. R. Pitney, Langport, Som. 1825-52, R. Sock Dennis, Som. 1852 to death (West Charlton House, Charlton Mackrell) 23/7/1881, leaving £5,736-2s-11d [C40257] Married (1) Pitney, Som. 1825 Polyxena Ann Michell (d.1864), with issue (2) Eton, Berks. 25/6/1867 Mrs Myra (Battisombe) Loxmore.

PYNE (William [Masters]) Born Waters-field, Essex, s. Arthur Pyne (Ball-volane Castle, Co. Cork) and Mary Masters. Pembroke, Oxford 1818 (aged 18), BA1822, MA1823, dn23, p24 [NiV]. R. Oxted, Surrey 1828 to death 22/5/1869, leaving £1,500 [C108626] Married (2) Paddington, London 24/4/1841 Marian Jane Mayfield (a minor, d.1853), with issue (3) Marylebone, London 5/3/1863 Ann Tamplin, with further issue. One son was an Irish nationalist M.P.

PYRKE (George) From Littledean, Glos., s. Joseph Pyrke. Queen's, Oxford 1801 (aged 18), BA1805, MA1806, dn06 (Glos.), p07 (Bristol), Fellow to 1816. R. Ganarew w. Whitchurch >< Ross, Heref. 1814 to death 3/12/1852 [C53710]

QUALTROUGH (Joseph) Bapt. Rushen, IoM 14/11/1780, s. John Qualtrough and Margaret Crebbin. Literate: dn03 (S&M), p06 (S&M). S/M Douglas, IoM 1810-16; V. Rushen 1816-24, V. Lonan, IoM 1824 to death 23/6/1853 aged 72 [C7314. Gelling] Married Braddan 19/3/1812 Agnes McCullough (of Dumfries), 12 ch. (inc. clerical son John).

QUARINGTON (John) Bapt. Gloucester 25/9/1770, s. Edward and Eleanor Quarington. Pembroke, Oxford 1788, BA1792, dn02 (Wor.), p04 (Bristol), MA1808, BD1808. V. Shopland, Essex 1803 to death 30/3/1844 aged 73 [C53713] Married Westminster, London 16/4/1808 Mrs Susanna Shadwell (d.1828) (2) Clerkenwell, London 1/11/1831 Catherrine Wise.

QUARTLEY (Henry) Born Huntsham, Devon 25/1/1754, s. William Quartley ad Grace Boughton. Magdalen, Oxford: chorister 1766-70; matr. 1770, BA1773, dn76 (Ex.), MA1778, then Queen's, Fellow 1778. R. Maids Moreton, Bucks. --, R. Stapleford, Herts. 1790, V. Wolverton, Bucks. 1794, R. Wicken, Northants. 1806 to death. Dom. Chap. to 2nd Earl of Roslyn 1806. Died Wolverton 26/1/1838 [C148633] Married Spitalfields, London 15/7/1782 Constantia Reade, w. s. below, and Heny Reade Quarterly.

QUARTLEY (William Walter) Born 3/12/1792, s. Rev. Henry Quartley (above?). [In Indian army 1807-17, 'struck off, having been absent beyond the prescribed period']. St Catharine's, Cambridge 1818 (a Ten Year Man), dn19 (Nor.), p20 (Nor.). V. Keynsham, Som. 1825-48, R. Washfield, Devon 1857 to death 15/7/1859, leaving £1,500 [C21291] Widow Dinah, and issue.

QUEKETT (William) Born Langport, Som. 3/10/1802, s. William Queckett and Mary Jane Bartlett. St John, Cambridge 1821, dn25 (B&W), BA1826, p26 (B&W), MA1831. R. Goose Bradon, Som. 1833 [blank in ERC], (founder and first) PC. Christ Church, Watney Street, East London 1841-65, R. Warrington, Lancs. [income in CR65 £1,290] 1854 to death 30/3/1888, leaving £2,786-14s-6d. [C40387. ODNB. Boase] Married (1) London 1835 Harriet Foulger (d.1849) (2) North Cadbury, Som. 2/7/1851 Mrs Mary (Clutterbuck) Williams (d.1851 - 4 months later), a clergy widow (3) Paddington, London 28/4/1855 Mrs Louisa (Dodgson) Webster. He was Charles Dickens's model curate; his philanthropic works are described in 'What a London Curate can do if he tries' (*Household Words*, Nov. 16 1850) and 'Emigration' (*ibid.*, 24 Jan 1852). The first clergyman to start Penny Readings, Dorcas and Mothers' Meeting Societies, and women's emigration to the Colonies. *My sayings and doings* … (1888) is his autobiography.

QUICKE (Andrew) Bapt. Newton St Cyres, Devon 12/1789, s. John Quicke and Emelia Cumming. New, Oxford 1805, BA 1809, dn10 (Ox.), Fellow to 1832, p11 (Glos.), etc.; Fellow of Winchester College. R. Ashbrittle, Som. 1811-24, V. Newton St Cyres 1825, R. Biddeston w. Slaughterford, Wilts. 1832 to death 14/1/1864, leaving £10,000 [C21292] Brother below.

QUICKE (William Henry) Born Newton St Cyres, Devon, s. John Quicke and Emilia Cumming. Pembroke, Cambridge 1813 (aged 18), then Jesus BA1814, BA1817, dn17 (B&W), p18 (Salis.). R. Stoke Pero, Som. 1818, V. Newton St Cyres 1818-24, R. Ashbrittle, Som. 1825-9, R. Chelwood, Bristol 1829 and V. Corston, Som. 1829 to death (Winchester, unm.) 31/10/1832, aged 38 [C40388] Brother above.

QUILTER (George) Bapt. Monks Hadley, Middx. 15/7/1793, s. James Quilter and Mary Ann Vokins. Peterhouse, Cambridge 1810, BA 1815, dn16 (Ely), Fellow 1816, p17 (Ely), MA 1818. V. Canwick, Lincs. 1818 to death 15/11/1871, leaving £16,000 [C73956] Married Richmond, Surrey 4/10/1818 Arabella Maria Julius, with issue.

RABBITTS (Cicero) Bapt. Maiden Bradley, Wilts. 8/1/1801, s. Hugh Rabbitts and Sarah Slade. Worcester, Oxford 1817, BA1821, dn22 (London for Salis.), p23 (Chester for Salis.). R. Wanstrow, Som. 1825 to death 28/7/1881 aged 84. Will not traced [C40289] Married Uphill, Som. C.1824 Harriet Susan Deacle (a clergy dau.)., w. clerical son Francis Deacle Rabbitts.

RABETT (Reginald) Born Bramfield Hall, Saxmundham, Suffolk 11/7/1785, s. Reginald Rabett and Mary Kerrison. St Edmund Hall, Oxford 1814, then Queens', Cambridge 1818, BA1819, MA1822, p24 (Heref.). PC. Aldershot, Hants. 1828, V. Thornton w. Bagworth, Leics. 1831-57, R. Passenham, Norfolk 1857 to death there 10/9/1860, leaving £1,000 [C73985] Married Roden, Shropshire 29/8/1828 Mary Bickerton (w).

RACKETT (Thomas) Bapt. Covent Garden, London 6/3/1`756, s. Thomas and Mary Rackett. University, Oxford 1773, BA1777, MA1780, dn80 (Ox. for Bristol), p80 (Ox. for Bristol). R. Spetisbury, Dorset 1780 to death 29/11/1840 [C37388]

RADCLIFFE (Charles Delmé-) Born Hitchin Priory, Herts. 1/2/1896, s. Emilius Henry Delmé (later Radcliffe) and Anne Millicant Clarke. Magdalene, Cambridge 1824, BA1828, dn29 (Lin.), p30 (Lin.), MA1832. R. Holwell, Beds. 1830 to death 14/7/1865, leaving £14,000 [C73987] Married Titchfield, Hants. 15/9/1831 Elizabeth Delmé, with clerical son Henry Eliot Delmé Radcliffe.

RADCLIFFE (George) Bapt. East Dean, Hants. 29/12/1802, s. Rev. George Radcliffe, sen. and Mary Wrigley. St Mary Hall, Oxford 1818, BA1822, MA1824, dn26 (Salis.), p27 (Salis.). V. Chute, Wilts. 1828 to death (Kensington, London) 20 or 22/5/1862. Will not traced [C89138] Married Marylebone, London 22/12/1827 Fanny Auchmuty, and had issue.

RADCLIFFE (James) Bapt. Worcester 12/4/1789, s. John [*pleb.*] and Elizabeth Radcliffe. Christ Church, Oxford 1807, BA 1811, dn12 (Salis.), MA1813, p14 (Salis.), Chap. New College 1814-15. PC. Whitechapel, Kirkham, Lancs. (with H/M Kirkham G/S) 1815 to death 11/2/1836, leaving £3,000 [C891139] Married Kirkham 7/3/1826 Mary Elizabeth King (w) (a niece of a Bishop of Rochester), with clerical son.

RADCLIFFE (John) Bapt. Bolton, Lancs. 24/10/1764, s. James Radcliffe and Anne Kirkall. BNC, Oxford 1781, BA1785, MA1787, dn87 (Ox.), Fellow and Tutor, p89 (Chester). Chetham's Librarian, Manchester 1787-92; R. Limehouse, London 1801-50, V. Dodington, Kent 1807 and Teynham, Kent 1811 to death 31/5/1850 [C37391] Married Holborn, London 27/7/1802 Anne Leigh, with clerical son Houstoune Radcliffe.

RADCLIFFE (John) Bapt. Oldham, Lancs. 22/10/1784, s. John and Nancy Radcliffe. Wadham, Oxford 1803, then St Mary Hall, BA1807, dn07 (Ex.), p08 (Bristol), MA1809, Chap. Merton 1835-52. V. Bramham, Yorks. 1823 and V. Radley, Berks. 1825 to death 22/2/1852 [C53736]

RADFORD (John) Bapt. Sheffield, Yorks. 18/7/1781, s. Rev. Thomas Radford and Elizabeth Gunning. Lincoln, Oxford 1800, BA1804, dn04 (Ox.), p05 (Ox.), MA1807, Fellow to 1834, BD 1815, Tutor 1822, DD1834, Rector of Lincoln College, Oxford 1834-51. Curate Oxford All Saints 1823, R. Twyford, Bucks. 1834 to death 21/10/1851 [C21296] A widower in 1851 Census.

RADFORD (John Arundel) Bapt. Lapford, Devon 10/4/1799, s. Rev. William Radford and Harriet Prestwood Froude. Queen's, Oxford 1817, then St Alban Hall, BA1823, p24 (Ex.). R. Nymet Rowland, Devon [blank in ERC] 1825 (and patron and 'brutal') R. Lapford 1825 [blank in ERC] to death 18/5/1861, leaving £2,000 [C146274] Married Aston on Trent, Derbys. 15/4/1824 Thomasin Elizabeth Dawson, with issue.

RAIKES (Robert Napier) Born Gloucester 3/11/1783, s. Robert Raikes ('promoter of Sunday Schools', *q.v.* ODNB) and Ann Trigg. Oriel, Oxford 1802, BA1806, dn06 (Ex. for Win.), p07 (Ex.), MA1813. V. Gayton, Norfolk 1811-12, R. Hellesdon w. Drayton >< Norfolk 1812, V. Longhope, Glos. 1837, V. Old Sodbury, Glos. to death 22/3/1851 [C108629] Married Longhope 10/9/1810 Caroline Probyn, with issue.

RAILTON (William) Literate: dn85 (Car.), p87 (Car.). PC. Cumberworth, High Hoyland, Yorks. 1792-1828, V. Bywell St Andrew, Northumberland 1828 to death 1/9/1840 aged 77

[C6214] Married Caldbeck, Cumberland 19/6/1820 Mary Robinson.

RAINE (James) Born Ovington, Wycliffe, Yorks. 23/1/1791, s. James Raine (blacksmith) and Anne Moore. S/M Durham G/S 1812-27. Literate: dn14 (Durham), then Trinity, Cambridge 1816 (a Ten Year Man), p18 (Durham), MA1825 Lambeth, incorporated at Durham DCL1857. Librarian to Dean and Chapter of Durham 1816-58; R. Meldon, Northumberland 1822-58 [but contested until 1846], R. Durham St Mary le Bow w. St Mary the Less South Bailey 1828 to death (Crook Hall, Durham) 6/12/1858, leaving £2,000 [C131337. ODNB. Boase. D. Cross, *Joseph Bouet's Durham: drawings from the age of reform* (Durham, 2005)] Married Denton, Durham 20/1/1828 Margaret Peacock (a clergy dau.), 3 dau, 1 clerical son. Principal Surrogate for the Diocese; antiquarian and topographer; friend of Surtees, and one of the founders of the Surtees Society. entry online with port: en.wikipedia.org/wiki/James_Raine

RAINE (William) Bapt. Batsford, Glos. 27/2/1774, s. Joseph and Jane Raine. Queen's, Oxford 1791, Fellow, BA1795, dn97 (Cant. for unspecified bishop), MA1798, p98 (Ox.). PC. Lemington, Warwicks. 1810, R. Widford, Glos. 1812, PC. Swinbrook, Oxon. 1838 to death (Lemington) 5/1/1858, leaving £14,000 [C37396]

RAINES (Francis Robert) Born Whitby, Yorks. 22/2/1805, s. Isaac Raines (physician) and Ann Robertson. [Apprenticed to a surgeon 1818-23] St Bees adm. 1826, dn28 (Chester), p29 (Chester), then Queens', Cambridge 1840, a Ten Year Man (MA1845 Lambeth). PC. Milnrow, Lancs. 1832 (with RD of Rochdale 1846 and Hon. Canon Manchester Cathedral 1849) to death. Dom. Chap. to Lord Dunmore 1841. Died (Scarborough, Yorks.) 17/10/1878 aged 73, leaving £10,000 [C170279. ODNB. Boase] Married Rochdale 19/11/1836 Honora Elizabeth, dau. Maj. John Beswicke (Pike House, Littleborough, Lancs.), with issue. J.P. 1849. F.S.A. A major Lancashire historian and author, and one of the founders of the Chetham Society.

RAMSDEN (Edward) From Ovenden, Halifax, Yorks., s. John Ramsden. St John's, Cambridge 1813, BA1813, dn17 (Chester for C&L), p19 (Wor. for C&L), MA1820. PC. Grantham Manthorpe w. Londonthorpe, Lincs. 1822, PC. Lower Darwen, Blackburn, Lancs. 1829-39, PC. Ovenden 1838, PC. Bradshaw, Bolton, Lancs. 1839 to death (Halifax) 6/6/1853 aged 62 [C19068]

RAMSDEN (Henry) Born Carlton Hall, Worksop, Notts. 10/9/1788, s. Robert Ramsden and Mrs Elizabeth (Uppleby) Smith. Queens', Cambridge 1807, dn12 (York for C&L), then Trinity Hall 1813, LLB1813, p13 (Win. for C&L). R. Brandsby, Yorks. 1825, R. Cherry Burton >< Yorks. 1828 to death 3/7/1837 aged 45 [C19423. YCO] Married Askham Richard, Yorks. 30/1/1821 Mary Swann., *s.p. J.P.* East Riding.

RAMSDEN (William) Born Whitechapel, London, s. Capt. George Ramsden and Lucy Carpenter. Christ Church, Oxford 1808 (aged 18), BA1812, p16 (Salis.), MA1828. PC. Leconfield, Yorks. 1823-35, R. Linwood, Lincs. 1827-60, R. Ashurst, Kent 1835-60, PC. Usselby, Lincs. 1835. Died (St Leonards on Sea, Kent) 4/11/1860 aged 73, leaving £12,000 [C135964] Married Selby, Yorks. 5/4/1815 Elizabeth Jane Bell (w), with issue.

RAMSDEN (William Benson) Born London 5/2/1763, s. Rev. William Ramsden (Master of Charterhouse School) and Elizabeth Parker. Christ's, Cambridge 1781, BA1785, dn85 (Ely), p87 (Ely), Fellow 1787-1800, MA1788, BD1812. V. Croxton, Norfolk 1797, V. Witcham, Cambs. 1800, V. Great Stambridge, Essex 1801, V. Little Wakering, Essex 1812 to death. Dom. Chap. to 2nd Earl of Liverpool 1812. Died 29/3/1838 [C100174] Married London 15/3/1800 Louisa Dowse, with issue.

RAMSHAW (Christopher) Born Scorton, Yorks. 14/1/1761, s. Rev. Richard Ramshaw and Elizabeth Jackson. Trinity, Cambridge 1779, dn83 (Peterb. for York), BA1784, p85 (York). R. Stainburn, Yorks. 1785-1815, V. Fewston, Yorks. 1790 to death 8/9/1843 [C108757. YCO] Married (1) Harewood, Yorks. 23/12/1788 Ann Robinson (d.1798), with issue (2) Fewston 28/1/1807 Elizabeth Curtis, many ch.

RAMSHAY (Thomas) Bapt. Brampton, Cumberland 20/5/1770, s. Thomas Ramshay. Queens', Cambridge 1791, dn93 (Car.), p94 (Car.), LLB1797. V. Brampton, Cumberland 1794 and R. Nether Denton, Cumberland 1794 to death 20/12/1840 aged 70 [C6217. Platt]

Married (1) Brampton 18/1/1798 Margaret Ewart (who d. aged 18) (2) Bishopwearmouth, Durham 22/8/1799 Maria Maling, with clerical son.

RANDALL (James) Born Winchester 18/10/1790, s. Peter James Randall and Sophia Goldfinch. Trinity, Oxford 1809, BA 1813, MA 1816, Fellow 1818-30 [barrister, Lincoln's Inn 1818] dn27 (Win.), p29 (Win.). S/M Rugby School 1813; V. Binfield, Berks. 1831-59, Archdeacon of Berkshire 1855-69, Canon of Bristol Cathedral 1867-75. Died Binfield rectory (w. his son-in-law) 19/11/1882 aged 92, leaving £15,744-10s-4d [C89143] Married Dorking, Surrey 12/6/1821 Rebe [sic] Lowndes. Two clerical sons (the first Bishop of Reading, and a Dean of Chichester). Online port. of R. w. four-year old son in a dress; and a very unflattering photo. of his wife.

RANDALL (John) Bapt. Wilton, Wilts. 17/10/1794 (Independent Chapel), s. James Randall (merchant) and Frances Worsfold. Magdalene, Cambridge 1813, then Trinity 1815, BA1817, dn17 (Heref.), p18 (Heref.). V. Lyonshall, Heref. 1826 to death 8/7/1859, leaving £3,000 (not administered until 1877) [C173598] Married Bristol 10/10/1841 Elizabeth King (w), and had issue.

RANDOLPH (Charles) Born Milverton, Som. 20/10/1794, s. Rev. James Randolph. Clare, Cambridge 1812, BA1816, dn18 (B&W), p19 (Bangor), MA1828. R. Holmpton and Welwick, Yorks. 1826, R. Lyme Regis, Dorset 1826-32, R. Kimpton, Hants. 1832 to death 29/7/1871, leaving £3,000 [C40392] Married Mary Anne Foyle, with issue.

RANDOLPH (George) Born Oxford 16/1/1797, s. Rev. John Randolph (Regius Professor of Divinity, later Bishop of Oxford, then of Bangor, then of London) and Jane Lambard. Christ Church, Oxford 1815, Student [Fellow] 1815-22, BA1819, dn20 (Ox.), p21 (Ox.), MA 1821. PC. Sevenoaks, Kent 1821-41, V. Eastry w. Worth Chapel, Kent 1821-41, R. Stanton on the Wolds, Yorks. 1827, R. Coulsdon, Surrey 1841-63. Died London 10/6/1880 aged 83, leaving £2,000 [C21301] Married Sevenoaks 20/8/1822 Catharine Elizabeth Drummond (a clergy dau.), with clerical son. Brothers John Honywood, and Thomas, below.

RANDOLPH (Henry Jones) Born Bristol 15/7/1778, s. William Randolph and Elizabeth Little. St Edmund Hall, Oxford 1796, BA1800, dn02 (Win.), p03 (Glos.), MA1804. R. Newington Bagpath, Glos. 1805-11 (res.), V. Great Badminton, Glos. ---, V. Hawkesbury, Glos. 1813 to death. Dom. Chap. to 6th Duke of Beaufort 1816. Died (Yate House, Glos.) 13/5/1860 aged 82, leaving £17-10s-0d. [C108634] Married Frances Cater, with clerical son William Cater Randolph.

RANDOLPH (Herbert) Born/bapt. Wimbledon, Surrey 3/11/1789, s. Rev. Herbert Randolph, sen. and Diana Knapp. Christ Church, Oxford 1806, BA1810, dn12 (Ox.), MA1813, p13 (Ox.). PC. Hawkhurst, Sussex 1817-19, V. Marcham, Berks. 1819 to death 13/3/1875, leaving £14,000 [C21302. CR65 as Henry James] Married Camberwell, Surrey 27/3/1806 Jane Wilson, with issue.

RANDOLPH (John Honywood) Born Oxford 8/3/1791, s. Rev. John Randolph (Regius Professor of Divinity, later Bishop of Oxford, then of Bangor, then of London) and Jane Lambard. Christ Church, Oxford 1809, Student [Fellow] 1809-14, BA1813, dn14 (Ox.), MA 1815, p15 (C&L for Win.). R. Wainfleet All Saints, Lincs. 1815-17, R. Burton Coggles, Lincs. 1816-22, R. Fobbing, Essex, 1822, Canon and Ealdland Prebend in St Paul's Cathedral 1822-68 [value £2-10s-0d.], R. Northolt (o/w Northall), Middx. 1822-34 (res.), PC. Hollington, Hastings, Sussex 1834, R. Mistley cum Bradfield, Essex 1839, R. Sanderstead, Surrey 1845-66. Died 31/6/1868, leaving £30,000 (CCEd date wrong here; and Fasti says 2/6/1868). Chap. to HRH Duke of Sussex 1815; Chap. of the British Factory at St Petersburg 1818; Proctor in Convocation for the Clergy of the Archdeaconry of Surrey [C19424. Bennett2] Married 30/8/1814 Sarah Wilson, with clerical sons George Augustus Frederick, and John. Brothers George (above), and Thomas (below). Photo online LNCP.

RANDOLPH (Thomas) Born Oxford 8/11/1788, s. of Rev. John Randolph (Regius Professor of Divinity, later Bishop of Oxford, then of Bangor, then of London) and Jane Lambard. Christ Church, Oxford 1806, Student [Fellow] 1806-13, BA1810, dn12 (London), MA1812. Cantlers Prebend in St Paul's Cathedral, London 1812-75 [value £1,500], R. Much Hadham and Little Hadham, Herts. [net income £1,761] (and Preacher throughout the Diocese of London) 1812 to death. Royal Chap. 1825; Dom. Chap. to Bishop of Carlisle, later Abp of York 1814. Died 2/5/1875, leaving £80,000 [C121129] Married Westminster, London 28/5/1813 Caroline Diana Macdonald, w. clerical sons Edward John, and Leveson Cyril Randolph.

RANKING (George) Bapt. Hampstead, London 8/8/1797. Christ's, Cambridge 1822, SCL, dn26 (B&W), p26 (Nor.), LLB1829. PC. Altrincham, Cheshire 1832-4, R. St Pancras, Chichester 1840-57, V. Wimbish w. Thundersley, Essex 1860-5. Died Tunbridge Wells, Kent 29/5/1871 aged 78, leaving £7,000 [C40395] Married Brighton, Sussex 8/10/1828 Eliza Maitland (of Lyndhurst, Hants.).

RAPER, *later* RAPER-HUNTON (John) Born Baldersby, Yorks. 25/6/1784, s. George Raper (a yeoman farmer) and Elizabeth Hunton. Clare, Cambridge 1802, BA1806, dn07 (Car. for York), p16 (Car.), then Trinity, Cambridge 1819, MA1819. R. Pickhill, Yorks. 1819-22, PC. Armathwaite, Cumberland 1822 (and Dom. Chap. to Countess Powlet) to death. Dom. Chap. to 7th Earl of Coventry 1819. Died 17/2/1838 (as Hunton) [C3417. Foster under his son Timothy. YCO. Platt] Married 23/2/1813 Mrs Isabella Agnes Milbourne (Armathwaite Castle), with clerical son.

RASHLEIGH (George) Bapt. Boughton, Kent 19/7/1784, s. Rev. Peter Rashleigh and Frances Burvill. Oriel, Oxford 1801, BA1805, dn07 (Cant.), p08 (Cant.), MA1809. V. (and patron) of Horton Kirby, Kent 1818 and V. Lower (*or* Little *or* Nether) Hardres, Kent 1827 to death 19/2/1874 aged 89, leaving £8,000 [C2158] Married IoW 21/11/1813 Maria D. Worsley, and clerical son Henry Burville Rashleigh.

RASHLEIGH (George Cumming) Bapt. Silverton, Devon 12/7/1791, s. Rev. George Rashleigh and Jane Cumming. New, Oxford 1809, Fellow 1809-29, BA1813, dn15 (Ex.), p15, MA1817, etc. Fellow of Winchester College. V. Andover w. Foxcott, Hants. 1829, PC. Hound, Hants. 1850 and Chap. of the Donative of Hamble-le-Rice, Hants. 1850 to death 1/4/1874, leaving £40,000 [C108635]

RASHLEIGH (Jonathan Stackhouse) Born Wickham, Hants. 6/10/1782, s. Rev. Jonathan Rashleigh and Catherine Stackhouse. Wadham, Oxford 1801, BA1805, dn05 (Win.), p06 (Ex.), MA1811. (succ. his father as) R. Wickham 1807 to death 15/5/1863, leaving £5,000 [C108636] Married Wickham 7/7/1807 Caroline Stanhope, many issue. Doubtless related to the man below.

RASHLEIGH (Peter) Born Wickham, Hants. (bapt. Fulham, London 14/9/1746), s. Jonathan Rashleigh (annuitant) and Mary Clayton. University, Oxford 1765 (aged 20), then All Souls, Fellow, BA1772 [barrister Middle Temple 1772] dn75 (Roch.), MA1775, p75 (Roch.). R. Wouldham, Kent 1775-88 (res.), V. New Romney, Kent 1781-93, R. Barking, Essex 1781 [net income £1,428], R. Southfleet, Essex 1788 to death. Dom. Chap. to Bishop of Rochester. Died 8/2/1836 [C1173] Married Boxley, Kent 13/11/1881 Frances Burvill, w. issue. Doubtless related to the man above.

RASTALL (Robert) Bapt. Newark on Trent, Notts. 22/6/1794, s. Rev. William Rastall and Mary Winthorpe. Jesus, Cambridge 1813, dn17 (York), BA1818, p18 (York), MA1822. (succ. his father as) R. Winthorpe, Notts. 1818 and R. Stubton, Lincs. 1819 to death. Dom. Chap. to 8th Lord Rollo 1819. Died 20/11/1856 [C74002. YCO] Married Whitby, Yorks. 12/5/1846 Annie Peters (Larpool Hall, Whitby).

RATHBONE (David) Bapt. Gawsworth, Cheshire 25/11/1787, s. Peter Rathbone and Esther Rathbone. Literate: dn11 (Chester), p14 (Chester). PC. Newchurch in Rossendale 1811-25, PC. Ashworth, Middleton, Lancs. 1832 (living at Ashworth Hall) to death 10/2/1871 aged 83, leaving £16,000 [C170281] Married (1) Newchurch 22/11/1814 Mary Ashworth (d.1816), with issue (2) Altham, Lancs. 23/11/1830 Eliza Ann Walker, with further issue. Surrogate.

RATHBONE (John Egerton) Bapt. Oxford 6/11/1778, s. Rev. John Rawbone [*sic*] and Jane Mary Egerton. New, Oxford 1795 (aged 16), BA1803. Fellow to 1829, dn15 (Ox.), p17 (Ox.), etc. Curate Romford, Essex 1828 to death. Chap. to HRH Duke of Sussex 1818. Died Witney, Oxon. 31/5/1838 [C21304] Married Minchampton, Sussex 13/11/1828 Arabella Colston (Filkins Hall, Oxon.).

RAVEN (Thomas) From Norfolk. Queens', Cambridge 1818, then Corpus Christi 1818, dn19 (Nor.), BA1822, p22 (Nor.), MA1825. PC.

Preston Holy Trinity, Lancs. 1824-49. Living at St Leonards on Sea, Sussex in 1851; living at Cheyne House, Chelsea 1860; died Lansdowne Hall, Torquay 16/3/1868 aged 75, leaving £3,000 [C114535] Married (1) Preston 23/11/1824 Susanna (dau. of Samuel Horrocks, *M.P.* and cotton manufacturer, she d.1842) (2) Jane (r.). An excellent water colourist, his son John Samuel Raven was a professional artist.

RAVENHILL (John) Bapt. Hackney, London 22/3/1753, s. Timothy Ravenhill. University, Oxford 1775, dn78 (C&L), BA1779, p79 (C&L), MA1813, BD and DD1813. R. Cattistock, Dorset 1792-1805 (res.), R. Tooting Graveney, Surrey 1805 to death 14/2/1833 (CCEd says 11/3/1833) [C19432]

RAVENSHAW (Edward) From Bracknell, Berks., s. John Ravenshaw. BNC, Oxford 1800 (aged 18), BA1804. MA1808. R. West Kington, Wilts. 1816 to death 13/12/1854 [C89151]

RAWLINGS (William) Bapt. St Columb Major, Cornwall 16/5/1761, 's. of a prosperous merchant'. Exeter, Oxford 1780, BA1783, dn84 (Ex.), p85 (Ex.). V. Padstow, Cornwall 1790-1836 and R. (and patron) of Lansallos, Cornwall 1822-36. Died Padstow 20/12/1836 aged 76 [C146278. DEB] Clerical son.

RAWLINS (Henry William) From Martock, Somerset, s. Rev. Henry Rawlins and Elizabeth White. Balliol, Oxford 1801 (aged 18), MA1805, dn06 (B&W), p07 (B&W), MA1808. R. Staplegrove, Som. 1810-26, R. Fiddington, Som. 1821-55, PC. Bishops Hull, Som. 1825, V. Kilton, Som. 1844 to death 21/6/1855 aged 71. Married Liverpool 2/7/1819 Eliza Nash, w. clerical son Francis John [C40398]. A great walker, with a keen knowledge of country and folk lore. Photo. of Mrs Rawlins online.

RAWNSLEY (Thomas Hardwicke) Born Bourne, Lincs. 31/10/1789, s. Thomas Hardwicke Rawnsley and Deborah Hardwicke. Exeter, Oxford 1807, BA1811, dn12 (Nor,), p13 (Lin.), MA1814. R. Belleau w. Claythorpe, Aby and Greenfield 1813-19 (res.), PC. Spilsby, Lincs. 1813-19 (res.), R. Folkingham w. Loughton, Lincs. 1814-61 (non-res.), R. Partney, Spilsby, Lincs. 1819-25 (res.), R. Halton Holegate, Lincs. 1825 to death. Dom. Chap. to Priscilla, 21st Baroness Willoughby de Eresby 1814. Died Spilsby 2/7/1861, leaving £16,000 [C74360. Bennett1] Married 6/11/1816 Sophia Walls (a clergy dau., Boothby Hall, Lincs.), w. clerical s. Robert Drummond Burell Rawnsley. Photo. online.

RAWSON (William) Born Blackwell, Derbys., s. John Rawson. Magdalene, Cambridge 1811 (aged 23), BA1815, dn15 (B&W), p15 (Chester), MA1818. (first) PC. Seaforth, Liverpool 1815 to death 23/12/1872 aged 84, leaving £25,000 [C40401] In 1851 had a wife Elizabeth and dau.

RAWSTORNE (Robert Atherton) Born Hutton Hall, Penwortham, Lancs. 2/12/1779, s. Laurence Rawstorne. BNC, Oxford 1796, BA 1800, dn02 (Chester), p03 (Chester), MA 1803. PC. Penwortham 1803-9, R. Warrington St Elphin, Lancs. 1807-31 (and S/M Warrington G/S) [blank in ERC], R. South Thoresby, Lincs. 1807-52, PC. Penwortham w (Curate) Longton 1831 to death 12/5/1852 [C74361] Married Clifton, Bristol 8/5/1823 Mary Gwillym, of Warrington, with clerical son of same name at Penwortham 1852-8.

RAY (William Carpenter) Bapt. Westbury on Trim, Somerset 29/3/1768, s. Rev. William and Arabella Ray, Redland, Somerset. Pembroke, Oxford 1786, BCL1795. V. Boreham, Essex 1795 and V. Pakenham, Suffolk 1805 to death 8/1/1845 [C114547] Married by 1811 Ann Rishton, with issue.

RAYER (William) From Middx., s. Willliam Rayer and Mary Hanmer. Trinity, Oxford 1803 (aged 18), BA1807, dn08 (Win.), p09 (Win.), MA1810. R. Tiverton (Tidcombe Portion), Devon 1811-64. Died Chevithorne, Devon 3/12/1868 aged 81. No will traced [C108641] Married July 1816 Jane Carew, w. issue.

RAYMOND, *born* SYNDERCOMBE (Gregory) Born Symondsbury, Dorset 3/12/1781, s. Rev. Gregory Syndercombe, sen. and Elizabeth Fort. Balliol, Oxford 1799, BA 1802, MA1828, LLD. R. Symondsbury 1806 to death (a bachelor) 2/2/1863, leaving £100,000 [C53746]. Name changed 1804.

RAYMOND (John) Born Wimbish, Essex 14/12/1791, s. Rev. John Raymond, sen. St Catharine's, Cambridge 1809, BA1814, dn15 (London), p16 (London). V. Wimbish 1828. Died? [C106630. Venn has date of father's death, but there is still confusion here]

RAYMOND (Oliver) Born Belchamp Hall, Belchamp Walter, Suffolk 1794, s. Rev. Samuel Raymond and Margaretta Bridges (a clergy dau.). Trinity Hall, Cambridge 1810, LLB1816, dn17 (Salis.), p18 (Salis.). (succ. his father as) R. (and patron) of Middleton, Essex 1823-89, V. Bulmer w. Belchamp Walter, Essex 1826-90. RD of Belchamp. Died (Middleton) 15/9/1889, leaving £9,198-18s-7d. [C89154. Boase] Married Belchamp Walter 4/2/1817 Ann Andrewes (a clergy dau.), with clerical son Charles Andrewes Raymond.

RAYMOND (Samuel) Probably from Co. Kerry, s. Samuel Raymond. TCD1812 (aged 16), BA1816, MA1849. R. Swindon, Glos. 1829, Hon. Canon of Gloucester Cathedral 1850-64-. Died Leamington 29/4/1872. Untraced will in Ireland [C161851. Al.Dub.] Married 4/9/1832 Jane Elliott, w. issue (incl. dau. Adamina).

RAYMOND, *born* FORBES (William Forbes) Son of Lt.-Col. William Forbes (Deputy Adjutant-General of the Forces in Ireland) and Anne Raymond. Trinity, Cambridge 1803 (aged 17), BA1807 [adm. Middle Temple 1807] MA1810, dn10 (London), p11 (London). R. Strethall, Essex 1820-56, Coleworth Prebend in Chichester Cathedral 1832-42, R. Howick, Northumberland 1842-6, Archdeacon of Northumberland 1842-53. Died London 21/3/1860, leaving £45,000 [C65043]

RAYNES (Michael Minnett) Bapt. Marylebone, London 14/4/1772, s. Samuel Raynes (Gainsborough, Lincs.) and Katharine Minnett. Jesus, Cambridge 1791, BA1795, dn95 (Bristol). V. Newton on Trent, Lincs. 1807, PC. Torksey, Lincs. 1809 to death 1852 (1st q. as Minnitt) [C53748] Wife Elizabeth.

RAYNES (Thomas) Bapt. 3/4/1788, s. Rev. Edward Robert and Harriot Raynes. Trinity, Cambridge 1806, BA1810, dn11 (B&W). R. Waldron, Sussex 1821 to death 3/1850 aged 62 [C48158] Brother below.

RAYNES (William) Bapt. Lewes, Sussex 21/4/1799, s. Rev. Edward Robert and Harriot Raynes. Jesus, Cambridge 1817, BA1821, dn22 (Bangor), p24 (Chester). (succ. his father as) R. Ripe (or Rype, o/w Eckington), Sussex 1824-52, R. Chalvington, Sussex 1849 to death 27/8/1852 aged 53 [C65046] Clerical son, also William. Brother above.

READSHAW (Caleb) Bapt. Richmond, Yorks. 15/9/1763, s. of Cuthbert Readshaw (an alderman). Trinity, Cambridge 1781, BA1786, dn86 (Durham), p88 (Durham for Chester), MA1789. PC. Eryholme, Gilling, Lancs. 1793-1835, V. Easby, Yorks. 1795-1838, R. Swettenham, Cheshire 1807-[14], R. Covington, Hunts. 1815-35. Died Richmond, Yorks. 24/2/1838 aged 74 [C133497] Married Bedale, Yorks. 31/1/1821 Elizabeth Prest (w). *J.P.* North Riding.

REDE, *born* COOPER (Robert Rede) Bapt. Great Yarmouth, Norfolk 11/4/1794, s. Rev. Samuel Lovick Cooper and Sarah Leman Rede. Trinity, Oxford 1814 (as Cooper), no degree, dn17 (Nor.), p18 (Nor.). R. Ingoldisthorpe, Norfolk 1818-25 (res.), R. Colchester St Leonard, Essex 1826. Died Dover, Kent 18/8/1852, living at Beccles, Suffolk [C121148 as Rede - C112334 as Cooper] Married Broxbourne, Herts. 17/11/1821 Louisa Henshaw (of Moor Hall, Essex), with issue.

REDHEAD (John Roberts) Bapt. Saffron Walden, Essex 4/1/1805, s. William and Jane Redhead. St Edmund Hall, Oxford 1824, BA 1828, p30 (Chester). V. Thurnby w. Stoughton, Leics. 1832 to death (a widower) 7/1/1872, leaving £300 [C74393] Married by 1831 Harriet Blundell, with clerical son Theodore John Redhead.

REDHEAD (Samuel) Born Clitheroe, Lancs. 24/12/1778, s. Robert (a deceased excise officer) and Frances Daws. Literate: dn01 (York), p03 (York). V. Haworth, Yorks. 1819 (but for three weeks only; as Patrick Bronte's predecessor he was 'ignominiously treated by the congregation'), V. Calverley, Yorks. 1822 (and H/M Bradford G/S, Yorks. at some date) to death (Bradford) 26/8/1845 [C116958. YCO] Married Bradford 20/12/1808 Mary Rand, with issue.

REDMAN (Thomas) Bapt. Orton, Westmorland 28/5/1761, s. of the schoolmaster and Parish Clerk there. Literate: dn87 (Car.), p88 (Car.). S/M Orton 1790; R. Kirkharle, Northumberland 1805 (non-res.) to death (unmarried) 25/5/1855 aged 94 [C6223]

REED (Christopher) Born Chipchase Castle, Northumberland 1/10/1797, s. Col. John Reed (sometime High Sheriff of Northumberland) and Mary Neville. Exeter, Oxford 1815 [barrister, Middle Temple 1824] BA1828, dn28 (Durham), p29 (Durham), MA1829. PC. Newcastle upon Tyne St Andrew 1828, V. Tynemouth, Northumberland 1830 to death (Kingston, Surrey) 21/7/1868, leaving £4,000 [C131345] Married Tynemouth 25/7/1837 Ann Collingwood (niece of Admiral Lord Collingwood), *s.p.* Brother John, below.

REED (James) Bapt. Barnstaple, Devon 21/9/1768, s. James and Martha Reed. Merton, Oxford 1787, then Exeter 1789, BA1791, Fellow 1792-1811, MA1794, BD1803. R. Eversholt, Beds. 1810 and V. Hamstead Norreys, Berks. 1819 to death. Chap. in Ordinary 1803. Died 10/1/1843 [C37420. Boase]

REED (Jeremiah) Literate: dn78 (Chester), p80 (Car.). PC. Rockcliffe, Cumberland 1780 to death 18/5/1833 (CCEd thus) [C3472. Platt]

REED (John) Born Chipchase Castle 6/2/1803, s. Col. John Reed (sometime High Sheriff of Northumberland) and wife Mary. Trinity, Cambridge 1821, BA1825, dn26 (Durham), p27 (Durham). R. and V. Newburn, Northumberland 1832 to death (unmarried) 4/9/1884 aged 81, leaving £4,608-17s-7d. [C131453] Brother Christopher, above.

REES (Thomas) [NiVoF] R. Garthorpe, Leics. 1820-[38]. Died? [C74392]

REES (William) [NiVoF] Born Aberavon, Glamorgan 21/6/1787 (CCEd thus), s. Rev. William Rees, sen. Jesus, Oxford 1809 (aged 21), no degree, p11 (Nor.). R. Horsey, Norfolk 1826 to death 6/11/1835 (CCEd thus) [C114776]

REES (William) Born Haverfordwest, Pembroke 10/5/1793, s. Rev. James Rees. Pembroke, Oxford 1811, BA1816, dn16 (Ox.), p17 (Ox.), MA1821. Minor Canon of Carlisle Cathedral 1819-63, PC. Carlisle St Mary 1819 (and S/M Carlisle Free School 1819-42) and R. Talbenny, Pembroke 1831 (non-res.) to death (Car.) 19/7/1865 aged 72, leaving £2,000 [C3473. Platt] Married before 1826, with issue. J.P. Cumberland.

REEVE (James) Born Lambeth, London, s. James Reeve and Elizabeth Cufler. St John's, Cambridge 1782 (aged 18), BA1786, dn86 (Glos. for London), p87 (Cant.), MA1789. PC. Maidstone All Saints, Kent 1800 to death 22/3/1842 aged 78 [C121151]

REEVE (Thomas) Literate: dn16 (Nor.), p17 (Nor.). R. (and patron) of Raydon, Norfolk 1817 to death 13/5/1865, leaving £8,000 [C114782]

RELPH (Joseph) Born/bapt. Lazonby, Cumberland 11/4/1784, s. Thomas Relph and Mary Dixon. St John, Cambridge 1802, then Peterhouse 1804, BA 1807, dn07 (Peterb.), p08 (Lin.), Fellow 1809, MA1810. R. Exford, Som. 1822 to death 13/1/1865, leaving £2,000 [C6228] Married Everton, Liverpool 12/8/1823 Barbara Dixon.

RELTON (John Rudge) Born Watlington, Oxon. 28/1/1789, s. Rev. James Relton and Elizabeth Rudge. Queen's, Oxford 1809, BA 1812, dn12 (Win.), p13 (Salis.), MA1817. PC. Marston Meysey, Wilts. 1817 to death (Cheltenham, Glos.) 27/1/1856 [C89160] Married (1) Colne Engaine, Essex 14/4/1814 Sophia Boyer (d.1832), with issue (2) Oxford (?) 10/7/1833 Mary Lawrance (d.1834) (3) Kemerton, Glos. 6/12/1834 Zepherine Anne Tonge.

RENAUD (George Daniel) From Hannington, Hants., s. Rev. David Renaud. St Mary Hall, Oxford 1793 (aged 22), no degree, p93 (Salis.). V. Chidham, Sussex 1805, V. Dewsall w. Callow, Heref. 1808, PC. Aconbury, Heref. 1808, V. Messengham w. Bottesford, Lincs. 1827. Died Southampton 2/12/1857 [C65057] Married Havant, Hants. 17/7/1806 Rebecca Bennett, with issue.

RENDLESHAM (William Thellusson, 3rd Baron) Born 6/1/1798, s. Peter Isaac Thellusson, 1st Baron Rendlesham and Elizabeth Eleanor Cornwall. Trinity, Cambridge 1816, BA, MA1818, dn21 (Nor.), p22 (Nor.). V. Aldenham, Herts. 1825 to death 13/9/1839 aged 41 [C74398] Married 10/1/1826 Lucy Pratt (Ryston Hall, Norfolk), *s.p.* Succ. to title 1832.

RENNELL (George) Born Stokenham, Devon 20/11/1772, s. Rev. Thomas Rennell. Exeter, Oxford 1791, BA1795, dn95 (Ex.), p97 (Ex.), then Emmanuel, Cambridge 1804, MA 1804. Chaplain R.N. (and on St Helena with Napoleon at some date), R. Greystead, Northumberland 1818-41. Died Newcastle (unm.) 31/10/1844, 'a lunatic' - but a memorial to him in (the now redundant) Greystead Church [C146285]

RENNELL (Thomas) Born Barnack, Northants. 8/2/1754, s. Rev. Thomas Rennell, sen. (Prebend of Winchester Cathedral). King's, Cambridge 1773, Fellow 1776-9, BA1777, MA1779, DD1794. Canon of 5th Prebend in Winchester Cathedral 1779-98 (res.), R. St Magnus the Martyr London Bridge, City of London (and Preacher throughout the Diocese of London) 1792-1808 (res.), V. Alton, Hants. 1795-1814 (res.), Master of the Temple [Church], London 1798-1828, Harleston Prebend in St Paul's Cathedral 1802-40, Dean of Winchester 1805-40, V. Barton Stacey, Hants. 1814 to death 31/3/1840 [C108644. ODNB] Married Winchester 21/7/1785 Sarah Blackstone (dau. of the judge), with issue.

RENOUARD (George Cecil) Born Stanford, Lincs. 7/9/1780, s. Peter Renouard and Mary Ott. Trinity, Cambridge 1797, then Sidney 1800, BA1802, Fellow 1804, dn04 (Lin.), p04 (Lin.), MA1805, BD1811, Lord Almoner's Professor of Arabic, Cambridge 1815-21. R. Swanscombe, Kent 1818 to death. British Chap. at Constantinople 1804-6; at Smyrna 1810-14. Died (unm.) 15/2/1867, leaving £4,000 [indexed as Renoiard] [C2173. ODNB. Boase] A major classical scholar, linguist, geographer and writer.

RENTON (William) From Knaresborough, Yorks., s. William and Frances Renton. Literate: dn19 (York), p21 (York). PC. Tilstock, Whitchurch, Shropshire 1828 [to death] 1857 (2nd q.) [C135700. YCO] Wife Agnes [*q.v. A brief memorial of Mrs Agnes Renton*, by A. R[enton]. For the private use of her family. (Kelso, 1866)].

REPTON (Edward) Born Sustead, Norfolk (bapt. Norwich 25/6/1782), s. Humphry Repton (the landscape gardener, *q.v.* ODNB) and Mary Clarke. Wadham, Oxford 1800, then Magdalen 1801-8, BA1804, dn05 (Glos.), MA 1806, p06 (Ox.). R. Miningsby, Lincs. 1817, Curate St Philip Chapel Regent Street, London 1820, Canon of Westminster Abbey 1838, V. Shoreham, Kent 1843 to death. Chap. to House of Commons. Died (St Leonards on Sea, Sussex) 6/8/1860, leaving £16,000 [C21309] Married Leyton, Essex 27/11/1808 Mary Ellis Herbert, with issue.

REVELL, REVEL (Samuel) From Sheffield, s. Samuel Revell. St John's, Cambridge 1822, BA1826, dn27 (C&L), p27 (C&L), MA1829. PC. Wingerworth, Derbys. 1828 to death 2/7/1869 aged 69, leaving under £200 [C19107] Widow Dorothy.

REYNARD (William) Bapt. Ripon, Yorks. 31/12/1776, s. William Reynard. Trinity, Cambridge 1792, then Magdalene 1794, BA1797, dn98 (York) p98 (York), MA1800. PC. Bishop Thornton >< Yorks. 1798, V. Stainley, Yorks. 1800 to death 7/1841 aged 75 [C116894. YCO] J.P. Ripon.

REYNOLDS (Charles) Bapt. Great Yarmouth, Norfolk 27/2/1800, s. Francis Riddell Reynolds (a brewer) and Anne Elizabeth Preston. Caius, Cambridge 1818, BA 1822, dn23 (Nor.), p24 (Nor.). V. Horningtoft, Norfolk 1826-9, R. Little Brandon (Brandon Parva), Norfolk 1830 and R. Great Fransham, Norfolk 1834 to death 28/11/1852 [C114789] Married (1) St Mary in the Marsh, Norfolk 6/12/1821 Rebecca Theodora Hansell (a clergy dau.), w. issue (2) Little Fransham, Norfolk 20/4/1837 Mary Swatman (a clergy dau.). Brother below.

REYNOLDS (John Preston) Born Great Yarmouth, Norfolk 27/10/1794, s. Francis Riddell Reynolds (a brewer) and Anne Elizabeth Preston. Caius, Cambridge 1812 (aged 18), BA 1817, dn17 (Nor.), p18 (Nor.), MA1825. R. Little Munden, Herts. 1819-31, R. Beeston St Andrew, Norfolk 1831-44, R. Necton, Norfolk 1845 to death 22/5/1861, leaving £20,000 [C73865] Married Swanton Morley, Norfolk 6/10/1818 Frances Elizabeth Collett (a clergy dau.), with issue. Brother above.

REYNOLDS (Osborne Shribb) Bapt. Kelsale, Suffolk 9/1/1782, s. Rev. Robert Reynolds (R. Boulge, Suffolk) and Sarah Shribb. Caius, Cambridge 1799, BA1804, dn05 (Nor.), p06 (Nor.), MA1807. PC. Letheringham, Suffolk 1806, PC. Hoo, Suffolk 1806, R. Boulge w. Debach 1817 to death 1848 (3rd q.) [C114788] Married Elizabeth Geater Sterne, w. clerical son Henry. A friend of Edward Fitzgerald, the poet.

RHAM (William Lewis) Born Utrecht, Holland, s. Wilhelm (de) Rham (of Leiden) and Anne Kincloh. Marischal College, Aberdeen, MA1799, then Trinity, Cambridge 1802 (aged 23), dn03 (Salis.), p03 (Salis.), BA1806, MA1810. V. Broad Hinton, Wilts. 1804-7 (res.), R. Fersfield, Norfolk 1808-43, Prebend of Bitton in Salisbury Cathedral 1806-7 (res.), then of Yetminster Secunda, Dorset 1807, R. Winkfield, Berks. 1808 to death 31/10/1843 [C85947. ODNB] 'Member of the Royal Agricultural Society, contributing many important articles on practical agriculture to its *Journal*. Started a school of agriculture and domestic work at Winkfield'.

RICE (Edward, Hon.) Born London 19/11/1779, s. George Rice, *M.P.*, and Cecil de Cardonnel, Baroness Dynevor. Christ Church, Oxford 1794, BA1798, then All Souls, dn00 (Ox.), p01 (Ox.), MA1802, BD and DD1820. Prebend of Driffield (and Precentor) in York Minister 1802-62, V. Sutton in the Forest (o/w Sutton-in-Galtres), Yorks. 1803-10 (res.), R. Great Rissington, Glos. 1810, R. and V. Great Barrington, Glos. 1810-20, Prebend of 9th Canon in Worcester Cathedral 1815-26 (res.), R. Oddington, Glos. 1820, Dean of Gloucester 1826 [*not* Archdeacon as in CCEd] to death 15/8/1862 aged 82, leaving £45,000 [C37431] Married Marylebone, London 9/7/1800 Charlotte Lascelles (dau. of a general), with clerical son Francis William below.

RICE (Edward) Born Stratford on Avon, Warwicks. 24/5/1795, s. Bernard Rice. Trinity, Cambridge 1813, BA1817, dn18 (London), p19 (London), MA1820, DD1839. S/M Christ's Hospital [School] 1818-36, H/M 1836-53 ('a very great headmaster who set the highest standard'); V. Horley, Surrey 1827 to death ('*hanged himself* to the post of his bed' six days after handing in his resignation) 20/6/1853 [C108646. Boase] Had issue.

RICE (Francis William, 5th Baron Dynevor) Born 10/5/1804, s. Rev. Hon. Edward Rice (above) and Charlotte Lascelles. Christ Church, Oxford 1822, BA1826, MA1847. V. Fairford, Glos. 1828 (and RD) to death (London) 3/8/1878 aged 74, leaving £60,000 [under Francis William Dynevor]. Lived at Newton House, Dynevor [Dinefwr], Carmarthen [C162018. Boase] Married (1) 3/2/1830 Harriet Ives Barker (d.1854), w. son the 6th Baron (2) 18/11/1856 Eliza Amelia Knox (w) (a clergy dau.). Succ. to title 1869.

RICE (Henry) [Trinity, Cambridge 1796, BA. MA?]. PC. Sandhurst, Berks. 1806, PC. Swingfield, Kent 1809-14 (res.), R. Great Holland, Essex 1812-60, PC. Buckland near Dover, Kent 1813-21. Died Bath 17/9/1860, leaving £12,000 [C108647. Venn entry is chaotic!]

RICE (Richard, sen.) Born Sherborne, Glos. 21/4/1759 (bapt. 4/9/1759), s. Rev. Richard Rice (V. Farrington, Berks.) and Dorothy Wintle. Merton, Oxford 1781, BCL1795. R. Eaton Hastings, Berks. 1789 to death (Swansea) 16/12/1835 [C37433. In ERC as R. Price] Married Charlotte Harriet Dickson, with s. below as successor.

RICE (Richard, jun.) Bapt. Eaton Hastings, Berks. 15/8/1792, s. Rev. Richard Rice (above) and Charlotte Harriet Dickson. Merton, Oxford 1810, BA1814, dn15 (Salis. for Win.), p16 (Salis.), MA1818. R. Compton Beauchamp, Berks. 1816, R. Hayton, Cumberland 1820-36 and V. Kirkland, Cumberland 1820-36, R. (and patron) of Eaton Hastings 1836 to death 29/9/1868 aged 75, leaving £450 [C3475. Platt] Married 1821 Mary Goodenough (a clergy dau.), with clerical son. Splendid port. online.

RICH (John) Born Farnham, Surrey 27/9/1789, s. Rev. Sir Charles Bostock Rich, 1st Bart. (of Shirley House, Hants.) and Mary Frances Rich [*thus*]. [H.E.I.C. 1805-13 (res.)] St John's, Cambridge 1812, dn15 (C&L for Salis.), BA1816, p16 (Heref. for Win.), MA1819. R. Cheddington, Bucks. 1819-46, V. Ivinghow, Bucks. 1821-46, R. Newtimber, Sussex 1846 to death 24/6/1856 aged 66 [C19110] Married St Pancras, London 3/8/1825 Georgiana Gordon, with clerical s., also John Rich.

RICHARDS (Charles, sen.) From Bradninch, Devon, s. Charles Richards. Corpus Christi, Oxford 1772 (aged 18), dn76 (Win.), p78 (Win.), BA1781, MA1783. Founder and H/M Hyde Abbey School for 50 years; V. Winchester St Bartholomew Hyde 1797-1833, R. Chale, IoW 1806-33, Canon of 5th Prebend in Winchester Cathedral 1827-33, V. Wansborough, Hants. 1830 to death. Dom. Chap. to Bishop of Norwich 1803. Died 20/1/1833 [C89287] Wife Susan, and sons Charles (below), George Pierce, and Henry, below.

RICHARDS (Charles, jun.) Bapt. Winchester St Bartholomew Hyde 16/1/1783, s. Rev. Charles, sen. (above) and Susan Richards. Christ Church, Oxford 1801, then Magdalen 1801-7, BA1805, dn06 (Win.), p07 (Ex.), MA 1808. S/M Hyde Abbey School, Winchester; 'Perpetual V'. South Stoneham, Hants. 1815-35, R. Nunney, Som. 1817-30 [C40409], R. (and patron) of Chale, IoW 1830 to death. Dom. Chap. to 13th Marquess of Winchester 1817. Died 27/12/1834 (CCEd thus) aged 51 [C108649 and 40409] Serious confusion with father above. Brothers George Pierce, and Henry, below.

RICHARDS (Edward Tew) Bapt. Farlington, Hants. 19/2/1798, s. Rev. Griffith Richards and Anne Longcroft. Corpus Christi, Oxford 1816, BA1819, dn22 (Heref.), MA1822, p22 (Ox.), Fellow 1822-4. R. Terwick, Sussex 1826, (succ. his father as) R. (and patron) of Farlington 1826 to death 17/3/1887, leaving £23,799-16s-0d. [C31313] Married (1) St Pancras, London 10/4/1823 Laura Page (d.1`833), w. issue (2) Farlington 9/6/1836 Horatia Haslewood, with clerical s. Arthur James Richards. Brother Henry Richards, below. Fine photo. online.

RICHARDS (George) From Hasleworth, Suffolk, s. Rev. James Richards. Trinity, Oxford 1785 (aged 17), BA1788, then Oriel, Fellow 1790, MA1791, dn92 (Ox.), p92 (Ox.), BD and DD1820. R. Lillingstone Lovell, Oxon. 1795-1825, R. Bampton, Oxon. 1796-1824, R. London St Martin in the Fields [net income £1,258] 1824 to death. Dom. Chap. to Elizabeth, Countess Harcourt 1809. Died 30/3/1837 [C21314]

RICHARDS (George Pierce) Bapt. Winchester 10/9/1785, s. Rev. Charles sen. (above). and Susan Richards, King's, Cambridge 1804, Fellow 1807-30, BA1809, dn08 (Win.), p09 (Win.), MA1812. H/M Leeds G/S 1813-18; V. Tiverton (Priors Portion) 1818-20, R. Sampford Courtenay, Devon 1829 to death 28/2/1859 [C108652. Boase] Married Beverley, Yorks. 6/1/1831 1831 Emma Mary Sara Antoinetta Eyre (a clergy dau., Kirk Ella, Yorks.). Brothers Charles (above), and Henry (below).

RICHARDS (Henry) Born Farlington, Hants. 1799, s. Rev. Griffith Richards and Anne Longcroft. Exeter, Oxford 1818, BA1822, dn22 (Chich.), MA1824, p24 (Chich.), BD1834. PC. Horfield, Dorset 1828 to death 1864 (3rd q.). No will traced [C53755] Married Bristol 23/10/1823 Caroline Daubeny (or Danberry?) (w), with issue. Brother Edward Tew Richards (above). Fine port. online.

RICHARDS (Henry) Born Winchester, s. Rev. Charles, sen. (above) and Susan Richards. Magdalen Hall, Oxford 1817 (aged 24), dn20 (Glos. for Win.), BA1824, p24 (Win.), MA1829. V. Keevil, Wilts. 1830-9. Died? [C89290] Brother Charles, jun. (above).

RICHARDS (Richard George) Born Hambledon, Hants., s. John Richards (schoolmaster). St John's, Cambridge 1792 (aged 18), then Christ's 1793, BA1797, dn97 (Win.), p98 (Win.), MA 1805. V. Hambledon 1800 to death 1841 (2nd q.) [C108655]

RICHARDS (Russell) Born London, s. John Richards (of Datchet, Bucks.). Educ. at Boulogne, France. Trinity, Cambridge 1817 (aged 17), BA1822 [adm. Middle Temple 1822] dn24 (Nor.), p25 (Nor.), MA1825. R. Ilketshall St John, Suffolk 1832-5, R. Wootton Courtney, Som. 1825 to death 23/10/1863 aged 62, leaving £10,000 [C21327] Widow Caroline Ann.

RICHARDS (Simon Slocombe) Bapt. Chipstable, Somerset 9/9/1785, s. Rev. Simon Richards. Emmanuel, Cambridge 1806, SCL, dn08 (B&W), p09 (B&W). R. Chipstable 1809 to death (unmarried) 1853 (2nd q.) [C48220]

RICHARDS (Thomas) From Aller, Somerset, s. James Richards (farmer). Emmanuel, Cambridge 1808, then to St John's 1810, BA1813, dn13 (Salis. for Chich.). V. Icklesham, Sussex 1817 to death ('suddenly while walking in George Street, Hastings') 6/12/1843 aged 52 [C65218] Married (1) Icklesham, Surrey 25/4/1818 Eliza Frances Hollingbury, with clerical s. (2) Winchester 5/8/1823 Ann Corbet, w. further clerical son Thomas Watkin, below.

RICHARDS (Thomas Watkin) Born City of London, s. Thomas Richards (above) and Ann Corbet. Queen's, Oxford 1811 (aged 17), BA 1815, MA1818, Fellow 1818-20. V. Seighford, Staffs. 1820, R. Puttenham, Surrey 1823 to death 30/10/1859. No Will Traced [C19535] Married Grendon Underwood, Bucks. 5/11/1819 Marian Pope, and had issue.

RICHARDS (William Page) From Bradninch, Devon, s. Charles Richards and Hannah Page. New, Oxford 1792 (aged 19), dn95 (C&L for Win.), BCL 1805, DCL1822. R. Stoke Abbas (o/w Stoke Abbot ><), Dorset 1811 (and H/M Blundell's School, Tiverton), PC. East Teignmouth, Devon 1823 to death 2/4/1861. Will not traced [C19536] Married Loders, Dorset 29/12/1813 Amelia, dau. Sir John Strachan, 1st Bart., with issue.

RICHARDSON (Benjamin) Bapt. Halifax, Yorks. 11/6/1775, s. William Richardson. Literate: dn01 (C&L for York), p01 (York). PC. Egton and PC. Glaisdale, Yorks. 1806-[44], PC.

Goatland, Yorks. 1831-[47]. Died? [C19537. YCO] Clerical son of same name at Glaisdale.

RICHARDSON (Harling) Bapt. Killington, Westmorland 8/3/1763, s. Robert Richardson and Elizabeth Harling. S/M Kendal. Literate: dn89 (Chester), p90 (Chester). PC. Barbon, Kirkby Lonsdale, Westmorland 1790 (and S/M) to death 22/5/1837 aged 78 [C170301] Married Kirkby Lonsdale 22/11/1794 Nancy Hewetson, with clerical son of same name.

RICHARDSON (James) Born St Bees, Cumberland 29/7/1760, s. William [*pleb.*] Richardson. Queen's, Oxford 1779, BA1783, dn84 (Ox. for York), p85 (York), MA1786. Probationer 1785 then Vicar Choral, York Minster 1786, R. York Holy Trinity Goodramgate w. St Maurice and St John del Pyke 1801-3, V. Ferry Fryston, Yorks. 1801-4, V. York St Martin, Coney Street 1803-29, PC. York St John Micklegate (o/w Ousebridge) 1804-50, V. Huntington, Yorks. 1804 and PC. Heslington, Yorks. 1822 to death 22/12/1850 aged 90 [C37438. YCO] Married York 14/12/1788 Charlotte Tait, w. clerical s. William (below).

RICHARDSON (John) Bapt. Warcop, Westmorland 19/5/1774, s. Christopher Richardson. Literate: dn98 (York), p98 (York). PC. Norton, Yorks. 1806 to death 16/10/1834 (CCEd thus) [C98708 / C136865. YCO]

RICHARDSON (Richard) Bapt. Worcester 23/8/1752, s. Richard Richardson. BNC, Oxford 1774, BA1778, dn77 (Wor.), p78 (Durham), MA1782, BD and DD1810. Minor Canon of Durham Cathedral 1777-84 (res.), PC. Witton Gilbert w. Kimblesworth, Durham 1780-1839, R. Mestham, Surrey 1784-91, R. Elwick Hall, Durham 1790-1828, Chancellor St Paul's Cathedral, London 1792-1839, Precentor St David's Cathedral 1816-39. R. Brancepeth, Durham 1828-39. Died Witton Gilbert 27/9/1839 aged 87 [C122059] Married Durham 2/4/1781 Mary Eden (dau. Sir Robert Eden, 3rd Bart.?).

RICHARDSON (Thomas) Born St Bees, Cumberland 1/11/1796, s. Henry (a cooper) and Ann Richardson. Literate: dn19 (York), p20 (York). V. Warthill, Yorks. 1831, V. Bugthorpe, Yorks. 1843-57, R. York St Martin Micklegate 1857 (with Chap. York Lunatic Asylum and S/M). Died York 24/3/1877, leaving £19,000 [C136206. YCO] Married York 1/1/1827 Mary Grainger, with issue.

RICHARDSON (William) Born Middleton in Lonsdale, Yorks. 3/8/1755, s. of a cooper. Schoolmaster. Literate: dn78 (Chester), p79 (Chester). V. Chester St John the Baptist 1785 to death 22/12/1837 [C180309]

RICHARDSON (William) Born St Bees, Cumberland 15/9/1779, s. John (a farmer) and Betty Richardson. Lincoln, Oxford 1800, BA 1804, dn04 (Chester for York), p04 (York). V. Ferry Fryston, Yorks. 1804 to death before 7/7/1852 [C98723. YCO] Married Halifax, Yorks. 19/4/1808 Charlotte Horton, with issue.

RICHARDSON (William) Born 17/11/1795, s. Rev. James Richardson (a Vicar Choral of York Minster, above) and Charlotte Tait. Trinity, Cambridge 1813, then St John's, 1817, BA1819, dn19 (Ex. for York), p20 (Ex. for York), MA1822. Vicar Choral of York Minster with R. York St Michael le Belfry 1829-32, R. Huttons Ambo, Yorks. 1832 and V. Crambe, Yorks. 1832 to death 14/7/1837 aged 41 [C136207. YCO] Married Aston, Warwicks. 27/12/1823 1823 Mary Darwell (a clergy dau.).

RICHINGS (Benjamin) Born Oxford 11/5/1788, s. Thomas Richings [*pleb.*] and Mary Haynes. Lincoln, Oxford 1805, BA1811, dn11, MA1812, p12 (Salis.). V. (and patron) of Mancetter, Warwicks. 1816 to death 30/4/1872, leaving £1,500 [C19543] Married Claybrook, Leics. 16/5/1815 Harriet Jane Goodacre, with clerical s. Frederic Hartshill Richings.

RICHMOND (Christopher George) Born Lancaster 23/2/1798, s. John (a surveyor) and Jane Richmond. Magdalene, Cambridge 1819, then St John's 1820, then Caius 1821, BA1825, dn26 (Lin.), p27 (Lin.). R. Donington on Bain, Lincs. 1829-31 (res.), V. Great Ludford (Ludford Magna), Lincs. 1831-42, V. Legsby, Lincs. 1832 and V. Sixhills, Lincs. 1838 to death 12/1842 [C75141] Married 24/8/1826 Frances Dixon (a clergy dau.), and had issue.

RICHMOND (Henry Sylvester) Bapt. Turvey, Beds. 20/4/1808, s. Rev. Legh Richmond (*q.v.* ODNB) and Mary Chambers. Queens', Cambridge 1827, BA1831, dn31 (Lin.), p33 (Lin.), MA1834. V. Breedon on the Hill, Lincs. and V. Ratby cum Groby, Lincs. 1833-41, R. Wyck Rissington, Glos. 1853 to death

4/7/1872 aged 64, leaving £7,000 [C75142. Boase] Married Guestling, Sussex 3/1/1837 Caroline Eliza Close (w), with issue.

RICKARDS (George) Born Leicester 23/5/1789 (nonconformist baptism), s. Thomas and Mary Rickards. Literate: dn13 (York), p14 (Car. or Ex. for York). PC. Wortley, Leeds, Yorks. 1814 to death 9/12/1843 [C135966. YCO] Married Leeds 11/2/1817 Hannah Bateson, with issue.

RICKARDS (Samuel) Bapt. Kettering, Northants. 6/12/1794 (nonconformist baptism) s. Thomas and Elizabeth Rickards (of Leicester). Oriel, Oxford 1813, BA1817, Fellow 1819-22, dn20 (Glos.), p21 (London for Cant.), MA1829. R. Stowlangtoft, Suffolk 1832 to death 24/8/1865, leaving £7,000 [C114851] Married Lucy Maria Wilmot (w), with issue. Brother below.

RICKARDS (Thomas Ascough) Born Leicester 8/10/1790, s. Thomas and Elizabeth Rickards (nonconformist baptism). Oriel, Oxford 1810, BA1814, dn14 (Salis.), p15 (London), MA1817. V. Cosby, Leics. 1816-72. Died 15/1/1878, leaving £3,000 [C75146] Married (1) Darley Dale, Derbys. 29/6/1819 Caroline Anne ('Cally') Gisborne (d.1823), w. child (2) Clapham, London 21/1/1830 Eliza Sophia Spicer (w), w. clerical s. Thomas. Brother above.

RICKETTS (Frederick) Born Marylebone, London 10/11/1788, s. George Poyntz Ricketts and Sophia Watts. Christ Church, Oxford 1805, Student [Fellow] 1805-12, BA1809, MA 1812, dn12 (York). R. Eckington w. Killamarsh, Derbys [net income £1,595] 1814 and R. Shaftesbury St James (o/w Shaston, Dorset 1818 to death. Dom. Chap. to 2nd Earl of Liverpool 1814; Chap. to Princess of Wales 1817. Died 23/3/1843 [C19545. YCO] Married Marylebone, London 1813 Mary Anne Sturt ('a niece of the Earl of Shaftesbury'), with issue.

RIDDELL (James) Born Little Govan, Renfrew 1796, s. Henry Riddell (Glasgow merchant) and Anne Glassford. Glasgow Univ. 1811-13, Snell Exhibitioner Balliol, Oxford 1813, BA1816, MA1819. R. Easton, Hants. 1826-36, V. Hanbury, Staffs. 1836-63. Lived and died Leamington, Warwicks. 13/5/1878. Will not traced [C19547. Snell] Married Northampton 15/1/1822 Dorothy Foster, with issue.

RIDDING (Charles Henry) From Winchester, s. John Ridding. New, Oxford 1815 (aged 18), Fellow 1815-24, BCL1823. S/M and Fellow of Winchester College. R. Rollestone, Wilts. 1824, V. Andover w. Foxcott, Hants. 1835 to death 5/5/1871, leaving £40,000 [C108664] Married Clifton, Bristol 29/7/1824 Charlotte Stonhouse Vigor (d.1832), w. clerical s. George Ridding (Headmaster of Winchester College, and first Bishop of Southwell).

RIDEOUT (John) From Woodmancote, Sussex, s. Rev. John Rideout, sen. Jesus, Cambridge 1785, BA1790, dn90 (Glos.), p92 (London), MA1795. (succ. his father as) R. Woodmancote 1795 to death 6/4/1838 aged 70 [C65227]

RIDEOUT (Philip) Bapt. Farnham, Dorset 15/8/1775, s. Rev. Philip Rideout, sen. and Anna Susanna Hinxman. Exeter, Oxford 1793, BA1797, p99 (Salis.). R. Farnham 1799 and V. Shapwick, Dorset 1811 to death 26/6/1834 (CCEd says 19/12/1834) [C53759] Married St George's Hanover Square, London 14/10/1805 Sarah Royall, with issue.

RIDEOUT see also under **RIDOUT**

RIDER, *later* CARR-RIDER (Ralph Carr-) Born Leeds 9/8/1767, s. Ingram Rider and Ann Carr. Merton, Oxford 1786, BA1789, dn90 (Cant.). R. Stoke, Kent 1811 to death 8/4/1839 [C2177. Foster as Carr-Rider] Married St Martin in the Fields, London 15/11/1802 Mary Inskip, with issue.

RIDLEY (Charles John) Born Newcastle upon Tyne 5/9/1792, s. Sir Matthew White Ridley, 2nd Bart. and Anne Colborne. University, Oxford 1809, BA1813, Fellow 1813-54, MA1817, dn17 (Ox.), p17 (Ox.), Rawlinson Professor of Anglo Saxon, Oxford 1820-27. R. Larling, Norfolk 1826, R. West Harling, Norfolk 1826 to death 8/10/1854 [C21332]

RIDLEY (Henry John) Born Wallsend, Northumberland 28/12/1789, s. Rev. Henry John Ridley, sen. and Frances Surtees. Christ Church, Oxford 1807, BA1811, dn13 (Win.), MA1813, p15 (Glos. for Win.). Canon of 1st Prebend in Bristol Cathedral 1816-32 (changed for 5th Prebend of Norwich Cathedral 1832), R. Abinger, Surrey 1821-34, R. Kirkby Underdale, Yorks. 1827 to death (*shot himself*) 11/11/1834 [C1108] Married (1) by 1813 Elizabeth Margaret

Antoinette Ellis (d.1816), 1s. (2) Marylebone, London 26/6/1823 Elizabeth Steere (who remarried 1st Lord Abinger in 1843).

RIDLEY (Richard) Born Newcastle upon Tyne 28/7/1782, s. Sir Matthew White Ridley, 2nd Bart. and Sarah Colborne. University, Oxford 1799, BA1803, dn05 (York), MA1806, p06 (York). PC. Cramlington, Northumberland 1806-38 (non-res.), V. Hart, Durham 1808 (non-res.), V. Leathley, Yorks. 1826 to death (Knaresborough, Yorks.) 21/1/1845 aged 62 [C98880. YCO] Married Ashton-on-Mersey, Cheshire 8/11/1810 Katherine Lucy Johnson (a clergy dau.).

RIDLEY (Thomas Yates) Born Lancaster 3/5/1796, s. Jacob Ridley (a merchant) and Jane Yates. [Trained as a physician at Edinburgh University] St John's, Cambridge 1815, then Peterhouse 1816, BA1820, dn19 (London), p21 (London), MA1823. R. Heysham, Lancs. 1824 (where he acted as doctor to his parishioners, '6 miles from all medical aid') to death 1/2/1838 aged 42 [C121310] Married (1) Heysham 20/3/1820 Margaret Hadwen (d.1823), w. issue (2) Liverpool 8/1/1825 Jane, widow of Rev. Thomas Clarkson, and owner of the avowdson.

RIDOUT (George) Born London 11/4/1788, s. John Ridout, Balliol, Oxford 1805, dn12 (Glos.), BCL1812, p12 (Glos.). R. Lamyat, Som. 1825-33 [C40413], V. Newland, Glos. 1832 to death 26/1/1871, leaving £4,000 [C50515/ 161992] Married Bristol 30/4/1816 1816 Mary Anne Dowell, with clerical sons.

RIDOUT (John Honyfield) Born Blandford, Dorset 17/7/1768, s. John Ridout and Honyfield Coker. Merton, Oxford 1775, dn90 (Bristol). R. Langton Long >< Dorset 1792. Probate granted 14/4/1855 [C53760] Married Bristol 15/4/1848 Jane Knight.

RIDOUT see also under **RIDEOUT**

RIDSDALE (Edward) Born Wakefield, Yorks. 22/5/1798, s. John and Ann Ridsdale. Trinity, Cambridge 1817, BA1821, dn22 (York), p23 (York). V. Ditton Priors, Shropshire 1825-[62]. Died a bachelor 12/8/1872, leaving £800 [C135706. YCO]

RIDSDALE (Robert) Bapt. Kirby Overblow, Yorks. 7/4/1791, s. William Ridsdale and Sarah Harland. Clare, Cambridge 1811, BA 1815, dn15 (Lin.), p16 (Lin.), Fellow 1816-26, MA1818. R. Knockin, Shropshire 1826-64-, V. Kirdford, Sussex 1826-31, R. North Chapel, Sussex 1831-34, R. Tillington, Sussex 1834 (and Fittleworth Prebend in Chichester Cathedral 1835) to death 21/5/1876 [total income £1,108], leaving £7,000 [C65231] Married Hertford 10/10/1826 Lady Audrey Harriet Townshend (dau. of 1st Marquess of Townshend, and who was 'granted the rank and style of a daughter of a Marquess'), with issue.

RIGBY (Joseph) Bapt. Beverley, Yorks. 19/4/1790, s. Rev. Robert Rigby and Sarah Carnley. Literate: dn15 (Ex. for York), p16 (York). V. Holme in Spalding Moor, Yorks. 1817, V. Hutton Cranswick, Yorks. 1819 and PC. Beswick, Yorks. 1819 to death 2/7/1870 aged 80. Will Not Traced [C135707. YCO] Married Hutton Cranswick 8/2/1826, with issue.

RIGG (Hugh) Bapt. Crosby Ravensworth, Westmorland 10/2/1782, s. Jonathan Rigg and Margaret Brown. H/M Crosby Ravensworth G/S 1801. Literate: dn05 (Car. for York), p06 (Chester). PC. Patrick Brompton >< w. PC. Brompton Hunton, Bedale, Yorks. 1811 to burial 10/2/1866 aged 84, leaving £1,500 [C6236. YCO] Married Crosby Ravensworth 18/5/1808 Maria Addison, with issue.

RIGG (Joseph) Born Burgh by Sands, Cumberland 14/7/1794, s. Robinson Rigg and Jane Peat. St John's, Cambridge 1816, then Corpus Christi 1816, BA1820, dn20 (Chester [for C&L?]), p21 (Chester for C&L), MA1827. PC. Preston St Paul, Lancs. 1829 to death (Burgh by Sands, unmarried) 3/10/1847 aged 53 [C19480]

RIGG (William) Born Little Strickland, Westmorland 28/5/1792, s. John Rigg and Jane Harrison. [NiVoF] dn16 (Chester), p17 (Chester). PC. Flookburgh, Cartmel, Lancs. 1822 to death 11/10/1863 aged 71. Will not traced [C170318] Married Flookburgh 2/3/1818 Mary Postlethwaite, with clerical son.

RIGG (Wilson) Bapt. Lancaster 11/7/1784, s. John and Sally Rigg. Literate: dn15 (York), p16 (Ely for York). PC. St John in the Wilderness, Hebden Bridge, Yorks. 1816-18, Incumbent of Ellenbrook Chapel, Worsley, Eccles, Lancs. 1819-56, (first) PC. Grange over Sands, Lancs. 1856 to death 16/10/1857, leaving £4,000

[C109209. YCO] Married Manchester 22/3/1810 Mary Bennett, and had issue.

RILEY (Richard) From Staffs. St John, Cambridge 1781, BA1785, dn87 (Peterb.), Fellow 1787-1806, MA1788, BD1795. V. Shrepreth, Cambs 1790-1804, R. Marwood, Devon 1803 to death 3/4/1853 aged 90 [C100178] Married Little Gransden, Cambs. 14/8/1805 Sarah Gower, w. clerical s. Richard Edward.

RIPLEY (Thomas Hyde) Born Fulham, London 13/11/1782, s. Rev. Thomas Ripley and Sophia Pemberton. King's, Cambridge 1802, BA1806, MA1809, Fellow 1805-14, dn06 (Bristol), p09 (Salis.). V. Wootton Bassett, Wilts. 1813-65, (succ. his father as) R. Tockenham, Wilts. 1828-65, PC. Chester le Street, Durham 1828 [total income £1,390] to death. Dom. Chap. to 1st Earl of Durham 1828. Died Tockenham 25/2/1865 aged 82, leaving £800 [C53761] Married (1) St George's Hanover Square, London 17/1/1815 Caroline Honeywood (d.1821), w. issue (2) Bloomsbury, London 26/2/1822 Caroline Augusta Tyndale, of Hayling, with further issue. Surrogate.

RIPPON (John) Born Stansfield, Yorks., s. Thomas Rippon. Trinity, Cambridge 1775 (aged 20), BA1780, dn81 (Ely), Fellow 1781, MA1783, p89 (Ely). V. Hitchin, Herts. 1794-1804, R. Long Marton, Westmorland 1803-33 (living at Long Marton Hall) and R. Kirkby Thorpe, Westmorland 1803 (non-res.) to death. Dom. Chap. to HRH Dowager Duchess of Cumberland and Strathearn 1819. Died 26/5/1833 (CCEd says 15/11/1833) aged 78 [C6237. Platt] Married (1) Holborn, London 7/5/1794 Maria Roycroft (d. Padua May 1798 aged 24) (2) London 18/2/1802 Hannah Harriet Diana Fearn. *J.P.* Westmorland and North Riding of Yorks.

RISLEY (John) Bapt. Tingewick, Bucks. 1/7/1771, s. Rev. John and Elizabeth Risley. New, Oxford 1787, BA1791, dn93 (Lin.), p96 (Ox.), MA1808. R. Ashton, Northants. 1799 and R. Thornton, Bucks. 1819 to death 29/4/1853 [C37464] Step-brother below.

RISLEY (William Cotton) Born Tingewick, Bucks. 22/10/1798, s. Rev. John Risley and Sarah Ann Cotton. New, Oxford 1816, BA1821, MA1824, etc. V. Whaddon, Wilts. 1829-48, V. Deddington, Oxon. 1836-48. Died there 1/6/1869, leaving £16,000 [C21346. IE and Will as William only] Married Adderbury, Oxon. 8/10/1828 Susanna Wells, with clerical sons Robert Wells Risley, and John Cotton Risley. Step-brother above. Photo. online.

RITSON (Bartholomew) Bapt. Waltham Abbey, Essex 30/8/1767, s. Daniel and Deborah Ritson. St John's, Cambridge 1786, BA1791, dn91 (Nor.), p92 (Nor.), MA1796. PC. Hopton, Yarmouth Norfolk 1801 to death 29/3/1835 (having been 'seized with apoplexy in the pulpit and died a few hours afterwards in an adjacent cottage') [C114890] Married Lowestoft, Suffolk 21/12/1792 Anne Ramsay, w. child.

RIVERS (Henry, Sir, 9th Bart.) Bapt. Winchester Cathedral 25/1/1770, s. Rev. Sir Peter Rivers, 6th Bart. (R. of Chelmsford, Essex) and Martha Coxe. St John's, Cambridge 1797, BA 1801, dn02 (Win.), p04 (Glos.), MA1805. R. Winchester St Peter 1804-18, V. Netheravon, Wilts. 1808-9, R. Walcot, Bath 1808-9, R. Winchester St Swithin 1813-39, R. Martyr Worthy, Hants. 1817-51, R. Farley Chamberlayne, Hants. 1839 to 'sudden' death 7/7/1851 'while crossing Easton Common alone' [C48235. Boase] Married 2/5/1812 Charlotte Eales (Cranbury, Hants.). Succ. to title 1805.

ROBERSON (Hammond) Bapt. Cawston, Norfolk 6/2/1757, s. Henry and Sarah Roberson. Magdalene, Cambridge 1775, BA 1779, dn79 (York) ('before he reached the canonical age' on the recommendation of Henry Venn), p81 (York), MA1782, Fellow. V. Hartshead cum Clifton, Yorks. 1795-1803, (builder and first) PC. Liversedge, Yorks. 1816 (w. Prebend of Apesthorpe in York Minster 1830 (w. PC. Apesthorpe, Notts. 1830 appended) to death 9/8/1841 aged 84 [C98889. YCO. DEB. J.T.M. Nussey, 'Hammond Roberson of Liversedge … bully or gentleman?' *Yorks. Archaeological J*, 53 (1981) 97-109] Married Batley, Yorks. 22/12/1787 Phoebe Ashworth. Charlotte Bronte saw him when she was 10 years old and carried away a vivid impression of his 'stern martial air'; she used him as the prototype of Matthewson Helstone in *Shirley*; he 'took delight in breaking-in difficult horses, but opposed bull-baiting'; 'he rode, armed with a sword, to help defend Rawfold's Mill during the Luddite riots'.

ROBERSON (Henry William Moncrieff) Born Oxford 26/8/1802, s. Thomas Roberson and Lucy Cox. Christ Church, Oxford (chorister 1812-18), matr. 1819, Lincoln 1821-25, BA1825, dn26, dn27 (Lin.), p29 (Ox.), MA1836. V. Tytherington, Glos. 1830 to death 8/7/1881, leaving £641-15s-0d. [C21353] Married 4/10/1832 Mary Field (w), with son of same name.

ROBERTS (Alfred William) Bapt. City of London 16/8/1763, s. William Roberts and Mary Barnes. Trinity, Cambridge 1782, BA 1787, dn87 (Cant.), p90 (Car.), MA1792. R. Coln St Denis, Glos. 1793-7, V. Barkston, Lincs. 1796-1801 (res.), PC. St Albans St Peter, Herts. 1801-20 (res.), R. Little Burstead (o/w Bursted Parva) w. Chap. Billericay, Essex 1820 to death 2/7/1843 [C6238] Married Barnes. Surrey 10/12/1794 Jean Bean, w. issue.

ROBERTS (Arthur) Bapt. London 22/12/1800, s. William (barrister and author, q.v. ODNB) and Elizabeth Ann Roberts. Oriel, Oxford 1819, BA1823, dn24 (Glos.), p24 (Win.), MA 1829. V. Woodrising, Norfolk 1831 to death 3/9/1886, leaving £4,516-18s-6d. [C108666. Boase] Married Norwich 21/11/1832 Elizabeth Hicks, and had issue.

ROBERTS (Christopher) Bapt. Grasmere, Westmorland 25/12/1760, s. Christopher Roberts and Francis Rigge. Literate: dn86 (Chester), p86 (Glos. for London). V. Great Edstone, Yorks. 1788 and PC. Bugthorpe, Yorks. 1808 to death 14/3/1843 [C121320] Married Hawkshead, Lancs. 3/11/1788 Mrs Elizabeth (Bownas) Patrickson, with issue.

ROBERTS (George) [NiVoF] V. Gretton w. Duddington Chapel, Northants. 1819 to death 24/10/1843 aged 73 [C89357]

ROBERTS (James) Bapt. LeekWootton, Warwicks. 13/12/1767, s. Rev. James Roberts, sen. Trinity, Oxford 1783, BA1787, dn90 (C&L) p91 (Wor.), MA1800. R. Wolverton, Warwicks. 1791 [C110790], R. Witherley, Leics. 1805-33 (res.). Died 6/1/1842 [C19587]

ROBERTS (James) Literate: p21 (Chester). PC. Quarnford (o/w Flash), Staffs. 1821-50. Died? [C19588]

ROBERTS (James Corall) Born Stoneleigh. Warwicks. 21/7/1795, s. Rev. James Roberts, and Mabel Corall. Trinity, Oxford 1813, BA 1818, MA1833. R. Wolston, Warwicks. 1819-71 [blank in ERC], R. Witherley, Leics. 1833. Dom. Chap. to 2nd Viscount Hood 1833. Died 6/9/1871, leaving £5,000 [C19589]

ROBERTS (John Phillips) From Oakingham, Berks., s. William Roberts. New, Oxford 1817 (aged 18), Chap. 1820-6, BA1821, dn22 (Ox.), p23 (Ox.), Chap. Christ Church 1824-28, MA 1826. Priest-Vicar Exeter Cathedral 1826-7 ('given notice'), Minor Canon of Chichester Cathedral and V. Chichester St Peter the Great 1831, R. Eastergate, Sussex 1849 to death 12/12/1882, leaving £772-3s-7d. [C21349] Married Exeter 19/7/1827 Margaret Cornelia Ford.

ROBERTS (John Richards) Bapt. Barnstaple, Devon 6/7/1795, s. John Roberts and Elizabeth Horwood. Trinity, Oxford 1794, Fellow to 1825, BA1798, dn99 (Peterb.), MA1801, p04 (Ox.), BD1810, etc. R. Hornblotton, Som. 1805-24, St Bartholomew the Great, Smithfield, London 1814-19, R. Rotherfield Greys, Oxon. 1824 to death 20/6/1843 [C21350] F.S.A.

ROBERTS (Robert) [NiVoF] V. Stewkley, Lincs. 1830 to death 1833 [C75167] Could be either of the two below?

ROBERTS (Robert) Born Cambridge 24/10/1787, s. William Roberts and Lettice King. St John's, Cambridge 1805, BA1809, dn11 (Ely), MA1812, p13 (Ely). V. Haverhill, Suffolk 1815-73, R. Little Thurlow, Suffolk 1819-24 (res.), V. Blyton cum Wharton, Lincs. 1824 to death 25/12/1875, leaving £30,000 [C75168] Married Wixoe, Suffolk 26/10/1819 Emily Nottidge (w), w. clerical son Josiah Pepys Roberts.

ROBERTS (Robert) From Stoke Doyle, Sussex, s. Rev. Robert Roberts, sen. Corpus Christi, Cambridge 1826, BA1830, dn30 (Peterb.), p31 (Peterb.). R. (and patron) of Wadenhoe, Northants. 1831 and R. Aldwincle All Saints, Northants. 1838 to death 27/3/1891 aged 84, leaving £1,754-3s-10d. [C110792] Widow Anne.

ROBERTS (Thomas) From Llandemog, Denbigh, s. Foulk Roberts. Hertford, Oxford 1800 (aged 17), then Jesus, BA1804, dn05 (Lin.), migrated to Magdalene, Cambridge MA1807. V. Barholme w. Stowe, Lincs. 1815-47, V. Deeping

St James, Lincs. 1815-30, V. Stamford St Mary, Lincs. 1828 to death (Greatford House, Stamford) 13/4/1847 [C75173. Kaye]

ROBERTS (William) Bapt. Eton, Berks. 29/5/1762, s. Rev. William Hayward Roberts (Provost of Eton College) and Jane Pitt. King's, Cambridge 1781, BA1786, Fellow 1784-6, p86 (Salis.), MA1786 (Lambeth). S/M Eton College 'for a short time', Fellow of Eton 1786-1833, Vice-Provost of Eton 1818-33. R. Clewer, Berks. 1791, R. Farnham Royal, Bucks. 1791, R. Worpleston, Surrey 1801 to death 1/1/1833 aged 71 (CCEd says 8/2/1833) [C75175. ODNB under his father] Clerical son William Henry, below.

ROBERTS (William) [NiVoF] V. Dunton Bassett, Lincs. 1829-[47]. Died? [C75177]

ROBERTS (William) [NiVoF] V. Sporle w. Palgrave, Norfolk 1831-[45]. Died? [C114900]

ROBERTS (William Henry) Born Eton, Berks. 1/9/1795, s. Rev. William Hayward Roberts (Provost of Eton College) and Jane Pitt. King's, Cambridge 1815, Fellow 1818-28, dn18 (Ely), BA1819, p19 (Salis. for Win.), MA1822. R. Clewer, Berks. 1827-43, V. Aldbourne, Wilts. 1832. Died 4/10/1843 [C89361]

ROBERTSON (John) Marischal College, Aberdeen, MA, p96 (London). R. Salcot, Essex 1796-1809 (res.), V. Great Bentley, Essex 1806 [C1213334], V. Brightingsea, Essex 1809 to death 5/5/1836 aged 77 [C121331. ERC links]

ROBERTSON (Love) Bapt. Ormesby, Norfolk 21/10/1764, s. George Robertson (a London mercer). Caius, Cambridge 1782, BA 1786, dn87 (Nor.), p88 (Nor.), MA1789. Prebendary of Moreton and Whaddon in Hereford Cathedral 1804-41, V. Bridstow, Heref. 1808 and V. Sellack w. King's Capel, Heref. 1831 to death (Bridstow) 22/8/1841 aged 77 [C48257]

ROBERTSON (Robert) [NiVoF] V. Boxted, Essex 1812 to death 4/10/1835 aged 81 (CCEd says 20/11/1835) [C121338]

ROBINS (Sanderson) Born Newington, Surrey 6/9/1801, s. Matthew Robins and Peggy Parratt Rose. Exeter, Oxford 1818, BA1823, dn24 (Nor. for Bristol), MA1825, p25 (Bristol). R. Edmondsham, Dorset 1826, Min. Maryle-bone Christ Church 1834, R. Dover St James, Kent 1854-6, V. St Peter in the Isle of Thanet, Kent 1856 to death (London) 5/12/1862, leaving £600 [C53762. ODNB as an educational writer] Married (1) Camberwell, London 27/12/1825 Elizabeth Holland (d.1834), w. issue (2) 18/4/1835 Caroline Gertrude Foster Barham, w. issue. Port. online: www.thekingscandlesticks.com/webs/pedigrees/14682.html

ROBINSON (Christopher) Bapt. Lanchester, Durham 20/4/1794, s. Rev. Christopher Robinson, sen. and Agnes Wallis. Lincoln, Oxford 1812, dn17 (Durham) BA1819, p19 (Durham). V. Kirknewton, Northumberland 1827 to death 1/2/1855 aged 61 [C133510] Married Bishop Auckland, Durham 21/1/1832 Elizabeth Culley, *s.p.*

ROBINSON (Disney) Born Harborne, Staffs. 10/9/1804, s. Rev. Richard George Robinson and Mary Woodhouse. St John's, Cambridge 1822, BA1828, dn28 (York), p30 (York), MA 1831. PC. Woolley, Yorks. 1833 ('absentee for last 22 years' in 1864, living at Henbury, Bristol) to death (Torquay, Devon) 7/9/1869 aged 69, leaving £30,000 [C135711. Boase. YCO] Married Darton, Yorks. 7/3/1833 Frances Rebecca Hodgson (w) (of Haigh Hall, Wakefield Yorks.). Brother of Hastings below.

ROBINSON (Francis) Born Oxford 29/10/1804, s. Thomas Robinson. Corpus Christi, Oxford 1819, BA1823, MA1826, Fellow 1826-31, dn28 (Ox.), p29 (Ox.). R. Little Staughton (Staughton Parva), Beds. 1831, R. Stonesfield, Oxon. 1834. Died Oxford 17/11/1886, leaving £20,858-10s-7d. [C21356] Married Highworth, Wilts. 10/9/1831 Sophia Elizabeth Rowden (w), and issue. Surrogate.

ROBINSON (George) Bapt. Giggleswick, Yorks. 12/1/1772, s. John and Mary Robinson. Literate: dn95 (York), p98 (Lin.). V. Tutbury, Staffs. 1818. Dead by 1841 [C75913. YCO]

ROBINSON (George Alington) Bapt. Market Rasen, Lincs. 28/8/1804, s. Rev. John Robinson (b.1773, below) and Sarah Alington (a clergy dau.). Christ's, Cambridge 1825, dn29 (Lin.), BA1830, p30 (Lin.). R. Bag Enderby, Lincs. 1831-6, R. Somersby, Lincs. 1831-41, R. Thorganby, Lincs. 1841-86, R. Irby on Humber, Lincs. 1842-80. Died (Louth, Lincs.) 22/1/1888 aged 83, leaving £823-11s-7d. [C75195] Married

West Rasen, Lincs. 8/12/1840 Sarah Penelope Alington (a clergy dau., Swinhope, Lincs.), with issue.

ROBINSON (George Stamp, Sir, 7th Bart.) Born Grafton Underwood, Northants. 29/8/1797, s. Rev. William Villiers Robinson (Cranford Hall, Northants.) and Anne Brooksbank. New, Oxford 1815, Fellow 1815-27, BA 1819, MA1824. R. Cranford St Andrew 1822-53, R. Shawell, Leics. 1827-34 (res.), R. Cranford 1840-53, Hon. Canon of Peterborough Cathedral 1845-64. Dom. Chap. to 2nd Earl of Lucan 1827. Died 'at the lunatic asylum, Cheadle', Cheshire (without clerical title) 9/10/1873 aged 76, leaving £12,000 [C75196. Boase] Married 24/5/1827 Emma Blencowe, with issue. Succ. to title 1833.

ROBINSON (Gilmour) Born Plumstead, Kent 8/12/1795 (bapt. Scotch Church, Woolwich 11/12/1795), s. Richard (a Scottish soldier) and Christian Robinson. A soldier. Literate: dn23 (Chester for York), p23 (York). PC. Tockholes, Blackburn, Lancs. 1830 to death (unmarried) 30/12/1856 aged 60 [C135712. YCO]

ROBINSON (Hastings) Born Lichfield 7/12/1793, s. Rev. Richard George Robinson and Mary Woodhouse. St John's, Cambridge 1811, BA 1815, dn16 (Bristol), Fellow 1816-28, MA1818, p19 (Ely), BD1826, DD1836. R. Great Warley, Essex 1827-66, RD, Hon. Canon of Rochester Cathedral 1862 to death 18/5/1866, leaving £20,000 [C53763. ODNB. Boase. DEB] Married Burton on Trent, Staffs. 9/5/1828 Margaret Ann Clayton. Brother of Disney, above. *J.P.* Essex; *F.R.S., F.G.S., F.R.A.S., F.S.A.*

ROBINSON (Henry) Born and bapt. Kendal, Westmorland 15/10/1791, s. Rev. Henry, sen. and Catherine Robinson. Trinity, Cambridge 1809, then Emmanuel 1812, BA1814, dn15 (York), p16 (Chester for York). PC. Farnley, Otley, Yorks. 1816-34, V. Otley 1816-27 (and H/M Otley G/S). Died Heysham, Lancs. 14/8/1834 aged 43 [C135713. YCO. Platt]

ROBINSON (John) [NiVoF] V. Hockliffe w. Chalgrave, Lincs. 1791 to death 15/2/1842 aged 74 [C75214]

ROBINSON (John) [NiVoF] Chap. of Donative of Woodcott, Hants. 1827-[52]. Died? [C108671]

ROBINSON (John) Bapt. Louth, Lincs. 14/1/1773, s. John Robinson ('Warden of Louth') and Elizabeth Baxter. Corpus Christ (Bennet Hall), Cambridge 1790, BA1795, dn95 (Lin.), p97 (Lin.), MA1801. R. Ulceby w. Fordington, Lincs. 1797, V. Nun (North) Ormesby, Lincs. 1802-48, V. Middle Rasen Tupholme, Lincs. 1804 and R. Faldingworth, Lincs. 1814 to burial 4/4/1848. Dom. Chap. to Elizabeth, Baroness Monson 1814 [C75208] Married Swinhope, Lincs. 7/9/1797 Sarah Alington (a clergy dau.), with clerical son George Alington Robinson (above). He was 'one of the members of the University who went to St James's Palace on Jan. 23, 1806, to present to the King an address on the victory gained at Trafalgar; states in his *Journal*, that he wore his gown, cassock, hood, bands and cap'.

ROBINSON (John) Born Temple Sowerby, Westmorland 4/1/1774, s. Henry and Agnes Robinson. Literate: dn97 (Car.), p98 (Car.), then Christ's, Cambridge 1807, a Ten Year Man (BD Lambeth 1833, DD?). PC. Swaledale, Westmorland 1798, PC. Ravenstonedale, Westmorland 1813-33 (and S/M there 1795-1818), R. Clifton, Westmorland 1818-40 and R. Cliburn, Westmorland 1833 to death. Dom. Chap. to 7th Viscount Ranelagh 1833. Died Clifton 4/12/1840 [C6251. ODNB] Married Raven-stonedale 10/4/1797 Mary Raisbeck, with issue. *J.P.* and *D.L.* Westmorland.

ROBINSON (John) Bapt. Linby, Notts. 22/3/1790, s. James and Ann Robinson. Trinity, Oxford 1812, BA1813, dn14 (Salis.), p16 (York). R. Widmerpool, Notts. 1830 to death 13/11/1869 aged 79, leaving £30,000 [C89362. YCO] Married (1) Derby 15/5/1823 Arabella Savile Foljambe (d. 1858), with issue (2) St George's Hanover Square, London 1861 (3rd q.) Martha Walker Freer.

ROBINSON (John) Born and bapt. Hinderwell, Yorks. 7/11/1790, s. John and Elizabeth Robinson. Literate: dn13 (York), p14 (York). R. Newbiggin, Westmorland 1818 to death (a widower) 29/10/1879 aged 89, leaving £600 [C6252. YCO. Platt] Married Hawkshead, Lancs. 14/12/1820 Isabella Dobson, with issue.

ROBINSON (John) Born Skipton, Yorks. 14/8/1797, s. Richard (an 'innholder') and Ellen Edmondson. St John, Cambridge 1828, then St Catharine's 1828, BA1832, dn32 (Lin. for York), p33 (York, but note two men of this name priested on the same day), MA1839. PC. Dewsbury St Paul, Hanging Heaton, Yorks. 1832, PC. Broughton in Furness, Lancs. 1844 to death 25/3/1870 aged 72, leaving £1,000 [C75215. YCO] Married with issue.

ROBINSON (John) Born York 21/10/1798, s. Rear-Admiral Hugh Robinson and Mary Myers. Corpus Christi, Cambridge 1816, BA 1820, dn21 (York for Durham), p23 (Durham), MA1826. Chaplain R.N. 1824-5; R. York St Denys Walmgate w. St George Naburn 1830-40, V. Amberley, Sussex 1840-3, V. St Lawrence, York 1843-67. Buried there (a widower) 29/12/1879 aged 81, leaving £25,000 [C21358. YCO] Married Bothal, Northumberland 2/2/1831 Elizabeth Otter (a clergy dau., Bothal, Yorks.). with clerical son.

ROBINSON (Nicholas) Born Liverpool 22/1/1801, s. of Alderman Nicholas Robinson and Ellen Yaite. Trinity, Cambridge 1819, BA 1824, dn24 Chester), MA1827. (first and joint) PC. Liverpool St Martin in the Fields 1829 to death 21/11/1834 [C170359]

ROBINSON (Nicholas Waite) Bapt. 8/10/1753, s. Henry Robinson (formerly Waite), Thicket Hall, Thorganby, Yorks. Trinity, Cambridge 1773, then Peterhouse 1777, BA1777, Fellow 1777, dn77 (York), p77 (York), MA1799 (Lambeth). R. Cadeby, Lincs. 1788, V. Clifton upon Dunmore, Warwicks. 1789-94, R. Suckley, Worcs. 1794 and V. Bodenham, Heref. 1799 to death. Dom. Chap. to 5th Earl of Essex 1799. Died 19/11/1842 aged 91 [C19605. YCO]

ROBINSON (Thomas) From Greystock, Cumberland, s. Joseph Robinson. Queen's, Oxford 1803 (aged 18), BA1807, dn09 (Salis.), p09 (Salis.), MA1810, Fellow 1815-24. V. Milford (cum Hardie), Hants. 1823 to death 2/8/1857 [C89366]

ROBINSON (William) Bapt. Selside, Westmorland 22/5/1790, s. of a farmer. Literate: dn14 (Chester), p15 (Chester). PC. Burneside, Westmorland 1817 (and S/M 1814) to death 4/4/1854 [C170364] Married 27/10/1816 Agnes Dodd (a clergy dau.), with issue.

ROBINSON (William) Literate: dn18 (Car.), p19 (Car.). Chap. of Donative of Kirkstead, Lincs. 1827, PC. Wood Enderby >< Lincs. 1830-56, V. Stickford, Lincs. 1856-75. Died before 1881 [C75236. ERC links]

ROBINSON (William) From Ridware, Staffs., s. Charles Robinson. Worcester, Oxford 1805 (aged 17), BA1809, MA1812, Fellow 1812-36. R. Wishaw, Warwicks. 1816-51-. Died? [C19627]

ROBINSON (William) [NiVoF] PC. Thornton-le-Fen, Lincs. 1825-51-, PC. Langriville, Wildmore (Fen), Lincs. 1829-51-. Died? [Not yet in CCEd. ERC links]

ROBINSON (William Beauclerk) Bapt. Holborn, London 12/12/1782, s. Daniel (a lawyer). and Hester Robinson. Magdalen Hall, Oxford 1802, BA1806, MA1811. R. Litlington, Sussex 1823-63. Died Eastbourne, Kent 5/10/1864, leaving £1,500 [C65248] Married Brighton, Sussex 5/11/1811 Harriet Wigney, w. clerical s. Leighton Robinson.

ROBINSON (William Scott) Born Dyrham, Glos. 9/1/1804 (bapt. Marylebone, London 13/3/1805), s. Sir George Abercrombie Robinson, 1st Bart. H.E.I.C., and Margaret Southwell (natural dau. of 14th Earl of Suffolk and Berkshire). Exeter, Oxford 1823, BA1826, MA1829. R. Dyrham 1828 and R. Farleigh Hungerford, Som. 1832 to death 9/1/1875 aged 71, leaving £2,000 [C53762. ODNB as an educational writer] Married Bishopsgate, City of London 12/2/1828 Matilda Maxwell Innes (w), with issue.

ROBSON (Jacob) Literate: dn22 (Chester), p23 (Chester), then Emmanuel, Cambridge 1824, a Ten Year Man (BD1834). (first) PC. Tyldesley cum Shakerley, Leigh, Lancs. 1828 to death 19/1/1851 aged 52 [C170366] Married by 1835 Tomasine Pennington (who died three weeks after their marriage, aged 28).

ROBSON (James) Born Sherburn, Westmorland 26/8/1776, s. Rev. James Robson, sen. Lincoln, Oxford 1794, then University, BA 1800, dn00 (C&L for Durham), p01 (Durham), MA1801. V. Owthorne, Yorks. 1812-21, V. Ainderby Steeple, Yorks. 1822-40 (res.). Died Heighington, Durham 27/2/1865 aged 87, leaving £600 [C19628 / 135973] Married Stockton, Co. Durham 9/4/1814 Charlotte Barbara Stuart (dau. of an H.E.I.C. naval officer), with issue. J.P.

ROBSON (John Evans) Bapt. Richmond, Yorks. 19/11/1798, s. William Robson. Literate: dn25 (Bristol for York), p25 (York). PC. Hartwith cum Winsley, Kirkby Malzeard, Yorks. 1825 to death 10/3/1874 aged 75, leaving £200 [C53764. YCO] Married Lee, Kent 19/2/1839 Harriet Williams (w).

ROBSON, *later* BROOKE (Richard Swann) Born Doncaster, Yorks. 3/1/1800, s. Richard Robson (a wine merchant) and Mary Nicholl. St Catherine's, Cambridge 1818, BA1822, dn23 (York), p24 (York), MA1827. PC. Rawcliffe (in Snaith), Yorks. 1824-37, PC. Whitgift, Yorks. 1832-7, V. Sutton on the Forest (o/w Sutton Galtries), Yorks. 1837-49. Died at Gateforth House, Gateforth, Yorks. 1/6/1871 aged 71, leaving £160,000. Dom. Chap. to Earl of Balcarres [C135717. YCO] Married Bromley, Kent 20/12/1836 his cousin Jane Brooke (w) (dau. of Lt.-Col. Brooke Hutchinson, Wold Newton, Yorks.), *s.p.*

ROBY (John) Bapt. Anstey, Leics. 5/4/1769, s. Thomas Roby (Ulverscroft, Leics.). Emmanuel, Cambs. 1786, BA1791, dn91 (Lin.), p93 (Lin.), MA1821. S/M Market Bosworth Free G/S 1823; R. Congerstone, Leics. 1793 and V. Austrey, Warwicks. 1825 to death (Market Bosworth) 10/10/1839 [C19629] Had issue.

ROBYNS (Thomas) Bapt. Madron, Cornwall 4/12/1772. Corpus Christi, Cambridge 1789, BA1794, dn97 (Ex.), p97 (Ex.), MA1820. V. Colebrooke, Devon 1816-31, V. Marystowe, Devon 1819 to death 1/1840 aged 67. Dom. Chap. to 1st Earl of Falmouth 1819 [C146206] Married Madron 17/4/1811 Ann Hitchens.

ROCHESTER (Bishop of) see under **MURRAY, George**

ROCKE (John) Born Shrewsbury, Shropshire 30/8/1783, s. Rev. John Rocke, sen. St John's, Cambridge 1802, BA1806, dn08 (Heref.). (succ. his father as) R. Clungunford, Heref. 1814 to death 14/6/1849 [C173688] Married Leintwardine, Heref. 18/2/1812 Anne Beale (Heath House, Shropshire), w. clerical son Thomas Owen Rocke.

ROCKETT (Caleb) Bapt. Honiton, Devon 4/2/1766, s. Caleb and Susanna Rockett. Balliol, Oxford 1785, dn88 (Lin. for B&W), p91 (B&W), then Jesus, Cambridge, MA1803. S/M Bridgwater G/S 1810; V. Stokenham, Devon (and Preacher throughout the Diocese of Exeter) 1803, V. Townstall, Devon 1804, Prebend of Timberscombe in Wells Cathedral 1807-19 (res.), V. Western Zoyland, Som. 1808-37, V. Timberscombe, Som. 1815-19, V. East Brent, Som. (and Preacher throughout the Diocese of B&W) 1819 to death. Dom. Chap. to Bishop of Gloucester / Bath and Wells 1804-19. Died 9/6/1837 [C40421] Clerical son of same name. J.P. Somerset.

RODBER (William Johnson) Born Melcombe Regis, Dorset 11/4/1792, s. Thomas Rodber and Catherine Pemberton. Literate: dn15 (London), p16 (St Davids). R. St Mary at Hill w. St Andrew Hubbard, City of London 1825 to death. Dom. Chap. to 2nd Baron Muncaster 1813. Died 21/12/1844 aged 53 [C121347] Married 1/9/1822 Isabella Mary Dunn (dau. of the 'eminent tailor of Bedford Street'). Secretary of 'The Incorporated Society for Building and Enlarging Churches and Chapels' for 25 years.

RODD (Charles) Bapt. St Just, Cornwall 8/10/1807, s. Rev. Edward Rodd (below) and Harriet Rashleigh. Exeter, Oxford 1826, BA 1829, dn31 (B&W), p32 (Ex.). R. North Hill, Cornwall 1832 to death 16/1/1885 aged 77 [C40423 / 195886]

RODD (Edward) Bapt. 1/9/1768 Trebartha Hall, Northill, Cornwall, s. Francis Rodd and Jane Hearle. Oriel, Oxford 1785, BA1789, dn91 (Ex.), then Exeter, Fellow 1791-1805, MA1792, p93 (Ex.), BD1803, DD1816. R. Dittisham, Devon (and Preacher throughout the Diocese of Exeter)1802, R. St Just in Roseland, Cornwall 1804-42, V. Lamerton, Devon 1816-42, Prebend in Exeter Cathedral 1826. Died (Trebartha) 23/7/1842 aged 73 [C146307. Boase] Married 25/4/1805 Harriet Rashleigh, w. son Charles (above).

RODNEY (Henry, Hon.) Born London 30/9/1790, s. Lt.-Col. George Rodney, 2nd Baron Rodney and Anne Harley. Jesus, Cambridge 1811, then Trinity 1812, BA, MA1814, dn15 (Heref.), p16 (Heref.). V. Eye, Heref. 1817-78, Prebend of Huntington in Hereford Cathedral 1825-78, PC. Kimbolton w. Middleton on the Hill, Heref. 1830-41, V. Llangattock Lingoed and Llanfihangel Crucorney, Monmouth 1828-73. Lived at Berrington House, Leominster, Heref. and died

(Eye) 21/12/1878 aged 88, leaving £14,000 [C171751] Brother below.

RODNEY (Spencer, 5th Baron Rodney) Born 30/5/1785, s. Lt.-Col. George Rodney, 2nd Baron Rodney and Anne Harley. Christ Church, Oxford 1803, then All Souls, Fellow 1807-44, BA1807, dn08 (Ox.), p09 (Ox.), MA1811. R. Elmley, Kent 1805-18, R. Luddenham, Kent 1812-13 (res.), V. Kenchester, Heref. 1813-33, V. New Romney, Kent 1821-33, R. Chelsfield, Kent 1833-4 (res.). Died unm. 15/5/1846 aged 52 [C7024] Brother above. Succ. to title 1843.

ROE (James) From Macclesfield, Cheshire, s. Rev. James Roe, sen. BNC, Oxford 1777 (aged 18), BA1781, dn81 (Ox.), MA1793. PC. Dorchester, Oxon. 1787-79, R. Newbury, Berks. (and Preacher throughout the Diocese of Salisbury) 1797 to death 9/7/1838 [C37486]

ROE (Thomas) Bapt. Exeter 15/4/1777, s. Robert Roe. Balliol, Oxford 1796, BA1799, dn99 (Ex.), p04 (Ex.). R. Elworthy, Som. 1818-35 [C40426], R. Brendon, Devon 1831-44, R. Oare, Som. 1842 to death 3/1/1855 [C146308]

ROE, *born* TURNER (Thomas Turner) From Whitchurch, Shropshire, s. William Turner. Trinity, Oxford 1806 (aged 16), BA 1810, dn13 (C&L), MA1814, p14 (C&L). R. Benington, Lincs. 1820-34, R. Swerford, Lincs. 1834 to death 14/7/1836 [C19634] Married Scalby, Scarborough, Yorks. 20/6/1826 Susannah Caroline Howard.

ROGERS (Alexander) Literate: p05 (Chester). V. Rolvenden, Kent 1812 to burial 26/1/1833 (CCEd says died 19/2/1833) [C1485]

ROGERS (Arthur) Literate: dn13 (Nor.), p14 (Nor.). PC. Sapiston, Suffolk 1815, PC. Hunston, Suffolk 1835. Died? [C114918]

ROGERS (Charles) Born Newark on Trent, Notts. 4/5/1793, s. Rev. Thomas Rogers (H/M Wakefield G/S, Yorks.) and Elizabeth Long. Literate: dn16 (Salis. for York), p17 (York). PC. Sowerby Bridge, Yorks. 1829 to death 11/1/1863, leaving £3,000 [C89372. YCO] Married Wakefield 1/2/1820 Cecilia Cawood, with issue.

ROGERS (Edward) Born Helston, Cornwall 18/2/1778, s. Edward and Christian Rogers. Jesus, Cambridge 1794, BA1799, dn01 (Lin.), p02 (Lin.), MA1802, then Magdalene, Fellow and Tutor 1802. Prebend of Bishopstone in Salisbury Cathedral 1804-21 (res.), V. Bishopstone, Wilts. 1816-17, V. Constantine, Cornwall 1817 to death there 25/8/1856 aged 79 [C75295. Boase] Married (2?) Mawnam, Cornwall 22/11/1821 Catherine Groube Boulderson, with issue. Brother Thomas Ellis, below?

ROGERS (George) From Bury St Edmunds, Suffolk, s. Peter Rogers (silversmith). Trinity Cambridge 1760 (aged 18), BA1764, dn64 (Lin. for Nor.), Fellow 1765, p65 (Nor.), MA1767. R. Horninger, Suffolk 1764-84, R. Little Whelnetham, Suffolk 1766-7, R. Sproughton, Suffolk 1784 to death 1835 aged 94 [C75296]

ROGERS (George) From Leek, Staffs., s. Rev. John Rogers. Christ Church, Oxford 1790 (aged 19), BA1793, p95 (Ox.), MA1796, Chaplain 1796-1806-. V. Market (or East) Lavington, Wilts. 1805 to death 29/5/1836 [C37487]

ROGERS (George Henvill) Bapt. Iwerne Courtenay, Dorset 21/4/1770, s. Rev. Richard and Elizabeth Rogers. Wadham, Oxford 1787, BA1791, dn93 (Ox.), p94 (Ox.), MA1796, Fellow to 1813, Chap. 1813-47. V. Southrop, Glos. 1812 to death 25/7/1847 [C37488] Brother below.

ROGERS (Henry Hody) Bapt. Iwerne Courtenay, Dorset 10/12/1774, s. Rev. Richard Colmer and Elizabeth Rogers. Wadham, Oxford 1792, dn97 (Bristol), p98 (Bristol), BCL1799. Chap. of Donative of Tarrant Crawford (o/w Tarrant Antioch), Dorset 1812, R. Iwerne Stapleton >< Dorset 1810, R. Pylle, Som. 1826 to death 17/4/1840 [C40428] Married (1) By 1801 Mary Edgar (d.1810), with issue (2) East Pennard, Som. 28/3/1826 Sarah Phelps. Brother above.

ROGERS (Hugh) Bapt. Sithney, Cornwall 4/1/1781, s. John Rogers, *M.P.*, and Margaret Basset. Jesus, Cambridge 1799, BA1804, dn04 (Lin.). R. Redruth, Cornwall 1804-41 and R. Camborne, Cornwall 1816 to death 10/7/1858, leaving £14,000 [C75297] Married Truro, Cornwall 4/9/1815 Frances Jenkins (a clergy dau.), w. clerical son Hugh St Aubyn Rogers. Brother below.

ROGERS (John) Bapt. Sithney, Cornwall 19/8/1778, s. John Rogers, *M.P.*, and Margaret Basset. Trinity, Oxford 1797, BA1801, dn03

(Ex.), p04 (Ex.), MA1810. R. Feniton, Devon 1805, R. (and patron) of Mawnan, Cornwall 1807, Prebend 1810 then Canon of Exeter Cathedral 1820 to death 12/6/1856 [C146310] Had clerical son. Brother above. For this 'priest, mine-owner, botanist, mineralogist, and scholar of Hebrew and Syriac':
https://en.wikipedia.org/wiki/John_Rogers_(divine)

ROGERS (John) Born Kington, Heref., s. William Rogers [*pleb*.]. Balliol, Oxford 1800 (aged 20), BA1804, dn04 (Heref.), p05 (Heref.), MA1807. V. Stowe, Heref. 1808 and R. Bedstone, Heref. 1809 to death 1/8/1840 aged 60 [C173704] *J.P.* Heref. and Shropshire.

ROGERS (John) Born Wentnor, Shropshire 21/9/1789, s. Thomas Rogers and Mary Powys. St John's, Cambridge 1808, BA1812, dn14 (Heref.), p15 (Heref.), MA1815. R. Myndtown (or Mindtown), Shropshire 1820 and R. Mainstone Chapel, Clun, Shropshire 1831 to death 9/6/1866. Venn and CR65 continue: V. Aymestrey. w. Leinthal Earles. Heref. 1850-[66] [C173705] Married 29/8/1816 Marianne Bodenham, with issue.

ROGERS (John) [NiVoF] PC. Elstead w. Frensham, Surrey 1815-[45]. Died? [C108677]

ROGERS (John Methuen) Born Warminster, Wilts. 27/1/1748, s. Rev. John and Wilhelmina Gratiana Rogers. Queen's, Oxford 1767, dn72 (Ox.), then New, BCL1776, p76 (Salis.). R. Berkley, Som. 1793 and R. Rodden, Som. 1801 to death 22/8/1834 (CCEd says 12/11/1834) [C37492]

ROGERS (Robert Green) Born Yarlington, Som. 6/11/1800, s. John Rogers and Anne Reynolds. Oriel, Oxford 1818, BA1822, dn24 (Chester), p25 (B&W), MA1825. R. (and patron) of Yarlington 1826 to death 19/3/1876, leaving £10,000 [C40429] Married (1) Yaxham, Norfolk 21/2/1834 Mary Theodora Johnson (a clergy dau., d.1836) (2) Barnstaple, Devon 30/12/1841 Lucy Judith Pine-Coffin (a clergy dau., d.1846) (3) Sherborne, Dorset 28/9/1852 Elizabeth Harbin Goodden (w); clerical son.

ROGERS (Thomas) Born King's Norton, Leics. 23/5/1786, s. Rev. Thomas Rogers, sen. (H/M Wakefield G/S). Trinity, Cambridge 1804, then Clare 1806, BA1808, dn09 (York), p10 (York). PC. Flockton, Thornhill, Yorks. 1810 to death 1848 (3rd q.?) aged 63 [C116920. YCO] Married Pontefract, Yorks. 3/12/1811 Harriet Leidger, with 4 ch. in 1832.

ROGERS (Thomas) Born London 17/3/1789, s. Daniel Rogers (Stourbridge, Worcs.). Sidney, Cambridge 1805, BA1811, MA1814, Fellow, p16 (Bristol). H/M Walsall Free G/S 1824; PC. Walsall St Paul, Staffs. 1827-39. Chap. of the Norfolk Island Convict Establishment, Australia 1846 to death there 1860 [C19640] Reference to a manuscript diary.

ROGERS (Thomas Ellis) From London, s. Edward and Christian Rogers. Trinity, Cambridge 1799 (aged 17), BA1805, dn05 (London), p06 (Ex. for London), MA1808. R. Hessett, Norfolk 1813 and R. Lackford, Suffolk 1807 to death 22/9/1844 aged 63 [C114920] Married (1) Sudbury, Suffolk 3/2/1822 Merielina Agnes Le Heup [*sic*] (d.1818), 1 ch. (2) Bury St Edmunds, Suffolk 28/4/1823 Sophia Mills, w. issue. Brother of Edward, above?

ROKEBY (Henry Ralph) Born Spratton, Northants. 8/4/1788, s. Rev. Langham Rokeby. Commander, *R.N.*, and Maria Isabella Davies. Downing, Cambridge 1826 (aged 37), BA1830, dn30 (Peterb.), p30 (Peterb.). R. (patron and Lord of the Manor) Arthingworth, Northants. 1830 to death 20/5/1870, leaving £3,000 [C110805] Married (1) Great Oxenden, Northants. 26/7/1827 Caroline Boulton (a clergy dau., d.1832), with clerical s. Henry Ralph, jun. (2) Market Harborough, Leics. 6/9/1837 Harriet Walley, with further issue. Surrogate 1838.

ROLES (William) From Waddington, Wilts., s. James Roles. Oriel, Oxford 1803 (aged 16), BA 1808, dn09 (Salis.), p10 (Salis.), MA1812. V. Sharncote, Northants. 1815-34, V. Raunds, Northants. 1817, R. Upton Lovell, Northants. 1820 to death 6/1/1834 (CCEd says 10/3/1834) [C53769]

ROLFE (Robert Rose) Bapt. Hilborough, Norfolk 9/5/1767, s. Rev. Robert Rolfe and Alice Nelson. Caius, Cambridge 1783, BA1788, dn89 (Nor.), p92 (Nor.). R. Cockley Cley, Norfolk 1795-1850, V. Yaxley, Norfolk 1796-1850, R. Thurgarton, Norfolk 1804-50, R. [sequestrator] Caldecote, Norfolk 1815-50, V. Hempnall, Norfolk 1819 to death (Norwich) 2/11/1850 aged 83 [C114923] Married (1) Frances Crever (a clergy dau., d.1803), 1 dau (2)

6/12/1808 Elizabeth Rose (a clergy dau., d.1838), with clerical son Edmund Nelson Rolfe (3) Bloomsbury, London 8/12/1839 Harriet Ann Child.

ROLLESTON (George) Bapt. City of London 4/6//1791, s. Robert Rolleston and Margaret Thormhill. Merton, Oxford 1810, BA1814, dn14 (Chester for York), p15 (York), MA1820. V. Maltby, Yorks. 1816-68 (living at Maltby Hall), V. Stainton le Street (o/w Great Stainton), Yorks. 1816-68, R. Stainton by Langworth, Lincs. 1823. Dom. Chap. to 5th Earl of Scarborough 1815 (the patron of both livings). Died (Maltby) 21/2/1868 aged 76. Will not traced [C75308. YCO] Married 1818 Anne Nettleship, with issue. Photo. online.

ROLLESTON (John) Born City of London 22/2/1787, s. Christopher Rolleston (Watnall Hall, Notts.) and Ann Duncan. Christ Church, Oxford 1805, BA1808, dn10 (York), p11 (York). PC. Annesley, Notts. 1811-14, V. Burton Joyce w. Bulcote, Notts. 1822-62, PC. Shelford, Notts. 1827. Died Burton Joyce 17/11/1862, leaving £6,000. Chap. to Prince of Wales 1810 [C116922. YCO] Married Gedling, Notts. 21/3/1814 Elizabeth Smelt (a clergy dau.), w. clerical son William Lancelot.

ROLLS (Henry) Born Southam, Warwicks. 19/6/1782, s. William Henry Rolls and Mary Lyndon. Christ's, Cambridge 1810, dn13 (Bristol), p13 (Bristol), BA 1816, migrated to Balliol, Oxford, MA1819. R. Barnwell St Andrew w. Barnwell All Saints, Northants. 1819-20, R. Aldwinckle All Saints, Northants. 1820 to death. Chap. to 4th Duke of Buccleuch; to 6th Duke of Queensberry 1819. Died Paris 24/7/1838 [C19643] Married (1) Liverpool 16/7/1810 Mary Hillary (d.1825), many ch. (2) 18/6/1838 Sarah Anne Rolls, with child.

ROMNEY (Francis Henry) Bapt. Whitbourne, Heref. 22/11/1804, s. James Wates and Elizabeth Romney, Worcester, Oxford 1826, BA1830, dn31 (Glos.), p32 (Glos.), MA1833. R. Ashchurch, Glos. 1831. Died Worcester 7/3/1871, leaving under £300 [C162553] Married (1) Clifton, Bristol 15/11/1831 Rebecca Harriette West (d.1833 aged 21) (2) 12/7/1834 Jane Lesingham, with issue.

ROOKE (George) From Langham, Essex, s. George Rooke. St John's, Cambridge 1795, BA 1799, dn00 (Peterb.), p02 (Peterb.), MA1803. R. Yardley Hastings, Northants. 1805 to death (Canterbury) 24/8/1856 aged 79 [C110809]

ROOKE (George) Born Lymington, Hants. 5/6/1796, s. Sir Giles Rooke (a judge) and Harriet Sophia Burrard. Merton, Oxford 1814, BA1816, Fellow 1821-31, dn22 (Ox.), p23 (Ox.), MA1822. V. Great Wolford, Warwicks. 1823-30, PC. Wolvercott, Oxon. 1829, V. Embleton, Northumberland 1830 (and Hon. Canon Durham Cathedral 1852) to death 17/8/1874 aged 78, leaving £8,000 [C21399] Married Embleton 11/4/1835 Clara Frances Moffatt, with issue.

ROOPER (Thomas Richard) Born Berkhamsted, Herts. 3/2/1782, s. John Rooper and Harriet Bonfoy. St John's, Cambridge 1800, BA1804, dn05 (Lin.), p06 (Lin.). V. Abbots Ripton ><, Lincs. 1806-53. Lived latterly and died Hove, Sussex 7/4/1865, leaving £40,000 [C75342] Married Little Paxton, Hunts. 6/11/1806 Persis Standly (Paxton House, Hunts.), with issue.

ROPER (John Riddall) Born London 19/1/1798, s. David Riddall Roper (architect) and Mary Davison. Bapt. as an adult 8/3/1822. Corpus Christi, Cambridge 1818, BA1822, dn22 (Lin.), p23 (Lin.), MA1825. PC. Brighton (or Lewes) St Margaret, Sussex 1832-7. Resided latterly at Ventnor, IoW, dying there 22/7/1886 aged 88, leaving £3,141-4s-6d. [C478]

ROSDEW (Joseph) Born Yealmpton, Devon 15/7/1768, s. Richard and Elizabeth Rosdew. Exeter, Oxford 1786, BA1790, dn91 (Ex.), Fellow 1792-1837, MA1793, p94 (Ox.), BD 1804, etc. V. South Newington, Oxon. 1808-18 (res.), R. Bushey, Herts. 1826 to death 1/6/1835 [C21310]

ROSE (Charles) From Daventry, Northants., s. Rev. William Lucas Rose (born Lucas) and Ann Rose. Lincoln, Oxford 1807 (aged 19), BA1810, dn11 (Peterb.), p12 (Ox.), Fellow 1812-36, MA 1812, Tutor 1814-34, BD1819, Lecturer in Greek 1822. R. Slapton, Northants. 1816, R. (Long) Combe, Oxon. 1820, R. Cublington, Bucks. 1835 to death 12/2/1845 [C21400] Brother Henry, below.

ROSE (Francis) Bapt. Boyndie, Aberdeenshire 14/7/1791. Aberdeen Univ., dn15 (Nor.), MA1815, p16 (Nor.), DD1846. R. Woughton on the Green, Bucks. 1823, PC. Baulking, Berks.

1856 to death 4/5/1870, leaving £2,000 [C114927]

ROSE (Henry) Born Daventry, Northants. 24/10/1781, s. William Lucas Rose (born Lucas). Clare, Cambridge 1808, Fellow 1812-31, BA1813, dn13 (Lin.), p14 (Lin.), MA1815. R. Whilton, Northants. 1814 and R. Brington, Northants. 1830 to death 24/2/1855 [C75347] Brother Charles, above.

ROSE (Henry John) Born Uckfield, Middx. 3/1/1800, s. Rev. William (V. Glynde, Sussex, below) and Susanna Rose. Peterhouse, Cambridge 1817, then St John's 1818, BA1821, MA 1824, Fellow 1824-38, dn25 (Ely), p26 (Ely), BD1831, incorporated at Oxford 1851. R. Cambridge St Edmund King and Martyr 1832-4, R. Houghton Conquest, Beds. 1837 and RD and Archdeacon of Bedford 1866 to death (at the 'Swan Hotel', Bedford) 31/1/1873, leaving £4,000 [C109207. ODNB. Boase] Married St Pancras, London 24/5/1838 Sarah Caroline Burgon, w. clerical sons Hugh James, and William Francis Rose. Brother, below. Editor of the *Encyclopaedia Metropolitana*.

ROSE (Hugh James) Born Horsted, Surrey 9/6/1795, s. Rev. William (V. Glynde, Sussex, below) and Susanna Rose. Trinity, Cambridge 1812, BA1817 [President of the Union 1817], dn17 (London), p18 (London), MA1820, BD 1827, Professor of Divinity Durham University 1833-4 (res. ill-health), (second) Principal of King's College, London 1836. V. Horsham, Surrey 1821-30, Middleton Prebend in Chichester Cathedral 1827-33 (res.), R. Hadleigh, Shropshire 1830-3, PC. Southwark St Thomas, London 1833-8, R. Fairstead, Essex 1833-7. Died (Florence) 22/12/1838, Chap. to Bp of London 1829 [C65307. ODNB] Married Richmond, Surrey 24/6/1819 Anna Cuyler Mair, *s.p.* Early leader in the Oxford Movement. Brother, above. Fine port in D. Cross, *Joseph Bouet's Durham ...* (Durham, 2005). anglicanhistory.org/bios/kindly/rose.html

ROSE (Robert) Born Eye, Suffolk, s. John Rose (surgeon). Caius, Cambridge 1789 (aged 17), BA1794, dn95 (Nor.), MA1797, p97 (Nor.). R. Palgrave, Suffolk 1799 and R. Frenze, Norfolk 1824 to death 18/5/1840 [C114928] Married Eye 6/1800 Mary Jacob, with issue.

ROSE (William) [NiVoF] Literate: dn92 (London for Cant.). V. Glynde, Sussex 1824 to death 1844 aged 78 [C121560]Wife Susanna, w. clerical sons Hugh James, and Henry John, above.

ROSENBERG (Charles [Bulkeley]) Born Bath 19/7/1792 (bapt. 16/1/1794), s. Charles Christian Rosenberg and Elizabeth Woolley. Wadham, Oxford 1811, SCL ('name removed'). Chap. R.N. 1825 (?). Sinecure R. Orgarswick, Kent 1829 [pop.10, income £39] to death (Paris) 26/4/1867 leaving under £100. 'Late' of Chelsea, London [C40434] Possibly married City of London 27/8/1817 Elizabeth Dodd.

ROTHWELL (Richard Rainshaw) Born Sefton, Liverpool 27/1/1771 s. Rev. Richard Rothwell (Sharples Hall, Lancs.). BNC, Oxford 1792, BA1799, MA1800, p02 (Chester). (succ. his father as) R. (and patron) of Sefton [net income £1,378] 1801 to death. Chap. at some date to Lord Palmerston. Died (unm.) 5/4/1863 aged 92, leaving £160,000 [C170374] Lived a very reclusive 'and most penurious' life; very athletic, he was a sea swimmer and boxer.

ROUCH (Frederick) From Bristol, s. Thomas Rouch. St John's, Cambridge 1817 (aged 18), BA1820, dn22 (Glos. for Bristol), p23 (Bristol), MA1824. Minor Canon of Bristol Cathedral 1825-7, Minor Canon of Canterbury Cathedral 1827-85, R. Canterbury St George the Martyr w. St Mary Magdalen 1829, V. Lower Halstow >< Kent 1840-59, R. Littlebourne, Kent 1859-81. Died (Canterbury) 9/6/1885, leaving £27,699-0s-10d. [C53772] Married Bristol 15/2/1825 Martha Pearce Emra, with issue.

ROUND (James Thomas) Born Birch Hall, Colchester, Essex 14/7/1798, s. Charles Round and Charlotte Green. Balliol, Oxford 1816, BA 1820, Fellow 1820-5, dn22 (Ox.), MA1823, p23 (Ox.), BD1830, etc. R. Colchester St Runwald 1824-51, R. Colchester St Nicholas 1830-46, R. Colchester All Saints 1851 to death (Hammersmith, Middx.) 27/8/1860 (named on the Lunacy Patients Admission Register for 1860), leaving £16,000 [C21410] Married 19/1/1836 (Caroline) Louisa Barlow (w), with issue. Brother below.

ROUND (Joseph Green) Born Birch Hall, Colchester 14/6/1803, s. Charles Round and Charlotte Green. Balliol, Oxford 1821, BA 1825, dn26 (London), MA1827, p27 (London). R. Woodham Mortimer, Essex 1830 to death (Leamington, Warwicks.) 12/9/1835 (CCEd says 24/10/1835) [C121561] Married Gillingham, Norfolk 2/10/1828 Elizabeth Martha Lewis, w. issue. Brother above.

ROUNDELL (Henry Dawson) Born Gledstone House, Marton, Yorks. 5/9/1785, s. Rev. William Roundell. BNC, Oxford 1804, BA1808, dn09 (Ox.), then Magdalen, Fellow 1809, MA1810, p10 (Ox.), BD1818. R. Fringford, Oxon. 1815 to death 17/12/1852 [C21412] Married Gargrave, Yorks. 2/11/1818 Elizabeth Garforth. 'A little huffish' (Wilberforce).

ROUQUET (James) Born Bristol, s. Rev. James Rouquet, sen. and Sarah Fenwick. Magdalen Hall, Oxford 1781 (aged 19), then Hertford 1785, BA1785, dn84 (B&W), p85 (B&W). V. West Harptree, Som. 1789 to death. Dom. Chap. to Elizabeth, Countess of Deloraine 1784. Died 22/3/1837 [C48319] Married Bath 31/10/1787 Jane Kite.

ROUS (George) Bapt. Westminster, London 28/3/1785, s. George Rous (barrister) and Charlotte Thomas (dau. of a Dean of Ely and Master of Christ's, Cambridge). Trinity, Cambridge 1802 [Adm. Inner Temple 1807] BA 1807, MA1810, dn11, p13 (B&W). R. Laverton, Som. 1817 to death (Bath) 5/7/1857 aged 71 [C48321]

ROUSE (Oliver) Bapt. Pyworthy, Devon 18/10/1780, s. Rev. John Rouse and Catherine Hart. Pembroke, Oxford 1796, no degree, dn03 (Ex.), p04 (Ex.). R. Tetcott, Devon 1811 to death 12/3/1846 aged 65 [C146317] Married Othery, Som. 30/4/1806 Priscilla Amelia Rouse [*thus*], with issue (incl. son Ezekiel Athanasius Rouse).

ROUTH (Martin Joseph) Born South Elmham, Beccles, Suffolk 18/9/1755, s. Rev. Peter Routh and Mary Reynolds. Queen's, Oxford 1770, then Magdalen 1771-5, BA1774, Fellow 1775-91, MA1776, dn77 (Nor.), BD 1786, DD 1791, President of Magdalen College, Oxford 1791-1854, p10 (Salis., after 33 years). R. & V. Tilehurst (cum Theale), Reading, Berks. [blank in ERC] 1810 to death 22/12/1854 (7.30pm; 'in his hundredth year') [C89378. ODNB has a long and sympathetic entry. R.D. Middleton, *Dr Routh* (Oxford, 1938)] Married Walcot, Bath 18/9/1820 (aged 65) Eliza Agnes Blagrave (35 years his junior), s.p. His great theological library went to the University of Durham. Extraordinary daguerrotype of him online.

ROUTLEDGE (John) Born Glasgow 31/7/1798, s. Very Rev. William Routledge (Dean of Glasgow and Galloway in the Scottish Episcopal Church, *q.v.* Bertie) and Mrs Jane Ovington. Glasgow University 1812-18, then Snell Exhibitioner at Balliol, Oxford 1818-19, dn21, p21. V. Cransley, Northants. 1831-62. Died (Bootle, Liverpool) 29/4/1864, leaving £1,000 [C7322. Snell] Married Wallasey, Cheshire 25/10/1836 Clementina Matilda Anne Boultbee, and had issue.

ROW (William) Bapt. Plymouth 21/2/1776. Exeter, Oxford 1794, BA1798, dn98 (Ex.), p00 (Ex.). R. St John, Cornwall/Devon 1808 to death 1/12/1842 [C146318]

ROWDEN (Edward) Born Cuxham, Oxon. 27/8/1780, s. Rev. Francis Rowden and Sophia Goodenough. New, Oxford 1798, BA1802, dn03 (Ox.), p04 (Glos.), MA1806, Fellow to 1812. V. Highworth w. Severnhampton, Wilts. 1804 to death 27/3/1869, leaving £25,000 [C21414] Married Cowley, Oxford 13/8/1811 Elizabeth Wetherall, with clerical s. Francis Marmaduke Rowden. Brother below. Surrogate.

ROWDEN (Francis) Born Cuxham, Oxon. 8/2/1782 (or 11/3/1783), s. Rev. Francis Rowden, sen. and Sophia Goodenough. Merton, Oxford 1798, BA1802, dn05 (Ox.), MA1805, p06 (Ox.), BD1816, Fellow to 1824. PC. Oxford St Cross (o/w Holywell) 1816-23, R. Cuxham 1823 and R. Ibstone (or Ibeston), Oxon. 1823 to death 18/9/1852 [C21415] Married by 1828 Catherine Charlotte Benson, and had issue.

ROWE (John) Bapt. Great Torrington, Devon 6/2/1755, s. John Rowe. Pembroke, Oxford 1774, p77 (B&W for Ex.), BA1778, dn78 (Ox.), BA1780. R. Alverdiscott (o/w Alscot), Devon 1787-1833 and R. Bow (o/w Nymet Tracey), Devon 1828 to death 13/7/1833 [C48396]

ROWE (John) Bapt. Launceston, Cornwall 12/11/1777, s. William Rowe. Exeter, Oxford 1796, BA1800, dn00 (Ex.), p01 (Ex.). V. Stratton, Cornwall 1816 and PC. Launceston St Mary Magdalen, Cornwall 1808 and V. St Clether, Cornwall 1832 to death. Chap. to Prince of Wales 1816. Died 8/3/1837 aged 60 [C146323]

ROWLAND (William Gorsuch) Bapt. Shrewsbury, Shropshire 16/8/1770, s. Rev. John Rowland and Mary Gorsuch. Christ Church, Oxford 1786, BA1790, MA1793, dn93 (C&L), p94 (C&L). Prebend of Curborough in Lichfield Cathedral 1814-51, PC. ('Ordinary and Official Principal of the Peculiar of') Shrewsbury St Mary 1816 to death 28/11/1851 [C19656]

ROWLANDSON (John) Bapt. Bampton, Cumberland 5/4/1793. [NiVoF] dn18 (Car.), p19 (Chester). V. Shap, Westmorland 1819 and PC. Mansergh, Westmorland 1830 to death 28/6/1857 aged 64 [C6270. Platt] Married 1825 Isabella Garnett ('of the 'King's Arms'), with issue. 'A sonorous and impressive preacher, a sagacious farmer'.

ROWLEY (George) Born Richmond, Yorks. 4/4/1782, s. George Rowley. University, Oxford 1799, BA1803, dn05 (Bristol), p06 (Bristol), MA1806, Fellow 1807-21, BD and DD1821, Master of University College, Oxford 1821-36, Vice-Chancellor of the University 1832-6. R. Stanwick, Northants. 1823 to death 5/10/1836 [C53774] *F.R.S.* (1811).

ROWLEY (Joseph) Born Kirkburton, Yorks. 20/3/1773, s. Benjamin Rowley [*pleb.*]. Queen's, Oxford 1791, BA1795, dn96 (Chester), p97 (Chester), MA1804. Usher Lancaster Royal G/S 1793, then H/M 1802-12; PC. Stalmine, Lancs. 1799 (w. Chap. Lancaster Castle Gaol 1804-58) to death 3/1/1864 aged 90, leaving £4,000 [C170379] Married Lancaster 29/5/1801 Jane Butler (Bentham, Yorks.), with issue.

ROWLEY (Joshua) Born Petersham, Surrey 16/10/1769, s. Rear-Admiral Sir Joshua Rowley, 1st Bart. (*q.v.* ODNB) and Sarah Burton. St John's, Cambridge 1787, BA1791, MA1794, dn97 (Nor.), p98 (Nor.). V. Brent Eleigh, Suffolk 1803-8, V. Stoke by Nayland, Suffolk 1808-32, R. Newbourne, Suffolk 1810-24, R. (and patron) of Brantham w. East Bergholt, Suffolk 1819-54 [net income £1,117], R. Holton St Mary, Suffolk 1824-36. Died 28/12/1854 [C114975] Married Brent Eleigh, Suffolk 2/4/1799 Mary Scourfield (Roberton Hall, Pembroke), and had issue.

ROWLEY (Thomas) Born Middleton Scriven, Shropshire 24/8/1797, s. Rev. Richard Rowley and Mary Falkner. Christ Church, Oxford 1815, BA1819, dn21 (Heref.), BA1822, p22 (Heref.), BD and DD1839. R. Frodesley, Shropshire 1822-4, H/M Bridgnorth G/S and (succ. his father as) R. Middleton Scriven 1822-54, R. Willey, Heref. 1854 to death 11/11/1877, leaving £5,000 [C19659. Boase] Married Wroxeter, Shropshire 30/12/1823 Mary Anne Farmer (w), with issue.

ROY (Thomas) [MA by 1828 but NiVoF] dn21 (London), p22 (Durham for Car.). PC. Bassenthwaite, Cumberland 1822-35, Chap. of the Donative of Woburn, Beds. 1823, V. Goldington 1828 to death 24/2/1835 (CCEd thus) [C3482. Platt] Married with issue.

ROYDS (Charles Smith) Born Summer Castle, Rochdale, Lancs. 20/9/1799, s. James Royds and Mary Smith. Christ's, Cambridge 1818, BA 1822, dn23 (Chester for C&L)), p24 (Chester), MA1825. R. (and patron) of Haughton, Staffs. 1831-79, R. Brereton, Cheshire 1836-43, Prebend of Bishop's Hull in Lichfield Cathedral 1857, PC. Derrington, Staffs. 1866 to death. Dom. Chap. to Marquess of Abercorn. Died 24/4/1879, leaving £50,000 [C19494] Married Betley, Staffs. 20/6/1837 Mary Anne Twemlow (w) (Betley Court), w. clerical son Charles Twemlow Royds. *J.P.* Staffs. Port online. Brother below.

ROYDS (Edward) Born Summer Castle, Rochdale, Lancs. 23/8/1790, s. James Royds and Mary Smith. Christ's, Cambridge 1816, dn17 (Ex. for Chester), p17 (Chester), BA1820, MA 1823. PC. Hundersfield, Lancs. 1817-27, R. Brereton cum Smethwick, Cheshire 1819-36, R. Haughton, Staffs. 1822-31. Died 11/4/1836 aged 45 [C19660] Married Walton 28/12/1819 Mary, dau. of Thomas Molyneux (a Mayor of Liverpool), 10 ch. (2 clerical) listed in a very full online entry: *entry*www.fitzwalter.com/afh/Royds/roydshist2.html . Brother above.

ROYLE (James) Born Crimplesham, Norfolk 27/8/1787, s. William Royle and Mary Bidden. St John's, Cambridge 1806, BA1811, dn11 (Nor.), p12 (Nor.), MA1814. V. Islington, Norfolk 1821-46, PC. Wereham w. Wretton, Norfolk 1823-59, R. Stanfield, Norfolk 1825 to death there 23/6/1864, leaving £600 [C114976] Married Holborn, London 13/10/1789 Elizabeth Patrick (w), and issue.

ROYLE (John) From Denbigh. St John's, Cambridge 1779 (rusticated 1782), p86 (St Asaph). R. Hilhay, Norfolk 1782 and 1786-1816,

R. Compton Martin, Som. 1816 to death 13/3/1840 aged 79 [C48404]

ROYSE (Nathaniel Thomas) Born Dunterton, Devon. Corpus Christi, Cambridge 1816, BA1821, dn22 (Glos.), p22 (Glos.). R. (and patron) of Dunterton 1833 [blank in ERC] to death 4/4/1853 aged 56 [C40488]

RUDALL (Edward) Born Crediton, Devon 30/3/1800, s. Rev. John Rudall (below) and Susanna Browning. Pembroke, Oxford 1819, BA1823, dn23 (Bristol), p24 (Ex.), MA1843. PC. Boyton, Cornwall 1826 to death (Lew-annick, Cornwall) 23/12/1862, leaving £1,000 [C53777] Married Holsworthy, Devon 7/6/1826 Elizabeth Robinson Camm (w).

RUDALL (John) Bapt. Stoke Damerel, Devon 25/1/1753. Exeter, Oxford 1771, dn75 (Ex.), p79 (Ex.). V. Crediton, Devon 1793-1832. Died 7/9/1835 [C146328] Married Sandford, Devon 8/2/1783 Susanna Browning, with son above.

RUDD (Eric) Born and bapt. 6/11/1773, s. Rev. James Rudd (St Paul's Qualified Chapel, Edinburgh) and Elisabeth (dau. Lord Duffus, and widow of both Capt. Alexander Sinclair, and of Charles Sinclair of Olrig). Literate: dn96 (Bristol for York), p98 (York). V. Appleby, Lincs. 1807, PC. Thorne, Yorks. 1816 to death 19/4/1856 [C75455. YCO. Bertie] Married York 30/12/1800 Sarah Brook, with issue.

RUDD (John) Born Cockermouth, Cumberland 23/12/1770, s. of John Rudd (attorney). Trinity, Cambridge 1787, BA1792, Fellow 1794, MA1795, dn95 (Car.), p96 (Ely). V. Blyth, Yorks. 1813-30, Master of St Mary Magdalen Hospital [almshouses], Bawtry, Yorks. 1816-34 (and Prebend of Halloughton in Southwell Collegiate Church 1827), R. Waltham, Lincs. 1830 to death. Dom. Chap. to Anna-Maria, Dowager Duchess of Newcastle 1821. Died 4/7/1834 aged 68 [C135975] Married Bath 19/4/1813 ('having been jilted by Miss Browne') Elizabeth Ferris, dau. of the Dean of Battle [Abbey], with issue. J.P. Notts. and Yorks. and Chairman of Quarter Sessions.

RUDDOCK (Noblett) Born Bristol 5/5/1777, s. Noblett Ruddock and Katherine Creagh. Trinity, Oxford 1795, BA 1799, dn00 (Bristol), MA1802, p03 (Bristol). V. Stockland Bristol, Som. 1814 and V. Westbury, Som. 1814 to death. . Dom. Chap. to 2nd Earl of Charlemont 1814. Died 27/4/1851 [C40491] Married Bristol 4/5/1803 Ann Grevile, with issue.

RUDDOCK (Richard Hastwell) Born Sedgefield, Co. Durham 3/5/1801. St John's, Cambridge 1819, BA1824, dn24 (Durham), p25 (Durham), MA1827. PC. All Saints Bishopsgate, City of London 1830 to death. Dean 1847, then President of Sion College, London 1852-3. Died 20/12/1857, leaving £600 [C21420]

RUDGE (Frederick) Born Haresfield. Glos. 2/10/1787, s. Rev. Thomas Rudge and Sarah King. Pembroke, Oxford 1805, dn14 (Heref. for Llandaff), p15 (B&W). V. Eardisland, Heref. 1816 to death (Tenbury, Worcs.) 5/2/1867, leaving under £200 [C40492 corrected] Had issue.

RUDGE (James Horace) Born Cromhill House, Cromhill, Glos. 27/4/1785, s. James Rudge. Pembroke, Oxford 1801, BA1808, dn08 (Glos.), then St Catharine's, Cambridge, MA 1813, DD. R. Hawkchurch, Dorset 1828 to death. Chap. to HRH Prince Leopold (later King of the Belgians) 1820; and to HRH Duke of York 1825; and to HRH Duke of Sussex 1831. Died 2/7/1852 [C53779] Was married. F.R.S. (1814).

RUFFORD (Francis) Bapt. Worcester 18/2/1755, s. Philip and Margaret Rufford, Wadham, Oxford 1772, BA1775, dn77 (Wor.), p79 (Wor.), MA1781. R. Lower Sapey, Worcs. 1784-1831, R. Kinwarton, Warwicks. 1787 to death 22/1/1833 (CCEd says 19/2/1833) [C122071] Married Westminster, London 26/5/1785 Sarah Squire, with son below.

RUFFORD (William Squire) Bapt. Lower Sapey, Worcs. 27/9/1785, s. Rev. Francis Rufford (above) and Sarah Squire. Christ Church, Oxford 1804, BA1808, MA1811. R. Binton, Warwicks. 1820 and R. Lower Sapey, Worcs. 1831 to death 17/4/1836 [C122073] Married West Bromwich, Staffs. 17/3/1814 Anne Barber, with issue.

RUSBY (Samuel Stones) Bapt Leeds 25/11/1799, s. Thomad Rusby and Elizabeth Stones. St Catharine's, Cambridge 1819, BA 1823, Fellow 1824, MA1826, dn27 (Ely), p27 (Ely). R. Coton, Cambs. 1827 to death 22/4/1862 aged 63, leaving £300 [C109206]

RUSH (John) Bapt. Heckfield, Hants. 5/10/1769, s. Rev. Montague Rush and Mrs Jane (Baker) Toovey (a clergy dau.). St John's, Oxford 1788, dn94 (Bristol for Win.), BCL 1795, p95 (C&L for Win.). R. Hartwell, Bucks. 1803, Min. Chelsea Old Church, London 1824 to death 4/6/1855 [C19661] Married Lowestoft, Suffolk 15/10/1801 Honor Chambers, with issue.

RUSHOUT-BOWLES (George, Hon.) see under **BOWLES**

RUSHTON (John) Born Newchurch in Rossendale, Lancs. 5/5/1798, s. of a yeoman farmer. Literate: dn22 (Chester), p23 (Chester), DDLambeth 1844. PC. Newchurch in Pendle, Lancs. 1825-47, Archdeacon of Manchester 1843-54 (when he compiled a detailed survey of the whole of the Archdeaconry of Manchester), R. Prestwich, Manchester 1847-54 (and Hon. Canon of Manchester Cathedral 1849), V. Blackburn 1854 to death 21/2/1868 aged 69, leaving £25,000 [C170380. Boase] Married (1) Newchurch 27/8/1823, Alice Hoyle Ashworth (d.1832), w. issue (2) Derby 5/12/1843 Henrietta Newton, with further and clerical son (also John).

RUSSELL (Arthur Tozer) Born Northampton 20/3/1806, s. Rev. Thomas Russell (formerly Cloutt, an Independent Minister, *q.v.* ODNB) and Elizabeth Tozer. St John's, Cambridge 1824, dn29 (Lin.), p30 (Lin.), LLB1831. V. Caxton, Cambs. 1830-52, V. Whaddon, Cambs. 1852-63, PC. St Thomas, Toxteth Park, Liverpool 1863-8, R. Wrockwardine Wood, Shropshire 1868-74, R. Southwick, Sussex 1874 to death 18/11/1874, leaving £800 [C75473. ODNB. Boase] Married (1) Southwark, London 28/1/1834 Mrs Emma (Howard) Deloughry (d.1850), with issue (2) Linton, Cambs. 1851 (3rd q.) Eliza Baynes.

RUSSELL (Charles) Born Wimborne, Dorset, s. Rev. William Russell. New, Oxford 1761 (aged 19), dn64 (Ox.), p66 (Ox.). R. Thurloxton, Som. 1768-1833, Chap. of the Donative of Thurlbere, Som. 1763, R. Lydeard St Lawrence 1768-1833, PC. Stoke St Mary, Som. 1768 to death 26/3/1833 (CCEd thus) [C27154]

RUSSELL (Isaac) Born St Bees, Cumberland 12/10/1788, s. Isaac (yeoman farmer) and Elizabeth Russell. Literate: dn11 (York), p12 (York). S/M Spilsby G/S 1818-56 (30 boarders); PC. Hagnaby, Lincs. 1835, V. Stickford, Lincs. 1845 to death. Chap. Spilsby House of Correction 1827. Died 1856 (1st q.) [C75476. YCO. Kaye] Clerical son John Russell.

RUSSELL (John) Born Meeth, Devon 17/3/1760, s. Rev. Michael Russell. Sidney, Cambridge 1778, BA1782, dn82 (B&W), p84 (Ex.), MA1785. R. Dittisham, Devon 1804-15, PC. St Juliot, Cornwall 1810-37, V. Hurstbourne Tarrant, Hants. 1814-18, R. Burbage, Wilts. 1814-41, R. Iddesleigh, Devon 1823-47, R. Jacobstowe, Devon 1836 to death 3/3/1847 aged 86 [probably C299048] Perhaps with clerical son of same name in same place?

RUSSELL (John) Born Helmdon, Northants., 23/9/1786, s. Rev. John Russell, sen. and Harriet Edmunds. Christ Church, Oxford 1803, BA1806, MA1809, dn09 (Cant.), p10 (London), BD1817, DD1830. H/M Charterhouse [School] 1811-32; Canon of 11th Prebend in Canterbury Cathedral 1827-63, R. St Michael Queenhithe w. Holy Trinity the Less, City of London 1829, R. St Botolph without Bishopsgate, City of London 1832 to death 3/6/1863, leaving £35,000 [C121568 - 121567] Clerical son William Russell.

RUSSELL (Whitworth) Born Eltham, Kent 17/9/1795, s. Sir Henry Russell, 1st Bart. and Anna Barbara Whitworth (dau. of a baronet). St John's, Cambridge 1814, BA1818, dn18 (Lin.), p19 (Lin.), MA1822. V. Chiddingly, Dorset 1825 to death. Inspector of Prisons and Chap. of Millbank Penitentiary 1830. Died (*by shooting himself* in the Board Room of the Millbank Penitentiary, London) 2/8/1847 [C65319] Married 6/4/1824 Frances (dau. of Vice-Admiral Charpentier), and had issue.

RUSSELL (William) Born London, s. John Russell (portrait painter, *q.v.* ODNB) and Hannah Faden. An artist himself, he gave up painting fearful lest 'his love of art might interfere with or displace his spiritual duties'. Clare, Cambridge 1810, BA 1814, dn14 (Glos. for Win.), p15 (C&L for Win.). R. Shepperton, Middx. 1817 (and RD Hampton 1847) to death (Highgate, London) 24/9/1870, leaving £14,000 [C19497. ODNB. Boase] Married Shepperton, Surrey 5/6/1820 Letitia Ann Nicholls, with issue. An exhibited artist.

RUSSELL (Wriothesley, Lord) Born London 11/5/1804, s. John, 6th Duke of Bedford and Georgiana Gordon (dau. of 4th Duke of Gordon), and thus half-brother of Lord John

Russell, Prime Minister. Trinity, Cambridge 1823, MA1829, dn29 (Lin.), p29 (Lin.). R. Chenies, Bucks. 1829-86, R. Streatham, Surrey [net income £1,136] 1830-5 (res.), Prebend of 9th Stall and Canon Residentiary St George's Chapel, Windsor 1840 to death. Deputy Clerk of the Closet 1850-86 and Chap. in Ordinary 1862-6; 'Confidential' Chap. to Prince Albert. Died 6/4/1886, leaving £2,069-10s-10d. [C75484. Boase. DEB. Francis W.B. Dunne, *Personal recollections of Lord Wriothesley Russell and Chenies* (1888 and photo.)] Married his cousin Elizabeth Laura Henrietta Russell (dau. of Lord William Russell) 23/6/1839, 2s., 1 dau. Temperance worker.

RUST, *later* RUST-D'EYE (Edgar) Born Abbots Hall, Stowmarket, Suffolk 1/3/1795, s. John Edgar Rust and Anne Sarah Rout. Caius, Cambridge 1812, BA1817, dn18 (Nor.), p19 (Nor.), MA 1820. R. Drinkstone, Suffolk 1824 to death (at Abbot's Hall) 22/11/1852 [C114989] Married Thrandeston, Suffolk 16/11/1821 Ann Dioness D'Eye (a clergy dau.), w. issue. Assumed additional surname 1852.

RYCROFT (Henry) Born Farnham, Surrey 28/2/1797, s. Sir Nelson Rycroft, 2nd Bart. and Charlotte Read. Trinity Hall, Cambridge 1815, BA1819, MA1822, p22 (Lin.). PC. Melton Ross, Lincs. 1822-5, Prebend of Scamblesby in Lincoln Cathedral 1822, R. Greetham, Lincs. 1825-32, V. Mumby, Lincs. 1823-40, V. Wyvell w. Hungarton, Lincs. 1824-40, R. Trusthorpe, Lincs. 1832 to death. Dom. Chap. to Bishop of Bristol, etc. 1825; to 4th Earl of Pomfret 1832. Died (unm., at Santa Luca de Barrameda, Cadiz) 6/4/1840 [C75485]

RYDER (Edward) Born London 28/4/1784, s. Thomas Ryder (Registrar of Charterhouse School) and Mary Croft. St John's, Cambridge 1802, BA1806, dn07 (Ex. for Lin.), p08 (Win. for Salis.), MA1810. R. Oaksey, Wilts. 1808 and R. Wendens Ambo, Essex 1814 to death 8/5/1857 aged 74 [C75488] Married 4/10/1817 Eliza Howard (natural dau. of Viscount Andover).

RYDER (Hon. Henry, Bishop of Gloucester *then of* Coventry and Lichfield) Born Streatham, Surrey 21/7/1777, s. Daniel Ryder, 1st Baron Harrowby and Elizabeth Terrick (dau. of a Bishop of London). St John's, Cambridge 1795, BA, MA1798, dn01 (Lin. for C&L), p01 (Glos.), DD1813. R. Lutterworth, Leics. 1801-16 (and Preacher throughout the Diocese of Lincoln 1805), V. Claybrook w. Wibtoft, Leics. 1805-16, Canon of Windsor 1808, Dean of Wells 1812-31 (and Canon Residentiary 1812-17), Bishop of Gloucester 1815-24 (the first-ever Evangelical appointment, 'vigorously opposed' by the Archbishop of Canterbury and the Dean and Chapter of Gloucester), Bishop of Coventry and Lichfield 1824 to death (Hastings, Sussex) 31/3/1836 aged 58 [C41548. ODNB] Married Thorpe Acre, Leics. 15/12/1802 Sophia Phillips, w. distinguished issue, and below. Kneeling statue by Francis Legatt in Lichfield Cathedral, and online.

RYDER (Henry Dudley) Born Garendon Park, Leics. 13/10/1803, s. Rt. Rev. Hon. Henry Ryder (above) and Sophia March Phillipps. Oriel, Oxford 1821, BA1825, dn27 (C&L), p28 (C&L), MA1828. R. Tarvin, Cheshire 1827-36, R. High Offley, Staffs. 1828-33, 4th Residential Canon of Lichfield (with Prebendal Stalls of Ryton and of Pipe Minor) 1833 to death. Dom. Chap. to two successive Bishops of Coventry and Lichfield (one his father). Died (Brussels) 19/1/1877 aged 73, leaving £20,000 [C19667. Boase] Married (1) Salcombe Regis, Devon 8/5/1828 Cornelia Sarah Cornish (d.1840), w. issue (2) Paris 27/3/1841 Eliza Julia Tucker, w. further issue.

RYDER (Thomas Richard) Born Hendon, Middx., s. Thomas Ryder and Mary Croft. Exeter, Oxford 1812 (aged 17), then Pembroke BA1817, dn17 (Salis. for London), p18 (London), MA1821. V. Ecclesfield, Yorks. 1825 to death 24/7/1839 [C89387] Married Bedale, Yorks. 23/1/1826 Anne Pulleine, with issue.

SABIN (John Edward) Bapt. Towcester, Northants. 11/1/1793, s. Edward Sabin and Sarah Heath. Lincoln, Oxford 1809, BA1814, dn15 (Lin.), p17 (Lin.). R. Preston Bissett, Bucks. 1823, Min. St Peter's, Eaton Square ('Eaton Chapel'), London 1835 to death 27/7/1863. No will traced [C75494. DEB] Married Drayton, Oxon. 24/10/1821 Mary Ann Humprhrey, w. clerical son of same name.

SADLER (Samuel Farmer) Bapt. Sandhurst, Glos. 13/6/1794, s. Rev. Samuel Farmer Sadler, sen. and Catherine Ann Parsons. Balliol, Oxford 1812, SCL, dn18 (Heref.), p21 (Glos.). R. Sutton under Brailes, Glos. 1823. Died Blackpool, Lancs. 31/10/1862, leaving £300 [C162800] Married Shipston on Stour, Warwicks. 21/4/1840 Ann Beatrix Hulton (of Preston, Lancs.), with issue.

SADLER (William) Bapt. Great Horkesley, Essex 19/4/1765, s. William Sadler and Mary Lay. Sidney, Cambridge 1783, BA1788, dn88 (Nor.), MA1791, p04 (London). V. Clare, Norfolk 1804-19, V. Poslingford, Norfolk 1804-33. Died Great Horkesley 15/11/1837 [C114998] Married Clare, Suffolk 30/12/1788 Sarah Stebbing, with issue.

SAFFORD (James Cutting) Born Weybread, Suffolk 10/7/1799 (bapt. 27/9/1818), s. Samuel Safford (farmer and *J.P.*, Mettingham Castle, Suffolk) and Mary Cole. Caius, Cambridge 1818, BA1822, dn23 (Lin.), p23 (Lin.). V. (and patron) of Mettingham 1824 and V. Ilketshall St Lawrence, Suffolk 1840 to death 2/8/1871, leaving £5,000 [C75496] Married Repton, Notts. 11/7/1825 Louisa Chartres (w) (a clergy dau., of Godmanchester, Hants.), with issue. *J.P.* Suffolk.

SAGE (Charles Arthur) From London, s. Alderman Joseph Sage (an Assay Master at the Royal Mint) and Sarah Shakespear. Trinity, Cambridge 1804 (aged 17), BA1808, dn11 (B&W), p17 (London). V. Brackley St Peter, Northants. 1825 (and RD 1826) to death 20/12/1867 aged 70, leaving £1,000 [C48429] Married Monken Hadley, Barnet, Middx. 28/12/1819 Caroline Quilter, with issue. Surrogate 1826.

SAINSBURY (Henry) From Newbury, Berks., s. Henry Sainsbury. St John's, Cambridge 1786 (aged 18), BA1790, p91 (Nor. for Win.), p92 (Salis.). R. Beckington w. Standerwick, Som. 1792 to death 31/10/1841 [C48433]

SAINT (John James) Bapt. Speldhurst, Kent 3/7/1800, s. John James Saint and Elizabeth Gable. BNC, Oxford 1818, BA1821, dn23, MA1825, p25. R. and V. (and patron) of Speldhurst, Kent 1830-89, RD of South Melling. Dom. Chap. to Earl of Rosslyn. Died Groombridge Place, Kent 6/6/1889, leaving £32,833-5s-6d. [C481] Married London 24/11/1826 Sophia Heath Wilson, with issue. Surrogate for the Diocese of Chichester. Good online photo.

SALE (Thomas) Born Clifton upon Dunsmore, Warwicks. 29/3/1804, s. Edward Sale and Mary Norman. Worcester, Oxford 1822, then Magdalen 1823-33, BA1825, dn27 (Ox.), p28 (London), MA1828, BD and DD1856. Curate Weld Chapel, Southgate, Edmonton, Middx. 1830-51, V. Sheffield 1851-73, RD, Prebend of Husthwaite in York Minster 1855 to death 20/9/1873, leaving £40,000 [C21425. DEB] Married Edmonton 7/8/1824 Lydia Rawlinson Walker, with clerical son Thomas Walker Sale.

SALISBURY (Bishop of) see under **BURGESS (Thomas)**

SALKELD (Edward) Born Sleagill, Westmorland (bapt. Morland 1/3/1801), s. Thomas Salkeld (a farmer) and Agnes Richardson. Trinity, Cambridge 1822, BA1826, dn28 (C&L), p29 (C&L), MA1831. PC. Carlisle Holy Trinity 1832-38, V. Crosby on Eden, Cumberland 1833-8, V. Aspatria, Cumberland 1838 to death 6/9/1872 aged 71, leaving £3,000 [C6278. Platt] Married (2?) Wrexham 19/7/1859 Esther Clark (w). *J.P.* Cumberland. Surrogate.

SALKELD (Robert) Bapt. Fifehead Neville, Dorset 26/7/1795, s. William Salkeld and Ann Clitherow. Exeter, Oxford 1812, then Corpus Christi (Ox. *or* Cam.?), BA1818, dn18 (Salis.), MA1819, p19 (Salis.). R. Great Fontmell (Fontmell Magna), Dorset 1819 to death 22/1/1866, leaving £600 [C53802] Married St George's Hanover Square, London 9/5/1820 Elizabeth Henrietta Wilson, with issue.

SALMON (George) Born Bath, Somerset 6/2/1789, s. of Harry Salmon (attorney) and Denne Colborne. Clare, Cambridge 1808, BA 1813, dn13 (Salis.), p14 (B&W), MA1816. V. Shustoke, Warwicks. 1831 to death (Bath) 18/2/1872, leaving £4,000 [C19670] Married (1) Weston super Mare, Som. 16/10/1814 Elizabeth Lannsdowne (d.1836), with issue (2) Batheaston, Som. 4/8/1846 Mary Ann Crook.

SALMON (Henry) Born Odiham, Hants. 16/12/1799, s. Rev. Thomas Peter Dod Salmon and Sarah Adams (a clergy dau.). Emmanuel, Cambridge 1817, BA1822, dn22 (Win.), p23 (Win.), MA1825. V. Hartley Wintney, Hants. 1829-31, R. Swarraton, Hants. 1831 to death (Milford, Surrey) 11/6/1874, leaving £6,000 [C108712] Married (1) Odiham 12/7/1825 Charlotte Washington (d.1830), with clerical s. Thomas Henry (2) Iffley, Oxon. 1/11/1831 Emily Charlotte Noel/Nowell, with further issue.

SALMON (Henry Willson) Born Cambridge 9/12/1790, s. Thomas and Mary Salmon. St John's, Cambridge 1808, BA1812, dn13 (Lin.), MA1815, p15 (C&L). Priest-Vicar in Lichfield Cathedral 1815, V. Sproxton w. Saltby, Leics. 1818-20, R. Redmile, Leics. 1819-28, R. Sturmer, Essex 1828-9, R. Lydgate, Suffolk 1829-40, R. Oldberrow, Worcs. 1859 to death (Henley in Thames) 4/11/1871, leaving £2,000 [C19499]

SALMON (Thomas William) Bapt. Gorleston, Suffolk 14/12/1801, s. Thomas Salmon (of Great Yarmouth, Norfolk). Caius, Cambridge 1819 BA1823. dn25 (Nor.), p26 (Lin.), MA 1826. PC. (and patron) of Woodbridge, Suffolk 1831-8, PC. Hopton, Suffolk 1841 to death 16/7/1848 aged 46 [C115004] Married Great Yarmouth 20/7/1826 Sarah Worship [*sic*], with issue.

SALT (Francis, sen.) Born Wem, Staffs. 1768, s. John Salt and Elizabeth Woodhouse. Magdalen Hall, Oxford 1790, dn96 (Heref.), BA1811, p12 (C&L). PC. Broughton, Shropshire 1812, R. Grinshill, Shropshire 1814. Died Wem 1843 (2nd q.) [C19673] Married (1) Halesowen, Staffs. 30/9/1794 Mary Lilly (d.1812), w. clerical sons Francis (below), and George Salt (2) Bridgnorth, Shropshire 2/1/1813 Joice Bathes, with further issue.

SALT (Francis, jun.) Born Bridgnorth, Shropshire 18/5/1795, s. Rev. Francis Salt, sen. (above) and Mary Lilly. Christ Church, Oxford 1814, BA1819, dn19 (C&L), MA1821, p35 (C&L). S/M Wem Free G/S, Shropshire to death; PC. Leebrockhurst, Shropshire 1825-41. Died Islington, London (his home) 20/5/1870, leaving £3,000 [C19674] Married Windsor, Berks. 4/11/1821 Frances Higgins, with issue.

SALTER (Edward Montagu) Born Strathfield Saye, Hants 12/5/1790., s. Rev. Edward Salter and Delicia Barton. Christ Church, Oxford 1809, BA 1813, dn13 (Ox.), MA1815, p16 (London). R. Hawkhurst, Kent 1819-26, R. Wood Norton cum Swanton Newars, Norfolk 1825 to death 31/3/1845 [C21429] Brothers John, and Thomas, below.

SALTER (John) Born Exeter, Devon 1/4/1784, s. John Salter and Sarah Moon. Exeter, Oxford 1797, dn04 (Ex.), p06 (Ex.), BA1807, MA1808. S/M East Teignmouth, Devon 1808; 'Perpetual V.' Stratton St Margaret, Wilts. 1808-33, Prebend of Winterborne Earls in Salisbury Cathedral 1814 to death 19/3/1833 (CCEd says 29/3/1833) [C89393] Married before 1805 Dinah Adams, w. clerical son George John Ranking Salter.

SALTER (John) From Strathfield Saye, Hants., s. Rev. Edward Salter and Delicia Barton. Christ Church, Oxford 1810 (aged 18), Student [Fellow] 1812-29, BA1814, MA1817, dn18 (Ox.), p20 (Ox.), Chap. 1838-9 (as John Henry). R. Iron Acton, Glos. 1828 (and Hon. Canon of Bristol Cathedral 1857) to death 9/2/1877, leaving £12,000 [C21430] Brothers Edward Montague (above), and Thomas (below).

SALTER (Thomas) Bapt. Strathfield Saye, Hants. 14/8/1788, s. Rev. Edward Salter and Delicia Barton. Christ Church, Oxford 1807, Student [Fellow] 1807-14, BA1811, dn12 (Win.), p13 (Glos.). R. Ibberton, Dorset 1813 to death 1855 (1st q.) [C53804] Brothers Edward Montagu, and John, above.

SALTER (William) Bapt. Feniton, Devon 10/1/1759, s. Maximilian Salter [*pleb.*] and Martha Skinner. Christ Church, Oxford 1781, BA1785, dn85 (Ex.), p87 (Ex.). R. Northleigh, Devon 1797 and R. Cadleigh, Devon 1800 [to death] 23/1/1847 [C146343] Married (1) Farway, Devon 12/12/1789 Sarah Jenkins (d.1820), with issue (2) Sidmouth, Devon 13/2/1824 Susanna Sanders.

SALUSBURY (James Thelwall) Born Graveley, Herts. 16/9/1775, s. Rev. Thelwall Salusbury and Ann Cecil. Sidney, Cambridge 1794, then Trinity Hall 1795, BCL, LLB, dn99 (Lin.), p00 (Lin.). PC. St Mary the Virgin, Aldermanbury, City of London 1803, R. Holwell, Beds. 1829-30 (res.). Probate granted 22/6/1843 [C75499] Married City of London 12/5/1813 Mary Slack.

SALVADOR (John Lovell) Born Twickenham, Surrey 20/6/1771, s. Francis (alias Daniel, who was scalped by Native Americans in South Carolinba) and Sarah Salvador. Christ Church, Oxford 1788, BA 1793, MA1795, dn95 (Ox.), p96 (Ox.), Student [Fellow] to 1812. R. Staunton on Wye, Heref. 1810 to death 26/12/1836 (*or* 1838) [C37524] Married 10/9/1801 Frances Pratt, w. issue.

SALVIN (Joseph, *some say* James) Bapt. Elkesley, Notts. 26/11/1797, s. David and Ann Salvin. Queens', Cambridge 1827, a Ten Year Man, dn22 (York), p23 (York). PC. York St Mary Castlegate 1831 to death 31/1/1871 aged 73, leaving £4,000 [C135722. YCO] Married (1) York 2/8/1830 Dorothy Milner, then aged 40 (2) Cheltenham 31/1/1861 Lucy Revell, with issue.

SALWEY (Richard) Born Ludlow, Shropshire 1/10/1800, s. Theophilus Richard Salwey, (of Westminster, London) and Anna Maria Hill. Christ Church, Oxford 1820, BA1824, dn25 (Heref.), p26 (Chester). R. Fawkham, Kent 1829-73, R. Ash, Kent 1840-88-. Died Stonehouse, Glos. 6/2/1895, leaving £2,503-16s-7d. [C482] Married Ash 26/11/1835 Mary Lambard, with issue.

SAMPSON, SAMSON (George) Born Beverley, Yorks. 18/3/1780 (bapt. 2/4/1784), s. Joshua Sampson (a physician). Clare, Cambridge 1801, then St John's, 1801, dn03 (York), then St Catharine's 1806, BA1809, p09 (C&L). R. (and patron) of Leven, Yorks. [net income £1,190] 1815 to death (Bridlington, Yorks.) 3/9/1839 [C19500 corrected over deacon's dates. YCO] Married York 8/2/1806 Anna Story, with issue. *J.P.* East Riding.

SAMPSON (Henry) Bapt. Clapham, Surrey 7/11/1794, s. Rev. Thomas Sampson (Petersham, Surrey). Trinity Hall, Cambridge 1808, LLB1814, dn17 (Nor.), p18 (Nor.). V. Cudham, Kent 1830-75, R. High Halstow, Kent 1875 to death (Kensington, London) 10/11/1884, leaving £1,185-10s-0d. [C483] Had issue.

SAMPSON (John) Born Madron, Cornwall 4/3/1759. Trinity, Cambridge 1790 (a Ten Year Man), dn93 (Nor.), p94 (Nor.). S/M Kendal, Westmorland; R. Halstead, Kent 1821-36. Died 27/3/1843 aged 78 [C115031]

SAMPSON (Theophilus) Born Edwinstowe, Notts. 20/1/1796, s. Thomas Sampson and Elizabeth Sutton de Garencières. Literate: dn19 (Ex. for York), p20 (York), CCEd says MA by 1826 (so a Ten Year Man?). R. Wailesby, Notts. 1826-33, R. Eakring, Notts. 1830 to death (Whitby, Yorks.) 8/6/1864, leaving £3,000 [C135724. YCO] Married (1) East Retford, Notts. 20/9/1820 Sophia Sampson (2) Mattersley, Notts. 28/12/1824 Honor Pawson (d.1839), with issue (3) Nottingham 24/8/1841 Eliza Frances Huthwaite (w), with further issue.

SAMPSON (Thomas) Literate: dn86 (Lin.), p91 (Nor.), then Trinity, Cambridge (a Ten Year Man), BD1799, DD1804. 'Sometime' Minister Denmark Hill Chapel, London, R. Groton, Suffolk 1806-36. Lived at Petersham, Surrey (where he prepared pupils for university) 1807 to death 31/3/1839 [C76011] Had issue. *J.P.* and *D.L.* Surrey. *F.R.S.* (1811), *F.S.A.*

SAMS (Barwick John) Born Bury St Edmunds, Suffolk 1803, s. Rev. John Barwick Sams (below) and Sarah Hewitt. Christ's, Cambridge 1821, BA1826, dn27 (Nor.), p28 (Nor.), MA 1829. R. Great Fakenham, Suffolk 1829-35, R. Alderton w. Grafton Regis, Northants. 1838 to death 15/10/1885, leaving £473-8s-10d. [C115034] Married Greenwich, Kent 19/4/1838 Susan Louisa Sutton (w), and issue.

SAMS (John Barwick) Born Bury St Edmunds, Suffolk 1763, s. John Sams (linen draper, Bocking, Essex) and Grace Barwick. Caius, Cambridge 1780, BA1785, dn86 (Nor.), p88 (Nor.). R. South Wotton, Norfolk 1795 and R. Honington, Suffolk 1807 to death (Bury St Edmunds) 6/5/1842 [C115035] Married Bury St Edmunds 27/2/1797 Sarah Hewitt (dau. of a doctor), with clerical son above.

SANDBY (George, sen.) From Denton, Norfolk, s. Rev. George Sandby (Vice-Chancellor of Cambridge University; w. slave money? - not in LBSO) and Mary Acres. Merton, Oxford 1786 (aged 17), BA1790, MA 1793. R. Hawridge, Bucks. 1793, V. Camberwell, Surrey 1796, R. Earsham, Norfolk 1809-[31]. Dom. Chap. to Bp of Bristol, Norwich, then of St Asaph 1796. Died Denton 8/2/1852 (living at Denton Lodge [C108716] Married Ipswich, Suffolk 8/8/1797 Maria Willett, w. son below.

SANDBY (George, jun.) Bapt. Denton, Norfolk 11/9/1798, s. Rev. George Sandby, sen. (above) and Maria Willett. Merton, Oxford 1816, BA1820, dn24 (Nor.), MA1825, p25 (Nor.). R. South Elmham, Suffolk 1831, V. Flixton, Suffolk 1842 to death (at his London house) 23/11/1880, leaving £25,000 [C93589] Married Langham, Norfolk 19/3/1831 Elizabeth Catherine Hodgson, with issue.

SANDELANDS see under **SANDILANDS**

SANDERS (Charles) Bapt. Uxbridge, Middx. 17/11/1771, s. Edward and Christian Sanders. Queens', Cambridge 1790, BA1794, dn95 (Nor. for York), p00 (Lin.), MA1802. S/M Uppingham School, Rutland; V. Ketton w. Tixover, Rutland 1813 to death. Confrator of Browne's Hospital [almshouses], Stamford, Lincs. 1806. Died 23/11/1844 [C76014. YCO]

SANDERS (Daniel) Bapt. Pinhoe, Devon 25/3/1773, s. Daniel Sanders. Exeter, Oxford 1793, BA1797, dn01 (Ex.), p01 (Ex.), then Emmanuel, Cambridge 1802, MA1802. R. Lifton, Devon 1802, R. Cheriton Fitzpayne, Devon 1802-24. Dom. Chap. to 2nd Earl Talbot 1802. Died Bath 20/9/1833 [C146346]

SANDERS (George) Born Greasley, Notts. 8/4/1771, s. Richard and Dorothy Sanders. Clare, Cambridge 1790, BA1795, dn95 (Bristol for York), p96 (C&L), Fellow 1796, MA1798. R. Trowell, Notts. (both Medieties) 1798 and R. Wollaton, Notts. 1798 to death. Dom. Chap. to 5th Baron Middleton 1798. Died 17/3/1838 [C19502. YCO] Married Matlock, Derbys. 26/11/1801 Catherine Eaton, with issue.

SANDERS (Robert) From Worcester, s. Thomas Sanders. Magdalen Hall, Oxford 1819 (aged 18), BA1825, MA1826. Minor Canon and Precentor of Worcester Cathedral 1825-76, R. Tibberton, Worcs. 1826-35 (res.), R. Sedgeberrow, Worcs. 1834, R. Cropthorne, Worcs. 1853 to death 23/3/1892, leaving £1,503-4s-2d. [C122111] Widow Emma, and issue.

SANDERS (Thomas) From Begbrook, Oxon., s. John Sanders. Christ Church, Oxford 1795 (aged 23), BA1799, dn99 (Lin.), MA1803, p05 (York). PC. Darley Chapel, Derby 1819-25 (res.), R. Towcester, Northants. 1826-34 [C110855], V. Stanford in the Vale, Berks. 1835 to death 19/4/1850 [C19680. YCO]

SANDERS (William) Born Westminster, London 31/8/1762, s. Nicholas and Sarah Sanders. St Mary Hall, Oxford 1786 (aged 24), dn88 (York), p92 (York). V. Lissington, Lincs. 1830. Dead by 27/1/1837 [C76017 / 119434. YCO]

SANDERSON (Thomas) Born Little Addington, Northants. Clare, Cambridge 1804, LLB1810, dn10 (Peterb.), p12 (Peterb.). S/M Higham Ferrers School, Northants. 1814; V. (and patron) of Little Addington (Addington Parva) 1813 to death 11/3/1855 aged 69, *s.p.* [C110859] 'The last Sanderson of Little Addington, where the family had resided for over 300 years, and the living had been held from father to son in succession from the year 1719.'

SANDFORD, *later* WINSTON (Benjamin) Bapt. Childwall, Liverpool 5/6/1786, s. Benjamin Sandford (of the Island of Martinique, West Indies) and Rebecca Winston. St John's, Cambridge 1804, LLB1810, dn12 (Chester for Cant.), p16 (London for Cant.). V. Farningham, Kent 1816-48. Died (Rhyl, Flintshire) 16/4/1866, leaving £12,000 [C121902] Married (1) Ewell, Surrey 15/5/1813 Helen Reid (d.1817), with issue (2) Clifton, Bristol 15/12/1846 Anne Knight.

SANDFORD (Humphrey) Born Shrewsbury, Shropshire 12/12/1782, s. Folliott Sandford and Isabella Deuchars. St John's, Cambridge 1805 (did not reside), then Magdalene 1805, dn96 (Heref.), BA1809, p11 (Heref.). PC. Edgton, Shropshire 1812-56, PC. Bicton, Shropshire 1817-52. Died 13/9/1856 [C19555] Married 21/1/1811 Frances Holland (a clergy dau.), with issue. Brothers Richard, and William, below.

SANDFORD (John) Born Edinburgh 22/3/1801, s. Rt. Rev. Daniel Sandford (Bishop of Edinburgh in Scottish Episcopal Church) and Helen Frances Catherine Erskine Douglas. Glasgow Univ. 1817/20, then Snell Exhibitioner at Balliol, Oxford 1820-5, BA1824, dn24 (C&L), p26 (C&L for Ox.), MA1841, BD 1845. V. Chillingham, Northumberland 1827-33, Chap. Long Acre, London 1833-6, V. Dunchurch, Warwicks. 1836-53, Hon. Canon of Worcester Cathedral 1844-73, Archdeacon of Coventry 1851-73, R. Hallow 1853-4, V. Grimley, Warwicks. 1853-4, R. Alvechurch, Worcs. [income £1,200] 1854 to death. Examining Chap. to Bishop of Worcester 1853-60. Warden of Queen's College [Medical School], Birmingham. Died 22/3/1873 aged 72, leaving £12,000 [C133615. ODNB. Boase. Snell] Married (1) Wells, Som. 16/8/1825 Elizabeth Gabriel Poole (d.1853), 3 clerical sons (inc. Charles, Bishop of Gibraltar) (2) St James, Piccadilly, London 3/4/1856 Anna Cunningham Grahame (of Gartmore, Perthshire, her third marriage), with further issue (w). An active member of the Lower House of Convocation.

SANDFORD (Richard) Born Shrewsbury, Shropshire 18/7/1791, s. Folliott Sandford and Isabella Deuchars. St John's, Cambridge 1815, then Magdalene 1817, BA1819, dn20 (Glos.), p21 (Glos.). V. Eaton under Haywood, Shropshire 1831 to death (unmarried) 2/1/1860, leaving £1,500 [C163106] Brothers Humphrey (above), and William, below.

SANDFORD (Robert) Bapt. Crook, Kendal, Westmorland 24/4/1774, s. Rev. William Sandford and Isabel Birket. H/M Crosthwaite and Lyth G/S 1795. Literate: dn99 (Chester), p01 (Chester). PC. Crook 1801 to death 19/3/1839 aged 65 [C170399] Married 1799 Margaret Bell, 9 ch. in 1824.

SANDFORD (William) Born Shrewsbury, Shropshire 21/8/1793, s. Folliott Sandford and Isabella Deuchars. Clare, Cambridge 1812, BA 1816, dn16 (Salis.), p18 (Ely for Chich.), MA 1819. PC. Newport, Shropshire 1827 to death 21/3/1864, leaving £2,000 [C19556] Married 23/4/1817 Mary Ann Richman Webb, with issue. Brothers Humphrey, and Richard, above.

SANDIFORD (Peter) From City of London, s. Rev. Rowland Sandiford and Mary Roberts. Corpus Christi, Cambridge 1766, BA1771, Fellow 1772, dn74 (London), MA1774, p75 (London), DD1817 (Lambeth). Professor of Astronomy, Gresham College, London 1795. R. Fulmodeston cum Croxton, Norfolk [net income £1,135] 1778-1835, R. Thurning, Norfolk 1778-1811, V. Newton St Mary (in the Marsh), Cambs. 1810-35 (Sinecure R. Ashbury, Berks. 1820 to death. Dom. Chap. to Bishop of Rochester, then of Ely 1810. Died 13/9/1835 aged 85 (CCEd says 4/10/1835) [C89395]

SANDILANDS, SANDELANDS (Richard) From Upton, Worcs., s. Richard Sandilands. Balliol, Oxford 1780 (aged 18), then Sidney, Cambridge, dn82 (Heref.), LLB1787, p98 (Heref.). R. Turnastone, Heref. 1798, Min. of English Church, St Omer, France. Dom. Chap. to Henrietta Charlotte, Viscountess Hereford 1784. Died St Omer 29/5/1836 aged 77. [C159302]

SANDWITH (William) Bapt. Whicham, Cumberland 25/3/1789, s. Daniel Sandwith and Deborah Benson. Literate: dn12 (Chester), p15 (Chester). PC. Woodland (in Furness), Lancs. 1815 to death (unmarried) 15/4/1851 aged 62 [C170402]

SANDYS, *later* SANDYS-LUMSDAINE (Edwin) Bapt. Canterbury 8/9/1785, s. Edwin Humphrey Sandys and Helen Chick. St John's, Oxford 1803, BA1808, dn08 (Lin.), p10 (Lin.), MA1814. R. (and patron) of Upper Hardres, Kent 1815 to death (Edrom, Berwickshire) 3/7/1871, leaving £16,000 [C76070. Foster as Lumsdaine] Married St Paul's Cray, Kent 14/11/1816 Mary Lillias Lumsdaine, and changed surname. Clerical son Francis Gordon Sandys-Lumsdaine. Brother John below.

SANDYS (Edwin Windsor Bayntun, Sir, 2nd Bart.) Born Gosport, Hants. 31/10/1801, s. Sir Edward Bayntun Sandys, 1st Bart. (Missenden Park, Glos.) and Agnes Cornish Allen. Adm. Lincoln's Inn 1817. Trinity, Cambridge 1819, BA1825, dn25 (Bristol for Nor.), p26 (Nor.), then Peterhouse, Fellow 1828. R. Winstone, Glos. 1830 to death 21/12/1839 aged 37 [C53806] One of the last people to be knighted by right as the eldest son of a baronet 1825.

SANDYS (John) Born Kingston, Kent, s. Edwin Humphrey Sandys and Helen Chick. St John's, Cambridge 1819, then Queens' 1820 ('because of his attraction to the teaching of Simeon, frowned upon at St John's'), BA1823, dn23 (Ely for Cant.), p24 (London for Cant.), Fellow of Queens' 1825, MA1826. PC. Islington St Paul, London 1830-61, R. Pakefield, Suffolk 1861-5, R. Rockland St Mary, Norfolk 1865 to death 25/12/1879 aged 79, leaving £18,000 [C76072] Married Canterbury 29/5/1832 Mary Almeria Willyams (a clergy dau., Kingston), with clerical s. John Edwin Sandys. Brother Edwin, above. The Sandys Exhibition was founded at Queens' in 1861.

SANDYS (William Travis) Born Graythwaite Hall, Kendal, Westmorland 23/5/1800, s. Miles Sandys and Elizabeth Dalrymple. Pembroke, Cambridge 1819, BA1824, dn24 (Chester), p26

(Chester), MA1827. R. (Church) Coniston, Lancs. 1826-40 (res.), PC. Satterthwaite, Hawkshead, Lancs. 1826-30 (res.), V. Beverley St Mary, Yorks. 1833-56, R. Burton (le) Coggles, Lincs. 1856 to death. Chap. to Duke of Devonshire. Died 21/1/1883 aged 80, leaving £5,145-3s-2d. [C170404. Bennett2] Married Measham, Derbys. 6/8/1835 Catherine Elizabeth Abney (Measham Hall), w. many children.

SANFORD (John) Born Ninehead, Somerset, s. John Sanford. BNC, Oxford 1796 (aged 18), BA1800, MA1803, dn03 (B&W), p03 (Win. for Ex.). V. Burlescombe, Devon (and Preacher throughout the Diocese of Exeter) 1803, R. Shirwell, Devon 1803-34 (res.), V. Ninehead 1810-35 (res.). Chap. to HRH Duke of Cambridge 1803-10. Died 27/9/1855 [C146348]

SAREL (Henry Rule) Born London 1/11/1791, s. Andrew Lovering Sarel and Anne Rule. Trinity, Cambridge 1809, BA1814, dn14 (C&L), p16 (C&L)], MA1817. R. Balcombe, Sussex 1819 (and RD) to death 14/11/1868, leaving £10,000 [C19560] Married Rushton, Northants. 9/1/1823 Janet Booth, with military issue.

SARGEAUNT (John) Born City of London 14/2/1799, s. John Sargeaunt and Henrietta Birch. Christ Church, Oxford 1817, BA1821, MA1824, dn24 (Peterb.), p25 (Lin. for Peterb.). V. (Great) Doddington, Northants. 1825, R. Stanwick, Northants. 1837 to death there 22/1/1858, leaving £14,000 [C76075] Married Marylebone, London 3/7/1821 Sarah Heede, with issue (incl. Sir William Charles Sargeaunt).

SARGENT (John) Born Woollavington, Sussex 8/10/1780, s. John Sargent, *M.P.*, and Charlotte Bettesworth. King's, Cambridge 1799 [adm. Inner Temple 1803] Fellow 1802-4, BA 1804, dn04 (Chich.), p05 (Roch.), MA1807. R. Graffham, Sussex 1805 and R. Woolavington w. Puriton, Som. 1815 to 'natural death. Dom. Chap. to 1st Baron Barham 1813. Dom. Chap. to 1st Baron Barham 1813. Died 3/5/1833 (CCEd says 10/6/1833). [C2212. ODNB. DEB] Married Carlton-in-Lindrick, Notts. 29/11/1804 Mary Smith, w. daughters who married Samuel Wiberforce (Bishop of Oxford), Henry Manning (later a Cardinal, then Sargent's curate), Henry Wilberforce, and George Dudley Ryder.

SAUL (Joseph) Literate: dn11 (Chester), p13 (Chester). PC. Warrington Holy Trinity 1814-45. Died 1845? [C170408] Married Eliza Sawrey, Warton, Lancs., with children after 1811. Major confusion with the Quaker educationalist of the same name at the Greenrow Academy, Wigton, Cumberland.

SAUL (Thomas) Bapt. Lancaster 23/4/1771, s. George Saul and Mary Raincock. St John's, Cambridge 1790, BA1794, dn95 (Ely for Chester), p95 (Chester), MA1797. PC. Wilton in Cleveland (o/w Wilton Chapel in Ellerburn, Yorks. 1797-1844, PC. White Chapel, Lancs. 1808-13. Died Redcar, Yorks. 23/1/1844 [C100187]

SAUMAREZ (James, Hon., *later* **2nd Baron de Saumarez)** Born Guernsey, Channel Islands 9/10/1789, s. Admiral James Saumarez (later 1st Bart., then 1st Baron de Saumarez) and Martha Le Marchant. Christ Church, Oxford 1807, BA 1811, dn12 (Nor.), p13 (Ox.), MA1814. R. Huggate, Yorks. 1825 to death (Cheltenham, a widower) 9/4/1863 aged 73. Will not traced [C2143. Boase] Married 5/10/1814 Mary (dau. Vice-Admiral William Lechmere), *s.p.* Succ. to title 1836.

SAUMAREZ (Paul) Bapt. Newington, Surrey 13/5/1798 [but some say Guernsey, Channel Islands], s. Richard Saumarez and Martha Le Mesurier. Trinity, Oxford 1816, BA1819, dn21 (Glos.), p22 (Glos.). R. Great Easton, Suffolk 1827 to death (a bachelor, Kensington, London) 10/11/1876, leaving £1,500 [C121906]

SAUNDERS (Augustus Page) Born Lewisham, Kent 4/3/1801, s. Robert Saunders and Margaret Keble. Christ Church, Oxford 1819, Student [Fellow] 1823-33, BA1824, dn25 (Ox.), MA1825, p25 (Ox.), BD and DD1842. H/M Charterhouse [School], London 1832-53; V. Ravensthorpe, Northants. 1832-5, V. Tamworth, Warwicks. 1832-54, Dean of Peterborough 1853 [income £1,000] to death. Declined the Deanery of Winchester 1872. Dom. Chap. to Bishop of Oxford, and Bath and Wells 1832. Died 21/7/1878, leaving £30,000 [C21442. Boase] Married Edmonton, Middx. 28/7/1838 Emma Frances Walford, with issue. *F.R.S.* (1833).

SAUNDERS (George Eveleigh) Bapt. Bristol 15/9/1786 (aged 15 months.), s. William Saunders and Catherine Eveleigh. Worcester, Oxford 1803, BA1807, dn08 (B&W), p09 (B&W), MA1810. R. Tarrant Rushton, Dorset

1810 and R. Tarrant Hinton Dorset 1810 to death 8/1/1842 [C48546] Married Tarrant Hinton 22/11/1815 Leonora Diggle, with issue.

SAUNDERS (Isaac) From London, s. Thomas Saunders. St Edmund Hall, Oxford 1800 (aged 19), BA1804, dn04 (London), p05 (London), MA1807. R. St Andrew-by-the-Wardrobe w. St Anne Blackfriars, City of London 1816 to death 1/1/1836 [C121908] Married London 18/6/1805 Jane Dredge, with issue.

SAUNDERS (James) From Highgate, London, s. Thomas Saunders. St John's, Oxford 1788 (aged 18), dn92 (Ox.), p93 (Ox.), BCL 1796, DCL1800, Fellow to 1812. R. Kirtlington, Oxon. 1809 to death 12/7/1838 [C21445]

SAVAGE (Robert) From Dublin, s. Robert Savage. Pembroke, Oxford 1790 (aged 17), BA 1794, dn95 (Salis.), p97 (Peterb. for Salis.), MA 1797. R. Harford, Devon 1802 to death 29/5/1841 [C89399]

SAVILE (George) Bapt. Royston, Yorks. 14/4/1763, s. George Savile (schoolmaster). University, Oxford 1781, BA1785, dn85 (Glos. for York), p87 (York). (first) Curate Shireoaks, Notts. 1810 and R. Howell, Lincs. 1828 to death 17/12/1839 aged 77 [C76112. YCO]

SAWBRIDGE (John Sikes) Born Hackney, London 18/3/1765, s. Henry Sawbridge and Elizabeth Sikes. Christ Church, Oxford 1783 (aged 18), BA1787, dn88 (Salis. for Peterb.), p89 (Peterb.), MA1790. PC. Ryton on Dunsmore, Warwicks. 1814-21 (res.), V. East Haddon, Northants. 1814-30, V. Stretton upon Dunsmore and Princethorpe, Warwicks. 1817-30, R. Welford, Berks. 1830 to death 15/1/1836 [C19754] Married Marnhead, Devon 26/8/1805 Frances Jane Framingham Thruston, and had issue.

SAWYER (William George) Born Devonport, Plymouth 23/6/1802, s. Admiral Sir Herbert Sawyer (*q.v.* ODNB) and Louisa Maria Lloyd. Balliol, Oxford 1820, BA1824, dn25 (B&W), p26 (B&W). Chap. (and patron) of the Donative of Dalby-on-the-Wolds, Leics. 1830 to death (Rugby, Warwicks.) 15/5/1871. No will traced [C40499]

SAY (Francis Edward) Bapt. East Hately, Cambs. 29/9/1763, s. Rev. Francis Say and Diana Morgan. Corpus Christi, Cambridge 1783, BA1788, dn88 (Ely), p89 (Ely), MA1791. V. Ranworth w. Upton >< Norfolk 1793-5, V. Braughing, Herts. 1795 and V. Hately St George 1795 to death. Dom. Chap.. to Mary, Countess of Macclesfield 1795. Died 1846 aged 83. [C100190]

SAY (Henry) Bapt. Downham Market, Norfolk 22/9/1768, s. William and Elisabeth Say. Trinity, Oxford 1786, BA1790, dn92 (Nor.), p93 (Nor.), MA1795. R. North Pickenham w. Houghton on the Hill, Norfolk 1794 to death 10/2/1855 [C115072]

SAYER (John) From Doddington, Kent, s. John Sayer. Merton, Oxford 1805 (aged 17), BA 1811, dn11 (Ex.), p13 (Cant.), MA1829. V. Arlingham, Glos. 1814 to death 28/12/1836 [C146353]

SCALE (Bernard) Born Dublin 1770, s. Barnard Scale (of Boreham, Essex) and Henrietta Ann Letch. St John's, Cambridge 1789, BA1793, dn93 (London), p94 (London), MA1798. V. Braintree, Essex 1796 and R. Willingale Spain, Essex 1804 to death. Dom. Chap. to 2nd Earl of Carhampton 1804. Died 16/5/1852 [C121916] Married (1) Cambridge 24/7/1794 Hannah Goode (d.1846 (2) Braintree 9/1847 Anna Jemima Coote, with issue.

SCARBOROUGH (William) From Lyme Regis, Dorset, s. William Scarborough. Christ Church, Oxford 1821 (aged 20), BA1825, dn25 (Ox.), p25 (Ox.), Chap. 1825-6, MA1828. PC. Market Harborough, Leics. 1826-56. Alive 1875. No will traced [C21448]

SCHNEIDER (Henry) Born Putney, Surrey 14/8/1800, s. Richard William Ulrich Schneider and Mary Eliza Jenings. St John's, Cambridge 1818, BA1822, dn24 (Lin.), p24 (Lin.), MA1825. R. Carlton Scroope, Lincs. (and RD) 1830-75. Died Brislington House, Som. [a private lunatic asylum] 1/9/1880 aged 80, leaving £3,000 [C76116. Kaye] Married Leadenham, Lincs. 31/5/1842 Julia Smith (w) (a clergy dau.).

SCHOLEFIELD (James) Born Henley on Thames, Oxon. 15/11/1789, s. Rev. Nathaniel (an Independent Minister) and Mary Scholefield. Trinity, Cambridge 1809, dn12 (Nor.), BA1813, Fellow 1815-27, MA1816, Regius Professor of Greek, Cambridge 1825-53. PC. Cambridge St Michael 1823-52, Canon of Ely Cathedral 1849 to death (Hastings, Sussex) 4/4/1853 [C115076. ODNB. Boase. DEB. Romilly2. H. Scholefield, *Memoir of the late Rev. James Scholefield* (1844)] Married Luton, Beds. 27/8/1827 Harriet Chase (a clergy dau.), with issue. The Scholefield Greek Prize was established in his memory. 'He seems to have been of a reserved, remote ... even harsh personality' (DEB).

SCHOLEFIELD (Jeremiah) Bapt. Aberford, Yorks. 14/3/1765, s. Jeremiah Scholefield. Trinity, Oxford 1783, BA1787, dn89 (Chester for Ox.), MA1790, p94 (Ox.), BD1799. R. Barton-on-the-Heath, Warwicks. 1808 to death 11/11/1846 [C37557] Married Eltham, Kent 26/9/1809 Margaret Holmes, with issue.

SCHOLEFIELD (Richard Brown) Born Saxton in Elmet, Yorks. 25/1/1784, s. Charles Scholefield (a farmer) and Hannah Brown. Literate: dn18 (York), p19 (York). PC. Ganton, Yorks. 1830 to death 13/11/1841 [C135980. YCO] Married Filey, Yorks. 1/1/1814 Mary Welborn, with clerical son of same name.

SCHOMBERG (Alexander William) Bapt. Seend, Wilts. 26/6/1799, s. Capt. Isaac Schomberg, *R.N.*, and Amelia Brodrick. Magdalen Hall, Oxford 1818, dn22 (Nor.), p23 (Peterb.), SCL 1823, BA1824, MA1825. PC. Stoak, Cheshire 1825-36-, V. Feltham, Middx. 1832, V. and R. Felthorpe w. Ringland, Norfolk 1832-3, R. Edburton (w. Falking), Sussex 1833 to death 3/7/1840 aged 41 [C109438] Married Liverpool 1/2/1828 Anna Maria Randles. Brother below.

SCHOMBERG (John Bathurst) Born London 2/3/1803, s. Capt. Isaac Schomberg, *R.N.*, and Amelia Brodrick. Emmanuel, Cambridge 1821, BA1825, dn26 (Nor.), p27 (Nor.). R. Belton, Suffolk 1830 to death 9/2/1837 [C115078] MarriedWestminster, London 18/2/1836 Margaret Mary Ashworth. Brother above.

SCHREIBER (Thomas) Bapt. Wickham Market, Suffolk 19/10/1794, s. William Schreiber and Mary Sewell. St John's, Cambridge 1813, BA1817, dn18 (Nor..), p19 (Nor..), MA 1820. R. Bradwell on Sea, Essex [net income £1,624] 1820-48. Died Ipswich 15/1/1873 aged 78, leaving £16,000 [C115079] Married St George's Hanover Square, London 10/11/1825 Sarah Maria, (dau. Admiral Bingham, of Lymington, Hants.), with many children.

SCOBELL (Edward) Born Bodmin, Cornwall 20/4/1785, s. Rev. Peter Edwin Scobell and Hannah Sanford. Balliol, Oxford 1801, then Magdalen Hall, dn09 (Ex.), BA1814, MA1827. V. Turville (o/w Turfield), Bucks. 1823, Min. St Peter Vere Street, London (o/w Oxford Chapel) 1832. Died London 9/6/1860, leaving £9,000 [C146354] Married Marylebone, London 4/10/1820 Ann Carter Chessell, with clerical son Sanford George Scobell. Brother John, below.

SCOBELL (George) Born Penzance, Cornwall 24/12/1774, s. George Pender Scobell and Elizabeth Stark. Balliol, Oxford 1792, BA 1796, dn97 (Salis.), p98 (Ox.), MA1800, BD and DD1810. S/M Henley G/S 1814; R. Brattleby, Lincs. 1803, Sequestrator of Pishill, Oxon. and of Nettlebed, Oxon. 1812, V. Turville (o/w Turfield), Bucks. 1812-23, R. Henley on Thames, Oxon. 1823-5 (res.). Died 7/3/1837 [C2222] Married (1) Cheveley, Berks. 13/12/1803 Hannah Stephens (2) Turville 28/7/1825 Ellen Lansdale, with clerical son George Richard Scobell.

SCOBELL (John) Bapt. Bodmin, Cornwall 15/5/1791, s. Rev. Peter Edwin Scobell and Hannah Sanford. Wadham, Oxford 1810, then Balliol 1812-16, BA1813, dn14 (B&W), p15 (B&W for Win.), MA1838. R. Lewes All Saints, Sussex 1821 and R. Lewes St. John the Baptist, Southover 1821 to death 1/9/1867, leaving £25,000 [C40500] Married Silverton, Devon 26/6/1826 Emma Land. Brother Edward, above.

SCORESBY (William) Born Cropton, Whitby, Yorks. 7/10/1789, s. William Scoresby (whaler, arctic explorer and scientist, *q.v.* ODNB) and Lady Mary [*both forenames*] Smith. Before ordination saw naval and whaling service. Edinburgh University (no degree), then Queens', Cambridge 1824 (a Ten Year Man), dn25 (York), p26 (York), BD1834, DD1839. (first) Chap. Liverpool Floating Church for Seamen (o/w the Mariners' Church) 1827-32, PC. Bedford Proprietary Chapel Exeter 1832-9, V. Bradford, Yorks. 1839-47 ('left a broken and disillusioned man'), retired to Torquay, Devon, dying there 25/33/1857 aged 68 [C135727. ODNB and photo. Boase. YCO. DEB. B. Waites, 'William Scoresby, 1789-1857, *Geographers: Bibliographical Studies* 4 (1980). R.E. Scoresby-Jackson, *The life of William Scoresby* (1861)] Married (1) Whitby 25/9/1811 Mary

Eliza Lockwood, 3s (2) Whitby 1828 Eliza Fitzgerald (3) Whitby 1849 Georgiana Kerr [not in BMD]. Meteorologist and oceanographer, one of the founders of the British Association for the Advancement of Science; F.R.S.E. (1819). F.R.S. (1824).

SCOTMAN (Thomas) Bapt. Newmarket, Suffolk 21/6/1749, s. Thomas and Jane Scotman. Christ's, Cambridge 1771, BA1776, dn77 (Peterb.), p78 (C&L), MA1779. V. Fisherton Delamere, Wilts. 1778-93, R. Buckland, Glos. 1793 to death (Rougham, Suffolk) 14/1/1848 aged 93 [C19567] Married Islington, London 20/5/1788 Elizabeth Hand (a clergy dau.).

SCOTT (Alexander) Born Edinburgh 18/4/1781, s. Francis Scott (of Beechwood) and Mary Don. Christ Church, Oxford 1799, BA 1803, dn04 (C&L for Durham), p05 C&L for Durham), MA1810. R. Egremont, Cumberland 1814-35 (res.), R. Whicham, Cumberland 1832-46, R. Bootle, Cumberland 1835 to death. Dom. Chap. to 6th Baron Polworth 1835. Died 30/9/1847 [C19759. Venn notes an identically named man] Married 1807 Agnes, dau. Col. Robert Johnston (Hutton Hall, Berwickshire), with sons Robert Scott, Dean of Rochester (and an admiral).

SCOTT (Alexander John) Born Rotherhithe, London 23/7/1768, s. Lt. Robert Scott, *R.N.*, and Jane Comyns. St John's, Cambridge 1786, BA1790, dn91 (Chich.), p92 (Chich.), MA1806, DD1806. Chaplain *R.N.* 1793-1805 (HMS *Berwick* 1793-5, HMS *St George* 1795, HMS *Britannia*, present at Battle of Copenhagen 1801 on HMS *London*; Private Secretary, Interpreter and Chaplain to Nelson on HMS *Victory* 1803-5 (where he had a library of 650 books on board), and was present at his death ('taking with him a mirror, wardroom table, bureau and fireplace from the famous ship'). Incumbent St John's, Jamaica 1798-1801 (where he was struck by lightning); V. Southminster, Essex 1803 and V. Catterick, Yorks. 1816 to death. Chaplain to Prince of Wales 1801 and Chap. in Ordinary 1816. Died Ecclesfield, Yorks. 24/7/1840 aged 72 [C121924. ODNB] Married 9/7/1807 Mary Frances Ryder (aged 17), 2 dau. (incl. Margaret Gatty, the children's writer). *Wikipedia* has a detailed article with portrait.

SCOTT (Charles Leonard) Bapt. Watton, Norfolk 12/8/1768. King's, Cambridge 1788, dn91 (Lin.), Fellow 1791-9, BA1792, p92 (Lin.), MA1795. R. Wootton Courtenay, Som. 1800-35 (res.). Died (London) 18/4/1845 [C40503 - not Lionel] Wife Nerine (Noreen?), and issue.

SCOTT (George Mallet) Bapt. Plymouth, Devon 23/2/1781, s. James Scott. BNC, Oxford 1796, then Exeter BA1802, dn03 (B&W), p05 (Ex.). PC. Wembury, Devon 1805, PC. Plympton St Maurice, Devon at death 30/12/1850 [C48572]

SCOTT (John) Born Weston Underwood, Bucks. 14/4/1777, s. Rev. Thomas Scott (*q.v.* ODNB) and Jane Kell. Magdalene, Cambridge 1795, BA1799, dn99 (London for York), p01 (York), MA1803. V. North Ferriby, Hull, Yorks. (with S/M Hull G/S) 1801-34 and V. (Kingston upon) Hull St Mary 1816 to death 18/10/1834 (CCEd says 14/11/1834) aged 57 [C103138. ODNB under his father. YCO. DEB] Married St George's Hanover Square, London 21/7/1801 Frances Errington (Newcastle upon Tyne), with clerical son. Brother Thomas, below.

SCOTT (John) From Little Oakley, Essex, s. Rev. Thomas Scott (two below). Lincoln, Oxford 1817 (aged 19), BA1821. R. Little Kimble, Bucks. 1831 ['patronage in dispute'] to death 28/9/1834 [C76128]

SCOTT (Mark) Born *c.* 1771. [MA by 1825 but NiVoF] V. Slawston, Leics. 1825-[47]. Died? [C76129] Married Church Bampton, Northants. 27/8/1804 Jane Bryan, w. issue.

SCOTT (Thomas, sen.) Born Weston Underwood, Bucks. 24/6/1779 (*or* 9/11/1780), s. Rev. Thomas Scott, sen. and Jane Kell. Queens', Cambridge 1800, BA1805, dn06 (Lin.), p06 (Lin.), MA1809. PC. Gawcott, Bucks. 1806-33, R. Little Kimble, Lincs. 1830-31, R. Wappenham, Northants. 1833 to death 24/2/1835 [C76134. ODNB] Married Bledlow, Bucks. 25/3/1806 Euphemia Lynch (of Antigua, West Indies), 13 ch., incl. Thomas (below), and Sir George Gilbert Scott, architect (*q.v.* ODNB). Brother John, above.

SCOTT (Thomas) Bapt. Watton, Norfolk 28/1/1767, s. Thomas and Ann Scott. Corpus Christi, Cambridge 1784, BA1789, dn89 (Nor.). R. Weeley, Essex 1800-6, R. Little Oakley, Essex 1794-30, R. Wix (o/w Weeks), Essex (a family living) 1800-[37]. Died? [C115168] Great confusion with the other two Thomas Scotts here.

SCOTT (Thomas, jun.) Born Gawcott, Bucks. 21/4/ 1810, s. Rev. Thomas Scott, sen. (above) and Euphemia Lynch. Queens', Cambridge 1825, BA1829, Fellow 1830, dn30 (Nor.), p31 (Ox.), MA1832. R. Nether Broughton, Leics. 1831-46, V. Isleham, Cambs. 1831-56, (succ. his father as) PC. Gawcott, Bucks. 1833-4 (res.), R. Onehouse, Suffolk 1834-46, (succ. his father as) R. Wappenham, Northants. 1835 (and Hon. Canon of Peterborough Cathedral 1879) to death 7/6/1880 aged 73, leaving £6,000 [C21450] Married Aylesbury, Bucks. 2/1/1861 Eliza Langston, with clerical s. (another) Thomas Scott. Potential confusion here.

SCOTT (Thomas Hobbes) Born Kelmscott, Oxon. 17/4/1783, s. Rev. James Scott and Jane Elizabeth Hamood. St. Alban Hall, Oxford 1813, MA1818, dn21 (Glos.), p21 (Glos.). Secretary to the Commission on NSW 1819-21, Archdeacon of New South Wales (then in the Diocese of Calcutta) 1824-9, salary £2,000. R. Whitfield, Northumberland 1822 (and Hon. Canon of Durham 1845) to death (unm.) 1/1/1860, leaving £800 [C130565] *Australian Dictionary of Biography Online Edition* has further references.

SCRATTON (Thomas Scott) Bapt. Hackney, London 7/1/1800, s. John Scratton and Abigail Cotton. Christ's, Cambridge 1818, BA1824, dn24 (London), p26 (London), MA1827. R. (Great) Sutton, Essex 1826 to death (Southend, Essex) 27/3/1877, leaving £25,000 [C121944] Married 23/2/1830 Mary Swaine (North Shoebury, Essex), with issue.

SCURR (Thomas) Bapt. Wigton, Cumberland 23/11/1768, s. Jonathan Scurr and Elizabeth Robinson. Literate: dn93 (York), p94 (Car. for York). PC. Thockrington, Northumberland 1815, PC. Allendale, Northumberland 1822 (w. H/M Hexham Free G/S 1809-33) to death 26/1/1836 aged 68 at Broadwood Hall, Allendale (where he had a boarding school) [C6286. YCO] Married Carlisle 21/10/1795 Sarah Simpson, with issue.

SEAGER (John) Born Bristol 28/3/1776, s. John Seager. Pembroke, Oxford 1798 (aged 22), BA1802, dn02 (Glos.), p03 (Heref.). R. Welsh Bicknor, Monmouth 1808. Died 27/5/1849 [C163383] Married Evesbatch, Worcs. 3/4/1806 Mary Lingen (a clergy dau.), w. clerical sons John Osborne, and Charles (later RC) Seager.

SEAGRAM (John) From Warminster, Wilts., s. John Seagram. Exeter, Oxford 1791 (aged 17), BA1795, p96 (Salis.), p01 (Salis.), MA1803. PC. Stroud, Glos. 1804-33, R. Godmanston, Dorset 1815-24 (res.), V. Aldbourne, Wilts. 1832 to death 28/8/1852 [C53813]

SEAGRAVE (John) Born 15/1/1771, s. Rev. Edward Seagrave, Oxhill, Warwicks. Worcester, Oxford 1788, BA1792, dn93 (Wor.), MA1795. p95 (Wor.). R. Tysoe w. Compton Wynwates, Warwicks. 1795-1821 (res.), R. Whiston, Northants. 1801-5, R. Castle Ashby, Northants. 1805-36, R. Westcote Barton, Oxon. 1813 to death. Dom. Chap. to 9th Earl of Northampton 1801-13. Died 21/4/1836 [C122115]

SEAGRAVE (Samuel Young) From Halford Bridge, Warwicks., s. Rev. John Seagrave. Oriel, Oxford 1814 (aged 18), then Magdalen Hall, BA1818, dn18 (Peterb.), p19 (Peterb.), MA1820. V. Tysoe w. Compton Wynyates, Warwicks. 1821 and R. (and patron of) Westcote Barton, Oxon. 1836 to death 30/12/1851 [C110868] Married Wakefield, Yorks. 21/7/1821 Henrietta Tooke, w. clerical s. John Young Seagrave succeeding at Westcote Barton.

SEALE (John Barlow) Bapt. Derby 23/2/1753, s. Rev. John and Sarah Seale. Emmanuel, Cambridge 1769, then Christ's 1773, BA1774, dn74 (Cant.), Fellow 1774, p74 (Ely), MA1777, DD1789, etc. R. Great Poringland, Norfolk 1779-92, V. Stisted, Essex 1792 and R. Anstey, Herts. 1806 to death. Sometime Chap. to Abp of Canterbury. Died 11/8/1838 [C100193] *F.R.S.* 1786.

SEDGEWICK, SEDGWICK (James) From Dent, Yorks. [NiVoF] V. Caxton, Cambs. 1797-1830 (res.), V. Curry Rivel, Som. 1799 to death 8/5/1834 (CCEd says 27/5/1834) aged 91.[C40514] Married Whitehaven 23/5/1782 Elizabeth Watts, w. issue.

SEDGWICK (Adam) Born Dent, Yorks. 22/3/1785, s. Rev. Richard Sedgwick and Margaret Sturgis. Trinity, Cambridge 1803, BA1808, Fellow 1810, MA1811, dn17 (Nor. for Bristol), p18 (Salis.), Hon.DCL Oxford 1860, Hon.LLD1866. Woodwardian Professor of Geology, Cambridge 1818-73. V. Shudy Camps, Cambs. 1824-32 (res.), Canon of 5th Prebend in Norwich Cathedral 1834 to death. Chap. to HRH Duke of Sussex 1819. Died (unmarried)

27/1/1873, leaving £4,000 [C1111. ODNB. Boase. DEB. J.W. Clark & T.M. Hughes, *The life and letters of the Reverend Adam Sedgwick* (Cambridge, 1890. 2 vols.). C. Speakman, *Adam Sedgwick* (1982)] F.R.S. (1830), etc., etc. Brother John, below.

SEDGWICK (John) Born Horton in Ribblesdale, Yorks. 22/3/1749, s. Stephen Sedgwick and Jane Bateson. Literate: dn73 (Chester), p74 (Chester). Chap. Howgill Chapel, Sedbergh, Yorks. 1773 (with S/M Howgill Free G/S 1791) to death 26/3/1836 aged 87 [C170427] Married Sedbergh 23/7/1773 Mary Moore, with issue.

SEDGWICK (John) Bapt. Sedbergh, Dent, Yorks. 16/10/1791, s. Rev. Richard Sedgwick and Margaret Sturgis. St John's, Cambridge 1809, BA1814, dn15 (Lin.), p16 (Lin.), MA 1817. V. Dent 1822-59, PC. Crook, Westmorland 1840. Died Dent 9/2/1859 aged 67, leaving £2,000 [C76146] Married Dent 18/4/1822 Jane Davoren (w), with clerical son. *J.P.* West Riding; brother of Adam Sedgwick, the geologist (above.)

SELKIRK (Thomas) Born Beckermet, Cumberland, s. Robert Selkirk and Susannah Kitchin. Literate: dn12 (Chester), p13 (Chester). PC. Penwortham, Lancs. 1814-19 (res.), PC. Bury St John's, Lancs. 1822-32. Died 20/2/1834 aged 45 (CCEd says 16/4/1834) [C170434] Married Ponsonby, Cumberland 1/1/1810 Bridget Gunson, with issue.

SELWYN (Edward) Bapt. Gloucester 23/4/1793, s. Henry Charles Selwyn and Sarah Thomson. [In Royal Artillery 1808-14] St Catharine's, Cambridge 1814, dn23 (Chester), p23 (Win. for Roch.), BA1824, MA1840. V. Ruddington, Notts. 1823-38, PC. Edwalton, Notts. 1833-8, R. Hemingford Abbotts, Hunts. 1838-65. Died there 14/9/1867 aged 73, leaving £600 [C2220. Romilly2 entry for 23/8/1850] Married (1) Bromley, Kent 2/9/1818 Frances Simons (d.1848, a clergy dau., of Granborough, Warwicks.), with clerical son (2) Hemingford Gray, Hunts. 3/1/1850 Fanny Margetts.

SELWYN (Townshend) Born Gloucester 10/6/1782, s. Henry Charles Selwyn and Sarah Thomson. Christ Church, Oxford 1800, BA 1804, MA1806, dn07 (Glos.), p08 (Glos.). R. Melbury Bubb, Dorset 1810-11, V. Milton Clevedon, Som. 1811-53, Canon Gloucester Cathedral 1814-53, V. Churcham w. Bulley, Glos. 1824, R. Kilmington, Som. 1837 to death 31/5/1853 [C40516] Married Burnham, Bucks. 16/6/1812 Charlotte Sophia Murray (dau. of a Bishop of Rochester), with clerical son Sydney George Selwyn (and an admiral).

SELWYN (William) Born 19/2/1806, s. William Selwyn (barrister) and Letitia Frances Kynaston. St John's, Cambridge 1823, BA1828, dn29 (Ely), Fellow 1829-32, MA1831, p31 (Roch.), incorporated at Oxford 1831, BD 1849, DD1864, Lady Margaret Professor of Divinity, Cambridge 1855-75. R. Branston, Leics. 1831-46, 6th Prebend in Ely Cathedral 1833-75, V. Melbourne, Cambs. 1846-53. Chap. in Ordinary 1859. Died 24/4/1875, leaving £60,000 [C20278. ODNB. Boase] Married 22/8/1832 Juliana Elizabeth Cooke. *F.R.S.* (1866), *F.R.A.S.*

SENHOUSE (James Lowther) Born Barbados 12/12/1793, s. William Senhouse (Surveyor-General there) and Elizabeth Ward Wood (also of Barbados). Trinity, Cambridge 1811, BA1815, MA1818 [adm. Student Inner Temple 1818] dn21 (London), p22 (Chester for London). PC. Ponsonby, Cumberland 1822-9 (res.), PC. Wilne w. Draycott 1823 and V. Sawley, Derbys. 1823-44, R. Gosforth, Cumberland 1827-35 (res.). Died Sawley 5/9/1844 [C22054] Married Kingston upon Thames, Surrey 7/1/1824 Elizabeth Brooks, with issue.

SENKLER (Edmund John) Born Docking, Norfolk 4/3/1802, s. Charles Senkler and Mary Edwards. Trinity, Cambridge 1820, then Caius 1821, BA1824, MA1827, p27 (Nor.). V. Barmer, Norfolk [no church] 1829. Emigrated to Brockville, Toronto, Canada 1843, dying there 28/10/1872 [C115179] Married Westminster, London 18/1/1837 Eleanor Elizabeth Stevens (a clergy dau.), 9 ch. Astronomer and meteorologist:

SERGEANT (Oswald) Bapt. Manchester 28/5/1800, s. William Sergeant. St John's, Cambridge 1818, BA1823, dn23 (Lin.), p24 (Chester), MA1826. (first) PC. Salford St Philip 1825-33 (res.), Fellow Manchester Collegiate Church 1830, then Canon Residentiary Manchester Cathedral 1847 to death. Dom. Chap. to Marquess of Stafford 1830. Died 12/2/1854 aged 53 [C76157] Married 1/5/1835 Alice Hewett, with clerical son. Financially astute, he ran the financial affairs of the Collegiate Church; 'He was a spare, consumptive looking man, rather bald, and of an irritable temperament'.

SERGROVE (John Sympson) Born Hackney, London 26/6/2790, s. Thomas Cox Sergrove and Mary Usher. Pembroke, Oxford 1806, then Emmanuel, Cambridge 1811, LLB1813, dn13 (Ely), p15 (London). R. Cooling, Kent 1818, Chap. of Carlisle [Proprietary] Chapel, Lambeth 1821-35, R. St Mary Somerset w. St Mary Mounthaw, London 1823 to death. Dom. Chap. to 2nd Earl of Caledon 1814. Died 9/8/1857 [C2223] Married (1) Shoreditch, London 8/8/18122 Anna Smith (d.1837), w. issue (2) Bloomsbury, London 20/3/1838 Margaret Moseley.

SERJEANT (John) [NiVoF] PC. Egloskerry w. Tremaine, Cornwall 1826 to death 5/6/1846 aged 85 [C146363 and probably 233235]

SERJEANTSON (James) Bapt. Wakefield, Yorks. 13/8/1771, s. William Serjeantson (Hanlith Hall, Yorks.) and Elizabeth Hobson. Glasgow University 1786-90; St John's, Cambridge 1789, BA1794, dn95 (Bristol for York), p96 (York), MA1804. R. Kirby Knowle, Yorks. 1797-1842, PC. York St Denys with St George, Naburn 1815-30, R. Kildale, Yorks. 1830 to death. Dom. Chaplain to 1st Baron Curzon (later 1st Viscount Curzon) from 1815. Died Kirby Knowle 6/9/1842. Married York 17/10/1796 Mary Bell (dau. of Peter Bell, Thirsk Hall, Ripon), w. clerical s., also Peter. [C53816. YCO]

SERJEANTSON (Robert James) Born Hull 8/9/1803, s. Major Robert Serjeantson and Isabella Dorman. Literate: dn26 (York), p27 (York). V. Snaith, Yorks. 1829 to death 30/10/1861 aged 58 ('found dead in bed - paralysis - cerebral effusion without evidence of violence'), leaving £1,500 [C135729. YCO] Married Walcot, Bath 29/10/1828 Maria Charlotte, dau. Vice-Admiral Volant Vashon Ballard (Coutes Hall, Yorks.), with clerical son William James Serjeantson

SERLE (Philip) From Heckfield, Hants. 18/11/1783, s. Ambrose and Martha Serle. Trinity, Oxford 1800, BA1803, Fellow to 1818, MA1807, dn07 (Bristol for London), p09 (Ox.), BA1816. R. Oddington, Oxon. 1818 to death 31/3/1857 [C21460] Wife Elizabeth. 'A grumbling, ill-conditioned, indolent, old, undogmatical and ... rather sceptical priest' (Wilberforce).

SERRELL (Henry Digby) Bapt. Fulham, London 6/4/1807, s. John Serrell and Elizabeth Dean. Queen's, Oxford 1822, dn28 (Win.), BA 1828, p29 (Win. for Bristol), MA1833. R. Podimore, Som. 1832-90. Died (Bath) 17/12/1896 aged 91 years, leaving £945-7s-5d. [C52468] Married Bath 6/4/1843 Laura Anne Armstrong, with issue. 'A great huntsman'.

SERRELL (Samuel) Bapt. Portland, Dorset 12/6/1763, s. John Serrell. Magdalen, Oxford 1780, then Merton, BA1784, dn88 (Salis.), p89 (Salis.). V. Wells St Cuthbert 1798-1832 (res.), living at Durnford House, Langton Maltravers, Dorset. Died 21/3/1842 [C40520] Married Kilmington, Som. 2/9/1808 Harriet Digby (dau. of a Dean of Worcester), with issue.

SERRES (John Edmund Dominick) Born Marylebone, London 21/7/1791, s. Dominick Michael Serres and Lucretia Madden. Queens', Cambridge 1818, BA1822, dn22 (Chester for York), p23 (York). PC. Eastbourne, Sussex 1823 and R. Lynch, Sussex 1823 to death (Alton, Southampton) 8/10/1861, leaving £600 [C170435. YCO] Married Chichester 18/4/1842 his cousin Elizabeth Madden, with clerical son.

SETTLE (Samuel) Bapt. Batley, Yorks. 4/12/1767 (in a Congregational Chapel), s. Joseph and Mary Settle. Magdalene, Cambridge 1794, BA1798, dn98 (Car. for York), p99 (York), MA1801. V. Winterbourne Stoke, Wilts. 1816, and R. Berwick St James, Wilts. 1817 to death. Dom. Chap. to 2nd Baron Headley 1817. Buried 18/3/1847 [C76160. YCO]

SETTLE (William) Trinity, Cambridge 1787, BA1791, dn91 (Lin.), p92 (Lin.). V. Great Sturton, Lincs. 1796 to death 4/7/1848 [C76161] Married Tealby, Lincs. 1798 Ann Dunn, with issue.

SEVERNE (Francis) Bapt. Abberley, Worcs. 6/3/1785, s. Rev. Francis Severne, sen. and Jane Seward. Magdalen Hall, Oxford 1803, then Sidney, Cambridge 1808, LLB1810, dn10 (York for Heref.), p11 (Heref.). R. Abberley, Heref. 1828 and R. Kyre Wyard, Heref. 1828 to death 16/6/1865, leaving £3,000 [C122118. YCO] Was married.

SEWELL (William) Bapt. Brigham, Cumberland 26/10/1748. Literate: dn71 (Car.), p74 (Car. for Chester). PC. Setmurthy, Cumberland 1778-1834 (with S/M there) and PC. Wythop,

Cumberland 1792 to death (Lorton, Cumberland) 26/2/1834 aged 85 (CCEd says 13/3/1834) [C6295]

SEWELL (William) Born Shap, Westmorland 2/12/1781, s. James Sewell and Margaret Whitesmith. Literate: dn05 (Car.), p06 (Car.). S/M Ambleside Free G/S, Westmorland 1812-27-; PC. Troutbeck, Windermere, Westmorland 1828 to death 31/7/1869 aged 88, leaving £450 [C6296] Married Bowness, Windermere 2/7/1816 Mary Collinson, with issue.

SEWELL (William) Born Newport, IoW 23/1/1804, s. Thomas Sewell (solicitor). Merton, Oxford 1822, BA1827, then Exeter, Fellow 1827-74, MA1829, dn30 (Ox.), p31 (Win.), Tutor 1831-53, BD1841, DD1857, etc. Whyte's Professor of Moral Philosophy, Oxford 1836-41. PC. St Nicholas in the Castle, Carisbrooke, IoW 1831 to death. Died (unmarried, Litchford Hall, Manchester, the house of his nephew) 14/11/1874, leaving £600 [C21461. ODNB. Boase] An early Tractarian, he dissociated himself from them because of his intense anti-Catholicism! Helped found St Columba's College, Rathfarnham, Dublin 1843 ('a sort of Irish Eton', Warden 1853-61), and also Radley College, Oxon. 1847; but debts caused the sequestration of his Oxford fellowship, obliging him to live in Germany 1862-70. Enormous list of publications in CR65.

SEYMER (George Augustus) From Alresford, Hants., s. Henry Seymer and Grizelda Ker. Oriel, Oxford 1803 (aged 18), BA1808, dn09 (Salis.), p09 (Salis.), MA1810. R. Iwerne Courtney (o/w Shroton), Dorset 1810, R. Burton Bradstock w. Shipton George, Dorset 1812 (depr.), PC. Winchester Holy Trinity 1854 to death. Dom. Chap. to 2nd Baron Rivers 1811. Died Shroton (a widower) 9/6/1861, leaving £4,000 [C53818] Married (1) Stourpaine, Dorset 18/5/1812 Isabella Mary Bastard (d.1821) (2) Walcot, Bath 8/3/1826 Susannah Elizabeth Birch.

SEYMOUR, *later* CULME-SEYMOUR (John Hobart Culme-, Sir, 2nd Bart.) Born Plymouth 24/3/1800, s. Admiral Sir Michael Seymour, 1st Bart. and Jane Hawker. Exeter, Oxford 1817, BA1821, dn23 (Chester), MA 1824, p24 (Chester). V. Horley w. Hornton, Oxon. 1824-53, Prebend of Leicester St Margaret in Lincoln Cathedral 1827-80, Canon Residentiary of Gloucester Cathedral 1829-80, R. Berkhampstead St Mary (o/w Northchurch), Herts. 1830 to death. Chap. in Ordinary to Queen Victoria 1827-80. Died 17/9/1880 [total income £1,052], leaving £15,000 [C65371. Boase] Married (1) 12/4/1833 Elizabeth Culme (a clergy dau.), with military issue (2) 10/2/1844 Maria Laura Smith, with further issue. Succ. to title 1834; name changed 1842.

SEYMOUR (Thomas) Bapt. Bridport, Dorset 27/7/1763, s. Richard and Elizabeth Seymour. Wadham, Exeter 1784, BA1788, dn88 (Bristol), p91 (Lin.). R. Woodsford, Dorset 1802 and PC. Tincleton, Dorset 1802 to death 28/6/1849 [C53819] Married Gillingham, Dorset 16/12/1794 Jane Green, with issue.

SHACKLETON (Henry John) Bapt. Highgate, London 10/3/1803, s. Thomas Shackleton (an Enfield seed factor). Trinity, Cambridge 1823, BA1827, MA1830. V. Plumstead, Kent 1828-53, V. Rothley, Leics. 1853 to death (Scarbrough, Yorks.) 13/11/1869, leaving £60,000 [C488] Married Camden, London 25/1/1831 Anna Hallett (West Chalborough, Dorset), with issue.

SHAFTO (John Duncombe) Born Whitworth, Co. Durham 16/5/1807, s. Robert (Eden) Duncombe Shafto and Catherine Eden. BNC, Oxford 1826, BA1830, dn30 (Chester), p31 (Chester). MA1832. R. Buckworth, Hunts. 1831, R. Morborne, Hunts. 1833, R. Brancepeth, Durham 1840-54, Hon Canon of Durham Cathedral 1849. Dom. Chap. to Isabella Ann, Marchioness of Hertford 1833. Died Buckworth 6/8/1863, leaving £30,000 [C76163] Married Hunton, Kent 10/4/1834 Catherine Harriet Moore, with issue.

SHANN (Timothy Metcalf) Born Tadcaster, Yorks. 28/3/1766, s. Thomas Shann (surgeon and apothecary) and Mary Metcalf. St John's, Cambridge 1785, BA1789, dn89 (York), p90 (York), MA1790. V. Hampsthwaite, Yorks. 1790-1839, V. Wighill, Yorks. 1800-39, PC. Healaugh, Yorks. 1800-14 (res.). Died Hampsthwaite 3/6/1839, *s.p.* [C101768. YCO]

SHAPCOTT (Thomas Lawes) Bapt. Sutton Veney, Wilts 30/12/1795, s. James Shapcott and Ann Lawes. St Alban Hall, Oxford 1813, BA 1818, dn18 (Ex. for Win.), p19 (Chester for Win.), then Magdalen Hall, MA1826. S/M Southampton G/S 1819; PC. East Kennett, Wilts. 1821-3 (res.), V. Southampton St Michael

1825 to death. Chap. to Southampton Gaol and to Royal Southern Yacht Club. Died 22/8/1854 [C89413] Married (1) Sutton Veney 15/7/1825 Jemima Long (d.1833), w. issue (2) Axbridge, Som. 1847 (2nd q.) Jane Verney.

SHARP, born BOWLT (Andrew) Bapt. Hartburn, Northumberland 2/1/1757, s. William Bowlt. Literate: dn80 (Durham), p83 (Car. for Durham). PC. Tweedmouth 1790, PC. Bamburgh, Northumberland 1791 and PC. Lucker, Northumberland 1810 to death (Clare Hall, Herts.) 29/6/1835 (CCEd thus) aged 77 [C4529 as Bowlt / C130654 as Sharp] Married London 6/8/1817 Catherine Sharp, with issue.

SHARP (Reginald) Born Kentmere, Westmorland 23/3/1759, s. Reginald and Elizabeth Sharp. Literate: dn92 (Chester), p93 (Chester). S/M Crosthwaite cum Lyth G/S to 1795, PC. Copp, St Michael upon Wyre, Lancs. 1804-[41]. Buried Cockerham, Lancs. 20/9/1845 [C170455] Married Garstang, Lancs. 16/2/1801 Cicely Thornton.

SHARP (Samuel) Bapt. Gildersome, Leeds 3/9/1773, s. John Sharp and Margaret Hey. Magdalene, Cambridge 1791, BA1796, dn96 (York), p97 (Lin.), MA1799. PC. Edale, Derbys. 1807-10, V. Wakefield, Yorks. 1810 to death 9/3/1855 [C19776. YCO] Married Birkin, Yorks. 27/2/1810 Margaret Alderson, with clerical son John Sharp.

SHARPE (Francis William) Born Alfreton, Derbys., s. Rev. John Robert Sharpe and Mary Elizabeth Turbutt. Emmanuel, Cambridge 1821, BA1825, dn28 (C&L), p29 (C&L). PC. Monyash, Derbys. 1829-41, PC. Temple Normanton, Derbys. 1842 and V. Tibshelf, Derbys. 1849 to death 15/10/1873 aged 69, leaving £18,000 [C19570] Married Chesterfield, Derbys. 16/9/1834 Mary Ann Jebb (w), with issue.

SHARPE (John) Born Dorking, Surrey 11/6/1769, s. Rev. John (Independent Minister) and Mary Sharpe. Trinity, Oxford 1788, BA 1792. PC. Shipley, Sussex 1822, R. Castle Eaton, Wilts. 1847 to death 27/12/1859, leaving £800 [C65375] Married Clarissa Petrie (w.), w. issue.

SHARPE (John) Born Dunblane, Perthshire 5/11/1790, s. John and Jane Sharpe. Literate: dn13 (York), p16 (York), then Sidney, Cambridge 1816, a Ten Year Man (BD 1826), DD 1831. V. Doncaster St George, Yorks. (and Preacher throughout the Diocese of York) 1817 [the church burnt down in 1853 and was entirely rebuilt], V. Brodsworth, Yorks. 1827 (with Prebend of Grindal in York Minster 1841 and RD) to death (Doncaster, a widower) 25/7/1860 aged 69, leaving £3,000 [C135732. YCO] Married Thirsk, Yorks. 27/9/1814 Sarah Falconer, with 11 ch. (some clerical) all listed online: www.natgould.org/john_sharpe_1792-1860

SHARPE (Lancelot) Bapt. City of London 6/9/1774, s. Lancelot Sharpe (merchant) and Sarah Till. Pembroke, Cambridge 1792, BA 1796, dn97 (Cant.), p98 (Cant.), MA1800. S/M Merchant Taylors' School 1807-19; H/M St Saviour's G/S Southwark, Surrey 1829-45; PC. All Hallows Staining, City of London 1802-51, Prebend of St Pauls Cathedral, London 1843 to death. Chap. to the Grocers' and Salters' Company. Died 26/10/1851 [C121949. Boase] Married (1) before 1804 Jane Mary Harrison (d.1823), many ch. (2) Edmonton, Middx. 5/4/1825 Mary Tweed, with further issue. *F.S.A.* 1813.

SHARPE (William) Bapt. Holt, Norfolk 28/6/1779, s. Rev. Jeremiah Sharpe (R. West Newton, Norfolk) and Anne Brereton. Queens', Cambridge 1806, BA1810, p10 (Nor.), MA1813. V. Cromer, Norfolk 1831-52 (res. when his sight failed). Died 6/8/1862, leaving £3,000 [C109446. DEB] Married Weasenham St Peter, Suffolk 26/6/1810 his first cousin Mary Hewitt, *s.p.*

SHARPE (William) [MA but NiVoF]. Chap. of Donative of Pattiswick, Essex 1831 to death 22/4/1835 (CCEd thus) [C121951 and other possibilities such as the above?]

SHAW (Edward) Bapt. Clerkenwell, London 17/1/1756, s. of Edward (a printer) and Catherine Shaw. Pembroke, Cambridge 1775, BA1780, dn80 (London), p81 (Lin. for London), MA1784. R. Woodham Walter, Essex 1793, V. Kirkleatham, Yorks. 1811 to death (Leeds) 11/10/1838 [C76181 has 2 men here and the death date of another man]

SHAW (Edward Butterworth) Born Halifax, Yorks. 8/7/1797, s. George (a surgeon) and Ellen Shaw. Caius, Cambridge 1813, BA1819, dn20 (York), p21 (York), MA1823. (first) PC. Manchester St Matthew 1825-35, R. Narborough, Leics. 1835 (and RD of Guthlaxton) to death (Prinknash, Glos.) 25/5/1880 aged 82, leaving £7,000 [C76183. YCO] Married (1) Manchester 19/1/1826 Elizabeth Williams (2) 19/9/1872 Susan, dau. of Col. Ackers, of Prinknash Park.

SHAW (John) From Lancaster, s. John Shaw. Lincoln, Oxford 1792 (aged 19), BA1796, p98 (B&W), MA1800. V. Bengeworth, Worcs. 1803 to death 8/12/1854 [C48623] Wife Elizabeth Maria in 1851.

SHAW (John) From Leics., s. of a clergyman. St John's, Cambridge 1821 (aged 18), BA1826, then Jesus, dn26 (Ely), Fellow 1826-8 (res.), p27 (Ely), MA1834. R. Conington, Cambs. 1830-41, V. Stoke Poges, Bucks. 1841 to death (Fen Drayton, Cambs.) 23/5/1866, leaving £3,000 [C76186] Married Grantham, Lincs. 22/7/1828 Elizabeth Batson (w), with clerical son John Shaw (in Australia).

SHAW (John Campbell) Born Jamaica, s. David Shaw and Henrietta Campbell. Literate: dn28 (Car.), p29 (Car.). PC. Ennerdale, Cumberland 1831 to death. Buried 28/4/1847 aged 45 [C6303. Platt] Married Holme Cultram, Cumberland 24/4/1823 Rebecca Saul (dau. of a Quaker educationalist), 10 ch.

SHAW (Joseph) From Bexley, Kent, s. John Shaw. BNC, Oxford 1796 (aged 18), BA1799, dn00 (Salis.), p02 (Win.). R. High Ham, Som. 1803 to death 18/7/1851 [C40526]

SHAW (Robert William) Born Kenward, Kent 4/10/1804, s. Sir John Gregory Shaw, 5th Bart. and Hon. Theodosia Margaret Monson. Christ Church, Oxford 1822, BA1826, dn28 (London), p29 (London), MA1831. R. Cuxton, Kent 1831-73, Hon. Canon of Rochester Cathedral 1851 and first RD in the Diocese. Dom. Chap. to Lord Gardner. Died 28/12/1873 aged 69, leaving £3,000 [C7035] Married St George's Hanover Square, London 18/2/1830 Sophia Cornwall (w), with clerical son Robert John.

SHEATH (Martin) Born Boston, Lincs. 17/11/1773, s. Abraham Sheath and Martha Norman. Trinity, Cambridge 1792, BA1797, dn97 (Lin.), p98 (Lin.), MA1800. R. Wyberton, Lincs. (and Preacher throughout the Diocese of Lincoln) 1821 to death 4/4/1859, leaving £16,000 [C76194] Married Boston 30/12/1800 Catherine Kenrick (d.1810), with issue (2) St James, Westminster, London 29/5/1813 Mary Arnall Gerburgh.

SHEEN (Samuel) Born Covent Garden, London 17/11/1793, s. Samuel and Hester Sheen. Balliol, Oxford 1812, BA1815, MA 1818. R. (and patron) of Stanstead, Suffolk 1823 to death 23/8/1867, leaving £20,000 [C76197] Wife Louisa, and clerical son of his name.

SHEEPSHANKS (John) Bapt. Linton in Craven, Yorks. 16/6/1765, s. Richard Sheepshanks and Susanna Garside. Trinity, Cambridge 1782, BA1787, dn87 (Nor.), Fellow 1789, p93 (Lin.), MA1790, Tutor 1799. PC. Leeds Holy Trinity 1802-44, V. Wymeswold, Leics. 1802-25, Archdeacon of Cornwall 1826-44, Min. Torquay Proprietary Chapel, Devon 1823, V. St Gluvias w. St Budock, Cornwall [blank in ERC] 1824 to death 17/12/1844 aged 79 [C76198] Married St Gluvias Maria Anderson.

SHEFFIELD (Charles [Robert]) Born London 19/10/1797, s. Rev. Sir Robert Sheffield, 3rd Bart. and Sarah Ann Kennet. Christ Church, Oxford 1817, BA1820, dn20 (Lin.), p22 (Lin.), MA1824. R. Flixborough w. Burton on Stather, Lincs. (and RD) 1822 to death 20/2/1882, leaving £38,334-9s-11d. [C76200] Married Alkborough, Lincs. 2/11/1820 Lucy Smelt (a military dau.), w. issue.

SHEIL (John) Literate: dn04 (Heref.), p05 (Heref.). PC. Cannock, Staffs. 1811 to death 24/8/1841 [C22055]

SHEILD see also **SHIELD**

SHELFORD (William Heard) Born Tuddenham, Norfolk 9/1798, s. Rev. Leonard Shelford and Ellen Grigson. Emmanuel, Cambridge 1815, BA1820, Fellow 1822, MA1823, dn29 (Ely), p29 (Lin. for Ely). V. (and patron) of Preston, Suffolk 1829 to death 1854 (1st q.) [C76202] Married Brent Eleigh, Suffolk 3/5/1832 Emily Frost Snape (a clergy dau.), with son Sir William Shelford, civil engineer (q.v. ODNB).

SHEPHARD (Thomas) Born Speen, Berks., s. Rev. Thomas, sen. and Elizabeth Shephard. BNC, Oxford 1774 (aged 16), BA1778, then Magdalene, Cambridge 1782, MA1782, p82 (Lin.), DD1828. PC. Hadnall, Shropshire 1786-1835, R. Enborne, Berks. 1789-1816, R. West Woodhay, Berks. 1798, R. West Felton, Shropshire 1816-17 (res.), R. Crux Easton, Hants. 1827 [C108765], R. Inkpen, Berks. 1828. Died 1843 (1st q.) aged 85 [C19785. Foster corrected] Had issue.

SHEPHERD (Edward John) Born Beverley, Yorks., s. Francis Shepherd. Adm. Gray's Inn 1820. Caius, Cambridge 1821, then Trinity 1821, BA1825, dn27 (Lin.), p27 (Roch.), MA 1839. R. Trottiscliffe, Kent 1827-74, R. Luddesdown, Kent 1834-56. Dom. Chap. to 7th Viscount Torrington 1834. Died 28/11/1874, leaving £7,000 [C526. Boase] Married Wateringbury, Kent 30/4/1836 Catherine Heyman Lucas, 3s. LNCP photo. online.

SHEPHERD (George) Bapt. Faversham, Kent 29/8/1766, s. John and Frances Shepherd. University, Oxford 1784, BA1788, dn90 (Bristol), MA1790, p90 (Cant.), Fellow 1794, Tutor 1798-1808, BD1807, DD1820. R. St Bartholomew by the Exchange, City of London 1807 to death 3/9/1849 [C53823]

SHEPHERD (John) Born Beckermet, Cumberland, s. Richard Shepherd. Literate: dn73 (Car.), p74 (Car.). PC. Mungrisdale, Greystoke, Cumberland 1805 to death 8/10/1836 aged 88 [C6306. Platt] Married Greystoke 21/10/1793 Ann Buckbarrow, with issue.

SHEPHERD (Thomas Henry) Born Brandesburton, Yorks. 2/12/1778, s. Rev. Henry Shepherd and Naomi Colyman. St John's, Cambridge 1797, BA1801, dn01 (York), migrated to BNC, Oxford 1802, p02 (Ox.), Fellow1802-11, MA1803. R. Clayworth, Notts. 1810-73 (with RD of Southwell and Prebend of Beckingham in Southwell Collegiate Church 1830), R. South Wheatley, Notts. 1838 to death. Dom. Chap. to 1st Earl of Harewood 1812. Died Clayworth 11/2/1873 aged 94 (the last surviving member of the unreformed Chapter), leaving £16,000 [C21504]

SHEPHERD (William) Born Norton, Malton, Yorks. 24/1/1806, s. John Shepherd and Ann Harrison. Literate: dn19, p20, then Trinity, Cambridge 1822 (a Ten Year Man, BD1833). PC. Pitstone, Bucks. 1822-38, R. Margaret Roding, Bucks. 1838-60 (living at Paddox Hall), R. Stapleford Tawney, Essex 1861 (and RD) to death 3/10/1867, leaving £1,000 [C76404. Venn suggests possible conflation with another man here] Married Norton 1/1/1821 Catherine Ashton, with clerical son Francis Bernard Shepherd.

SHEPPARD (John Revett) Born Spexhall, Suffolk 25/10/1806, s. Rev. Revett Sheppard (C.Wrabness, Essex) and Sarah Cobb. Caius, Cambridge 1823, BA1829, dn30 (London), p30 (Win.). (succ. his father as) R. Thwaite, Suffolk 1830 to death ('*by his own hand* at a hotel in Wick, Caithness') 17/4/1841 [C108768]

SHEPPARD (Thomas) From Bath, s. Rev. Edward Sheppard. St Edmund Hall, Oxford 1780 (aged 17), BA1783, MA1786. PC. Clerkenwell St James, London 1814 to death 31/8/1839 [C122193]

SHERER (George) From Southampton, s. Joseph Sherer. New, Oxford 1795 (aged 18), BA 1799, MA1803, Fellow to 1823. V. Crondall, Hants. 1808, V. Wilcot, Wilts. 1810-23, V. Marshfield, Glos. 1822 to death (Bath) 21/3/1858, leaving £7,000 [C89419] Widow Mary Anne.

SHERIFFE (Thomas) Bapt. Bungay, Suffolk 21/10/1758. Trinity Hall, Cambridge 1781 dn83 (Nor.), p85 (Nor.), LLB1788. R. (and patron) of Uggeshall w. Sotherton, Norfolk 1786-1842, R. Kirstead, Norfolk 1793-4 (res.). Died 14/5/1842 aged 84 [C115213] Clerical son of same name in same parish.

SHERSON (Robert) Bapt. Fetcham, Surrey 29/1/1801, s. Robert Sherson and Catherine Taylor. St Mary Hall, Oxford 1821, BA1825, dn25 (Ox.), p26 (Cashel for Ox. - in Oxford), MA1828. R. Yaverland, IoW 1830 to death 21/8/1869, leaving £3,000 [C21507] Married Westminster, London 20/9/1836 Catherine James.

SHERWEN (Samuel) Born and bapt. Gosforth, Cumberland 27/7/1790, s. John Sherwen and Sarah Sharp. Literate: dn[13] (Chester), p14 (Chester), then Queens', Cambridge 1816, a Ten Year Man. PC. Mosser, Cumberland 1823-70, R. (and patron) of Dean, Cumberland 1825 to death 24/10/1870 aged 80, leaving £12,000 [C170469] Married (1) Cockermouth, Cumberland 25/4/1835 Hannah Robinson (d.1842) (2) Edinburgh 2/7/1846 Anne Eliza Grey. Good article at: sherwensofcumbria.weebly.com/sherwen.html

SHIELD, SHEILD (Henry) Born Preston, Rutland 8/3/1757, s. Henry Sheild and Mary Hames. St John's, Cambridge 1775, BA1780, dn80 (Lin.), p81 (Lin.), MA1788. Usher Uppingham School 1781-3; R. Stoke Dry, Rutland 1791-1840, R. Preston, Rutland 1802 to death. Dom. Chap. to 6th Earl of Dysart 1802. Died 28/2/1840 aged 83 [C76394]

SHIFFNER (George, Sir, 3rd Bart.) Born Coombe Place, Lewes, Sussex 17/5/1791, s. Sir George Shifner, 1st Bart., *M.P.*, and Mary Bridger. Christ Church, Oxford 1810, BA1814, dn16 (Ex. for York), MA1818, p18 (Salis.). R. Lewes St Anne, Sussex 1818-48, R. Hamsey, Sussex 1818-48, Eartham Prebend in Chichester Cathedral 1829 and V. Hamport, Hants. 1848 to death. Dom. Chap. to 4th Viscount Gage 1818. Died 14/12/1863, leaving £10,000 [C65757. Boase] Married Knutsford, Cheshire 10/7/1817 Elizabeth Johnson (a clergy dau.), with son Rev. Sir George Croxton Shiffner. Succ. to baronetcy 1859.

SHINGLEWOOD (Joseph) Caius, Cambridge 1776 (a Ten Year Man - NiV), dn76 (London), p77 (London). H/M Maldon G/S, Essex 1769-1810; R. Chignall St James and St Mary w. Mashbury, Essex 1780 [vacant in ERC] to death 16/9/1832 aged 89 (CCEd says 19/10/1832) [C122198]

SHIPLEY (Charles) Born Henllan, Denbigh 13/8/1783, s. Very Rev. William Davies Shipley (Dean of St Asaph, of West Woodhay House, Berks.) and Penelope Yonge. BNC, Oxford, 1802, then All Souls, BA1806, dn07 (St Asaph), p08 (Ox.). R. Finmere, Dorset 1812, R. Mappowder, Dorset 1814 to death 24/7/1834 aged 50 (CCEd says 4/2/1835) [C21508] Married West Woodhay 21/6/1821 Charlotte Sloper, w. clerical son Orby Shipley. Deprived from All Souls for supposed homosexual advances.

SHIPLEY (Samuel) Bapt. Ashbourne, Derbys. 18/2/1761, s. Daniel [*pleb*.] and Mary Shipley. Wadham, Oxford 1781, then Oriel, dn85 (C&L), p85 (C&L), BA1786, MA1788. R. and V. Ashbourne w. Mapleton, Derbys. 1806 to death 7/2/1850 [C19794. DEB] Had issue.

SHIPPERDSON, SHEPHERDSON (Thomas Richard) Born Durham 3/3/1789, s. Ralph Shipperdson. St John's, Cambridge 1808, BA 1812, dn12 (Durham), p13 (Durham), MA 1816, DD1858. R. Durham St Mary le Bow w. St Mary the Less 1815-42, V. Buckworth, Lincs. 1830-31, V. Woodhorn w. Newbiggen, Morpeth, Northumberland 1842 (with Minor Canon of Durham Cathedral) to death (Woodhorn) 18/6/1865 aged 76, leaving £1,500 [C76407] Married Durham 2/7/1825 Mary Anne Hutchinson (w).

SHIPTON (John) Bapt. Stantonbury, Bucks. 11/3/1758, s. John and Mary Shipton. Queen's, Oxford 1776, BA1779, dn80 (C&L), p83 (Heref.), MA1783, BD and DD1810. R. Stantonbury, Bucks. 1782 and R. Portishead, Bristol 1791 to death 11/4/1838 [C19797] Wife Jane, and son below.

SHIPTON (John Noble) Born Bristol, s. Rev. John (above) and Jane Shipton. Oriel, Oxford 1805 (aged 16), then Balliol, BA1809, dn11 (Win.), MA 1811, p12 (B&W), BD1818, DD1841. R. Hinton Blewitt, Som. 1830-2, V. Othery, Som. 1832-64, R. Nailsea, Som. 1834-9. Died 25/2/1864, leaving £14,000 [C40592. Boase] Married Bristol 9/9/1841 Mary Simmons (w).

SHIRLEY (James) Born London 15/1/1802, s. Evelyn Shirley and Phyllis Byam Wollaston. Trinity, Oxford 1819, BA1823, dn25, MA1826, p26 (Lin.). R. Antingham St Mary 1827-[30], R. Frettenham w. Stanninghall, Norfolk 1830 to death 7/1/1870, leaving £25,000 [C65761] Married London 29/12/1831 Catherine Louisa Dolphin, with issue.

SHIRLEY (Thomas Harward) Born Worcester 21/8/1783, s. John Shirley [*pleb*.]. Magdalen Hall, Oxford 1792, BA1796, dn96 (Wor.), p97 (Wor.). R. Berrow, Worcs. 1797-9 (res.), R. Bredicot, Worcs. 1799-1801 (res.), R. Worcester St Swithin, Worcs. 1801 to death 2/2/1842 [C122126]

SHIRLEY (Walter) Born London 11/10/1768, s. Rev. Hon. Walter Shirley, sen. (Loughrea, Co. Galway, a cousin of the Countess of Huntingdon) and Henrietta Maria Phillips. TCD1786, BA1791, dn92. Influenced by John Wesley. Irish curacies. V. Woodford cum Membris, Northants. 1814, V. Shirley, Derbys. 1815-28, PC. Winster, Derby. 1829. Died 9/4/1859, Irish will only [C19801. Al.Dub. DEB. D.W.T. Crooks (ed.), *Clergy of Tuam, Killala and Achonry* (Belfast, 2008)] Married Dublin 26/7/1796 Alicia, dau. Sir Edward

Newenham, *M.P.*, with son Walter Augustus Shirley (Bishop of Sodor and Man), below.

SHIRLEY (Walter Augustus, *later* **Bishop of Sodor and Man)** Born Westport, Co. Mayo 30/5/1797, s. Rev. Walter Shirley (above) and Alicia Newenham. New, Oxford 1816, BA1819, Fellow 1819, dn20 (Heref.), p21 (Heref.), DD 1846. (succ. his father as) V. Shirley, Derbys. 1828-47, R. Whiston, Yorks. 1838-9, R. (and patron) of Brailsford, Derbys. 1839, Archdeacon of Derby 1840, Prebend of Ufton Decani in Lichfield Cathedral 1841-9, Bishop of Sodor and Man 1847 to death (pneumonia) 21/4/1847 aged 49 (episcopate of two months and nineteen days) [C19800. ODNB. Gelling. DEB. T. Hill, *Letters and memoir of the late Walter Augustus Shirley, DD* (1849)] Married (at the British Embassy, Paris) 4/8/1827 Maria Waddington (of St Remy, Normandy; she left an unpublished diary 1846-8), with son Walter Waddington Shirley (Regius Prof. of Divinity, Oxford University).

SHORT (John) From Solihull, Warwicks., s. John Short and Jane Mashiter. Trinity, Oxford 1786 (aged 18), BA 1790, dn91 (Wor.), p93 (Salis.). R. Baddesley Clinton, Warwicks 1795, PC. ('Master' of) Temple Balsall, Warwicks. 1798 to death (w) 12/3/1855 [C19802] Clerical s. John Holbeche Short.

SHORT (Laurence) Born Dronfield, Derbys. 1/2/1769, s. John Short (formerly of Madras) and Caroline Emma Hay. Queens', Cambridge 1787, BA1791, dn91 (C&L), p93 (C&L). R. Ashover, Derbys. 1797 to death 30/6/1835 (CCEd thus) [C19574] Married Thornbury, Glos. 30/4/1801 Charlotte Elenora Holwell (a clergy dau.), with issue.

SHORT (Thomas Vowler, *later* **Bishop of Sodor and Man,** *then* **Bishop of St Asaph)** Born Dawlish, Devon 16/9/1790, s. Ven. William Short (Archdeacon of Cornwall) and Elizabeth Hodgkinson. Christ Church, Oxford 1809, BA1813, dn13 (Ox.), p14 (Ox.), MA1815, BD1824, DD1837, Tutor 1816-29 [where he was intimate with the Oxford Movement founders], etc. PC. Cowley, Oxford 1816-23, R. Stockley Pomeroy, Devon 1823-6, R. King's Worthy, Hants. 1826-34, R. Bloomsbury St George, London 1834-41, Bishop of Sodor and Man 1841-6, Bishop of St Asaph 1846-70. Deputy Clerk of the Closet 1837. Died Gresford, Denbigh 13/4/1872, leaving £14,000. [C21511. ODNB. Boase] Married Bathford, Som. 26/2/1833 Mrs Mary (Davies) Conybeare. Brother below.

SHORT (William) Born Dawlish, Devon 12/10/1792, s. Ven. William Short (Archdeacon of Cornwall) and Elizabeth Hodgkinson. Christ Church, Oxford 1810, Student [Fellow] 1813-23, BA1814, dn15 (Ox.), MA1817, p17 (Car.). V. Chippenham, Wilts. 1823, Prebend of Stratford in Salisbury Cathedral 1834-78, R. St George the Martyr, Queen Square, London 1836-58, R. Llandrinio, Montgomery 1858 to death 16/2/1878, leaving £25,000 [C6314. ODNB under brother Thomas Vowler, above. DEB] Married Lacock, Wilts. 5/6/1827 Jane Awdry, with clerical sons Walter Francis, and Ambrose Short.

SHRUBB (Charles) Born Thames Ditton, Surrey 29/5/1790, s. John Peyto Shrubb and Charlotte Elers. Exeter, Oxford 1808, BA1811, dn12 (Salis. for Win.), p14 (Salis. for Win.), MA1815. V. (and patron) of Boldre w. Lymington and Brocklehurst, Hants. 1819 to death 24/4/1875, leaving £90,000 [C89426] Married Little Ilford, Essex 4/12/1833 Charlotte Aubrey Bayliff, with issue. Brother below.

SHRUBB (Henry) Bapt. Esher, Surrey 19/7/1792, s. John Peyto Shrubb and Charlotte Elers. St John's, Oxford 1810, then Corpus Christi 1812-20, BA1814, MA1818, dn18 (Ox.), p19 (Ox.), Fellow 1820-33, BD1827. R. Stratford Tony, Wilts. 1833 to death (at 'The United Hotel', Westminster, London) 4/7/1879, living at Braboeuf Manor, Guildford, leaving £300,000 [C21512] Married Guildford, Surrey 1849 (2nd q.) Jane More Wight. Brother above.

SHUCKBURGH (Charles William) Born Downton, Wilts. 30/8/1772, s. John Shuckburgh and Diana Webb. Oriel, Oxford 1789, BA1793, dn96 (Salis.), p96 (Salis.), MA1813. R. Goldhanger w. Little Totham, Essex 1798 to natural death 29/8/1833 (CCEd says 31/1/1834) [C89427] Married Salisbury 16/7/1798 Henrietta Blake, with clerical son below.

SHUCKBURGH (Robert [Shirley]) Born Goldhanger, Essex, s. Rev. Charles William Shuckburgh (above) and Henrietta Blake. Trinity, Oxford 1820 (aged 17), BA1823, MA 1828, p28 (Win.). R. Aldborough, Norfolk 1832 to death 30/4/1860, leaving £3,000 [C108773]

Married Winchester 7/7/1834 Henrietta King, with issue.

SHULDHAM (John) Born 'Bengal, British India', s. Thomas and Sophia Shuldham. Christ Church, Oxford 1813 (aged 19), Student [Fellow] 1823-46, BA1817, MA1820, dn22 (Ox.), p23 (Ox.), Reader in Greek 1824 and Rhetoric 1825. PC. Cowley, Oxon. 1827, R. Wood Norton, Norfolk 1845-79. Died Cheltenham (unmarried) 23/11/1884, leaving £26,950-18s-5d. [C21561]

SHUTE (Henry) Born Stapleton, Glos. 30/6/1749, s. Rev. Henry Shute, sen. and Mary Nashe. Oriel, Oxford 1776, BA1779, MA1782, dn82 (Ox. for Bristol), p83 (Bristol). R. Brancaster, Norfolk 1785-1804, PC. Stapleton 1785 and R. Frampton Cotterell, Glos. 1804 to death. One of the Duke of Beaufort's chaplains. Died (a widower) 28/4/1841 [C37619] Married Stapleton 28/7/1788 Mary Devey, with issue.

SHUTTLEWORTH (Philip Nicholas, *later* **Bishop of Chichester)** Bapt. Kirkham, Lancs. 9/2/1782, s. Rev. Humphrey Shuttleworth ('an anti-papal writer') and Agnes Houghton. New, Oxford 1800, BA1806, dn06 (Ox.), MA1811, p14 (Ox.), Fellow to 1822, Tutor, BD and DD 1822, Warden of New College, Oxford 1822, (Sinecure R. Colerne, Wilts. 1824), R. Foxley, Wilts. 1824, Bishop of Chichester 1840 to death 7/1/1842 [C21563. ODNB] Married Hambleton, Bucks. 29/7/1823 Emma Martha Welch (Tunstall, Lancs.), with issue.

SIBLEY (Joseph) From London, s. Joseph Sibley. St John's, Oxford 1807 (aged 18), BA 1812, dn12 (Win.), p14 (Glos. for Win.), MA 1815. V. Enstone, Oxon. 1830 to death 28/4/1840 [C21564]

SIBSON (Edmund) Born Plumbland, Cumberland 3/2/1782, s. Rev. John (a schoolmaster, Darwen, Lancs.) and Anne Sibson. Literate: dn05 (Chester), p06 (Chester). PC. Ashton in Makerfield, Lancs. 1809-41. Died there 22/12/1847 aged 65 (from a cold) [C170488] Married Blackburn, Lancs. 8/11/1809 Betty Brandwood (of Darwen), with issue. 'A man of iron mould, an accomplished scholar, and a mathematician [who helped out George Stephenson], and who loved the work of a parish priest'. An important antiquary, and a good botanist: www.stthomasstluke.org.uk › Our Church › History

SIBTHORP (Humphrey Waldo-) From Canwick Hall, Lincs., s. Col. Humphrey Sibthorpe (afterwards Waldo Sibthorpe) and Susannah Ellison. University, Oxford 1804 (aged 17), then Exeter, Fellow 1806-18, dn09 (Ox.), BA1810, p10 (Ox.), MA1811. R. Washingborough w. Heighington, Lincs. 1817 [net income £1,554] and R. Hatton, Lincs. 1824 to death 4/11/1865, leaving £50,000 [C21565. Boase. Kaye] Married Beverley, Yorks. 6/1/1818 Mary Esther Ellison (w), with issue. *J.P.* The 'colourful and preposterous' *M.P.* Col. Charles de Laet Waldo Sibthorpe was his brother.

SIDMOUTH (William Leonard Addington, 2nd Viscount) see under **ADDINGTON**

SIDNEY (Robert [Parry]) Born Coity, Glamorgan, s. John Sidney. Jesus, Oxford 1789 (aged 18), BA1793, dn94 (Ox.), MA1795, p95 (Ox.), BD1803, Fellow to 1821. R. Llanharry, Glamorgan 1812 and R. Longworth, Berks. 1820 to death 10/12/1841 [C37606]

SIEVEWRIGHT, SIVEWRIGHT (George) From London, s. John Sivewright. Trinity, Cambridge 1816, LLB1824. V. Blakesley, Northants. 1828 to death (London) 24/1/1838 [C110882. Venn under Sivewright, CCEd under Sievewright]

SIKES (Thomas) Bapt. Hackney, London 16/3/1766, s. Thomas Sikes and Jane Barnston. St Edmund Hall, Oxford 1785, then Pembroke, BA1788, dn92 (Salis.), MA1792, p92 (Salis.). V. (and patron) of Guilsborough, Northants. 1792 to death 14/12/1834 (CCEd says 18/3/1835) [C89430]

SIKES see also under **SYKES**

SILVER (Thomas) Bapt. Winchester 8/12/1776, s. John Nicholas and Frances Silver. St John's, Oxford 1793, Fellow to 1828, BCL 1807, DCL1812, LLD1818. Rawlinson Professor of Anglo-Saxon, Oxford 1817-22. V. Great Staughton, Hunts. 1822-3 (res.), then 1831-53, PC. Fyfield, Oxon. 1827, V. Charlbury (o/w Chilson), Oxon. 1828 to death 8/3/1853 [C21568] 'Eccentric - poor' (Wilberforce).

SIMEON (Charles) Born Reading, Berks. 24/9/1759, s. Richard Simeon and Elizabeth Hutton. King's, Cambridge 1779, dn82 (Ely), BA1783, p83 (Peterb.), MA1786, Fellow 1782-

1836, etc. V. Cambridge Holy Trinity 1783 to death (unmarried) 13/11/1836 [C100184. ODNB. Kaye. DEB. W. Carus, *Memoirs of the life of the Rev. Charles Simeon* (1847 and reprints); H.H. Hopkins, *Charles Simeon of Cambridge* (1977)] 'The Prince of Evangelicals' and the outstandingly influential figure in the development of the evangelical movement (and of the Church Missionary Society).

SIMMONS (Charles Tynte) Born Churchill, Somerset 24/9/1798, s. Thomas Simmons and Frances Lintorn. Trinity, Cambridge 1818 (aged 20), BA1822, dn22 (Chester), p23 (Chester). R. East Lambrook, Som. 1825, R. Shipham, Som. 1825 to death (Clevedon, Som.) 22/1/1865 aged 66. Will not traced [C40594] Married Churchill 29/4/1835 Caroline Perry, with issue.

SIMMONS (Samuel) Bapt. Congresbury, Som. 3/11/1778, s. Samuel Simmons and Sarah Beakes. Pembroke, Oxford 1795 (aged 17), BA 1799, dn01 (Ex. for B&W), p04 (B&W). R. Bawdrip, Som. 1804, V. Bishop's Lydeard, Som. 1806-[36 Buried (Weston-super-Mare, Som.) 13/9/1844 aged 66 [C48677]

SIMONS (Edward) Born Hastingsleigh, Kent 25/11/1781, s. Rev. Nicholas Simons and Elizabeth Tucker. St John's, Cambridge 1800, BA1804, dn06 (Ely), MA1807, p07 (Ely), Fellow 1807-11. R. Ovington, Norfolk 1810 to death 11/4/1865, leaving £25,000 [C100195] Married Cambridge 16/4/1811 Susanne Maria Roberts.

SIMONS (John) Bapt. Eton, Berkshire 17/9/1755, s. Thomas and Anne Simons. Queens', Cambridge 1775, dn79 (London for Lin.), p79 (London), LLB1783. R. St Paul's Cray, Kent 1782 to death 8/8/1836 [C2246] Married (1) Marylebone, London 14/4/1777 Mary Ann Sturges (d.1800), with issue (2) Marylebone, London Isabella Fawcett 15/6/1809. F.L.S.

SIMONS (John) Born Hyderabad 1800/1. Queens', Cambridge 1821, BA1826, dn26 (Heref.), p26 (Heref.), MA1829. V. Dymock, Glos. 1827 to death 6/11/1866, leaving £800 [C164280] Married Bedwardine, Worcs. 13/2/1838 Hannah Wood Thompson

SIMONS (Nicholas) Born Chislet, Kent 5/1/1754, s. Rev. Nicholas, sen. and Elizabeth Simons. Christ's, Cambridge 1772, BA1776, dn76 (Peterb.), then Clare, MA1779, Fellow. V. Elmstead, Kent 1779-95, R. Hastingleigh, Kent 1779-95, V. Welton, Yorks. 1795-1807, R. Canterbury St Margaret 1806-22 (res.), V. Minster in Thanet, Kent (and Preacher throughout the Diocese of Canterbury) 1807-39, R. Ickham (o/w Weld Chapel), Kent 1822 to death. Chap. to Bishop of Norwich/Archbishop of Canterbury 1822. Died 20/4/1839 (CCEd date is of the father) [C110883] Married Chislet, Kent 8/1/1781 Elizabeth Tucker (a clergy dau.), with issue. J.P. Leics.; succ. to family property 1776.

SIMPKINSON, *later* KING (James) Born Kingston upon Thames, Surrey, s. Roger Simpkinson and Elizabeth King. Queen's, Oxford 1786 (aged 19), dn88 (Heref.), BA1790, p91 (Heref.), MA1793. R. St Peter Le Poer, City of London 1792 to death 13/7/1842, living at Staunton Park, Leominster, Heref. [C173854. F. as King] Married London 1/7/1802 Emma Vaux, with issue. Name changed 1837.

SIMPSON (Francis) Born Pendleton, Eccles, Lancs. 25/5/1790, s. John Simpson and Elizabeth Hawksley. Jesus, Cambridge 1812, SCL, dn14 (York), p15 (York). V. Carnaby, Yorks. w. PC. Boynton, Yorks. 1832, PC. Fraisthorpe, Yorks. 1832-40, 1856 to death (Boynton) 12/10/1869 aged 79, leaving £70,000. Lived at Foston Hall, Malton, Yorks. [C135736. YCO] Married Boynton 12/4/1814 Anne, dau. Sir William Strickland, 6th Bart. (of Boynton Hall), with clerical son (of same name in same place), and a dau. Mary, *q.v.* C. B. Freeman, *Mary Simpson of Boynton vicarage, teacher of ploughboys and critic of Methodism* (York, 1972).

SIMPSON (George) Born Sittingbourne, Kent 4/4/1784, s. Valentine Simpson and Sarah Hopper. Trinity, Cambridge 1808, BA1812, dn12 (Cant.), p13 (Cant.), MA1816. V. Bobbing, Kent 1818 and V. Warden, Isle of Sheppey, Kent 1821 to death 20/4/1854 aged 69 [C124392] Married Whitfield, Kent 6/7/1813 Lucy Stringer (Archer's Court, Kent), with issue.

SIMPSON (Henry Winckworth) Bapt. City of London 9/7/1792, s. James Simpson and Alice Holness. St John's, Cambridge 1808, BA1814, dn15 (Heref.), p16 (Heref.), MA1818. Min. Old Brentford Chapel, Ealing 1828, V. Horsham, Sussex 1830-9, R. Bexhill, Sussex and RD of Hastings 1840-76, Prebend of Heathfield in Chichester Cathedral 1841 to death 4/6/1876, leaving £8,000 [C530] Married Hardwicke, Glos. 28/11/1822 Elizabeth Bonella Macgregor

Skinner, w. clerical son Arthur Barwick Simpson.

SIMPSON (James) Born Reedness, Yorks. 28/4/1784, s. Rev. Henry Simpson (Chaplain of Whitgift School, Grimsby, Yorks.). St Catharine's, Cambridge 1804, BA1808, dn08 (Bristol for York), p09 (York), MA1811. R. Swinefleet, Whitgift, Yorks. 1809 to death 1843 aged 59 [C53835. YCO] Was married with clerical son. Confusion with the man below.

SIMPSON (James) Bapt. Disley, Cheshire 23/2/1788, s. James Simpson and Mary Platt. Literate: dn13 ([Chester]), p14 (Chester). PC. Great Sankey, Lancs. 1814 to death (a widower) 17/10/1871 aged 84, leaving £600 [C170496] Married Leigh, Lancs. Mary Guest 11/1/1841, with issue. Confusion with the man above.

SIMPSON (John) Bapt. Derby 9/1/1798, s. Robert (a jeweller) and Mary Simpson. St John's, Cambridge 1817 (aged 19), BA1821, dn21 (Chester for C&L), p22 (London for C&L), MA1824, DD1839. V. Alstonfield, Staffs. 1822 (and RD of Alstonfield 1837) to death 20/1/1870, leaving £14,000 [C19721. Boase] Married Great Faringdon, Berks. 1/11/1827 Emmeline Hawkins. Surrogate 1822-1870.

SIMPSON (Joseph) From London, s. Charles Simpson. St Edmund Hall, Oxford 1805 (aged 20), BA1809, dn09 (C&L), p10 (C&L), MA1812. R. (and patron) of Little Horsted (Horsted Parva), Sussex 1830 to death 25/11/1853 [C19813] Wife Ann in 1851.

SIMPSON (Maltyward) Born Mickfield, Suffolk, s. Rev. Maltyward Simpson, sen. and Catherine Seaman. Caius, Cambridge 1822 (aged 18), BA1826, dn27 (Nor.), p28 (Nor.). (succ. his father as) R. (and patron) of Mickfield 1829 to death 1/11/1872 aged 68, leaving £4,000 [C115291] Married Aldborough, Norfolk 19/8/1845 Frances Gay (w).

SIMPSON (Thomas) Bapt. Bolton upon Swale, Yorks. 21/12/1763, s. of Sarah Simpson. Literate: dn87 (York), p88 (York). V. Kirkleatham, Yorks. 1802, V. Ebberston, Yorks. 1810 to death 17/10/1836 aged 72 [C107201. YCO]

SIMPSON (Thomas) Bapt. Windermere, Westmorland 23/5/1789, s. George and Hannah Simpson. Literate: dn13 (York), p14 (York). V. Cold Kirby, Yorks. 1830 to death 23/6/1863 aged 74, leaving £800 [C135738. YCO] Married Helmsley, Yorks. 10/12/1822 Ruth Sandwith. Kept a school in Helmsley 1823.

SIMPSON (Thomas Wood) Born Hemsworth, Yorks., s. Rev. John Simpson and Mary Wood. Worcester, Oxford 1803, BA1806 (aged 19), dn07 (Ox.), p08 (Ox.), MA1809, Fellow 1812-18. R. Thurnscoe, Yorks. 1815 to death (probably a widower) 5/7/1868 aged 84, leaving £8,000 [C21570] Married Marylebone, London 23/7/1822 Mary Welch, w. clerical son John Curwen Simpson.

SIMPSON (William) Bapt. Tanfield, Durham 22/9/1794, s. Rev. Joseph Simpson. Literate: dn17 (Durham), p18 (Durham). PC. Tanfield 1824 and PC. Tynemouth, Northumberland 1824 to death 27/4/1857 aged 62 [C133654] Married Durham 30/6/1828 Margaret Sang (Dunbar, East Lothian), with issue.

SIMS (William Erratt) Born Pentlow, Essex, s. Robert Samuel Sims (farmer) and Jane Erratt. Pembroke, Cambridge 1792 (aged 22), BA1797, dn97 (London), p99 (Nor.), MA1801. PC. Nayland and Wissington, Suffolk 1800-15, R. West Tofts, Norfolk 1814-44, PC. Santon Downham >< Suffolk 1815 and R. West Bergholt, Essex 1817 to death. Dom. Chap. to 2nd Baron Rendlesham 1811. Died 27/2/1846 [C66799] Married (1) Thurston, Suffolk 16/9/1800 Susan Sturgeon (d.1834), and had issue (2) Camberwell, London 12/11/1839 Hannah Fairfax.

SIMSON (Robert) From Coventry, s. Rev. Robert Simson. Coventry. [In army: served at Siege of Gibraltar 1779]. St John's, Oxford 1785 (aged 22), Oxford 1791. V. Coventry St Michael, Warwicks. 1793 to death 16/5/1846 [C19814]

SINGLETON (John) From Suffolk, s. John Singleton. Suffolk. St John's, Cambridge 1789 (aged 18), BA1793, MA1796. R. Sutterby, Lincs. 1821 and PC. Haugh, Lincs. 1825 to death 1847 aged 84 [C76481. Venn rightly notes confusion here] Widow Mary.

SINGLETON (John) see also under **SINGLETON (William)**

SINGLETON (Richard Alexander) Born Liverpool 27/5/1775, s. John Singleton. S/M Garstang G/S, Lancs. Literate: dn03 (Chester), p04 (Chester), then St John's, Cambridge 1814, a Ten Year Man (BD1825). 'Sometime' S/M Wharton G/S, Cheshire; PC. Manchester St Peter, Blackley 1809 to death 2/1/1838 aged 62 [C170507] Married Warton, Lancs. 31/7/1805 Eleanor Harris, with clerical son John Benedict Singleton.

SINGLETON (Thomas) Born 25/7/1783 (bapt. Walton, Suffolk), s. (Thomas) Anketell Singleton (Governor of Fort Landguard, Suffolk) and Catherine Anna Maria Grose (dau. of the antiquary). Corpus Christi, Cambridge 1800, BA1804, dn07 (Nor.), p07 (Nor.), MA 1826, Hon. LLD1830 (TCD). [Tutor, later Private Secretary to Earl Percy, then Lord Lieutenant of Ireland]. R. Elsdon, Northumberland 1813-42, Archdeacon of Northumberland (with R. Howick annexed 1826) and Canon of 2nd Prebend in Worcester Cathedral 1829 to death. Dom. Chap. to 6th Duke of Northumberland 1812. Died unmarried (Alnwick Castle) 13/3/1842 [C115293. ODNB] This is the Archdeacon Singleton to whom Sydney Smith addressed his letters *against* church reform.

SINGLETON (William, *sometimes called* John) Literate: dn77 (Lin.), p78 (Lin.). V. Bole, Notts. 1811-36, R. South Witham, Lincs. 1820 to death 24/6/1836 aged 82 [C76485. Bennett2] Married Stroxton, Lincs. 22/12/1798 Martha Hardy.

SINGLETON (William) [NiVoF] V. Dunton, Beds. 1804-6, V. Hanslope w. Castlethorpe, Bucks. 1806. Died Drigg Hall, Cumberland 11/10/1841 aged 77 [C76486]

SISSMORE (Henry) Bapt. Portsmouth, Hants. 23/8/1756, s. John and Mary Sissmore, Queen's, Oxford 1774, then New, dn79 (Ox.), p81 (Ox.), BCL1783. Fellow of Winchester College 'fifty years'; R. Sydling St Nicholas, Dorset 1810-15, V. Portsmouth to 1814, R. Widley and Wymering, Hants. 1814-51 to death 6/7/1851 aged 95 [C37629]

SISSON (Thomas) Born Leeds 17/12/1752, s. John Sisson and Matha Sharp. Emmanuel, Cambridge 1771, BA1776, dn76 (Ely), Fellow 1778, p78 (Peterb.), MA1779, tutor. R. Wallington, Herts. 1782-1837, V. Shephall, Herts. 1792-1805 (res.), V. Chippenham, Cambs. 1805 to death. Dom. Chap. to 4th Earl of Orford 1792; to 1st Marquess of Camden 1805. Died Wallington 31/12/1837 aged 85 [C108856] Married Wisbech, Cambs. 7/2/1783 Elizabeth Oswin, with issue.

SITWELL (Hervey Wilmot) Born Stainsby, Derbys. 30/12/1794, s. Edward Sacheverel Sitwell (formerly Wilmot) and Lucy Wheler (dau. of a baronet). St. John's, Cambridge 1813, BA 1817, dn18 (C&L), p19 (Wor.). V. Leamington Hastings, Warwicks. 1821-62. Died (Stainsby House, Worsley, Derbys.) 13/2/1879, leaving £14,000 [C19725] Married Leamington Hastings 4/10/1820 Sophia Wheler, *s.p.* Brother below.

SITWELL (William) Born Stainsby, Derbys. 29/1/1783, s. Edward Sacheverel Sitwell (formerly Wilmot) and Lucy Wheler (dau. of a baronet). St. John's, Cambridge 1801, BA 1805, dn06 (C&L), p07 (C&L). R. Morley, Derbys. 1807 to death (unmarried) 24/6/1844 [C19726] Brother above.

SIVEWRIGHT (George) see under **SIEVEWRIGHT**

SKEELES (George John) Born Peterborough 17/12/1790, s. Rev. William Drury Skeeles. Christ's, Cambridge 1808, BA1813, dn13 (Ely), p13 (Nor.). V. Cranwell, 1833, R. Kirkby Underwood, Lincs. 1831 to death (Bury St Edmunds, Suffolk) 21/12/1833 (CCEd thus) [C76491]

SKELTON (Joseph) Bapt. Pudsey, Leeds 31/12/1800, s. George and Ann Skelton. Literate: dn24 (Chester for York), p25 (York). H/M Scarborough G/S 1835; Chap. of the Donative of Wykeham, Yorks. 1828-52, V. Wold Newton, Yorks. 1829 to death 29/6/1860, leaving £5,000 [C135740. YCO] Married Scarborough, Yorks. 21/8/1826 Alice Terry (w).

SKELTON (Robert) Born Aislaby, Yorks. 18/5/1791, s. Rev. Robert Skelton, sen. and Alice Watson. Literate: dn14 (York), p15 (York), then St Catherine's, Cambridge 1849 (a Ten Year Man). V. (and patron) of Levisham, Yorks. 1818-77, PC. (and patron) of Rosedale, Yorks. (living at Grove House, there)1818-74. Died 6/1/1877 aged 85. Will not traced [C135741. YCO] Married Levisham 24/10/1816 Jane Richardson, with issue.

SKEY (William) Bapt. Malmesbury, Wilts. 16/3/1774, s. William Skey and Mary Garlick. St John's, Cambridge 1792, BA1796, dn98 (Salis.), p98 (Salis.). V. Great Bedwyn, Wilts. 1799-1814,

V. Little Bedwyn, Wilts. 1814 to death (Malmesbury) 29/12/1842 aged 68 [C89433]

SKILLERN (Richard Solloway) Bapt. Gloucester 27/11/1773, s. Joseph Skillern [*pleb.*] and Mellina Solloway. Trinity, Oxford 1792, then All Souls, BA1796, dn96 (Glos), MA1800, p01 (Glos). Master of the Crypt Free G/S, Gloucester 1807 '20 years'; V. Chipping Norton, Oxon. 1808 to death 20/2/1836 [C21571] Freeman of the city of Gloucester.

SKILLICORNE, *born* NASH (Richard Skillicorne) Bapt. Cowley, Glos. 2/2/1779, s. Rev. Thomas Nash and Elizabeth Skillicorne (sister of 'the true founder of Cheltenham'). Worcester, Oxford 1797, BA1801, dn01 (Glos.), p10 (Glos). R. (and patron) of Salford, Oxon. 1826 to death 21/12/1834 (CCEd thus) [C21578. F. as Nash] Changed name 1803. http:// eynsham-pc.gov. uk

SKINNER (John) Born Cheshunt, Herts. 8/6/1772 , s. Russell Skinner and Mary Page. Trinity, Oxford 1790 [adm. Lincoln's Inn 1794] BA1794, dn96 (B&W), MA1797, p98 (B&W). R. Camerton, Som. 1800 to death (*shot himself*) 12/8/1839 [C48690. ODNB] Married Enfield, Middx. 1805 Ann Holmes (d.1812), with issue. A major antiquarian, he left 98 illustrated ms volumes, of which parts have been published, especially his *Journal of a Somerset Rector 1803-1834* (1971) which reveals perhaps better than any other diary the brutal realities of rural life in the early 19th century. s.spachman.tripod.com/Woolf/johnskinner.htm

SKINNER (Richard) Bapt. Gidleigh, Devon 27/10/1773, s. Rev. Richard, sen. and Jane Skinner. Queen's, Oxford 1791, migrated to Pembroke, Cambridge BA1795, dn96 (Ex.), p97 (Ex.), MA1822. R. Sampford Peverell, Devon 1821-35 res.), R. Uplowman, Devon 1821-32 (res.). Dom. Chap. to Bishop of Norwich 1821. Died Uffculme 4/7/1838 [C146371] Married (1) Crediton, Devon 30/3/1802 Mary Battishill Pidsley (d.1821), w. issue (2) Uplowman 13/1/1831 Anne Palmer Sweet, w. further issue.

SKIPWORTH (Thomas Richard) Bapt. Aylesby, Lincs. 15/10/1785, s. Philip Skipworth and Rosamond Borman. Literate: dn12 (Lin.), p13 (Lin.). R. Pickworth, Lincs. 1814 [totally blank in ERC] and PC. Belton, Grantham, Lincs. 1814 [totally blank in ERC] to death. Dom. Chap. to the Duke of St Albans. Died 10/5/1867. No will traced [C76501] Married Epworth, Lincs. 21/5/1821 Anne Hawksley Capes, with issue.

SKRIMSHIRE (Thomas) Bapt. Wisbech, Cambs. 29/4/1774, s. William Skrimshire (surgeon) and Elizabeth Fenwick. Clare, Cambridge 1791, then Magdalene 1794, LLB 1798, dn98 (Nor.), p99 (Nor.). R. Testerton, Norfolk 1800-36, V. Great and Little Hockham, Norfolk 1800-36, V. Houghton (juxta Harpley), Norfolk 1817-22 (res.), V. South Creake, Norfolk 1822-24 (res.). Dom. Chap. to Marquess of Cholmondeley. Died Hockham 23/3/1836 [C115274] Married Whissonsett, Norfolk 23/6/1797 Rose Raven, and had issue.

SKURRAY (Francis) Bapt. Beckington, Som., 24/10/1774, s. Francis Skurray and Mary Hales. Merton, Oxford 1792, BA1796, dn97 (Peterb. for Salis.), p98 (Salis.), MA1798, then Lincoln, Fellow to 1824, BD1808. PC. Imber, Wilts. 1804-5, R. Lullington, Som. 1805, PC. Horningsham, Wilts. 1806, R. Winterbourne Abbas w. Winterbourne Steepleton, Dorset 1823 to death (Warminster, Wilts.) 10/3/1848 [C48694] Married St George's Hanover Square, London 1811 Frances Jemima --, with issue. An art collector, there is an online painting of him in his parsonage gallery at Horningsham.

SKYNNER (William) Born Easton (by Stamford), Lincs. 23/11/1777, s. Rev. John Skynner and Sarah Lancaster. St John's, Cambridge 1796, BA1800, MA1803, dn01 (Peterb.), p03 (Peterb.). R. Bradley, Derbys. 1805-58, V. Rushden, Herts. 1806 and R. Cuxwold, Lincs. 1814 to death (Rushden) 13/4/1858, leaving £6,000 [C19817]

SLACK (Thomas) Literate: dn80 (London), p82 (Lin. for London). R. Margaret Roding, Essex 1790-1811, PC. Pleshey, Essex 1811, R. Little Leighs, Essex 1841 to death. Buried 1/1/1851 aged 93 [C76533]

SLADE (James) Born Daventry, Northants. 2/5/1783, s. Rev. James Slade, sen. and Elizabeth Waterfield. Emmanuel, Cambridge 1800, dn06 (Peterb.), BA1807, p07 (Peterb.), Fellow 1806, MA1807. R. Teversham, Cambs. 1811-16, V. Milton, Cambs. 1813-16, Canon of Chester Cathedral 1816-60, V. Bolton (le Moors), Lancs. (and King's Preacher throughout the County of Lancaster) 1817-56, R. Tattenhall, Cheshire 1818-26 (res.), R. Northenden, Cheshire 1826-9, R. West Kirby, Cheshire 1829 to death. Dom. Chap. to his father-in-law the Bishop of Chester 1812; to Bishop of Bath and Wells 1826-29. Died 15/5/1860, leaving £4,000 [C110888, ODNB. Boase. J.A. Atkinson, *Memoir of the Rev. Canon Slade* (Bolton, 1893); H.O. Fielding, *James Slade, Vicar of Bolton, 1817-1856* (Bolton, 1983, with fine port.)] Married (1) 28/5/1812 Augusta Law (d.1822) (dau. of the Bishop of Chester), their surviving dau. making a clerical marriage (2) 10/5/1824 Mary Bolling, dau. of a Bolton surgeon, *s.p.* A major figure in the life of Bolton as reformer and educationalist; some said he should have been the first Bishop of Manchester.

SLAPP (Thomas Peyton) Born Botesdale, Suffolk 1775, s. Thomas Slapp (attorney) and Anne Katherina Kendall. Christ's, Cambridge 1793, BA1798, dn99 (Nor.), MA1801, p08 (Nor.). R. Little Brandon (Brandon Parva), Norfolk 1811, R. Bracon Ash, Norfolk 1811-49, PC. Old Buckenham, Norfolk 1815 and R. Rickinghall Inferior w. Rickinghall Superior, Suffolk 1827 to death (Old Buckenham Lodge) 13/11/1849 [C115298] Married Dublin 21/12/1807 Olivia Beatty.

SLATER (Thomas) From Wilby, Northants., s. John Slater. Lincoln, Oxford 1782 (aged 17), BA1786, dn88 (Peterb.), p89 (Peterb.). R. Wilby 1790. Will proved 20/5/1837 [C110889]

SLATTER (George Maximilian) From Oxford, s. William Slatter. Chorister at Magdalen, Oxford 1798; matr. Hertford 1803 (aged 14), migrated to Peterhouse, Cambridge 1816 (a Ten Year Man, BD1826), dn16 (Chester for Salis.), p17 (Ex.), DD1850. Priest-Vicar Exeter Cathedral 1817 and V. West Anstey, Devon 1819 to death (Exeter) 27/4/1868 aged 77, leaving £3,000 [C89437. Boase] Married Anna Maria Ewart. Seems to have engaged in Cornish mining speculation.

SLATTER (William) Bapt. Oxford 15/8/1788, s. Rev. John Slatter and Lucy Gerard. Merton, Oxford 1803 (aged 14), BA 1809, BA1810, dn12 (Salis.), Chap. 1819-24. (succ. his father as) V. Cumnor, Berks. 1810 [blank in ERC] and V. Hethe, Oxon. 1823 to death (Cumnor) 8/11/1849 aged 66 [C21605] Married London 25/8/1814 his cousin Lucy Butler, with issue.

SLEATH (William Boultbee) Born Broughton, Leics. 14/2/1762, s. William Sleath and Mildred Liptrott. Literate: dn84 (C&L), then Emmanuel, Cambridge 1786 (a Ten Year Man), dn86 (C&L), BD1797, DD1802. S/M Rugby School; then H/M Repton School 1800-30; V. Willington, Derbys. 1809-20 (res.), then 1832-42, V. Thurnby w. Stoughton, Leics. 1825-32. Master of Etwall Hospital [almshouses], Derbys. 1832 to death 21/10/1842 [C11737. Long obit. in *Gentleman's Magazine*] Married (1) Rugby, Staffs. 5/6/1783 Louise Chartres (2) Leamington Spa, Warwicks. 4/1/1842 Mary Soden (w). *F.S.A.* Port. online.

SLEEMAN (Peter) Bapt. Tavistock, Devon 8/10/1773, s. Rev. Richard Sleeman and Alice Perring. Balliol, Oxford 1792, BA1796, dn97 (Ex.), p97 (Ex.), MA1799. V. (and patron) of Whitchurch, Devon 1823 to death 27/4/1848 [C146374] Married Whitchurch 4/6/1810 Elizabeth Grace Bedford, and had issue.

SLINGSBY (Henry James) Bapt. Windsor, Berks. 2/5/1786, s. John Slingsby and Hannah Roebuck. King's, Cambridge 1805, Fellow 1808-31, BA1809, dn09 (Win.), p10 (Win.), MA1812. R. (Great) Greenford, Middx. 1831-2 (res.), R. Stower Provost w. Todbere, Dorset 1833 to death 30/4/1844 [C53838]

SLOCOCK (Samuel) From Newbury, Berks., s. Samuel Slocock. St John's, Oxford 1798 (aged 18), SCL, dn02 (Salis.), p03 (Salis.), BCL. R. Wasing, Berks. 1812, Min. Portsea St Paul, Hants. 1829. Dom. Chap. to 2nd Earl of Carnarvon 1814. Died 20/8/1847 [C89442]

SLOPER (George) Born Middx. 24/9/1774, natural s. Lt.-Gen. Sir Robert Sloper. [Cornet in army 1795; Lt. 1796]. Emmanuel, Cambridge 1790, BA1795, MA1798, p98 (Salis.), dn98 (Salis.), incorporated at Oxford 1816. R. West Woodhay, Berks. 1798-1851-. Died Ostend 9/1/1855 [C89443] Wife Mary.

SMALL (Harry Alexander) Born 13/8/1803 (but bapt. 31/12/1822), s. Alexander Small (Clifton Reynes Hall, Olney, Bucks.) and Ann Shewen. Downing, Cambridge 1823, dn27 (Lin.), p27 (Ely for Lin.), LLB1830. R. Haversham, Bucks. 1827 and R. Clifton Reynes 1832-53. Died Solden House, Bletchley, Bucks. 6/1/1867, leaving £800 [C76560. Venn corrected] Married All Souls, Marylebone,

London 13/5/1848 Elizabeth Greaves, and had issue. Brother below.

SMALL (Henry) Bapt. Clifton Reynes Hall, Olney, Bucks. 23/7/1777, s. Alexander Small and Ann Shewen. BNC, Oxford 1796, no degree? R. St Albans Abbey Church 1817-35 (res.). Dom. Chap. to 1st Earl of Verulam 1817. Died 27/10/1852 [C122425] Married Llanelli, Carmarthen 19/3/1800. Brother above. The Reverend Henry Small, appointed rector of St Albans Abbey parish in 1817, found himself dealing with a decrepit building, declining congregation and low income. In 1826, he took up the post of Headmaster of Dixie Grammar School in Market Bosworth and tried to combine this with his duties as rector. This was not a success; he was sacked after 18 months. When the St Albans Savings Bank was established in 1828, Small took charge and, over the next few years, he embezzled some £20,000 of the money deposited in the bank by the local 'labouring classes'. He absconded to Boulogne in 1835 from where he could not be extradited. Largely through the good offices of several wealthy local men, including Lord Verulam, all the depositors got their money back. Astonishingly, Small reappeared in St Albans in 1845, requesting money from the Guardians of the Poor'.

SMALLEY (Cornwall) Born and bapt. City of London 14/10/1789, s. Cornwall Smalley and Eleanor Tierney. Queens', Cambridge 1807, BA 1812, dn12 (Salis.), p13 (Salis.), MA1822. V. Brailes, Warwicks. 1816-56, Min. Bayswater Proprietary Chapel, Paddington, London 1829 to death (Worthing, Sussex) 11/8/1859 aged 69, leaving £2,000 [C89445] Wife Mary Wallace, and clerical son of same name. Brother below.

SMALLEY (George) Bapt. Hampstead, London 4/8/1798, s. Cornwall Smalley and Eleanor Tierney. Trinity, Oxford 1816, BA 1820, MA1823, p23 (Nor.). V. Debenham, Suffolk 1823 to death. Buried 16/7/1840 [C115301] Married Brailes, Warwicks. 4/8/1798 Frances Jane Hay, and had issue. Brother above.

SMELT (Maurice) Bapt. Slindon, Sussex 6/7/1784, s. Rev. John and Ann Smelt. Trinity, Oxford 1802 (aged 18), BA1806, dn07 (Glos.), p08. Sequestrator of Barnham, Surrey 1815, R. Slindon, Sussex 1815 and V. Binsted, Suffolk 1815 to death. Dom. Chap. to 12th Baron Zouche 1815. Died Cheltenham 18/10/1867, leaving £10,000 [C137371] Married Lambeth, Surrey 10/6/1817 Mary Anne Williams, with clerical sons Maurice Allen, and Henry Smelt.

SMIJTH, *later* **BOWYER-SMIJTH (Edward, Sir, 10th Bart.)** Born Hill Hall, Theydon Mount, Essex 1/3/1785, s. Sir William Smyth, 7th Bart. and Anne Bowyer. Trinity, Cambridge 1803, BA1807, dn08 (Win.), p09 (Win.), MA1811. V. Camberwell, Surrey 1809-23 (res.), Chap. Manchester St Clement 1811-[17], R. Stow Maries, Essex 1823-36, R. Stapleford Tawney w. Theydon Mount 1837-9. Chap. to Prince Regent 1811. Died 15/8/1850 [C108808] Married St George's Hanover Square, London 29/5/1813 Letitia Cicely Weyland (Woodrising Hall, Norfolk), with issue. Succ. to title 1838; changed name 1839.

SMITH (Alexander James) Literate: dn81 (Cant.), p82 (Lin. for Cant.). V. (Temple) Ewell, Kent 1786, V. Alkham w. Capel le Ferne, Kent 1786, R. Little Carlton w. Castle Carlton 1790 to death 19/2/1835 (CCEd thus) [C76569] Married Dover, Kent 31/10/1791 Ann Hammond.

SMITH (Alfred) From Oxford, s. Roger Smith. Queen's, Oxford 1817 (aged 18), BA 1821, dn21 (Ox.), p22 (Ox.). PC. South Broom, Wilts. 1832 to death 29/10/1877, living at Old Park, Devizes, leaving £25,000 [C21611] Married City of London 6/7/1823 Harriot Smith (w), w. clerical s. Alfred Charles Smith.

SMITH (Cecil Robert) Born Madras, s. Cecil Smith. Balliol, Oxford 1817 (aged 18), BA 1821, dn21 (Glos.), p23 (Chester), MA1823. PC. Withiel Florey, Som. 1827 to death 12/5/1861, living at Lydiard House, Taunton, Som., leaving £16,000 [C40601] Married Seaton, Devon 15/7/1825 Mary Jane Warren, one child. J.P.

SMITH (Charles Adam John) Born London 16/4/1802, s. Charles Smith and Caroline Hakewill. St John's, Cambridge 1819, BA1823, dn25 (London), p26 (London for Win.), MA 1827. (first) PC. Birch, Middleton, Lancs. 1829-33, Chaplain of the London Episcopal Floating Church off the Tower of London (and of the Sailors' Home, Well Street, London Docks, and of the Destitute Sailors' Asylum) 1842-7, PC. Macclesfield, Cheshire 1847 to death 13/1/1878 aged 76, leaving £20,000 [C106756] Married (1) by 1836 Lydia Grenfell Hitchins (d.1847), with issue (2) York 19/12/1850 Emily Parker Salmond, with further issue.

SMITH (Charles George Whitaker) Born Barrowby Hall, Garforth, Leeds 2/1/1797, s. Charles and Elizabeth Smith. St Bees, Cumberland adm. 1819, dn21 (Chester for unspecified bishop - probably York), p21 (York). PC. Knottingley, Pontefract, Yorks. [C135985] 1827-40-, R. Carlton in Lindrick, Notts. 1849 to death. Dom. Chap. to Lord Galway in 1864. Died 6/7/1875 aged 78, leaving £4,000 [C135742. YCO] Married Pontefract 6/8/1827 Mary Trueman, with issue.

SMITH (Courtney) Bapt. Edensor, Derbys. 18/2/1808, s. Richard and Charlotte Smith. Trinity, Cambridge 1826, MA1830, dn31 (C&L), p32 (C&L). PC. Barlow, Staveley, Derbys. 1832-55, R. Pleasley, Derbys. 1856 to death 17/8/1867, leaving £1,000 [C19732] Married Old Brampton, Derbys. 18/8/1835 Emily Barnes, with clerical son Gerald Hyde Smith.

SMITH (Digby) Bapt. City of London 1/8/1752, s. William Smith. Merton, Oxford 1768, BA1772, MA1775, dn75 (Ox.), p76 (Wor.). Minor Canon of Worcester Cathedral 1775-1832, V. Himbleton, Worcs. 1777-94 (res.), R. Worcester St Swithin 1794-1801, R. Worcester St Martin 1801 to death. Chap. St Oswald's Hospital [almshouses], Worcester 1789-1833. Dom. Chap. to Anne, Countesss Dowager Ferrers 1781. Buried 21/1/1833 aged 80 (CCEd says 29/6/1833) [C37644] Married 1783 Catherine Charlotte Ann Maria Teresa Gray, with issue.

SMITH (Edward) Bapt. Cotgrave, Notts. 24/11/1765, s. Rev. William and Judith Smith. Sidney, Cambridge 1785, BA1789, dn89 (London for York), p90 (Win. for York). V. Camberwell, Surrey 1809-16, V. Egmanton cum Tollerton, Notts. 1816 to death 21/10/1840 [C134630. YCO]

SMITH (Edward) [BA but NiVoF]: dn27 (Chester), p28 (Chester). PC. Harty, Isle of Sheppey, Kent 1831-6. Died? [C137002]

SMITH (Edward Grose) Born London 29/6/1795, s. Edward Grose Smith (attorney) and Mary Grose. Caius, Cambridge 1813 [adm. Lincoln's Inn 1815] BA1819, dn19 (Salis.), p20 (Lin.), MA1821. PC. St Helens, IoW 1832 to death 13/9/1833 aged 37 [C2271] Married Canterbury 17/9/1792 Mary Fielder Heathfield, and had issue.

SMITH (Edward Orlebar) Bapt. Holcot, Beds. 10/5/1788, s. Rev. Edward Orlebar Smith, sen. and Charlotte Hervey. Corpus Christi, Oxford 1806, BA1810, MA1814, dn14 (Ox.), p15 (Ox.), Fellow 1818-20. R. (and patron) of Hulcote w. Salford, Beds. 1819 to death 24/6/1865, leaving £20,000 [C21613] Married Marylebone, London 14/5/1822 his cousin Mary Willis. J.P. Beds. Photo. online.

SMITH (Francis) [NiVoF] R. Grindon, Warwicks. 1793-4, V. Eardisley w. Bollingham, Heref. 1793-[1845] [ERC links]. Died? [C173882]

SMITH (George) Bapt. Clyst Honiton, Devon 6/1/1762, s. Abraham Smith. Balliol, Oxford 1780, BA1784, dn84 (Ex.), p86 (Ex.). V. Salcombe, Devon 1794, V. Ottery St Mary, Devon 1794-1841, V. Braunton w. Saunton and Knowle, Devon 1796, R. Charleton w. Buckland Tout Saints, Devon 1807 to death. Chap. to HRH Duke of Clarence 1794-1807. Died 1/11/1841 [C159363]

SMITH (George) Bapt. Askham, Northumberland 22/10/1762, s. Wade Smith [*pleb.*]. St Alban Hall, Oxford 1790, dn92 (Salis.), p93 (Salis.). V. Norton Bavant, Wilts. 1794-[1837], R. Hill Deverill, Wilts. 1798-[1838] [ERC links them]. Died? [C89449]

SMITH (George) [Literate]. PC. Bridlington, Yorks. 1809 to death 1848 (1st q.) aged 80 [C135131] Wife Hannah and issue in 1841.

SMITH (George William) Caius, Cambridge 1791 (a Ten Year Man), dn92 (Nor.), p93 (Nor.). V. Bawdsey, Suffolk 1825-41. Dom. Chap. to Earl of Stradbroke. Died *c*.1841? [C115365]

SMITH (Harry) From Clerkenwell, London, s. Harry Smith. BNC, Oxford 1809 (aged 17), BA 1812, MA1815, dn17 (London), p17 (Lin.). R. Crundale, Kent 1828-68. Died London 17/2/1881, leaving £60,000 [C76617]

SMITH (Henry) From London, s. Rev. Samuel Smith. Christ Church, Oxford 1791 (aged 17), BA1795, MA1798, dn99 (Chester), p00 (Ox.). V. Alconbury w. Alconbury Weston, Hants. 1803-9 (res.), V. Kilsby, Northants. 1809, Prebend of North Leverton in Southwell Collegiate Church 1807 to death 17/1/1844 [C21614] Clerical son Henry.

SMITH (Henry Curtis) Born Bath, Somerset 25/1/1806, s. Sir John Wyldbore Smith, 2nd Bart. and Elizabeth Ann Marriott. Balliol, Oxford 1824, BA1828, dn30 (Bristol), MA1832, p32 (Bristol). R. Tarrant Rawston (o/w Tarrant Antioch), Dorset 1832 to death (Rushton, Northants) 12 *or* 19/12/1834 aged 28 (CCEd says 1/3/1835) [C53840] Married 25/10/1832 Elizabeth Green (w), of Hinxton Hall, Cambs. (she remarried).

SMITH (Henry John) Born Ireland 6/6/1802. [MA but NiVoF nor Al.Dub.]. R. Birkenshaw cum Hunsworth, Birstall, Yorks. 1833 to death 16/12/1862, leaving £4,000 [Not yet in CCEd] Married Halifax, Yorks. 1841 Anne Emmet (w), and had issue.

SMITH (Henry Richard Somers) Born St Pancras, London, s. William Henry Smith. Trinity, Cambridge 1813 (aged 18), BA1817, dn19 (Durham), p20 (Durham). R. Little Bentley, Essex 1824 (and RD of Adleigh 1851) to death 5/1/1871, leaving £4,000 [C122439] Widow Caroline, with issue.

SMITH (Hugh) Born London 13/6/1778, s. Hugh Smith (Lincoln's Inn). [Adm. Lincoln's Inn 1797]. Trinity, Cambridge 1791, BA1815, dn15 (Chester), MA1818. R. Weston sub Edge, Glos. 1815, R. Stoke d'Abernon, Surrey 1846-62. Boarding in Kensington 1861. Died? Will not traced [C164720] Wife Eleanor, and issue.

SMITH (Jeremiah) Born Brewood, Staffs. 23/8/1771, s. Jeremiah and Ann Smith. Hertford, Oxford 1790, then Corpus Christi, BA 1794, dn94 (C&L), p95 (Wor.), MA1797, BD 1810, DD1811. S/M King Edward V1 School, Birmingham 1798-1807, High Master Manchester G/S 1807-37; PC. Manchester St Peter 1813-25, R. Manchester St Ann 1823-37 (with King's Preacher for Lancashire 1824, a sinecure: abolished 1845), V. Great Wilbraham, Cambs. 1832-47. Died Brewood 21/12/1854 aged 84, leaving £6,926-3s-3d. [C19835. ODNB. Boase] Married Birmingham 27/7/1811 Felicia Anderson, with clerical son. The *Admission Register* of Manchester G/S (Vol. 3, Part 1. 1874) has port. but no biography.

SMITH (John) Christ's, Cambridge 1788, BA 1792, dn94 (Lin.), p95 (Lin.), MA1795. S/M Dilhorne School, Staffs.; V. Bicester, Oxon. 1800 to death 21/7/1835 aged 65 (CCEd says 16/12/1835) [C19838]

SMITH (John) [NiVoF] R. Newhaven (o/w Meeching), Sussex 1805, V. Rougham, Norfolk 1809 [C115378.]. Died? [C72279. ERC links them]

SMITH (John) [NiVoF] R. Deane, Hants. 1805. Died? [C108797] Perhaps one of the others here?

SMITH (John) Born Manchester 27/3/1798, s. Rev. Thomas Smith and Ann Hartley. St John's, Cambridge 1817, BA1822, dn24 (London), p25 (Win.), MA1836. R. Pwllcrochan, Pembroke 1832-4, R. Baldock, Herts. 1832 to death 3/3/1870, leaving £2,000 [C167936. Boase] Married Marylebone, London 6/2/1815 Elizabeth Frances Cross, with issue. His income was derived from reporting for the *Cambridge Chronicle*. It was he who actually deciphered the shorthand of Samuel Pepys' *Diary*, Lord Braybrook taking the credit.

SMITH (John) From Bury St Edmunds, Suffolk, s. John Smith (surgeon). St John's, Cambridge 1811, BA1815, Fellow 1816-23, MA1818, dn19 (Bristol), p21 (Nor.), BD1826. R. Great Dunmow, Essex 1829-34, R. Kirkby w. Asgarby, Lincs. 1823-9, Chiswick Prebend in St Paul's Cathedral 1830-59, V. Ealing, Middx. 1834-53, R. Acton, Middx. 1853 to death there 16/2/1859, leaving £25,000 [C122512] Married 10/7/1823 Frances Mary Blomfield (w) (sister of the Bishop of London, here), w. clerical son John Charles Smith. 'Never recovered' from the disappointment of not succ. his uncle as V. Holt, Norfolk.

SMITH (John Bainbridge) Formerly a compositor in York. Literate: dn19 (Lin.), p20 (Lin.), then Christ's, Cambridge 1821 (a Ten Year Man), BD1832, DD1837. H/M Horncastle G/S, Lincs. 1818-54; R. Martin, Lincs. 1824-54, PC. Baumber, Lincs. 1824 and R. Sotby, Lincs. 1827 to death (Martin) 10/3/1854 ('from injuries received in a railway accident') [C76651. Boase] Clerical son of same name.

SMITH (John Tetley) Bapt. Repton, Derbys. 6/6/1806, s. John Smith and Dorothy Greaves. Queen's, Oxford 1823, BA1828, dn28 (C&L), p29 (C&L). Chap. of the Donative of Bretby, Repton 1832 [to death] (Repton) 7/2/1873, leaving £1,500 [Blank in ERC] [C19840] Married Burton-on-Trent 1849 Sarah Greaves (w).

SMITH (Joseph) Born Rodborough, Glos. 25/6/1794, s. Peter Smith and Mary Playne. University, Oxford 1811, then Trinity 1814-24, BA1815, MA1818, dn18 (Glos.), Fellow 1824-52, p25 (Ox.), BD 1827, etc. R. East Bradenham, Norfolk 1832, V. Rotherfield Greys, Essex 1851-66. Died Worthing, surrey 23/2/1886. Will not readily traceable [C21617] Married St George's Hanover Square, London 12/7/1862 Mrs Jane (Goodden) Moore.

SMITH (Martin Stafford) Bapt. Churchdown, Glos. 27/6/1746, s. Martin Smith. BNC, Oxford 1764, then Corpus Christi, BA1768, MA1772, dn72 (London), p72 (London), BD 1781. PC. Maisemore, Glos. 1776-93, V. Cirencester, Glos. 1778-89, R. Uphill, Som. 1789-90, R. Breane, Som. 1789-1831 (res.), R. Alvechurch, Worcs. 1790-3, R. Fladbury, Worcs. 1793 to death (Bath) 6/1/1834 (CCEd thus), leaving £200,000 [C40605] Married (1) Wyke Regis, Dorset 9/10/1781 the much older Mrs Gertrude (Tucker) Warburton (Prior Park, Bath, the relict of a Bishop of Gloucester, she d.1796 aged 69) (2) Walcot, Bath 7/1797 Mary Elizabeth Plaisted.

SMITH (Michael) From Prince William Town, South Carolina, s. Rev. Haddon Smith. Worcester, Oxford 1792 (aged 19), BA1797, dn97 (Ox.), p98 (Ox.), MA1799. Minor Canon in Rochester Cathedral 1803, V. Stockbury, Kent 1810-27, V. Sutton at Hone, Kent 1827 [to death]. Buried 12/11/1835 [C1488]

SMITH (Richard) From London, s. Thomas Smith. Trinity, Cambridge 1784 (aged 17), BA1789, dn89 (Peterb.), Fellow 1791-1804, MA1792, p92 (Lin.), etc. R. Kingsley, Staffs. 1804-8, Chap. of the Donative of Edensor [Chatsworth], Derbys. 1804, V. Westham, Sussex 1808-21, R. Jevington, Sussex 1808, R. Staveley, Derbys. 1821. Dom. Chap. to 5th (1808) and 6th (1811) Dukes of Devonshire. Died? [C76666. Venn is wrong in attributing Sutton and Bicknor (below) to this man, and the death date is of the man below]

SMITH (Richard) Born Westminster, London, s. Rev. Richard Smith, sen. and Elizabeth Mary Mapp. St Alban Hall, Oxford 1793 (aged 25), BA1808, MA1809. R. Sutton, Sussex 1815 and R. Bicknor, Kent 1824 to death. Dom. Chap. to 3rd Earl of Egremont 1824. Died 23/10/1848 aged 82 [C108798. Venn mixes with man below. LBSO - awarded £1,259-6s-11d for 'half the compensation for 123 enslaved people in Barbados'] Married Mary Evatt, with issue.

SMITH (Robert) Born Alnwick, Northumberland 31/8/1774, s. of George (innkeeper) and Mary Smith. Literate: dn12 (York), p13 (York). PC. Kyloe, Durham 1830 to death 28/9/1851 [C135744. YCO] Married 1814 Esther Stopford.

SMITH (Robert) Born Waddington, Yorks. 1/5/1778, s. Rev. Robert Smith, sen. Literate: dn01 (York), p02 (York). PC. Honley w. Brockholes, Almondbury, Yorks. 1802. Died 1845 aged 67 [C126980. YCO]

SMITH (Robert [Crawforth]) Born Painswick, Glos., s. Robert Smith. Pembroke, Oxford 1816 (aged 19), BA1820, dn21 (Glos.), p21 (Glos.), MA 1824. PC. Gloucester St Catherine 1825-70, PC. Churchdown, Glos. 1826, R. Whaddon, Glos. 1831, R. Cowley, Cheltenham 1837. Died (Gloucester) 20/9/1870, leaving £3,000 [C164868]

SMITH (Robert Ralph) From Aksey, Wilts., s. Rev. Ralph Smith. New, Oxford 1791 (aged 17), BA1795, dn96 (Salis.), MA1799, p02 (Glos.), etc. V. Colerne, Wilts 1814-15 (res.), V. Adderbury, Oxon. 1823 to death 1836 [C21618]

SMITH (Samuel) Bapt. Westminster Abbey, London 15/10/1765, s. Rev. Samuel Smith (H/M Westminster School) and Anna Morris. Christ Church, Oxford 1782, BA1786, dn89 (Chester for Ox.), MA1789, p90 (Ox.), BD1797, DD1808, etc., PC. Oxford St Thomas the Martyr 1792-5, Prebend of Leverton North in Southwell Minister 1800, Prebend of Grindal in York Minister 1801-41, PC. Daventry, Northants. 1803, Canon of 2nd Prebend in Christ Church Cathedral, Oxford 1807-24, (succ. his father as) R. Dry Drayton, Cambs. 1808-28 then again 1831-41, Dean of Christ Church Cathedral, Oxford 1824-31, 11th Prebend of Durham Cathedral 1831 to death. Chap. to Speaker of the House of Commons 1802. Died 19/1/1841 [C17378 mixes in father. ODNB] Married Weybridge, Surrey 9/8/1803 Ann Brady Barnett, with clerical sons Samuel, Henry, and Charles Smith.

SMITH (Samuel) Born Shalden, Hants. 12/7/1794, s. Thomas Smith and Martha Badgen. Kings, Cambridge 1814, Fellow 1817-32, p17 (Ely for Win.), BA1818, p19 (Heref.), MA1821. R. Tiverton (Priors Portion), Devon

[blank in ERC] 1830-2, V. Weedon Lois ><
Northants (and RD) 1832 to death (Brighton)
6/2/1867 aged 74, leaving £4,000 [C17377].
Married (1) Harriet Dickinson (2) Lichborough,
Northants. 26/10/1843 Ann Grant.

SMITH (Samuel) Born London, s. Samuel
Smith. Trinity, Cambridge 1822, BA1827, dn27
(London), p28 (London). PC. Camberwell St
George's District Church 1832-85 [blank in
ERC], R. Kingdown w. Mappowder, Kent 1885-
94, living latterly at Penge, Surrey, dying there
25/9/1897 aged 93, leaving £3,490-6s-1d. [Not
identifiable in CCEd] Married Clerkenwell,
London 4/6/1841 Ann Catherine Camroux.

SMITH (Samuel) [BA but NiVoF] V. and R.
Astwick w. Arlesey >< Beds. 1830-3 (res.).
Died? [C76673] Above?

SMITH (Samuel Colby) Bapt. Great
Yarmouth. Norfolk 4/1/1775, s. William
(surgeon) and Elizabeth Smith. Caius, Cam-
bridge 1792, BA1797, dn97 (Nor.), p99 (Nor.),
MA1800, Fellow 1801-22. R. Denver (1st
Moiety, o/w West Hall), Norfolk 1820 to death
18/4/1852 [C115391. Venn as Coleby] Married
Gunthorpe, Melton Constable, Norfolk
11/11/1822 Lucy Maria Collyer (a clergy dau.,
Gunthorpe Hall).

SMITH (Sumner) Born Monken Hadley,
Middx. 5/3/1777, s. William Smith and Sarah
Sumner. Queen's, Oxford 1795, BA1799, dn00
(Salis.), MA1802. R. Ashill, Som. 1805, R. Ham,
Wilts 1831 to death (Hungerford, Berks.)
12/6/1843 [C40608] Married Bath 7/10/1807
Mary Anne Spry, and had issue.

SMITH (Sydney) Born Woodford, Essex
3/6/1771, s. Robert Smith (merchant) and
Maria Olier. New, Oxford 1789, Fellow 1791,
BA1792, dn93 (Lin.), p96 (Ox.), MA1796. V.
Netheravon, Wilts. 1794-1809, R. Foston-le-
Cley, Yorks. 1809-29 (res.), R. Londesborough,
Yorks. 1823-9, R. Combe Florey, Somerset
1829-34, V. Halberton, Devon 1829, Canon of
3rd Prebend of Bristol Cathedral 1828-31,
Prebend of Neasden and Canon Residentiary in
St Paul's Cathedral, London 1831 to death.
Dom. Chap. to Anne, Dowager Baroness
Somerset 1823. Died 21/2/1845 (maximum
total income £2,900) [C37656. ODNB. (port.).
Saba Holland [dau.], *A memoir of the Rev. Sydney
Smith* (1855); P. Virgin, *Sydney Smith: a biography*
(1994) provides the context for many of the the
clergy here; and many other titles] Married
(happily) Cheam, Surrey 2/7/1800 Catharine
Amelia Pybus, 3s., 2 dau. In Edinburgh 1798-
1803, he was one of the founders of, and major
contributors to, the *Edinburgh Review*; wit;
progressive political and social writer; The
Wikipedia entry is a model one.

SMITH (Thomas) Peterhouse, Cambridge,
[BA. MA but NiV], dn92 (Ely for Win.). PC.
Norton Mandeville, Essex 1810-15, R. Bobbing-
worth, Essex 1812. Dom. Chap. to 6th Viscount
Ranelagh 1810-12. Died? [C100198]

SMITH (Thomas) Born Clay Coton,
Northants. 11/4/1774, s. Rev. Thomas Smith.
Sidney, Cambridge 1792, BA1796, dn96
(Peterb.), p98 (Peterb.), MA1804. R. (and
patron) of Clay Coton 1798, V. Lilbourne,
Northants. 1804 to death. Dom. Chap. to Lord
Tara 1804. Died 6/12/1851 aged 77 [C110928]
Had issue.

SMITH (Thomas) From Farnham, Surrey, s.
Thomas Smith. Wadham, Oxford 1805 (aged
20), BA1808, dn11 (Glos.), p12 (Glos.). S/M
Chipping Sodbury Free G/S 1819; Curate Old
Sodbury Chapel, Chipping Sodbury, Glos. 1822.
Died? [C164872]

SMITH (Thomas) [NiVoF] V. Winterton,
Lincs. 1829 to death 17/12/1856 aged 68 (succ.
by his son who later became a Baptist Minister)
[C76683]

SMITH (Thomas) Born Preston, Lancs.
3/11/1791, s. William and Mary Smith. Literate:
dn15 (York), p16 (York). PC. Owthorpe, Notts.
1825-64, R. Stanton-on-the-Wolds, Notts. 1848
to death (a widower, at the Nottingham General
Hospital) 7/9/1875, leaving £1,000 [C135992.
YCO] Wife Sarah and issue.

SMITH (William) Bapt. Ripon, Yorks.
24/2/1772, s. of William Smith (a mercer).
Trinity, Cambridge 1791, BA1795, dn95 (York),
p96 (York), MA1801. PC. Pool, Yorks. 1796-
1834 and PC. Burley, Yorks. 1813 to death
14/11/1834 aged 62 [C134639. YCO]

SMITH (William) [NiVoF] R. Badger [as
Bagsore in ERC], Shropshire 1795 to death
9/12/1837 aged 70 (monumental tablet online
identifies) [C173916] Never absent from the
parsh for more than two weeks in 42 years.

SMITH (William) [NiVoF] (Sinecure R. Abingdon St Nicholas, Berks. 1804). Chap. at Abingdon Bridewell [a House of Correction] 1826. Will probably for this man 3/2/1846 [C89470] One of the others here?

SMITH (William) Trinity, Cambridge 1809, BA1813, dn14 (Nor.), p14 (Nor.), MA1816. R. Brome w. Oakley, Suffolk 1819-21, R. Honingham w. East Tuddenham, Norfolk 1831 to death 7/12/1850 [C115402] Had issue.

SMITH (William Henry) Born York 4/4/1806, s. of Henry Smith (attorney) and Sarah Prowde. Emmanuel, Cambridge 1824, then Queens' 1825, BA1828, dn29 (York), p30 (Rochester for York). R. Hinderwell, Yorks. 1830-50. Died after 1857. Will not traced [C135747. YCO] Married (1) Scalby, Yorks. 14/10/1835 Elizabeth Mary Howard (a clergy dau., Throxenby Hall, Scarborough, Yorks., d.1839), with issue (2) Hinderwell 28/12/1839 Mary Jane Hopkins, with further issue.

SMITH see also under **SMYTH**

SMITH-MARRIOTT (William Marriott) see under **MARRIOTT**

SMITHSON (John) Bapt. Leeds, Yorks. 1752, s. Henry Smithson. Trinity, Cambridge 1771, BA1775, dn76 (C&L), MA1778, p81 (C&L). PC. Headingley cum Birley, Leeds 1782 and PC. Kirkheaton, Yorks. 1785 to death 1/1/1836 [C19863] Married Leeds 1798 Ruth Hainsworth.

SMYTH, SMYTHE (Charles Bohun) Bapt. Euston juxta Thetford, Suffolk 20/4/1793, s. Rev. Charles John Smyth (V. Catton, Norfolk). Chorister Magdalen, Oxford 1802-8; matr. Wadham, Oxford 1810, BA1815, dn20, p21. V. Alfriston, Sussex 1832-70. Died Eastbourne, Sussex 19/7/1872, leaving £5,000 [C72253. Boase] Married (1) Catton, Norfolk 29/7/1825 Rachel Eloisa Harvey (d.1832) (2) Wingfield, Suffolk 28/6/1833 Harriet Cotton Sumpter (w).

SMYTH (Edmund) Born Great Linford, Bucks. 14/3/1793, s. Rev. William Smyth and Susannah Ray. Literate: p15 (Lin.), then St John's, Cambridge 1818, BA1822, MA1825. V. North Elkington, Lincs. 1823 and V. East Haddon, Northants. 1830 to death 7/12/1853 aged 61 [C110930] Married Louth 8/6/1826 Ann Mary Bellwood.

SMYTH (John Hill) [BD but NiVoF]. PC. Liverpool St Stephen 1796, PC. Liverpool St Thomas, Toxteth Park 1825 to burial 11/5/1834 (CCEd says died 6/11/1834) aged 72 [C170550]

SMYTH (Joshua) Born Swefling, Suffolk 23/3/1792, s. James Smyth and Hannah Ann Kemp. Literate: dn18 (York), p19 (York). PC. Keyingham, Yorks. 1821-73, V. Burton Pidsea, Yorks. 1832-65. Died Colchester, Essex 24/3/1878, leaving £1,000 [C135994. YCO] Married (1) Sculcoates, Hull, Yorks. 2/12/1824 Hannah Collinson (d.1845), w. clerical s. John G. Smyth (2) Woodbridge, Suffolk 1865 (3rd q.) Amelia Wolton.

SMYTH (Philip) From Weston, Norfolk, s. Philip Smyth. New, Oxford 1777 (aged 17), dn81 (Ox.), BCL1784, p85 (Ox.). R. Worthen, Shropshire 1811 to death 21/7/1840 [C37653]

SMYTH (Richard) Born Stapleford Tawney, Essex 4/3/1756, s. Rev. Sir William Smyth, 6th Bart. (Hill Hall and Horham Hall, Essex) and Abigail Wood. St John's, Cambridge 1774, re-adm. 1777 and 1800, dn78 (C&L for London), p80 (London), LLB1801. R. Stapleford Tawney w. Theydon Mount 1780 and R. Little Warley, Essex 1800 to death 3/1/1837 [C19865] 'Married Charlotte, dau. of James Montague, of Lackham House, Wilts., who was perhaps the most celebrated person of her time for exquisite beauty and symmetry of form'.

SMYTH (Thomas Scott) Born Liverpool 19/4/1777, s. Thomas Smyth (Irish-born Lord Mayor of Liverpool) and Elizabeth Blagg. BNC, Oxford 1794, BA1797, Fellow of Oriel 1800-13, dn05 (Ox.), p06 (Ox.), MA1801. V. St Austell w. St Blazey, Cornwall 1815-54, Canon of 3rd Prebend in Bristol Cathedral 1828-31, Prebend of Exeter Cathedral 1829 to death (Clifton, Bristol) 14/11/1854 aged 77 [C21630] Married (1) Prestbury, Cheshire 28/1/1812 Frances Ryle (d.1820), w. issue (2) St James's, Piccadilly, London 21/11/1822 Georgiana Theophila Metcalfe, w. further issue.

SMYTH (William, sen.) Bapt. Tyningham cum Filgrave, Bucks. 20/5/1761, s. Rev. Edmund Smyth and Dorothea Shan. Christ Church, Oxford 1780, BA1783, dn84 (Lin.), p85 (Nor.), MA1786. R. Great Linford, Bucks. 1786, R. Broughton, Bucks. 1790-1815, R. Tyringham w. Filgrave 1815-22. Chap. to HRH Duke of

York and Albany 1790-1815-. Died 9/12/1837 [C76712] Married 1790 Susannah Ray, with son William, below.

SMYTH (William, jun.) Born Great Linford, Bucks. 17/6/1791, s. Rev. William Smyth, sen. (above) and Susannah Ray. BNC, Oxford 1809 (aged 17), BA1813, MA1815, p15 (Lin.). PC. Little Linford, Lincs. 1815, R. Broughton, Lincs. 1821, V. North Elkington, Lincs. 1818-23, V. South Elkington, Lincs. 1821. Dom. Chap. to 1st Baron Glastonbury 1816. Died 21/1/1873, leaving £60,000 [C76713] MarriedTannington, Suffolk 13/6/1820, w clerical s. James Grenville Smyth.

SMYTH (William Watson) Bapt. Marylebone, London 19/1/1806, s. Rev. George Watson Smyth and Phoebe Vaine. Trinity Hall, Cambridge 1822, BA1827, dn28 (Nor.), p28 (Nor.), MA1830. V. Manton, Rutland 1828-59. Latterly of Colsterworth, Lincs.; in 1861 Census 'boarding' at the Great Western Railway Hotel, Paddington, London; living with his brother at Wadhurst Castle, Sussex in 1871. Died (unmarried) and buried Wadhurst 20/8/1873. Will not traced [C110931]

SMYTH see also under **SMITH**

SMYTHIES (Henry Yeates) Born South Moreton, Berks. 15/2/1765, s. Rev. Humphrey Smythies (V. Blewbery, Berks.) and Katharine Carter. Merton, Oxford 1780, then Emmanuel, Cambridge 1781, BA1786, dn87 (Nor.), MA 1789, p92 (Nor.), BD1796, Fellow 1788, etc. V. Stanground, Hunts. [net income £1,299] 1809 to death 20/6/1842 [C76715] Married Belchamp Walter, Essex 14/11/1809 Isabella Raymond (a clergy dau., Belchamp Hall), with issue. J.P. for Hunts.

SNAPE (Richard) Born Billinge, Wigan, Lancs. 9/3/1771, s. Thomas Snape and Nancy Martlew. Magdalene, Cambridge 1789, BA 1793, dn96 (London), p97 (London). R. (and patron) of Brent Eleigh, Suffolk 1808 to death 4/5/1860, leaving £30,000 [C66843] Married 20/11/1806 Letitia Anne Frost (w) (dau. of a solicitor, Sudbury, Suffolk), with issue.

SNELL (Thomas) From Bloomsbury, London, s. William Snell. St John's, Oxford 1797 (aged 18), Fellow 1797-1803, dn02 (Glos.), BCL 1803, p03 (Ox.). R. Windlesham w. Bagshot, Surrey 1807 (and RD 1834) to death 2/4/1843 (within a week of his wife) [C21632] Married Richmons, Ssurrey 23/2/1804 (the Irish) Barbara Cooke, 10 ch.

SNELSON (Richard Filewood) Born Hanbury, Staffs. 28/7/1780, s. Rev. Jeffrey Snelson and Mary Filewood. Trinity, Oxford 1798, BA 1802, dn03 (London), p04 (London), MA1805. (succ. his father as) V. Reigate, Surrey 1812 to death 6/3/1847 [C122557] Married Epsom, Surrey 16/5/1820 Elizabeth Davies.

SNEYD (John) Born Keele, Staffs. 7/10/1763, s. Ralph Sneyd and Barbara Bagot. Christ Church, Oxford 1782, BA1786, dn87 (by Bp of St David's for Bp of Oxford - in Oxford), MA 1788, p88 (Ox.). R. Bramshall, Staffs. 1788-1835, PC. Capesthorne, Cheshire 1788-1811 (res.), PC. Keele, Staffs. 1789-1829 (res.), R. Elford, Staffs. 1792 to death 2/7/1835 (CCEd says 29/8/1835) [C19873]

SNEYD (Lewis) Born Keele, Staffs. 14/7/1788, s. Rev. Ralph Sneyd and Penelope Moore. Christ Church, Oxford 1805, BA1809, then All Souls, Fellow 1809-27, dn12 (Ox.), p12 (C&L), MA1813, Warden of All Souls, Oxford 1827-58. R. East Lockinge, Berks. 1827 to death 21/2/1858, leaving £50,000 [C19875]

SNEYD (Wetenhall) Born Dublin c.1752. [NiVoF] V. Newchurch, IoW 1816 and R. Bletchingley, Surrey 1838. Died Merston, IoW 21/11/1840 aged 88 [C53882] Married (1) Dublin July 1777 Margaret Cullen (d.1797), w. issue (2) Newchurch 24/9/1801 Mrs Harriet Cleader, w. further issue.

SNOW (Thomas Lambert) Bapt. Tidmington, Worcs. 23/2/1772, s. Thomas Snow and Ann Banbury. Worcester, Oxford 1789, BA1793, dn97 (Ox.), p98 (Ox.). R. (and patron) of Barcheston, Warwicks. 1800 to death 22/6/1839, living at Tidmington [C37665] Married Ann Robins, w. clerical s. Thomas.

SNOWDEN (William) Born Hemingbrough, Yorks. 1/3/1785, s. of Richard (a farmer) and Jane Snowden. Literate: dn08 (Bristol for York), p09 (York), then St John's, Cambridge 1827, then St Catharine's 1828 (a Ten Year Man, BD1829). PC. Horbury, Yorks. 1818-34, R. Swillington, Yorks. 1837 to death (Gateforth, Yorks.) 5/4/1847 [C53886. YCO] Married Skelbrooke, Yorks. 22/12/1809 Elizabeth England, with clerical son.

SOAMES (Henry) Born City of London 15/1/1785, s. Nathaniel Soames (shoemaker) and Sarah Aldwin. Wadham, Oxford 1803, BA 1807, dn08 (Bristol), MA1809, p09 (London). R. Shelley, Essex 1812-60, R. Little Laver, Essex, 1821-4 (res.), R. Furneaux Pelham w. Brent Pelham >< Essex 1831-9, R. Stapleford Tawney w. Theydon Mount, Essex 1839 and Chancellor of St Paul's Cathedral 1842 to death. Dom. Chap. to 4th Earl of Dartmouth 1821-31. Died 21/10/1860, leaving £4,000 [C53846. ODNB. Boase] Wife Mary, and issue.

SOCKETT (Thomas) Bapt. Worcester 15/12/1764, s. Richard and Anne Elizabeth Sockett. Worcester, Oxford 1787, BA1791, dn91 (Wor.), p91 (Wor.). R. Ombersley, Worcs. 1791 to death 1837 [C122161]

SOCKETT (Thomas) Born London 20/11/1777, s. Thomas Sockett and Sarah Brightman. Exeter, Oxford 1806, SCL, dn08 (Win.), p08 (Win.), BA1811, MA1813. R. North Scarle, Lincs. 1811, R. Duncton, Sussex 1815, R. Petworth, Sussex 1816 to death 17/3/1859, leaving £3,000 [C64328] Married (1) Westminster, London 27/7/1810 Sarah Gray (d.1814), w. clerical son Henry Sockett (2) Petworth, Susex 21/3/1816 Sarah Herrington, w. further issue. Photo. online.

SODOR AND MAN (Bishop of) see under **WARD (William)**

SOLLIS (William) Bapt. Chipping Camden, Glos. 19/10/1792, s. William Sollis and Mary Emms. Pembroke, Oxford 1809, BA1812, MA 1815, dn15 (Glos.), p17 (Glos.). PC. West Woolfardisworthy, Devon 1822, R. West Putford, Devon 1835, V. Fenton, Staffs 1839 to death (Newcastle under Lyme, Staffs.) 14/2/1873 aged 80, leaving under £100 [C146389] Married Blockley, Worcs. 17/2/1817 Ann Wheatcroft, and had issue.

SOMERSET (Villiers Plantagenet Henry) Born 12/2/1803, s. Gen. Lord Charles Henry Somerset (s. of the 5th Duke of Beaufort) and Lady Elizabeth Courtenay (dau. of 2nd Viscount Courtenay). Christ Church, Oxford 1820, BA 1826, dn26 (Bristol for Llandaff), p27 (Ex.). R. Honiton, Devon 1827 to death 3/2/1855 [C53848] Married 7/7/1844 Frances Dorothy Ley, with clerical son Henry Plantagenet Somerset.

SOMERSET (William George Henry, Lord) Bapt. 2/10/1784, s. 5th Duke of Beaufort and Elizabeth (dau. of Admiral the Hon. Edward Boscawen). [In army 1801-11-]. Literate: dn14 (Nor.), p15 (Salis. for Nor.), then Jesus, Cambridge 1815, BA, dn14 (Nor.), p14 (Salis.), MA 1818. V. Stoke Gifford, Glos. 1814-26 (res.), R. Llangattock w. Llanelly, Brecon 1814-51, R. Magor w. Redwick, Mon. 1821-6, (Sinecure R. Llanfihangel w. Crickhowell, Brecon 1823-51), R. Tormarton w. Acton Turville, Glos. 1826-51, 6th Prebend in Bristol Cathedral 1822 to death (Clifton) 14/1/1851 aged 66 [C53847] Married (1) 29/6/1813 Elizabeth Molyneux (dau. of a military baronet), w. clerical sons William, and Boscawen George Henry (2) 22/9/1844 Mrs Frances Westby (Brady) O'Callaghan (Raheen Manor, Co. Clare). 'It was stated by those who knew him that he never wrote a sermon; but there is a tradition that he preached twice in the Cathedral [Bristol] in the course of twenty-three years. On the other hand, he had all the skill of his family for driving a coach and four, which it was his constant practice to do after morning service during his periods of residence; and where the stables he built at Tormarton were much more imposing than was the rectory'.'

SOMERVILLE (William) Born 14/10/1789, s. Lt.-Col. Hon. Hugh Somerville and Mary Digby. Peterhouse, Cambridge 1814, dn17 (Glos.), BA1818, p18 (C&L), MA1826. R. Aston Somerville, Glos. 1828-41, R. Barford, Warwicks. 1841 to death. Dom. Chap. to 15th Baron Somerville 1818. Died Birkenhead, Cheshire 6/7/1857 [C19879] Married Blithfield, Staffs. 5/5/1830 Charlotte Bagot (a clergy dau.), 5s.

SOUTH (Thomas [Horner]) [NiVoF] PC. Burton Hastings, Warwicks. 1797 to death (Fittleton, Wilts.) 28/12/1842 aged 80 [C19880. No mention of any degree in *Gentleman's Magazine* obit.]

SOUTHALL (Henry) Bapt. Stoke Prior, Worcs. 9/11/1763, s. Rev. Henry Southall, sen. Magdalen Hall, Oxford 1785, BA1789, dn89 (Wor.), p91 (Wor). V. Upton Snodbury, Worcs. 1797-1802, PC. Dormston, Worcs. 1800-50, R. Kington, Worcs. 1804 and R. Bishampton, Worcs. 1820 to death 5/4/1850 [C122165]

SOUTHBY (--) Chap. of the Donative of Bulford, Wilts. 1830-[53] [a family living;

forname blank in CL1851]. Died? [Not in CCEd] It has proved impossible to identify this man, but possibilities in Foster].

SOUTHCOMB (Edmund) Bapt. Rose Ash, Devon 29/7/1792, s. Rev. John Southcomb and Susannah Granger. Sidney, Cambridge 1811, BA1815, dn15 (Ex.), p16 (Ex.), MA1818, Fellow. (succ. his father as) R. (and patron) of Rose Ash 1822 to death 5/5/1854 [C40610]

SOUTHMEAD (William) Bapt. Chagford, Devon 11/3/1762, s. Rev. John Southmead. Balliol, Oxford 1781, BA1785, dn85 (Ex.), p88 (Ex.). R. Gidleigh, Devon 1791 to death 25/12/1832 [C146394]

SOUTHWELL (Marcus Richard) Born Stoke Damerel, Devon, s. Richard Hayes Southwell and Ann Batty. Exeter, Oxford 1823 (aged 18), BA1827, dn28 (B&W), p29 (Ex.), MA1839. V. (and patron) of St Albans, St Stephen, Herts. 1830 to death 1/9/1880 aged 75, leaving £60,000 [C122569] Married Tamerton Foliott, Devon 28/9/1825 Cecilia Jane Johnson, w. clerical s. of same name.

SPARKE (Bowyer Edward, Bishop of Chester, *then of* Ely) Born Chelsea, London 17/4/1759, s. Major William Sparke and Mary Lambert. Pembroke, Cambridge 1777, BA1782, Fellow 1784, MA1785, dn89 (Roch.), p89 (Lin.), BD and DD1803. R. Waltham, Leics. 1789, V. Scalford, Leics. 1800-5, R. Redmile, Leics. 1800-9, Dean of Bristol 1803-9, V. St Augustine the Less, Bristol 1803-9, R. Leverington, Ely 1806, Bishop of Chester 1809-12, Bishop of Ely 1812 to death 4/4/1836, leaving £149,000. He was the last bishop to exercise civil jurisdiction in the Isle of Ely [C2277. Not in ODNB] Married 8/12/1790 Hester Hobbs (of Blandford Forum, Dorset), w. clerical sons Edward Bowyer, and John Henry (both below). 'It was said that one could find one's way in the Fens at night by the little Sparkes planted in good livings.' *F.,R.S.; F.S.A.*

SPARKE (Edward Bowyer) Son of Rt. Rev. Bowyer Edward Sparke (above) and Hester Hobbs. Pembroke, Cambridge 1821, BA1826, Fellow 1826-30, dn28 (Ely), MA1829, p29 (Ely). R. Hagworthingham, Lincs. 1829 (only), R. Conington, Cambs. 1829-30, R. Barley, Herts. 1829-31, Prebend of 4th Canon in Ely Cathedral 1829, then 7th 1831-79, V. Littleport, Ely, Cambs. 1830-65, R. Feltwell, Cambs. [net income £1,207] 1831 to death. Registrar of the Diocese of Ely. Dom. Chap. to his father the Bp of Ely 1829. Died 28/6/1879, leaving £160,000 [C19613] Married 7/3/1833 Catherine Maria Newcombe (w) (a clergy dau., Hockwold Hall, Norfolk). Brother below.

SPARKE (John Henry) Born Blandford Forum, Dorset 12/8/1794, s. Rt. Rev. Bowyer Edward Sparke (above) and Hester Hobbs. Pembroke, Cambridge 1810, BA1815, then Jesus, Fellow 1815, MA 1818, dn18 (Ely), p18 (Ely). R. Stretham, Cambs. 1818-28, Canon of 6th Prebend in Ely Cathedral 1818 (5th Prebend 1824 to death), (Sinecure R. Littlebury, Essex [income £2,190] 1818-39), R. Cottenham, Cambs. 1819-27, R. Leverington, Cambs. 1827-70, R. Benwell, Norfolk 1829-31, R. (and patron) of Gunthorpe w. Bale, Norfolk [net income £2,099] 1831 (living at Gunthorpe Hall) to death ('The Brunswick House Hotel', London) 8/2/1870, leaving £140,000 [C19614] Married Westminster, London 10/9/1825 Agnes (dau. of Sir John Dugdale Astley, 1st Bart., Melton Constable Hall, Norfolk), with issue. Brother above.

SPEARE (James) Bapt. Westminster, London 5/3/1774, s. James and Mary Speare. Clare, Cambridge 1792, BA1797, dn99 (Peterb.), Fellow 1799, MA1800, p02 (Ely). R. Rotherhithe, Surrey 1816-17, R. Elmsett, Suffolk 1817 to death 22/5/1850 aged 76 [C100315] Probably married Cambridge 1/8/1817 Sarah Headley.

SPEIDELL (Thomas) Bapt. Barnes, Surrey 4/11/1776, s. Jacob Thomas Speidell and Elizabeth Jellicoe. St John's, Cambridge 1795, BA1799, MA1803, dn05 (Ox.), BD 1808, etc. PC. Northmoor, Oxon. 1810-14, R. Handborough, Oxon. 1824-29, R. Crick, Northants. 1829 to death 21/1/1836 [C21633]

SPEKE (Hugh) From Ilminster, Somerset. Emmanuel, Cambridge 1821, BA1825, dn26 (B&W), p27 (B&W), MA1828. United R. West Dowlish and Dowlishwake >< Som. 1827 and V. Curry Rivel, Som. 1834 to death. Dom. Chap. to 2nd Baron Crewe 1832. Died (Marseilles) 25/12/1856 aged 53 [C40612] Married Chard, Som. 22/7/1828 Mary Weekes Coles (Parrocks Lodge, Chard), with issue.

SPENCE (Hugh Maltby) Born Hackney, London 6/8/1802, s. Sawyer and Margaret Spence. Lincoln, Oxford 1821, BA1824, dn25

(Peterb.), p26 (Peterb.), MA1829. V. West Haddon, Northants. 1826 to death 25/7/1855 [C110937] Married (1) West Haddon 25/5/1826 Elizabeth Harding. (d.1827) (2) Greenwich, Kent 25/11/1830 Margaret Millicent Webb, and had issue.

SPENCE (John) Born Bedale, Yorks. (bapt. Leicester 25/6/1781), s. John Spence and Ann Gale. Trinity, Cambridge 1801, BA1805, dn05 (Lin.), p08 (Lin.), MA1809. R. East Keal, Lincs. 1824 and R. Winceby, Lincs. 1829 to death 12/2/1860 aged 81, leaving £10,000 [C76784. Kaye. Bennett2] Married Spalding, Lincs. 17/11/1811 Mary Pine Gates ('with consent of her mother' - the patron), and son Joseph Spence, following his father at East Keal.

SPENCE (John) Born West Ham, Middx. Clare, Cambridge 1809, then Trinity 1810, BA 1814, dn14 (Ely for Lin.), p15 (Lin.), MA1817. R. and V. Culworth, Northants. 1829-52, V. West Haddon, Northants. 1823-6, dying there 21/10/1852 [C76789]

SPENCER (Charles) From Westminister, London, s. James Spencer. Queen's, Oxford 1802 (aged 18), BA1806, MA1809, dn06 (Ex. for London), p07 (Salis. for London). V. Bishop's Stortford, Herts. 1817 to death. Dom. Chap. to 1st Baron Hotham 1812. Died 7/7/1849 [C89480] Married Westminster, London 28/9/1813 Emma Amilia Beechey, w. clerical son William Henry Spencer.

SPENCER (George [John] Trevor, *later* **Bishop of Madras)** Born Mayfair, London 4/12/1799, s. Hon. William Robert Spencer and Susan Gräfin von Jenison-Walworth ('widow of Count Spreti'). University, Oxford 1817, BA 1822, dn23 (Ely for Salis.), p23 (Salis.), DD 1847. PC. Buxton, Derbys. 1824-37 (res.), R. Leaden Roding, Essex 1828-32 (res.), Bishop of Madras 1837-49, Coadjutor (Assistant) Bishop of Bath and Wells, Chancellor of St Paul's Cathedral 1860, R. Walton on the Wolds, Leics. 1861 to death. Min. of the Marbeuf (Anglican) Chapel in Paris. Died (of dropsy, Edge Moor, Buxton) 16/7/1866, leaving £16,000 [C26156. ODNB. Boase] Married 27/5/1823 Harriet Theodora Hobhouse (dau. of a baronet), 2s. (inc. Rev. Almeric John Spencer), 3 dau. Good photograph (showing him badly in need of a haircut) at: www.19thcenturyphotos.com/George-Spencer,-Bishop-of-Madras-123476.htm

SPENCER (Houghton) Bapt. Stowmarket, Suffolk 1/8/1778, s. James and Elizabeth Spencer. Trinity, Cambridge 1796, no degree? dn20 (Nor.), p20 (Nor.). PC. Crimplesham, Norfolk 1829 to death (Wereham, Norfolk) 5/1/1850 aged 71 [C115567] Married Suidbury, Suffolk 22/9/1807 Amelia Sarah Strutt, w. clerical son John Spencer.

SPENCER (James) Bapt. Leighton Bromswold, Hunts. 19/12/1773, s. George Spencer and Hannah/Dinah Jackson. Literate: dn11 (Chester), p12 (Chester). PC. Turton, Bolton-le-Moors, Lancs. 1815-59. Died there 23/1/1866 aged 92. Will not traced [C170555] Married Bolton-le-Moors 23/1/1826 Mary Ann Scholes, w. issue (inc. a clerical son who succeeded him).

SPENCER (Nicholas) Bapt. Kilkeel, Co. Down 26/6/1759, s. Brent Spencer. TCD 1775, dn83 (Ex.), p84 (Ex.), MA1786. V. Halse, Som. 1793-1843, V. Burlescombe, Devon 1803-[19], PC. Ash Priors >< Som. 1821-34 (res.). Dom. Chap. to Earl Spencer. Died 11/10/1843 aged 84 [C40613. Al.Dub.]

SPENCER (Thomas) From Bradford on Avon, Wilts., s. Rev. Edward Spencer and Susannah Lowe. St Edmund Hall, Oxford 1793 (aged 18), BA1796, dn96 (Salis.), p98 (Salis.), MA1799. V. Wingfield, Wilts. 1819-33, 1835 to death 11/6/1842 aged 62 [C89481] Wife Fanny A., with issue.

SPENCER (Thomas) Bapt. Derby 18/10/1796. St John's, Cambridge 1816, BA1820, dn20 (Ely for Nor.), p21 (Nor.), MA1823, Fellow 1823-9. PC. Hinton Charterhouse, Som. 1826-48. Resided latterly in London. Died 26/1/1853 [C40614. ODNB. Boase] Married Dublin 1829 Anna Maria Brooke, *s.p.* Evangelical; writer on social subjects; uncle of Herbert Spencer; Sec. of the National Temperance Society. A 'decidedly fine-looking man, with a commanding figure, a good voice and a ready utterance'.

SPENCER (William) From Burslem, Staffs., s. Thomas Spencer. Trinity, Cambridge 1790 (aged 18), BA1794, dn94 (C&L), p96 (C&L). R. Cranleigh, Surrey 1805-12, V. Dronfield w. Alcaston, Derbys. 1809 to death 10/12/1845 aged 74 [C19891] Had issue.

SPENCER (William Packenham [Maxwell]) Born India 1/2/1800, s. Lt.-Gen. William

Spencer (Bramley Grange, Ripon, Yorks.) and Charlotte Swann. St John's, Cambridge 1817, BA1821, Fellow 1823-8, dn24 (Bristol), MA 1824, p25 (Lin. for Ely). R. Starston, Norfolk 1827-44, R. Badley, Suffolk 1835-7. Died (Merton House, Grantchester, Cambridge) 16/8/1845 [C53858]

SPENCER-STANHOPE (Charles) see under **STANHOPE**

SPERLING (Harvey [James]) Bapt. Theydon Garnon, Essex 12/11/1795, s. Henry Piper Sperling and Anne Grace. Trinity, Cambridge 1813, BA1818, dn19 (Nor.), p20 (Nor.), MA 1821. R. Papworth St Agnes, Cambs. 1821 to death (St Ives, Hunts.) 24/5/1858, leaving £20,000 [C109279] Married London 27/6/1822 Anne Irving McNabb (of Stirling), with issue. Doubtless related to the man below.

SPERLING (James) Born Dynes Hall, Great Maplestead, Essex, s. Henry Sperling and Mary Piper. Adm. to Middle Temple 1783. Trinity, Cambridge 1791 (aged 19), BA1795, dn96 (London), p97 (London), MA1798. V. Great Maplestead (living at Monks Hall) 1797 and R. Lamarsh, Essex 1803 to death. Dom. Chap to Catherine, Dowager Lady Howard de Walden and Braybrooke 1803. Died 31/10/1850 aged 78 [C122576] Married Holborn, London 2/5/1797 Elizabeth Bullock (Shelley House, Ongar. Essex). with issue. Related to man above.

SPETTIGUE (Edmund) Bapt. Launceston, Cornwall 6/6/1776, s. Solomon and Grace Spettigue. Exeter, Oxford 1794, BA1798, dn98 (Ex.), p01 (Ex.). R. Michaelstow, Cornwall 1818-47. Latterly infirm and living in Launceston, dying there 1848 (3rd q.) [C146397] Married by 1822 Mary Bosisto, w.issue.

SPOONER (John) Born Birches Green, Warwicks. 10/1/1785, s. Isaac Spooner and Barbara (dau. of Sir Henry Gough, 1st Bart.). St John's, Cambridge 1805, then Corpus Christi 1805, re-adm. St John's 1806, BA1810, dn10 (Lin.), p11 (Win.). R. Elvetham, Hants. 1811 to death Marne, France 20/4/1841 [C76843]. Brother William, below. Their sister Barbara Spooner married William Wilberforce.

SPOONER (John Bourryau) Bapt. City of London 4/6/17861, s. Hungerford and Jane Spooner. [NiVoF] R. Blyborough, Lincs. 1795 to death. Buried 10/6/1846 [C76844. LBSO]

Married Boston, Lincs. 15/11/1810 Dorothy Lawrence.

SPOONER (Robert Denny Rix) Bapt. Lingwood, Norfolk 1/11/1763, s. Denny (a farmer) and Mary Spooner. Caius, Cambridge 1782, BA1786, dn86 (Nor.), p88 (Nor.), MA1789. S/M Anwick, Lincs. 1791; V Brauncewell w. Dunsby and Anwick >< Lincs. 1812-26 (res.), V. Rushall, Staffs. 1792-1807 (res.), V. Worlaby, Lincs. 1806 to death (Hastings, Sussex) 1836 aged 73 [C19895] Married Finsbury, London 5/12/1811 Sarah Manning, with issue.

SPOONER (William) Born Aston-Juxta-Birmingham 20/8/1778, s. Isaac Spooner and Barbara (dau. of Sir Henry Gough, 1st Bart.). St John's, Cambridge 1796, BA1800, dn01 (London), p02 (C&L), MA 1803. R. Elmdon, Warwicks. 1802, V. Chipping Camden, Glos. 1815-24, R. Acle, Norfolk 1824, Archdeacon of Coventry and Canon Residentiary in Lichfield Cathedral 1827-51 (res.), Prebend of Bishophull and Canon Residentiary in Lichfield Cathedral 1828 to death. Dom. Chap. to 3rd Baron Calthorpe 1810. Died (Elmdon) 2/9/1857 [C19896] Married Newington, Kent 7/9/1810 Anna Maria Sidney O'Brien (dau. of an Irish baronet), with clerical son Edward Spooner. Brother John, above. Their sister Barbara Spooner married William Wilberforce.

SPRAGG (Francis Roach) Born Ferham Longcot, Berks. 1/9/1782, s. Samuel Spragge and Ann Stratton. Queens', Cambridge 1803, BA1808, dn08 (Bristol), dn09 (B&W), Fellow 1809, MA1811. V. ('Treasurer') Combe St Nicholas, Som. 1823 and Swallowclift Prebend in Heytesbury Collegiate Church, Wilts. 1835 to death (and burial in) Paris 31/5/1838 [C49028] Married Clapham, London 21/7/1812 Eliza Elliott, and had issue.

SPRANGER (Robert) Born Holborn, London 26/11/1777, s. John Spranger and Jane Roughsedge. Jesus, Oxford 1799, dn03 (Nor.), p03 (Nor.), then Trinity Hall, Cambridge 1808, LLB1809, incorporated at Oxford, DCL 1834. R. Ilston, Glamorgan 1804-5, R. Pwllchrochan, Pembroke 1804, V. Tamerton Foliot, Devon 1806-20, R. Low Toynton, Lincs. 1820 and R. Creeton, Lincs. 1820 (non-res.) to death (London) 13/2/1850 [C76846. V. only. Kaye. Bennett2] Married Castor, Northants. 9/5/1809 Sarah Maria White (a clergy dau.), with issue.

SPRIGGE (James Dewhurst) Born Leicester 29/2/1780, s. William Sprigge and Martha Leavis. Clare, Cambridge 1819, then Peterhouse 1819, dn20 (Nor.), p21 (Nor.), LLB1830. R. (and patron) of Brockley, Suffolk 1824 to death 1846 (4th q. as Dewhirst) [C115569] Married Stamford, Lincs. 12/12/1802 Mary Ann Shepherd, and had issue.

SPROSTON (George) Perhaps born Stratford-on-Avon, Warwicks. 28/12/1792, s. John and Mary Sproston. Literate: dn15 (Lin.), p16 (Lin.). PC. Oldbury, Shropshire 1832, PC. Trimdon, Durham 1846-75-. Buried 3/10/1883 aged 92. No will traced [C76849] Married Market Harborough 9/8/1812 Susannah Rice Moses, and issue.

SPRY (John) Bapt. Stoke Damerel, Devon 20/6/1764, s. John Spry and Margaret Brooking. Christ Church, Oxford 1778, then St Alban Hall, BA1786, dn86 (Salis. for Ox.), p89 (Ex.). V. Ugborough, Devon 1810. Died 12/6/1845 aged 81 [C89487] Married Stoke Damerel, Devon 8/1/1789 Ann Crappe [*sic*].

SPRY (John Hume) Born Bristol, s. Rev. Benjamin Spry and Harriet Bromfield. Oriel, Oxford 1796 (aged 18), BA1799, dn00 (London), p01 (Bristol), MA1802, BD and DD1824. (first) Min. Birmingham Christ Church 1813-24 (res.), V. Hanbury, Staffs. 1816-32 (res.), PC. All Souls Langham Place, Marylebone, London 1824 [net income £1,898], R. St Marylebone 1825 and 8th Prebend in Canterbury Cathedral 1828 to death 11/11/1854 [C19897. Kaye] Married (1) Marylebone 14/5/1833 Anne Elizabeth Spence (d.1846), with issue (2) Old Church St Pancras, London 17/8/1848 Mrs Emily Anne (Allen) Chapman.

SPRY (William) Bapt. Plymouth, Devon 2/4/1787, s. Diggory Morris and Anna Maria Spry. Exeter, Oxford 1806, BA1810, dn10 (Ely for Ex.), p11 (Ex.), MA1814. R. (and patron) of Botus Fleming, Cornwall 1826 to death 26/8/1844 [C100318] Married Anne Conely, w. issue.

SPURGEON (John) Born Harpley, Norfolk 20/10/1801, s. Christopher Spurgeon and Eleanor Palgrave. Corpus Christi, Cambridge 1820, BA1824, dn25 (Nor.), p26 (Nor.). V. (and patron) of Twyford, Norfolk 1829 and V. Guist, Norfolk 1833 to death (Twyford) 29/1/1860 aged 58, leaving £800 [C115576] Married Norwich 21/6/1832 Frances Norris, and clerical son John Norris Spurgeon.

SPURGEON (Richard) Bapt. Great Yarmouth, Norfolk 25/8/1767, s. John Spurgeon and Sarah Baker. Pembroke, Cambridge 1786, BA1790, dn90 (Nor.), p91 (Nor.). R. Coppen-hall, Cheshire 1797-1805 (res.), R. Mulbarton w. Kinningham, Norfolk 1812 to death 19/5/1842 aged 74 [C115578] Married Martham, Norfolk 15/12/1800 Mary Cannon.

SPURWAY (John) Born Barnstaple, Devon 26/5/1790, s. Rev. William Spurway (below) and Avice Cutcliffe. Exeter, Oxford 1807, Fellow 1810-22, BA1813, dn13 (Ox.), MA1814, p15 (Ox.). R. Tiverton (Pitt's Portion), Devon (and Preacher throughout the Diocese of Exeter) 1821 to death 17/8/1874 aged 84, leaving £70,000 [C21663] Married by 1829 Margaretta Western, with issue.

SPURWAY (William) Bapt. Barnstaple, Devon 12/11/1742. Balliol, Oxford 1760, BA 1764, MA1766, dn67 (Ox.), p67 (Ex.). PC. Pilton, Devon 1772-1837, (Sinecure R. Broad Nymet, Devon 1781-1837), R. Tiverton (Clare Portion), Devon 1794 and R. Alwinghton, Devon 1794 to death, Dom Chap to 3rd Earl of Egmont 1794. Died 1/7/1837 aged 94 [C37726] Married Avice Cutcliffe, with clerical son John (above).

SQUIRE (Edmund) Born Wandsworth, Surrey 3/10/1780, s. John (physician) and Jane Squire. Christ's, Cambridge 1797, BA1801, MA 1804, dn11 (Lin.), p11 (Lin.). S/M Felsted G/S, Essex 1814-35; Curate of Great Waltham Black Chapel, Essex [a peculiar] at some date; V. Puttenham, Herts. 1831-5, R. Ashen, Essex 1835 to death 22/2/1853 aged 72 [C76851]

SQUIRE (John Franklin) Bapt. Bratton Fleming, Devon 23/12/1790, s. Rev. John Franklin Squire, sen. and Anne Snell. Caius, Cambridge 1808, BA1812, Fellow 1814-28, dn14 (Ex.), MA1815. R. Beachampton, Bucks. 1827 to death. Dom. Chap. to Bishop of Winchester 1823. Died 17/6/1834, aged 43 [C40616 has death date wrong] Married Beachampton 26/1/1829 Jane Harman.

ST AUBYN (Robert Thomas) Bapt. 6/8/1786, natural s. Sir John St Aubyn, 5th Bart. (St Michael's Mount, Cornwall, *q.v.* ODNB) and Martha Nicholls [thus a different mother to his step-brother, below]. Christ Church, Oxford

1806, BA1810, dn10 (Ex.), p14 (Ex.). R. Ruan Minor, Cornwall 1813-40-. Died Bow, London 26/9/1875 aged 89 (titled Esquire), leaving [as Staubyn] £3,000 [C122167] Married (1) 1813 Frances Fleming St John's (d.1863) (2) Gravesend, Kent 7/8/1866 Anne Catherine Russell (w); had issue. Step-brother, below.

ST AUBYN (William John) Born Croan, Cornwall 17/12/1794, natural s. Sir John St Aubyn, 5th Bart. (St Michael's Mount, Cornwall, *q.v.* ODNB) and Juliana Vinicombe [thus a different mother to his step-brother, above]. Christ Church, Oxford 1814, then Downing, Cambridge 1821, BA1824, dn23 (London), p28 (Ex.). R. Stoke Damerel (o/w Devonport), Devon 1828 [blank in ERC] to death 30/7/1877 aged 82, leaving £450 [C69113] Married 1/10/1822 Ann Dorothy (w) (dau. Sir Thomas Barrett-Leggett, 1st Bart.), with issue. Step-brother, above.

ST BARBE (Roger Frampton) Born Lymington, Hants. 3/8/1790, s. Charles St Barbe and Anne Hicks. St Catharine's, Cambridge 1812, BA1816, dn16 (Lin.), p17 (Lin.), MA1824. R. Sudbrook, Lincs. 1817, R. Stockton, Wilts. 1824 to death 13/11/1854 [C76854] Married Lincoln 13/10/1824 Harriet Money, *s.p.*

ST JOHN (George Frederick) Born 29/5/1795, natural s. (of the thoroughly disreputable) 3rd Viscount Bolingbroke/4th Viscount St John's and Baroness Hompesch (whom he married after the death of his first wife in 1819). Balliol, Oxford 1813, BA1816, then Jesus Cambridge 1816 (did not reside), dn19 (Nor.), p20 (Nor.), MA1823. R. Manston, Dorset 1820 to death 7/1/1867 aged 72, leaving £450 [C53860] Married Brighton 28/1/1830 Henrietta Frances Magrath, *s.p.* Freemason; artist; 'imprisoned for the debts of others; he was not so straight-laced as some would have their clergyman to be'.

ST JOHN (George William) Born Rockley, Wilts. 4/5/1796, s. Gen. Hon. Frederick St John's and Arabella Craven. Balliol, Oxford 1815, then Jesus, Cambridge 1816, MA1817, dn19 (Bristol), p20 (Salis.). V. Stanton Lacy, Shropshire 1820-47, R. Bladon cum Woodstock, Oxon. 1847 to death. Dom. Chap. to Marquess of Ailesbury 1821. Died (unmarried) 5/6/1876 aged 80, leaving £1,500 [C89493]

ST JOHN (Henry Ellis) Bapt. West Court, Finchampstead, Berks., s. Rev. Ellis St John and Anne Banister. Worcester, Oxford 1795 (aged 19), dn98 (Salis.), no degree, dn07 (Salis.). R. Finchampstead 1809 and R. (and patron) of Barkham, Berks. 1819 to death 27/8/1842 [C89494] Married (1) Godaling, Surrey 12/9/1802 Sarah Boxall (d.1832), w. issue (2) Walcot, Bath 1/8/1839 Elizabeth Alexander.

ST JOHN (Henry St Andrew) Bapt. Pirton, Worcs. 30/11/1796, s. Rev. John Francis Fleming Seymour St John (below) and Frances Fleming. Wadham, Oxford 1814, BA1818, dn20 (Wor.), MA1821, p21 (Wor.). PC. Putney, Surrey 1821-33 (res.), V. Addingham, Surrey 1834-8, V. Hilton, Dorset 1838 to death (Redhill, Surrey) 2/12/1874, leaving £6,000. Lived latterly at Tenby, Pembroke, then Redhill [C3492] Married Wimbledon, Surrey 12/5/1835 Emily Murray Belcher, with clerical son Henry Beauchamp St John (and bother JFSJ, below).

ST JOHN (John Francis Seymour Fleming, sen.) Bapt. Bletsoe, Beds. 16/11/1761, s. Very Rev. St. Andrew St John's (Dean of Worcester) and Sarah Chase. Christ Church, Oxford 1779, BA1783, MA1785. R. Grafton Flyford, Worcs. 1786-94 (res.), V. Powick, Worcs. 1792-1832, R. Croome D'Abitot w. Pirton, Worcs. 1794-1810, Canon of 10th Prebend of Worcester Cathedral 1804-32, PC. Putney, Surrey 1811-13, R. Severn Stoke, Worcs. 1815 to death. Master of St Oswald's Hospital [almshouses], Worcester 1828-32. Dom. Chap. to 7th Earl of Coventry 1792-1815. Died 4/12/1832 aged 71 (CCEd says 31/1/1833) [C159294 followed here] Married 26/5/1788 Frances Fleming, 6s. (2 clerical sons, one above, and one of same name - below - with major confusion), 5 dau.

ST JOHN (John Francis Seymour Fleming, jun.) Born Worcester 9/4/1789, s. Rev. John Francis Seymour Fleming St John's (above) and Frances Fleming. Christ Church, Oxford 1807, BA1811, MA1814. PC. Putney, Surrey 1813-21 (res.), V. Spondon, Derbys. 1814-33 (res.), R. Severn Stoke, Worcs. 1815-33, PC. Stanley, Derbys. 1830 (res.), PC. Chaddesden, Derbys. 1830. Living at Dinmore, Heref. Died 3/8/1848 [C122105 as Saint John and followed here. Austin. Major confusion with father, above] Married 5/6/1828 Cassandra Hurt. Brother Henry St John, above.

ST JOHN (Oliver D'Oyley) From Mottisfont, Hants., s. Rev. Oliver Goodyer St John and Hester Pollen (sister of a baronet). Merton, Oxford 1797 (aged 18), BA1800, dn02 (Win.), p03 (Win.). (succ. his father as) R. (and patron) of Mottisfont w. East Dean and Lockerley 1804 to death 21/3/1848 [C108823]

ST QUINTIN (George Darby) Born Speen, Berks. 18/3/1803, s. William Thomas St Quintin (born Darby) of Scampton Hall, Yorks. and Arabella Bridget Calcraft (dau. of a general). Christ Church, Oxford 1821, then Trinity, Cambridge 1821, BA1826, dn26 (Lin. for Chich.), p27 (C&L), MA1829. R. Broughton w. Bossington, Hants. (and Preacher throughout the Diocese of Winchester) 1827-41, Durham College [University] 1842-6, PC. St Leonard's on Sea, Sussex 1846-5. Dom. Chap. to Marquess of Salisbury 1847-72. Died 22/12/1872, leaving £45,000 [C19900] Married Chelsea, London 21/4/1827 Georgina Henrietta Louisa (dau. Hon. and Rev. Gerald Valerian Wellesley, *q.v.*), *s.p.*

STABBACK (Thomas) Bapt. Exeter 3/1/1771, s. Rev. John Stabback and Frances Mann. Oriel, Oxford 1788, dn92 (London), BA1793, p95 (Salis.). S/M Helston G/S, Cornwall 1814; military chaplain; R. Exeter St Edmund w. R. Exeter St Mary Steps 1801-[25], V. Cubert, Cornwall 1810 to death 29/1/1850 [C89497] Married Cheriton Fitzpayne, Devon 18/4/1802 Elizabeth Plomer, and had issue. Brother, below.

STABBACK (William) Bapt. Exeter 18/3/1760, s. Rev. John Stabback and Frances Mann. Balliol, Oxford 1778, BA1782, dn82 (Ex.), p84 (Ex.), then Jesus, Cambridge 1810, MA1810. V. Pagham, Sussex 1792-4, R. East Anstey, Devon 1809-[16], PC. Mariansleigh, Devon 1809-37, R. St Clether, Devon 1809-37, R. Exeter St Stephen 1816 and V. Sancreed, Cornwall 1816 to death. Dom. Chap. to 1st Earl of Harrowby 1809. Died Exeter 16/8/1837 [C146402] Married Bath 19/8/1800 Elizabeth Hoblyn (a clergy dau., Newton St Cyres, Devon). Brother, above.

STACEY (Daniel George) Born Oxford 27/7/1784, s. Rev. Henry Peter Stacey and Ann Keele. Pembroke, Oxford 1804, SCL, dn09 (Ox.), then New, Fellow 1809-32, p10 (Ox.), BCL1813, etc. V. Hornchurch, Essex 1831 to death (unmarried) 25/1/1863, leaving £600 [C21664. Foster as Stacy]

STACKHOUSE (William) Bapt. Probus, Cornwall 15/11/1773, s. William Stackhouse and Mary Rashleigh. Trinity, Oxford 1791, BA 1795, dn97 (Ex.), p97 (Ex.), MA1799. V. Modbury, Devon 1798-[1859], V. Antony, Cornwall 1802. Dom. Chap. to 8th Earl of Cork and Orrery 1802. Died Trehane House, Probus 21/11/1861 [dramatic picture of the shell of the house online], leaving £8,000 [C146403] Married Modbury, Devon 24/9/1800 Sarah Smith, with issue.

STACYE (Thomas) Born Bathfield, Sheffield 17/2/1757, s. Rev. John Stacye and Anne Jessop. Christ's, Cambridge, 1776, BA1780, dn80 (York), p81 (York), MA1783. V. Glossop, Derbys. 1781-92, V. Worksop, Notts. 1792 to death. Dom. Chap. to 3rd Earl of Dartmouth 1802. Died 28/1/1847 aged 90 [C19903. YCO] Married Worksop 23/1/1809 Maria Outram, with clerical son. Suspended in 1832 because of 'inefficiency and inaudibility'.

STAFFORD (Egerton) Born Penkridge, Staffs. 3/6/1763, s. Rev. James Stafford and Anne Biddulph. Christ Church, Oxford 1781, BA1785, dn86 (C&L), p87 (C&L), MA1788. R. Thenford, Northants. 1787 and V. Chacombe, Northants. 1802 to death 22/2/1843 [C19904] Clerical son (below).

STAFFORD (James Charles) Born Farthinghoe, Northants., s. Rev. Egerton and Mary Lucy Stafford (above). Trinity, Oxford 1811 (aged 17), then Lincoln 1813, then Magdalen 1815-32, BA 1816, dn17 (Ox.), p18 (Ox.), MA1818, BD 1832, Fellow 1832-42, etc. V. Penkridge, Staffs. 1830-33, 'Official Principal' of the Royal Free Chapel of Tettenhall Regis, Wolverhampton, Staffs. 1830, V. Dinton, Wilts. 1841-64-. Died Clifton, Bristol 15/12/1873, leaving £6,000 [C19905] Married 1841 (3rd q.) Susannah Judith >< Blencowe, with clerical sons Charles Egerton Fiennes Stafford, and John Richard Wykeham Stafford.

STAFFORD (John Herman) Born Dublin, s. Brabazon Stafford. TCD1819 (aged 15), BA 1826, dn28, p29. PC. Liverpool St Matthew 1832-5, Minister Liverpool St Paul 1835 to death 1868 (2nd q.) aged 64. A will is noted in Dublin [C170562. Al.Dub. as John] Married (1) Dublin before 1831 Thomasine Palmer (d.1842), with issue (2) Almoritia, Co. Westmeath 24/11/1846 Caroline Christiana Chamley, with further issue. Surrogate.

STAINES (William Tolbutt) Bapt. Canterbury 2/7/1775, s. Alderman Richard Staines and Sarah Tolbutt. St John's, Cambridge 1792, then Queens' 1795, BA1797, Fellow 1798, dn98 (Ely), p99 (Cant.), MA1800. Minor Canon of Rochester Cathedral 1801-32, PC. Strood, Kent 1803-5 (res.), V. Shorne, Kent 1805-32 (res.), V. Aylesford, Kent 1832 to death 24/9/1840 aged 65 [C1490] Married Leeds 10/4/1818 Jane Bolland (dau. of an attorney).

STAINTON (John) Born Egremont, Cumberland 6/8/1784, s. Edward Stainton (stonemason) and Mary Molly Burgess. Literate: dn08 (Chester), p11 (Chester). PC. Rampside, Dalton in Furness, Lancs. 1808-35 (depr.) [C170564] Married (1) 13/9/1808 Eleanor Haile (on whose death her father demanded the return of her dowry, and had Stainton imprisoned for 8 weeks for non-payment) (2) Dalton 31/3/1811 Ann Huddleston, a servant, 'just 16', 12 ch. Suspended for 3 years for intemperance 1820; charged with assault 1827; charged with 'drunkenness, immorality and excesses' 1830 and suspended for 3 years. Sentenced to transportation for life at Lancaster Assizes 1835 for forging a will. Died a beggar at West Maitland, NSW, Australia 28/12/1848 aged 59. M. Stainton, 'The Rev. John Stainton, of Rampside', *Cumbria Family History Society Newsletter*, No.98 (Feb. 2001) and No.99 (May 2001) is a compression of his 530pp manuscript in the Lancashire Record Office in Preston, this being the most detailed study of any of the clergy here [Note 'Riding the Stang' in 1830 to express the parishioners' disgust at his drinking and visits to Anne Pattie, the local prostitute; and compare the episode with a similar 'Skimmity Ride' in Thomas Hardy's *The Mayor of Casterbridge*].

STAMBURY (Henry) From Bridgwater, Som., s. Rev. Willoughby Stambury. Oriel, Oxford 1776 (aged 14), BA1780, dn84 (B&W), p86 (B&W), R. Hinton St George, Som. 1789 and R. Seavington St Michael, Som. 1789 to death 25/10/1837 [C49052]

STAMMERS (Robert) Bapt. Long Melford, Suffolk 14/12/1803, s. Joseph Stammers and Sarah Shepherd. St John's, Cambridge 1821, re-adm. 1822, BA1827, dn28 (C&L), p28 (C&L), MA1831. V. Woodhouse (in Barrow), Leics.

1832-82, V. Quorndon, Leics. 1832 to death 7/5/1888 aged 85, leaving £8,636-5s-1d. [C19773] Married Bury St Edmunds, Suffolk 17/6/1829 Sarah Dalton (dau. of a surgeon), with issue.

STANDLY (John) Born Little Paxton, Hunts. 30/4/1787, s. Henry Standly (born Poynter) and Persis Lens. Trinity, Cambridge 1804, then Caius 1805, BA1809, Fellow 1809-22, MA1812, dn16 (Lin.), p17 (Lin.). V. Buckden, Hunts. 1831-8, V. Southoe, Hunts. 1839 to death (Blaenporth, Cardigan) 5/6/1848 aged 61 [C76867] Married Blaenporth 16/4/1822 Caroline Frances Brigstocke, with issue.

STANE, *born* BRAMSTON (John Bramston) Bapt. Roxwell, Essex 21/5/1773, s. Thomas Berney Bramston and Mary Gardiner. Christ Church, Oxford 1791, BA1795, dn96 (London), MA1797, p97 (Glos.). R. Willingale Doe, Essex 1797-1806 (res.), R. Theydon Garnon, Essex 1799-1812 (res.), R. East Mersea, Essex 1806, (Sinecure R. Little Badow, Essex 1813). Dom. Chap. to 6th Earl Waldegrave 1799-1806-. Died Bath 21/2/1857, living at Forest Hall, Stansted, Essex [C66804] Married Marylebone, London 20/6/1801 Mary Elizabeth Newton, with issue.

STANGER (Edmund) Born Cambridge 17/10/1763, s. Hugh Stanger (butler to the Master of Peterhouse, Cambridge) and his wife Dorothy (a lady's maid in the same family). St John's, Cambridge 1781, BA1785, dn87 (Ely for Car.), p88 (Lin.), MA1788, Fellow 1788-1846, BD1796. PC. Wetheral cum Warwick, Cumberland (non-res.) 1787 to death 21/12/1846 aged 84 [C3493. Platt] 'A living sermon on the truths he taught.'

STANHOPE, *later* SPENCER-STANHOPE (Charles Spencer) Born Cawthorne, Yorks. 14/10/1795, s. Walter Spencer-Stanhope (formerly Stanhope), *M.P.*, and Mary Winifred Pulleine. Christ Church, Oxford 1813, BA1817, MA1819, dn19 (York), p21 (York). PC. Cawthorne 1822-74 (living at Cannon Hall there), V. Mattersey, Notts. 1834-35, V. Weaverham, Cheshire 1835 to death. Dom. Chap. to 1st Earl of Lonsdale 1820. Died 29/10/1874 aged 79, leaving £18,000 [C135750. YCO] Married 8/7/1840 Frederica Mary Goodenough (w) (a clergy dau.), with issue.

STANHOPE (Fitzroy Henry Richard, Hon.) Born 24/4/1787, s. Gen. Charles Stanhope, 3rd Earl of Harrington and Jane Fleming (Lady of the Bedchamber to Queen Charlotte). Trinity Hall, Cambridge 1810, MA (BA?) 1811, dn14, p15 (Glos.). V. Wressle, Yorks. 1814-56, R. Catton (w. Stamford Bridge), Yorks. 1814-58, 'Dean' and R. of Donative of St Buryan, Cornwall [a Royal Peculiar, net income £1,012] 1817-58. Dom. Chap. to his father 1815. Died Hans Place, London 11/4/1864 aged 76, leaving £1,500 [C135751 as Richard Henry. Boase] Married St George's Hanover Square, London 8/11/1808 Caroline Wyndham Hodges (w), the 17 year-old natural dau. of Hon. Charles Wyndham, with issue. Know as the 'Dean of Tattersalls' [a gambling club]; a member of the Garrick Club; and inventor of the Stanhope Phaeton (a two-wheeled gig). His equally worldly brother, below.

STANHOPE (Henry William, Hon.) Born London 2/8/1790, s. Gen. Charles Stanhope, 3rd Earl of Harrington and Jane Fleming (Lady of the Bedchamber to Queen Charlotte). Trinity Hall, Cambridge 1812, BA1812, MA 1814, dn15 (C&L), p15 (Roch.). V. and R. Chesham Woburn w. Chesham Leicester, Bucks. 1826-47, R. Gawsworth, Cheshire 1827 (non-res.) to death (London) 21/6/1872 aged 81, leaving £12,000 (but where he is not noted as a cleric) [C2281] Married (1) Grace Aguilar, with dau. (2) Camberwell, London 12/8/1862 Fanny Copère (r.), a French woman. His equally worldly brother, above.

STANIFORTH (Thomas) Born Liverpool 11/2/1807, s. Samuel Stanifirth (slave-trader) and Mary Littledale. Christ Church, Oxford 1826, BA1830, dn30 (York), p31 (York), MA 1833. R. Bolton by Bowland, Yorks. 1831-59 [blank in ERC]. Lived in and died at Kirk Hammerton Hall, Westmorland 8/7/1887 aged 80, leaving £150,492-16s-8d. [C135752. Boase. YCO. LBSO] Married (1) Tandridge, Surrey 26/9/1837 Harriet Turner (d.1874) (2) Northallerton, Yorks. 1880 (2nd q.) Caroline Wormald.

STANLEY (Edward) Born Workington, Cumberland 9/3/1776, s. Edward Stanley and Julia Christian. St John's, Cambridge 1794, BA1798, dn99 (Chester), p00 (Chester), MA 1822. H.E.I.C. Chap. Fort St George, Madras 1801; R. Plumbland, Cumberland 1802-34, R. Harrington, Cumberland 1822-23, R. Workington 1831 to death. Dom. Chap. to 1st Baron Dover 1831. Died (unm.) 1/4/1834 (CCEd thus) [C6353 thus. Platt] D.L. Cumberland

STANLEY (Edward, *later* Bishop of Norwich) Born London 1/1/1779, s. Sir John Thomas Stanley, 6th Bart. (of Alderley, Cheshire) and Margaret Owen. St John's, Cambridge 1798, BA1802, dn05 (Win.), p05 (Win.), MA1805, DD 1837. R. Alderley (Edge) 1805-37, Bishop of Norwich 1837 (and Clerk of Chapel Royal 1837) to death (Brahan Castle, Dingwall, Scotland whilst on holiday) 6/9/1849 aged 70 [C108829. ODNB. J.J. Adeane and M. Grenfel (eds.), *Before and after Waterloo: letters from Edward Stanley, 1802, 1814, 1816* (1908); *Memoirs of Edward and Catherine Stanley* ed. A.P. Stanley (2nd edn. 1880)] Married 8/5/1810 Catherine Leycester (a clergy dau.), 5 ch. (including A.P. Stanley, Dean of St Paul's). *F.R.S.*; 'A vigorous and fearless reformer'.

STANLEY (Joseph) Bapt. Broughton in Furness, Lancs. 19/6/1796, s. Thomas Stanley and Mary Stainton. St Bees adm. 1818, dn21 ( ), p23 (Chester). R. Waberthwaite, Cumberland 1826-47, PC. Muncaster, Cumberland 1826-44 (res.) Died (Ashton under Lyne, Lancs.) 17/2/1847 aged 51 [C170567] Married Waberthwaite 28/8/1828 Faith, dau. Capt. John Wood (of Whitehaven), with issue. 'Resident in Lord Lindsay's family' (as tutor) at some date.

STANNARD (Christopher) Born Norwich 6/9/1774, s. Joseph Stannard and Ann Karrin. St John's, Cambridge 1795, BA1799, dn99 (Ely), MA1802, Fellow 1805-33, p07 (Nor.), BD1809. R. Norwich St Peter Hungate 1811-39, R. Great Snoring w. Thursford 1831 to death 17/5/1851 [C100321. Boase] Married Norwich 10/7/1835 Maria Bedford.

STANTON (John) From Moulton, Northants., s. Rev. William Stanton. Chorister Magdalen, Oxford 1780-8; matr. 1789, BA1793, Fellow 1793-1801, MA1796, dn95 (Peterb.), p99 (Chester). R. Scaldwell, Northants. 1804 and V. (and patron) of Moulton 1830 to death. Dom. Chap. to 2nd Marquess of Northampton 1830. Died 12/1/1836 aged 63 [C37732]

STAPLETON (Ambrose) Born Bere Ferris, Devon 4/10/1770, s. William Stapleton and Sarah Skelton. Exeter, Oxford 1788, BA1792, dn93 (Ex.), p94 (Ex.), then Queens', Cambridge 1825, MA1825. V. East Budleigh, Devon 1795

and R. Halwell, Devon 1825 to death. Dom. Chap. to 1st Baron Rolle 1825. Died 10/11/1852 [C146408] Married by 1811 Mary Jackson, with issue.

STAPLETON (Francis Jarvis, Sir, 7th Bart.) Born London 6/8/1807, s. Sir Thomas Stapleton, 6th Bart. (later 22nd Baron le Despencer, also known confusingly as 12th Lord Despencer) and Elizabeth Elliot (of Antigua, West Indies). Trinity, Cambridge 1825, BA 1826, MA1831, dn31 (Nor.). R. Tudeley, Kent 1832 and R. Mereweorth, Kent 1832 to death (Merewoorth Court) 11/2/1874 aged 66, leaving £20,000 [C7167. Boase. LBSO] Married at Florence 17/5/1830 Margaret (w) (dau. Lt.-Gen. Sir George Airey), with clerical son Eliot Henry Stapleton. Succ. to title 1831.

STAPLETON, STAPYLETON (Martin) Born London 31/12/1800, s. Martin Bree (later Stapleton) and Sophia Parsons. Trinity, Cambridge 1818, BA1823, dn24 (York), p25 (York). R. Barlborough, Derbys. 1827 to death. Irish Will gives death as Co. Kerry 21/5/1868 and as Martin Stapleton Bree [C19918. YCO] Married York 17/7/1828 Elizabeth Henrietta Stote Donnison (a clergy dau., Felixkirk, Yorks.), with issue.

STARKIE (Matthew Yatman) Born Blackburn, Lancs. 8/2/1792, s. Rev. Thomas Starkie and Ann/Diane Yatman. St John's, Cambridge 1810, dn15 (Chester), LLB1816, p16 (Chester). PC. Over Darwen, Blackburn 1816 and R. Rushbury, Salop 1818 to death (Church Stretton, Shropshire) 11/9/1851 [C170570] Married Anne White.

STARKY (John) Bapt. Skelton, Cumberland 18/4/1770, s. Rev. Samuel Starky and Jane Wells. Queen's, Oxford 1787, BA1791, dn92 (Salis.), MA1809, BD and DD1810. R. Brown Candover and R. Chilton Candover, Wilts. 1798-[1807], R. Charlynch (Charlinch), Som. 1808 to death 1/4/1834 (CCEd says 23/10/1834) [C40618] Married Piccadilly, London 9/8/1797 Maria Barbara, dau. Sir Andrew Bayntun Rolt, 2nd Bart. (of Spye Park, Wilts.), and had issue.

STATHAM (Richard Jervis) Bapt. Liverpool 11/9/1805, s. William Statham and Harriet Heathcote. Corpus Christi, Oxford 1824, BA 1827, dn28 (Chester), p30 (Chester). R. Tarporley, Cheshire 1830-65, Min. Liverpool St Martin in the Fields 1830-[4]. Died 27/6/1865, leaving £5,000 [C170572] Married Walton on the Hill, Liverpool 26/4/1830 Mary Hannah Horner (w), with issue.

STAUNTON, born ASHPINSHAW (John Aspinshaw) Bapt. Ashby-de-la-Zouche, Leics. 29/5/1765, s. Edward Ashpinshaw Staunton (Hatton Gardens, London) and Sarah Locke. Emmanuel, Cambridge 1783, BA1788, dn88 (Nor.), p90 (York), MA1791, LLD1804. R. Nottingham St Peter 1797-1814, V. Hinckley, Leics. 1804-12 (res.), R. Elton on the Hill, Notts. 1812, R. Kilvington, Notts. 1813, R. (and patron) of Staunton, Notts. 1826 to death 2/6/1851 aged 86 [C76178. YCO] Married Staunton 23/5/1793 Elizabeth Brough, with clerical son (all predeceasing him). Inherited Staunton Hall 1807 and changed his name; J.P. Notts.

STAWELL (William Moggridge) Bapt. South Molton, Devon 12/8/1756, s. John Stawell and Mary Moggridge. Exeter, Oxford 1773, BA 1777, dn78 (Ex.), p80 (Ex.), MA1781. R. High Bickington, Devon 1780-1808, R. Creacombe, Devon 1822-[32], R. East Buckland w. Filleigh, Devon 1823-[31]. Died 9/2/1833 [C89500] Married South Molton 23/7/1782 Charlotte Palmer, w. clerical son, below.

STAWELL (William Palmer) Bapt. South Molton, Devon 7/5/1783, s. Rev. William Moggridge Stawell (above) and Charlotte Palmer. Exeter, Oxford 1801, BA1805, dn06 (Ex.), p07 (Ex.). R. High Bickington, Devon 1808 to death 8/6/1850 [C146412]

STEDMAN (John) Bapt. Godalming, Surrey 15/8/1784, s. Richard Stedman and Elizabeth Simmons. Trinity, Cambridge 1806, BA1810, dn10 (Win.), p11 (Win.), MA1816. V. Gosfield, Essex 1830 to death. Chap. to Guildford House of Correction 1821. Died 21/5/1837 [C108831] Married Guildford, Surrey 22/6/1818, w. issue.

STEEL (John) Bapt. Lincoln 12/9/1799, s. John Steel and Elizabeth Curtois. Christ's, Cambridge 1818, BA1822, dn22 (Lin.), p22 (Lin.). PC. Cowbit, Spalding, Lincs. 1827-62, R. Great Horkesley, Essex [income £1,075] 1862 to death. Chap. to Earl Cowper. Died 16/10/1876, leaving £6,000 [C76878] Married (1) Northallerton, Yorks. 10/9/1828 Elizabeth Blanshard (d.1843), with issue (2) St Pancras, London 6/12/1853 Maria Jessop, with further issue.

STEELE (John) Born and bapt. Westminster, London 9/8/1795 (but 'of Westmorland'), s. Charles and Jane Steele. St John's, Cambridge 1822, a Ten Year Man, dn23 (York), p24 (York). PC. Macclesfield Christ Church, Cheshire 1828 to death. Living on IoM in 1864. Died Clifton, Bristol 5/8/1876 aged 81. Will not traced [C135753. YCO] Wife Jane, and issue.

STEELE (Jonathan Walkden) Born East Harlsey, Yorks. 18/5/1794, s. Rev. Jonathan Steele and Teresa Walkden. Literate: dn17 (York), p18 (York). (succ. his father as) PC. East Harlsey 1818-54, PC. Ingleby Arncliffe, Yorks. 1818 to death (East Harlsey) 1854 (1st q.) [C136268. YCO] Married Northallerton, Yorks. 20/5/1823 Priscilla Jackson, with issue.

STEELE (Robert) Born Dublin, s. Sir Parker Steele, 2nd Bart. and Maria Verity [NiVoF nor Al.Dub.] R. Trimingham, Norfolk 1816 and R. Mundesley, Norfolk 1817 to death. Buried 22/12/1857 [C115593] Married 1806 Sarah --, and had issue.

STEELE (Thomas) Born Halifax, Yorks. 4/8/1785, s. of Alexander Steele (a farmer). St John's, Cambridge 1805, BA1809, dn09 (Chester), p11 (Chester). V. Littleborough, Lancs. 1816 [C170607] Married Kippax, Yorks. 16/9/1817 Jessy Mcintyre, with a dau.

STEELE (Thomas) Peterhouse, Cambridge 1819 (a Ten Year Man, aged 24). V. Coaley (o/w Cowley), Glos. 1832 to death 8/5/1835 (CCEd thus) [C165077] 'Accused of scandalising his Coaley parish'.

STEER (Charles) Born Wakefield, Yorks. 28/6/1757, s. Charles Steer (merchant). St John's, Cambridge 1777, BA1781, dn81 (Lin. for York), p81 (York). V. Axminster, Devon 1782 to death there 12/11/1835 [C76880. YCO] Twice married. 'A great walker and a great talker'.

STEGGALL (John [Heigham]) Bapt. Barking, Suffolk 8/5/1791, s. Rev. Charles (and Mary) Steggall. 'Ran away from school and lived for a time with gypsies at Wyverstone. Went to sea in a South Sea whaler. Ensign, 12th Madras Native Infantry (invalided home 1811; struck off for absence 1816). Also practiced as a surgeon! Corpus Christi, Cambridge 1813, no degree [but CCEd adds DD - possibly MD?], dn14 (Nor.), p15 (Nor.). PC. Great Ashfield, Suffolk 1823 to death 12/1/1881 [C115596. Boase. *John H. Steggall: a real history of a Suffolk man. Narrated by himself*, ed. Richard Cobbold] (1857 - possibly fiction?)] Married 19/10/1815 Sarah Weeding. Surrogate.

STEPHEN (Thomas) Born Ballaugh, IoM 16/1/1776, s. Daniel Stephen and Eleanor Corlett. Literate: dn98 (S&M). V. (Kirk) Marown, IoM 1809-27, Vicar General 1812-24, V. Patrick, IoM 1827 to death (Ballaugh) 29/4/1842 [C7324. Gelling - where he is described as being 'very caustic'] Married Ballaugh 13/4/1801 Charlotte Gelling (a clergy, dau.), with clerical son. For some years editor of the *Manx Advertiser*.

STEPHEN (William, or James) Born Middx. c.1782, natural s. of James Stephen. (q.v. ODNB). St John's, Cambridge 1798, BA1802, dn04 (Win. for Ely), MA1805, p05 (Ely). V. Bledlow, Bucks. 1808-67, V. Stagsden, Beds. 1811 to death. Chap. to 2nd Viscount Hood 1811. Died (unmarried) 1/1/1867 aged 85, leaving £4,000 [C76891]

STEPHENS, *later* LODER (Charles Loder) From Kencott, Oxon., s. Charles Stephens. Trinity, Oxford 1815 (aged 17), then St Mary Hall, BA1825, dn25 (Glos.), p26 (Glos.). V. Haresfield, Glos. 1826. Died Bath 31/1/1883 aged 85 (as Charles Loder Loder), leaving £1,760-1s-4d. [C165083] Married Wath, Ripon, Yorks. 14/10/1824 Mary Newton (a clergy dau.). Changed name 1844 'in compliance with the will of Charles Loder'.

STEPHENS (Darell) Bapt. Plymouth, Devon 13/4/1771, s. Edward Stephens. Exeter, Oxford 1790, dn93 (Ex.), BA1794, p95 (Ex.). V. Maker, Cornwall 1796-1848, V. St Petroc Minor, Cornwall 1834 to death. Dom. Chap. to 2nd Earl of Mount Edgecumbe 1834. Died (Trewornan Manor, Wadebridge) 2/2/1848 aged 77 [C137007] Married Bodmin, Cornwall 14/7/1802 Mary Bennett, with issue.

STEPHENS (Hugh) From Salisbury, s. Hugh Stephens. Jesus, Oxford 1782 (aged 20), BA 1791, MA1818, BD1818. V. Alderbury (w. Farley and Picton Chapels), Wilts. 1813 to death 22/3/1843. Chap. of St Nicholas Hospital [almshouses], Salisbury [C89166]

STEPHENS (Lancelot Pepys) Bapt. London 9/2/1766, s. Lancelot Stephens (shopkeeper and comb maker) and Mary West Bridell. Pembroke, Cambridge 1784, BA1788, MA1791, dn97 (London), p98 (London). S/M Clapton 1787-96; at Christ's Hospital School 1796-1817; V. Ugley. Essex 1815-17, PC. Berden, Essex 1815-17, V. Clavering w. Langley, Essex 1816 and R. North Cray, Kent 1823 to death 7/3/1834 (CCEd thus) aged 69 [C2286] Married City of London 16/5/1812 Mary Judith Wales, with issue.

STEPHENS (Richard) Born France ('a British subject') *or* Leicester 29/3/1785, s. Richard Stephens and Alice Lettice Pascoe. BNC, Oxford 1802, BA1806, MA1809, Fellow 1810-12?, dn10 (Ox.), p11 (Ox.), BD1816, etc. S/M Rugby School 1812-15; V. Belgrave, Leics. 1824 to death 29/5/1871, leaving £30,000 [C21689] Married Paris 7/1/1819 *and again* Westminster, London 1/8/1819 Anne Emilie Sievrac (w), with clerical son John Otter Stephens.

STEPHENSON, STEVENSON (George) Born Newcastle upon Tyne 16/4/1759, s. Rev. George Stephenson, sen. Lincoln, Oxford 1776, BA1779, then University, Fellow, dn81 (Durham), p83 (Durham), MA1783. R. Saltfleetby All Saints, Lincs. 1788-1807, V. Kelloe, Durham 1806-14 (res.), [R. Redmarshall, Durham 1814 to death 27/1/1844 aged 85?] [C76904. Foster as Stevenson] Had issue. J.P. Co. Durham.

STEPHENSON (John) Born Seathwaite, Lancs. 28/5/1768, s. John and Mary/Martha Gibson [NiVoF] dn93 (Chester), p94 (Chester). S/M Blencowe School 1797-1826; V. Dacre, Cumberland 1802 to death 4/9/1849 [C6358] Married Kendal, Westmorland 24/9/1796 Margaret Wilkinson, w.clerical son, also John.

STEPHENSON (John Hollier) Born City of London 10/12/1798, s. William Stephenson and Elizabeth Hollier. Trinity, Cambridge 1817, BA 1821, dn24 (Heref.), p24 (Heref.), MA1825. R. Dengie (Bacon's Portion), Essex 1825-41, PC. Elstead, Surrey 1836-41, V. Corringham, Essex 1841 (and RD) to death (London) 1/8/1861 aged 62, leaving £9,000 [C40620] Widow Mary.

STEPHENSON (Joseph [Adam]) Bapt. Rowley Regis, Staffs. 15/8/1783, s. Rev. Christopher and Elizabeth Stephenson. Queen's, Oxford 1799, BA1803, MA1806, p07 (Roch.). R. Lympsham, Som. 1809 to death 22/4/1837 [C2287] Married Asington, Suffolk 11/8/1812 Elizabeth Gurdon, with clerical s. Joseph Henry Stephenson here later. Brother William Rose, below.

STEPHENSON (Joshua) From Barton, Northants., s. Rev. George Stephenson. Pembroke, Cambridge 1796, then St John's 1786, BA1791, MA1795, dn98 (Peterb.), p98 (Lin. for Peterb.). R. Cranford St Andrew, Northants. 1798-1800, R. Selworthy, Som. 1802 to death 14/10/1863 aged 93, leaving £4,000 [C49103]

STEPHENSON (William Rose) Bapt. Rowley Regis, Staffs. 24/10/1779, s. Rev. Christopher and Elizabeth Stephenson. Literate: dn13 (London), p16 (London). R. Corringham, Essex 1818, R. Neenton, Shropshire 1821. Died 1841 aged 62 [C115646] Married City of London 10/5/1798 Elizabeth Hollier, with issue. Brother Joseph Adam Stephenson, above.

STEPHENSON see also under **STEVENSON**

STERKY (Frederic Alexander) Born London 1803, s. Rev. Alexander Sterky and Cattern Chitty [*sic*]. Christ Church, Oxford 1821, Student [Fellow] 1821-33, BA 1825, dn26 (Ox.), p27 (Ox.), MA1828. PC. of Donative of St Osyth, Essex 1831, V. North Ottrington w. Thornton-le-Street, Yorks. 1832 to death (Hastings, Sussex) 27/1/1866 aged 63, leaving £100 [C21669] Married (1) St James, Piccadilly, London 8/5/1833 Marion Collins (of Ipswich) (2) Northallerton, Yorks. 1852 (2nd q.) Mary Catherine Watson (w), (of Inveresk, Midlothian), w. issue.

STEUART, STEWART (Charles Augustus) Born Cavendish Sq., London 3/1/1777, s. James Steuart and Catherine Botham. University, Oxford 1794, BA1798, dn99 (Salis.), p01 (Salis.), MA1801. R. Edmondthorpe, Leics. 1804-8, V. Braithwell, Yorks. 1808-[51], R. Rawmarsh, Yorks. 1811 [C135997], R. Ewhurst, Surrey 1811-45. Lived at Sunningdale, Berks.; died Berkeley Square, London 25/5/1859 aged 82, leaving £60,000 [C89501] Married St George's Hanover Square, London 11/1/1831 Mrs Mary Elizabeth (Freshfield) Barclay, with issue.

STEVENS (Frederick Richard) Born Farnham, Surrey 5/7/1798 (bapt. 1/7/1806), s. James Stevens. Worcester, Oxford 1817, BA 1821, dn22 (Win.), MA1823, p24 (Win.). PC.

Seale, Surrey 1832 to death (unm.) 27/5/1861, leaving £7,000 [C108836]

STEVENS (Henry) Born Bradfield, Berks. 1766, s. Rev. Thomas Stevens and Jane Townshend. Trinity, Oxford 1784, BCL1791, dn91 (Ex. for Salis.), p25 (Salis.). R. (and patron) of Bradfield 1800 and V. Buckland, Berks. 1830 to death 17/10/1842 [C89504 is confused with clerical son of same name (who d.1830 and was R. Buckland 1828-30) Married Salisbury 21/1/1794 Maria Tinney, w. issue.

STEVENS (John) Bapt. Bicester, Oxon. 27/8/1768, s. John Stevens. New, Oxford 1787 (aged 19), Fellow 1789, BA1794, MA1795, DD. R. Birchanger, Essex 1807, V. Swalcliffe, Oxon. 1808 and R. (Great) Poringland, Norfolk 1813 to death 25/1/1837 [C21693]

STEVENS, *born* MOORE (John Moore) Born Great Torrington, Devon 7/9/1774, s. Rev. Thomas Moore and Christian Stevens. Exeter, Oxford 1802, BA1806, Fellow 1806-11, MA 1808, dn09 (Ex.), p10 (York for Ex.). Formerly private tutor to Earl Howe; R. Langtree, Devon 1810-22, Archdeacon of Exeter 1820-65 (w. Prebend of Exeter Cathedral 1821-65 and Canon Residentiary 1842-65), V. Otterton, Devon 1822 to death 30/3/1865, leaving £30,000 [C134739 as Moore. Boase. YCO] Had issue. Changed name 1832.

STEVENS (Robert) From Norwich, s. Robert Stevens. Trinity, Cambridge 1797, BA1801, dn01 (Nor.), p02 (London), MA1804, DD1821. R. St James Garlickhithe, City of London 1814-21, Prebend of Ketton in Lincoln Cathedral 1814-70, V. West Farleigh, Kent 1820-70, Dean of Rochester 1820 [income £1,400] to death. Chaplain to House of Commons 1816. Died 3/2/1870, leaving £25,000 [C546. Boase] Married 15/7/1806 Elizabeth Mason, with clerical sons Charles Abbot, and Henry.

STEVENS (Robert Stephen) From Ansford, Somerset, s. Robert Stevens. Wadham, Oxford 1796 (aged 18), BA1800, dn02 (Ox.), p04 (Ox.), MA1806, Fellow to 1824, etc.. PC. Denham St Mary, Suffolk 1813, V. South Petherwin, Cornwall 1824 to death 1/10/1856 [C21694] Married Bruton, Som. 28/7/1824 Catherine Burges.

STEVENSON (George) Born Eton, Berks. 14/4/1795, s. of the Very Rev. George Stevenson (Dean of Kilfenora, Co. Clare) and Lydia Thackeray (a relation of the novelist). Trinity, Cambridge 1812, BA1816, Fellow 1818, MA 1819, dn21 (Ely), p23 (Lin.). R. & V. Callan, Co. Kilkenny 1825-31, V. Backford, Cheshire 1831-8, V. Dickleburgh, Norfolk 1839-68, RD and Hon. Canon Norwich Cathedral 1847 to death 8/3/1868 aged 72, leaving £2,000 [C170618] Married Huntingfield, Suffolk 13/11/1814 Fanny (*or* Harriet) Salter, 3s, 4 dau. Brother below.

STEVENSON (Thomas) Born Callan, Co. Kilkenny 6/6/1804, s. Very Rev. George Stevenson (Dean of Kilfenora, Co. Clare) and Lydia Thackeray (a relation of the novelist). Trinity, Cambridge 1821, BA1825, dn27 (B&W for Win.), p28 (Win.). R. Winchester St Peter Chesil, 1832 to death. Master of St Mary Magdalen Hospital [almshouses], Winchester . Died 1844 [C40621] Married Egham, Surrey 13/6/1832 Louisa Georgiana Lardy. Brother above.

STEVENSON see also under **STEPHENSON**

STEWARD (Edward Tucker) Bapt. Melcombe Regis, Dorset 10/7/1774, s. Capt. Gabriel Steward (*H.E.I.C.* and *M.P.*) and Rebecca Tucker. Oriel, Oxford 1792, BA1795, dn03 (Win.), p03 (Win.). R. Wem, Shropshire 1804 to death 1846 (3rd q.) [C19927]

STEWARD (George William) Bapt. Heigham, Norfolk 10/3/1805, s. John Steward (attorney, High Sheriff and sometime Mayor of Norwich) and Anna Maria Richards. Corpus Christi, Cambridge 1822, BA1827, dn28 (Nor.), p29 (Nor.), MA1830. R. (and patron) of Caister St Edmund, Norfolk 1829 (and RD) to death 5/7/1878, leaving £6,000 [C19929] Married Caister 6/12/1831 Susan Branford, with clerical son Charles Edward Steward. Brother below. Photo. online.

STEWARD (John Henry) Born Heigham, Norfolk 9/12/1799, s. John Steward (attorney, High Sheriff and sometime Mayor of Norwich) and Anna Maria Richards. Trinity, Cambridge 1818, BA1822, dn22 (Peterb. for Nor.), p23 (Bristol for Nor.), MA1825, V. (and patron) of Swardeston, Norfolk 1824-63 [blank in ERC], V. Saxlingham Nethergate w. Saxlingham Thorpe, Norfolk 1824-33, R. (and patron) of Hethel, Norfolk 1835 to death (at his home, The Manor House, East Carleton, Norfolk)

22/3/1863, leaving £25,000 [C53888] Married North Walsham, Norfolk 5/7/1821 Harriet Wilkinson (a clergy dau.), with issue.

STEWART (Charles Augustus) see under **STEUART**

STEWART (James Haldane) Born Boston, Massachusetts 23/12/1778, s. Duncan Stewart (of Ardshiel, Argyll) and Anne Erving (both American Royalists who had returned to Britain). Student Lincoln's Inn 1793. Exeter, Oxford 1803, BA1806, dn06 (Ex. for Salis.), p07 (Salis.), MA1811. Minister of Percy [Proprietary] Chapel, London 1812-28 [breakdown 1817], (built and first) PC. Liverpool St Bridget (or Bride) 1830-40 (res.), V. Great Ouseburn, Yorks. 1830-46, R. Limpsfield, Surrey 1846 to death. Dom. Chap. to 1st Marquess of Bredalbane 1809; to 2nd Marquess of Bute 1811. Died 22/10/1854 [C89503. Boase. D.D. Stewart, *Memoir of the life of the Rev. Robert Haldane Stewart, MA, late Rector of Limpsfield, Surrey* (rev. edn. 1857)] Married Edinburgh 20/8/1816 Mary (dau. David Dale of New Lanark), with clerical son of same name.

STEWART, STEWARD (John) Born Bury St Edmunds, Suffolk 1/12/1769, s. Thomas and Mary Stewart. Trinity, Cambridge 1786 (as Steward), BA1792 (as Steward), p95 (London), MA1800 (Steward). S/M Charterhouse [School] 1793-1805, Usher 1805-11; R. Little Wigborough, Essex 1811-12, R. Little Hallingbury, Essex 1812 and R. Thwaite All Saints, Norfolk 1832 to death 22/4/1835 (CCEd thus) [C69167] Married Eliza Burdett (of Mowsley, Leics.).

STEWART (John Vanderstegen) Bapt. Portsea, Hants. 22/9/1794, s. John Henry Stewart and Fanny Desborough. Jesus, Cambridge 1817, p21 (London for Cant.), LLB1823. R. Gilston, Herts. 1821-38, V. Portsea 1838 to death there 12/1/1878 aged 83, leaving £2,000 [C122604] Married Portsea 22/9/1818 Caroline Gibson Drury, with issue. Stern port. online.

STEWART (William) Born Liverpool 11/11/1785 (nonconformist baptism), s. John and Elizabeth Stewart. BNC, Oxford 1805, BA1809, MA1811, dn12 (Chester), p13 (Chester). PC. Liverpool Hale St Mary, Childwall 1818 to death 1/12/1856 aged 72 [C170619] Married Manchester 8/11/1819 Elizabeth Bradshaw (w), 1s., 4 dau.

STEWART see also under **STUART**

STILL (John) Born East Knoyle, Wilts. 13/1/1761, s. James Still and Susannah Stent. Wadham, Oxford 1778, dn84 (Salis.), p85 (Ely for Salis.), BCL 1785. R. Chicklade, Wilts. 1786, R. Dumbleton, Glos. 1795-7, R. Fonthill Gifford, Wilts. 1797, RD of Chalke 1812, Prebend of Stratton in Salisbury Cathedral 1824, V. Inglesham, Wilts. 1825 [C37750] to death 1/4/1839 (CCEd says 24/6/1834) [C89509]

STILLINGFLEET (Henry Anthony) Bapt. Worcester Cathedral 18/10/1770, s. Rev. James Stillingfleet and Katherine Mackworth. Christ Church, Oxford 1788, BA1792, MA1795, p95 (Heref.). PC. How Caple w. Sollers Hope, Hereford 1795 to death 11/9/1846 [C174013] Married Bristol 17/7/1813 Lydia Venner, with clerical son Henry James William Stillingfleet. Brother below.

STILLINGFLEET (Robert Digby) Bapt. Worcester Cathedral 13/7/1779, s. Rev. James Stillingfleet and Katherine Mackworth. Worcester, Oxford 1798, then St Edmund Hall, BA1802, dn03 (Bristol). V. Cleeve Prior, Worcs. 1812 to death 3/12/1856 [C53892] Married Bristol 23/11/1815 Sarah Webb. Brother above.

STOCKDALE (Joseph) Bapt. Wragby, Lincs. 10/5/1784, s. Joseph Stockdale and Frances Sowerby. Corpus Christi, Cambridge 1803, BA 1807, dn07 (Lin.), p08 (Lin.), MA1811. V. Kingerby, Lincs. 1811 and R. Tetford, Lincs. 1820 (and RD of Walshcroft 1829) to death. Dom. Chap. to Mary Sophia, Viscountess Bridport 1820-8. Died 13/1/1874 aged 89, leaving £2,000 [C76983. Kaye] Married Wragby 14/6/1809 Frances Elizabeth Walter, with issue.

STOCKDALE (William) Bapt. Hayton, Yorks. 5/4/1767, s. Rev. Robert Stockdale and Katharine Minshull. Jesus, Cambridge 1784, BA1789, dn89 (York for Peterb.), p91 (Peterb.), Fellow 1791, MA1792. V. Hundon, Suffolk 1801-37, V. Mears Ashby, Northants. 1814-48, PC. Lincoln St Michael on the Mount 1826, R. Wilby, Northants. 1837 to death 28/2/1848 [C76993. YCO] Married St Albans 28/1/1802 Honor Wolley (a clergy dau.), with issue. *F.L.S.*

STOCKEN (Henry) Born Fulham, London 19/11/1796, s. Oliver Frederick and Ann Stocken. Literate: dn24 (York), p25 (York). PC. Arkendale, Yorks. 1832, PC. Wilton, Yorks.

1857 to death 13/5/1861, leaving £1,000 [C135755. YCO] Married York 16/10/1827 Charlotte Pullan (w).

STOCKWELL (Joseph Samuel) Bapt. Stratford Toney, Wilts. 10/6/1798, s. Thomas Stockwell and Ann Martin. Literate: dn21 (Salis.), p22 (Salis.), MA1829 (Lambeth). V. North Newnton, Wilts. 1829, R. and V. Wilton w. Netherhampton, Ditchampton and Bulbridge, Wilts. 1832, V. Wylye, Wilts. 1840 to death 8/2/1869, leaving £3,000 [C89512] Married Curry Malet, Som. 4/9/1832 Anne Cardew (a clergy dau. and relict), and had issue.

STODDART (John) Bapt. Aspley Guise, Beds. 3/5/1793, s. Rev. John, sen. (S/M Northampton G/S) and Ruth Stordy. Clare, Cambridge 1811, BA1816, dn16 (Salis. for Peterb.), p17 (Peterb.), Fellow 1817-20, MA1819, DD1826. V. Pattishall (1st Part), Northants. 1819-37, R. New Brentford, Middx. 1837-42, R. Lowick, Northants. 1842 and R. Islip, Northants. 1843 to death. Dom. Chap. to Duke of Dorset; Chap. to the Hanwell Lunatic Asylum, Norwood, Middx. 1831. Died 4/1/1855 aged 61 [C89513] Wife Ann, and issue.

STOKES (Henry) [MA but NiVoF. Al.Dub. has a possibility] V. Doveridge, Derbys. 1785 to death aged 77. Probate granted 26/9/1838 [C19933]

STOKES (James Calcott Hayes) Bapt. Tettenhall, Staffs. 28/8/1770, s. Francis Smith Stokes and Katherine Calcott, New, Oxford 1791, BA1795, d95 (Ox.), p96 (Ox.), MA1800. R. Birchanger, Essex 1808, V. Manuden, Essex 1829. Living at Kinton Hall, Shropshire at death. Dom. Chap. to Louisa, 7th Countess of Dysart 1829. Probate granted 3/4/1851 [C37757] Married Birchanger 16/2/1813 Susannah Frances Weldon, and had issue.

STOKES (John) Bapt. Elton. Hunts. 15/3/1774, s. John [*pleb.*] and Ann Stokes. Christ Church, Oxford 1792, BA1796, dn96 (Peterb.), Chap. 1796-1802, p98 (Ox.), MA1799. V. Cobham, Kent 1814 and R. Milton next Gravesend, Kent 1827 to death 23/12/1859, leaving £1,500 [C550] Married with clerical son Edward Stokes.

STONARD (John) Born Lambeth, London 10/3/1769, s. Jonathan and Frances Stonard. BNC, Oxford 1789, BA1793, dn94 (Cant.), p94 (Cant.), MA1796, BD and DD1817. R. West Deeping, Lincs. 1811, R. Aldingham, Lancs. [net income £1,093] 1814 (where he built Aldingham Hall) to death (unmarried) 22/4/1849 aged 80 [C159393] 'In the last year of his life he was awarded the North Lonsdale Agricultural Society's prize for the best field of mangle wurzels'. Left everything to his butler and to his adopted son Edward Jones Schollick.

STONE (George) Born Brimley, Dorset 4/11/1797, s. Daniel Stone. Sidney, Cambridge 1817, BA1822, dn22 (Bristol for Chich.), p23 (Chester), MA1825. V. Long Burton >< Dorset 1826-42, R. Bondleigh, Devon 1842 to death 29/9/1853 [C53897] Married 1836 Caroline Susanna Elkins (a clergy dau.), with issue.

STONE (James Henry) Born Richmond, Surrey 12/4/1803, s. Daniel Arthur Stone, *M.D.*, and Biddy Maria Clarke. Trinity, Cambridge 1823. BA1828, dn28 (Peterb.), p29 (Peterb.), MA1831. PC. Eye, Northants. 1832 to death 14/11/1842 aged 39 ('*hanged himself* in a fit of insanity') [C110971]

STONE (Samuel) Born Norwich, s. Samuel Stone (attorney). Caius, Cambridge 1821, BA 1826, dn27 (Nor.), MA1829, p29 (Nor.). R. Norwich St Augustine 1832-41, PC. Norwich St John's de Sepulchre 1841 to death 19/8/1848 [C1116]

STONE (Thomas) Bapt. Macclesfield, Cheshire 1/8/1776 (Presbyterian Chapel), s. Samuel and Elizabeth Stone. BNC, Oxford 1794, BA1797, MA1800, dn23 (Bangor), p24 (Ox.), BD1811, DD1813, Fellow to 1814. R. Wootton Rivers, Wilts. 1813 to death 26/10/1859, leaving £1,500 [C21748] Married w. issue.

STONE (William) From Prestbury, Cheshire, s. Samuel Stone. BNC, Oxford 1819 (aged 18), BA1822, Fellow 1822-30, MA1825, dn25 (Ox.), p26 (Ox.). R. Bethnal Green St John's, London 1829, R. Spitalfields Christ Church, London 1829-56, Canon of Canterbury Cathedral 1855-82, R. Canterbury St George the Martyr w. St Mary Magdalen 1858-66. Died 2/2/1882 aged 81, leaving £15,275-10s-8d. [C21749. Boase]

STONEHOUSE (William Brocklehurst) From Manchester, s. John Stonehouse. BNC, Oxford 1812 (aged 18), dn15 (Lin.), p16 (Lin.), BA 1816, MA1819, DCL1845. V. Owston (Ferry), Lincs. 1821 and Archdeacon of Stow

1844 to death 18/12/1862, leaving £12,000 [C77015] Married Owston Ferry, Lincs. 29/10/1832 Mrs Elizabeth (Sanders) Shipworth.

STONEY (Thomas Umfreville) Born Thorpe, Chelmsford, Essex 19/1/1790, s. Rev. John Stoney and Sarah Umfreville. Jesus, Cambridge 1808, BA1813, dn13 (London), p14 (London), MA1816. Curate Pateley Bridge, Yorks. 1826 to death 1/4/1864 aged 74, leaving £4,000 [C122612]

STONHOUSE VIGOR (Henry) Born Calcutta 20/3/1801, s. Rev. Timothy Vigor (born Stonhouse) and Charlotte Huntingford (a clergy dau.). St John's, Cambridge 1822, BA 1826, dn26 (Salis.), p27 (Salis.), MA1830. R. Eaton Bishop, Heref. 1830 to death 7/5/1838 [C89518 as Stonhouse. Foster has a confusing entry] Married Bath 24/3/1829 Louisa Burt Gordon, with issue.

STOPES (James) From Britwell Salome, Oxon., s. Rev. James Stopes, sen. St John's, Oxford 1773 (aged 18), BA1778, dn79 (Ox.), p80 (Ox.), MA1781. V. Worminghall, Bucks. 1795 to death 24/1/1837 [C21752]

STOPFORD (George Powys) Born Petersham, Surrey 4/10/1801, s. Rev. Hon. Richard Bruce Stopford (below) and Hon. Eleanor Powys (dau. 1st Baron Lilford). Christ Church, Oxford 1819, BA1823, then All Souls, Fellow 1823-7, dn25 (Ox.), p26 (Ox.), MA1831. R. Warkton, Northants. 1826 and R. Barton Seagrave, Northants 1864 to death 28/11/1867, leaving £2,000 [C21753]

STOPFORD (Joshua) Bapt. Ashton-under-Lyne, Lancs. 24/6/1759, s. Thomas Stopford (felt-maker and hatter) and Mary Hollingworth. St Catharine's, Cambridge 1778, BA 1782, dn84 (Lin. for Chich.). R. East Marden, Sussex 1805-15, Sequestrator of North Marden, Sussex 1806, V. & R. South Hayling, Hants. 1817-32 (w. R. North Hayling Chapel 1829), living at Emsworth, Sussex by 1830. Buried 24/12/1835. [C70479 and C108842] Wife Ann, s.p. Another identically named man in same area.

STOPFORD (Richard Bruce, Hon.) Born 2/4/1774, s. James, 2nd Earl of Courtown and Mary Powys. Christ Church, Oxford 1792, BA1796, dn98 (Ex.), p98 (Ex.), MA1799. R. Barton Seagrave, Northants. 1798-1800, V. Slawston, Leics. 1800-2, V. Nuneaton, Northants. 1803, Prebend of Bullinghope in Hereford Cathedral 1810 and Canon of Windsor 1812 to death. Chap to the Queen. Died 2/12/1844 aged 70 [C19937] Married 10/11/1800 Hon. Eleanor Powys (dau. of 1st Baron Lilford), w. clerical sons George Powys (above), and Charles.

STORDY (Joseph) Bapt. Kirkbampton, Cumberland 30/1/1763, s. Thomas Stordy. Literate: dn91 (Lin. for Car.), p92 (Car.). PC. Kirkbampton 1809 to death 2/4/1835 (CCEd thus) aged 72 [C6363]

STORER (John) Bapt. Nottingham 17/7/1782, s. John Storer (physician) and Mary Douglas. Christ Church, Oxford 1800, BA1805, dn05 (York), p06 (York), MA1808. R. Hawkesworth, Notts. 1808 (with 'Principal Official of the Royal Peculiar of Bridgnorth') to death (Clifton, Notts.) 4/2/1837 [C134689. YCO] Married (1) 13/7/1809 Charlotte Wylde (a clergy dau., d.1816), w. clerical son (2) 1818 Elizabeth, dau. Thomas Whitmore, *M.P.* (Apley Park, Shropshire), with further issue.

STORIE (John George) Born Camberwell, Surrey 8/6/1797, s. Rev. George Henry Storie and Elizabeth Jekyll Chalmers. Christ Church, Oxford 1815, then Magdalen, BA1819, dn20 (Glos. for London), p21 (London), MA1824. R. Stow Maries, Essex 1822-3 (res.), V. Camberwell St Giles, London [net income £1,820] 1823, PC. Peckham, Surrey 1850 to death 4/11/1858. No will traced [C108843] Married Marylebone, London 9/7/1822 Elizabeth Perring, w. issue. Freemason.

STORRY (John Bridges) Bapt. Colchester, Essex 18/12/1799, s. Rev. Robert Storry. Queens', Cambridge 1807, BA1811, dn13 (Nor.), p13 (Nor.), MA1814. V. Great Tey, Essex 1814 to death. Dom. Chap. to Lord Howden. Died 6/11/1854 aged 64 [C115672] Married (2?) Feb. 1849 Martha Mary Glover.

STOUGHTON (James) Bapt. Wymondham, Suffolk Dec. 1767, s. Peter Stoughton and Elizabeth Clarke. Corpus Christi, Cambridge 1786, BA1791, dn91 (Nor.), p92 (Ely for Nor.). R. Foxley, Norfolk 1792 and R. Sparham, Norfolk 1792-1839. Probate granted 9/12/1840 [C100326] Married 1806 Diana Lloyd (Bawdeswell Hall, Norfolk), with issue.

STOVIN (James) Bapt. Rossington, Yorks. 27/11/1754, s. James Stovin, *J.P.,* and Margaret Walker. Peterhouse, Cambridge 1771, BA1776, dn77 (Peterb.), p78 (Peterb.), MA1779, Fellow 1779-85, DD1800. R. Rossington 1783 to death (Chelsea, London) 13/8/1833 aged 78 [C108857] Married 16/10/1790 Eleanor Charlotte Rivington, with issue. *J.P.* West Riding and Lincs.

STOWELL (Hugh) Bapt. Douglas, IoM 7/12/1768, s. Thomas Stowell and Ann Brown. Literate: dn91 (S&M), p93 (S&M). Chap. St Matthew, Douglas (with S/M Douglas G/S) 1797-1802, V. Lonan, IoM 1802-17, R. Ballaugh, IoM 1814 to death 14/10/1835 [C7325. Gelling. DEB] Married Santan, IoM 20/9/1796 Amelia Callow, with clerical son Hugh Stowell, jun. [C135176] The Evangelical leader; and first PC. Christ Church, Salford, from 1831, but who is not included in ERC or here. Preached in Manx, and corrected the Manx New Testament; 'an evangelical of evangelicals'.

STRACEY (George, Sir, 3rd Bart.) Born Madras 12/1770, s. Sir Edward Stracey, 1st Bart. (Rackheath Hall, Norfolk) and Mrs Elizabeth (Lathom) Williamson. Jesus, Cambridge 1788 (a Ten Year Man?), no degree, dn94 (Nor.), p94 (Nor.), LLB. R. Rackheath 1797 to death 27/12/1854 [C115674. Boase] Married March 1814 Sophia Anne Mapes (Rollesby Hall, Norfolk), and had issue. Succ. to title 1851.

STRANGWAYS, *or* FOX-STRANGWAYS (Edward Fox) Born Maiden Newton, Dorset 2/4/1806, s. Rev. Hon. Charles Redlynch Fox-Strangways (*supra* under Fox-Strangways) and Jane Haines (a clergy dau.). St John's, Cambridge 1823, BA1827, dn29 (Ex.), p30 (Ex.). R. Melbury Osmund w. Melbury Sampford, Dorset 1830-2. Died 31/12/1838 at Government House, British Honduras [*sic*] aged 32 [C53907] Brother below.

STRANGWAYS, *or* FOX-STRANGWAYS (Henry Fox) Born Maiden Newton, Dorset. 25/2/1793, s. Rev. Charles Redlynch Fox-Strangways (*supra* under Fox-Strangways) and Jane Haines. Pembroke, Oxford 1810, BA 1814, dn16 (B&W), MA1817, p17 (Glos.). R. West Grimstead, Wilts. 1817-53- [blank in ERC], R. Rewe, Devon 1825-60, R. Moreton, Devon 1826. Dom. Chap. to 3rd Earl of Ilchester 1820. Died 'on or about' 25/2/1860, leaving £18,000 [C53908. ERC links] Married Downes, Crediton, Devon 26/6/1827 Esther Eleanora Buller, with clerical son. Brother above.

STRANGWAYS see also under **FOX-STRANGWAYS (Charles Redlynch. Hon.)**

STRATON (George William) Born Lisnawully, Co. Louth 28/8/1808, s. John Warde Straton and Lady Emilia Jocelyn (dau. of 1st Earl of Roden). Corpus Christi, Cambridge 1825, dn29 (Lin.), BA1830, p30 (Lin.). R. Somersal Herbert, Derbys. 1832-43, R. Thornton le Moor, Lincs. 1832-43, R. Aylestone, Leics. 1843 to death. Dom. Chap. to Viscount Powerscourt. Died (Upper Norwood, Surrey) 27/1/1891, leaving £3,199-6s-3d. [C19941] Married 2/4/1832 Elinor Katherine Norman, with clerical s. Norman Dumenil John Straton. Surrogate.

STRATTON (Joshua) From Princes Risborough, Bucks., s. John Young Stratton and Elizabeth Gilks. New, Oxford 1816 (aged 18), Chap. 1818-25, BA1819, dn21 (Cant.), p22 (Ox.), MA1823. Minor Canon and Precentor of Canterbury Cathedral 1825, V. Lower Halstow >< Kent 1825, V. Goodneston w. Graveney, Kent 1842 to death 15/6/1864, leaving £1,500 [C21756] Probably married East Grinstead, Sussex 8/12/1825 Susannah Head.

STREATFEILD, STREATFIELD (William) Bapt. Southampton 31/12/1790, s. Henry Bryan Streatfeild and Elizabeth Catherine Ogle. Wadham, Oxford 1809, then Trinity 1812-16, BA1813, dn14 (Cant), MA1816, Fellow 1819-28, p21 (Ox.), Lecturer in Philosophy. V. Broxted, Essex 1823-9, V. East Ham, Essex 1827 to death. Chap. to HRH Duke of Clarence 1816. Died (while preaching) 27/5/1860, leaving £8,000 [C124421. *Memoir of the Rev. W. Streatfield, MA, Vicar of East Ham, Essex*, by His Daughters (PPC, 1869. photo. port.)] Married (1) Westerham, Kent 4/9/1834 Harriet Jane Streatfeild (d.1837), with issue (2) Marylebone, London 2/6/1840 Jane Emma Larkins (w), and further issue. Sepia photo. online.

STREET (George) Bapt. London 30/4/1774, s. James Wallis Street and Sarah Bennett. St John's, Oxford 1794, BA1797, MA1806. R. Langton by Spilsby, Lincs. 1800 to death 4/8/1856 [C77069]

STREETEN (Henry Thomas) Born Lambeth, Surrey 12/10/1806, s. John Mitchell

Streeten. Queen's, Oxford 1825, BA1829, dn29 (Lin.), p30 (Lin.). (first) PC. Richmond St John's the Divine, Surrey 1831, V. Rodham Cheney, Wilts. 1848 to death (Lydiard Millicent, Wilts.) 15/11/1849 [C77071] Married Holborn, London April 1831 Sarah Paget, w. clerical s. Henry Robert Bradley Septimus Streeten.

STRICKLAND (Peter) Bapt. Windermere, Westmorland 6/9/1772, s. Thomas and Agnes Strickland. Literate: dn95 (Chester), p97 (Chester). S/M Old Hutton Free G/S, Kendal 1793-5, H/M ('Conduct') Windermere G/S 1795-1807; PC. Staveley, Kendal, Westmorland 1807 (and S/M) to death 16/7/1837 aged 64. Lived at Reston Hall, Ings, Westmorland [C170630] Married Whitehaven, Cumberland 13/9/1815 Dorothy Hilton, with issue.

STRICKLAND (Thomas Alfred) Born Ripon, Yorks. 6/1/1802, s. George Strickland and Jane Letitia Winn. Merton, Oxford 1820, BA 1824, dn25 (York), p26 (York), MA1831. R. Sherburn, Malton, Yorks. 1826-34 (res.), V. Bredon, Worcs. 1837 to death 7/11/1852 [C135757] Married Tewkesbury, Glos. 1840 (4th q.) Anne Catherine Fitzgerald (a clergy dau.), with clerical son.

STRONG (Charles) From Tiverton, Devon, s. Richard Henry Strong. Wadham, Oxford 1801 (aged 17), BA1805, dn07 (Ex.), MA1810, p11 (Ex.). R. Broughton Gifford, Wilts. 1811-48. Died Dawlish, Devon 27/1/1864, leaving £7,000 [C146423] Clerical son Charles Edward.

STRONG (Clement) Bapt. St Pancras, London 28/9/1790, s. Clement Samuel Strong and Anne Streatfeild. [Adm. Lincoln's Inn 1809]. St John's, Cambridge 1812, LLB1819, p16 (Chester for Chich.). (Sinecure R. Gedney, Lincs.) 1824 to death (Hayes Common, Kent) 15/4/1852 aged 62 [C2292] Married Limpsfield, Surrey 30/6/1816 Catherine Bridget Biscoe (Hookwood, Surrey). Brother Thomas Linwood Strong, below.

STRONG (Philip Thistlethwayte) Born London 4/5/1782, s. William Strong and Mary Ayling. Oriel, Oxford 1800, BA1803, MA1806. R. Myland St Michael, Essex 1817, V. Aston Abbots 1823 and PC. Wing, Bucks. 1823 to death. Dom. Chap. to 1st Marquess of Wellesley 1814. Died 28/11/1849 [C77075] Married Laleham, Surrey 10/7/1827 Charlotte Bridget Hartwell, w. issue.

STRONG (Robert, sen.) Bapt. Wandsworth, Surrey 7/5/1766, s. Thomas Strong and Sophia Alsop. Trinity, Oxford 1783, dn88 (Lin. for Heref.), BCL1792. (Sinecure R. Bromyard (1st Portion), Heref. 1794-1849), R. Brampton Abbots, Heref. 1799 to death 30/4/1849 [C77076] Married (1) Barnes, Surrey 3/4/1793 Caroline Radegund Roberts, w. clerical son (below) (2) St Albans, Herts. 14/6/1804 Sophia Margaretta Bean, w. further issue. [Note: St Radegund, a 6th century Frankish Queen]. Brother Thomas Strong, below.

STRONG (Robert, jun.) Born Barnes, Surrey 6/1/1796, s. Rev. Robert Strong, sen. (above) and Caroline Radegund Roberts. Wadham, Oxford 1813, BA1817, p20 (Glos.), MA1823. V. Painswick, Glos. 1823 to death 26/1/1856 [C165148] Married (1) Abenhall, Glos. 2/8/1821 Julia Grosvenor (d.1842), w. clerical son, another Robert Strong (2) Lechlade, Glos. 4/9/1849 Eleanor Herbert.

STRONG (Thomas) Bapt. Wandsworth, Surrey 2/1/1770, s. Thomas Strong and Sophia Alsop (dau of a Lord Mayor of London). St John's, Cambridge 1787, BA1792, dn93 (Nor. for Win.), p94 (Car. for Win.), MA1794. R. (and patron) of Clyst St Mary, Devon 1795-1851, R. Theberton, Suffolk 1819-41. Died Bath, Som. 14/3/1860 aged 90, leaving £18,000 [C108854] Married Hampstead, London 21/2/1802 Augusta Louisa Rundell (w), with clerical sons Edward Rundell Strong, and Thomas Augustus Strong. Brother Robert Strong, sen., above.

STRONG (Thomas Linwood) Born City of London 8/10/1786, s. Clement Samuel Strong and Anne Streatfeild. Oriel, Oxford 1803, BA 1807, dn09 (Win.), p10 (Win.), MA1810, BD 1817. R. Titsey, Surrey 1813-14, R. St Michael, Queenhithe w. Holy Trinity the Less, City of London 1822-9, R. Sedgefield, Durham 1829-56 [net income £1,802], Hon. Canon Durham Cathedral 1844. Died Egham, Surrey 26/9/1865 aged 79, leaving £50,000 (living at Portman Square, London) [C108846] Married Wandsworth, London 13/6/1812 Anna Maria Tritton, with clerical son. Brother Clement, above.

STRONG (William) Born Peterborough, Northants. 13/2/1756, s. Isaac Strong and Elizabeth de la Rue. Queens', Cambridge 1775, BA1779, dn81 (Peterb.), p81 (Peterb.), MA 1782, DD 1802. R. Bolingbroke w. Hareby, Lincs. 1782-1834 (non-res.), V. Billinghay, Lincs.

1785-1832 (res.), Archdeacon of Northampton 1797-1842, Canon of Peterborough Cathedral 1841 to death. Lived at Stanground, Peterborough. Chap. in Ordinary 1825; Dom. Chap. to Bishop of Lincoln; Dom. Chap. to Anne, Dowager Baroness Godolphin 1785. Died 8/9/1842 [C110973. Kaye. Bennett2] Married Peterborough 17/10/1785 Margaret Wakelin (a clergy dau., Fletton, Hants.), with issue.

STUART (Edmund Luttrell) Born Blandford, Dorset 21/2/1798, s. Hon. Archibald Stuart (grandson of the 9th Earl of Moray) and Cornelia Pleydell. Exeter, Oxford 1818, BA 1822, dn23 (Bristol), p23 (Ely for Bristol). R. Winterborne Houghton, Dorset 1823-[57]. Died 5/11/1869 aged 71, leaving £40,000 [C53913] Married Church Knowle, Dorset 2/9/1834 Elizabeth Jackson (a clergy dau.), with issue, their three sons becoming successive Earls of Moray.

STUART (Henry) From Essex. Peterhouse, Cambridge 1789, BA1793, dn94 (London), p95 (London), MA1796. V. Steeple Bumpstead, Essex 1801 and R. East Donyland, Essex 1801 to 'natural death'. Dom. Chap. to 3rd Earl of Mansfield 1801. Died (Lofthouse, Yorks., the home of his clerical son-in-law) 4/5/1834 (CCEd says 10/6/1834) [C66840] Had issue.

STUART (John Burnett-) Born Mintlaw, Aberdeenshire 1775, s. Theodosius Burnett-Stuart. MA (Aberdeen?). PC. Latchford, Cheshire 1807-9, R. (and patron) of Grappenhall, Cheshire 1808-47, (first) PC. Nottingham St James 1809-41 [blank in ERC]. Died Scarborough, Yorks. 12/10/1847 aged 72 [C170632] Married 1821 Elizabeth Sarah Horsfall, with clerical son of same name.

STUART (John Francis) Bapt. Westminster, London 9/2/1765, s. James Stuart and Ann Taylor. St John's, Oxford 1782, BA1786, dn88 (Salis.), MA1789, p89 (Salis.). R. Lower Gravenhurst, Beds. 1792-1833, R. Whitney, Heref. 1804 and R. Weston Market >< Suffolk 1805 to death 9/7/1833 (CCEd says 7/1/1834) [C77179] Married Kensington, London 25/8/1802 Caroline Stiell, and had issue.

STUART see also under **STEWART, STEUART**

STUBBIN (Newman John, sen.) Bapt. Roydon, Suffolk 12/1/1768, s. John Stubbin and Elizabeth Partridge. Trinity, Oxford 1785, BA 1789, dn90 (Nor.), p92 (Nor.), MA1792. V. Offton w. Little Brisset, Suffolk 1796-1832, R. Somersham, Suffolk 1803 and PC. Higham St Mary, Suffolk 1807 to death 25/7/1835 (CCEd says 27/8/1835) [C115679] Married Gosfield, Essex 16/1/1798 Martha Sparrow, w. son below.

STUBBIN (Newman John, jun.) Bapt. 21/6/1799, s. Rev. Newman John Stubbin, sen. (above) and Martha Sparrow. St John's, Oxford 1817, BA1821, dn22 (Nor.), p23 (Nor.), MA 1825. V. Offton w. Little Bricett, Suffolk 1832, R. (and patron) of Somersham, Suffolk 1833-75. Died Ipswich Suffolk 3/8/1881, leaving £23,928-6s-2d. [C115680]

STUBBS (John Pountney) From Wolverhampton, Staffs., s. Walter Stubbs and Elizabeth Pountney. Christ Church, Oxford 1782 (aged 16), BA1786, MA1789, dn89 (C&L), p91 (C&L). V. Market Drayton, Shropshire 1793 (w. S/M Market Drayton Parish School 1801) to 1833, PC. Wavertree, Liverpool 1806-20 (res.). Buried 11/1/1833 aged 67 (CCEd says died 29/3/1833) [C19944] Married (1) Adderley, Shropshire 7/10/1792 Martha Beedam (d.1812), with issue (2) Childwall, Liverpool 22/6/1813 Elizabeth Pole, w. further issue.

STUBBS (Phineas) Bapt. Ravenstonedale, Westmorland 25/10/1769, s. John Stubbs and Margaret Wilson. Literate: dn00 (York), p02 (York). PC. Hannah cum Hagnaby, Lincs. 1821, V. Well, Yorks, 1830 to death 7/11/1834 aged 65 (CCEd says 17/8/1835) [C77182. YCO] Married Firbeck, Rotherham, Yorks. 18/3/1800 Hannah (or Ann) Bradley, with clerical son of the same name (who succeeded him at Well).

STUDHOLME (Robert) Bapt. Carlisle 24/8/1795, s. John Studholme and Mary Matthews. St Bees adm. 1817, dn18 (Chester), p18 (Chester). PC. Goosnargh, Kirkham, Lancs. 1822 to death (Whittingham, Lancs.) 9/1/1867 aged 71, leaving £1,500 [C170636] Married Goosnargh 21/7/1828 Jane Cookson, with clerical son.

STYCHE (George) From Staffs. St John's, Cambridge 1814 (aged 25), BA1818, p18 (Chester for C&L), p20 (Chester for C&L), MA1824. PC. Keele, Staffs. 1830 to death 5/5/1839 aged 50 [C19951]

SUCKLING (Benjamin) Born Middx. 1768, s. William Suckling (Comptroller of the Customs, of Banham Haugh, Norfolk) and Elizabeth Browne. Trinity, Cambridge 1786, BA1791, dn91 (Nor.), p92 (Nor.), MA1794. R. Matlaske w. Plumstead >< Norfolk 1793 to death 1837 [C115684]

SULLIVAN (Frederick) Born Thames Ditton, Surrey 2/1797, s. Sir Richard Joseph Sullivan, 1st Bart. and Mary Lodge. BNC, Oxford 1814, BA1817, then All Souls, Fellow 1818-21, dn20 (Chester for Win.), p21 (Win.), MA1822. V. Kimpton, Herts. 1827-73, V. Weston, Herts. 1827-32 (res.) to death. Dom. Chap. to 20th Baron Dacre 1827. Died 28/7/1873 aged 76, leaving £18,000 [C77193. *A Family Chronicle: derived from notes and letters*, selected by [his dau.] Barbarina, The Honorable Lady Grey (1908)] Married (1) St George's Hanover Square, London 3/1/1821 Arabella Jane Wilmot (d.1839), with issue (2) St George's Hanover Square London 1843 (3rd q.) Emily Ames.

SUMNER (Charles Richard, Bishop of Llandaff, *then* of Winchester) Born Kenilworth, Warwickshire 22/11/1790 (CCEd says 29/12/1790 - perhaps baptism?), s. Rev. Robert Sumner and Hannah Bird, and brother to the Archbishop of Canterbury John Bird Sumner (below). Trinity, Cambridge 1812, BA 1814, dn14 (Nor.), p17 (Salis. for Win.), MA 1817, DD1825, Oxford 1841. V. Abingdon, Berks. 1821-2, Canon of 2nd Prebend Worcester 1822-5, Canon of 2nd Prebend Canterbury 1825-7, Dean of St Pauls and Portpoole Prebend 1826-*in commendam* with Bishop of Llandaff 1826-28, then a reforming and vigorous Bishop of Winchester (aged 37) 1827 to retirement 1869. Private Chap. to George 1V at Windsor and Chap. in Ordinary from 1823. Died Farnham Castle (where he was allowed to remain) 15/8/1874, leaving £80,000 [C85317. ODNB. G.H. Sumner, *Life of Charles Richard Sumner* (1876)]. Married Geneva 24/1/1816 Jenie Fanny Barnabine, 4s., 3 dau.

SUMNER (Charles Vernon Holme) Born Westminster, London, s. George Sumner and Louisa Premble. BNC, Oxford 1816, then Trinity, Cambridge 1817 (aged 17), BA1823, dn23 (York for Win.), p24 (Lin. for Win.). R. Farnborough, Hants. 1827-34, R. Newdigate, Surrey 1827-34, R. Byfleet, Surrey 1834-51, R. Ringwould, Kent 1853-66. R. West Cliffe, Dover, Kent 1854-64-. Chap. in Ordinary 1830.

Died (Swaffham, Norfolk) 4/12/1876, leaving £30,000 [C77194. YCO] Married 1825 Henrietta Katherine Mason (Necton Hall, Norfolk).

SUMNER (James) Born Hulme, Manchester 3/9/1799, s. William Sumner and Mary Cawley. Trinity Hall, Cambridge 1819, BA1823, dn24 (Chester), p25 (Chester), MA1827. PC. Pott Shrigley, Cheshire 1829-72. Died London 20/2/1878 aged 78, leaving £16,000 [C170639] Married Cheltenham, Glos. 1850 (2nd q.) Ellen Louisa King, w. issue.

SUMNER (John Bird, Bishop of Chester, *then* Archbishop of Canterbury) Born Kenilworth, Warwickshire 25/2/1780, s. Rev. Robert Sumner and Hannah Bird (and brother to Charles Richard Sumner, Bishop of Winchester, above). King's, Cambridge 1798, Fellow 1801-3, BA1803, dn03 (Salis.), p05, MA1807, DD1828. V. and R. Mapledurham, Oxon. 1818-88 ('a devoted, evangelical pastor'), Prebend of 9th, then 5th, then 2nd Prebendal Stall, Durham Cathedral 1820-8. Important Bishop of Chester (incl. all of industrial Lancs.) 1828-48 (233 new churches, 671 new day schools). As Archbishop of Canterbury 1848 to death (Addinton Park, Surrey 6/9/1862, leaving £60,000) he was a firm, gracious and statesman-like leader, 'a tall, imposing figure … an outgoing, gentle and gracious individual' (ODNB) [C217662. ODNB. N.A.D. Scotland, *John Bird Sumner, evangelical archbishop* (1995)] Married 31/3/1805 Marianne Roberton (dau. of an Edinburgh naval offier), and had issue.

SUNDERLAND (John) Born Ulverston, Lancs. 21/12/1769, s. Thomas Sunderland and Anne Dickson. Trinity, Cambridge 1787, BA 1792, MA1795. One of the original Cambridge 'Apostles'. V. St Mellons w. St Llanedeyrn, Glamorgan -1799-1807, V. Pennington, Lancs. 1806-37 (non-res.: in Lausanne?), V. Ulverston St Mary 1807-35, V. Wiveliscombe, Som. 1813-37, R. Norton, Kent 1816. Died Ulverston 23/12/1837 aged 68 [C49159] Married (1) Askham, Westmorland 17/12/1806 Anne King (dau. of the Vice-Chancellor of the Duchy of Lancaster), with issue (2) Moresby, Cumberland 21/2/1827 Mary Elizabeth Morland (of Capplethwaite Hall, Kendal).

SUNDERLAND (Thomas Lister Joseph) Bapt. Halifax, Yorks. 25/5/1808, s. Joseph Sunderland (surgeon) and Hannah Lister. Caius, Cambridge 1825 (aged 17), BA 1830, dn31

(Lin.), p32 (Lin.), MA1833. V. Tilsworth, Beds. 1833-45 [vacant in ERC]. Latterly of Ravensden Grange, Beds., dying there 15/10/1857 [C77197] Married Leighton Buzzard, Beds. 24/5/1837 Anne Wood, with son of same name.

SURTEES (John) Born Newcastle upon Tyne 11/5/1794, s. William Surtees and Elizabeth Catherine Lewis. University, Oxford 1801 (aged 18), BA 1806, dn07 (Ex.), p08 (Win. for Salis.), Fellow, MA1808. R. Edmondthorpe, Leics. 1808-11, R. Lullington, Derbys. 1810, R. West Deeping, Lincs. 1810, R. Sleaford, Lincs. 1810, R. East Farleigh 1811-12 (res.), R. Banham, Norfolk 1812, R. Taverham, Norfolk 1814, Canon of 2nd Prebend in Bristol Cathedral 1821-57, R. Bristol St Augustine 1825-32 (res.). Dom. Chap. to 2nd Earl of Sefton 1810. Died 23/12/1857 [C53919] Married Bath 12/1/1803 Mary Ann Hawkins ('a minor with consent'), with clerical son Scott Frederick Surtees.

SUTCLIFFE (Thomas) Bapt. Heptonstall, Yorks. 24/1/1762, s. John and Grace Sutcliffe. Literate: dn92 (York), p93 (York). PC. Luddenden, Yorks. 1796 to death 28/5/1834 aged 72 [C134713. YCO] Surrogate.

SUTLEFFE (Robert) Bapt. Norwich 3/1/1768. Corpus Christi St Benet, Cambridge 1784, BA1789, Fellow 1790, dn90 (Ely), MA 1792, p92 (Nor.), BD1800. R. Lambourne, Essex 1815 to death 20/9/1840 aged 72 [C100329] Married Norwich 13/8/1819 Judith Maria Woodhouse.

SUTTON (Charles) Bapt. Norwich 7/3/1756, s. Edward Sutton (a draper). St John's, Cambridge 1775, BA1779, dn79 (Nor.), p80 (Nor.), MA1782, Fellow 1784-1793, BD1790, DD1806. Usher at Norwich G/S 1789-93; PC. Norwich St George Tombland 1788-1841, R. Alburgh, Norfolk 1793 and V. Thornham w. Holme-next-the-Sea >< Norfolk 1794 to death (Norwich) 27/5/1846 aged 90 [C100330] Married 15/8/1793 Mrs Charlotte (Kirby) Meadows.

SUTTON (Evelyn Levett) Born Marylebone, London 10/6/1777, s. Evelyn Levett and Drusilla Sutton. Trinity, Cambridge 1796, BA 1801, dn01 (C&L for York), p02 (Nor. for York), MA 1807. R. Canterbury St Alphage 1806-12, V. High Halden, Kent 1806-35, V. Preston, Kent 1812-17, PC. Oare, Kent 1812-20, V. St Peter in Thanet, Kent 1820 and Canon of Westminster Abbey 1832 to death. Dom. Chap. to 19th Baron Grey de Ruthyn; to 1st Baron Manners 1812. Died 'suddenly attacked with apoplexy, whilst reading the 9th Commandment' 26/1/1835 [C19956. YCO] Married Westminster, London 10/6/1830 Amy Kynaston.

SUTTON (John Lucas) Born Weekley, Northants. 29/3/1793, s. Rev. John Sutton and Elizabeth Salmon. Balliol, Oxford 1811, BA 1815, MA1818. R. Weekley 1818 and R. Little Oakely (Oakely Parva), Northants. 1818 to death (Kettering, Northants.) 29/9/1870 aged 77, leaving £3,000 [C19958] Married St Pancras, London 11/6/1822 Letitia Bowan, with clerical son of same name.

SUTTON (Robert) Born Howden, Yorks. 20/5/1788, s. of Robert (a farmer) and Dorothy Sutton. St John's, Cambridge 1806, BA1810, dn11 (York), p12 (Salis. for York), MA1831. PC. Fulford, York 1812-58, R. York St Michael, Spurriergate 1817-58, Prebend (4th Stall) in Ripon Collegiate Church 1828, then Canon of Ripon Cathedral 1836 to death there 18/9/1858 aged 70, leaving £15,000 [C85319. YCO] Married York 11/7/1809 Harriot Buckle (w), with clerical son, also Robert.

SUTTON (Robert Wooding) Born Stambourne, Essex, s. Robert Sutton and Susannah Wooding. Clare, Cambridge 1819, BA1824, dn25 (London), p26 (London), MA1827. V. Norton, Herts. 1826-31 (res.), R. Layer Breton, Essex 1831 to death (Bonchurch, IoW) 4/7/1855 aged 57 [C122624] Married Layer Breton, Essex 26/6/1832 Sarah Wilson.

SUTTON (Thomas) From Leek, Staffs., s. Thomas Sutton. Worcester, Oxford 1795 (aged 17), BA1799, dn01 (Ox.), p02 (Ox.), MA1802, BD and DD1842. V. Sheffield St Peter, Yorks. 1805 (and Prebend of Riccall in York Minster) 1841 to death (Sheffield) 9/1/1851 aged 73 [C37773] Wife Elizabeth, with issue.

SUTTON, or MANNERS-SUTTON (Thomas Manners) Bapt. Lincoln 23/8/1789, s. Hon. John Sutton (of Kelham, Notts.) and Anne Manners. Trinity, Cambridge 1809, BA 1813, dn13 (Bristol for York), p13 (York), MA 1817. Prebend of Westminster Abbey 1817-31, R. Tunstall, Kent 1817-36, R. Great Chart, Kent 1818-36, Sub-Dean of Lincoln Cathedral (where he compsed and directed music) 1831-44, R.

Avenham w. Kelham, 1837 to death. Chap. to his cousin the Speaker of the House of Commons 1798. Died 27/10/1844 aged 49 [C135759. YCO both under Sutton. Venn under Manners-Sutton. Kaye] Married Kington Magna, Dorset 23/11/1826 Lucy Sarah Mortimer (a clergy dau.).

SWAIN (John) Bapt. Mottram in Longendale, Cheshire 15/12/1776, s. James and Mary Swain. Clare, Cambridge 1795, BA1800, dn00 (York), p00 (London for Chester). R. Taxal, Cheshire 1800 and V. Elvaston cum Thurlston and Ambaston, Derbys. 1806 to death. Dom. Chap. to Earl of Harrington. Died when returning on foot from Derby, he 'fell down and suddenly expired' 27/10/1841 [C19961. YCO]

SWAINSON (Charles Litchfield) Bapt. Hackney, London 27/6/1799, s. John Timothy Swainson and Betty Hammerton. St John's, Oxford 1815, Fellow 1818, BA1819, dn20 (Ox.), p21 (Ox.), MA1822, BD1829. PC. Liverpool St Mary, Edge Hill 1823-35, V. Oxford St Giles 1835-6, R. Crick, Northants. 1836 (and RD) to death 4/8/1871 aged 73, leaving £4,000 [C21763] Married Milverton, Warwicks. 23/5/1838 Harriet France, with clerical son.

SWAINSON (Christopher) Born Preston, Lancs. 12/7/1775, s. John Swainson (calico merchant) and Susannah Inman (of Manchester and Jamaica). Worcester, Oxford 1795 (aged 20), BA1797, MA1799, then St John's, Cambridge 1793, dn00 (Bristol), p01 (Bristol). Tutor to the sons of the 2nd Lord Clive (whom he accompanied to Eton, 1798); V. Hawkesbury, Glos. 1802-13, V. Clun, Shropshire 1805-54, Prebend of Cublington in Hereford Cathedral 1808 and R. Wistanstow, Shropshire 1816 to death there. Chap. to two Bishops of Worcester 1816. Died 19/12/1854 [C53922] Married 3/8/1809 Elizabeth Low (dau. of a Preston physician), and had issue.

SWALES (Christopher Easterby) Bapt. 17/2/1788, s. Edward Swales and Grace Easterby. Literate: dn12 (York), p15 (York). PC. Over Silton, Yorks. 1822 to death ('after a long and painful illness') 10/3/1848 aged 64 [C135761. YCO] Married 14/6 or 7/7/1823 Catherine Hodgson Faint, with issue.

SWAN (Francis, sen.) Bapt. Swinderby, Lincs. 6/9/1753, s. Henry Swan and Susanah Bellamy. Corpus Christi, Oxford 1771, BA 1775, MA 1779, dn79 (Win.), p80 (Lin.). R. Skegness, Lincs. 1781-5, R. Lincoln St Peter at Arches 1783-1830, R. Conisholme, Lincs. 1784-1809, V. Kirton in Holland, Lincs. 1785, Prebend of Dunham and Newport in Lincoln Cathedral 1804-25 (res.), R. Winteringham, Lincs. 1808, R. Lincoln St Benedict (--) [or this could be the son, below?] Chap. to 2nd Baron Vernon 1784-1808. Died Lincoln 23/2/1845 [C77217] Married Cambridge 26/9/1782 Susannah Maria Norris, with son below.

SWAN (Francis, jun.) Bapt. Lincoln 21/5/1787, s. Rev. Francis Swan, sen. (above) and Susannah Maria Norris. Exeter, Oxford 1803, then Magdalen 1807-10, BA1808, MA 1810, dn10 (Ox.), p11 (Ox.), Fellow 1810-24, LLB, BD1818. R. Conisholme, Lincs. 1811-19 (res.), R. Blyton cum Wharton, Lincs. 1811-24, R. Sausthorpe, Lincs. 1819-78 (living at Sausthorpe Hall), R. Swerford cum Shorwell, Oxon. 1824-33, Prebend of Dunham and Newport in Lincoln Cathedral 1825-78, R. Bennington, Lincs. 1833-69. Dom. Chap. to 4th Duke of Portland 1811, Died 5/1/1878, leaving £350,000 [C21764] Wife Susan Linton, w. clerical son.

SWANN (Charles) Born Wansford, Northants. 15/11/1772, s. John Swann, (merchant) and Mary Adams. St John's, Cambridge 1791, BA1795, dn96 (Lin. for Peterb.), p97 (Peterb.), MA1799. V. Ridlington, Rutland 1804, R. Stamford St Michael w. St Andrew and St Stephen, Lincs. 1808-11, V. Great Marlow, Bucks. 1811, R. Edmondthorpe, Leics. 1811 to death, Royal Chap. 1798; Chap. to 7th Earl of Cavan 1808. Died 2/5/1846 [C77218] Married Hemel Hempstead, Herts. 2/5/1805 Sarah Willan (a clergy dau.), many ch. *J.P.* for Rutland, Northants. and Leics., and Chairman of Quarter Sessions. Port. online.

SWANN (Robert) Born and bapt. York 13/8/1798, s. Robert Swann (a banker, Askham Hall, Yorks.) and Ursula Carr. Trinity, Cambridge 1815, BA1820, dn22 (York), p23 (York), MA1824. R. Brandsby, Yorks. 1823 and R. North (or Cherry) Burton, Yorks. 1837 [total income in CR65 £1,802] to death (Brandsby) 24/12/1872 aged 74, leaving £20,000 [C135762. YCO] Married 20/11/1832 Jane Cornelia Anne Percival, with clerical son.

SWANTON (Francis) Born Winchester, s. Rev. Francis Swanton, sen. Wadham, Oxford

1810 (aged 18), BCL1817. V. Piddletrenthide, Dorset 1826, 'Perpetual V.' Letcombe Regis, Berks. 1820, V. Winchester St John's 1826 and R. Barton Stacey, Hants. 1845 to death 2/11/1871, leaving £7,000 [C53923 and C108870 - where Foster is transcribed incorrectly]

SWATMAN (Edward) Bapt. King's Lynn, Norfolk 22/2/1778, s. William and Elisabeth Swatman. Trinity, Cambridge 1794, BA1798, dn00 (Ex. for Nor.), MA1801, p03 (Nor.), Chap. 1803-11. R. (and patron) of Little Fransham, Norfolk 1803-39, V. Dulverton, Som. 1826-9 (res.). Died 1840 (1st q.) aged 63 [C40639]

SWAYNE (George) Bapt. Pucklehurst, Glos. 27/11/1772, s. Rev. George Swayne, sen. and Sarah Rocke. Wadham, Oxford 1789, BA1793, dn95 (Bristol), p96 (Ox.), MA1798, Fellow to 1819, Chap. 1819-26, BD and DD1827. R. Langridge, Som. 1814-25, V. Hockley, Essex 1819, V. South Benfleet, Essex 1827. Dom. Chap. to 1st Viscount Hood 1814. Died 13/2/1837 [C37776]

SWEET (Charles) Bapt. Bradninch, Devon 24/6/1752, s. George Sweet and Catharine Richards. Wadham, Oxford 1771, dn74 (Ex.), BA1775, p76 (Ex.). R. (and patron) of Kentisbury, Devon 1776 to death 27/7/1833 [C146427] Married Exeter 3/10/1777 Jane Barter, w. son below.

SWEET (Charles Barter) Bapt. Kentisbury, Devon 6/11/1780, s. Rev. Charles Sweet (above) and Jane Barter. Balliol, Oxford 1798, BA 1802, MA1805. R. Kittisford, Som. 1824-31, R. Sampford Arundel, Som. 1831 to death 23/3/1862, leaving £18,000 [C40640 - not Barker] Married Alderbury, Wilts. 23/10/1810 Lucy Fort, with clerical son Charles Sweet.

SWEET-ESCOTT (Thomas) see under **ESCOTT**

SWETTENHAM (Thomas Swettenham Eaton) Bapt. Great Crosby, Lancs. 23/3/1786, s. John Eaton Swettenham (of Swettenham Hall, Eaton, Cheshire) and Sarah Crosby. Literate: dn13 (Chester), p14 (Chester). R. Swettenham 1814 to death (Corwen, Merioneth) 1868 (4th q.) aged 82. Will not traced [C170649] Married St Albans Abbey 14/5/1805 1805 Anna Antonia Heyes (of Kendal, Westmorland), with issue.

SWIRE (John) Bapt. Sculcoates, Hull, Yorks. 16/1/1797, s. of John Swire (a merchant, of Cononley Hall, Kildwick, Yorks.) and Mary Robinson. University, Oxford 1815, BA1819, dn22 (York), p23 (Chester), MA1823. V. Manfield, Yorks. 1823 to death 20/1/1860, leaving £20,000 [C135763. YCO] Married Northallerton, Yorks. 4/3/1819 Anne Robson (Richmond), w. clerical s. Frederick. J.P.

SWORDE (Thomas) Probably bapt. Norwich 31/8/1767, s. Wiliam and Sussanah Sworde. [NiVoF] PC. Thetford St Cuthbert w. Thetford St Peter, Norfolk 1829. Dom. Chap. to Duke of Grafton 1845. Probate granted 28/9/1854 [C115693]

SYER (Barrington) Bapt. Haverhill, Suffolk 10/11/1780, s. Rev. Benjamin Blomfield Syer (below) and Mary Moore. Caius, Cambridge 1798, BA1802, dn02 (Nor.), p04 (London). V. Gestingthorpe, Essex 1804-49, PC. Stoke by Clare, Essex 1807-15, V. Little Wallingford, Suffolk 1837 to death 30/10/1849 [C115694] Married Kedington, Suffolk 5/9/1814 Sophia Major (or Mayer), 1 dau.

SYER (Barrington Blomfield) Born and bapt. Little (o/w Earl) Stonham, Suffolk 15/8/1755, s. Rev. Dey [sic] Syer (R. Kedington, Suffolk) and Elizabeth Blomfield. Caius, Cambridge 1773, dn77 (Nor.), BA1778. V. (and patron) of Little Waldingfield, Suffolk 1787-1837, R. (and patron) of Kedington 1800-41, R. Great Wratting w. Little Wratting, Oxon. 1800-18. Died 19/4/1844 aged 89 [C115695] Married (1) Mary Moore (Kentwell Hall, Long Melford, Suffolk), 4s. (2) Marian Elizabeth Chevallier (Aspall Hall, Suffolk), 2s. J.P. Suffolk.

SYKES (Christopher) Born and bapt. Sledmere, Yorks. 18/10/1774, s. Sir Christopher Sykes, 2nd Bart. and Elizabeth Tatton. St John's, Cambridge 1792, BA1797, dn97 (London for York), p99 (York). PC. Scampston, Yorks. 1802-18 (res.), R. Hilston 1819, Yorks. and R. Roos, Yorks. 1819 to death 9/11/1857 aged 83 [C122628. YCO] Married Stockport 14/5/1799 Lucy Dorothea Langford, with issue.

SYKES see also under **SIKES**

SYMONDS (Robert) From Sellack, Heref., s. Thomas Powell Symons. BNC, Oxford 1786, BA1790, then Oriel, Fellow, dn91 (Ox.), MA

1792, p01 (Glos.). R. Hinton Waldrist, Berks. 1801 to death 6/12/1836 [C37785]

SYMONDS (Samuel) Born Falmouth, Cornwall 1792, s. of Samuel Symonds (a merchant) and Jane Bolitho. Clare, Cambridge 1811, BA 1815? dn15 (Ex.), p16 (Ex.), MA1819. R. Philleigh, Cornwall 1818 to death 12/5/1868 aged 76, leaving under £300 [C146433] Married (1) Budock, Cornwall 18/1/1813 Winifred Noye, with issue (2) Plymouth 1860 (4th q.) Elizabeth (Lizzie) Kivell/Kevill Worsley (w). J.P. for Cornwall. Engaged in a libel trial in 1831.

SYMONDS (Thomas) From Witney, Oxon., s. Thomas Symonds [*pleb.*]. Merton, Oxford 1790 (aged 17), BA1794, dn96 (Ox.), p97 (Ox.), MA 1797. V. Eynsham, Oxon. 1826 and V. Stanton Harcourt, Oxon. 1827 to death. Dom. Chap. to 1st Baron Clonbrock 1827. Died 7/1/1845 [C21765] Married Cowley, Oxon. 9/7/1803 Frances Nash, with issue.

SYMONS (Henry John) Bapt. Hackney, London 28/2/1781, s. Rev. Jelinger Symons and Juliana Lane. St John's, Oxford 1799, BA1803, dn04 (Ox.), p05 (Ox.), MA1808, BCL and DCL1813. Army Chap. (present at the Battle of Corunna); V. Hereford St Martin 1824 to death. Chap. to HRH Dukes of Kent, and of Cambridge. Died 22/3/1857. [C21767] Married St George's Hanover Square, Lonson 26/10/1807 Frances Issanchon (a minor).

SYMONS (Jelinger) Bapt. Low Leyton, Essex 13/8/1778, s. Rev Jelinger Symons, sen. (R. Hackney, London, and *not* above) and Juliana Lane. St John's, Cambridge 1793, BA1797, dn98 (Durham), p01 (Durham), MA1800. Min. Stamford Hill, Hackney, London 1802, V. Monkland, Heref. 1808-51, V. Wilcot, Wilts. 1823, R. Radnage, Bucks. 1833 to death. Chap. at Boulogne 1821. Died 20/5/1851 [C77257. ODNB] Married London 1/1/1805 Maria Henrietta Airey (Sniperley, Co. Durham), w. issue. Botanist.**NS (John Trehane)** Born St Ervan, Cornwall 23/5/1787, s. Rev. John Symons and Frances Walker Kedington, Suffolk. Exeter, Oxford 1805, BA1809, dn10 (Ex.), p11 (Ex.). R. Trevalga, Cornwall 1831 to death (Plymouth) 5/9/1867 aged 80, leaving £2,000 [C146435] Widow Betsy Bowen, with issue.

SYMPSON (Charles John) Born New Shrubland Hall, Barham, Suffolk 16/6/1803, s. Robert and Charlotte Sympson. Trinity, Cambridge 1822, BA1826, dn27 (York), p27 (York), MA 1829. V. East Drayton, Notts. 1831-45, R. Teversal, Notts. 1831-45, R. Kirkby Misperton, Yorks. 1845 to death. Dom. Chap. to 1st Baron Faversham 1831. Died 12/2/1870 aged 68, leaving £3,000 [C135765. YCO] Married Tonbridge, Kent 28/7/1838 Mrs Eliza Maria (Lubbock) Brown, with issue.

SYNDERSCOMBE (Gregory) see under **RAYMOND**

TACY (Henry) Bapt. Oakham, Rutland 24/4/1783, s. James Tacy and Jane Halford. Queens', Cambridge 1808, dn12 (Nor.), BA 1813, p13 (Nor.), MA1816. PC. Bylaugh, Norfolk 1818-26, R. Swanton Morley w. Worthing, Norfolk 1825 and Prebend of Norwich Cathedral 1841 to death (Semer, Suffolk) 10/4/1863 aged 80, leaving £3,000 [C112922] Wife Harriet, and issue. Pencil port. by Amelia Opie online.

TADDY (John) Born London 29/5/1783, s. Christopher Taddy (Buckland, Kent) and Mary Anne (dau. of Sir John Hopkins, a Lord Mayor of London). Trinity, Cambridge 1801, BA1805, dn06 (Cant.), p07 (Cant.), Fellow 1807-10, MA 1808. PC. Northill, Beds. 1811 to death 23/1/1858, leaving £80,000 [C77270] Married Wingham, Kent 1/110/1810 Catherine Latham, with clerical son, also John Taddy.

TALBOT (Arthur Chetwynd-, Hon.) Born London 12/11/1805, s. Charles, 2nd Earl Talbot and Frances Tomasine Lambart. Christ Church, Oxford 1822, BA1826, then All Souls, Fellow 1827-9, MA1829. R. Ingestre, Staffs. 1829 and R. Church Eaton, Staffs. 1829 (and RD of Lapney and Triezul) to death 13/1/1884 aged 78 [total income £1,500], leaving £9,602-12s-7d. [C19970] Married (1) Ingestre 17/7/1832 Frances Elizabeth Frances Hervey-Aston (d.1845), w. issue (2) Hull 19/10/1854 Mary Elizabeth Masterman, w. clerical s. Arthur Henry Talbot.

TALBOT (Thomas) Born Sutton Mandeville, Wilts. 4/9/1779, s. Thomas and Elizabeth Talbot. Hertford, Oxford 1800 (aged 20), then St Alban Hall, BA1805, dn05 (Glos.), p06 (Ex.). R. Hawling, Glos. 1808 to death. Died Fisherton Anger, Wilts. 24/9/1843 [C146464]

TALMASH (Hugh Francis, Hon.) see under **TOLLEMACHE**

TANNER (Robert) Bapt. Rose Ash, Devon 6/3/1770, s. Robert Tanner. Exeter, Oxford 1788, BA1792, dn93 (Ex.), p94 (Ex.), then Trinity, Cambridge 1814, MA1814. R. Ashreigny (o/w King's Ash), Devon 1812, R. Chumleigh Collegiate Church, Devon (with all 6 Prebends) 1814-23 (res.), R. Kingsnympton, Devon 1814 and V. Okehampton, Devon 1831 to death there. Dom. Chap. to 2nd Viscount Kilwarden 1814; to 2nd Viscount Clifden 1831.

Died 3/6/1834 aged 64 [C146469] Wife Maria, and issue.

TANNER (Thomas, sen.) Bapt. Cheldon, Devon 19/3/1754, s. Rev. William Tanner and Catherine Rule. Exeter, Oxford 1771, BA1775, dn76 (Ex.), p78 (Ex.), then Trinity, Cambridge, MA1779. PC. Bradninch, Devon 1780 to death 29/10/1843 aged 90 [C146470. Foster mixes father and son of same name (below)] Married Tiverton, Devon. 15/5/1783 Sarah Marder, w. issue (below).

TANNER (Thomas, jun.) From Bradninch, Devon, s. Rev. Thomas Tanner (above) and Sarah Marder. Balliol, Oxford 1806 (aged 18), BA1809, dn10 (Ex.), p12 (Ex.), MA1812. H/M Portsmouth G/S and Dartmouth G/S; PC. Kingswear, Devon 1812-18 (res.), Chap. of the Donative of Burlescombe, Devon 1819-65, Chap. of Donative of Ashford, Devon 1820, V. Ninehead, Som. 1835 to death. Dom. Chap. to 4th Earl Bathurst 1835. Died 1/12/1865, leaving £8,000 [C146471] Widow Mary.

TANQUERAY (Edward) Born Tingrith, Beds. 6/5/1762, s. Rev. Thomas Tanqueray and Mary Willaume. Clare, Cambridge 1781, dn85 (Lin.), p86 (Lin.), LLB1793. R. Newton Bromswold, Northants. 1786-8, R. Tingrith 1788-1846, V. Ridgmont, Beds. 1790-1833 [sequestrator], R. Tempsford, Beds. 1814 to death 31/12/1846 [C77313] Married Tingrith 8/2/1803 Frances Elizabeth Aveling (a clergy dau., Millbrook, Beds.), with issue.

TARLETON (John Edward) Born Liverpool 16/8/1783, s. Thomas Tarleton (slave trader, then landed proprietor of Bolesworth Castle, Tattenhall, Cheshire) and Mary Robinson. BNC, Oxford 1802, BA1806, then All Souls, dn08 (Ox.), p09 (Ox.), BCL11809, Fellow 1809-35, 849, leaving £600 [C7043. LBSO]

TARPLEY (Kenneth Mackenzie Reed) Born Jersey, Channel Islands 1781, s. Thomas Tarpley. Christ Church, Oxford 1798, Student [Fellow] to 1816, BA1802, MA 1805, p05 (Ox.). V. Oxford St Mary Magdalene 1808-15, PC. Ludford, Heref. 1811-25, V. Floore/Flower, Northants. 1815 to death. Dom. Chap. to 1st Earl of Effingham 1817. Died 1865 (1st q.). No will found [C21770] Wife Charlotte ?Hornsby, and issue.

TASKER (Henry) Bapt. Wilmington, Dartford, Kent 20/6/1794, s. John Tasker and Sarah Effield Chapman. Pembroke, Cambridge 1812, BA1816, Fellow 1817, MA1819, dn21 (Ely), p22 (Bristol for Ely). V. Soham w. Barway, Cambs. [net income £1,642] 1832 (and Hon. Canon of Ely Cathedral) to death 17/1/1874, leaving £25,000 [C53930]

TATE (James) Bapt. Richmond, Yorks. 11/6/1771, s. of Thomas Tate (a maltster). Sidney, Cambridge 1789, BA1794, dn95 (Ely), Fellow 1795-6, MA1797, p00 (York for Chester). 'The learned master of Richmond School' 1796-1833; PC. Bellerby, Yorks. 1802-8, R. Marske (in Craven), Yorks. 1808-34, R. Downholme, Yorks. 1808-34, Prebend of Consumpta per Mare and Canon Residentiary of St Paul's Cathedral, London 1833 and R. Edmonton, Middx. 1839 to death (Clifton, Bristol) 2/9/1843 [C100444. YCO] Married London 29/9/1796 Margaret Wallis (from Ireland), with clerical issue.

TATHAM (Arthur) Born London 22/9/1808, s. Charles Heathcote Tatham (architect) and Harriet Williams. Magdalene, Cambridge 1827, BA1831, dn32 (Roch. for Ely), p32 (Ex.), MA 1835. R. Boconnoc w. Broadoak, Cornwall 1832-74, Prebend of Exeter Cathedral 1860 to death (Liskeard, Cornwall) 22/2/1874 aged 65, leaving £1,000 [C109496. Boase] Married (1) St Martin's-in-the-Fields, London 23/10/1801 Harriet Edwards, 1 dau. (2) Egg Buckland, Devon 22/6/1853 Jemima Amabel Glanville, 4 ch. *J.P.* Cornwall. Leader in the movement for the creation of the Truro bishopric.

TATHAM (Edward) Bapt. Sedbergh, Yorks. 1/10/1749, s. James Tatham [*pleb.*]. Magdalene, Cambridge 1767 (did not reside), then Queen's, Oxford 1769, BA1772, MA1776, dn76 (B&W), p78, then Lincoln, Fellow, BD1783, DD1787, controversial Rector of Lincoln College, Oxford 1792-1834. R. Copp 1784-5 (res.), PC. Tilstock 1791-5 (res.), R. Twyford, Bucks. 1792, R. Whithurch w. Marbury, Shropshire 1829 to death 24/4/1834 (CCEd says 3/5/1834) [C20008. ODNB] Married 1801 Elizabeth Cook, of Cheltenham. 'In the closing years of his life, he chiefly lived at Combe rectory. He scarcely ever appeared at Oxford, unless it was to bring with him in his dogcart a pair of pigs of his own breeding for sale in the pig-market. Many caricatures and lampoons of him passed from hand to hand at Oxford, and he was known as "the devil who looked over Lincoln." '

TATHAM (John) Born Melling, Lancs., s. Rev. John Tatham, sen. and Elizabeth Dawson. Literate: dn86 (Chester), p87 (Chester). Curate Kendal St George, Westmorland 1791-1847 (res.), (succ. his father as) V. Melling 1794 (together they held the parish for 101 years) to death. Chap. to Duke of Hamilton 1818. Died 5/2/1851 aged 87 [C170657] Married (1) Lancaster 18/10/1796 Agnes Dawson (d.1813), with issue (2) Lancaster 4/4/1815 Mrs Margaret (Hodgson) Skirrow, with issue.

TATHAM (Ralph) Bapt. Barton, Whittingham, Northumberland 6/11/1778, s. Rev. Ralph Tatham, sen. and Ann Smith. St John's, Cambridge 1796, BA 1800, Fellow, 1802, MA1803, dn04 (Roch.), p04 (Roch.), BD1811, Tutor 1814-20, etc. DD1839, President of St John's College, Cambridge 1839-57, Vice-Chancellor of Cambridge 1839-40, 1845-6. R. Colkirk w. Stibbard, Norfolk 1816 to death (at College) 19/1/1857 aged 79 [C2400. Boase] 'He was well qualified for this office by his singular dignity of person, courtesy of manner, and a great skill in complimentary speeches. The wags said of him: "He brought forth butter in a lordly dish."'

TATTAM (Henry) Bapt. North Marston, Bucks. 7/1/1789, s. John Tattam and Jane Gurney. Literate: dn18 (Nor.), p19 (Nor), then Christ's, Cambridge 1823 (a Ten Year Man), LLD (TCD), DD (G4/9/1779 4/9/1779 Göttingen), DPhil. (Leiden) 1845. R. Bedford St Cuthbert 1822-49, R. Great Woolstone, Bucks. 1831-49, Archdeacon of Bedford 1845-66 (but 'lacked the commitment needed at a time of great change in the church' - ODNB), V. Stanford Rivers, Essex 1849 to death there. Min. English Episcopal Chapel, Amsterdam 1822. Chap. Bedford County Lunatic Asylum 1829. Chap. in Ordinary 1853-68. Died 8/1/1868, leaving £6,000 [C77320. ODNB. Boase. Kaye] Married Holborn, London 18/10/1820 Eliza Ann Platt, *s.p.* Coptic scholar and editor (for manuscripts he went to Egypt). *F.R.S.* (1835). Photo. online.

TATTERSHALL (Thomas) Bapt. Scarborough, Yorks. 6/7/1795, s. Rev. Thomas (a Methodist minister from Brampton, Hunts.) and Mary Tattershall. Queens', Cambridge 1811, BA1816, MA1819, dn20 (Nor.), p21 (Glos.), Fellow 1821-7, DD1838, incorporated at

Oxford 1844. PC. Liverpool St Matthew 1821-30, (first) PC. Liverpool St Augustine, Evertonl 1830 to death 29/10/1846 aged 51 [C115718. DEB] Married York 2/1/1828 Ann Murgatroyd, with clerical son.

TATUM (William Wyndham) Born Salisbury 24/10/1805, s. Thomas Tatum and Diana Shuckburgh. Queen's, Oxford 1823, BA1827, dn29 (Salis.), p30 (Salis.). R. Salisbury St Martin 1830 to death (Milford, Wilts.) 7/4/1870, leaving £3,000 [C85330] Married Plympton, Devon 1850 (1st q.) Mary Grace Adams (w), with issue.

TAUNTON (Robert Cropp) Bapt. Sydling St Nicholas, Dorset 23/9/1779, s. Rev. Robert Taunton and Frances Cropp. Corpus Christi, Oxford 1797, BA1800, MA1803, dn03 (Win.), p03 (Win.). R. Ashley, Hants. 1802. Died Bathwick, Som. 7/4/1860, leaving £30,000 [C108875] Married Claverton, Som. 19/4/1805 Lucy Eckersall.

TAYLER (Archdale Wilson) Bapt. Morcott, Rutland 14/10/1785, s. Archdale Wilson Tayler and Frances Elizabeth Hall. Christ Church, Oxford 1802, Student [Fellow] 1802-15, BA 1806, MA 1808, dn08 (Ox.), p11 (Ox.). *H.E.I.C.* Chap. Dacca, Bengal 1815-25; R. Stoke Newington, Middx. 1830 to death 11/10/1852 [C21805] Married (1) Wrexham, Denbigh 1815 Catherine Grace Briggs (d.1829), w. issue (2) Stepney, London 23/1/1832 Martha Ann Wilson (d.1841) (3) Camden London 3/10/1844 Elizabeth Heathfield. Brother below.

TAYLER (Henry Joseph) Bapt. Broughton Poggs, Oxon. 3/9/1787, s. Archdale Wilson Tayler and Frances Elizabeth Hall. Usher at Bury St Edmunds School, Suffolk. Literate: dn10 (Nor.), p11 (Nor.), then Emmanuel, Cambridge 1821 (a Ten Year Man, BD1822). R. Winnall, Hants. 1820-9, R. Raithby, Lincs. 1829-64, R. Kinwarton, Warwicks. 1833-4, R. Upton on Severn, Worcs. 1834-64, Canon of Worcester Cathedral. Died (Upton) 5/1/1864, leaving £8,000 [C77321. Bennett] Married 22/7/1820 Jemima Maria (dau. Sir William Fraser, 1st Bart.), with clerical son Henry Carr Archdale Tayler. Brother above.

TAYLOR (Charles) From Oxford, s. John Taylor [*pleb.*]. Chorister Magdalen, Oxford 1788-94; matr. Balliol 1796 (aged 16), BA1800, dn03 (Heref.), p04 (Heref.), MA1807, BD and DD 1822. H/M Ludlow G/S 1800, and of Hereford Cathedral School 1807; V. Staunton Long >< Shropshire 1815, Prebend of Moreton Magna in Hereford Cathedral 1820-36 and Chancellor 1825, V. Madeley cum Tiberton, Heref. 1821 and V. Almeley, Heref. 1830 to death 9/6/1836 [C53937]

TAYLOR ([Charles]) [NiVoF] Curate Bethell [Proprietary Chapel], Guernsey, Channel Islands --. Died before 1842 [Not in CCEd]

TAYLOR (Charles) From Yorkshire. St John's, Cambridge 1804, BA1809, dn10 (Nor.), p11 (Nor.). R. Marlingford, Norfolk 1814 and R. (and patron) of Clopton, Suffolk 1829 to death there 9/12/1847 aged 60 [C 115726] Had issue.

TAYLOR (Charles) [BA but NiVoF] R. Biddesham, Som. 1831-[58]. Probate (Bath) to some cleric of this name 24/3/1857 [C40711]

TAYLOR (George) Bapt. London 7/11/1793, s. John Taylor (silversmith). Pembroke, Cambridge 1811, BA1815, dn16 (Nor.), p18 (Nor.), MA1821, incorporated at Oxford 1826, DCL. H/M Dedham Free G/S, Essex 1823-40; PC. Stoke by Clare, Suffolk 1818-38, V. Dedham, Essex 1840 (and RD) to death (White Colne, Essex) 5/12/1871, leaving £9,000 [C115727] Married Hawkwell, Essex 25/1/1813 Martha Deeks (d.1818), with dau.

TAYLOR (Henry) From Kensington, London, s.Rev. Richard Taylor. Lincoln, Oxford 1796 (aged 18), BA1799, MA1802. V. Liddington, Wilts. 1801-24, R. North and South Stoke w. Easton (o/w Stoke Rochford), Lincs. 1824, R. Ashby by Partney, Lincs. 1824. Dom. Chap. to 9th Earl of Kellie 1824. Died 19/6/1842. [C108884. Bennett2]

TAYLOR (Henry) From Purbrook, Hants., s. William Taylor. Worcester, Oxford 1822 (aged 19), BA1826, dn26 (B&W), p28 (Win.). R. South Pool, Devon 1826 and V. Stokenham, Devon 1829 to death (Torquay, Devon) 24/4/1861, leaving £4,000 [C40713] Widow Marianne.

TAYLOR (Henry) [MA but NiVoF] PC. Aldeby, Norfolk 1811-[43]. Died? [C115724]

TAYLOR (Henry) [MA but NiVoF] R. North Moreton, Berks. 1824-[58]. Died? [C85334]

TAYLOR (Henry Joseph) [NiVoF] R. Winnall, Hants. 1828-33. Died? [C108885]

TAYLOR (James) From Clifton, Bristol, s. Rev. John Taylor. Oriel [Foster as St John's], Oxford 1790 (aged 18), SCL, dn95 (Bristol), p95 (Bristol). PC. Clifton, Bristol 1795 to death 5/3/1847 aged 63 [C53938] Was married.

TAYLOR (John) From Ashley Moor, Heref., s. William Taylor [*pleb*.]. Queen's, Oxford 1783 (aged 21), then Balliol, BA1787, p88 (Heref.), MA1791, BD and DD1809. PC. Ford, Heref. 1802-43, PC. Hope under Dinmore, Heref. 1807, R. Wigmore, Heref. 1831-[42]. Died 24/7/1843 [C174110

TAYLOR (John) From Carmarthen, s. Thomas Taylor. Wadham, Oxford 1801 (aged 19), BA 1805, dn05 (Ox.), p06 (Glos.). R. Imber, Wilts. [blank in ERC] 1817-52, V. Llanarthney, Carmarthen 1816-52, PC. Willand, Devon 1817 to death 28/6/1852 [C85336]

TAYLOR (John) Bapt. Eye, Suffolk 7/6/1791, s. Robert and Sophia Taylor. Caius, Cambridge 1809, BA1815, dn16 (Nor.), p17 (Nor.). R. Haynford, Norfolk 1817-36, PC. Norwich St Michael at Thorne 1828-36, R. Diptford, Devon 1828 to death (Norwich) 19/12/1836 [C115731] Married Ipswich 2/8/1815 Mrs Sophia Toosey.

TAYLOR (Joseph) Born All Hallows the Great, London, s. Joseph Taylor [*pleb*.]. St John's, Oxford 1781 (aged 16), no degree. H/M Heskin School, Chorley, Lancs.; PC. Coppull, Lincs. 1801 to death 9/11/1839 aged 74 [C170673]

TAYLOR (Joseph) Born Bowes, Yorks, s. George Taylor. St Edmund Hall, Oxford 1793 (aged 19), BA1797, then King's College, Cambridge 1802, MA. S/M Stourbridge Free School, Worcs. 1808; V. Snittersfield, Warwicks. 1802-33, PC. Stourbridge Chapel, Old Swinford 1810 (w. S/M Old Swinford Parish School 1810). Died 2/5/1833 (CCEd says 29/5/1833) [C122215]

TAYLOR (Mascie Domville) Born Lymm Hall, Cheshire 22/7/1783, s. Thomas Taylor and Ann Massey. BNC, Oxford 1802, BA1806, dn06 (Chester), p07 (Chester), MA1809. Minor Canon of Chester Cathedral, R. (Great) Langton, Yorks. 1812 and R. Moreton Corbet, Shropshire 1819 to death. Dom. Chap. to 2nd Earl of Orford 1809. Died Great Broughton, Cheshire 9/10/1845 [C20032] Married (1) Childwall, Liverpool 15/1/1812 Diana Houghton (d.1824), w. issue (2) Chester 27/9/1825 Patty Jemima Ffoulkes, w. further issue.

TAYLOR (Montague James) Born Madras, s. James and Frances M. Taylor. BNC, Oxford 1824 (aged 17), BA1828, dn29 (Chich.), p30 (Chich.). V. Harrold, Beds. 1831. Died Brompton, London 29/6/1896 aged 89, leaving £24,259-9s-5d. [C70590] Married Marylebone, London 29/8/1832 Louisa Anne Curtis, with military issue.

TAYLOR (Richard) Born Sevenoaks, Kent, s. Jeffery Taylor. Jesus, Cambridge 1792 (aged 17), BA1797, dn99 (Nor.), MA1800, p01 (Nor.). R. East Grinstead, Sussex 1815 to death 20/3/1835 (CCEd says 27/5/1835) [C70594]

TAYLOR (Robert) Born Aberhavest, Montgomery, s. Rev. Joseph Taylor. Pembroke, Oxford 1768 (aged 18), BA1771, dn72 (Heref.), p73 (Heref.), MA1774 (Worcester). R. Shelve, Shropshire 1775 and R. More, Shropshire 1776 to death 10/10/1833 (CCEd thus) [C174122]

TAYLOR (Robert) From City of London, s. Robert Taylor. Trinity, Cambridge 1802 (aged 22), BA1806, MA1810 [barrister, Lincoln's Inn 1811] dn23 (London), p23 (London). R. Clifton Campville w. Chilcote, Staffs. [net income £1,287] 1824 to death 19/5/1850 [C20034]

TAYLOR (Robert) Bapt. Ulverston, Lancs. 9/5/1795, s. Thomas Taylor. St Bees, Cumberland 1818-19, dn19 (Chester), p20 (Chester). PC. Underbarrow, Kendal, Westmorland 1822-39. Alive 1844 [C170676] Married (1) 4 ch. (2) Underbarrow 17/8/1835 Elizabeth Clark, with further issue. 'He would appear to have been hardly ever sober.'

TAYLOR (William) Probably bapt. Kingsland, Heref. 2/1/1790, s. William and Mary Taylor. Magdalen Hall, Oxford 1817, SCL, dn19 (Chester for York), p23 (York). V. Bishop Burton >< Beverley, Yorks. 1826-41 (res.), PC. Longton, Staffs. 1826-33. Died? [C135770. YCO]

TAYLOR (William Addington) From Bath, s. William Joshua Taylor. Exeter, Oxford 1815 (aged 18), BA1819, dn20 (B&W), p21 (Chester for B&W). R. (and patron) of Litchborough, Northants. 1821 to death (Siston, Bristol) 28/7/1881, leaving £760 [C40715] Widow Anne Catherine, and clerical son of same name.

TAYLOR (William Robert) Bapt. Earl Stonham, Suffolk 22/5/1803, s. Rev. William Taylor. Jesus, Cambridge 1821, BA1826, dn26 (Nor.), p27 (Nor.). PC. West Beckham, Norfolk 1829 and R. Barningham Town >< Norfolk 1832 to death (Holt, Norfolk) 23/8/1843 aged 40 [C1126] Married Holt 23/6/1828 Rebecca Beckwith.

TELLET, TELLIT (Edward) Born Lezayre, IoM 6/4/1796, s. Daniel Tellet and Elizabeth Crellin. [NiVoF] dn20 (S&M as 'academic student'). PC. Monkhopton Chapel, Much Wenlock, Shropshire 1820 and V. Much Wenlock 1835 to death 1841 (3rd q.) [C7325] J.P.

TEMPLE (Isaac) Born Harrington, Cumberland, 9/3/1793, s. Henry and Dinah Temple. Queens', Cambridge 1813, dn16 (Chester), BA 1817, p21 (Nor.), MA1821. PC. Longton (o/w Lane End), Stoke on Trent, Staffs. 1826-33, Chaplain of Donative of Plemstall, Cheshire 1833 to death. Dom. Chap. to 8th Earl of Dalhousie 1828. Died 5/12/1880 aged 87, leaving £7,000 [C20039] Married Stafford 27/8/1826 Sarah Jane Tomkinson, with issue.

TEMPLE (Robert) Born Harrington, Cumberland 1792. [NiVoF] PC. Stafford St Mary, Staffs. 1831-64-. Died Castlechurch, Staffs. 14/3/1872, leaving £5,000 [C20041] Wife Sarah in 1851.

TEMPLE (William Smoult) Born and bapt. South Shields, Durham 31/8/1788, s. Simon Temple (a shipbuilder) and Eleanor Smoult. Trinity, Cambridge 1807, dn14 (Durham), p15 (Durham). R. Meldon, Durham 1820-2, Minor Canon Durham Cathedral 1821-31, V. Dalton le Dale, Durham 1822-32, V. Aycliffe, Durham 1831-5, R. Dinsdale, Durham 1835 to death (Leamington, Warwicks.) 25/3/1859 aged 71, leaving £1,500 [C130752. LBSO] Married York 28/8/1827 Mary Waldy (w), of Jarrow, with clerical issue.

TEMPLEMAN (John) Born Merriott, Somerset, s. Thomas Templeman. Wadham Oxford 1770 (aged 17), BA1774, dn74 (Ex. for Bristol), p75 (B&W), then King's, Cambridge 1782, MA1792. PC. Lopen, Som. 1783-1835, PC. Cudworth, Som. 1788-98, R. Buckland St Mary, Som. 1788-1830, R. Cricket St Thomas, Som. 1798 to death. Dom. Chap. to 1st Viscount Bridport 1798. Died Lopen 20/4/1835 (CCEd says 4/5/1835) aged 85 [C40718] Married Lopen 7/1/1788 Sarah Weare/Nease, with clerical son.

TEMPLER (George Henry) Born Calcutta 4/1/1782, s. George Templer and Jane Paull. Merton, Oxford 1800, BA1804, dn06 (B&W), p06 (B&W), MA 1808. V. Shapwick, Som. 1806, R. Thornford, Dorset 1810 and Prebend of Combe IX in Wells Cathedral 1811 to death (Shapwick) 8/4/1849 [C49576] Married Piccadilly, London 1807 Anna Maria Graham. Brother below.

TEMPLER (James Acland) Born Shapwick House, Som., s. George Templer and Jane Paull. Merton, Oxford 1814 (aged 17), BA1819, dn21 (Salis.), p22 (Chester for Bristol), MA1822. PC. St Michaelchurch, Som. 1822, V. Puddletown, Dorset 1822 to death (Weymouth, Dorset) 18/6/1866, leaving £3,000 (left unadministered) [C40720] Married Walcot, Bath 26/6/1828 Ann Mason (w), w. child. Brother above.

TEMPLER (John) Born Rotherhithe, Kent 1751, s. James Templer (of Stover Lodge, Devon) and Mary Parlby. Trinity, Cambridge 1770, BA1774, dn74 (Peterb. for London), p75 (Win.), MA1778. R. Trusham, Devon 1792 (res.), R. Paignton, Devon 1793-1832, V. Cullompton, Devon 1819-[30], R. Teigngrace, Devon 1827-32, R. West Ogwell, Devon 1830 to death 6/2/1832 aged 81, living at Lindridge House, Devon ('one of the finest houses in the south-west') [C108868] Married Devon 2/5/1778 Mrs Jane (Shubruck) Line (of South Carolina).

TENCH (John) Born Davenham, Cheshire 11/12/1865, s. Rev. John anf Mary Tench, sen. BNC, Oxford 1783 (aged 17), BA1787, MA 1789, dn89 (Chester), p90 (Chester), BD1808, Fellow to 1813, etc. R. Great Rollright, Oxon. 1811 to death 22/1/1848 [C21808]

TENNANT (Francis) From Bentham, Yorks., s. John Tennant. Cambridge 1772 (aged 17), BA1776, Fellow 1777, MA1779. R. Orton Waterville, Lincs. 1799 to death 15/12/1837 aged 84 [C77379]

TENNANT (Ottiwell) Born Castle Bolton, Yorks. 20/6/1780, s. Edward Tennant and Rebecca Bailey. Trinity, Cambridge 1798, then St Catharine's 1800, BA1803, dn03 (Chester), p05 (Chester), MA1806. R. Winwick, Hunts. 1812-63, R. Caldecote, Hunts. 1814-22, R. Upton w. Copmanford >< Hunts. 1821 to death 10/3/1863 aged 82, leaving £45,000 [C77380] Married St George's Hanover Square, London 22/7/1830 Mary Ellis.

TENNANT (Sanderson) Bapt. Leeds 26/4/1802, s. James Tennant (a broker) and Harriet Catley. Trinity, Cambridge 1819, BA 1824, MA 1827, Chap. 1827-37, p27 (Ely). (first) H/M Blackheath Proprietary School; V. Orwell St Andrew, Cambs. 1830, V. Hatfield Broad Oak, Essex 1834-5 (res.). Died (Kensington, London) 16/2/1872, leaving £30,000 [C109502] Married (1) Scarborough, Yorks. 26/12/1837 Charlotte Ogden (d.1845), with issue (2) Liverpool 26/3/1849 Jane Fleming Drysdale, with further issue.

TERRY (Michael) Born Dummer, Hants. 22/10/1775, s. Thomas and Elizabeth Terry. St John's, Cambridge 1794, BA1797, MA1797, dn98 (Win.), p00 (Win.). PC. Wield, Hants. 1804 and R. Dummer 1811 to death (Brancaster, Norfolk) 22/4/1848 [108889] 2 other Oxford men of this name.

THACKERAY (John Richard) Born Cambridge 17/5/1772, s. Thomas Thackeray (surgeon) and Lydia Whish. Pembroke, Cambridge 1789, BA 1794, dn96 (Ely), p96 (Ely), MA1797, then Emmanuel 1802. R. Broxted, Essex 1810, R. Downham Market, Norfolk 1810-46, V. Wiggenhall St Mary Magdalen, Norfolk 1810 and Chap. Hadley, Middx. 1829 to death 19/8/1846 [C77409] Married Barnet, Herts., 13/12/1810 Marianne Franks, w. clerical s. Richard William Thackeray.

THACKWELL (Stephen) Born Berrow, Worcs. 26/5/1776, s. John Thackwell. Trinity, Oxford 1795, BA1799, dn99 (Wor.), p00 (Wor.). R. Birtsmorton, Worcs. 1800. Died 1857 (3rd q.) [C122221] Married Berrow 17/6/1824 Susannah Clarke, w. clerical son William Henry.

THARP (Augustus James) Born Chippenham, Cambs. 17/9/1805, s. John Tharp and Anna Maria Phillips. Christ's, Cambridge 1824, BA 1828, dn29 (Nor.), p30 (Nor.). PC. Denston, Suffolk 1830-8, V. Chippenham, Cambs. 1838 and R. Snailwell, Cambs. 1854 to death. Dom. Chap. to Lord Keane. Died 7/9/1877, leaving £3,000 [C115748] Married 22/12/1840 Juliet Bond (a clergy dau.), with issue.

THEED (Edward Rutter) Born Hilton, Hunts. 10/12/1786, s. Edward Theed and Jane Searle. Sidney, Cambridge 1804, BA1808, dn09 (Nor.), p11 (Nor.), MA1812. R. Fletton, Hunts. 1830 and V. Selling, Kent 1831 to death 18/3/1851, leaving under £100 (probate granted April 1855) [C77411] Married Stanford Baron, Northants. 24/5/1810 Frances Phillips (w), w. clerical s. John Vernon Theed.

THELLUSON (William, 3rd Baron Rendlesham) see under **RENDLESHAM**

THELWALL (John Hampden) Born Derby 25/5/1797 (nonconformist baptism), s. John Thelwall and Susannah Vellam. Trinity, Cambridge 1818, BA1823, MA1826, dn26 (Nor.), p28 (B&W). R. Oving, Bucks. 1831 to death (Bath) 19/7/1874, leaving £1,000 [C40722]

THEOBALD (George) Bapt. Kirkby Lonsdale, Westmorland 14/3/1762, s. George Theobald and Dorothy Dobson. Literate: dn85 (Chester), p86 (Chester). S/M Whittington, Lancs. to 1795; PC. Old Hutton, Kendal, Westmorland 1793 to death 10/2/1834 (CCEd says 7/11/1835) aged 72 [C170690] Married Whittington 12/6/1783 Margaret Dixon, with clerical issue.

THEOBALD, born POOLE (Thomas John) Bapt. Bishopstoke, Hunts. 14/1/1803, s. Thomas John Poole (*after 1816* Theobald) and Charity Smith. Christ's, Cambridge 1822, BA 1829, dn30 (Nor.), p30 (Nor.), MA1834. R. Nunney, Som. 1830 to death. Dom. Chap. to Viscount Palmerston. Died Clifton, Bristol 3/4/1877, leaving £6,000 [C40723] Married St George's Hanover Square, London 21/9/1824 Elizabeth Lavinia Gostling (w), w. issue.

THEODOSIUS (Theodosius) Formerly Minister of Ruiton Congregational Church, Upper Gornal. Staffs. Literate: dn15 (B&W), p16 (B&W). (first) PC. Gornal 1824-48, R. Burwarton, Staffs. 1850. Died 1853 (1st q.) [C20045] Married Darlaston, Staffs. 3/1/1809 Catharine Fletcher, with clerical son James Henry Theodosius.

THEXTON (Joseph) Bapt. Beetham, Westmorland 18/3/1764, s. Thomas Thexton (a maltster) and Catherine Thornbarrow. Literate: dn86 (York), p88 (York). PC. Preston Patrick, Westmorland 1811, V. Beetham 1811 to death 27/6/1844 aged 81 [C110582. YCO] Married 1818 Janet Yeats, Ashton House, Beetham, with issue.

THICKINS (John) St John's, Cambridge 1819 (a Ten Year Man). V. Exhall, Warwicks. 1805-55, V. Fillongley, Warwicks. 1826 to death 15/12/1855 aged 82 [C19975] Wife Sarah, and clerical son William Thickins.

THIRLWALL (Thomas Wigzell) Born Bowers Gifford, Essex 29/4/1793, s. Rev. Thomas Thirlwall (*q.v.* ODNB). St John's, Cambridge 1811, BA1815, Fellow 1816-33, MA 1818, dn19 (Salis. for Ely), p21 (London), BD 1826. Curate Enfield St James, London 1831, R. Ickleford w. Pirton, Herts. 1835 to death (Baldock, Herts.) 21/12/1846 aged 54 (apoplexy) [C77418] Married Vange, Essex 14/7/1832 Helen French (a clergy dau.).

THISTLETHWAITE (William) Born Kirkby Fleetham, Yorks. 11/4/1776, s. Rev. Robert Thistlethwaite and Elizabeth Bowes. Sidney, Cambridge 1793, BA1798, dn98 (Lin.), p00 (Lin.), MA1814. R. Little Bolton St George, Lancs. 1808 to death 2/1/1838 [C77420. DEB. G. Thistlethwaite, *Memoirs of the Rev. William Thistlethwaite, MA* (1838)] Married 1798 Henrietta Knowsley, w. clerical s. George.

THOMAS (Edward) From London, s. David Thomas. St Edmund Hall, Oxford 1779 (aged 19), dn82 (Ox. for London), p84 (Chester for London), BA1786, MA1813, BD and DD1816. V. Billesdon cum Goadby and Rolleston, Leics. 1793 and R. Skeffington, Leics. 1816 to death. Dom. Chap. to 4th Earl of Tyrconnell 1816. Died 3/12/1836 [C37841]

THOMAS (John) From Carno, Montgomery, s. Rev. John Thomas, sen. Jesus, Oxford 1786 (aged 18), Wadham 1789, BA1790, dn90 (Heref.), p92 (Heref.), MA1793. H/M Ludlow G/S 1790. PC Lucton, Heref. (and S/M Lucton G/S) 1802-31, (succ. his father as) PC Carno 1793 and V. Orleton, Heref. 1816 to death 5/2/1838 [C158547 differs from ERC]

THOMAS (John) Born Westminster London, s. of John Thomas (merchant). Magdalene, Cambridge 1813 (aged 23), then Trinity 1816, BA1818, dn18 (Ely), p19 (Ely), MA1821. V. Great Burstead, Essex 1822 to death. Chap. to HRH Duke of Sussex. Died 10/10/1856. [C109508] Had issue.

THOMAS (John Godfrey, Sir, 6th Bart.) Born 1/9/1784, s. Sir John Thomas, 5th Bart. and Mary Parker. St Mary Hall, Oxford 1800, then Wadham, BA1803, MA1806. V. Bodiam, Sussex 1809 and R. Wartling, Sussex 1811 to death 7/5/1841 aged 56 [C70646] Married (1) Walcot, Bath 1/4/1808 Frances Ram, w. issue (incl. 7th Bart.) (2) 10/3/1817 Elizabeth Anne Vignoles (a clergy dau.), w. further issue (incl. 8th Bart). Succ. as 6th Bart. 1828.

THOMAS (Richard) Literate. p13 (Lin.), p14 (Lin.). PC. Hemswell, Lincs. 1823 to death 1848 [C77470]

THOMAS (Thomas) From Pennant, Montgomery, s. Thomas Thomas. Christ's, Cambridge 1782 (a Ten Year Man, BD1793). PC. Kingswood, Glos. 1777-1833. Died Wotton under Edge, Glos. 23/6/1834 aged 86 [C165410 which has complex alternatives]

THOMAS (Thomas) [MA but NiVoF?] V. Tidenham, Glos. 1802 to death 16/12/1839 aged 70 [C165414] J.P. for Glos.

THOMAS (Vaughan) Bapt. Kingston, Surrey 20/9/1775, s. John Thomas and Frances Wotton. Oriel, Oxford 1792, then Corpus Christi, Fellow to 1811, BA1796, MA1800, dn00 (Ox.), p01 (Ox.), BD1809, Chap. 1832-44. V. Yarnton, Oxon. 1803-58, V. Stoneleigh, Warwicks. 1804 and R. Duntisbourne Rouse, Glos. 1811 to death. Dom. Chap. to 1st Baron Somers 1804. Died Oxford 26/10/1858, leaving £18,000 [C20063. ODNB. Boase] Wife Catharine in 1851 (born East Indies).

THOMAS (William) From Anglesey. St John's, Cambridge 1809, BA1813, dn14 (Bangor), p15 (Bangor), MA1816. R. Llanbedrgoch, Anglesey 1814, PC. Orlestone, Kent 1828, R. Llansadwrn, Anglesey 1829 to death 10/4/1845 [C158553] Married Anglesey 7/7/1829 Anne Roberts, 4 ch.

THOMAS (William Garnett) Born Barbados, s. Lynch Thomas. Trinity, Cambridge 1818 (aged 19), BA1822, MA1825, dn26 (Chester), p27 (Chester). PC. Burtonwood, Warrington,

Lancs. 1829-76. Died there (a lodger) 17/1/1881 aged 82, leaving £8,000 [C170702]

THOMAS (William Prockter/Procter) From Bishop's Hull, Somerset, s. Prockter and Susannah Elizabeth Thomas. St Mary Hall, Oxford 1801 (aged 17), migrated to Trinity Hall, Cambridge 1805, dn06 (B&W), LLB1808, p08 (B&W). V. Sampford Arundel, Som. 1819-27, Prebend of Holcombe in Wells Cathedral 1821-50, V. Holcombe Burnell, Devon 1822-7, V. Witheridge, Devon 1832-43, V. Wellington, Som. 1843 to death. Dom. Chap. to HRH Duke of Sussex 1815. Died 29/10/1850 [C49611] Married (1) Sampford Arundel 29/4/1811 Arabella Maria Bayley, 3 ch. *Parliamentary divorce* 12/5/1819, 3 ch. [Arabella was a minor when she married Thomas. She went on to marry Robert Tyser, the doctor who had delivered her children, with whom she had been conducting an affair! She was Tyser's 3rd wife. Salacious details in the divorce proceedings in the House of Lords Journal online] (2) Northam, Devon 1/5/1823 Mrs Ann (Husbands) Benson.

THOMPSON (Cyprian) Bapt. St Bees, Cumberland 3/4/1788, s. Thomas Thompson and Jane Richardson. S/M Whicham and Millom G/S Cumberland to 1811 [NiVoF] dn12 (Car.), p13 (Car.). PC. Fazeley, Staffs. 1818 to death 22/10/1869 aged 81, leaving £800 [C6380] Wife Eleanor, and issue.

THOMPSON (Edward) Born Acaster Malbis, Yorks. 1807, s Jonathan Thompson and Ellin Norfolk. [NiVoF] V. Lambourn, Berks. 1832-51, V. Chaddleworth, Berks. 1851-81-. Died Winchester 27/2/1891, leaving £94.0s-4d. [C85353] Wife Frances (b. Jamaica), and issue.

THOMPSON (Francis, *formerly* **Christopher Francis)** Bapt. Warden, Northumberland 16/8/1787, s. Rev. John and Mary Thompson. St John's, Cambridge 1805 (aged 18, as Christopher Francis), dn11 (Durham), LLB 1812, p13 (Dur.). PC. Shrewsbury St Julian, Shropshire 1832-40, PC. Durham St Giles 1841, PC. Carham, North-umberland 1844 to death there 26/7/1865, leaving £450 [C20070] Wife Mary, and clerical s. Frederick Brewster Thompson.

THOMPSON (Francis Edward) Born Winch-more Hill, Middx. 24/6/1804, s. Francis Thompson. Trinity, Cambridge 1822, BA1826, dn28 (London for Chich.), p29. V. Old Brentford, Middx. 1830 to death (Isleworth, Middx., a bachelor) 31/12/1873, leaving £1,500 [C70650]

THOMPSON (George) Bapt. Morland, Westmorland 15/8/1784, s. of a schoolmaster. Literate: dn21 (Durham), p23 (Durham for Chester). PC. Heatherycleugh, Stanhope, Durham 1825 (non-res.) to death (Cheltenham, Glos.) 11/11/1864 aged 80, leaving £600 [C133673] Married(1) Margaret in 1841, w. issue (2) Anna Isabella in 1861.

THOMPSON (George Hodgson) Born Tottenham, London 14/12/1794, s. John Thompson. Pembroke, Cambridge 1813, BA 1818, dn18 (London), p19 (London), MA1821. PC. Tottenham Holy Trinity, London 1830-44, R. Friern Barnet, Middx. 1846 to death 8/5/1850 [C123125] Had issue.

THOMPSON (Henry) From Bradfield, Essex, s. Matthew Thompson. Trinity, Cambridge 1803 (aged 18), BA1808, dn09 (Salis.), p10 (London). V. Long Preston, Yorks. 1809-11, V. Mistley cum Manningtree and Bradfield, Essex 1811-39, R. Fobbing, Essex 1839 to death ('in his chaise at Orsett, when returning from a Protectionist meeting at Grays') 1/3/1850 [C85354]

THOMPSON (Henry, Sir, 3rd Bart.) Born Gosport, Hants. 5/11/1796, s. Admiral Sir Charles Thompson, 1st Bart. and Jane Selby. Oriel, Oxford 1814, BA1819, dn19, MA1821, p27 (B&W). Min. Bembridge, IoW 1829, PC. Trinity Church, Fareham, Hants. to 1844, R. Frant, Sussex 1844 and Prebend of Thorney in Chichester Cathedral (and RD) 1854 to death. Proctor in Convocation for the Archdeaconry of Lewes. Died Bournemouth 1/7/1868, leaving £8,000 [C40729. Boase] Married (1) 26/2/1826 Hannah Jane Grey (niece of the Prime Minister, 2nd Earl Grey, she d. in childbed) (2) Brighton 10/1835 Emily Frances Anne Leeke (Longford Hall, Shifnal, Shropshire), with further issue. Succ. to title 1799; baronetcy extinct on his death.

THOMPSON (John) Born Patterdale, Westmorland 28/1/1777, s. Rev. Thomas Thompson. Literate: p00 (Car.), p01 (Car.). (succ. his father as) PC. Patterdale 1804-61 (96 years in the parish between them), PC. Holm Cultram, Westmorland 1809-14. Died Patterdale 7/6/1861 aged 84, leaving £100 [C159454. Platt] Married Patterdale 3/9/1818 Dorothy

Mounsey (dau. of the last 'King of Patterdale'), w. issue.

THOMPSON (John) Born Stanwick, Yorks. 28/5/1779. Sidney, Cambridge 1797, BA1802, dn02 (Chester), p02 (Chester), MA1806, then Christ's 1808. V. Thornton Steward, Yorks. 1826 to death 30/11/1842 [C136715] Wife Margaret, married before 1813, with issue.

THOMPSON (John) Born Seal, Kent, s. Thomas Thompson. Jesus, Cambridge 1798, BA 1803, dn03 (B&W for Cant.), p04 (Roch. for Cant.), MA1806. V. Meopham, Kent 1816 to death. Dom. Chap. to 3rd Baron Hotham 1816. Died 30/8/1854 aged 74 [C2410] Below?

THOMPSON (John) [NiVoF] V. Horton, Dorset 1816-[1838] [C53957 - and presumably some other number?] Above?

THOMPSON (Joseph, sen.) Born Greystoke, Cumberland 9/10/1768, s. Joseph Thompson and Mary Hunter. Literate: dn94 (London for Durham), p98 (Durham). PC. Lanchester, Durham 1806 to death 6/5/1842 aged 72 [C134540] Married (1) Crosthwaite, Cumberland 28/3/1789 Ann Todd (d.1791), 1 dau. (2) 1791 Mary Byers, with clerical son of same name (two below)

THOMPSON (Joseph) [NiVoF] PC. Marfleet, Hull, Yorks. 1828 to death (a widower) 1845 (2nd q.) [Possibly in YCO] Married Jane Hall, of Hull, with issue.

THOMPSON (Joseph, jun.) Bapt. Lanchester, Northumberland 28/7/1806, s. Rev. Joseph Thompson, sen. (above) and Mary Byers. St Bees adm. 1826, dn28 (Durham), p29 (Durham). PC. Esh, Northumberland 1832-5 (res.), PC. Satley, Durham 1832 to death 27/9/1867 aged 66, leaving £3,000 [C130783] Married Newcastle upon Tyne 11/9/1836 Mary Fenwick, s.p.

THOMPSON (Marmaduke) Born London 5/4/1776, s. Thomas William Thompson (silk merchant) and Charlotte Augusta Steers. Pembroke, Cambridge 1796, BA1800, dn00 (Nor.), p00 (Nor.), MA1803. One of the first 5 chaplains nominated by Rev. Charles Simeon as *H.E.I.C.* Chaplains at Cuddalore, India 1806-9, then Fort St George 1809-15, then St George, Madras 1815-19 (returned to England after the death of his first wife). R. Brightwell, Berks.

1831 to death 12/4/1851 [C77495. DEB] Married (1) City of London 1/5/1806 Eliza Maria Cowling (d. India 1819), 2 ch. (2) Cheriton, Kent 1/9/1825 Albinia (dau. of John Sullivan, *M.P.*, and Lady Henrietta Anne Barbara Hobart, she d.1827), w. further issue (3) Taplow, Bucks. 9/12/1828 Lucy Birs, with yet further issue.

THOMPSON, TOMPSON (Matthew Carrier) Bapt. Iver, Bucks. 1/10/1800, s. Carrier Thompson and Margaret Ann Smith. Trinity, Oxford 1819, BA1822, dn29 (Lin.), p29 (Lin.), MA1830. R. Woodston, Peterborough 1829-71 and V. Alderminster, Warwicks. 1830 (and RD of Kineton) to death 10/1/1882, leaving £37,123-12s-3d. [C77497] Married North Berwick, East Lothian 23/10/1829 Eliza Dalrymple (a military dau.), with clerical son Reginald Tompson.

THOMPSON (Richard) Born Selby, Yorks. 7/8/1800, s. John Thompson. Literate: dn26 (York), p27 (York), then St John's, Cambridge 1830 (A Ten Year Man?). Chap. of Donative of Barlow, Brayton, Yorks. 1826, V. (and patron) of Sutton on Trent, Notts. 1833 to death (Weymouth, Dorset) 21/9/1858, leaving under £300 [C135777] Married King's Norton, Worcs. 3/19/1832 Sophia Taylor (w).

THOMPSON (Robert) Bapt. Orton, Cumberland 22/8/1792, s. John Thompson (innkeeper) and Agnes Potter. Literate: dn15 (Durham), p16 (Durham). S/M (Bishop) Auckland Free School, Durham 1814-47; PC. Eggleston, Durham 1828-35 (res.), PC. Escomb, Auckland 1827 to death 13/3/1847 [C133507. YCO] Married Heanor, Derbys. 28/7/1825 Jemima Grammer, w. clerical s. Grammer Thompson.

THOMPSON (Robert Stephen) Bapt. Ouseburn, Yorks. 11/10/1778, s. Henry Thompson and Mary Spence. University, Oxford 1796, BA1800, dn01 (York), p02 (York). V. Myton on Swale, Yorks. 1804-60, V. Askham Bryan, Ainsty of York 1807 [blank in ERC] and V. Askham Richard, Ainsty of York 1816 to death 7/1/1862, leaving £14,000 [C102610. YCO] Married York 27/2/1808 Harriet Walbanke-Childers (Carr House, Ampleforth, Yorks.), with issue.

THOMPSON (Thomas) Born 1770, s. Rev. Thomas Thompson, sen. [NiVoF] dn96 (Car.), p97 (Car.). PC. Allhallows, Cumberland 1812 to death 28/12/1858, leaving under £100 [C6394. Platt] Married Anne Clarke (w), with issue.

THOMPSON (Thomas) [NiVoF]. V. Adlingfleet, Yorks. 1821 to death 19/10/1835 (CCEd thus) aged 81 [C136009]

THOMPSON (William) Bapt. City of London 20/7/1794, s. Nathaniel Thompson. Trinity, Cambridge 1817 (aged 22), BA1821, dn21 (Lin.), p22 (Lin.), MA 1825. PC. Halstock, Dorset 1826-43, Curate Finsbury St Barnabas, London 1827. Died ('in the City Road, London') 28/4/1843 aged 48 [C77519] Wife Eliza, w. issue.

THOMPSON see also under **THOMSON, TOMPSON**

THOMSON (James) Born Stamfordham, Northumberland 9/2/1755. Literate: dn85 (Durham), p86 (Durham). S/M Newcastle upon Tyne for 7 years, then at Morpeth; V. Ormesby, Yorks. 1816 to death 5/2/1837 aged 82 [C136011] Married Thornton in Craven, Yorks. 24/11/1785 Ann Nelson (a clergy dau.), w. issue.

THOMSON (John Boyle) Born Kensington, London, s. Rev. Robert Thomson. [Adm. Inner Temple 1798]. Jesus, Cambridge 1798, BA1803, Fellow 1804-9 (marriage), MA1806, dn09 (Ely), p09 (Ely). R. Luddesdown, Kent 1809-34. Died St Lawrence, Isle of Thanet, Kent [not IoW] 9/12/1859 aged 78, leaving £8,000 [C2511] Married Lyme Regis, Dorset 26/10/1809 Alicia Rothwell (w), and had issue.

THOMSON see also under **THOMPSON, TOMPSON**

THORNBER (William) Born Poulton le Fylde, Lancs. 2/12/1803, s. Giles Thornber and Elizabeth Harrison. Trinity, Oxford 1824, BA 1828, p28 (Chester). PC. Blackpool, Lancs. 1829-46, then living there without cure. Died Coton Hill Asylum ('for the upper and middle classes'), Stafford 6/12/1885 aged 82, leaving £1,805-13s-1d. [C170722] Married Bispham, Lancs. 13/12/1831 Alice Banks, with issue. Historian and populariser of Blackpool, he was also a heavy drinker who gave boxing lessons and *may* have frequented brothels in the town.

THORNTON (John) From Horsham, Sussex, s. John Thornton. Wadham, Oxford 1804 (aged 16), BA1808, dn10, p11, MA1813, Fellow 1813-20, BD and DD1824. V. Wisborough Green, Sussex 1820 and R. Coombes, Sussex 1824 to death 9/3/1866, leaving £1,000 [C70662] Widow Jane.

THORNTON (Philip) Born Leicester 9/5/1782, s. Thomas Lee Thornton (Brockhall, Leics.) and Mary Reeve. Sidney, Cambridge 1800, BA 1804, dn05 (Peterb.), p06 (Peterb.), MA1807, then Clare 1818, incorporated at Oxford 1826. R. Brockhall, Northants. 1806 and Hon. Canon of Peterborough Cathedral 1844 to death. Dom. Chap. to Bishop of Gloucester, then of Lichfield 1815. Died (unm.) 9/7/1869, leaving £12,000 [C111533]

THOROLD (Charles) Bapt. Grimsby, Lincs. 12/2/1799, s. Rev. William (Kirton House, Boston, Lincs.) and Frances Thorold. Emmanuel, Cambridge 1819, BA1823, dn23 (Lin.), p24 (Lin.), MA 1826. R. Ludborough, Lincs. 1825 to death. Buried Bakewell, Derbys. 17/1/1854 aged 55 [C77525]

THOROLD (Edward) Born 6/1/1779, s. Sir John Thorold, 9th Bart. *M.P.*, and Jane Hayford. Trinity, Oxford 1798, BA1802, dn04 (Lin.), p05 (Lin.). then Clare, Cambridge 1805, MA1805. R. Grayingham, Lincs. 1805-20 (res.), R. Hougham w. Marston, Lincs. (and Preacher throughout the Diocese of Lincoln) 1823-36, R. (and patron) of Morcott, Rutland 1829-34. Dom. Chap. to Bishop of Ely 1816. Died 22/4/1836 aged 57 [C77526] Married Grantham, Lincs. 20/6/1807 Mary Wilson, with issue (incl. Anthony Wilson Thorold, Bishop of Rochester, then of Winchester).

THOROLD (Henry Baugh) Bapt. Rauceby, Lincs. 23/4/1805, s. Rev. George Thorold and Elizabeth Baugh. Trinity, Oxford 1823, BA 1827, dn28 (Lin.), p29 (Lin.). V. North w. South Rauceby 1830-6, V. Hougham w. Marston, Lincs. 1836 to death 29/11/1885, leaving £34,000-8s-4d. [C77529] Married Barrowby, Lincs. 2/7/1829 Julia Ellis, with issue.

THOROLD (James) Born IoW, s. Richard Thorold. St Alban Hall, Oxford 1791 aged 19, then Pembroke, BA1805. R. Kencot, Oxon. 1801 to death. Buried (w) Kencot 23/2/1857 aged 88 [C37868 as John] Married (1) 31/12/1800 Mary Rogers (d.1818), 4 dau. (2) Caroline in 1841.

THOROLD (Michael) Born Clarborough, Notts. 28/3/1776, s. Samuel Thorold and Susanna Goodacre. St John's, Cambridge 1794, BA1798, dn99 (Ex. for York), p00 (London for York). R. Aunsby, Lincs. 1800 and R. Heydour w. Kelby and Culverthorpe, Lincs. 1800 to death 27/12/1835 [C77530. YCO]

THOROTON (Charles Roos) Bapt. Belvoir Castle, Knipton, Lincs. 15/1/1771, s. Col. Thomas Thoroton (Screveton Hall, Newark, Notts.) and Roosilia Drake Manners (actually Drake, being a natural dau. of the 3rd Duke of Rutland and 'Mrs [Elizabeth] Drake'). Peterhouse, Cambridge 1789, BA1793, MA1796, dn00 (York), p01 (C&L for York). R. Screveton 1801-17 (and living at Screveton Hall), (Sinecure R. Llanstanffraid-ym-Mechain, Montgomery 1817-46), R. Bottesford, Leics. (and Preacher throughout the Diocese of Lincoln) 1821 to death. Chap. to the Duke of Rutland. Died unm. 14/2/1846 aged 76 'whilst visiting at Belvoir Castle' [C20076. YCO] Step-brother below?

THOROTON (Levett Edward) Born Dalham, Suffolk 8/9/1789, s. Thomas Thoroton (of Screveton Hall and Flintham Hall, Notts.) and Anne Bowes. Trinity, Cambridge 1808, BA 1812, dn13 (York), p14 (York). R. Ingoldmells, Lincs. 1815, R. Colwick, Notts. 1818-34, R. West Bridgford, Notts. 1818-31, R. Rowley, Yorks. [net income £1,465] 1831 to death. Chap. to Earl Grey 1831. Died (Brighton) 1852 (4th q.) [C135779. YCO] Married Lambeth Palace, London 6/6/1816 Caroline Sarah, dau. of Sir Alexander Grant of Dalvey, 7th Bart., with issue. Step-brother above?

THORP (Charles) Born Gateshead, Durham 13/10/1783, s. Ven. Robert Thorp (Archdeacon of Northumberland) and Grace Alder. Peterhouse, Cambridge 1799, then University, Oxford 1799, BA1803, Fellow 1803, dn06 (Ox.), MA1806, p07 (Durham), BD1822, DD1835 (all Oxford). (succ. his father as) V. Ryton, Durham 1807-62, Prebend of Llandrindod in Brecon Collegiate Church 1826, Canon of 4th Prebend of Durham Cathedral 1829-62, Archdeacon of Durham (w. R. Easington annexed 1831-2) 1831-62 (res.), (first) Warden of Durham College (later University) 1832 to death (Ryton) 10/10/1862, leaving £45,000 [C21822. ODNB. Boase] Married (1) 5/7/1810 Frances Wilkie Selby, s.p. (2) 7/10/1817 Mary Robinson (w), with issue. F.R.S.; 'He was one of the Crewe Trustees, an active church restorer, philanthropist and art collector'; as well as actively promoting bird life on the Inner Farne Islands by buying them; at Ryton he established the first savings bank in the North of England; promoted the new University of Durham by channelling former Cathedral funds into it. Portrait in D. Cross, *Joseph Bouet's Durham* (Durham, 2005).

THORP (Henry) From Southwick, Hants. Christ's, Cambridge 1815 (aged 21), dn18 (Ex.), BA by 1819, p19 (Ex.), MA1826. PC. Topsham, Devon 1825 (and Chap. to his patron the Marchioness of Headfort) to death 13/2/1857 [C146491] Married Honiton, Devon 4/8/1818 Margaret Courtenay Gidley, with issue.

THORP, THORPE (Henry) From Oxted, Surrey, s. Rev. Thomas and Maria Thorpe. St John's, Oxford 1822 (aged 18), Fellow 1822-32, BA1826, dn26, p28, MA1830, etc. R. Aston le Walls, Northants. 1831 to death 14/6/1886. No Will traced [C21830 as Thorpe]

THORP (Thomas) Born Leics. 1786. Emmanuel, Cambridge 1804, BA1808, dn09 (Salis. for Win.), p11 (Win. for C&L), MA1811. R. Burton Overy, Leics. 1811-45, R. Calton Curlieu w. Ilston on the Hill, Leics. 1819 to death. Dom. Chap. to 2nd Earl of Onslow 1819. Died 26/7/1846 aged 59 [C19981] Married 27/8/1811 Frances Lee 27/8/1811, clerical sons Thomas, and Frederick succeeded him at Burton Overy.

THORP, THORPE (Thomas) Born Loughborough, Leics., s. John Thorp. Emmanuel, Cambridge 1809, BA1813, dn14 (Lin.), p15 (Lin.), MA1816. R. Wilford, Notts. 1819 to death 25/2/1864 aged 73, leaving £60,000 [C77587]

THORP (William) From Oxford, s. William Thorp. Trinity, Oxford 1779 (aged 16), BA 1782, MA1785, dn85 (Ox. for Salis.), p86 (Salis). V. Sandford St Martin, Oxon. 1807 to death 16/3/1835 (CCEd thus) [C21825]

THORPE (William) Born Newmarket, Suffolk 31/12/1775 (bapt. 20/10/1777), s. William Thorpe (woollen draper). Caius, Cambridge 1795, BA1800, dn00 (Ex. for Nor.), p01 (Nor.), MA1803. V. Stetchworth, Cambs. 1809 and 'Perpetual V.' Chattisham, Suffolk 1830 to death 20/3/1830 [C100455] Married East Dereham, Norfolk 11/5/1819 Elizabeth Smyth.

THRELKELD (Philip) Bapt. Milburn, Westmorland 13/1/1799, s. Rev. Philip and Isabella Threlkeld, sen. [NiVoF] Literate: dn22 (Car.), p23 (Car.). PC. Milburn, 1830 to death 26/1/1842 aged 43 [C6398] Married Wetheral, Westmorland 22/12/1821 Ann Collin, with issue.

THRESHER (William) Born Fareham, Hants. St John's, Cambridge 1815, BA1820, dn21 (Chester for Win.), p22 (Chester for Win.), MA1823. V. Titchfield, Hants. 1826 to death (Fareham) 10/2/1857 aged 59 [C108914] Married 1/12/1831 Lucy, dau. of Admiral Stair Douglas.

THRING (John Gale Dalton) Born Bishopstrow, Wilts. 27/9/1784, s. John Thring (banker, Alford House, Warminster, Wilts.) and Elizabeth Everett. St John's, Cambridge 1803, dn08 (Bristol), p08 (B&W), LLB1809. R. Alford, Lincs. (living at Alford House) 1808-68, R. Bishopstrow, Wilts. 1831-45, RD of Cary. Died (Clevedon, Som.) 11/12/1874 aged 90, leaving £3,000 [C43895] Married 2/10/1811 Sarah Jenkyns (a clergy dau., *q.v.* Boase), w. issue (incl. Edward Thring, the great headmaster of Uppingham School). *J.P., D.L.* Somerset

THRING (William Davison) Bapt. Sutton Veney, Wilts. 18/1/1783, s. Rev. Brouncker Thring [*sic*] and Mary Bayly. Wadham, Oxford 1800, BA1804, dn06 (Ex.), p07 (Ex.), MA1825, BD and DD1830. R. Sutton Veney 1813 and V. Fisherton Delamere, Wilts. 1830 to death 2/9/1854 [C85364] Married St James, Westminster, London 28/7/1814 Jane Dugdale, and had issue.

THURLOW (Charles Augustus) Born Norwich 9/7/1802 (bapt. 24/7/1805), s. Rev. Edward South Thurlow (below) and Elizabeth Mary Thompson. Balliol, Oxford 1820, BA 1824, dn27 (Nor.), p27 (Nor.), MA1828. V. Scalby, Yorks. 1827-40, PC. Beverley St John 1837-40, R. Malpas (Upper Mediety), Cheshire 1840-73 [income £1,050], RD. Hon. Canon Chester Cathedral 1844 (and Chancellor of Diocese 1854), Prebend of Husthwaite in York Minster 1845-55. Died Malpas 5/7/1873 aged 70, leaving £60,000 [C1119. Boase] Married St George's Hanover Square, London 1/3/1836 Frances Margaret, dau. Sir Thomas Buckler Lethbridge, 2nd Bart., at least 8 ch. Brother below.

THURLOW (Edward) Bapt. Norwich 21/10/1788, s. Rev. Edward South Thurlow (below) and Elizabeth Mary Thompson. Christ's, Cambridge 1804 (did not reside), then St John's 1806, LLB1812, dn12 (Nor.), p12 (Lin. for Nor.). R. Lound, Suffolk 1816-59, R. Ashby, Suffolk 1817-52, R. Langham, Suffolk 1824; no further cures. Died London 14/12/1883 aged 95, leaving £47,249-19s-8d. [C77594] Married Gosfield, Essex 7/7/1812 Susannah Elizabeth Alston, with issue. Brother above.

THURLOW (Edward South) Born Norwich 29/5/1764, s. John Thurlow and Josepha Morse. Magdalen, Oxford 1781, BA1785, dn88, MA 1828. Canon of 3rd Prebend in Norwich Cathedral 1788-1847, (Sinecure R. Eastyn (o/w Hope), Flintshire 1789-1806, Sinecure R. Llandrillo, Merioneth 1789-1806), R. Houghton-le-Spring, Durham 1789 [net income £2,157] and R. Stamfordham, Northumberland 1792 to death. Dom. Chap. to 1st Baron Thurlow. Died St Faith, Norfolk 17/2/1847 aged 82 [C1120] Married (1) 17/7/1786 Elizabeth Mary Thompson (d.1808), with clerical issue (above) (2) 10/4/1810 Susanna Love (a clergy dau.), with further issue.

THURLOW (Thomas) Born 6/10/1788, s. Rt. Rev. Thomas Thurlow (Bishop of Durham, and brother of Lord Chancellor Thurlow) and Anne Beere. St John's, Cambridge 1806, BA 1811, dn12 (Lin.), p14 (Lin.), MA1816. R. Boxford, Suffolk 1816-39. Sometime of Cranby, Surrey, but latterly of Baynard's Park, Horsham, Surrey, dying there 26/9/1874, leaving £180,000 [C77595. Boase] Married 4/6/1811 Mary Frances Lyon, with issue. In 1829 he succeeded to three judicial sinecures, which were abolished 1831, and for which he received 'an equivalent life annuity' of £11,734-2s-5d.

THURSBY (George Augustus) Born Sutton, Wilts., s. Walter Harvey Thursby and Dorothy Pigott. Oriel, Oxford 1789 (aged 18), BA1792, dn94 (C&L), p94 (C&L), MA1795. R. Abington, Northants. 1795 and V. Penn, Northants. 1808 to death. Dom. Chap. to Anne Dorothea, Baroness Alvaney 1819 Died 17/1/1836, living at Cound Hall, Shrewsbury/ [C20080] Married St George's Hanover Square, London 24/5/1800 Francis Cresset Pelham, w. clerical son Henry, below.

THURSBY, *later* **THURSBY-PELHAM (Henry)** Son of Rev. George Augustus Thursby (above) and Frances Cresset Pelham. Oriel, Oxford 1818 (aged 17), BA1821, MA1824, dn24 (Peterb.), p25 (Peterb.). R. Isham Inferior (actually 'Comportioner of Lower Isham'), Northants. 1825-31, R. Bonnington, Kent 1828-31 (res.), R. Cound, Shrewsbury, Shropshire (living at Cound Hall) 1839-64. Died 19/12/1878, leaving £50,000 [C20081. Foster as Pelham] Clerical son Augustus Thursby Pelham. Took additional name 1852.

THURSBY (William) Born Pitsford, Northants. 27/4/1795, s. John Harvey Thursby and Emma Pigott. Oriel, Oxford 1814, BA 1818, dn19 (Ox. for Peterb.), p20 (Peterb.), MA1820. V. Northampton All Saints 1822-33 (res.), V. Hardingstone, Northants. 1822-34 (res.), R. Worsthorne, Burnley, Lancs. 1835-69 (living at Ormerod House, Burnley). Dom. Chap. to HRH Duke of Cambridge 1822. Died Brighton 10/8/1884, leaving £225,200-11s-6d. [C111538] Married Burnley 9/9/1824 Eleanor Mary Hargreaves, w. issue (incl. s. Sir John Harvey Thursby, Bart.).

THURSFIELD (Richard) Bapt. Benthall, Shropshire 21/5/1771, s. John Thursfield and Sarah Browne. Christ Church, Oxford 1788, BA 1792, dn94 (C&L), MA1795, dn95 (C&L). PC. Patsull, Staffs. 1803, V. Pattingham, Staffs. 1819. Died 1847 (2nd q.) [C20082] Married by 1797 Letitia Periam, w. issue. And yet: In 1838 Archdeacon Hodson reported to Bishop Butler that 'the wretched incumbent was brought home drunk in a cart last Saturday night - is frequently seen lying in the roads in a state of intoxication - lives like a pig, in a poor house, with a pauper as his companion, in one room of a large vicarage house which is sadly out of repairs ... The parish registers have not been filled up for the last two or three years, and are lying about in all directions ... Your Lordship will judge how the duties are performed by a drunkard of sixty-seven.'

THURTELL (Edward) Born Hobland Hall, Hopton, Suffolk 7/4/1794, s. John Thurtell (a bankrupt naval officer) and Anne Browne. Literate: dn19 (Nor.), p20 (Nor.). PC. Leck, Tunstall, Lancs. 1827, PC. Thornton le Fylde, Lancs. 1837-41, PC. Caton, Suffolk 1841 to death 13/2/1852 aged 57 [C115783] Married Gorleston, Suffolk 1/1/1818 his cousin Sarah Browne, with issue: www.thurtellfamily.net/uk/hoblandhall.html

THYNNE (John, Hon., *'commonly called Lord John Thynne'*) Born 7/11/1798, s. 2nd Marquess of Bath and Hon. Isabella Elizabeth Byng (dau. of 4th Viscount Terrington). St John, Cambridge (as a nobleman), MA1819, dn22 (Ely for Salis.), p22 (Salis.), DD1838, (Sinecure R. Backwell, Som. 1823-72), R. Kingston Deverill, Wilts. 1823-36, R. Street, Som. 1823-50 (w. Prebend of Crackpole St Mary and Sub-Dean Lincoln Cathedral, 1828-31), Canon 1831 and Sub-Dean of Westminster Abbey 1835 to death 9/2/1881 aged 82, leaving £60,000. Lived at Haynes Park, Beds. [C49629. Boase] Married 2/3/1824 Anna Constantia ('who invented the domestic aquarium' in 1846), dau. Rev. Charles Cobbe Beresford, with issue.

TICKELL (John Ambrose) Born 1753, s. John Tickell (Glasnevin, Dublin) and Esther Pierson. Literate: dn84 (unspecified bishop for St David's), then Queens', Cambridge 1786 (a Ten Year Man), p87 (St David's). V. Hempstead, Norfolk 1787-1835, V. Wighton, Norfolk 1787 and V. Castleacre, Norfolk 1796-1835 [all three blank in ERC], Chancellor of Norwich Cathedral. Died 26/3/1835 (CCEd says 20/4/1835) [C115786] Married Sarah Cumberland, and had issue.

TIFFIN (William) Literate: dn00 (Car.), p01 (Car.). PC. Stapleford, Notts. 1811-15, PC. Annesley, Notts. 1811, V. Kirkby in Cleveland 1812-16, V. Ormsby, Yorks. 1814-16, V. Hayton, Notts. 1815-33, V. Mattersey, Notts. 1815-34, V. Beeford w. Lissett and Dunnington, Yorks. 1833 to death. Dom. Chap. to Mary, Dowager Countess of Lonsdale 1811. Died 5/12/1844 [C136013] Married Greasley, Notts. 6/1/1819 Dorothy Rolleston (Watnall Hall, Notts.)

TILBROOK(E) (Samuel) From Bury St Edmunds, Suffolk, s. John Tilbrook. Peterhouse, Cambridge 1801 (aged 19), BA1806, dn08 (Nor.), p08 (Nor.), MA1809, Fellow 1810-28, BD1816, etc. S/M Bury St Edmunds School 1807; R. and V. Freckenham, Suffolk 1829 to death 20/5/1835 aged 52 (CCEd says 14/10/1835) [C7048 - not James] Married 15/12/1829 Frances Ayling (Tillington, Sussex), w. issue. 'Famous for his geniality and social gifts', etc.

TILLARD (Richard) Born York 16/7/1765, s. Rev. Richard Tillard, sen. (V. Wirksworth, Derbys.) and Sarah Yoward. St John's, Cambridge 1784, BA1788, dn88 (Ely), Fellow 1790-98, p91 (Ely), MA1791. V. Madingley, Cambs. 1791-6, R. Bluntisham, Hunts. [net income £1,010] (and Preacher throughout the Diocese of Lincoln) 1796-1841. Retired to Canterbury, and died Hastings, Sussex 4/1/1850 [C77597] Married 31/12/1810 Margaret Smelt (a clergy dau., and the granddaughter. of the 5th Earl of Chesterfield), with issue. J.P. for Hunts. 'Since the present wealthy incumbent became allied to the house of Stanhope, the rectorial table is not infrequently the easy and fascinating resort of the principal nobility of this country.'

TILNEY (Henry) Born Harleston, Norfolk, s. Henry Tilney (schoolmaster). Caius, Cambridge 1789 (aged 20), dn95 (Wor.), BA1794, MA1795, Fellow 1795, p97 (Nor.). R. Hockwold and Wilton, Norfolk 1806 to death there 1/11/1834 (CCEd says 2/4/1835) [C115792]

TIMBRILL, *later* **TIMBRELL (John)** Born Pershore, Worcs. 9/8/1770 (CCEd thus), s. Thomas Timbrill. Worcester, Oxford 1790, BA 1793, dn93 (Wor.), p95 (Wor.), MA1796, BD 1803, DD1816. V. Beckford w. Ashton under Hill, Glos. 1797-1865, R. Bretforton, Worcs. 1816-45, R. Dursley, Glos. 1825 and Archdeacon of Gloucester 1825 to death (Beckford) 7/1/1865 [Foster 8/12/1834], leaving £25,000 [C122234. Boase] Had issue. Surrogate 1825.

TIMS (John) From Folkestone, Kent, s. Rev. John Tims . University, Oxford 1796 (aged 17), BA 1800, dn02 (London for Cant.), p03 (B&W for Cant.), MA1804. V. Tonge, Kent 1803 to death 9/4/1857 [C49639]

TIMSON (Edward) Born Eling, Southampton, Hants., s. Henry Thomas Timson (of Tackley, Hants.) and Susanna Plumtree. Trinity, Oxford 1815 (aged 18), BA1819, dn20 (Glos. *or* Chester), p21 (Win.), MA1823. PC. Chilworth, Hants. 1823-[40]. Died Eling, Hants. 27/2/1873, leaving £40,000 [C108916] Married Cheltenham 6/5/1830 Margaret Angelina Green, with issue.

TINDALL (James) Born Scarborough, Yorks. 17/3/1790, s. James and Mary Tindall, St John's, Cambridge 1808, BA1812, dn13 (York), p14 (Ex. for York), MA1815. R. Knipton, Leics. 1814-17, R. Woolsthorpe with Stainworth, Lincs. (and Preacher throughout the Diocese of Lincoln) 1815-17, R. Knaptoft, Leics. 1817 to death (Mowsley, Leics.) 26/5/1852 aged 62 [C77599. YCO] Married Bridlington, Yorks. 19/10/1819 Mary AnnWaite.

TINSLEY (William Calcroft) Bapt. 30/6/1780, s. John and Mary Tinsley. [NiVoF] dn10 (Ely for York), p18 (C&L). V. Scarcliffe, Derbys. 1818 and V. Bolsover, Derbys. 1818 (living at Bolsover Castle) to death 29/10/1833 (CCEd thus) [C20086. YCO. Austin] Married Sheffield 23/1/1805 Sarah Frith, w. issue.

TIREMAN (Thomas) Born York 30/11/1791, s. Thomas Tireman (a glover) and Ann Wilbor. Literate: dn14 (York), p15 (York). V. Acomb, Ainsty of York 1816-36, V. York Holy Trinity Micklegate 1818-22. Probate granted (Chepstow, Monmouth) 18/5/1852 [C135782. YCO] Married Overton, Yorks. 3/2/1819 Catharine Place.

TITLOW (Samuel) Born Redenhall, Norfolk 15/6/1793, s. George Titlow and Susanna Vipond. St John, Cambridge 1811 (as Tittilowe), BA1817, dn17 (London), p18 (London), MA 1820. V. Norwich St John Timberhill 1831 and R. Norwich St Peter Hungate 1839 to death 21/4/1871, leaving £7,000 [C115797]

TODD (Henry John) Bapt. Britford, Salisbury 13/2/1763, s. Rev. Henry Todd and Mary Smith. Chorister Magdalen, Oxford 1771-9; matr. 1779, BA1784, dn85 (Ox.), then Hertford, Fellow, MA1786, p87 (Ox.), Tutor and Lecturer. PC. Beckermet St John w. Beckermet St Bridget, Cumberland 1787-1803, Minor Canon of Canterbury Cathedral (w. Sinecure R. Ogarswick, New Romney, Kent 1791-2), V. Milton, Kent 1792-1801, R. All Hallows, Lombard Street, London 1801-10, V. Ivinghoe, Bucks. Nov. to Dec. 1803, R. Woolwich, Kent 1803-5, V. Edlesborough, Bucks. 1805-7, R. Little Gaddesden, Herts. 1805, R. Coulsdon, Surrey 1807-20, V. Addington, Surrey 1813-21, then moved north ('giving up all Lambeth connections'), R. Settrington, Yorks. 1820-46, Prebend of Husthwaite in York Minster 1830 and Archdeacon of Cleveland 1832 to death. Keeper of MSS at Lambeth Palace, then Librarian and Chap. to Archbishop Manners-Sutton. Chap. in Ordinary 1812 to death; Dom. Chap. to 11th Viscount Kilmorey 1782; to 2nd Earl of Fife; to 7th Earl of Bridgewater 1803-7. Died 24/12/1845 aged 82

[C2521. ODNB] Married 1788 Ann Dixon, 8 dau. A major editor, especially of Milton.

TODD (Isaac) Bapt. Dacre, Cumberland 30/5/1798, s. Joseph Todd (a joiner, Wreay, Carlisle) and Dinah Mounsey. St Bees, Cumberland adm. 1820, dn24 (Chester), p25 (Chester). (first) PC. Shincliffe, Durham 1826 to death 12/6/1872 aged 74, leaving £2,000 [C131090] Married Cambridge 20/6/1870 Lucy Philadelphia Penson.

TODD (Nicholas) [NiVoF] dn83 (Chester), p05 (Chester). S/M Corby G/S, Lincs. 1798-1836; PC.Rampside, Lancs. 1795-9- (res.), V. Bitchfield, Lincs. 1806 to death 24/6/1836 aged 76 [C77606]

TOKE (Thomas) Born Barnston, Essex 15/11/1772, s. Rev. Nicholas Toke and Catherine Bruce. Christ's, Cambridge 1792, BA1796, dn96 (London), MA1799, p00 (London), Fellow 1802-14. R. Little Canfield, Essex 1813 to death (Dunmow, Essex) 26/10/1838 [C123145] Wife Dorothy.

TOKE (William) Born Ashford, Kent 1769, s. John Toke (Godinton House) and Margaretta Eleanor Roundell. Emmanuel, Cambridge 1788, LLB, dn91 (Salis.), p93 (Salis.). V. Felsted, Dunmow, Essex 1797-8 (res.), V. Patrixbourne w. Bridge, Kent 1799-1800 (res.), R. Barnston, Essex 1807-37, PC. Little Dunmow 1824. Died Dover 2/5/1855, leaving £25,000 [C89562] Married Castle Combe, Wilts. 18/3/1793 Sarah West (a clergy dau.), w. clerical son Nicholas. Succ. to the family seat of Godinton 1837.

TOLLEMACHE, *born* TALMASH (Hugh Francis, Hon.) Born Petersham, Surrey 19/9/1802, s. Sir William Talmash (formerly Manners), Lord Huntingtower (of Buckminster, Leics.), *M.P.*, and Catherine Rebecca Gray. Pembroke, Cambridge 1823, then Peterhouse 1827, BA1831, dn31 (Peterb.), p31 (Peterb.). R. Harrington, Northants. 1831 to death 2/3/1890 aged 87, leaving £76,929-0s-11d. [C109512] Married Paddington, London 22/6/1824 Matilda Hume, with clerical sons Clement Reginald Tollemache and Ernest Celestine Tollemache. Name changed 1821.

TOMBLIN (Charles) From Edith Weston, Rutland, s. Robert Tomblin. Emmanuel, Cambridge 1820, BA1825, dn25 (Lin.), p25 (Glos. for Lin.), MA1828. V. Walcot, Lincs. 1828-58 and V. Langtoft, Lincs. 1834-56. Died 20/12/1858, leaving under £300 [C77611] Widow Elizabeth, and issue.

TOMES (Robert) From Long Marston, Glos., s. John Tomes and Ann Fisher. Magdalen Hall, Oxford 1826 (aged 19), BA1830, MA 1862. V. Coughton w. Sambourne, Warwicks. 1831-73. Died Cheltenham 27/7/1897, leaving £16,639-1s-2d. [C122237] Married Kidderminster 2/11/1831 Sarah Washborne Perry, w issue.

TOMKINS (Frederick) From City of London, s. Martin Tomkins. University, Oxford 1781 (aged 17), BA1785, MA1790, BD and DD1810. R. South Perrot, Dorset 1794, V. Harmonsworth w. West Drayton, Middx. 1810 to death 27/11/1843 [C54018]

TOMKINS (Thomas) Bapt. Alton St Pancras, Dorset 22/5/1761, s. Edwin Tomkins and Betty Hore. Balliol, Oxford 1780, BA1783, dn83 (Ox.), p86 (Ox.), then Emmanuel, Cambridge 1793, MA1794. R. Chilton Cantelo, Som. 1788-1839, R. West Coker, Som. 1795-1802, R. Thorn Falcon, Som. 1836 to death. Dom. Chap. to 2nd Earl of Carnarvon 1795. Died (Yeovil, Som.) 18/7/1839 [C37921] Married Wincanton, Som. 7/10/1788 Mary Messiter, with issue.

TOMKINSON (Henry) Born Reaseheath Hall, Nantwich, Cheshire 29/4/1795, s. Henry Tomkinson and Anne Darlington. Trinity, Cambridge 1804, [called to the Bar Middle Temple 1813] re-adm. 1814, then Trinity Hall 1819, dn20 (Glos.), p20 (Nor. for Chester), LLD1823. V. Acton, Cheshire 1820 and R. Davenham, Cheshire 1822 to death (Reaseheath Hall) 9/6/1838 [C115800] Married Manchester 8/7/1824 Harriet Sophia Philips, with issue.

TOMKYNS (John) Bapt. Broxbourne, Herts. 19/1/1783, s. Rev. William Moore and Letitia Tomykns. [Capt. 1st Royal Dragoons in Spain]. [Adm. Inner Temple 1802] King's, Cambridge 1802, BA1805, Fellow 1805-28, MA1809, p24, Tutor 1826-8, etc. R. and V. Stower Provost w. Todbere, Dorset 1827-32, R. Greenford, Middx. 1833 to death 16/12/1849 [C54019] Married Marylebone, London 30/12/1845 Isabella Frederick Coore, 1 ch.

TOMKYNS (Richard Bohun) From Buckinghill, Heref., s. Thomas Tomkyns. New, Oxford 1789 (aged 18), dn94 (Ox.), p95 (Ox.),

BCL1797, Fellow to 1826, etc. R. Great Horwood, Bucks. 1816 and R. Saham Toney, Norfolk 1825 to death 19/4/1833 aged 66 [C37922] Married Holborn, London 14/12/1826 Elizabeth Dipper. Name changed 1832.

TOMLINSON (George, *later* Bishop of Gibraltar) Born Newton, Manchester 12/3/1794, s. John Tomlinson. St John's, Cambridge 1818 [where he was a founder of the Cambridge Apostles], dn22 (Lin.), BA1823, p23 (Lin.), MA1826, DD1842. Tutor to the family of Sir Robert Peel; Curate St Matthew Spring Gardens, London 1832-42, first Bishop of Gibraltar 1842 [based initially in Malta] to death (Malta) 6/2/1863 aged 62, leaving £9,000 (as George Gibraltar). Secretary to S.P.C.K. 1832-42 [C77616. Boase. F. Blackburn, *George Tomlinson: a biography* (1954)] Married (1) Bolton, East Lothian 21/11/1848 Louisa (dau. Gen. Hon. Sir Patrick Stuart, she d.1850) (2) St James, Westminster, London 6/1/1855 Eleanor Jane (dau. Col. Charles Mackenzie-Fraser, *M.P.*), with issue. Missionary tour to the Levant 1840.

TOMLINSON (John Wick(e)s) Born Hanley, Staffs., s. John Tomlinson. Trinity, Oxford 1817 (aged 16), BA1821, MA1823, dn23 (Chester), p25 (C&L). R. Stoke on Trent, Staffs. 1831 to death 13/10/1857 [C563] Married (1) Rugby, Warwicks. 1/7/1831 Caroline Humer (2) Paddington, London 28/9/1848 Jemima Winton Read.

TOMPSON (James Browne) Born Norwich 15/2/1776 (bapt. in an Independent Chapel), s. Samuel (a linen draper) and Hannah Tompson. Caius, Cambridge 1793, LLB1799, dn99 (Nor.), p00 (Nor.). V. Shropham, Norfolk 1801 and PC. Tompson, Norfolk 1816 to death 13/8/1849 aged 73 [C115801] Married 24/10/1794 Elizabeth Anne Leathes (at Cornhill, Northumberland *or* at Horseheath, Cambs.), with issue.

TOMPSON (Matthew Carrier) Bapt. Iver, Bucks. 1/8/1800, s. Carrier Tompson and Mary Anne Smith. Trinity, Oxford 1819, BA1822, MA 1830. R. Woodstone, Hunts. 1829-71, V. Alderminster, Warwicks. 1830 (and RD of Kineton) to death 10/1/1882, leaving £37,123-12s-3d. [C122238] Married North Berwick, East Lothian, 23/10/1829 Eliza Dalrymple, with clerical son Reginald Tompson.

TOMPSON see also under **THOMPSON, THOMSON**

TOMS (William) Bapt. Bishopsnympton, Devon 22/2/1755, s. Lewis Toms. Wadham, Oxford 1773, BA1777, dn77 (B&W for Ex.), MA1783. PC. South Molton, Devon 1794 and R. (and patron) of Combe Martin, Devon 1794 to death 21/2/1833 [C49663]

TONKIN, *born* MOORE ['*which name he abandoned*'] (Uriah) Born Falmouth, Cornwall 30/12/1789. s. Rev. William Moore and Juliana Tonkin. Exeter, Oxford 1807, BA 1811, p14 (Ex.). V. (Ewny juxta) Lelant, Cornwall 1832 to death 12/1/1869 aged 79, leaving £6,000 [C146498] Married Barnstaple, Devon 17/7/1812 Louisa Squire, with clerical son John Tonkin.

TONYN (John Frederick) From London, s. George Tonyn. Queen's, Oxford 1791 (aged 20), BA1795, MA1800. R. Alvechurch, Worcs. [net income £1,025] 1801 to death 28/4/1854 [C122239] Married St George's Hanover Square, London 16/7/1802 Anna Price.

TOOGOOD (John James) Bapt. Kingston Magna, Dorset 11/12/1770, s. Rev. John and Ann Toogood, Trinity, Oxford 1788, BA1793, dn93 (Ex. for Bristol), p95 (Bristol for Salis.), MA1795, BD and DD1815. R. Milston, Wilts. 1801-34, R. Writhlington, Som. 1802-16, V. Broad Hinton, Wilts. 1815 to death 14/7/1834 (CCEd says 19/8/1834) [C49649]

TOOKE (Alfred) Born Manchester 22/11/1795, s. Edward and Sarah Tooke. BNC, Oxford 1813, then St Mary Hall, BA1818, dn19 (Chester for York), p19 (York), MA1820. R. Thorne Coffin, Som. 1824-43. Died Croydon, Surrey (but formerly of Balham, Surrey) 5/2/1872, leaving £4,000 [C136269. YCO] Married Weymouth, Dorset 22/6/1825 Eliza Poole (a clergy dau., from Bath).

TOOKEY (Charles) From Birmingham, s. of John Tookey and Jane Darby. Magdalen Hall, Oxford 1814 (aged 22), BA1822, MA1825. R. Oddingley, Worcs. 1824-[52]. Died 16/3/1882, leaving £3,842-19s-2d. [C122240] Wife Elizabeth, and issue.

TOPHAM (John) Bapt. Darlington, Yorks. 7/12/1794, s. Rev. John James Topham and Mary Allison. Sidney, Cambridge 1814, re-adm.

St John's 1814, BA1818, dn18 ([Wor.]), p19 (Wor.), MA1821. S/M Bromsgrove G/S 1818-32; R. Droitwich St Andrew w. St Mary Witton, Worcs. 1828-80. Died 24/6/1881, leaving £15,359-11s.-2d. [C122241. Boase] Married Selby, Yorks. 1/2/1820 Isabella Bowes, and issue.

TOPLIS (John) Bapt. Nottingham 25/5/1775, s. John (a mercer) and Susanna Toplis. Queens', Cambridge 1797, BA1801, dn01 (York), p02 (York), MA1804, Fellow 1810, BD1813, Tutor. H/M Nottingham G/S 1806-19; R. South Walsham St Lawrence, Norfolk 1824 to death 20/11/1857 aged 82, leaving £8,000 [C110669. YCO] Married South Walsham 24/3/1829 Elizabeth Smith (w).

TOPP (John) Born 21/10/1791, s. Richard Topp (Whitton Hall, Shropshire) and Anne Hughes. St John's, Cambridge 1809 (as Top), LLB1816, p16 (Heref.). PC. Wolstaston Chapel, Alberbury, Heref. 1824 to death (Pisa, Italy) 22/12/1837 [C174224] Married 12/8/1828 Maria Harley (of Shrewsbury), 2 dau.

TOPPING (John) Born Haydon Bridge, Northumberland 2/12/1764, s. Michael Topping and Elizabeth Green. Literate: dn97 (Car.), p03 (Car.). V. Irthington, Brampton, Cumberland 1811 to death 18/4/1847 aged 84 [C5647. Platt] Married Mary Hindhaugh by 1794. In 1804 when his stipend was £35 he had 7 ch. (inc. clerical son) 'Held in the highest estimation by his parishioners', etc.

TOPPING (Jonathan) Bapt. Shap, Westmorland 21/10/1781, s. John Topping (a 'head husbandman' from Bampton, Cumberland) and Mary Bird. Literate: dn05 ([Carlisle]), p06 (Car.). V. Leigh, Lancs. 1826 to death (*suicide*, 'with a horse pistol') 1839 (3rd q.) [C5649] Married Shap 7/9/1808 1808 Mary Wilkinson, 14 ch. (6 living at his death).

TORDIFFE (Thomas) Bapt. Plumbland, Cumberland 28/11/1765, s. William Tordiff [*pleb.*] and Elizabeth Wilkinson. Queen's, Oxford 1785, BA1789. dn90, p90. R. Holcombe St Andrew, Som. 1805 to death (Ilfracombe) 17/5/1845 [C122242] Married Joyce Wolferstan.

TORLESSE (Charles Martin) Bapt. Bloomsbury, London 26/6/1795, s. Charles Torlesse and Anna Maria Robinson. Trinity, Cambridge 1814, BA1818, dn21 (Lin.), MA1821, p22 (Lin.). V. Stoke by Nayland, Suffolk 1832 to death 12/7/1881 aged 86, leaving £4,676-15s.-0d. [C77639] Married Ipswich, Suffolk 7/4/1823 Catherine Gurney Wakefield, with issue. Photo. online.

TORR (John) Born Westleigh, Devon 15/9/1771, s. James Torr and Rebecca Hooley. Exeter, Oxford 1790, BA1792, dn94 (Ex.), p95 (B&W for Ex.). V. Westleigh 1803 to death 25/7/1835 [C49667] Married Uffculme, Devon 27/6/1803 Jane Tuplin, with issue.

TORRE (Henry) Born Bridlington, Yorks. 17/9/1780, s. James and Esther Torre. University, Oxford 1798, BA1804, dn04 (York), p06 (York). PC. Sledmere, Yorks. before 1825, R. Thornhill, Dewsbury, Yorks. 1824 [income £1,004] to death. Dom. Chap. to 2nd Earl of Mexborough 1815. Died (a widower) 25/12/1866 aged 90, leaving £4,000 [C110670. YCO] Married (1) Brighton, Sussex 11/3/1816 Mary Ellen Hodgson, of Stapleton Park, Yorks., with issue (2) Kirkheaton, Yorks. 1/2/1827 Caroline Sarah (dau. Sir John Lister Kaye, 1st Bart., Wakefield, Yorks.), with further issue; a clerical son.

TORRE (John) Bapt. Normanton, Yorks. 16/11/1760, s. Rev. James Torre and Betty Holme. Trinity, Cambridge 1778, BA1782, dn83 (York), MA1786, p87 (Chester). R. Catwick, Yorks. 1799 to death 13/4/1835 [C110672. Venn does not mention ordination. YCO] Married Lymm, Cheshire 30/10/1792 Harriet Leigh. Brother below.

TORRE, *later* HOLME (Nicholas) Born Sandal, Yorks. 14/12/1753, s. Rev. James Torre and Betty Holme. Trinity, Cambridge 1770, BA1775, Fellow 1777, dn77 (C&L for York), MA1778, p79 (York). R. Rise, Hull 1782 and V. Aldbrough (1st Mediety), Yorks. 1794 to death. Dom. Chap. to 12th Earl of Derby 1794. Died (Rise) 14/11/1833 (CCEd thus). [C19988. YCO] Married (1) Kippax, Yorks. 6/1793 Isabella Barker (d.1808, a clergy dau.), *s.p.* (2) 10/5/1809 Dorothy Worsley (a clergy dau.), *s.p.* Assumed the name Holme in 1811 on inheriting the estates and arms of Paull-Holme. Brother above.

TORRIANO (Josias) Born Nellore, Madras 12/3/1788, s. William Harcourt Torriano (Madras Civil Service) and Lydia Fraser /Frazier.

[In Madras Infantry 1804-20 (res.)] Trinity, Cambridge 1819, then St Catharine's 1819, dn23 (Salis.), p24 (St David's), BA1824, MA1830. Chap. Bengal Presidency 1824; V. Stanstead Mountfitchet, Essex 1828-51, then lived in Bayswater, London. Died 14/3/1877 aged 88 (but buried Southampton June 1880) [C66837] Married Reading, Berks. 8/6/1824 Louise Hooper, with issue (incl. an insane dau. who kept his embalmed body in a glass-topped coffin in the bathroom, *q.v.* an extraordinary online entry).

TOTHILL (John) Bapt. Exeter Cathedral 8/10/1764, s. John Tothill and Alice Miner. Exeter, Oxford 1784, BA1788, dn88 (Ex.), p89 (Ex.). R. Hittisleigh, Devon 1799-[45]. Perhaps died 8/12/1844 [C146499] Married Kenton, Devon 18/1/1794 Mary Disting, with issue.

TOTTON (William Jurin). Born Edgware, Middx. 30/8/1769, s. Rev. William Totton and Frances Jurin. Oriel, Oxford 1789, dn93 (Ex.), BA1793, p94 (Lin.), MA1796. R. Meldreth, Cambs. 1794 and R. Debden, Essex 1796 to death 1/1/1850 [C77641] Married (1) Islington, Middx. 2/12/1796 Frances Mary Ann Church (d.1842), w. issue (2) Holywell, Oxford 10/10/1815 Eleanor Rudge.

TOTTY (Hugh) From Holywell, Flintshire, s. John Totty and Mary Lloyd. Christ Church, Oxford 1774 (aged 17), BA1778, dn79 (Ox.), MA1781, p81 (Ox. for Chester), BD1791, DD1823. PC. Wyken, Warwicks. 1788-1823 (res.), R. Etchingham, Sussex 1795 and V. Fairlight, Sussex 1823 to death. Chap. to Prince of Wales, then George 1V. Died (Bath) 21/12/1857 aged 101 [C20098. Boase] Wife Sarah Margaret.

TOWERS (James) [NiVoF] V. Wherwell, Hants. 1820. Died 1838 [C108925. ERC as J.A.] Married Salisbury Cathedral 15/5/1800 Anne Delicia Iremonger (of Wherwell Priory).

TOWNLEY (Charles) Born Fulbourne, Cambs. 17/3/1795, s. Richard Greaves Townley and Margaret Gale. Trinity, Cambridge 1812, BA1817, dn19 (Ely), p20 (Peterb.), MA1820. V. Little Abington, Cambs. 1828 and R. Hadstock, Essex 1838 to death. Dom. Chap. to Duke of Leeds. Died Hadstock 29/4/1870, leaving £1,500 [C109516. CR65 as two people] Married Hemingstone, Suffolk 8/11/1831 Elizabeth Sarah Martin.

TOWNLEY (Edmund) Born Outwell, Norfolk 3/10/1804, s. Rev. Jonathan Townley (below) and Elizabeth Johnson. St Bees: dn27 (Nor.), p27 (Nor.). PC. Staveley in Cartmel, Lancs. 1828-71 (and S/M 1829), RD of Cartmel 1871 to death. Dom. Chap. to Earl of Stair in 1840. Died 7/11/1881 aged 77, leaving £8,206-0s-10d. [C115827] Married Cartmel 9/7/1836 Margaret Catherine (dau. James Losh, Newcastle, *q.v.* ODNB, *et al*), with clerical son.

TOWNLEY (George Stepney) Bapt. City of London 10/8/1747, s. Rev. James Townley and Jane Bonnin. St John's, Oxford 1766, Fellow 1766, BA1770, dn70 (Ox.), p71 (Cant.), MA 1774. V. Great Totham, Essex 1777, R. St Stephen Walbrook w. St Benet Sherehog, City of London 1784 to death 14/2/1835 (CCEd says 6/3/1835) [C37939] Left a child.

TOWNLEY (Jonathan) Born Rochdale, Lancs. 27/12/1774, s. Col. Richard Townley (Belfield Hall) and Mary Penny. Clare, Cambridge 1792, BA1797, MA1801. R. Upwell, Norfolk 1798-1812, R. Gaywood, Norfolk 1817-27, V. Stradsett, Norfolk 1817-45, PC. Colton, Lancs. 1824-34, V. Steeple Bumpstead, Essex 1834 to death (North Pickenham, Norfolk) 17/12/1848 aged 74 [C115828] Married (1) Lancaster 24/8/1799 Elizabeth Johnson, with clerical s. Edmund Townhead Townley. Parish sequestrated 1831 because of a debt of £1,200; 'and [he] has absconded'.

TOWNLEY (William) St John's, Cambridge 1810 (a Ten Year Man) [but *Gentleman's Mag.* says Trinity, Cambridge, BA1792, MA1795]. V. Orpington w. St Mary Cray, Kent 1816 to death (intestate) 24/9/1847 aged 67? [C77650 is a literate] 3 men of this name here?

TOWNLEY (William Gale) Bapt. Westminster, London 31/1/1788, s. Richard Greaves Townley (Baupré Hall, Outwell, Norfolk) and Margaret Gale. Trinity, Cambridge 1805, BA 1809, dn12 (Ely), p12 (London), MA 1812. R. Upwell w.Welney [net income £3,855], Norfolk 1812 to death 15/5/1862 aged 74, leaving £8,000 [C100462] Married Ryston, Norfolk 17/6/1845 Harriet Gale Pratt, *s.p.* J.P. and Chairman of Isle of Ely Quarter Sessions.

TOWNSEND, TOWNSHEND (Abraham Boyle) Born Castle Castletownshend, Cork, s. Richard Boyle Townsend and Henrietta Frances Newenham. Christ Church, Oxford 1809 (aged

18), Student [Fellow] 1809-27, BA1815, MA 1816. R. Easthampstead, Berks. 1826 to death 5/2/1860, leaving £2,000 [C89609] Married Abingdon, Berks. 17/6/1826 Sarah Maria Payton, with issue. Brother Maurice Fitzgerald Stephens Townsend, below.

TOWNSEND (Charles) Born London 19/6/1780, s. Rev. Joseph Townsend (R. Pusey, Wilts.) and Joyce Nankivell. BNC, Oxford 1796, then Magdalen, Fellow, BA1800, MA 1803, dn03 (Ox.), p04 (Glos. [for Salis.?]). R. Calstone Wellington, Wilts. 1804-33, PC. West Bromwich, Staffs. 1815. Died 10/11/1865, leaving £12,000 [C20101] Married Melton Mowbray, Leics. 6/7/1807 Lucy Jesse, with issue.

TOWNSEND (Edward James) Born Honington, Warwicks. 28/8/1786, s. Gore Townsend and Lady Elizabeth Windsor (dau. 4th Earl of Plymouth). Merton, Oxford 1805, BA1809, Fellow 1812-17, MA1813. V. Honington 1812-17, R. Rawmarsh, Yorks. 1816-31, (Sinecure R. Heyes, Middx. 1827-58), R. Ilmington, Warwicks, 1831 to death. Dom. Chap. to 6th Earl of Plymouth 1812. Died (Leamington, Warwicks.) 19/4/1858, leaving £8,000 [C122244] Married St George's Hanover Square, London 4/3/1818 Mary Catherine Hambrough (w), and had issue.

TOWNSEND (George) Born Ramsgate, Kent 12/9/1788, s. Rev. George Townsend (an Independent Minister) and Susanna Morris. Trinity, Cambridge 1808, BA1812, dn13 (Ely), p14 (Ely), MA1816, DD(Durham) 1845. [Professor at Sandhurst Military College 1816-22], Canon of 10th Prebend in Durham Cathedral 1825-57, V. Northallerton, Yorks. 1826-39, PC. Durham St Margaret 1839-42. Dom. Chap. to Bishop of Durham 1822-57. Died Durham University 23/11/1857 [C109517. ODNB. Boase] Married (1) Brighton 8/7/1813 Elizabeth Tyler (dau. of a barrister, she d.1835), with clerical son (2) St George's Hanover Square, London 19/12/1838 Charlotte Charlten Hollingbery, with further issue. Met the Pope in 1850 - to convert him to Protestantism!

TOWNSEND, *later* WILLIAM-POWLETT (Henry, 3rd Baron Bayning) Born 8/6/1797, s. Charles, 1st Baron Bayning, M.P., and Annabella Powlett Smyth (a clergy dau.). St John's, Cambridge 1816, MA1818, dn20 (Nor.), p21 (Nor.). R. Brome w. Oakley, Suffolk 1821-47, R. (and patron) of Honingham w. East Tuddenham, Norfolk 1851-66, Hon. Canon of Norwich Cathedral (and RD) 1844. Died (of paralysis) Honingham Hall 5/8/1866 aged 69, leaving £20,000 [will under Bayning] [C115832] Married Ramsey, Hunts. 9/8/1842 Emma Fellowes, *s.p.* Succ. to title 1823; title thereafter extinct. Photo. LNCP. as Rev. Lord Henry Bayning.

TOWNSEND (John Charles) From Newbury, Berks, s. Richard Townsend. St John's, Oxford 1802 (aged 18), BA1806, dn07 (Ex.), MA1809. R. (and patron) of Ickford, Bucks. 1808-46. Died 13/12/1850 [C77655] Married Greenham, Berks. 13/9/1805 Sarah Argyle ?Syerinson, w. issue.

TOWNSEND (John Haynes) Bapt. Alderley, Glos. 10/4/1782, s. John Townsend (London). Magdalen, Oxford 1797, BA1801, dn01 (Ox.), p02 (Ox.), MA1804. PC. Marazion, Cornwall 1819, R. Parkham, Devon 1856 to death 18/5/1864, leaving £6,000 [C21844] Married Tamworth, Staffs. 24/9/1805 Sarah Wright.

TOWNSEND (Maurice Fitzgerald [Stephens]) Born Cork 7/5/1791, s. Richard Boyle Townsend and Henrietta Newenham. Christ Church, Oxford 1808, Student [Fellow] 1808-24, BA 1812, MA1815, dn16 (Ox.), p17 (Ox.). V. Thornbury, Glos. 1823 to death 21/3/1872, leaving £7,000 [C21845] Married 16/5/1826 Alice Elizabeth Shute, with issue. Brother Abraham Boyle Townsend, above.

TOWNSEND (Richard Lawrence) Born Ashton under Lyme, Staffs. 17/3/1799, s. William Townsend (Liverpool). St Mary Hall, Oxford 1822, BA1828, MA1828. (joint) PC. Liverpool St Philip 1828, Inc. Wandsworth All Saints, London 1847-50, then V. 1850 to death 26/12/1855 [C170742] Married Prestbury, Cheshire 30/10/1828 Helen Wood, with issue.

TOWNSEND (Samuel Thomas) Born Ireland, s. Capt. Samuel Irwin Townsend and Katherine Thomas. Trinity, Cambridge, 1821 (aged 24) [adm. Lincoln's Inn 1822] BA1826, dn28, p29, MA1830. R. Farndish, Beds. 1830-52, V. Chicheley, Bucks. 1830-52. Dom. Chap to 3rd Earl of Clarendon 1830. Lived latterly and died London 12/1874, *s.p.*, leaving £30,000. [C564] Married (1) St George's Hanover Square, London 18/2/1828 Catherine Louisa St Leger (d. 1854 1st q.) (2) Thornbury, Glos. 1859 (3rd q.) Eliza Frances Cadogan (w).

TOWNSEND (Thomas) Born London, s. Thomas Townsend and Mary Davis. Magdalen Hall, Oxford 1780 (aged 32). R. Aisthorpe w. Thorpe in the Fallows, Lincs. 1803 to death. Dom. Chap to 1st Earl Beauchamp 1815. Died 15/7/1833 (CCEd says 29/11/1833). [C77657]

TOWNSEND (William Lawrence) From Alderton, Glos., s. Rev. Robert Lawrence Townsend. Worcester, Oxford 1816 (aged 18), BA1821, dn21 (Glos.), MA1823, p24 (Glos.). R. Alderton 1830 and R. Bishop's Cleeve [net income £1,574], Glos. 1830 to death 10/9/1883 [C137016]

TOWNSHEND (Frederick Patrick, Hon., 'commmonly called Lord Frederick Townshend') Born Dublin 30/12/1767, s. 1st Marquess Townshend (Lord Lieutenant of Ireland) and Charlotte Compton, 15th Baroness Ferrers. St John's, Cambridge 1787, MA1788, dn92 (Nor.), p92 (Nor.). R. Stiffkey, Norfolk 1792 (nominally) to death 28/6/1836 [C115830]. Insane: he *murdered* his brother in a coach while travelling to London 27/5/1796.

TRAGETT, TRAGITT (Thomas Heathcote) Born Walworth, Surrey, s. Reuben Groom Tragitt and Elizabeth Whithorne. Exeter, Oxford 1816 (aged 17), then Corpus Christi 1816-23, BA1819, MA1822, dn23 (Ox.), Fellow 1823-5, p24 (Ox.). (first) PC. Coventry Christ Church 1832, V. Timsbury, Hants. 1843-53. Died Danes House, Awbridge, Hants. 1/10/1887 aged 88, leaving £33,070-16s-11d. [C21849] Married Leamington, Warwicks. 17/8/1825 Louisa Lane, with issue. Jane Austen connections.

TREBECK (Jonathan) Bapt. Wath upon Dearne, Yorks. 11/9/1798, s. Rev. Thomas Trebeck (below) and Eloise Burward. Christ Church, Oxford 1817, Student [Fellow] 1817-27, BA1821, dn21 (Ox.), p22 (Ox.), MA1823. V. Cople, Beds. 1826 and V. Melbourn, Cambs. 1833 to death 2/4/1846 [C21850] Married York 7/9/1826 Charlotte Cooke (described by Romilly as 'an ugly cold piece of aristocratical ice!'), with clerical s. James John Trebeck. 'A dull Oxonian' (also Romilly).

TREBECK (Thomas) Born London 26/1/1765, s. Rev. James Trebeck and Mary Davies. Christ Church, Oxford 1782, BA1787, dn87 (Ox.), p89 (Ox.), MA1790. R. Wath upon Dearne, Yorks. 1793-1822, 4th Prebend of Ripon Collegiate Church 1805, R. Chailey, Sussex 1821 to death. Dom. Chap to Bishop of Bristol 1796-7. Died 8/7/1851 [C37963] Married Marylebone, London 22/12/1794 Eloise Burward, with son above.

TREDCROFT (Robert) Bapt. Horsham, Surrey 12/1/1792, s. Nathaniel Tredcroft and Sarah Steele. Christ Church, Oxford 1810, BA 1814, dn15 (Chester), p16 (Salis. for Chich.), MA1818. Sequestrator of Westhampnett, Sussex 1815, R. Whatlington, Sussex 1821, Prebend of Centum Solidorum in Lincoln Cathedral 1821-2 (res.), Hampstead Prebend in Chichester Cathedral 1822-46, R. Fittleworth, Sussex 1824, R. West Itchenor, Sussex 1824, R. Coombes, Sussex 1824, R. Tangmere, Sussex 1828 to death 18/12/1846 [C70922] Married Hampton, Surrey 3/8/1824 Frances Katherine Pechell, with issue.

TREFUSIS (John) Bapt. Aldenham, Hants. 2/2/1772, s. Robert George Trefusis, Newbury, Bucks. Oriel, Oxford 1791, BA1795, dn96 (Ex.), p97 (Ex.), MA1802. R. St Columb Major [net income £1,296], Cornwall 1798-1841 and R. South Hill w. Callington, Cornwall 1802 to death. Dom. Chap. to 4th Baron Clinton 1802. Died 14/2/1841 [C146503] Married Bodmin, Cornwall 5/5/1801 Elizabeth Cory.

TRELAWNY (Charles Trelawny Collins) see under **COLLINS**

TREMENHEERE (William) Born Penzance 19/10/1757, s. William Tremenheere (attorney) and Catherine Borlase (a clergy dau.). Pembroke, Cambridge 1775, BA1779 [usher at Oakham School 1778-83] dn80 (Peterb.), p82 (Lin.), MA1830. Sometime Chaplain *R.N.*; V. Madron w. Morvah, Cornwall 1812 to death. Dom. Chap. to Viscount Torrington 1814. Died (unm.) 3/7/1838. [C77661]

TREMLETT (Daniel) Bapt. Sutton Sandford, Devon 4/6/1798, s. Elias Tremlett and Nancy Twiner. St John, Cambridge 1816, BA1820, MA1824. R. Rodney Stoke (o/w Stoke Gifford), Som. 1822 to death (Wells, Som.) 19/2/1846 aged 49 [C49687] Married Richmond, Yorks. 2/10/1826 Isabella Mary Simpson, with issue.

TRENCHARD born ASHFORDBY (John Ashfordby) Born Cheshunt, Herts. 1771, s. John Ashfordby and Ellen Hippisley-Trenchard. Trinity, Oxford, 1789, dn97 (Ex. for Salis.), p97 (Bristol for Salis.), BCL and DCL 1802. R.

(and patron) of Stanton Fitzwarren, Wilts. 1822 (living at Stanton House) 1822 to death 10/3/1838 aged 66 [C83237 under Ashfordby] Married (1) City of London 1793 Martha Cook (d.1832), with clerical sons John Trenchard Craven Ashfordby-Trenchard, and Walter Ashfordby-Trenchard (2) 1832 Mrs Sarah (Baker) Brookes. Name added on inheriting estates in 1831.

TRENOW (Frederick Joseph Cox) Bapt. Wolborough w. Newton Abbot, Devon 28/12/1787. Literate: p12 (B&W), then Sidney, Cambridge 1818 (a Ten Year Man, MA1825 Lambeth). Ran a private school in Dorchester, Dorset; R. Langton Herring, Dorset 1824 to death 12/10/1855 aged 68 [C49691] Married (1) Dorchester 14/6/1815 Mary Pearce (d.1826), with issue (2) Bristol 28/2/1828 Mrs Hannah (Baker) Dare, with further issue (including one son a RC priest).

TRENOWETH (Samuel) Bapt. Covent Garden, London 16/9/1749, s. Samuel and Ann Trenoweth (Emmer Green, Berks.) Trinity, Oxford 1766, dn71 (Win.), p72 (Win.). R. North Benfleet, Essex 1778-1839 aged 94. Probate granted 8/2/1839 [C108938]

TREVELYAN (George) Born Nettlecombe, Som. 29/11/1795, s. Ven. George Trevelyan, sen. (Archdeacon of Bath) and Harriet Neave. Balliol, Oxford 1813, BA1818, MA1820, dn20 (B&W), p20 (B&W). V. Stogumber, Som. 1820-71 (non-res.), V. Milverton, Som. 1822-5, R. Treborough, Som. 1828. Dom. Chap. to Harriet, Countess of Errol 1822. Died (Colyton, Som.) 25/4/1871, leaving £7,000 [C40743] Married 2/4/1833 Frances Ann Lumsden. Brother John Thomas below.

TREVELYAN (George) Born Hartburn, Northumberland 22/5/1802, s. Rev. Walter Trevelyan and Charlotte Hudson. Oriel, Oxford 1820, BA1824, then Merton, Fellow 1826-35, dn27 (B&W), MA1827, etc. PC. Wolvercott, Oxon. 1831, V. Malden w. Chessington, Surrey 1834 to death 3/6/1850, leaving £260-18s-9d (unadministered until 1885) [C21851] Married Epsom, Surrey 14/5/1835 (w) Anne Gosse, w. clerical son Walter Henry Trevelyan.

TREVELYAN (John Thomas) Born Nettlecombe, Som. 26/2/1799, s. Ven. George Trevelyan (Archdeacon of Bath) and Harriet Neave. St Mary Hall, Oxford 1822, dn24 (Nor), p24 (Nor), BA1826, MA1829. V. Milverton, Som. 1825, R. Huish Champflower >< Som. 1833 to death. Dom. Chap. to Bishop of Llandaff 1833. Died Madeira 16/8/1844 (unm.). Brother George (two above) [C40744. LBSO]

TREVENEN (Edward) Bapt. Helston, Cornwall 22/4/1785, s. (alderman) John Trevenen and Lydia Johns. Pembroke, Oxford 1803, BA1808, dn08 (Ex.), p09 (Ex.). R. Drewsteignton, Devon 1810 to death (London) 10/6/1846 [C146512] Married (1) Hackney, London 27/8/1818 Mary Anne Cazenove (d.1829), with issue (2) Brightwell, Oxon. 12/3/1835 Emma Strickland.

TREWEEKE (George) Bapt. Penzance, Cornwall 23/4/1779, s. Rev. George Treweeke, sen. and Mary Sandys. Trinity, Oxford 1796, BA1800, MA1811, dn12 (Nor.). V. St Minver, Cornwall 1817 and R. Illogan, Cornwall 1822 to death there. Dom. Chap. to 1st Baron de Dunstanville 1822. Died 15/2/1851 [C21852] Married Madron, Cornwall 15/8/1815 Marianne Napleton, w. clerical son Charles Napleton Treweeke.

TRIM (William Hewlett) From Bere Regis, Dorset, s. George Trim. Wadham, Oxford 1814 (aged 18), BA1819, dn20 (Glos.), MA1821, p21 (Ex.). R. Sandford Orcas, Som. 1832 to death (Bristol) 25/3/1870 aged 74, leaving £1,000 [C40747] Married East Coker, Som. 29/4/1822 Martha Bullock.

TRIMMER (Henry) Bapt. North Cray, Kent 2/9/1798, s. Joshua Kirby Trimmer and Eliza Willet Thompson. Exeter, Oxford 1819, BA 1822, dn22 (Win.), p23 (Lin.), MA1830. V. Buckminster w. Sewstern, Leics. 1823-34 (res.). Died Norwich 20/7/1842 [C77671] Married St Pancras, London 5/6/1823 Mary Deacon, with issue.

TRIMMER (Henry Scott) Bapt. Ealing, Middx. 26/8/1778, s. James Scott and Sarah Kirby. Merton, Oxford 1798, BA1802, dn02 (London), p02 (London). V. Heston, Middx. 1804 to death. Dom. Chap. to 6th Duke of Devonshire 1811. Died 25/11/1859, leaving £25,000 [C123368] Married Sudbury, Suffolk 3/7/1805 Mary Driver Syer, with clerical son Harrington James Trimmer.

TRIPP (Charles) Born Spofforth, Yorks. 20/4/1784, s. Rev. John Tripp and Sarah

Burchell. Trinity, Cambridge 1801, BA1806, dn07 (Ely for York), p08 (York), MA1809, DD 1825. (Sinecure R. Bondleigh, Devon 1814-35), R. Kentisbeare, Devon 1825-33-, (Sinecure R. North and South Bradon, Som. 1829-65), R. Sampford Brett, Som. 1830-39, R. Blackborough, Devon 1835-39, R. Silverton, Devon 1839 [income £1,014] to death 9/4/1865, leaving £9,000 [C40748. YCO] Married Bathwick, Som. 15/6/1815 his first cousin Frances Owen (dau. of a general), with clerical sons Henry, and John Tripp. J.P. for Somerset and Devon. Some dates here may be confused.

TRIPP (James) Born Petworth, Sussex 25/4/1787, s. James Upton Tripp and Sarah Edshaw. Christ's, Cambridge 1804, BA1810, dn10 (Win.), p11 (Win.). R. Up Waltham, Sussex 1813-40, Sequestrator of Hardham, Sussex 1829, Sequestrator of Cold Waltham, Sussex 1830, R. Kirby Overblow, Yorks. 1840-47, R. Spofforth, Yorks. 1847 (and RD) to death there 8/11/1879, leaving £16,000 [C70928] Married (1) Marylebone, London 19/2/1818 Frances Martha Buckle (d.1820), with issue (2) Marylebone 24/5/1823 Eliza Howard Harvey, with further issue.

TRIPP (Robert Henry) Born Rewe, Devon 3/7/1801, s. Rev. Robert Tripp and Mary Leigh. Exeter, Oxford 1818, BA1822, dn24 (Ex.), p25 (Ex.), MA1826. R. Exeter St Sidwell 1828-42, V. Altarnun, Cornwall 1842 to death there 13/3/1880 aged 79, leaving £1,500 [C146514] Married Nettlecombe, Somerset 27/10/1831 his first cousin Elizabeth Ann Tripp, w. clerical son of same name (and also the botanical writer Fanny Tripp, *q.v.* online).

TRIST (Samuel [Peter] John) Bapt. Veryan, Cornwall 25/12/1791, s. Rev. Jeremiah Trist and Elizabeth Charlotte Fincher. Oriel, Oxford 1809, BA1813, MA1816, dn16 (Ex.), p17 (Ex.). V. Veryan 1829 to death (unm.) 8/6/1869 aged 76, leaving £3,000 [C146518] Photo. online.

TRISTRAM (Henry Baker) Born Great Ponton, Lincs. 9/9/1795, s. Rev. Thomas Tristram and Louisa Barrington. Christ Church, Oxford 1813, Student [Fellow] 1813-21, BA 1817, dn18 (Durham), p19 (Durham), MA1820. V. Bramham, Yorks. 1820-3, V. Eglingham, Northumberland 1821 to death 30/5/1837 [C131095] Married (1) Stroud, Glos. 11/7/1820 Charlotte Jocelyn Mary Smith (dau. of a barrister, she d.1830), with clerical s. of same name (ornithologist and Darwinian) (2) Edinburgh 17/7/1833 Anne Wood, of St Kitts, West Indies.

TRIVETT (William) Born London 26/3/1776, s. William Trivett and Frances Farquhar. Trinity, Cambridge 1795, BA1799, dn00 (Ex.), p01 (Roch.), MA1808. R. Bradwell, Suffolk 1810 to death 28/11/1863, leaving £4,000 [C2527] An Oxford man of same name.

TROLLOPE (Henry) Born Easton, Northants., s. Thomas Middleton Trollope and Isabella Thorold (dau. of a baronet). Clare, Cambridge 1791, BA1795, dn95 (Peterb.), p96 (Peterb.), MA1798. R. Harrington, Lincs. 1802 and R. Brinkhill, Lincs. 1821 to death 24/7/1839 [C77676] Married Cottered, Herts. 12/5/1803 Diana Trollope (a clergy dau.), *s.p.*

TROTMAN (Fiennes Samuel) Born Harbury, Warwicks. 25/10/1796, s. Rev. Edward Trotman and Lucy Newsham. Sidney, Cambridge 1815, BA1819, dn20 (Chester for C&L), p21 (Chester for C&L). V. Dallington, Northants. 1822 and R. Stoke Goldington w. Gayhurst >< Bucks. 1822 to death (Brighton) 30/1/1863 aged 66, leaving £7,000. Lived at Dallington Park (Hall?), Northants. [C19990] Married (1) Steeple Ashton, Oxon. 21/4/1826 Mary Earle (a clergy dau., she d.1841), with clerical son Edward Fiennes Trotman (2) Winchester 23/11/1842 Caroline Short.

TROUGHTON (James) Bapt. Coventry, Warwicks. 1/9/1795, s. James and Sarah Troughton. Christ Church, Oxford 1814, BA 1818, dn18 (Chester for C&L), MA1827. Chap. of Donative of Binley, Warwicks. 1821-36, PC. Wyken, Warwicks. 1824-36, R. Yelvertoft, Northants. 1824-8, R. Ashley, Staffs. 1827 to death 1/3/1836 [C20108]

TROUGHTON (John) Bapt. Whicham, Cumberland 21/1/1776, s. William Troughton and Agnes Armer. Literate: dn99 (Chester), p00 (Chester). PC. Walney, Dalton in Furness, Lancs. 1805 (and S/M 1804) to death 29/9/1839 aged 63 [C170749] Married Dalton in Furness 3/10/1807 Mary Hunter. 'An ardent sportsman and judge of athletic contests.'

TROYTE (Edward [Berkeley]) Bapt. Huntsham, Devon 16/10/1763, s. William Troyte. Oriel, Oxford 1781, dn87 (B&W), p87 (B&W), BCL and DCL 1796. R. Puckington,

Som. 1787 and R. (and patron) of Huntsham 1796 to death 9/5/1852 (unmarried) [C49743] A sporting parson.

TRUEMAN (Edward) Born Pontefract, Yorks. 13/5/1803, s. of Edward Trueman (a banker). Worcester, Oxford 1822, BA1826, dn26 (York), p27 (London for York), MA1829. V. Langtoft, Yorks. 1827 and V. North Grimston, Malton, Yorks. 1827 to death 4/11/1884 aged 81, leaving £3,149-19s-0d. [C123373. YCO]

TRUMPER (John) From Grosmont, Monmouth, s. Thomas Trumper. Jesus, Oxford 1790 (aged 19), BA1794, p94 (Heref.), p95 (Heref.). V. Clifford, Heref. 1808 to death 7/12/1854 [C174251] Married Hay on Wye. Heref. 1838 (1st q.) Mrs Anne Lloyd.

TRYE (Charles Brandon) Born Gloucester 11/6/1806, s. Charles Brandon Trye and Mary Lysons. BNC, Oxford 1824, BA1829, dn29 (Glos.), p30 (Glos.), MA1832. R. (and patron) of Leckhampton, Glos. 1830 (living at Leckhampton Court) and Hon. Canon of Gloucester 1877 to death 22/2/1884, leaving £9,116-13s-11d. [C150781] Married Gloucester 22/5/1832 Jane Riland Pickard, with issue.

TRYON (John Thomas) Bapt. Cottingham, Northants. 28/5/1788, s. George Tryon and Elizabeth Wingfield. St John's, Cambridge 1806, BA1810, dn11 (Peterb.), p12 (London). R. (and patron) of Bulwick, Northants. 1812 to death there 2/11/1861 aged 73, leaving £18,000 [C111542] Married Streatham, Surrey 3/6/1819 Sarah Whalley (w), and had issue: https://www.wikitree.com/wiki/Tryon-2017

TUCKER (Andrew) Bapt. Fifehead, Dorset 17/5/1778, s. Rev. Andrew, sen. and Sarah Tucker. Wadham, Oxford 1796, BA1800, dn01 (Ox.), p03 (Bristol), MA1818. R. Wootton Fitzpaine, Dorset 1817, R. Catherston Leweston, Dorset 1818 to death 15/3/1858. No will traced [C37979] Married (1) Hawkchurch, Devon 1/8/1803 Agnes Domett (d.1823), with issue (2) Wootton Fitzpaine 9/8/1825 Mary Anne Corpe, with further issue; about 20 ch. in all.

TUCKER (George) Born Axminster, Devon, s. Rev. George Tucker, sen. Wadham, Oxford 1815 (aged 17), SCL, dn21 (Ex.), p22 (Lin. for Ex.). R. Musbury, Devon 1821 to death there, leaving £600 [C77790] Married Musbury 29/3/1797 Elizabeth Symes, with son below.

TUCKER (Henry Tippetts) Born Musbury, Devon 24/7/1799, s. Rev. George Tucker (above) and Elizabeth Symes. St John, Oxford 1816, BA1820, dn22 (Ex.), p23 (Ex.), MA1823. R. Uplyme, Devon 1823-42, R. (and patron) of Angersleigh, Som. 1842-64-, R. Clayhidon, Devon 1848-[73], RD of Dunkeswell in 1864. Died (Leigh Court, Angersleigh) 1870 aged 71, leaving £16,000 [C146522] Married Cotleigh, Devon 19/1/1825 Charlotte Michell (w).

TUCKER (John) Bapt. Drewsteignton, Devon 9/4/1787, s. William Tucker (farmer) and Susanna Dadd. Pembroke, Oxford 1806, no degree, dn10 (Ex.), p22 (Glos.). S/M Moretonhampstead G/S, Devon 1815; Min. Portland St. Proprietary Chapel, Cheltenham, Glos. 1818-19, PC. Southborough, Kent 1830, PC. Charlton Abbots, Glos. 1831. Lived and died Ham House, Cheltenham 17/1/1859, leaving £600 [C146523] Married (1) Moretonhampstead Mary Ann Kinsman (d.1830), with issue (2) Bradninch, Devon Jane Rogers Shepherd (d.1847), with further issue (3) St Pancras, London 6/1/848 Amy Whitton Malpas. His complicated teaching career is noted in CCEd.

TUCKER (Marwood) Born Kilmington, Devon 1/11/1763, s. Benedict Marwood Tucker and Mary Frances Pester. Balliol, Oxford 1781, BA1785, dn86 (Ex.), p88 (Ex.). V Harpford w. Venn Ottery, Devon 1811 to death 12/5/1845 [C146525] Married Charlotte Jane Foulkes (Coryton Park, Kilmington, Devon), w. clerical sons Marwood, jun., and William Marwood Tucker (below)

TUCKER (Robert Hardy) Bapt. Marlborough, Wilts. 31/3/1763, s. Samuel [*pleb.*] and Elizabeth Tucker. Oriel, Oxford 1782, BA1785, dn85 (Salis.), p87 (Salis.). V. Marlborough 1796. Died (unm.) 18/2/1843 aged 80 [C89623]

TUCKER (Stephen) Bapt. Canterbury Cathedral 20/1/1764, s. Rev. John Tucker and Jane Gurney. Trinity, Cambridge 1780, BA 1785, dn86 (Lin. for Cant.), p88 (Glos. for Cant.), MA1788. V. Lympne, Kent 1789-94, V. Lynsted, Kent 1793, V. Borden, Kent 1797 and R. Markshall, Kent 1800 to death (Welling, Kent) 8/7/1838 [C77793] Married City of London 2/10/1787 Jane Frend, with issue.

TUCKER (William Comyns) Bapt. Morchard Bishop, Devon 29/4/1772, s. Rev. Peter Tucker and Agnes Reeve. Balliol, Oxford 1789, BA 1793, dn94 (Ex.), p96 (Ex.). R. Washford Pyne, Devon 1796 to death. Buried 29/3/ 1838 [C146529] Married (1) Tiverton, Devon 11/9/1797 Elizabeth Smale (2) Washford Pyne 24/12/1836 Hannah Maria Leash.

TUCKER (William Marwood) Born Exmouth, Devon, s. Rev. Marwood Tucker (above) and Charlotte Jane Foulkes. Balliol, Oxford 1810 (aged 16), BA1814, dn16 (Salis. for Ex.), p17 (Ex.), Fellow 1817-27, MA1818. R. Colchester All Saints, Essex 1827, R. Colchester St Botolph, Essex 1827, R. Widworthy, Devon 1831 to death 8/1/1851 [C89624] Married West Malling, Kent 19/5/1829 Agnes Sophia Bax.

TUCKNISS (Benjamin Fuller) Born Essequibo, British Guiana 13/2/1797 (bapt. Philadelphia, USA 12/4/1801), s. Abraham Tuckniss and Frances Reading. St Catharine's, Cambridge 1826, dn30 (Chester), BA1831, p31 (Chester). PC. Raskelf, Yorks. 1832 to death 28/7/1845 [C136905 *but not Suckniss*] Married 21/2/1822 in Barbados Mary Jane Austin (a clergy dau.), with clerical issue.

TUFNELL (George) Bapt. Great Waltham, Essex 10/1/1796, s. William Joliffe Tufnell (Langleys House) and Anne Close. [In a Guards Regiment 1814-21] Emmanuel, Cambridge 1821, BA1825, dn25 (Bristol for London), p25 (London). V. Wormingford, Essex 1825-40, V. Uffington, Berks. 1847-52, R. Thornton Watlass, Yorks. 1852 to death (Banstead, Surrey) 16/1/1868, leaving £1,000. Chap. at Boulogne 1842 (debt?) [C54053] Married St George's Hanover Square, London 22/1/1821 Maria Newton Kortwright (Hylands House, Chelmsford, Essex), with clerical son Frederick Tufnell.

TUFNELL (Samuel Joliffe) Born 1/12/1773, s. George Forster Tufnell and Mary Farhill. Trinity, Cambridge 1792, BA1796, p98 (London for Chester), MA1800. PC. Nun Monkton, Yorks. 1798-1809 (res.), R. West Stoke, Sussex 1803-4, V. North Mundham, Sussex 1803-50, V. (and patron) of Hunston, Sussex 1803-50, Firle Prebend in Chichester Cathedral 1804 to death. Dom. Chap. to 4th Viscount Midleton 1803. Died 7/11/1850 [C123377] Married North Mundham 7/3/1811 Charlotte Diggins (of Chichester), one dau.

TUGWELL (Lewis) Bapt. Bradford on Avon, Som. 2/1/1802, s. George Hayward Tugwell and Sarah Clutterbuck. BNC, Oxford 1819, BA 1823, dn24 (Salis.), MA1825, p26 (Lin. for York). V. Longridge Deverill >< w. Crockerton, Wilts. 1829. Lived latterly in the Royal Hotel, Bath; probably died 1880 [C77795. YCO] Married Nottingham 25/7/1827 Sarah Godfrey, with issue.

TUNNICLIFF (Francis) From Etwall, Derbys., s. James Tunnicliff [*pleb.*]. Trinity, Oxford 1792 (aged 17), BA1796, dn98 (C&L), p01 (C&L). R. Hartshorne, Derbys. 1803 [vacant in ERC] to death 14/8/1832 (CCEd says 8/3/1833) [C20112] Married Hartshorne 28/1/1806 Frances Sophia Taylor, with issue.

TUNSTALL (Matthew) [NiVoF] dn90 (Chester), p91 (Chester). S/M Bolton cum Redmire, Yorks. 1798; PC. Belper, Derbys. 1807-44, PC. Turnditch, Derbys. 1807. Died 1844 (4th q.) aged 79 [C20113]

TURBERVILLLE (George) Bapt. Tewkesbury, Glos. 21/10/1756, s. George Turberville (and Mrs Elizabeth Ellis?). Trinity, Oxford 1779, dn79 (Glos.), p85 (Ox.), BA1787, MA 1787. V. Hanley Castle, Worcs. 1789 (w. S/M Hanley Castle G/S 1790), V. Eldersfield, Worcs. 1810-13 (res.), R. Bromsberrow, Glos. 1812-23, R. Whichford, Warwicks. 1823 to death. Dom. Chap. to 1st Earl of Beauchamp 1810-23. Died 27/8/1839 [C159511] Married Bristol 16/11/1780 Elizabeth Osborne, with issue. *J.P.*

TURBUTT (Richard Burrow) Born Morton, Derbys. 19/5/1770, s. William Turbutt and Elizabeth Burrow. BNC, Oxford 1790, BA1794, dn94 (C&L), p95 (C&L). R. Morton 1795 (w. Brackenfield, Derbys. 1808-24) to death 30/1/1841 [C20115. Austin 126 notes this 'very slovenly man' and his filthy church - 'filthy even to disgust'] Married City of London 8/8/1802 Isabella Sharpe, with clerical son Richard Tarbutt.

TURMINE (Henry) Bapt. Canterbury 29/1/1784, s. Noah Turmine and Susanne Briault. Sidney, Cambridge 1806, BA1811, dn11 (Bristol), p12 (Salis. for Cant.), MA1814. PC. Minster (in Sheppey), Kent 1819 to death 4/12/1846 [C54057] Married Chatham, Kent 19/1/1823 Susannah Atkinson.

TURNER, *later* **FARLEY (Charles)** From Lambeth, Surrey, s. George Matthew Turner and Frances Melton. Magdalene, Cambridge 1818 (aged 24), BA1822, dn22 (London), dn23 (London), MA1825. R. Eastham w. Orleton, Worcs. 1830-[38]. Lived at Moor Hall, Stourport, Worcs. Died (a bachelor) Calverley Park, Tunbridge Wells, Kent ['a gated villa development'] 16/5/1867 aged 65, leaving £45,000 [C123381] Took the name Farley 1848.

TURNER (Daniel) Born Meerbrook, Staffs. 3/3/1799, s.Rev. James Turner and Mary Ashton. Literate: dn22 (Chester), p23 (Chester). PC. Endon, Staffs. 1832 to death 1864 (4th q.). No will traced [C20119] Married Leek, Staffs. 1843 (3rd q.) Ann Phillips. Brother James below.

TURNER (Edward) From Eton, Berks., s. Henry Turner. Pembroke, Oxford 1771 (aged 18), BA1774, dn75 (Ox.), p76 (Ox.), MA1777. R. Evedon, Lincs 1774 and R. Noke, Oxon. 1804 and to death 18/12/1836 [C21861]

TURNER (George) From Felpham, Sussex, s. Fulham Turner. Merton, Oxford 1776 (aged 18), then Christ Church BA1781, dn82 (Ox.), p83 (Ox.), MA1783. PC. Hook Norton, Oxon. 1783, PC. Drayton Chapel, Dorchester, Oxon. 1792, V. Spelsbury, Oxon. 1792 to death 1/12/1840 [C37985]

TURNER (George) Bapt. Pulham, Norfolk 14/4/1767, s. George and Mary Turner. Jesus, Cambridge 1783, BA1788, dn88 (Nor.), p93 (Nor.). R. Monewden, Suffolk 1803 and R. Kettleburgh, Suffolk 1806 to death 9/11/1839 aged 72 [C115847. LBSO] Had issue.

TURNER (James) Bapt. Meerbrook, Staffs. 28/5/1797, s. Rev. James Turner, sen. and Mary Ashton. Christ Church, Oxford 1816, BA1820, MA1823. PC. Meerbrook 1826 to death 29/10/1863, leaving £2,000 [C20124] Married Elizabeth Cruso (w). Brother Daniel above.

TURNER (John) From Sherston, Wilts., s. Rev. Thomas Turner. Pembroke, Oxford 1792 (aged 17), BA1796, dn98 (Nor. for Salis.), MA 1799, p99 (Bristol). V. Sherston Magna w. Sherston Parva, Wilts. 1802-30 (res.), R. Luckington, Wilts. 1821 and V. Horton, Glos. 1830 to death 14/5/1848 [C137020] J.P.

TURNER (John) From Clent, Staffs., s. John Turner. Oriel, Oxford 1793 (aged 17), BA1796, dn99 (Glos.), MA1801, p03 (Bristol). R. Hagley, Worcs. 1804, Inc. Halesowen St Kenelm, Staffs. 1836 to death 13/1/1847 [C54065] Had issue.

TURNER (John) From Little Wenlock, Shropshire, s. Rev. John, sen. and Ann Turner. St John, Cambridge 1801, BA1806, dn06 (Lin.), p08 (Lin.). V. Hennock, Devon 1828 to death 5/11/1846 aged 67 [C77810] Married w. iaaue.

TURNER (John) Bapt. Cadbury, Devon 23/11/1791, s. John Turner and Mary Tremlett. Sydney, Cambridge 1812, 'expelled from the University 1815', dn15 (B&W), p15 (B&W). R. Chelwood, Som. 1817-29, R. Stoke Pero, Som. 1829-55, V. Corston, Som. 1829, R. Ashbrittle, Som. 1829 to death 11/2/1855, aged 63 [C40755] Married (1) Okehampton, Devon 5/4/1817 Caroline Mary Hawkes (d.1850), 6 ch. (2) Tiverton, Devon 1851 (4th q.) Mrs Isabella Mary Alder, with further issue.

TURNER (John Fisher) Bapt. Exeter 11/10/1805, s. Thomas Turner and Harriott Hodge. Christ Church, Oxford 1824, then Worcester 1825-9, BA1828, dn28 (Ex.), p29 (Ex.), MA1834. R. Exeter St Mary Major 1829-56, V. Winkleigh, Devon 1856 to death 1/12/1871 aged 66, leaving under £600 [C146533] Married Devon 1832/3 Emily Arthur (w), with issue.

TURNER (Richard) Born Great Yarmouth, Norfolk 18/10/1751, s. Rev. Francis Turner and Sarah Dawson. Pembroke, Cambridge 1777 (a Ten Year Man, BD1787), dn78 (Nor.), p79 (Nor.). R. Sweffling, Norfolk 1785-1835, Prebend of Empringham in Lincoln Cathedral 1796-1835, PC. Great Yarmouth 1800-30, V. Ormesby St Margaret and Ormesby St Michael w. Scratby, Norfolk 1813 death 13/10/1835 [C77826] Married (1) Great Yarmouth 30/8/1773 Frances Kentish (d.1777) (2) Beccles, Suffolk 20/3/1783 Elizabeth Rede (d.1805), w. clerical s. Joseph Richard Turner (3) Great Yarmouth 30/12/1817 Sarah Parish (a clergy dau.). Port. online.

TURNER (Samuel) Born Caistor, Lincs. 28/12/1755, s. John and Mary Turner. Queens', Cambridge 1772, BA1777, dn78 (Ely), p80 (Lin.), MA1780. R. Low Toynton, Lincs. 1782-7, R. Rothwell, Lincs. 1783-1835, V. Attenborough w. Bramcote, Notts. 1790-1835, R. West Torrington, Lincs. 1794 and V. Tealby, Lincs. 1816 to death. Dom. Chap. to 5th Earl of

Scarborough 1783. Died 9/3/1835 (CCEd says 16/5/1835) [C77820. Kaye] He lodged as a bachelor at 'The George Inn' at Caistor, marrying the landlord's widow (a former barmaid) Barbara Bullock, *s.p.* Great-uncle of the Tennyson brothers (born Turner), of whom Charles Tennyson became his heir.

TURNER (Samuel) Born Nettleton House, Caistor, Lincs. 1/3/1797, s. Samuel Turner and Mary Swan. University, Oxford 1816, BA1820, dn20 (York for Lin.), p21 (Lin.). MA1822. R. Nettleton, Lincs. 1823 and V. Cadney cum Howsham, Lincs. 1823 to death 1/5/1877, leaving £30,000 [C77822. YCO] Married Binbrook, Lincs. 21/6/1832 Margaret Wright (w), their son changing his surname to Wright.

TURNER (Samuel Blois) Born Bloomsbury, London 12/12/1805, s. Thomas Turner (physician) and Lucretia Grace Blois (dau. of a baronet w. West Indian connections). Pembroke, Cambridge 1824, BA1828, dn29 (Nor.), p30 (Nor.). PC. Little Linstead (Linstead Parva) 1832-61, PC. Great Linstead (Linstead Magna), Lincs. 1838-61, R. South Eltham, Lincs. 1861 to death 1/11/1882 aged 77, leaving £2,771-0s-11d. [C115850] Married Hethersett, Norfolk 20/10/1835 Marian Day, 2 ch. (2) Halesworth, Suffolk 7/1/1852 Marian Hankinson; clerical sons Thomas Day Turner, and Samuel Hankinson Turner.

TURNER (Stagg) Bapt. Bolton, Cumberland 14/5/1775, s. John and Ann Turner. Trinity, Cambridge 1794, dn00 (Car.), p00 (Car.). S/M Bassenthwaite, Cumberland 1800, PC. Rennington w. Rock, Northumberland 1822 to death 25/1/1834 aged 59 [C5658]

TURNER (William) From Whitchurch, Shropshire, s. William Turner. Christ Church, Oxford 1809 (aged 17), BA1813, dn15 (Chester), MA1816, p16 (Chester for Chich.). V. Chidham, Sussex 1823-33, Seaford Prebend in Chichester Cathedral 1832-57, R. New Fishbourne, Sussex 1833. Died 19/11/1857 [C70950]

TURNER (William Hamilton) Bapt. Cambridge 5/6/1803, s. Rev. Joseph Turner (Master of Pembroke College) and Mary Derbyshire. Pembroke, Cambridge 1819, BA 1824, dn26 (Nor.), MA 1827, p27 (Nor.). V. Dilham w. Honing, Norfolk 1828-30, R. Barley, Herts. 1831-8, V. Banwell, Som. 1838 to death 21/6/1896, leaving £10,932-6s-10d. [C109521] Married Bury St Edmunds, Suffolk 10/6/1823 Emily Blackley, with issue.

TURNER A'BECKETT (Thomas) see under **A'BECKETT**

TURNOR (Charles) Born Stoke Rochford, Grantham, Lincs., s. Edmund Turnor. Trinity, Cambridge 1787, BA1791, dn91 (York), p94 (London for Peterb.), MA1794. V. Kirmond-le-Mire, Lincs. 1794-1825 (res.), V. Timberland, Lincs. 1799-1802, R. Holton cum Beckering, Lincs. 1800-02, V. Wendover, Bucks. 1802-36, V. Deeping St James 1811-18 (res.), Prebend of Sutton in Marisco in Lincoln Cathedral 1818-53, V. Milton Ernest, Beds. 1825-32 (res.). Latterly of Cheltenham. Dom. Chap. to 1st Baron Carrington 1800-25. Died Leamington, Warwicks. 12/1/1853 [C77848. YCO. Boase] Had issue. *F.R.S.* (1839), *F.R.A.S.*, *F.S.A.* 'Presented certain [Isaac] Newton material to the Royal Society and erected an obelisk to Newton in the park at Stoke Rochford, 1847'.

TURNOUR (Adolphus Augustus, Hon.) Born London 31/8/1789, s. Charles, Edward, 2nd Earl Winterton and Jane Chapman. Queen's, Oxford 1810 (but at United College, St Andrews University 1811- 12), no degree, dn13 (Nor.), p14 (Nor.). 'Perpetual V'. Docking, Norfolk 1817-19 (res.), R. Garveston, Norfolk 1825-8 (res.), V. Besthorpe, Norfolk 1825, R. Little Melton, Norfolk 1830-2 (res.), R. Tatterset w. Tatterford, Norfolk 1832 to death 5/3/1857. Dom. Chap. to Bishop of Norwich 1814 [C1220. Smart] Married 9/11/1812 Janet Dewar (dau. of an Edinburgh surgeon), w. clerical s. of same name.

TURTON (Henry) Bapt. Eccleshall, Staffs. 7/6/1785, s. John Turton (Sugnall Hall, Staffs.) and Mary Meysey. [Officer in Indian Army 1803-15 (retired)]. Sidney, Cambridge 1815, BA1820, dn20 (Chester), p20 (Chester), MA 1824. PC. Betley, Staffs. 1820 to death 25/10/1861, leaving £4,000 [C20132] Married (1) Newcastle under Lyme, Staffs. 28/1/1830 Harriet Elizabeth Northen (d.1834), with issue (2) Mortlake, Surrey 19/8/1838 Amelia St George Smyth, with further issue.

TURTON (Thomas, *later* **Bishop of Ely)** Born Hatfield, Yorks. 25/2/1780, s. Thomas Turton and Ann Harn. Queens', Cambridge 1801, then St Catharine's 1804, Fellow 1806,

BA1805 [Senior Wrangler], Tutor 1807. MA 1808, dn13 (Nor.), p13 (Nor.), BD1816, DD 1828 Lucasian Professor of Mathematics, Cambridge 1822-6, Regius Professor of Divinity, Cambridge (w. Prebend of Heydor w. Halton in Lincoln Cathedral) 1827-42, R. Gimingham w. Trunch, Norfolk 1826-33, R. Somersham, Hunts. [net income £1,770] 1827-42, Dean of Peterborough, 1830-42 (w. 2nd Prebend of Peterborough Cathedral 1830 only), Dean of Westminster 1842-5, Bishop of Ely 1845 to death (unm.) 7/1/1864, leaving £40,000 (mainly to charities, as Thomas Ely) [C77852. ODNB. Boase] Polemical writer; composer.

TUSON (George Baily) Born Langport, Som. 9/4/1788, s. George Baily and Frances Baily. Trinity Hall, Cambridge 1815 (a Ten Year Man, BD1825), p16 (London for Roch.). V. Huish Episcopi w. Langport 1824-39, R. Little Stanmore, Middx. 1850 to death. Chap. Royal Artillery, Woolwich 1839-49. Died (Hanham, Bristol) 25/4/1868 aged 80, leaving £1,000 [C569] Married East Barnet, Herts. 12/6/1811 Letitia Dodge, with issue.

TWEDDELL (Robert) Born Haydon Bridge, Northumberland 2/10/1772, s. Francis Tweddell and Jane Westgarth. Trinity, Cambridge 1792, BA1796, MA1799, dn00 (York for Chester), p01 (Chester). V. Lyddington w. Caldecote, Rutland 1827-30, V. Halton, Runcorn, Cheshire 1830 to death 3/7/1850 [C77858. YCO] Married 1818 Eliza Smyth, Limerick (a clergy dau., 'then residing at Chorlton Hall, Manchester'), with issue.

TWEED (Joseph) Bapt. Capel and Little Wenham, Suffolk 2/5/1787, s. the Rev. Joseph Tweed, sen. and Sarah Powell. Caius, Cambridge 1804 (aged 17), BA1810, dn10 (Nor.), p11 (Nor.). R. Hintlesham, Suffolk 1819-22 (res.), (succ. his father as) R. Capel St Mary w. Little Wenham 1828 to death 14/6/1867, leaving £800 [C115852] Married Capel 31/5/1828 Caroline Frances Barthorp (Hollesley, Suffolk), with issue.

TWENTYMAN (Joseph) Born Carlisle 29/5/1804, s. Joseph Twentyman and Elizabeth Wilson. St Bees?: dn27 (York), p28 (York). Curate Thornes, Wakefield, Yorks. 1831-8, Minor Canon Carlisle Cathedral 1838-43 (license revoked by the Bishop for drinking). Died Carlisle 13/2/1854 aged 49 (having crashed his gig - Platt says while drunk) [C135786. YCO.

Platt] Married (1) Thornes 16/10/1826 Mary Burgess (d.1833) (2) Carlisle 4/9/1838 Arabella Fawcett (a clergy dau.), with issue. In 1851 living alone in a Kendal hotel.

TWIGG (William) Born Scurff Hall, Drax, Yorks. 23/4/1796, s. William Twigg and Betty Dowson. Trinity, Cambridge 1814, BA1818, MA1821, dn21 (Ely), p22 (Ely). V. Pickhill, Yorks. 1825 to death 13/6/1859 aged 63, leaving £7,000 [C109522] Married Whitby, Yorks. 6/7/1849 Mary Younghusband, with issue.

TWINING (Daniel) Bapt. Twickenham, Surrey 4/8/1777, s. Richard Twining (of Isleworth, London, and a member of the tea importing family) and Mary Aldred. Pembroke, Cambridge 1795, BA1800, dn00 (Salis.), p01 (Salis.), MA1803, Fellow 1803, etc. R. Stilton, Hunts. 1806-52, R. Therfield, Herts. 1832 to death there. Dom. Chap. to Duke of Sussex 1832. Died 5/3/1853 aged 75 [C77871] Married 5/6/1810 Jane Wing (Thorney Abbey, Cambs.).

TWISLETON (Charles Samuel, Hon.) Born Ceylon 4/7/1806, s. Hon. & Ven. Thomas James Twisleton (Archdeacon of Colombo, Ceylon) and Anne Ashe. Balliol, Oxford 1824, BA1828, dn29 (C&L), p30 (C&L), MA1831. R. Ashow, Warwicks. 1831-65. Died Kenilworth, Warwicks. 13/9/1890 aged 84, *s.p.*, leaving £78,028-19s-0d. [C20139] Married (1) Marylebone, London 26/9/1837 Caroline Carr (d.1873) (2) Kenilworth 24/1/1878 Susan Dorothea Thicknesse-Touchet (w). Brother below. 'Granted the rank of a baron's younger son'.

TWISLETON, *later* TWISLETON-WYKEHAM-FIENNES, 16th Baron Saye and Sele (Frederick Benjamin) Born Gayton, Northants. 4/7/1799, s. Ven. the Hon. Thomas James Twisleton (Archdeacon of Colombo, Ceylon) and Anne Ashe. New, Oxford 1817, BCL1826, DCL1832. R. Broadwell w. Adelstrop, Glos. 1825-52, Master of St Ethelbert's Hospital [almshouses], Hereford 1844, Prebend of Eigne and Canon Residentiary Hereford Cathedral 1849 and Archdeacon of Hereford 1863 to death 26.5/1887 aged 87, leaving £14,122-6s-5d. Lived at Broughton Castle, Banbury, Oxon. [C165995. F. as Fiennes] Married (1) Cheriton, Kent 4/6/1827 Hon. Emily Wingfield (dau. 4th Viscount Powerscourt, she d.1837), with clerical sons Cecil Brownlow, and Wingfield Stratford Twistleton-Wykeham-Fiennes (2) Adelstrop 18/8/1857 Hon. Caroline Leigh (dau. 1st Baron Leigh of Stoneleigh). Assumed the title 1847 (but some authors call him 10th or 13th Baron); name changed 1849. Brother above. Port. online.

TWOPENNY, TWOPENY (Richard) Born Rochester, Kent 11/8/1757, s. William Twopenny and Charlotte Soan. Oriel, Oxford 1773, BA1777, MA1780, dn80 (Ox.), p83 (Glos. for Peterb.), BD? V. Little Casterton, Rutland 1783-1843, V. Allhallows, Kent 1795, V. North Stoke, Oxon. 1829 to death. Dom. Chap. to 11th Baron Teynham 1781. Died 23/11/1843 aged 87 [C1496] Married Ifley, Oxon. 19/10/1786 Margaret Nowell, w. issue (inc. Rev. Richard Twopeny). Port. online.

TWOPENY, TWOPENNY (David) Bapt. Rochester, Kent 12/1/1803, s. Edward and Susanna Twopeny. Oriel, Oxford 1820, BA 1824, dn25 (London), MA1827, p27 (London). V. Stockbury, Kent 1831 to death (St Leonards on Sea, Sussex) 22/10/1875, leaving £6,000 [C1497] Married Little Casterton, Rutland 29/5/1834 Mary Twopeny [*thus*].

TWYFORD (Charles Edward) Bapt. Trotton, Surrey 28/7/1788, s. Samuel Twyford (of Wotton Place, Midhurst, Sussex) and Susanna Charlotte Callaway. Emmanuel, Cambridge 1805, LLB1811, dn12 (Win.), p13 (Salis. for Win.). R. Trotton 1813-50. Probate granted 23/8/1850 [C70958] Married Fareham, Sussex 7/2/1828 Georgina Purvis (dau. of the naval Secretary to Earl Howe and Earl St Vincent), with issue.

TYLDEN (Richard Osborne) Born Milstead, Kent 25/9/1783, s. Richard Tylden and Mary Rolphe. Caius, Cambridge 1802, BA1806, dn06 (Cant.), Fellow 1806-10, p07 (Cant.), MA1809. V. Chilham, Kent 1809-62, R. Milstead, Kent 1819-21 (res.). Died 2/3/1862, leaving £1,000 [C159522] Married (1) Lynsted, Kent 11/12/1809 Frances Fairman (d.1849, 2nd q.), and had issue (2) Brompton, London 6/5/1852 Harriet Leonora Frances Ireland (w), with further issue.

TYLER (James Endell) Born Monmouth 30/1/1789, s. James Tyler and Ann Endell. Oriel, Oxford 1805, BA1809, Fellow 1811-28, MA1813, dn13 (Glos.), p14 (Ox.), BD1823, Tutor 1818-26, etc. PC. Moreton Pinckney, Northants. 1818-27 (res.), R. St Giles in the Fields, London 1826, Canon of St Paul's Cathedral, London 1845 to death 5/10/1851 [C21866. Boase] Married Dixton Newton, Monmouth 18/4//1827 Elizabeth Ann Griffin, and had issue.

TYLEY (James) Bapt. Streatley, Beds. 4/1/1776, s. Rev. Edward Tyley and Penelope Smyth. St John's, Cambridge 1794 (did not reside), then Trinity, Oxford 1794 (aged 18), BA1799, dn99 (Peterb.), p99 (Peterb.). R. (and patron) of Great Addington, Northants. 1799-1830 and V. 1832-56, R. Claydon w. Akenham, Suffolk 1830-2. Died 2/5/1856 [C111544] Wife Mary.

TYNDALE (Thomas George) Born Bathford, Som. 17/6/1777, s. George Booth and Elizabeth Annesley. Trinity, Oxford 1795, BA1799, dn00 (Salis.), p01 (Salis.), MA1802. V. Wooburn, Bucks. 1805, V. Tadlow, Cambs. 1811-20, R. Holton, Oxon. 1820-56. Dom. Chap. to 14th Viscount Hereford 1815. Died Oxford 19/5/1865, leaving £1,500 [C21868] Married Swallowfield, Berks. 22/2/1809 Mary Anne Earle, with clerical son Henry Annesley.

TYNDALL (George) Born Bristol 11/11/1798, s. Thomas Tyndall and Marianne Schimmelpenning (*q.v.* ODNB). Christ Church, Oxford 1815, BA1819, then Merton, Fellow 1823-40, MA1824, dn26 (Ox.), p26 (Ox.), etc. PC. Holywell, Oxford (o/w Oxford St Cross) 1828, R. Lapworth, Warwicks. 1839 to death 23/2/1848 [C21867]

TYNER (William) Born Croydon, Surrey 22/4/1763, s. William Tyner. St John's, Cambridge 1781, BA1785, dn96 (Lin.), p97 (Salis.), MA1806. V. Compton w. Up Marden, Sussex 1815 to death (Lee Park, Blackheath, Sussex, the home of his son in law) 26/9/1854 [C70962] Married (1) Portsea, Hants. 16/2/1792 Nancy Maria Howell (d.1806), and had issue (2) 25/4/1811 Sarah Colston.

TYRELL, TYRRELL (Charles Tysson Jenner) Born Lowestoft, Suffolk 22/6/1804, s. Sir John Tyrell, 1st Bart. (Boreham House, Essex) and Sarah Tysson. Oriel, Oxford 1821, BA1825. R. Midley, Kent 1833 and R. Buckland Feversham, Kent 1833 [both vacant in ERC] to death (Pimlico, London) 3/11/1858, leaving £459 [C123395] Married Lowestoft 19/8/1805

Elizabeth West, with issue. Name Jenner added 1828.

TYRWHITT (James Bradshaw) Born Pentre, Carmarthen, s. John Tyrwhitt and Sophia Dymoke. Jesus, Cambridge 1824, re-adm. 1827, BA1828. R. Wilksby, Lincs. 1831 and R. Claxby Pluckacre, Lincs. 1838 to death (Arundell, Sussex) 24/1/1873 aged 66, leaving £1,500 [C77882. *Notices and remains of the family of Tyrwhitt* (*c.*1872)] Married Petersham, Surrey 25/1/1827 Anne Frances Barrett.

TYRWHITT (Thomas) Born Astley Abbotts, Shropshire 11/1/1802, s. Richard Tyrwhitt and Elizabeth Lipyatt. Christ Church, Oxford 1819, BA1823, dn25 (Bristol), p26 (Bristol). Prebend of Gillingham Minor in Salisbury Cathedral 1828-49, V. Turnworth, Dorset 1830 and V. Winterbourne Whitchurch, Dorset 1830 to death (Den Haag, Holland) 11/8/1849 [C52612] Married Henstridge, Som. 20/6/1837 Margaret Anne Bridges, w. issue.

TYRWHITT-DRAKE (George) see under **DRAKE**

TYSON (Edward) Bapt. Eskdale, Cumberland 6/7/1771, s. Thomas Tyson and Esther Russell. Literate: dn94 (Chester), p95 (Chester). PC. Seathwaite, Kirkby Ireleth, Lancs. 1802 to death 3/9/1854 aged 83 [C170769] Married (1) Garstang, Lancs. 22/10/1793 Betty Varlow (2) Eskdale 27/1/1806 Elizabeth Porter, with issue,

TYSON (John) Bapt. Egremont, Cumberland 24/7/1784, s. William and Dorothy Tyson. Literate: dn07 (Carlisle for York), p08 (York). H/M Anchorage School, Gateshead 1809-15-; V. Merrington, Durham 1831 to death 19/7/1864 aged 80, leaving £600 [C110819. YCO] Married Beckermet, Cumberland 31/7/1809 Mary Smith, with issue. 'The Rev. Tyson will always be remembered in Merrington for his prodigious appetite'.

UHTHOFF (Henry) Born London 19/7/1758, s. Henry Uhthoff (a German merchant from Bremen) and Anna Maria Cornelia Vanneck (dau. of a baronet). Emmanuel, Cambridge 1776, BA1781, dn82 (Nor.), p82 (Nor.). R. Huntingfield w. Cookley, Norfolk 1782 and R. Aldham, Norfolk 1782 to death 9/2/1848 [C115858] Married Bloomsbury, London 22/10/1783 Mary Farrer (dau. of a lawyer), with issue.

UMPLEBY (John) Bapt. Heslington, York 3/11/1761, s. William and Cicely Umpleby. Lincoln, Oxford 1780, BA1784, dn84 (Ox. for York), p86 (Ox. for York). V. Pannal, Yorks. 1789-1816, PC. Airmyn, Yorks. 1798 to death, V. Yarburgh, Lincs. 1813-34 (res.). Died 26/2/1839 aged 77 [C37992. YCO] Married Pannal 18/8/1796 Ann Crosby, with clerical son.

UNDERWOOD (John Hanmer) Bapt. Ross-on-Wye, Heref. 6/3/1803, s. Rev. Thomas Underwood (below) and Elizabeth Mary Morgan. BNC, Oxford 1819, BA1823, dn26 (Herf.), p27 (Heref.), MA1825. V. Bosbury, Heref. 1830 and Prebend of Hereford Cathedral 1850 to death 30/8/1856 [C174282] Married Exeter 14/6/1832 Harriet Smith Dowell.

UNDERWOOD (Thomas) Bapt. Hereford 18/3/1772, s. Richard Underwood and Elizabeth Mary Edwards. Merton, Oxford 1790, BA1794, MA1796. V. Pipe and Lyde, Heref. 1801-14 (res.), R. Ross-on-Wye, Heref. [net income £1,284] 1801, Prebend of Wellington in Hereford Cathedral 1800-39 (Residentiary Canon 1804-39), V. Fownhope and Woolhope, Heref. 1814-21 (res.), V. Wellington, Heref. 1826, V. Upton Bishop, Heref. 1831 [to death] 24/8/1839 Dom. Chap. to 1st Earl of Yarborough 1801; to Catherine, Countess de la Warr 1801; to Bishop of Gloucester and Hereford 1803-31; to Bishop of Bristol 1813 [C137022] Married Woolhope, Heref. 3/1/1801 Elizabeth Mary Morgan (a clergy dau.), 14 ch. including clerical sons Thomas, and John Hamner (above). Port. online.

UNWIN (Edward) Bapt. Great Baddow, Essex 19/5/1767, s. James Unwin and Frances Stephenson. Pembroke, Oxford 1784, BA1788, MA1792, dn92 (C&L for Salis.), p94 (Salis.). V. Buckland, Berks. 1802-05, V. Derby St Werburgh 1809 to death 18/11/1847 [C20143] Married (1) Marylebone, London 19/6/1809 Elizabeth Preston (d.1843), with issue (2) Marylebone, London 26/7/1843 Penelope Sarah Ellis.

UNWIN (Joseph Rolling) Bapt. Pleasley, Derbys. 6/8/1797, natural son of Elizabeth Unwin. Literate: dn24 (Chester for York), p24 (York). PC. Langar-cum-Barnestone, Notts. 1824 - resigned as rector in 1834 ('a broken man'), he 'lived for a few years in poverty until, on Saturday 13 May 1837, he walked to Nottingham, sold his spoons, which was all he had left, for £5. The next morning he was found dead, drowned in the Nottingham canal' [C135787. YCO]

UPJOHN (Thomas) Bapt. Launceston, Cornwall 13/5/1766, s. Thomas Upjohn and Charlotte Anna Rouse. Pembroke, Oxford 1784, dn88 (Ex.), BA1789, p90 (Ex.). R. Honeychurch, Devon 1832-43, R. Highbray, Devon 1836 to death 2/5/1843 [C146558] Married Othery, Som. 6/6/1793 Elizabeth Rose, with issue.

UPJOHN (William) Bapt. Laleham, Middx. 3/4/1774, s. Robert Upjohn [*pleb.*] and Sarah Glover. St Edmund Hall, Oxford 1801, dn04 (Nor.), BA1805, p05 (Nor.), MA1820. R. Field Dalling, Norfolk 1811 and V. Binham, Norfolk 1822 to death 10/7/1855 [C115860] Married Field Dalling 1/11/1824 Anna Maria Lecount, with issue.

UPPLEBY (William) Born Barrow upon Humber, Lincs. 4/4/1764, s. John Uppleby and Dorothy Crowle. Sidney, Cambridge 1780, BA 1784, dn84 (Lin.), p85 (Lin.), MA1787. V. Wootton, Lincs. 1785-1803, V. Barton upon Humber, Lincs. 1789 to death 7/4/1834 (CCEd says 20/5/1834) [C77897] Married Barrow 30/1/1786 Margaret Midgley, and had issue.

UPTON (James) Bapt. Yeovil, Som. 26/6/1763, s. James Upton. Merton, Oxford 1779, BA 1783, dn84 (Lin. for Bristol), p87 (C&L for B&W). R. Beer Crocombe w. Stocklinch Magdalen, Som. 1787 to death 23/7/1844 aged 82 [C20144]

UPTON (Robert) Born Bramhope Manor, Leeds 17/9/1800, s. Thomas Everard Upton (solicitor) and Mary Bramley. Trinity, Cambridge 1818, BA1123, dn24 (York), p25 (York). PC. Moreton Say(e), Shropshire 1831-67, then V. 1867-74, then R. 1874 to death. Chap. to

Market Drayton Poor Law Union, Shropshire. Died 19/9/1881, leaving £1,397-10s-10d. (left unadministered) [C20146. YCO] Married Market Drayton 9/10/1838 Sally Emily Wilkinson (dau. of a naval Commander), and had issue (inc. a dau. Apelina).

URQUHART (Frederic) Born Gainsborough, Lincs. 5/12/1800, s. Rev. David Henry and Elizabeth Urquhart, BNC, Oxford 1820, BA 1824, dn24 (Bristol), p24 (Bristol), MA1826. R. West Knighton, Dorset 1829 to death (Paris) 22/12/1859, leaving £800 [C54073] Wife Margaret by 1829, w. clerical s. William. Brother below.

URQUHART (Henry John) Bapt. Gainsborough, Lincs. 12/6/1797, s. Rev. David Henry and Elizabeth Urquhart. BNC, Oxford 1817, then New, Fellow 1817-28, BA1821, MA1825. Min. Brighton Chapel Royal [then a Proprietary Chapel], Sussex 1831-4 (res.), V. Fleet, Dorset 1849-58. Lived latterly at Cheltenham, Glos. Died Eastbourne, Sussex 16/12/1862, leaving £300 [C70970] Married Lanark 9/7/1827 Hannah Urquhart [*sic*] (w), with issue. Brother above.

USKO (John Frederick) Königsberg University. A German Lutheran Minister, working mainly in Smyrna; dn08 (London), p08 (Win. for London). R. Orsett, Essex 1808. Died 31/12/1842 aged 81 [C108932. An exceptional linguist, his full and adventurous life is recorded in his autobiography *Narrative of the travels and literary life of Rev. John Frederick Usko, late Chaplain to the factory at Smyrna* (1808). A lengthy obituary in *Gentleman's Magazine*, which fails to mention his reception into the CoE] Married Henrietta Elizabeth Zimmermann (born Smyrna).

UTHWATT (William) see under **ANDREWES**

UTTERSON (Alfred Gibson) Bapt. Fareham, Wilts. 30/11/1792, s. John Utterson and Elizabeth Rowe. St John's, Oxford 1810, then St John's, Cambridge 1814, BA1815, MA1820. PC. Apuldram, Sussex 1818-20, R. Layer Marney, Essex 1828 to death (Frankfurt-on-Main, Hesse) 29/7/1841 aged 48 [C70971] Married Thornbury, Glos. 26/4/1829 Mary Susannah Kelso (of Kilmarnock), with issue.

UVEDALE (Robert) Bapt. Langton-by-Spilsby, Lincs. 13/1/1772, Rev. Robert Uvedale, sen. and Diana Langton. Trinity, Cambridge 1790, BA1795, dn96 (Lin.), p98 (Lin.), MA 1798. V. Fotherby, Lincs. 1808 and V. Hogsthorpe, Lincs. 1824 to death (Louth, Lincs.) 28/7/1846 [C77901] Brother below.

UVEDALE (Washbourne) Born and bapt. Langton by Spilsby, Lincs. 8/6/1777, s. Rev. Robert Uvedale and Diana Langton. Trinity, Cambridge 1796, BA1800, dn01 (Lin.), p02 (Lin.). PC. Markby, Lincs. 1808-33, V. Kirmond-le-Mire, Lincs. 1825 and V. Stixwold, Lincs. 1831 to death 2/4/1833 (CCEd thus) [C77902] Brother above.

VAILLANT (Philip) Bapt. Westminster, London 12/11/1767, s. Paul Vaillant and Theodosia Whichcott. Christ Church, Oxford 1784, BA1789, dn90 (Ox.), MA1791, p91 (Ox.). R. Stoke d'Abernon, Surrey 1801 to death there 14/5/1846 [C37997] Married Stoke 17/7/1805 Elizabeth Balchin, with issue.

VALE (William Humphrey) Bapt. Birmingham 2/8/1786, s. Humphrey and Ann Vale. Trinity, Cambridge 1811, then Magdalene 1813, BA1815, dn15 (Lin.), p17 (Lin.), MA1818. PC. Eccleshall Bierlow, Sheffield, Yorks. 1829-53, V. Tideswell, Derbys. 1858 to death (Wormhill, Derbys.) 26/6/1864, leaving £16,000 [C77903] Married Dronfield, Derbys. 4/9/1821 Emily Spencer.

VALENTINE (John) From Oadby, Leics. Emmanuel, Cambridge 1771, BA1775, dn75 (Lin.), p76 (Lin.). PC. Tintinhull, Som. 1816 to death. Probate 9/3/1847 [C40758 says d.1828 aged 76] Clerical son George M. Valentine. Confusion with another cleric of this name.

VALENTINE (Thomas) Bapt. Portsmouth, Hants. 16/12/1787, s. John Valentine and Mary Ann O'Farrell. Magdalen Hall, Oxford 1806, BA1810, MA1813. V. South Hayling, Sussex 1813-18, R. Nuthurst, Surrey 1817-19, 1822, R. Wanstrow, Som. 1818-23, V. Cocking, Essex 1823, Selsey Prebend in Chichester Cathedral 1824 to death (a widower) 6/3/1859, leaving £600. Dom. Chap. to Bishop of Chichester 1823 [C49788] Married West Dean, Sussex 3/12/1816 Anne Charlotte Webb, with issue.

VALLACK (Benjamin William Salmon) Bapt. St Budeaux, Cornwall 4/2/1804, s. William Vallack and Judith Smith. Exeter, Oxford 1821, BA1825, dn29 (Nor. for Bristol), p29 (Win. for Bristol). PC. St Budeaux 1832 to death 21/2/1875 aged 72, leaving £6,000 [C54074] Married '1834 Devon' Amelia Millett Rawle, with issue.

VALLANCEY (Henry Edward Francis) Born New Windsor, Berks. 26/9/1807, s. George Preston Vallancey and Isabella Humphries. King's, Cambridge 1827, Fellow 1830-49, BA 1831, dn31 (Lin.), MA1834, p35 (Chich. for Nor.). Curate Great Bricet, Suffolk 1832-8, PC. Wattisham, Suffolk 1832, (first) V. Sutton, St Helens, Lancs. 1849 to death. Chap. to first Bishop of Guiana 1843-9. Died 19/9/1888 aged 82, leaving £2,089-8s-5d. [C70972] Important article (w. photos.) also reveals a pair of twins with his housekeeper in 1831: www.suttonbeauty.org.uk/suttonhistory/vallancey/

VALPY (Richard) Born Jersey, Channel Islands. 7/12/1754, s. Richard Valpy and Catherine Chevalier. Pembroke, Oxford 1773, BA1776, dn77 (Heref.), p80 (Nor.), MA1784, BD and DD1792. S/M Bury St Edmunds 1777; 'very sucessful' H/M King Henry VII School Reading 1781-1836. R. Stradishall, Suffolk (non-res.) 1787 to death 28/3/1836 [C86914. ODNB as educationalist] Married (1) 1778 Mary Cornelius (d.1780) (2) Caversham, Oxon. 30/5/1782 Mary Benwell, and had issue.

VAN DER MEULEN (John) Born St Albans, Herts. 15/3/1778, s. Joseph Pomfret Van der Meulen and Susanna Hitch. Caius, Cambridge 1803, dn06 (Peterb. for Nor.), p06 (Nor.), LLB 1810. V. Messing, Essex 1807-19 (res.), V. Belchamp St Paul, Essex 1812 to death, Minor Canon or 10th Prebend of St Paul's Cathedral 1812-17. Priest in Ordinary 1814-15; Dom. Chap. to Lord Grimston. Died Versailles 6/5/1863, leaving £200 [C110548]

VAN MILDERT (William, Bishop of Llandaff, *then* of Durham) Born London 6/11/1765, s. Cornelius Van Mildert (a gin manufacturer of Dutch extraction, from Newington, Surrey) and Martha Hill. Queen's, Oxford 1784, BA1787, dn88 (Oxford), p89 (London)MA1790, BD and DD1813. R. Bradden, Northants. 1795-7, R. St Mary-le-Bow, City of London 1807, Dom Chap. to 4th Marquess of Queensbury and V. Farningham, Kent 1807-15. A conservative Regius Professor of Divinity (w. Canon of Christ Church Cathedral and R. Ewelme), Oxford 1813-20. Bishop of Llandaff (resident and conscientious) with Dean of St Paul's Cathedral *in commendam* 1820-6. Bishop of Durham 1826 to death. A militant conservative and last of the 'Prince Bishops', he founded the University of Durham to pre-empt government confiscation of his ecclesiastical revenues. Died Auckland Castle (his official residence) 21/2/1836 [C37998. E.H. Varley, *The last of the Prince-Bishops: William Van Mildert and the high church movement in the early nineteenth century* (1992). G.F.A. Best, 'The mind and times of William Van Mildert', *J. Theological Studies*, ns, 14 (1963), 355-70] Married 22/12/1795 Jane Douglas (dau. of general), *s.p.*

Fine drawing in D. Cross, *Joseph Bouet's Durham* … (Durham, 2005).

VANBRUGH (George) Born Lancashire c.1756. Queens', Cambridge 1775, dn79 (Chester), p81 (Chester), LLB1783. R. Aughton, Ormskirk, Lancs. 1786-1834 (res.), Prebendary of Timberscombe in Wells Cathedral 1825 to death. Dom. Chap. to 1st Baron Rivers 1785; Dom. Chap. to Bishop of Chester 1812. Died Waterloo, Liverpool 16/10/1847 aged 91 [C40761] Married Chester 23/2/1786 (or 1789) Frances Ravenscroft.

VANE (John) Born Durham, the natural son of 1st Duke of Cleveland (*or* 'the acknowledged natural son of Lord Castlereagh'). Trinity, Cambridge 1809, BA1814, Fellow of Magdalene 1814-23, dn15 (Ely), MA1817, p17 (Ely); Fellow of Dulwich College 1818-48. PC. Speeton, Yorks 1819-32, V. Wroxeter, Salop 1823-8, R. Wrington, Som. 1828-66 [patron: Duke of Cleveland, *thus*; entry blank in ERC], PC. Burrington, Wrington, Som. 1831 to death. Dom. Chap. to 5th Earl Cowper 1815; Chap. in Ordinary to 1831-70 (and Dep. Clerk of the Closet); Chap. to House of Commons 1835-9. Died (unm.) 29/12/1870 aged 80, leaving £45,000 [C20152. Boase]

VANE (Robert Morgan) Born Bilby Hall, Notts. 4/10/1785, s. Morgan Vane and Catherine Brookes. Emmanuel, Cambridge 1804, BA 1808, dn09 (Lin. for Peterb.), MA1811, p12 (Peterb.). R. Lowick, Northants. 1816 and R. Islip, Northants. 1816 to death. Dom. Chap. to Duke of Dorset. Died Margate, Kent 27/8/1842 aged 56 [C77940] Married Lowick, Northants. 24/7/1832 Sarah Tolson (Birkby, Cumberland), and had issue.

VANSITTART (Edward) see under **NEALE**

VANSITTART (William) Born Westminster, London 30/11/1779, s. Col. Arthur Vansittart and Hon. Ann Hanger (dau. 1st Baron Coleraine). Christ Church, Oxford 1798, BA 1802, dn03 (Ox.), p03 (Salis.), MA1805, BD and DD1826. R. and V. White Waltham w. Shottesbrooke >< Berks. 1803, Canon of 1st Prebend in Carlisle Cathedral 1824 to death. Master of Wigston Hospital [almshouses], Leicester Died 22/11/1847 [C3506] Married 11/2/1817 Charlotte Teresa Warde, and had issue.

VASHON (James Volvant) Bapt. Ludlow, Shropshire 17/4/1784, s. Admiral James Vashon and Jane Bethell. Oriel, Oxford 1802, BA1806, MA1810. R. (and patron) of Salwarpe, Worcs. 1808 to death 2/7/1845 [C122252] Married St Lawrence, Kent 21/11/1821 Mary Ann Mayhew, with issue.

VAUGHAN (Benjamin Kerr) Born Ireland, s. Benjamin Vaughan and Martha Kerr. Trinity, Oxford 1785 (aged 21), no degree, p87 (Ox.). V. Wilcote, Oxon. 1788-1810. R. Aveton Gifford, Devon 1788 to death (a widower) 12/1/1847 aged 87 [C38001] Married Lambeth, Surrey 9/12/1796 Julia Strachey.

VAUGHAN (James) Born Bristol, s. Richard Vaughan and Elizabeth Berrow. St Edmund Hall, Oxford 1794 (aged 20), BA1798, MA 1804. R. Wraxall, Som. 1801-57, R. Walton in Gordano, Som. 1824. Died 5/6/1857 [C40763] Married Bristol 1/1/1799 Sarah Protheroe, w. clerical s. of same name (*q.v.* Boase).

VAUGHAN (John) Born Bristol 28/10/1792, s. of John Vaughan (a shipping merchant) and Mary Biven. St John's, Cambridge 1820, re-adm. 1821, re-adm. again 1825, SCL1828, dn28 (Bristol), p28 (Nor.), DCL1844. R. Holmpton, Yorks. 1831-4, R. Upton Lovell, Wilts. 1834-41, PC. Brixton St Matthew, South London 1841-55. Died Regent's Park, London 24/2/1860, leaving £25,000 [C54075] Married Bristol 15 *or* 17/4/1817 Elizabeth Marychurch (w), with clerical issue. Indicted 1850 for 'feloniously inserting' a false burial entry into the parish register: www.oldbaileyonline.org › Deception › fraud

VAUGHAN (Thomas) Born Thruxton, Heref., s. Rev. Richard and Isabella Vaughan. Worcester, Oxford 1784 (aged 21), p88 (Heref.), BA1789. PC. Stoke Prior w. Docklow, Heref. 1788 to death 30/5/1840 (C174839]

VAUGHAN (Thomas) From Llanville, Brecon, s. William Vaughan [*pleb*]. Jesus, Oxford 1795 (aged 19), BA1799, dn99 (Oxford), p00 (Oxford), MA1803 R. Hope Bagot, Shropshire 1817, R. Billingsley, Shropshire 1823, R. Llantevailog, Brecon 1830, all to death 3/1/1855 [C20155]

VAUGHAN (William) Born Shrewsbury, Shropshire 1799, s. John Vaughan. St John's, Cambridge 1817, BA1822, dn23 (Heref.), p24

(Heref.), MA1825. PC. Astley, Warwicks. 1828-61, R. Pontesbury (3rd Portion), Heref. 1829 to death (Hinton Hall, Shropshire) 26/11/1866, leaving £2,000 [C32451. CR65 links]. Married Aldborough, Yorks. 4/6/1836 Jane Fletcher (Minskip Lodge, Boroughbridge, Yorks.) (w), with issue.

VAUGHTON (Roger Ryland) Bapt. Handsworth, Warwicks. 27/9/1790, s. Roger Vaughton and Elizabeth Hall. Emmanuel, Cambridge 1808, BA1812, dn13 (Chester), p14 (C&L), MA1815. V. Maxstoke 1814-18 (res.), R. Arley, Warwicks. 1815-49, R. Westborough (1st Mediety) w. Dry Doddington, Lincs. 1861-64-. Rented Yeldersley Hall, Derbys. 1850-61; then living at Regent's Park, London to death (Torquay, Devon) 25/6/1868, leaving £7,000 [C19999] Married Lincoln 1814 Elizabeth Wray, with issue.

VAUSE (John) Bapt. Wigan, Lancs. 29/8/1769, s. Rev. John Vause, sen. and Margaret Rainford. King's, Cambridge 1789, Fellow 1792-1800, BA1793, dn92 (Lin.), p93 (Nor.), MA 1796. S/M Eton College 1796-99; PC. Liverpool Christ Church 1800 (with Chap. of Donative of Garston, Lancs. 1812) to death 31/12/1835 at Boulogne (so in debt?) [C77916] Married Liverpool 5/3/1800 Ann Fisher (of Ditton Lodge, Lancs.).

VAUX (William) Bapt. Hackney, London 12/8/1784, s. Edward Vaux and Mary Johnson. Christ Church, Oxford 1803, BA1806, then Balliol, Fellow 1809-16, MA1810, dn10 (Ox.), p12 (Ox.), BD1826. R. Long Crichel, Dorset 1815-20, R. Sutton Waldron, Dorset 1816-22, R. Patching (and Sinecure R. 1823) w. West Tarring, Sussex 1822-44, Canon of 6th Prebend in Winchester Cathedral 1831-44, R. Romsey, Hants. 1834-[40]. Dom. Chap. to Bishop of Peterborough 1816; to Archbishop of Canterbury 1828. Died 30/12/1844 [C21876] Married Romsey 10/9/1839 Elizabeth Jane Loring, with issue.

VAVASOUR (Marmaduke) Bapt. Rochdale, Lancs. 29/3/1797, s. Thomas Hippon Vavasour and Penelope Smith. BNC, Oxford 1816, BA 1820, MA1822, dn22 (Glos.), p23 (Glos.). V. Ashby de la Zouche, Leics. 1833-75, PC. Smisby, Leics. 1834-75, Hon. Canon of Peterborough Cathedral 1851 to death (Clifton, Bristol) 6/11/1879, leaving £2,000 [C77918] Married Severn Stoke, Worcs. 19/10/1826 Mary Anne St John, with clerical son Francis Stukeley Vavasour.

VAVASOUR (Richard Frederick) Born Dublin, s. William Vavasour (advocate). TCD 1801 (aged 16), BA1806, MA1823, incorporated at Oxford 1834. R. Stow on the Wold, Glos. 1822 [blank in ERC] to death 27/1/1853 [C159239. Al.Dub.] Married Rochdale, Lancs. 1/7/1823 his cousin Julia Vavasour, and had issue.

VAWDREY (Gilbert) Born Moresbarrow Hall, Middlewich, Cheshire 28/12/1778, s. Daniel Vawdrey and Mary Seaman. [NiVoF]. PC. Wrenbury, Cheshire 1810 to death (unmarried) 4/2/1844 [C170781] Brother two below.

VAWDREY (William) Born Bristol 22/1/1771, s. George Vawdrey. St Edmund Hall, Oxford 1789, BA1793, dn93 (Heref.), p95 (Heref.). R. Kennerleigh, Devon 1811 to death 28/3/1838 [C174846]

VAWDREY (William) Born Moresbarrow Hall, Middlewich, Cheshire 28/3/1784, s. Daniel Vawdrey and Mary Seaman. Literate: p13 (Chester). PC. Burwardsley, Cheshire 1824, PC. Harthill, Cheshire 1833 to death 1850 (3rd q.) [C146564] Married by 1823 Frances Brabant, Middlewich, with issue. Brother, above.

VEALE (William) Bapt. Gulval, Cornwall 21/4/1782, S. Richard Veale and Mary Grigg. New, Oxford 1803, BA1806, dn08, p09, Fellow 1809-16, MA1819. V. Ashbrittle, Som. 1810-11, V. St Keverne, Cornwall 1817, V. Zennor, Cornwall 1824. Died 8/9/1867 aged 85, leaving £12,000 [C49803] Married Madron, Cornwall 23/4/1808 Loveday Tonkin, and had issue.

VECK (Henry Aubrey) Bapt. Bishop's Waltham, Hants. 16/4/1785, s. Richard Beck and Elizabeth Bulpett (?). Magdalen Hall, Oxford 1818, BA1822, dn22 (Win.), p23 (Lin. for Win.), MA1825. PC. Alverstoke, Hants. 1831 to death (Bishop's Waltham) 3/6/1866, leaving £1,500 [C77919] Married Portsea, Hants. 1/6/1837 Dorothy Barthomley.

VENABLES (James) From Londonderry, s. Thomas Venables. Worcester, Oxford 1796 (aged 17), then Corpus Christi BA1801, p05 (Cant.), MA1803. V. Buckland Newton, Dorset 1805 (and Canon of Salisbury Cathedral 1841) to death 18/12/1851 [C54078] Married Camden,

London 15/2/1821 Mary Caroline Lewis, with clerical sons Edmund Burke, and James Lewis Walker Venables.

VENABLES-VERNON, *later* **HARCOURT (Edward, Bishop of Carlisle,** *then* **Archbishop of York)** Born Sudbury Hall, Derbyshire 10/19/1757, s. George Venables-Vernon, 1st Baron Vernon, and Martha Harcourt. Christ Church, Oxford 1774, Fellow of All Souls 1778-83, BCL1780, dn81 (Ox.), p81 (Peterb.), DCL 1786. R. Sudbury (family living) 1782-1802, Canon of Christ Church 1785, Canon of Gloucester 1785-92, pastoral Bishop of Carlisle (aged 34) 1791-1808, Archbishop of York 1808 to death 5/11/1849 (from a chill following a fall from a bridge into a pond at Bishopthorpe Palace, York), leaving £66,000. In 1831 he inherited the estates (but not the title) of his cousin 3rd Earl Harcourt, and changed his name solely to Harcourt, moving to Nuneham Courtney House, Oxon. [C3508 under Vernon, ODNB - followed here under Venables-Vernon. Foster under Harcourt. A.M.G. Stephenson, 'Archbishop Vernon Harcourt', in *Studies in Church History* 4, ed. G.J. Cuming (Leiden, 1967)] Married 5/2/1784 Lady Anne Leveson-Gower (dau. 2nd Earl Gower, later 1st Marquess of Stafford), 16 ch. (including 3 sons here under Vernon).

VENN (Henry) Born Clapham, London 10/2/1796, s. Rev. John Venn and Katherine King. Queens', Cambridge 1814, BA1818, dn19 (Ely), Fellow 1819-29, p21 (Nor.), MA1821, etc., BD1828. R. Drypool, Hull, Yorks. 1827-34, R. St John, Holloway, London 1834-46, Prebend of Caddington Minor in St Paul's Cathedral 1846 [value £2] to death (East Sheen, Surrey) 13/1/1873 aged 76, leaving £6,000 [C109529. ODNB. Boase. DEB] Married North Ferriby, Yorks. 21/1/1829 Martha Sykes, with clerical son (and also John Venn, the logician). W. Knight, *Memoir of the Rev. Henry Venn, BD, Prebendary of St Paul's, and Honorary Secretary of the Church Missionary Society* (new edn. 1882) Evangelical leader; friend of Charles Simeon; highly efficient Hon. Sec. of Church Missionary Society in London 1841-73. Brother below.

VENN (John) Born Clapham, London 17/4/1802, s. Rev. John Venn, sen. and Katherine King. [Went to India as a cadet 1818-20, invalided home]. Queens', Cambridge 1823, BA1827, dn28 (London), p29 (London), Fellow 1829-34, MA1830. PC. Pinner, Middx. 1830-3, V. Hereford St Peter w. St Owen 1833-70, Prebend of Withington Parva in Hereford Cathedral 1843-68 (res.). Died unmarried 12/5/1890, leaving £7,399-13s-1d. [C123707] 'Provided a steam cornmill for the benefit of the poor and started an Industrious Aid Society'. Brother above.

VENOUR (John) Born Wellesbourne, Warwicks. 24/5/1768, s. John Venour and Catherine Landour. Worcester, Oxford 1785, BA1789, MA1792, dn93 (C&L), p96 (C&L for Wor.). R. Bourton on Dunsmore, Warwicks. 1818 to death 11/7/1839 [C20157] Married Sherborne, Dorset 1/3/1808 Maria Briggs, with issue.

VENTRIS (Edward) Bapt. Cambridge 9/9/1802, s. William Richmond and Mary Ventris. Peterhouse, Cambs. 1821, BA1825, dn25 (Lin. for Ely), p25 (Ely), MA1828. PC. Stow cum Quy, Cambs. 1825 to death. Sometime Chap. to Lord St Leonards; and to the County Gaol. Died Cambridge 12/9/1886 aged 85, leaving £1,963-19s-2d. [C77924] Married (1) Cambridge 6/7/1831 Mary Ann Raye (d.1833), with clerical son Edward Favell Ventris (2) West Hackney, London 19/11/1839 Elizabeth Sarah Bullen Nicholson, with further issue.

VENTRIS (James) Born Buddesden, Suffolk, s. Rev. Edward Ventris and Martha Elmis. St Mary Hall, Oxford 1778 (aged 18), then Magdalen 1781-6, BA1782, dn84 (Ox.), MA 1786, Fellow 1786-1814, BD1793. V. Upper Beeding, Sussex 1813 to death (Chawton, Hants.) 31/1/1841 [C38008] Married 22/8/1816 Jane Hinton.

VERELST (Arthur Charles) Born Aston Hall, Sheffield, Yorks. 5/12/1779, s. Harry Verelst (former Governor of Bengal, *H.E.I..S., q.v.* ODNB) and Anne Wordsworth. Clare, Cambridge 1800, dn02 (York), BA1802, p05 (York), MA1806. R. Withycombe, Som. 1819-42 and V. Wadworth, Yorks. 1820 to death. Dom. Chap. to 17th Earl of Erroll. Died 24/11/1842 [C40764. YCO] Married Wellington, Salop 4/4/1818 Charlotte Anne, dau. Col. William Charlton, Apley Castle, Shropshire, with issue. Brother below.

VERELST (William) Born Aston Hall, Sheffield, Yorks. 4/10/1784, s. Harry Verelst (a former Governor of Bengal, *H.E.I.C.S., q.v.* ODNB) and Anne Wordsworth. Pembroke,

Cambridge 1803, BA1807, then St Catharine's, Fellow 1807, MA1810, dn11 (B&W), p12 (B&W). V. Rauceby, Lincs. 1823-30, R. Grayingham, Lincs. 1820 to death. Dom. Chap. to 18th Earl of Erroll 1819. Died West Retford, Notts. 4/7/1851 [C49814] Married Darrington, Yorks. 1/5/1844 Sophia Lee (Grove Hall, Yorks.), *s.p.* Brother above.

VERNON, *later* **VERNON HARCOURT (Charles George Venables)** Born 14/11/1798, s. Edward Vernon (later Harcourt) (Bishop of Carlisle and later Archbishop of York, above) and Lady Anne Leveson-Gower (dau. of 1st Marquess of Stafford). Christ Church, Oxford 1816, BA1820, dn22 (York), p22 (York), MA 1822. R. Rothbury, Northumberland 1822-70 [income in CR65 £1,106] (and Preacher in and throughout the Diocese of Durham 1822), (Sinecure R. Headon, Notts. 1830-7), Prebend of Norwell Overhall in Southwell Collegiate Church 1830-48, Canon Residentiary (with 3rd Prebend) of Carlisle Cathedral 1837 [value £1,000] to death (Rothbury, unmarried) 10/12/1870 aged 72, leaving £18,000 [C6404 (blank) and YCO under Vernon, Foster under Harcourt] Brothers Leveson Venables Vernon, and William Venables Vernon, here.

VERNON (Henry Garioch) From Born Jamaica, s. Bowater Vernon. Queen's, Oxford 1777 (aged 18), dn81 (Wor.), BA1784, p84 (Ox.), MA1784. V. White Ladies Aston, Worcs. 1794-1808, R. London St Clement Danes 1795-1807, R. Great Bromley, Essex 1807 to death 12/6/1837 [C38010] Married St George's Hanover Square, London 28/6/1792 Henrietta Anne Warren, with clerical son Mark Henry (below).

VERNON (John) Born Belbroughton Worcs. 30/8/1802, s. Thomas Shrawley Vernon and Elizabeth Taylor. Emmanuel, Cambridge 1821, BA1826, dn--(Worc.), p--(Worc.). R. Shrawley, Worcs. 1827-62. Lived in Bayswater, London, then Potton, Beds. to death 6/12/1875 aged 73, leaving £800 [C122256 is confused with an Oxford namesake] Married Lillington, Warwicks. 6/10/1853 Mrs Elizabeth (Morris) Harris, with issue. Brother William, below.

VERNON, *or* **VENABLES VERNON (John [Sedley] Venables-, Hon.)** Bapt. 8/3/1789, s. 3rd Baron Vernon (Nuthall Hall, Notts.) and Alice Lucy Sedley. Christ Church, Oxford 1816, Student [Fellow] 1816-22, BA 1820, dn21 (York), p22 (Chester for York), MA1823. R. Molesworth, Hunts. 1822-6, R. Kirkby in Ashfield, Notts. 1829-75, R. Barton in Fabis, Notts. 1826-29, V. Dunham, Notts. 1829, Prebend of Dunham in Southwell Collegiate Church 1826 and V. Nuthall 1837 [total income £1,168] to death 12/12/1875 aged 78, leaving £16,000 [C77928. YCO] Married (1) Copgrave, Yorks. 24/11/1830 Frances Barbara Duncombe (d.1848), dau. of Lord Feversham, 1s. who died (2) Pimlico, London 15/12/1853 Caroline, dau. Gen. Hon. Sir Edward Paget.

VERNON, *later* **VERNON HARCOURT (Leveson Venables)** Born Sudbury, Derbys. 20/3/1788, s. Edward Vernon (later Harcourt), Bishop of Carlisle (later Archbishop of York, above) and Lady Anne Leveson-Gower (dau. of 1st Marquess of Stafford). Christ Church, Oxford 1806, BA1810, Student [Fellow] 1806-13, dn12 (York), p12 (York), MA1813. V. Sutton on the Forest, Yorks. 1812-13, R. Rothbury, Northumberland 1813-22, (Sinecure R. Kirby in Cleveland 1819), V. Stokesley, Yorks. [net income £1,220] 1822-35, V. Stainton in Cleveland 1824-33, Sub-Dean of York Minster 1826-7, Chancellor of York 1827-60 (w. Prebend of Laughton-en-le-Morthen annexed), Archdeacon of Cleveland 1828-32 (w. V. Stainton, Stockton on Tees, Yorks. 1828 annexed), R. Beckenham, Kent 1835-51. Died Newsells Park, Herts. 26/7/1860, leaving £40,000 [C6735, ODNB (port.), Foster under his father. YCO under Vernon. Boase under Harcourt] Married St George's Hanover Square, London 19/8/1815 Hon. Caroline Mary Peachey (w), dau. 2nd Baron Selsey, *s.p.* His brothers Charles George Vernon, and William Venables Vernon here. Surname added 1831.

VERNON (Mark Henry) Bapt. White Ladies Aston, Worcs. 3/9/1797, s. Rev. Henry Garioch Vernon (above) and Ann Warren. Trinity, Cambridge 1812, BA1817, dn21 (London), MA 1822, p22 (London). R. Colchester St Martin, Essex 1825-36, V. Lyminster, Sussex 1833-6, V. Westfield, Battle, Sussex 1836 to death 6/5/1881 aged 84, leaving £10,847-12s-11d. [C71108] Married Marylebone, London 30/5/1833 Mary Martha, dau. Sir William Horne (Epping House, Little Berkhampstead, Herts.), with issue.

VERNON (Robert) Bapt. Worcester 9/2/1761, s. Robert Vernon. Worcester, Oxford

1780, dn83 (Glos), dn83 (Glos.), BA1784, p85 (Wor.), MA1787. PC. Huddington, Worcs 1790 and R, Heythrop, Oxford 1800 and of R. Grafton Flyford, Worcs 1831, all to death 4/4/1845 [C38011] Married Claverley, Shropshire 16/4/1789 Catherine Batty, with issue.

VERNON (William) Born Clitheroe, Lancs. 11/7/1792, s. John Joseph James Vernon and Hannah Mason. St John's, Cambridge 1816, a Ten Year Man, dn16 (Chester), p17 (Chester). PC. Grindleton, Clitheroe, Yorks. 1822-32. Died Southall, Middx. 14/5/1871, leaving £5,000 [C136019. LBSO] Married (1) Sarah Kemball, with issue (2) Preston, Lancs. 8/5/1827 Elizabeth Raven, w. clerical s. William James Vernon.

VERNON (William) Born Hanbury Hall, Worcs. 30/8/1793, s. Thomas Shrawley Vernon and Elizabeth Tayler. Emmanuel, Cambridge 1813, BA1818, MA 1821. R. Hanbury, Worcs. [net income £1,188] 1820 to death 24/4/1855 aged 61 [C122259] Married 3/11/1823 Emily Angel Foley (Narberth, Pembroke), with issue. Brother John, above.

VERNON, *later* VERNON HARCOURT (William [Venables]) Born Sudbury, Derbys. 1/6/1789, s. Edward Venables Vernon (Harcourt after 1831), (Bishop of Carlisle, later Archbishop of York, above) and Lady Anne Leveson-Gower. [R.N. in the West Indies 1801-6] Christ Church, Oxford 1807, Student [Fellow] 1807-15, BA1811, dn13 (York), p13 (York), MA1814, incorporated at Cambridge, MA1833. V. Bishopthorpe, Ainsty of York 1814-24, R. Nunburnholme, Yorks. 1816-18, R. Etton, Yorks. 1816-34, Canon Residentiary of York Minster (w. Prebend of North Newbald annexed) 1821-71, (Sinecure R. Kirkby in Cleveland, Yorks. 1823-71), R. Wheldrake, Yorks. 1824-34, V. Bishopthorpe (again) 1834-8, R. Bolton Percy, Yorks. 1837-65 [gross income in CR65 £3,083] Died Nuneham Park, Oxon. 1/4/1871 [Fasti says 3/4/1871] aged 81, leaving £30,000 [C135790 as Vernon. ODNB (port.). Boase. F. as Harcourt] Married 'quickly' in 1824 Matilda Mary, dau. Col. William Gooch, issue included the politician Sir William Harcourt, Chancellor of the Exchequer. Harcourt surname added 1831. *F.G.S.* (1823), *F.R.S.* (1824). Important amateur chemist and geologist; reformer; founder and general secretary (1831) and President (1839) of the British Association for the Advancement of Science; his brothers Charles, and Leveson Vernon Harcourt here: https://m.youtube.com/watch?v=39XqJL8SAFc&feature=youtube_gdata_player

VEVERS, *born* WILKINSON (Richard) Bapt. Rothwell, Yorks. 23/3/1756, s. Thomas Wilkinson and Elizabeth Broadhead. Literate: dn83 (York), p84 (Lin.), then St John's, Cambridge 1786 (a Ten Year Man, BD1796). V. Croft, Lincs. 1784-92, R. Bucknall, Lincs. 1791-1804, V. Gunthorpe, Leics. 1800-13, R. Saxby w. Stapleford, Leics. 1804-35, R. Stoke Albany, Northants. 1813-31, V. Wilbarston, Northants. 1813-31, R. Kettering, Northants. 1831 to death 17/1/1838 [C77930] Married Kilnwick Pervy, Yorks. 1/1/1778 Theodosia Dorothy, dau. of Rev. Sir William Anderson, 6th Bart., with son, below. Changed name to inherit.

VEVERS (Richard William) Born 25/11/1778, s. Rev. Richard Vevers (above) and Theodosia Dorothy Anderson. Trinity, Cambridge 1797, BA1801, dn08 (Lin.), p10 (Lin.), MA1816. V. Marton, Lincs. 1812-32, V. Great Carlton, Lincs. -1812, R. Somersal Herbert, Derbys. 1821-32, R. Cubley w. Marston Montgomery, Derbys. 1832 to death. Dom. Chap. to 3rd Baron Sondes 1813. Died 24/1/1858, leaving £1,500 [C20158] Married Frances Stanhope Darby (natural dau. of 5th Earl of Chesterfield).

VICARS (Matthew) Born Eskdale, Cumberland 1773, s. John Vicars and Jane Moore. Literate: dn96 (Car.), p97 (Car.). R. Exeter Allhallows, Goldsmith Street 1821-43, R. Godmanstone w. Nether Cerne, Dorset 1843 to death 25/5/1853 aged 79 [C5664] Married (1) York 21/11/1796 Harriott Atkinson (d.1823), w. issue (2) Crediton, Devon 20/4/1829 Ann Roberts, w. clerical s. John.

VICARY (Abraham Thomas Rogers) Bapt. Exeter 27/11/1797, s. William and Jane Vicary. Jesus, Cambridge 1821, BA1826, dn27, p28 (Ex.), MA1829. Priest-Vicar of Exeter Cathedral, R. Exeter St Paul 1832 to death there 7/12/1842 aged 44 [C146569] Married Heavitree, Devon 24/1/1824 Barbara Templer, with issue.

VICKERS (John) Bapt. Ecclesfield, Yorks. 19/3/1766, s. William Vickers. Queens', Cambridge 1783, BA1788, dn89 (York), Fellow 1790-3, MA1791, p91 (Ely), then Trinity Hall,

Fellow 1793, etc. R. Swannington w. Wood Dalling, Norfolk 1803 to death 1839 (3rd q.) [C100471. YCO] Married (1) Ecclesfield 7/2/1804 Harriet Dixon (d.1814), w. issue (2) Norwich 13/8/1818 Judith Baker; with issue.

VICKERS (William) Born Worfield, Shropshire 19/1/1789, s. Valentine Vickers and Susanna Gittins. Trinity, Cambridge 1807, BA 1811, dn12 (Heref.), MA1814. R. Chetton w. Deuxhill and Glazeley, Shropshire 1813, and Archdeacon of Shropshire 1838 to death 10/5/1851 aged 62 [C174302. Boase] Wife Anne Parry.

VICKERY (Francis William Johnson) Born City of London 25/12/1788, s. William and Catherina Isabella Vickery. University, Oxford 1803, BA1809, dn12 (Win.), MA1812. V. Buckland Filleigh, Devon 1821-31. Died (Bloomsbury, London) 28/5/1866 aged 77, leaving under £100 [C108962] Married (1) St Pancras, London 2/11/1814 Eliza Sharpe, w. issue (2) Derby 16/1/1844 Charlotte Josephine Davenport (w).

VIGOR (Henry Stonhouse) see under **STONHOUSE VIGOR**

VILETT (John Wayte) Bapt. Swindon, Wilts., 22/9/1790, s. Rev. Thomas Goddard Vilett and Margaret Southby. St John's, Oxford 1807, Fellow 1807-34, BA1812, MA1816. V. Fyfield, Berks. 1830, R. Fyfield Bavant, Berks. at death 4/10/1834 (CCEd thus) [C86818]

VILLERS (William) Born Wolverhampton, Staffs., s. Simon Villers and Elizabeth Salt. Balliol, Oxford 1809 (aged 18), BA1813, dn15 (London), p17 (Glos.), MA1847. V. Chelmarsh, Heref. 1821-35, PC. Kidderminster St George, Worcs. 1825, V. Bromsgrove, Worcs. 1846 to death 15/1/1861, leaving £1,500 [C122261] Married Altham, Lancs. 14/7/1825 Susannah Peel (w), with clerical sons William Richard, and Robert John Villers.

VINCE (Samuel Berney) Born Fressingfield, Suffolk 2/4/1781, s. Ven. Samuel Vince (Archdeacon of Bedford) and Mary Paris. King's, Cambridge 1799, Fellow 1802, BA1804, dn05 (Lin.), p06 (Lin.), Tutor 1816-26, etc. Inc. Cambridge St Edward 1813-16, V. Ringwood, Hants. 1826 to death 14/6/1845 [C77932]

VINCENT (Edward) Bapt. Cheshunt, Herts. 24/3/1787, s. Robert Vincent and Susan Phillimore. St John's, Oxford 1805, then Exeter, BA1809, dn10 (Salis. for Win.), MA1811. V. Rowde, Wilts. 1816 and V. Chirton, Wilts. 1826 to death 28/3/1864, leaving £1,500 [C86828] Married Stanstead, Essex 20/2/1819 Margaret McKay, with issue.

VINCENT (Frederick, Sir, 11th Bart.) Born London 8/1/1798, s. Henry Dormer Vincent (Lily Hill Park, Bracknell, Berks.) and Isabella Elizabeth Hervey. BNC, Oxford 1815, dn18 (Salis. for Win.), p19 (Salis. for Win.), BA1819, MA1823. V. Hitchenden, Berks. 1825-36, R. Slinfold, Sussex 1844-68, Prebend of Seaford in Chichester Cathedral 1860-83, living at Bracknell, Berks. Chap. to Bishop of Chichester 1852-70. Died and buried Cannes 8/1/1883 aged 85, leaving £221,526-14s-5d. [C71398. Boase] Married (1) Hughenden, Bucks. 26/10/1826 Louisa Norris (d.1841), with issue (2) Hurstpierpoint, Sussex 4/9/1844 Maria Copley Young (w), with further issue (incl. 1st Viscount D'Abernon and Rev. Sir William Vincent, 12th Bart.). Succ. to title 1880.

VINCENT (Matson) Born Leeds 26/10/1790, s. John Tunnadine Vincent and Catherine Fourness. University, Oxford 1808, BA1812, dn13 (York), MA1815, p15 (York). PC. Clayton w. Frickley, Yorks. 1817-20 (res.), PC. Brampton St Thomas, Derbys. 1832 to death 12/6/1846 [C135791. YCO] Married Brampton 3/11/1835 Tabitha Longson, with issue.

VINCENT (William St Andrew) Bapt. Westminster Abbey, London 31/12/1772, s. Rev. William Vincent and Hannah Wyatt. Christ Church, Oxford 1791, BA1795, dn97 (Ox.), dn98 (Roch.), MA1798, BD1827. Prebend of Hova Villa Chichester Cathedral 1801-49, R. Allhallows the Great w. Allhallows the Less, City of London (and Preacher throughout the Diocese of London) 1803, V. (and patron) of Bolney, Sussex 1827 to death 22/7/1849 [C2535] Married Oakham, Rutland 1/8/1803 Frances Elizabeth Gayfrere Jones, w. issue.

VINK (Charles George Frederick) Born Bethnal Green, London 1/10/1803, s. Wynand Adriaen de Gruiter Vink and Martha Lorani. Magdalen Hall, Oxford 1822, BA1826, dn26 (B&W), p28 (Bristol), MA1833. Chap. of the Donative of Bothenhampton, Dorset 1826-[40].

Died (Hastings, Kent) 28/9/1868, leaving £3,000 [C40765]

VIVEN (James William) see under **VIVIAN, below**

VIVIAN (Charles Pasley) Bapt. Friern Barnet, Middx. 26/7/1800, s. John Vivian (Claverton, Somerset) and Marianne Edwards. Trinity Hall, Cambridge 1816 [adm. Inner Temple 1817] LLB1822. V. Wellingborough, Northants. 1825 (living at Hatton Hall there) to death 14/12/1841 (Colworth House, Sharnbrook, Beds., 'at dinner with a party of friends, and was in the act of offering the wing of a fowl to one of the guests, when he suddenly fell back on his chair [and] life was extinct') [C110989. Boase] Married Heighington, Co. Durham 21/10/1828 Grace Anna Aylmer (dau. of a general), with issue.

VIVIAN, *born* VIVEN (James William) Bapt. Bishopsgate, City of London 6/2/1785, s. John Viven and Ann Bliss. All Souls, Oxford 1803, BA1807, dn08 (Win.), p09 (Ex. for London), MA1810, BD and DD1823. 10th (1817), 12th (1821), then 6th Minor Canon (1825) in St Paul's Cathedral, London to death, R. St Augustine w. St Faith, City of London 1821-42, V. Mucking, Essex 1824-42, R. St Peter le Poer w. St Benet Fink, City of London 1842 to death. Priest in Ordinary 1815; Dom. Chap. to 1st Earl of Guilford 1809. Died 17/4/1876, leaving £70,000 [C108966 under Viven. Boase] Married Bishopsgate 14/5/1814 Katherine Ann Griffin (d.1836), with issue.

VIVIAN (William Henry) Bapt. Cornwood, Devon 6/7/1756, s. Rev. Thomas Vivian and Mary Hussey. Exeter, Oxford 1773, BA1777, dn78 (Ex.), p80 (Ex.). R. Charles [the Martyr] Cornwall 1780 to death (Chelsea, London) 28/10/1840 [C146574] Married Shoreditch, London 1/6/1805 Frances Wingrove, *s.p.*

VOLLANS (William) Born Cridlen Park, Pontefract, Yorks. 25/10/1761, s. William Vollans. Sidney, Cambridge 1785, BA1789, dn88 (London), p90 (Lin.), MA1793, DD. R. Hemsworth, Yorks. 1790 [income in 1831 £1,064] to death (London) 1840 aged 82, *s.p.* [C77939]

VYE (John) Born Exeter 5/1/1764, s. Rev. John Vye, sen. Exeter, Oxford 1781, BA1785, Fellow 1785-1810, dn86 (Ex.), p88 (Ex.), MA 1791, BD1801. V. Morthoe, Devon 1795-1805, R. Wootton, Northants. 1806 to death 28/6/1833 (CCEd says 3/10/1833) [C146576]

VYNER (William Phillips) Bapt. Wappenbury, Warwicks. 2/11/1806, s. Robert Vyner and Laura Glover. University, Oxford 1825, BA 1829, dn29 (C&L), p31 (C&L). V. Marton, Warwicks 1831, V. Authorpe, Lincs. 1836-76, R. Withern, Lincs. 1863-76, RD. Died Louth, Lincs. (unm.?) 20/7/1878, leaving £5,000 [C20163]

VYVYAN (Thomas Hutton) Born Trelowarren, Helston, Cornwall 3/3/1803 (bapt. 4/3/1805), s. Sir Vyell Vyvyan, 7th Bart. and Mary Hutton Rawlinson. Trinity, Cambridge 1821, no degree, dn29 (Ex.). PC. Penzance St Mary, Cornwall 1832-40. Died Harwich, Essex 7/9/1844 [C146579] Married Trelowarren 8/9/1835 Mary William Grenfell (of Penzance), w. clerical s. Thomas Grenfell Vyvyan. Brother, below.

VYVYAN (Vyell Francis) Bapt. Trelowarren, Helston, Cornwall 29/9/1803, s. Sir Vyell Vyvyan, 7th Bart. and Mary Hutton Rawlinson. St John, Cambridge 1820, then Trinity, Oxford 1821, dn25 (Ex.), p25 (Ex.), BA1826, MA1839. R. Withiel, Cornwall 1825 to death 30/1/1877 aged 75 [C146580] Married 21/7/1825 Anne Taylor, with 2 clerical sons (incl. 9th Bart.). Brother above.

WADDINGTON (George) Born Padiham, Lancs. 1790, s. Rev. Thomas Waddington. St John's, Cambridge 1806, re-adm. 1811, BA1811, dn13 (Ely), p14 (Chester), MA1814. (succ. his father as) R. Northwold, Norfolk 1814 to death 29/4/1833 aged 43 (CCEd says 11/6/1833) [C109530] Married St George's Hanover Square, London 4/3/1817 Jane Cocks (a niece of Lord Somers).

WADE (Arthur Savage) Bapt. Warwick 19/9/1787, s. Charles Gregory Wade (attorney and mayor) and Susanna Savage. St John's, Cambridge 1806, BA1810, MA1813, DD1825. V. Warwick St Nicholas 1811 to death (apoplexy) 17/11/1845 in a shop in Regent's Street, London ('to order a greatcoat'), 'although he had been absent from his clerical duties for many years, living in London and devoting himself to [Chartist] politics'. Probate of £1,000, all left to a Miss Mary Ann Crafter, Norfolk [C122262. Long obit. in *Gentleman's Magazine*] Brother below.

WADE (Charles Gregory) Born Warwick 25/8/1784, s. Charles George Wade (attorney and mayor) and Susanna Savage. Merton, Oxford 1803, BA1806, dn07 (Heref.), MA1810. R. Great Hanwood, Shropshire 1810 to death 4/4/1835 (CCEd says 10/8/1835) [C122263] Married Shrewsbury 10/5/1821 Anna Maria Burton, w. issue. Brother above.

WADE (Ellis) Born Orford, Suffolk 27/12/1796, s. Mark Farley Wade and Elizabeth Ellis. Sidney, Cambridge 1813, BA1817, dn20 (Glos.), MA1820, p21 (Nor.), incorporated at Oxford 1839. PC. Wantisden, Suffolk 1832 and R. Blaxall, Suffolk 1836 to death 8/10/1864, leaving £8,000 [C115888] Married Leiston, Suffolk 12/10/1825 Sarah Josselyn, with issue.

WADE (Thomas) Bapt. Rickmansworth, Herts. 14/3/1753, s. Thomas and Ann Wade. Literate: dn81 (Lin. for York), p82 (York). PC. Tottington, Bury, Lancs. 1799 to death 19/3/1834 (CCEd thus) aged 80 [C77949. YCO] Married Bradford 9/8/1797 Elizabeth Bridges, Horton Old Hall, Bradford, with issue.

WAGNER (Henry Michell) Bapt. Westminster, London 15/12/1792, s. Melchior Henry Wagner and Anne Elizabeth Michell (a clergy dau.). King's, Cambridge 1812, Fellow 1815-24, BA1816, MA1819, dn21 (Ely), p24 (Ely). Tutor to Duke of Wellington's two sons 1816-24; V. Brighton, Sussex 1824 [net income £1,041] (w. Blatchington annexed 1825) to 1870, Treasurer of Chichester Cathedral 1834 to death 'at lunchtime' 7/10/1870, leaving £100,000 [C81121. Boase] Married (1) Westminster, London 1823 Elizabeth Douglas (d.1829), with clerical son Arthur Douglas Wagner (the notorious ritualist) (2) 2/7/1838 Mary Sykes Watson (d.1840).

WAINWRIGHT (Latham) Born London 31/7/1772, s. Robert Wainwright (a Clerk in Chancery) and Ann Arnold. Christ's, Cambridge 1798, then Emmanuel, BA1802, dn02 (Nor.), p03 (Lin.), MA1806. R. Great Brickhill, Bucks. 1803 to death (London, 'where he normally resided') 21/12/1833 (CCEd says 14/5/1834). 'The rheumatic gout which rendered him a cripple, ultimately destroyed him' [C77971. Long *Gentleman's Magazine* obit.] F.S.A. 'A studious, friendly and inoffensive man'; 'his means were ample and easy'.

WAIT (Daniel Guildford) Bapt. Bristol 3/12/1789, s. Daniel Wait and Mary Jago. University, Oxford 1809, then St John's, Cambridge 1812, dn12 (B&W), re-adm. Oxford 1813, p13 (B&W), LLB Cambridge 1819, LLD Cambridge 1824. [Catalogued the oriental mss. in the Bodleian Library 1825-] R. Blagdon, Som. 1819 to death 30/9/1850 aged 61. A prisoner in the Fleet Prison for debt 1833 [C49845. ODNB] Married Westbury-on-Trim, Glos. 10/2/1814 Priscilla Morgan Thorne (d.1819), with issue (2) Burrington, Som. 9/12/1819 Elizabeth Mary Wilde, with further issue.

WAIT (William Piguenit) Born Bristol 1792, s. Rev. William Wait and Wilhelmina Piguenit. Wadham, Oxford 1812 (aged 20), no degree, dn16 (B&W), p17 (Glos.). R. Chew Stoke, Som. 1819 and R. Norton Malreward, Som. 1819. Died Christchurch, Hants. 22/10/1870, leaving £35,000 [C40792] Married (1) 9/12/1816 Elizabeth Palmer Matthews (d.1867), with issue (2) Clifton, Bristol 25/4/1867 Mrs Alice Agnes (Wylde) Prowse (his 2nd cousin, aged 31, a clergy dau.; she remarried after Wait's death).

WAITE (John) Born Barwick in Elmet, Yorks. 3/2/1781, s. Richard Waite (a tailor) and Alice Barker. St John's, Cambridge 1799, BA1803, dn03 (Lin.), p05 (Lin.). MA1806. Usher Louth G/S 1812, H/M 1814-51 (Tennyson was among his pupils); R. Stewton, Lincs. 1817-41, V. Tathwell, Lincs. 1841 to death (Manby, Lincs.)

18/1/1872. No will traced [C77973] Married 1804 Mary Phillips (dau. of a Louth solicitor), with clerical son, below.

WAITE (John Deane) Born Louth, Lincs. 16/3/1805, s. Rev. John Waite (above) and Mary Phillips. Clare, Cambridge 1824, BA1828, dn28 (Lin.), p29 (Lin.), MA1831. V. Little Cawthorpe, Lincs. 1832-51, R. Manby, Lincs. 1852 to death 18/6/1885 aged 80, leaving £1,889-12s-3d. [C77972]

WAITE (Joseph) Born Morpeth, Northumberland 5/9/1782 (bapt. Wigton, Cumberland 8/6/1783), s. John Waite and Ann Robinson. Literate: dn17 (Durham), p18 (Durham). PC. Weardale St John, Auckland, Co. Durham 1821-51. Died Gainford, Durham 13/2/1865 aged 82. Will not traced [C131182] Married (1) Wigton 19/11/1803 Mary Rook (2) Washington, Durham 5/1/1821 Jane Humble, with issue.

WAKE (Henry) Bapt. East Knoyle, Wilts. 12/2/1770, s. Rev. Charles Wake and Barbara Bathsua Beckford. St John's, Cambridge 1788, dn92 (Salis.), BA1793, p94 (Salis.), MA1813. V. Mere, Wilts. 1812 and R. Over Wallop, Hants. 1813 to death. Dom. Chap. to 13th Marquess of Winchester 1813. Died 1/12/1851 aged 81 [C87085] Married Southampton 26/3/1813 Urania Catherine Camilla (dau. Hon. and Rev. Barton Wallop, she d.1814).

WAKE (Richard William) Born 16/7/1775, s. Sir William Wake, 8th Bart. and Mary Fenton. St John's, Cambridge 1793, BA1797, dn99 (London), p99 (London), MA1803. R. Courteenhall, Northants. 1813 to death. Dom. Chap. to Philadelphia Hannah, Viscountess Cremone 1813. Died Bushy Park, Inniskerry, Co. Kerry 29/11/1850 aged 85 (and was buried in Ireland) [C111484] Married (1) 17/11/1798 Jane Eliza (d.1823), dau. Sir William Dunkin (a judge in Calcutta), with issue (2) Tunbridge Wells, Surrey 6/4/1836 Harriet, dau. of Henry Grattan, the Irish statesman.

WAKEFIELD (William) Bapt. Curdworth, Warwicks. 18/10/1791, s. William Wakefield and Elizabeth Swift. St John's, Oxford 1808, BA1812, dn14 (C&L), p15 (C&L), MA1815. V. (and part patron of) Curdworth 1817 to death (unm.) 19/2/1875 aged 84, leaving £5,000 [C20173]

WAKEHAM (Henry) Bapt. Ingham, Suffolk 12/5/1763, s. Very Rev. Nicholas Wakeham (R. and Dean of Bocking, Essex - a Peculiar) and Harriet Perryman. Pembroke, Cambridge 1781, BA1786, dn96 (Glos.), p87 (Chester for Cant.), MA1789. R. Ingham w. Tilworth and Colford 1790-1839, R. West Stow, Suffolk 1801-29 (res.). Died 23/1839 [C115906] Married Bocking 28/6/1791 Jane Nottidge. Brother below.

WAKEHAM (Perryman) Born Ingham, Suffolk 12/8/1764, s. Very Rev. Nicholas Wakeham (R. and Dean of Bocking, Essex - a Peculiar) and Harriet Perryman. Caius, Cambridge 1783, BA1787, dn87 (C&L), p88 (C&L), MA1790. R. Little Saxham, Suffolk 1790-1841 (non-res.). Died Braintree, Essex 25/10/1852 aged 89 [C20053] Married Bures, Essex/Suffolk 17/7/1809 Mary Elliston. Brother above.

WAKEMAN (Edward Ward) Born Claines, Worcs. 13/5/1801, s. Sir Henry Wakeman, 1st Bart., *H.E.I.C.*, and Sarah Offley. Wadham, Oxford 1820, BA1823, MA1827 (as Edward). R. Claines 1825 to death 8/9/1855 aged 54, living at Coton Hall, Shropshire [Not yet in CCEd] Married Cheltenham 28/4/1835 Louisa Thompson, with issue.

WALBANKE-CHILDERS see under **CHILDERS**

WALCOT (Charles) Bapt. Powick, Worcs. 23/1/1794 or 1795, s. Rev. John Walcot (below) and Sarah Dashwood King. Trinity, Oxford 1813, BA1817, p19 (Heref.), MA1820. R. (and patron) of Hopton Wafers, Shropshire 1820-34 (res.), R. (and patron of) Bitterley w. Middleton, Shropshire (while living at Bitterley Court) 1835 to death 18/12/1875, leaving under £100 [C174307] Married (1) Stoke Milborough, Shropshire 23/2/1818 Anne Walcot (Perry Park, Dublin, she d.1824), w. clerical son John (2) 1828 Charlotte Catherine Molyneux (d.1848) (3) Clun, Shropshire 1851 (2nd q.) Mary Anne Rocke, with further issue. *J.P.*

WALCOT (John) Bapt. Astley, Worcs. 22/2/1766, s. Charles Walcot and Ann Levett. Christ's, Oxford 1783, then St Mary Hall, LLB 1791, dn93 (Heref. for Nor.). R. (and patron of) Bitterley w. Middleton, Shropshire 1795 and R. Hopton Cangeford, Shropshire 1822 to death 23/11/1834, living at Bitterley Court [C115907] Married (West Wycombe, Bucks.?) 2/12/1788

Sarah, dau. Sir John Dashwood King, with clerical son Charles Walcot (above).

WALDY (Richard) Bapt. Yarm, Yorks. 12/8/1795, s. John Waldy and Ann Garmondsway. Clare, Cambridge 1814, BA1818, dn19 (Heref.), p19 (Salis.), MA1821. R. Turnerspuddle w. Affpuddle, Dorset 1824 (and Prebend of Gillingham Minor in Salisbury Cathedral 1849) to death. Dom. Chap. to Dowager Lady Vernon 1821. Died (Affpuddle) 19/12/1868, leaving £1,500 [C54082] Married Christchurch, Hants. 19/8/1823 Isabella Greenwood (w) (a clergy dau.), with clerical son (and a dau. Frances Helen, a minor novelist, writing under the pseudonym of Beatrice Yorke).

WALE (Alexander Malcolm) Born Shelford, Cambs. 12/5/1797, s. Gen. Sir Charles Wale and Louisa Sherard (a clergy dau.). St John's, Cambridge 1814 [adm. Inner Temple 1819] BA 1819, Fellow 1821-31, MA1822, dn27 (Lin.), p27 (Ely), BD1830, etc. V. Sunninghill, Berks. 1830 to death 26/5/1884, leaving £2,818-15s-7d. Succ. to his father's estates at Shelford, which he sold to his brother 1850 [C77996] Married 1/1/1835 Caroline Ardrighetti (b. Fribourg, Switzerland) and had issue. 'In April 1829 [as Senior Proctor] he was mobbed by undergraduates who pursued him from the Senate House to the gates of St John's, hissing and groaning, and though some of the offenders were summoned before the Vice-Chancellor's Court, the Proctors were not satisfied and sent in their resignations.'

WALFORD (Edward Gibbs) Bapt. Banbury, Oxon. 28/4/1778, s. William Walford and Agnes Gibbs. Lincoln, Oxford 1795, BA1799, dn00 (Peterb.), then St Mary Hall, MA1801, p02 (Peterb.). V. Elsfield, Oxon. 1804-32, V. Frieston w. Butterwick, Lincs. 1805-16 (res.), V. Shotteswell, Warwicks. 1805 and R. Chipping Warden, Northants. 1832 to death 15/5/1864, leaving £450 [C20176] Married (1) Mitcham, Surrey 6/5/1830 Mrs Elizabeth (Lancaster) Smith (d.1843) (2) Jane Fowler (w) - but not in FreeBMD.

WALFORD (Ellis) Bapt. Long Stratton St Mary, Norfolk 15/5/1803, s. Rev. William Walford (below) and Diana Burroughes (a clergy dau.). Corpus Christi, Cambridge 1821, BA1825, dn26 (Nor.), p28 (Nor.), MA1829. R. (and patron) of Dallinghoe, Suffolk 1830-81, R. Bucklesham, Suffolk 1833-69. RD of Wilford 1842. Died 11/10/1881 aged 78, leaving £7,811-4s-0d. [C115909] Married (1) Marylebone, London 20/1/1832 Henrietta Hall Colvin (d.1841), with issue (2) Kelsale, Suffolk 22/11/1842 Frances Matilda Brown (a clergy dau.), with clerical son Lancelot Charles Walford.

WALFORD (William) Bapt. Woodbridge, Suffolk 6/3/1753, s. William Walford (ironmonger) and Mary Davy. Caius, Cambridge 1769, BA1774, dn75 (Nor.), MA1777, p77 (Nor.), Fellow 1777, etc. R. Weeting All Saints w. St Mary, Norfolk 1794-5 (res.), R. Bucklesham, Suffolk 1794-1833, R. Long Stratton St Mary, Norfolk 1795, R. Norwich St Clement 1795-1839. Died 25/6/1842 [C115912] Married Long Stratton 20/10/1796 Diana Burroughes (a clergy dau.), with son Ellis (above)

WALKER (Adam John) From Newry, Co. Down, s. Adam Walker. Trinity, Cambridge 1786 (aged 17), BA1791, MA1794. R. Llangua, Monmouth 1808-30, V. Yazor, Heref. 1809-39, R. Bedstone, Shropshire 1809, R. Bishopstone, Heref. 1809 to sudden death (Weobley, Heref.) 1/1/1839 aged 69 [C2538] Married Brampton Abbottts, Heref. 11/6/1799 Loveday Whitmore, w. child.

WALKER (George) Bapt. Eye, Suffolk 14/7/1779, s. Rev. William Walker (R. Stuston, Suffolk, below). Caius, Cambridge 1796, BA 1801, dn01 (Nor.), p03 (Nor.), MA1804. R. Scole, Norfolk 1812 to death 12/2/1845 [C115913] Married Eye 21/6/1820 Elizabeth Denny, w. issue.

WALKER (Jeremiah) St Bees adm. 1817 (first intake): dn17 (Chester), p18 (Chester), then Sidney, Cambridge 1819 (a Ten Year Man, BD). V. Ulpha, Cumberland 1828 to death 15/1/1881, leaving £800 [C20506. B.S.W. Simpson, *A mountain chapelry* (1950 and port.) adds DCL] Surrogate.

WALKER (John) Bapt. Shap, Westmorland 14/4/1771, s. Richard Walker and Agnes Bousfield. Trinity, Cambridge 1792, then Peterhouse 1793, BA1797, dn97 (London), p98 (London), MA1800, Fellow 1800, then Trinity Hall, Fellow 1802, Tutor, etc. R. Cottered, Herts. 1806 and V. Wethersfield, Essex 1814 to death 30/11/1853 [C78010] Married Cottered 2/6/1813 Sophia Mary Sisson (a clergy dau., Wallington, Herts.), with issue.

WALKER (Robert) Bapt. Lanlivery, Cornwall 25/11/1754, s. Rev. James Walker and Susanna Hussey. Balliol, Oxford 1772, BA1775, dn78 (Ox. for Ex.), MA 1778, p79 (Ex.). V. St Winnow, Cornwall 1782 to death 1835 aged 80 [C38099] Married St Clement, Cornwall 29/1/1782 Sophia Warrick, with issue.

WALKER (Robert) Literate: dn99 (Car.), p00 (Car.). PC. Swaledale Westmorland 1815 and R. South Otterington, Yorks. (both Medieties) 1828 to death (unm.) 27/8/1833 aged 62 [C136020]

WALKER (Robert) Born Cosgrove, Notts. 29/9/1780, s. Rev. Charles Walker. Trinity, Cambridge 1798, BA1802, dn03 (Lin.), p04 (Lin.), MA1805. V. Dunton, Beds. [blank in ERC] 1806 to death 20/1/1852 [C78061]

WALKER (Robert) [NiVoF] V. Eaton, Leics. 1814 [C78062] and V. Utterby, Lincs. 1830-[54]. Died? [C78064. ERC links them]

WALKER (Samuel Masterson) Born London, 11/2/1802, s. Maj.-Gen. Joseph and Eleanor Walker. Caius, Cambridge 1820, BA1824, dn25 (Ex.), p26 (Ex.), MA 1843, incorporated at Oxford 1851. V. St Enoder, Cornwall 1828 to death there 6/2/1874 aged 70, leaving £2,000 [C146591] Married (1) Cubert, Cornwall 25/1/1835 Maria Hosken (d.1856), with issue (2) Honiton, Devon 1862 (4th q.) Augusta Gardiner (w). Surrogate.

WALKER (Thomas) From Wolverhampton, s. James Walker. St Edmund Hall, Oxford 1785 (aged 22). Sacrist (1789), Prebend of Hatherton 1799 (then of Featherstone 1806), then Inc. Wolverhampton Collegiate Church 1799 to death 5/4/1834 aged 72 (living at Merridale House) [C20512] Wife Diana, and clerical son, also Thomas. Confusion here.

WALKER (Thomas) Born Wragby, Lincs. 12/6/1793, s. Edward and Martha Walker. Jesus, Cambridge 1814, BA1819, dn19 (Lin.), p21 (Lin.). R. Offord d'Arcy, Hunts. 1828 to death 1859 aged 72. No will traced [C78068] In 1851 wife Jane, 2 dau.

WALKER (Thomas) From Staffs. Peterhouse, Cambridge 1806, dn11 (C&L), LLB1812, p12 (C&L). R. Standon, Staffs. 1812, R. Tixall, Staffs. 1823-8. Died? [C20060] Had issue.

WALKER (Thomas Gregory Warren) Born Stanford Dingley, Berks. 22/6/1763, s. Rev. Benjamin Walker and Isabella Warren. Magdalen, Oxford 1782, BA1786, dn86 (York), p87 (York), MA1789. V. Hartlip, Kent 1795-1810, V. Rickling, Essex 1810 to death 3/10/1834 (CCEd thus) [C1501. YCO. F. as Thomas only] Married 8/8/1792 Mary Harridge.

WALKER (Thomas Horatio) Born Redland, Bristol 26/2/1799, s. Thomas Walker and Harriet Ludlow. Oriel, Oxford 1816, BA1821, dn22 (Ely for Salis.), p23 (Ely for Salis.), MA 1824. V. Stoke Gifford, Glos. 1826-34, V. Bickleigh, Devon 1832 to death 18/10/1841 [C54116] Married 25/11/1828 Ann Stevens, with issue.

WALKER (William) Born Wakefield, Yorks. 30/7/1750, s. Thomas Walker. Clare, Cambridge 1768, BA1772, dn72 (Nor.), p74 (Nor.), MA 1798. R. Ilketshall St John 1786-1832, R. Stuston, Suffolk 1792-1832, Prebend of Sandiacre, Lichfield Cathedral 1798-1832, R. Bessingham, Cromer, Norfolk 1820 to death 15/8/1832 [assumed from C115915 as parish not in ERC] Son George, above.

WALKER (William) Born Ashbourne, Derbys., s. Edmund Walker. St John's, Cambridge 1783 (aged 18), BA1788, dn88 (C&L), p89 (Roch.), MA1791, Fellow 1792-1814, BD 1798. R. Layham, Glos. 1812-35, R. Monksilver, Suffolk 1812 to death 1/12/1835 aged 70 [C2540]

WALKER (William) [NiVoF]. PC. (and patron) of Eskdaleside (o/w Sleights) w. Ugglebarnby, Whitby, Yorks. 1824-[54]. Died? [C136022] A Thomas Walker succ. him here 1854.

WALKER (William Fullerton) Born Edinburgh 3/8/1802, s. Alexander Walker and Christian Boswall. Magdalen Hall, Oxford 1824, BA1828, dn28 (Chester), p29 (Chester), MA 1831. (first) PC. Oldham St James, Lancs. 1829 to death 31/8/1857 [C170804. DEB] Married Prestwich, Lancs. 24/05/1832 Mary Ann Hague.

WALKER (William Henry) Born London, s. William Walker (Amwell, Herts.). Pembroke, Cambridge 1805 (aged 18), BA1810, dn10 (London), MA1810, p11 (London). V. Great

Wigston, Leics. 1813 to death (Sutton, Surrey) 16/5/1834 aged 47 [C78072]

WALKEY (Charles Collyns) Born Exeter 25/7/1804, s. Rev. Charles Elliott Walkey (R. Clyst St Lawrence, Devon, below) and Elizabeth Collyns. Balliol, Oxford 1821, then Worcester 1823-30, BA1825, MA1828, dn28 (Ex.), p30 (Ex.), Fellow 1830-2. V. Lucton, Heref. (and H/M Lucton G/S) 1831-73. Died Cheltenham, Glos. 4/6/1887, leaving £9,010-16s-0d. [C146592. Boase] Married 25/1/1832 Milborough Ann Huyshe, with clerical son Charles John Elliot Walkey.

WALKEY (Charles Elliott) Born London 19/6/1780, s. Benjamin Walkey and Mary Elliott. Balliol, Oxford 1798, BA1802, dn03 (London for Ex.), p03/4 (Ex.). R. Clyst St Lawrence, Devon 1804 to death there 4/9/1865, leaving £14,000 [C123736. Boase] Married Exeter 27/9/1803 Elizabeth Collyns, with clerical son Charles Collyns Walkey (above).

WALL (James) Literate: dn13 (Nor.), p14 (Nor.). PC. Norton Subcourse, Norfolk 1814, PC. Raveningham, Norfolk 1814, PC. Heckingham, Norfolk 1816 and PC. Hales, Norfolk 1816-[44]. Probably died 1850 (4th q.) [C115919]

WALL (John) Bapt. Leominster, Heref. 20/5/1751, s. John and Ann Wall. Christ Church, Oxford 1772, dn75 (Heref.), p75 (Heref.), BA1777, then Christ's, Cambridge MA1782. V. Kington w. Huntington, Heref. Radnor 1782 (and Prebend of Pratum Minus in Hereford Cathedral 1782) to death 27/11/1834 aged 84 [C174324] Married Quatt, Malvern, Shropshire 3/8/1802 Elizabeth Whitmore (of Dudmarton), w. issue.

WALLACE (Thomas) Born Great Braxted, Essex 19/8/1764, s. Rev. Job Wallace and Elizabeth Chaplyn. Corpus Christi, Cambridge 1782, BA1787, dn88 (London for Win.), MA 1790. R. Liston, Essex 1800 to death 15/2/1855 aged 91 [C123743] Married Liston 4/10/1821 Sarah Berson, w. issue.

WALLAS (Edmund) Bapt. Hesket in the Forest, Cumberland 26/4/1750, s. Robert (a yeoman farmer) and Catherine Wallas. [NiVoF] dn73 (Lin.), p74 (Car. for Lin.). V. Laneham, Yorks. 1781 to death 10/12/1841 aged 92 [C6412]

WALLER (Bryan) Born Lancaster 1/6/1765, s. of Richard Waller (tallow chandler and soap boiler) and Eleanor Atkinson. Trinity, Cambridge 1784, BA1788, MA1791, dn93 (Car.), p95 (Peterb.). V. Burton in Kendal, Westmorland 1806 to death 17/8/1842 aged 78 [C6414] Married Burton 13/12/1834 Jane Clark (w), with issue.

WALLER (Charles) Bapt. Sutton, Suffolk 8/5/1804. Queens', Cambridge 1826, dn30 (Nor.), BA1831, p31 (Nor.). R. (Great) Waldringfield, Suffolk [blank in ERC] 1833-9. Died (Woodbridge, Suffolk) 17/8/1842 [C115921] Married Trimley St Mary, Suffolk 29/12/1830 Catharine Julian (a clergy dau.), w. clerical son Charles Edward.

WALLER (Richard) From Middx. s. Ven. James Waller, Archdeacon of Essex ('*killed* when in bed by the fall of a chimney-stack'). Jesus, Cambridge 1787, BA1791, dn93 (Ex. for London), MA 1794, p95 (London). R. Great Birch w. Little Birch), Essex 1795 to death 6/4/1848 [C123746]

WALLER (William) Bapt. Tunstall, Lancs. 17/12/1763, s. Rev. John (PC. Ingleton, Yorks.) and Isabella Waller. Literate: p88 (York), then Pembroke, Cambridge 1794 (a Ten Year Man, BD1804). PC. Ingleton 1805 to death. Dom. Chap. to 6th Marquess of Queensbury 1817. Died 19/10/1844 aged 80 [C125537. YCO. 'A highly cultured, stern-looking old gentleman, he wore a very dark wig which added solemnity to the austerity of his aspect. Sometimes he would cease from speaking … to take a drink of wine from a pretty large glass or goblet which he had on a shelf within the pulpit'. A. Hewitson, *The story of my village 1840-1850* (new edn. 1982)].

WALLINGTON (Charles) Bapt. Dursley, Glos. 30/10/1750, s. Charles Wallington and Elizabeth Neale. Christ Church, Oxford 1770, BA1773, dn76 (St David's), MA1776, p77 (Heref. for Glos.). R. Lashborough, Glos. 1778, R. Harescombe w. Pitchcombe, Glos. 1791-1804, R. Hawkwell, Essex 1789 to death 28/3/1843 [C123748] Married (1) Wotton-under-Edge, Glos. 27/11/1774 Mary Watkins (d.1791), w. issue (2) Rugby, Warwicks. 14/1/1782 Frances Russell Harris, w. further issue. .

WALLIS (John) Bapt. Bodmin, Cornwall 9/3/1790, s. John (attorney and Town Clerk) and Isabella Wallis. Solicitor. Exeter, Oxford 1813, dn17 (Ex.), p17 (Ex.), BA1820, MA1821. V. Bodmin 1817 (and 'official of the Archdeacon of Cornwall' 1840) to death 6/12/1866 aged 77, leaving £1,500 [C146594. Boase] Surrogate. Mayor of Bodmin 1822.

WALLIS (Samuel) Born Dorset 20/6/1741, s. Samuel Wallis and Mary Porter. Jesus, Cambridge 1761, BA1765, dn66 (London), p67 (London), Fellow 1767-73, MA1768. R. Compton Valence, Dorset 1773, PC. Chaldon Herring, Dorset 1800-20, V. Loders, Dorset 1820 and V. Bradpole, Dorset 1820 to death. Dom. Chap. to 13th Marquess of Winchester 1820. Died 8/1/1835 aged 93 (CCEd says 21/1/1835) [C51753] Married Owermoigne, Dorset 9/2/1773 Molly Ingram, with issue.

WALLS (Joseph) Bapt. Spilsby, Lincs. 16/1/1779, s. Rev. Edward Walls (formerly Codd), Boothby Hall, Welton-le-Marsh, Lincs. and Mary Booth. BNC, Oxford 1797, then Magdalen 1798-1804, BA1801, dn02 (Ox.), p03 (Ox.), MA1804. V. East Kirkby, Leics. 1805-57 (non-res.), R. Gayton-le-Wold, Lincs. 1811 and PC. Welton-le-Marsh, Lincs. 1825 to death 1/1/1857, living at Boothby Hall [C21894. Bennett2. Kaye] Married Gamston, Notts. 21/8/1804 Elizabeth Wright, with clerical son Richard George Walls.

WALM(E)SLEY (Tindal Thompson) Bapt. New Malton, Yorks. 6/9/1758, s. Geoffrey Walmsley. St John's, Cambridge 1777, BA1781, dn81 (Lin. for Nor.), p82 (Peterb.), Fellow 1783-1806, MA1784, BD1792, DD1819. R. Ludgate St Martin, City of London 1805-19, R. St Vedast Foster Lane w. St Nicholas le Querne, City of London 1815 and R. Hanwell, Middx. 1819 to death. Dom. Chap. to Prince of Wales 1786. Died 27/1/1847 aged 88 [C78298]

WALPOLE (Robert) Born 8/8/1781, s. Robert Walpole (Envoy to Portugal and Clerk of the Privy Council) and Diana Grosset. Merton, Oxford 1797, then Trinity, Cambridge 1799, BA1803 [adm. Lincoln's Inn 1803], dn08 (Nor.), MA1809, p09 (Nor.), BD1828. R. Itteringham w. Mannington, Norfolk 1809-56, R. Tivetshall St Margaret, Norfolk 1815-28, R. Marylebone Christ Church, London 1828 to death 16/4/1856 [C115926] Married 6/2/1811 Caroline Frances Hyde (dau. of a judge in Calcutta), with issue.

WALPOLE (Thomas, Hon.) Born Woodmanstone, Surrey 30/9/1805, s. Thomas Walpole and Lady Margaret Perceval (dau. of 2nd Earl of Egmont). Balliol, Oxford 1822, BA1826, dn29 (Nor.), MA1829, p29 (Lin. for Nor.). R. Beach-amwell St Mary, Norfolk 1830, R. Alverstoke, Hants. 1846 (and Hon. Canon of Winchester Cathedral 1871) to death 7/2/1881 aged 75, leaving £14,000 [C78299] Married 15/1/1833 Margaret Isabella Mitchell, with issue.

WALSH (John Henry Arnold) Born Taunton, Som., s. John Walsh and Cassandra Arnold. Balliol, Oxford 1822 (aged 17), BA1827, dn27 (Salis.), MA1829, p29 (Salis.). PC. Warminster, Wilts. 1831-59, R. Bishopstrow, Wilts. 1859 to death 17/5/1871 aged 66, leaving £25,000 [C89682] Married Walcot, Bath 30/9/1830 Ann Bury, and had issue.

WALSINGHAM (Thomas de Grey, 4th Baron). Born Chelsea, London 10/4/1778, s. Thomas, 2nd Baron Walsingham and Hon. Augusta Georgina Elizabeth Irby (dau. of 1st Baron Boston). St John's, Cambridge 1796 [as a nobleman], MA1799, p02. R. (and patron) of Merton, Norfolk 1803-39, R. Fawley, Hants. 1806 [net income £1,179], R. Calbourne, IoW 1807, Archdeacon of Surrey 1814-39, Canon of 1st Prebend in Winchester Cathedral 1807 to death 8/9/1839 aged 61 [C109008. Long obit. in *Gentleman's Magazine*] Married Chelsea, London 12/8/1802 Elizabeth North (dau. of Brownlow North, Bishop of Winchester), 6s, 4 dau. Succ. to title 1831 (after his elder brother and his wife were burnt to death in a fire in their London house).

WALTER (Edward) Born Brigg, Lincs. 13/11/1801, s. Rev. James (V. Market Rasen, Lincs., below) and Frances Maria Walter. Christ's, Cambridge 1819, BA1824, dn24 (Lin.), p25 (Lin.). V. Woodhall, Lincs. 1827 and R. Langton by Horncastle, Lincs. 1828 to death 11/11/1877 ('of a chill caught by walking six miles in a snow storm after a meeting at Woodhall Spa') [C78302. Boase] Married Pontefract, Yorks. 30/10/1828 Anne Keeling Pyemont (Tanshelf House, Pontefract), with issue. Brothers Henry, and Weever Walter, below. 'Invented a bicycle many years before such machines came into use'.

WALTER (Edward Newton) Born Hoebridge Manor, Woking, Surrey 1/10/1763, s. Rev.

Alleyne Walter (R. Crowcombe, Som.) and Sarah Bird. St John's, Cambridge 1782, BA 1789. R. Leigh, 1808 to death. Chap. to HRH Duke of Clarence 1812. Died East Dulwich, Surrey 7/2/1837 aged 74 [C49880] Married Ann Keats before 1813, and had issue.

WALTER (Henry) Born Louth 28/1/1785, s. Rev. James (below) and Frances Maria Walter. St John, Cambridge 1802, BA1806, Fellow 1806-24, MA1809, dn09 (Nor.), p10 (Bristol for Ely), BD1816, Prof. of Natural Philosophy and Mathematics, *H.E.I.C.*'s Haileybury College, Herts. 1806-30. R. Hazelbury Bryan, Dorset 1821 to death. Dom. Chap to Duke of Northumberland ('with whom he travelled abroad in 1817'). Died 25/1/1859, leaving £1,000 [C54117. ODNB. Boase. Kaye. DEB] Married Bayford, Herts. 3/6/1824 Emily Anne Baker (w). *F.R.S.* (1819). Brothers Weever (below), and Edward (above). Distantly related to Jane Austen.

WALTER (James) Bapt. Shipborne, Kent 10/3/1759, s. William Hampson Walter and Susannah Weaver. Corpus Christ, Cambridge 1777, BA1781, Fellow 1783, dn83 (Lin.), p84 (Lin.). S/M Louth G/S 1783-7; H/M Brigg G/S, Lincs. 1787-9; V. Market Rasen 1792 to death 8/2/1845 [C78304] Married Oxted, Surrey 3/5/1784 his cousin Frances Maria Walter, w. clerical sons Edward, Henry (above), and Weever (below).

WALTER (Richard) Born Milton Damerel, Devon 23/1/1764, s. George Walter. Exeter, Oxford 1781, BA1785, dn86 (Ex.), p88 (Ex.). R. (and patron) of Parkham, Devon 1785 to death 11/5/1842 [C146597] Married North Tamerton, Cornwall 12/3/1787 Honor Cary, and had issue.

WALTER (Weever) Born Brigg, Lincs. 29/1/1797, s. Rev. James (above) and Frances Maria Walter. St John's, Cambridge 1814, then Sidney 1817, BA1818, MA1821, dn21 (Ely for London), p21 (London for Bristol). H/M Brigg G/S 1834-5; R. Gate Burton, Lincs. 1828-35 (w. Chap. of the Donative of Knaith, Lincs. 1828), R. Bonby, Lincs. 1835-60, Prebend of Lincoln Cathedral 1846. Died 12/1/1860, leaving £1,000 [C54118. Boase. Kaye] Married (1) Dirleton, East Lothian 1/7/1822 Lilias Cochrane (d.1843), with clerical son William Hampson Walter (2) Edinburgh 8/10/1845 Susan Coutts (w). Brothers Henry, and Edward Walter (above).

WALTER (William) Bapt. Monkleigh, Devon 12/9/1776, s. Rev. John and Elizabeth Walter. Exeter, Oxford, 1794, BA1798, dn99 (St Asaph), p03 (B&W), then Peterhouse, Cambridge, MA1807. V. Abbotsham, Devon 1807 and R. Bideford, Devon 1812 to death. Chap. to HRH Duke of Clarence 1812. Died 2/4/1844 aged 68 [C49885] Married Ann Keats before 1813, and had issue.

WALTERS (Charles) Born Bishops Waltham, Hants. 29/5/1784, s. Rev. Charles Henry Walters (H/M) and Sarah Budd. Magdalen Hall, Oxford 1805, BA1808, dn08 (Win.), p08 (Win.), MA1822. R. Bramdean, Hants. 1831-45, R. Weeke (o/w Wyke), Hants. 1845 to death. Chap. to the Wyke Poor Law Union. Died Winchester 7/6/1869, leaving £16,000 [C109011. Boase] Married East Meon, Hants. 24/7/1816 Anna Sophia King, with clerical son of same name. *F.R.A.S.* (1838).

WALTON (Jonathan) Born Farnacres, Durham 7/10/1774, s. Nicholas Walton and Ruth Airey. Trinity, Cambridge 1792, BA1796, MA1799, dn00 (Durham), p00 (Durham), BD 1813, DD 1825. R. Birdbrook, Essex 1801 to death there 20/4/1846 [C6416] Married City of London 4/1/1804 Judith Fenn.

WALTON (William) [NiVoF] dn15 (Car.), p16 (Car.). PC. Allendale St Peter w. Allenheads Chapel, Northumberland 1822-51 (and S/M there 1822-27). 'Late of Moulton, Norfolk.' Died London 20/10/1865, leaving £1,500 [C6419] Married Allendale 31/11/1827 Jane Crawhall.

WANE (John) Literate: dn78 (C&L for Chester), p80 (Chester). V. Whiteparish, Wilts. 1800, and R. Sherfield English, Hants. 1802 to death 3/7/1835 aged 80 [C20551]

WAPSHARE (Charles) Born Salisbury, Wilts. 11/9/1775, s. Charles William Wapshare (a lawyer) and Mary Sandford. Merton, Oxford 1793, BA1797, dn01 (Salis.), p01 (Salis.). R. Sproatley, Yorks. 1806-58 (non-res.), V. Kilmersdon, Som. 1806, R. East Hendred, Berks. 1806 to death 22/8/1858 aged 82, leaving £35,000 [C49907] Married Salisbury 18/11/1795 Ann Dyneley (London), w. issue. Port. online.

WARBURTON (Henry) Bapt. Hackney, Middx. 10/5/1791, s. Thomas (physician) and

Susanna Warburton. Caius, Cambridge 1808, BA1813, dn14 (Salis.), p16 (London for Salis.), MA1816. R. Little Peatling, Leics. 1816-22, R. Sible Hedingham >< Essex 1822 to death (Colchester, Essex) 6/12/1837 [C78313] Had issue.

WARBURTON, or EGERTON-WARBURTON (James Francis Egerton-) Born Barrow, Cheshire 15/4/1807, s. Rev. Rowland Warburton and Emma Croxton. BNC, Oxford 1824, BA1828, dn30 (Chester), MA1831, p31 (Chester). R. (and patron) of Lymm (2nd Mediety w. Donative of Warburton), Cheshire 1832 to death. Chap. to Col. and Mrs. Beaumont at Allenheads in 1827. Died 12/9/1849 aged 42 [C17817] Married Blisworth, Northants. 19/2/1819 Anne Stone, w. clerical sons Francis, and Geoffrey; and dau. Katherine Anne, *aka* the Anglican Mother Superior Kate, St Saviour's Priory, Haggerston, London Docks.

WARBURTON, *born* JOBSON (Robert) Born Leeds 1/1/1773. St Catharine's, Cambridge 1793, dn96 (York), p99 (York). R. Holtby, Yorks. 1799 to death 1845 (3rd q.) [C110055. YCO]

WARD (Anthony) Bapt. Orton, Cumberland 29/6/1788, s. of Thomas (a farmer) and Elizabeth Ward. Literate: dn12 (York), p12 (York) Some say BA? V. Eastrington, Yorks. 1825 (living at Methley Park, Leeds) to death 26/10/1841 aged 52 [C135797. YCO] Married Orton 11/6/1828 Mary Milner (a clergy dau.) 'He was a man of meek and kind disposition', etc.

WARD (Benjamin) Born Tong, Shropshire 24/10/1791, s. (Rev.?) John Ward and Mary Andrews. Literate: dn17 (Glos.), p17 (Glos.). Missionary with the new CMS Mission to Ceylon 1817; (first) PC. Carlisle Christ Church 1831-60 (and military chap.), Hon. Canon of Carlisle 1857-79, R. Meesden, Herts. 1859-75 (res.). Died Chester 8/5/1879 aged 87, leaving £1,500 [C167123. Platt] Married Wellington, Shropshire 4/9/1815 Mary Meire, with 2 clerical sons.

WARD (Charles) Born Marlborough, Wilts. 28/4/1799, s. John Ward and Hannah Hawkes. BNC, Oxford 1816, BA1820, dn22 (London), MA1822, p23 (Chester for Salis.). Minor Canon of Bristol Cathedral 1824-5, R. Maulden, Beds. 1825 (and RD Fleete 1840) to death 15/3/1879, leaving £30,000 [C78502] Married Westbury-on-Trim, Glos. 15/8/1825 Susanna Foster, with clerical sons Charles Bruce, and Philip Gordon.

WARD (Charles Richard) Bapt. Bristol 15/8/1799, s. Danvers and Florence Ward. Magdalen Hall, Oxford 1818, BA1822, dn22 (Glos.), p23 (Glos.), MA1825. V. Wapley w. Codington, Glos. 1824 to death (a bachelor) 22/3/1858, leaving £25,000 [C40795]

WARD (Edward) Bapt. Stannington Bridge, Northumberland 15/8/1771, s. William and Susannah Ward. Wadham, Oxford 1789, BA 1793, dn95 (Ox.), p95 (Ox.), MA1799. PC. Iver, Bucks. 1805 to death 19/3/1835 (CCEd says 20/9/1835) [C38113]

WARD (Edward) [Born *c*.1788] Bapt. Haughley, Suffolk 30/11/1797, s. James Ward and Mary Edwards. Jesus, Cambridge 1805, BA1809, dn10 (Nor.), p11 (Nor.), MA1812. V. Haughley 1812 to death 18/4/1868 aged 80, leaving £4,000 [C115931]

WARD (Edward John) Bapt. City of London 28/2/1804, s. John Ward and Mary Ward. Trinity, Oxford 1823, BA1826, dn27 (B&W), p27 (Win.), MA1830. R. East Clandon, Surrey 1832-81. Lived latterly and died Brunswick House Hotel, Hanover Square, London 20/11/1883, leaving £4,026-2s-3d. [C40796] Married Guildford, Surrey 25/10/1831 Frances Sarah Skurray, with clerical s. John Martyr Ward.

WARD (George) Born Croxdale, Co. Durham 9/5/1795, s. Robert Ward. Trinity, Cambridge 1813, BA1818, dn18 (Durham), p19 (Durham), MA 1821. Chap. *H.E.I.C.* Bengal 1831. R. Hope Bagot, Shropshire 1826 to death (Bareilly, India) April 1840 aged 44 [C123755] Married Gainsford, Co. Durham 6/10/1825 Catherine Isabella Garnett.

WARD (Henry) Bapt. Castle Church, Staffs. 14/12/1756, s. Abraham Ward and Margaret Tunnicliffe. Worcester, Oxford 1774, BA1778, dn79 (Ox.), p80 (C&L), MA1781. PC. Havering-atte-Bower, Essex 1784 and R. Little Thurrock, Essex 1786 to death 29/11/1837 [C20554]

WARD (Henry Davis) Born London, s. William Ward. Trinity, Cambridge 1821 (aged 18), BA1825, dn26 (Lin.), p27 (Lin.), MA1828. V. Felmersham w. Pavenham, Beds. 1827 to death (Exmouth, Devon) 19/4/1846 [C78507]

Married Woburn, Beds. 15/1/1828 Mary Ann Land, with issue.

WARD (James Thornborrow) Born Tebay, Westmorland 12/6/1799, s. of Jonathan Ward (a small farmer) and Nancy Fawcett. Literate: dn22 (Car.), p23 (Car.). H/M Lowther G/S 1829-32; V. Askham, Cumberland 1832 to death 13/4/1863 aged 64 (having been ill for 12 years), leaving £6,000 [C6421/C6396 wrongly as James Thornborrow. Platt] Married West Ward, Westmorland 1840 (2nd q.) Elizabeth Brunskill (w), Mansergh Hall, Westmorland, with issue. J.P. for Cumberland and Westmorland.

WARD (John) Born Barking, Essex 29/8/1763. St John's, Cambridge 1781, BA 1785, dn85 (Lin. for London), MA1790, p91 (Nor.). R. (and patron) of Stoke Ash, Suffolk 1794 and R. Occold, Suffolk 1805 to death 12/9/1845 aged 84 [C78509] Had issue. J.P. Suffolk.

WARD (John) From Bristol, s. John Ward. Wadham, Oxford 1802 (aged 19), BA1806, dn06 (London for Salis.), p06 (Glos. for Salis.), MA 1809. R. Littleton on Severn, Glos. 1807-29, R. Compton Greenfield, Glos. 1810 to death. Dom. Chap. to 7th Baron Reay 1811. Died (Bristol) 22/9/1842 [C54119]

WARD (John) Born Marlborough, Wilts. 8/5/1795, s. John Ward (attorney) and Hannah Hawkes. Christ's, Cambridge 1821, dn24 (Salis.), BA1825, p26 (Salis.), MA1828. V. Great Bedwyn, Wilts. 1826-50, R. Wath upon Dearne, Yorks. 1850 to death. Dom. Chap. to Marquess of Ailesbury 1826-50. Died 4/12/1861, leaving £9,000 [C89687. Boase] Married (1) St George's Hanover Square, London 9/1/1823 Ann Merriman (of Rodbourne Cheney, Wilts., she d.1844), with issue (2) Notting Hill, London 21/7/1846 Helen Duncan (dau. of a clergyman who was also 'Superintendent of Military Accounts at the War Office'!), with further issue. An original member of the Council of Marlborough College. Surrogate 1829, 1836.

WARD (John Giffard) From Southampton, s. John Ward and Anne Marr. New, Oxford 1797 (aged 18), BA1801, dn02 (Win.), p08 (Bristol), MA1811, Fellow to 1816. R. Chelmsford, Essex 1817-26 (res.), R. St James, Piccadilly, London 1825 [net income £1,468], Dean of Lincoln 1845 to death. Dom. Chap. to 2nd (1810) and 3rd (1825) Earls of Courtown. Died 28/2/1860, leaving £3,000 [C54120] Married St James, Piccadilly, London 29/5/1816 Amelia Catherine Lloyd, and had issue.

WARD (Michael) From Islip, Oxon., s. Richard Ward [*pleb*]. St Alban Hall, Oxford 1779 (aged 20), then Worcester, BCL1805. V. Lapley, Staffs. 1806, R. Stiffkey and Marston, Norfolk 1836 to death 8/12/1841 [C20559] Widow Amelia Catherine, and issue.

WARD (Philip) Born Trunch, Norfolk 1/9/1795, s. Rev. Marmaduke Ward and Eleanor Smyth. Trinity, Oxford 1813, BA1817, dn18 (Nor.), p19 (Nor.), MA1820. V. Tenterden, Kent 1830 to death 16/1/1859, leaving £600 [C115933] Married Burnham Market, Norfolk 19/2/1822 Horatia Nelson Hamilton (the natural dau. of Admiral Lord Nelson and Emma Hamilton, *q.v.* W. Gerin, *Horatia Nelson* (Oxford, 1970)) (w), with clerical son Horatio Nelson Ward.

WARD, *later* **PORTER (Poyntz Stewart)** Bapt. Barford, Warwicks. 18/12/1766, s. Charles Ward and Elizabeth Packwood. Lincoln, Oxford 1783, BA1788, dn89 (C&L), p92 (Wor.). PC. Bearley, Warwicks. 1802 and PC. Henley in Arden, Warwicks. 1806 to death 17/11/1846 [C20560] Married Wootton Wawen, Warwicks, 11/10/1797 Mary Welch, w. issue. Name changed 1824 on inheriting.

WARD (Richard) [NiVoF] PC. Cromford, Staffs. 1797 and PC. Dethick (CCEd as Ashover, Dethick and Lea Chapel), Staffs. 1799. Died 11/9/1834 [C20563. ERC links them]

WARD (Richard) Born Sedbergh, Yorks. 6/11/1794, s. Richard and Eleanor Ward. St John's, Cambridge 1814, BA1818, dn18 (Glos. for C&L), p20 (Chester for C&L), MA1821. PC. Cauldon, Staffs. 1829, Chap. of Donative of Calton, Staffs. 1832, PC. Waterfall, Staffs. 1832 to probable death 1849 (2nd q.) [C20012. CCEd links them] Was married.

WARD (Richard Rowland) Bapt. Derby 17/7/1763, s. Richard Ward and Rebecca Cotton. Wadham, Oxford 1784, BA1788, dn87 (C&L), p88 (C&L). V. Derby St Peter w. Normanton by Derby 1787 and V. Sutton on the Hill, Derbys. 1795 to death 11/9/1834 [C20564. F. as Richard only. Austin says Rowley] Married Derby 4/12/1792 Anne Mellor, with issue.

WARD (Robert) Born Weybread, Suffolk. Clare, Cambridge 1818, BA1822, dn22 (Peterb. for Nor.), MA1825. S/M Thetford G/S 1827-48; R. Santon, Norfolk 1829-48, PC. Breckles, Norfolk 1837-46. Died Thetford 13/6/1848 aged 50 [C109538] Married 28/12/1825 Mary Umphalby.

WARD (Samuel Broomhead) Born Sheffield 12/4/1798, s. Samuel Broomhead Ward and Hannah Watkinson. Caius, Cambridge 1816, BA1820, BA1823 (Chester), p27 (B&W). R. Teffont Evias, Wilts. 1830 to death 20/4/1866 aged 68, leaving £4,000 [C20015] Married Eccles, Lancs. 9/12/1830 Ellen Chadwick (Hathersage Hall, Derbys.), with issue.

WARD (Walter Mather) Bapt. Derby 9/12/1780, s. William Ward and Anne Mather. Emmanuel, Cambridge 1799, BA1804, dn04 (C&L), p05 (C&L), MA1827. V. Hartington, Derbys. 1827 and PC. Wetton, Staffs. 1828-55. Buried Hartington 7/4/1855 [C20017]

WARD (William, Bishop of Sodor and Man) Born Saintfield, Co. Down 29/9/1762, s. Adam Ward. Literate: dn 88 (Glos), p89 (London), then Caius, Cambridge 1797 (a Ten Year Man, BD1798), DD1828. R. Myland St Michael, Essex 1796-1817, Prebend of Wilsford and Woodford in Salisbury Cathedral 1811-38, R. Alphamstone, Essex 1812, R. Great Horkesley, Essex 1817, Bishop of Sodor and Man 1828 to death (Great Horkesley) 26/1/1838, aged 75 [C8709. Gilling. E. C. Wilson, *An island bishop: 1762-1838: memorials of William Ward, D.D. Bishop of Sodor and Mann 1828-1838* (1931). Not in ODNB] Married Oct. 1805 Anne Hammersley (a banker's dau.), 1s, 5 dau.

WARDALE (John Reynolds) Born Whitby, Yorks. 10/2/1776, s. Francis (an attorney) and Ann Wardale. Clare, Cambridge 1793, BA1798, dn98 (York), p00 (York), Fellow 1800-13, MA 1802. R. Higham Gobion, Beds. 1813-57. Died Hitchin, Herts. 28/12/1859 aged 83, leaving £35,000 [C78523. YCO] Married Pirton, Herts. 30/9/1833 Mary Hanscombe, with clerical son John Wardale.

WARDE (Richard) Bapt. Yalding, Kent 12/6/1763, s. Rev. Richard, sen. and Anne Warde. St John's, Cambridge 1781, BA1785, dn86 (Roch.), p87 (Roch.), MA1788. R. Ditton, Kent 1796 w. R. Yalding [net imcome £1,184] 1798 to death. Dom. Chap. to 7th Baron Reay 1798. Died 26/3/1840 aged 75 [C582. LBSO] Married Aylesford, Kent 4/2/1790 Sarah Ramsay (a clergy dau., Teston, Kent).

WARDE (Thomas) Born Leamington, Warwicks., s. Rowley Warde and Mary Lenton. Magdalen Hall, Oxford 1788 (aged 18), BA1792, dn93 (C&L). V. Weston under Wetherley, Warwicks. 1806 to death 1/2/1850 [C20642] Married Offchurch, Warwicks. 4/5/1802 Charlotte Lloyd, and had issue.

WARDELL (Henry) Born Guisbrough, Yorks. 28/3/1800, s. John Wardell and Eleanor Martin. Trinity, Cambridge 1819, dn23 (Durham), BA 1824, p24 (Ox. for Durham), MA1827. R. Winlaton, Newcastle upon Tyne 1833 to death 4/10/1884 aged 84, leaving £1,000 [C21898] Married 16/10/1826 Mary Newby (a clergy dau.), with clerical son. One of his sons married the actress Ellen Terry.

WARDLE (Joseph) Born City of London 8/2/1782, s. William Wardle and Prudence Carpenter. St Edmund Hall, Oxford 1806, no degree, dn10 (York), p11 (York). PC. Gildersome, Dewsbury, Yorks. 1811-21, PC. Beeston, Yorks. 1831 to death. Chaplain to The Retreat, York ('for the reception and recovery of persons afflicted with disorders of the mind'). Died 31/3/1855 [C125548. YCO] Married Batley, Yorks. 17/6/1815 Lydia Jane Loveday, with issue.

WARE (George) Bapt. Tiverton, Devon 12/7/1798, s. John (merchant) and Ann Ware. St Edmund Hall, Oxford 1817, then Peterhouse, Cambridge 1819, BA1823, dn22 (Ches.), p22 (C&L), MA1832. V. Winsham, Som. 1831-70, R. (and patron) of Ashton, Devon 1832-61. Died 5/6/1870 aged 71, leaving £12,000 [C40797. Boase] Wife Elizabeth, 8 ch. Brother below.

WARE (Henry) Bapt. Tiverton, Devon 3/9/1806, s. John (merchant) and Ann Ware. Magdalen Hall, Oxford 1824, BA1828, dn30 (B&W), MA1831, p31 (Ex.). R. Ladock, Cornwall 1832 to death 28/1/1844 aged 37 [C40798] Wife Elizabeth. Brother above.

WARE (James) Born London, s. James Ware. Trinity, Cambridge 1812 (aged 21), BA1816, dn18 (London), p22 (London), MA1823. R. Wyverstone, Suffolk 1829-55. Probate granted 23/3/1855 [C115938] Wife Mary.

WARING (Francis John, *or* John Francis) Bapt. Clerkenwell, London 13/4/1771, s. Rev. Henry Waring and Elizabeth Thompson. Emmanuel, Cambridge 1789 (as J.F.), dn93 (Lin.), BA1794, p95 (Nor.), MA 1797. V. Heybridge, Essex 1798 (and H/M Maldon G/S, Essex 1815-32, 'though he did little teaching') to death 7/6//1833 aged 62 [C78529] Married 1833 Abra Maria Polley, 9 ch. Wikipedia notes: He was notorious for the extraordinary way he performed the duties of his office. He would read church lessons at breakneck speed, give a very quick sermon of one or two sentences and then run down the aisle and leap onto a horse to gallop off and repeat the performance at two other churches in the area. His domestic arrangements were equally peculiar. Although he wasn't poor, his vicarage was furnished with rough-hewn logs, instead of chairs. His children ate their meals from a trough next to the split-log dining table. He and his wife slept in an enormous wicker cradle suspended from the ceiling. Another website repeats the story and also says: Francis Waring …. was noted, too, for an idiosyncratic dress sense, appearing in church in hats of his own devising, and on one occasion being loudly rebuked by his bishop for wearing purple at important ecclesiastical functions. The bishop was handed a card - kept in readiness for just such a purpose - on which was written, "How very good of you to notice. Do let me recommend my tailor."

WARING (William) Born Barnes, Middx. 5/12/1801, s. John Edward Waring and Mary Scott. Trinity, Cambridge 1819, then Magdalene 1822, Fellow 1823-32, BA1823, dn24, p25, MA 1826. PC. Southampton Jesus Free Chapel (o/w St Mary Extra) 1829, V. Sibbertoft, Northants. 1835-7, V. Welford, Northants. 1835-42, V. Shobdon, Heref. 1847-54, Archdeacon of Salop 1851-77, R. Burwarton, Shropshire 1865-71, Canon Residentiary in Hereford Cathedral 1870-7. At Abington Abbey, Northants. (a private mental institution) 1844-7. Chap. to Bishop of Hereford 1862-68. Master of St Catherine's Hospital [almshouses], Ledbury, Heref. 1870-77. Died Hemel Hempstead 1/3/1877, leaving £14,000 [C109021. Boase] Wife Mary.

WARKMAN (Henry) Bapt. Earsdon, Northumberland 22/12/1782, s. Rev. William Warkman. St Andrews University, MA1801, dn06 (Durham), p09 (Durham). PC. Earsdon 1811-57 (and Minor Canon and Precentor of Durham Cathedral to 1849). Died 12/3/1857 aged 74 [C134196. Smart] Married Newcastle upon Tyne 3/7/1822 Anne Hawthorne Atkinson, with issue.

WARNEFORD (Edward) Bapt. Winterbourne, Glos. 19/12/1778, s. Rev. Edward Warneford and Frances Cater. Chorister Magdalen, Oxford 1793-8; matr. St John's 1797, BA1801, dn01 (Ox.), p03 (Ox.), MA1823. Prebend of Milton Manor in Lincoln Cathedral 1826 and R. Ashburnham w. Penshurst, Sussex 1830 to death 15/1/1840 aged 61 [C21901] 'He has left eleven children, of whom only one is provided for'.

WARNEFORD (Samuel Wilson) Born 1763, s. Rev. Francis Warneford (Warneford Place, Highworth, Wilts.) and Catherine Calverley. University, Oxford 1779, BA1783, MA1786, dn86 (Ox.), p87 (Ox.), BCL1790, DCL1810. R. Lydiard Millicent, Wilts. 1809-55, R. Bourton on the Hill w. Moreton in the Marsh, Glos. 1810 and Hon. Canon of Gloucester Cathedral 1844 to death 11/1/1855 aged 92 [C38119. ODNB. Boase. Vaughan Thomas, *Christian philanthropy exemplified in a memoir of the Rev. Samuel Wilson Warneford, LL.D., late Rector of Bourton-on-the-Hill, and Honorary Canon of Gloucester and Bristol* (1855)] Married 27/9/1796 Margaret Loveden (dau. of an *M.P.*), *s.p.* A philanthropist on a massive scale, he built schools, hospitals and a lunatic asylum [The Wareford Hospital, Oxford], at an estimated total of £200,000. Fine port. at: artuk.org/discover/artworks/reverend-dr-samuel-wilson-warneford-17631855-43017

WARNER (Daniel Francis) Born Antigua, West Indies 9/6/1795, s. Thomas Warner and Dorothy Frye. Magdalen Hall, Oxford 1813, BA 1817, dn19 (Chester), p20 (Ely for Salis.), MA 1820, BD 1828. R. Kingsdown w. Mappicombe, Kent 1831, V. Hoo St Werburgh 1835 to death 17/11/1870, leaving £450 [C1502] Married St Pancras, London 15/7/1818 Sylviana Maria Vaughan, with issue.

WARNER (George Henry Lee-) Bapt. Boxwell, Glos. 9/4/1804. St John's, Cambridge 1822, BA1826, dn27 (Nor.), p28 (Nor.), MA 1829. V. Canterbury St Mary Bredin 1828 to (burial) 1/1/1840 [C116001. Venn as Lee-Warner] Brother below?

WARNER (James Lee) [NiVoF] V. Houghton St Giles, Walsingham, Norfolk 1807 and Chap. of the Donative of Great and Little Walsingham,

Norfolk 1807 to death 8/5/1835 (CCEd thus) [C116003] Clerical son of same name. Brother above?

WARNER (Richard) Born Marylebone, London 18/10/1763, s. Richard Warner (tradesman) and Rebecca Sawyer. St Mary Hall, Oxford 1787, no degree, dn89 (York). R. Great Chalfield, Berks. 1809-57, V. Norton St Philip w. Hinton Charterhouse, Som. 1817-19, V. Timberscombe, Som. 1825-6, R. Croscombe, Som. 1826-8 (res.), R. Chelwood, Som. 1832 to death 27/7/1857 aged 93 [C40880. ODNB. Boase.YCO] Married Tettenhall Regis, Staffs. 5/10/1801 Ann Pearson (w), with issue. Antiquarian and prolific miscellaneous writer.

WARNER (William) From Rotherhithe, Kent, s. John Warner. St John's, Oxford 1795 (aged 18), BA1799, dn99 (Salis.), p01 (Salis.), MA1803. V. Chiseldon, Wilts. 1801-14, R. Widford, Essex 1814 to death (Bath) 3/1/1840, aged 62 [C89691]

WARRE (Francis) Bapt. Cheddon Fitzpayne, Som. 4/11/1775, s. Rev. Francis Warre, sen. [*q.v.* Boase] and Joanna Bliss. Oriel, Oxford 1793, dn98 (B&W), BCL1799, p99 (Ex. for B&W), DCL 1829. R. Cheddon Fitzpayne 1800, R. Hemyock, Devon 1829, Prebend of Combe XIV in Wells Cathedral 1823 to death 16/1/1854 [C49925] Married Walcot, Bath 24/2/1800 Louisa Charlotte Popham, with clerical son.

WARREN (Dawson) Bapt. Westminster, London 14/1/1771, s. of James and Martha Warren. Trinity, Oxford 1790, BA1794, dn94 (Lin.), p95 (London), MA1799. V. Edmonton, Middx. 1795 [net income £1,550] (w. St John Weld's Chapel, Southgate 1813) to death 17/12/1838 aged 68 [C78542. Broadley, A.M. (ed.), *The journal of a British chaplain in Paris during the peace negotiations of 1801-2* (1913)] Married City of London 14/1/1796 his cousin Charlotte Lucy Jackson, 13 ch. (incl. Revds Edward Blackburn, and Charles Edward Dawson Warren, and an Anglican nun).

WARREN (Henry) Born London 4/9/1772, s. Richard Warren (physician to George III) and Elizabeth Shaw. Trinity, Cambridge 1790, BA 1794, dn96 (Bangor), p97 (Bangor), MA1797. Prebend of Llanfair in Bangor Cathedral 1797, R. Ashington w. Buncton, Sussex 1799 and V. Farnham, Surrey 1799 to death. Dom. Chap. to Bishop of St David's/Bangor 1799. Died 21/6/1845 [C158577] Married Wiggonholt, Sussex 24/6/1799 Eliza Mason, with issue.

WARREN (John) Born Bangor 4/10/1796, s. Very Rev. John Warren, sen. (Dean of Bangor) and Elizabeth Crooke. Jesus, Cambridge 1814, BA1818, dn19 (Bangor), Fellow 1818-29, p20 (Bangor), MA1821, Tutor. R. Caldecote, Hunts. 1822 and R. Graveley, Cambs. 1822 (which two parishes he amalgamated). Died Bangor 16/8/1852 [C109539. ODNB under Charles Warren. Boase] Married Brighton 27/8/1835 his cousin Caroline Elizabeth Warren (a military dau.), *s.p.* Brother William, below. *F.R.S.* (1830).

WARREN (John Crabb [Blair]) Born Greenstead, Essex, s. Rev. William Hamilton Warren and Elizabeth Shrapnel. Sidney, Cambridge 1820, BA1826, dn27 (London), p28 (London), MA1830. PC. Little Horkesley, Essex 1829 to death. Probate granted 31/10/1856 [C123767] Brother Zachariah Shrapnel Warren, below.

WARREN (Thomas) Born Westminster, London 29/9/1769, s. Ven. John Warren (Archdeacon of Worcester) and Mary Noyes. Christ Church, Oxford 1787, BA1791, MA1794. V. Tolpuddle, Dorset 1805 to death 18/11/1851 [C54125] Married Clifton, Bristol 3/10/1805 Jane Powell. This is the man who 'betrayed' the Tolpuddle Martyrs.

WARREN (Thomas Alston) Born Dunstable, Beds. 18/12/1768, s. Thomas Warren and Catherine Manley. St John's, Oxford 1787, BA 1791, dn91 (Ox.), p93 (Ox.), MA1795, BD1808, Fellow to 1814, Chap. 1834-53. PC. Randwick, Glos. 1800-14, R. South Warnborough, Hants. 1814 to death 26/12/1853 [C38120] Married Bampton, Oxon. 27/8/1825 Catherine Manley.

WARREN (William) Born Bangor 1/8/1803, s. Very Rev. John Warren, sen. (Dean of Bangor) and Elizabeth Crooke. Jesus, Cambridge 1822, BA1826, dn27 (Bangor), p28 (Bangor), MA1829. Llanfihangel Yscefiog w. Llanffinan, Anglesey 1828-32, R. Wroot, Lincs. 1832 to death (Brighton) 29/12/1877, leaving £3,000 [C78547] Married Eton, Bucks. 11/4/1844 Ann Sarah Bethell (w) (a clergy dau., Womplesdon, Surrey). Brother John, above.

WARREN (Zachariah Shrapnel) Born Greensted, Essex 2/4/1796, s. Rev. William Hamilton Warren and Elizabeth Shrapnel.

Sidney, Cambridge 1812, BA1818, dn19 (Salis.), p20 (Peterb. for York), MA1821. Usher at Oakham School 1819, H/M Beverley School, Yorks. 1828-42; V. Dorrington, Lincs. 1823 and V. Ancaster, Lincs. 1841 to death 19/8/1861, leaving £18,000 [C78548] Married Stretton, Rutland 14/10/1823 Maria Lamb (a clergy dau.) (w), with clerical son John Shrapnel Warren. Brother John Crabb Blair Warren, above.

WARRENER (Robert) Born Dalton, Lancs., s. James W. and Sarah Park. Magdalen Hall, Oxford 1805 (aged 19), BA dn10 (Chester), p11 (Chester). R. Snave, Kent 1832-51-, R. Snargate w. Snave ><, Kent 1832 to death. Buried Hertford 16/12/1869 aged 84 [C71438] Married Rye, Sussex 8/4/1817 Catherine Sarah

WARRINER (Enoch Hodgkinson) Born Westminster, London, s. George Warriner and Elizabeth Grubb. Lincoln, Oxford 1801 (aged 17), BA1806, dn06 (Lin.), MA1808, p08 (Lin.). R. Foots Cray, Kent 1823 to death 17/9/1861 aged 67, leaving £4,000 [C583] Married Camberwell, London 21/6/1806 Elizabeth Hartley.

WARRINGTON (William) Born Acton, Wrexham, Denbigh 18/10/1772, s. Rev. George Warrington and Mary Strudwick. Wadham, Oxford 1791, BA1794, dn96 (Ox.), p96 (Ox.), then Balliol MA1800. V. St Lawrence Jewry w. St Mary Magdalen, Milk Street, City of London 1809-15, V. Leake w. Nether Stilton, Northallerton, Yorks. 1815 [blank in ERC] to death 28/4/1852 aged 79 [C38368] Married St George's Hanover Square, London 27/1/1810 Anne Priscilla Mainwaring. In King's Bench Prison for debt 1834.

WARTNABY (Thomas) Born Leics. c.1768, s. William Wartnaby and Ann Wade. Queens', Cambridge 1786, dn90 (Peterb.), LLB1793, p95 (Lin.). PC. Irby-in-the-Marsh, Lincs. 1813 [C78537 as Warmanby], R. Knossington, Leics. 1817 to death 30/11/1845 aged 77 [C78550. ERC links] Married Gumley, Leics. 22/2/1796 Ann West, with issue.

WASEY (George) Born Westminster, London 3/1/1773, s. William John Spearman and Elizabetha Honora Wasey. Oriel, Oxford 1791, then All Souls, Fellow 1795-1812, BA1795, dn96 (Ox.), MA1799, BD1809. R. Whittington, Glos. 1801-11, R. Wytham, Berks. 1802-11, R. Albury, Oxon. 1802-11, R. Ulcombe, Kent 1811 to death. Chap. to Prince of Wales 1802. Died Banbury, Oxon. 24/3/1838 [C21902] Married Marylebone, London 2/6/1810 Ann Sophia Frodsham, w. clerical sons William George Leigh Wasey, and John Spearman Wasey.

WASNEY (William Atkinson) Bapt. Hull 9/2/1769, s. Thomas Wasney and Mercy Atkinson. Trinity, Cambridge 1786, BA1791, dn91 (York), p93 (York), MA1794. V. Bracewell, Yorks. 1814-36. Died there 1842 (2nd q.) aged 73 [C111000. YCO] Married Thornton in Craven, Yorks. 19/10/1796 Ellen Wilkinson, with issue.

WASS(E) (Samuel) Born Sheffield, Yorks. 19/12/1798, s. Robert Wasse and Jane Wrathall. Literate, dn22 (York), p29 (York). H/M Sherborne G/S, Yorks. 1828; R. Hayfield, Derbys. 1832 to death 1856 (2nd q.) [C135801. YCO] Married Epworth, Lincs. 1828 Mary Gervas. Brother below.

WASS(E) (William) Born Handsworth, Yorks. 2/6/1792, s. Robert Wasse and Jane Wrathall. St Edmund Hall, Oxford 1815, then St Catherine's, Cambridge 1816, a Ten Year Man, dn16 (York), p17 (York). PC. Preston in Holderness w. Headon, Yorks. 1828 to death 19/2/1839 aged 46 [C135802. YCO] Brother above.

WATERS (John) From London, s. Richard Waters. St John's, Oxford 1772 (aged 17), dn78 (Ox.), BCL1779, p79 (Ox. for Win.). R. Tandridge, Surrey 1809. Died 12/4/1834 [C38375]

WATERS (Mark) Bapt. Great Yarmouth, Norfolk 24/3/1807, s. Mark Waters (merchant) and Margartta Maria Tolver. Emmanuel, Cambridge 1825, BA1829, dn30 (Nor.), p31 (Nor.). (joint) Min. Great Yarmouth St George 1833 to death 19/10/1864 aged 57, leaving £5,000 [C116013] Married Great Yarmouth 22/10/1833 Katherine Maria Preston (w), with issue.

WATERS (William Thomas) Bapt. Stamford, Lincs. 17/10/1771, s. William (apothecary and surgeon) and Susanna Waters. St John's, Cambridge 1789, BA1793, dn94 (Lin. for Peterb.), p97 (Lin.), MA1815. R. Dunsby, Lincs. 1802-53, V. Sempringham w. Pointon and Birthorpe, Lincs. 1813-26 (res.), R. Rippingale, Lincs. 1825 to death. Dom. Chap. to 17th Baron Saltoun 1813. Buried 11/2/1853 [C78308] Married Stamford 1798 Catherine Fothergill, and had issue.

WATKIN (Edward) Bapt. Northampton 6/1/1789, s. Rev. George Watkin and Frances Thompson. Lincoln, Oxford 1807, BA1811, p12 (Peterb.), MA1814. V. Northampton St Giles, 1812, V. (and patron) of Cogenhoe, Northants. 1812 to death. Dom. Chap. to 1st Marquess of Northampton 1812. Died 18/5/1864, leaving £600 [C111499] Married (2) Cogenhoe 20/1/1860 Ann Arden.

WATKINS (Charles Frederick) Bapt. Corsley, Wilts. 16/1/1795, s. Rev. William Watkins (R. Port Eynon, Glamorgan) and Jane Cradock Nowell. [In Royal Navy 1810-15]. Christ's, Cambridge 1818 (a Ten Year Man), dn18 (Salis.), p18 (Salis.). Warden of Farley Hospital [almshouses], Wilts. 1822-32; V. Brixworth, Northants. 1832 to death 15/7/1873, leaving £600 [C87092. ODNB. Boase] Married (1) Berks. 26/4/1822 Matilda Opfferman (d.1824), 2 ch. (2) Bloomsbury, London 12/2/1825 Caroline Rebecca Aldridge (d.1827), 2 ch. (3) Farley 30/7/1828 Elizabeth Parsons (w), at least 14 ch. Fossil collector and author.

WATKINS (Charles Kemeys) Born Odiham, Hants., s. Rev. George Watkins. Corpus Christi, Oxford 1794 (aged 16), BA1798, MA1802, dn02 (Win.), p02 (Win.), Fellow 1803-22, BD1811. R. Fenny Compton, Warwicks. 1821 to death 22/4/1840 [C20661] 'Mr Watkins gave more than £700 a year to acts of charity'.

WATKINS (George Nowell) Bapt. Froyle, Hants. 10/2/1771, s. Rev. George Watkins and Ann Baldwin. St Mary Hall, Oxford 1788, BA 1792, dn94 (Bristol), p95 (Peterb.), MA1795. PC. Long Sutton, Hants. 1806 to death (Froyle) 5/6/1844 [C40805] Married Bloomsbury, London 24/5/1810 Mary Boswell Aston, with issue.

WATKINS (Henry) Born Conisbrough, Yorks. 6/7/1775, s. Rev. Henry Watkins, sen. and Ann Marian Wilmer. Christ's, Cambridge 1794, BA 1798, dn00 (York), p01 (York). V. Beckingham, Notts. 1802 and V. Silkstone, Yorks. 1835 to death 13/12/1844 aged 69 [C111003. YCO] Married Tickhill, Yorks. 15/3/1803 Frances Mary Bower (Killerby Hall, Yorks.), w. clerical son.

WATKINS (Henry George) Bapt. Holborn, London 21/2/1765, s. Henry Watkins (auctioneer) and Mary Judkins. St Edmund Hall, Oxford 1788, dn91 (Nor. for Win.), BA1791, p91 (C&L for Win.), MA1794. R. St Swithin London Stone w. St Mary Bothaw, City of London 1805 to death 9/1/1850 [C20662. DEB] Married Islington, London 22/10/1800 Sarah Long, with clerical son, also Henry George Watkins,

WATKINS (John) Born Fulham, Middx, s. John Watkins. Jesus, Oxford 1811 (aged 18), BA1815, dn16 (Ox.), p17 (Ox.), MA1818. V. Auborne, Lincs. 1821 to death 11/3/1834 (CCEd says 6/8/1834) [C21904]

WATKINS (Morgan) Born Llanthetty, Brecon 24/4/1800, s. Philip Watkins. Jesus, Oxford 1820, BA1824, dn25 (Glos.), p26 (Glos.). V. Southwell, Notts. 1831 and V. Bleasby, Notts. 1838 to death 1841 aged 40 [C167276] Married (1) Bexley, Kent 9/3/1831 Henrietta Auriol (d.1832), dau. Very Rev. Edward Auriol Hay-Drummond (2) Bloomsbury, London 1834 Eliza Hunter (a minor), of Kirkton, Perthshire.

WATKINS (Thomas) Born Hereford 1775, s. Thomas Watkins [*pleb*]. Christ Church, Oxford 1793, BA1797, dn99 (Heref.), MA 1801. Vicar Choral Hereford Cathedral 1797-1802, V. Eaton-under-Haywood, Shropshire 1799-1805, Chap. Winchester College 1810 (w. Minor Canon and Minor Canon and Precentor Winchester Cathedral '37 years'), V. Minety, Wilts. 1810, V. Wootton St Lawrence, Hants. 1829-34, Perpetual Vicar Collingbourne Kingston, Wilts. 1833. Died 9/4/1839 aged 64 [C89699] Married Winchester 20/12/1825 Elizabeth Pipon.

WATKINS (William) Born Hereford, s. William Watkins [*pleb*]. New, Oxford 1807 (aged 18), BA1811, Chap. 1812-14, p13 (Heref), MA 1818. Vicar Choral in Hereford Cathedral 1812, OC. Sutton St Michael, Heref. 1815-29, R. Racton w. Lordington, Sussex 1817, Minor Canon of Chichester Cathedral (w. R. Chichester St Olave) 1825, R. Rumboldswyke, Sussex 1828. Dom. Chap. to 4th Baron Brandon 1817. Died 21/3/1865, leaving £800 [C159612] Wife Frances, and issue.

WATKINSON (Robert) Born Essex 18/10/1775. Trinity, Cambridge 1793 (did not reside), re-adm. Emmanuel 1794, BA1798, Fellow 1800, MA1801, dn01 (Nor.), p02 (Nor.), BD1808. Usher and S/M Charterhouse School 1799-1826 [but not continuously]; R. Newland St Lawrence, Essex 1827-9, V. Earls Colne,

Essex 1829-67. Died 21/2/1869, leaving £70,000 [C116017. Boase] Married St Pancras, London 13/1/1827 Catherine Harby (w). 'An active and popular vicar.'

WATLING (Charles Henry) Born Leominster, Heref. 22/11/1794, s. Robert Watling and Mary Brewer. Merton, Oxford 1813, then Jesus, Fellow 1817-34, BA1817, dn18 (Ox.), p18 (Ox.), MA1820, BD1827, Tutor, Latin 1822 & Greek lecturer 1823. Curate Charlton Regis (o/w King's Charlton), Glos. 1830 and R. Tredington, Worcs. 1839 to death (Norton Bavant, Wilts.) 1/3/1871, leaving £4,000 [C21905] Married Childwall, Liverpool 22/8/1833 Emily Porter, with clerical son Henry Fairchild Watling.

WATSON (Anthony) Bapt. Bridekirk, Cumberland 19/5/1793, s. Anthony Watson and Jane Irvine. Literate: dn17 (Chester), p19 (Chester). PC. Holy Island, Northumberland 1822 to death 23/10/1867 aged 74, leaving £1,500 [C134605] Married Bridekirk 24/6/1813 Frances Messenger (a clergy dau.), with issue.

WATSON (Christopher George) Born South Weald, Essex 21/12/1787, s. Lt.-Col. Christopher Watson (3rd Dragoon Guards, Westwood House, Great Horkesley, Essex) and Catherine Marlam. Pembroke, Cambridge 1806, BA1810, dn10 (Nor.), p11 (Nor.), MA1814. R. Salcot, Essex 1812-9, R. Melton, Suffolk 1814 to death (Woodbridge, Suffolk) 3/2/1870, leaving £16,000 [C116018] Married Marylebone, London 4/6/1819 Elizabeth Lant Bullock, with clerical son Frederick Watson.

WATSON (John) Bapt. Wigton, Cumberland 6/12/1753, s. John Watson. Literate: dn79 (York), p80 (York), then Queens', Cambridge, BA1781, MA1784. PC. Coley, Halifax 1791. Died Wigton ('the patrimonial estate of his ancestors') 1841 (1st q.) aged 86 [C101948. NiV. YCO]

WATSON (John) Born Greystoke, Westmorland. [NiVoF] dn19 (Car.), p20 (Car.). PC. Cumrew, Cumberland 1828 and R. Renwick, Cumberland 1832 to death 4/12/1866 aged 78, leaving £200 [C3531. Platt says also an amateur architect] Wife Margaret (w), married before 1851.

WATSON (John) From Prestbury, Cheshire, s. Rev. John Watson, sen. BNC, Oxford 1809 (aged 19), BA1813, Fellow 1813-32, MA1815, etc. R. Selham, Sussex 1832-42. Died Oxford 21/1/1875 aged 86, leaving £140,000 [C71448 Boase]

WATSON (John Hewlett) Bapt. Tytherley, Hants. 24/6/1801, s. William Watson and Mary Hewlett. Wadham, Oxford 1819 (aged 17), BA 1823, dn24 (Lin. for Cant.), p25 (Lin.), MA 1828. V. West Wratting, Cambs. 1829, R. Tydd St Giles, Cambs. 1829 to death (Gravesend, Kent) 15/3/1862, leaving £3,000 [C78568] Married (1) City of London 24/3/1831 Clarissa Ann Gregory (d.1834) (2) Cambridge 18/1/1837 Elizabeth Mary Wilson, with issue.

WATSON (John James) Born Hackney, London 15/12/1767, s. John Watson and Dorothy Robson. University, Oxford 1787, BA1790, p92 (Salis. for Win.), MA1793, BD and DD1808. R. Hackney St John, Middx. 1799 [net income £1,082], R. Digswell, Herts. 1811, Archdeacon of St Albans 1816-39, V. Denford w. Ringstead, Northants. 1822, Broomesbury Prebend in St Paul's Cathedral, London 1825 to death 9/6/1839 [C109032] Married Hackney 12/1/1803 Caroline Powell, with clerical son John David Watson.

WATSON (Joseph Burges) Born Lambeth, South London 30/1/1801, s. Joseph Watson (Surbiton Hill House, Kingston-upon-Thames, Surrey) and Mary Burges. Emmanuel, Cambridge 1820, BA1824, dn24 (London), p25 (Nor.), MA1827. V. Norton, Herts. 1831-42. Died Edmonton, Essex 10/4/1881 aged 79, no will traced [C20667. Venn death date is wrong] Married Kensington, London 3/5/1837 Margaret Louisa Ford, with issue.

WATSON (Robert) From Yeovil, Som., s. George Watson. Trinity, Oxford 1779 (aged 21), no degree, dn80 (Ely for B&W), p91 (Glos.). V. Bristol Temple Church 1791-1816, V. Bristol Christ Church w. St Ewen 1816 to death 11/8/1842 [C54128]

WATSON (Robert) [NiVoF]. PC. Wyresdale, Lancs. 1829 to death (Islington, London) 17/5/1863, leaving £300 [C170839] In 1841 Census aged '65', living with wife Mary only.

WATSON (Samuel) From Holborn, London, s. James Watson. Christ Church, Oxford 1781 (aged 17), BA1785, dn87 (Roch.), p88 (Roch.), MA1792, BD and DD1806. S/M Shooters Hill,

Greenwich, Kent; R. Gravesend, Kent 1811 and Sen. Chap. in the Ordnance Dept., Woolwich, Kent to death 9/4/1837 [C2544]

WATSON (Thomas) [NiVoF]. PC. Elland, Yorks. 1793-1802, V. Edenhall w. Langwathby, Cumberland 1801 to death 15/5/1833 aged 74 [C3532. Platt] Married there 5/8/1807 Mary Johnson, with issue.

WATSON (Thomas) Bapt. Norwich 12/11/1780, s. Thomas Watson. Caius, Cambridge 1798, dn03 (Nor.), BA1804, p05 (Nor.), MA1807. R. Thurlton, Norfolk 1821-45, PC. Hardley, Norfolk 1821-45, PC. Costessy, Norfolk 1821-45, PC. Tottenhill, Norfolk 1832, V. Newton-by-Castle Acre, Norfolk 1834-41. Died 20/3/1845 aged 64 (Venn says 11/4/1845) [C109547]

WATSON (Thomas) Born Easton, Cumberland 3/7/1796 (bapt. 28/7/1799), s. Christopher Watson and Mary Young. St Edmund Hall, Oxford 1818, BA1823, dn23 (Peterb.), p24 (Peterb.), MA1839. (first) Curate Clerkenwell St Philip, London 1834-50, V. East Farleigh, Kent 1850 to death 12/9/1880, leaving £10,000 [C111507. Boase] Married 11/5/1837 Frances Marian Springett, with clerical sons Christopher Stowell Watson, Howard Aylwin Watson, and Thomas Springett Watson.

WATTS (James) Born Tewksbury, Glos., s. John Watts [*pleb*.]. Christ Church, Oxford 1795 (aged 19), BA1799, MA1802, p09 (Bristol). V. Easton Maudit, Heref. 1806, V. Weston Beggard, Heref. 1809, V. Ledbury, Heref. 1810 to death. Dom. Chap. to Anne. Countess of Galloway 1809. Died 1847 (1st q.) [C54129. F. as John - scribal error] Clerical son James George Watts.

WATTS (John) Bapt. City of London 8/3/1795, s. Robert and Harriet Watts. University, Oxford 1812, BA1816, Fellow 1817-29, dn18 (Ox.), MA1819, p20 (Ox.), Tutor 1821-7, etc. R. Tarrant Gunville, Dorset 1828-72. RD of Pimperne 1835, Prebend of Netheravon in Salisbury Cathedral 1846 to death 2/6/1872. Died 2/6/1872, leaving £20,000 [C21912] Married Hazlebury Bryan, Dorset 7/6/1816 Charlotte Upshall, with clerical son. Surrogate.

WATTS (Robert) From Middx. Literate: dn75 (London), p76 (London), then St John's, Cambridge 1778 (aged 24, a Ten Year Man), MA 1797 Lambeth. V. St Helen's Bishopsgate, City of London 1795, Prebend of Ealdstreet in St Paul's Cathedral 1797-1842, R. St Alphege London Wall, City of London 1799-42, R. St Benet Gracechurch w. St Leonard Eastcheap, City of London 1829 to death. Assistant 1785-9, then Librarian 1799 Sion College. Died Sion College 19/1/1842 aged 92 [C123859] Clerical son of same name.

WAY (Charles John) Born Spaynes Hall, Great Yeldham, Essex 23/1/1796, s. Gregory Lewis Way (barrister) and Ann Frances Paxton (a clergy dau.). Trinity, Cambridge 1814, BA1818, dn19 (Lin.), p22 (London), MA1822. R. Middleton, Lancs. 1832-5 [net income £1,070], V. Boreham, Essex 1850 to death. Chap. to Duke of Atholl at some date. Lived latterly at Spaynes Hall. Died 9/11/1873 aged 77, leaving £2,000 [C78579] Married 1/8/1832 Hemel Hempstead, Herts. Georgiana Augusta Grover, with issue.

WAY (Henry Hugh) Bapt. Denham, Bucks. 13/4/1807, s. Benjamin Way (High Sheriff of Bucks.) and Mary Smyth. Merton, Oxford 1825, BA1829, dn30 (Lin.), p31 (B&W). V. Henbury, Glos. 1831-60 (living at Alderbourne Manor, Langley, Bucks.) to death 23/2/1890, leaving £37,923-3s-4d. [C40808] Married (1) Henbury 22/10/1823 Susanna Daniel (d.1875), with clerical sons John Hugh, and William Henry Broadley Way (2) Steyning, Sussex 1876 (2nd q.) Annie Poore. J.P. Step-brother below.

WAY (William) Bapt. St James, Westminster, London 8/4/1773, s. Benjamin Way (High Sheriff of Bucks.) and Elizabeth Ann Cooke. Christ Church, Oxford 1791, BA1795, dn95 (Lin.), p97 (Lin.), MA1798. R. Denham 1797 and R. Hedgerley, Bucks. 1797 to death 12/8/1845 [C78584] Married 5/2/1816 Elizabeth Lloyd Wheate. Step-brother above.

WAYET (John) From Boston, Lincs., s. John Wayet and Ann Wheldale. Queen's, Oxford 1786 (aged 19), BA1790, dn90 (Lin.), p91 (Lin.). V. Frampton, Lincs. 1796-1804 (res.), V. Pinchbeck, Lincs. 1821-34. Died 12/7/1841 aged 74 [C78586] Married Boston 7/5/1805 Elizabeth Flowers, with issue (inc. son Field Flowers Wayet!).

WAYLAND (Daniel Sheppard) Bapt. Frome, Somerset 29/3/1782 (in a Baptist meeting house), s. Daniel Wayland and Sophia Sheppard. St Edmund Hall, Oxford 1801, BA1805, dn06

(B&W), p07 (Cant. for B&W), MA1808. PC. Kirton in Lindsey, Lincs. 1812-59, V. North Kelsey, Lincs. 1819-20, PC. Thurlby (by Bourne), Lincs. 1823 to death (Bassingham, Lincs.) 8/4/1859, leaving £7,000 [C49992. Kaye] Married Jane Boyce, w. issue by 1819.

WAYNE (William Henry) Born Quorndon, Derbys. 1/5/1803, s. William Henry Wayne (Quorndon House) and Anne Salmon. St John's, Cambridge 1821 (as Henry: kept four terms), then Peterhouse 1823, BA1825, dn27 (C&L), p28 (C&L), MA1828. PC. Heage, Derbys. 1828-41, PC. Alsop en le Dale, Derbys. 1834-41, V. Much Wenlock. Shropshire 1842-72, PC. Benthall, Heref. 1842. Died 20/12/1872, leaving £5,000 [C20672] Married Brighton 10/2/1829 Jane Mitford, with clerical son of father's name.

WEBB (Elias) Born Sherbourne, Warwicks. 30/3/1775, s. Thomas Webb and Margaret Nanfan. St John's, Cambridge 1793, BA1797, dn97 (Wor.), MA1800, p02 (Wor.), DD? V. Warwick St Nicholas 1810-11, PC. Bishopton, Warwicks. 1813-17, PC. Sherbourne 1822 to death (Sladnor, Devon) 4/6/1848 aged 75 [C122277] Married Daventry, Northants. 7/9/1797 Ann Watkins.

WEBB (John) Bapt. City of London 19/4/1776, s. William Webb and Ann Sise. Wadham, Oxford 1794, BA1798, dn99 (C&L), p01 (C&L), MA1802. PC. Waterfall, Staffs. 1801, Minor Canon of Worcester Cathedral 1811, R. (and patron) of Tretire and Michaelchurch, Heref. 1812-69, Minor Canon of Gloucester Cathedral (and V. Cardiff St. Mary) 1821-63 (non-res.), PC. Hardwick, Heref. 1861 to death. Dom. Chap. to 2nd Earl Romney 1822. Died 18/2/1869 aged 92, leaving £9,000 [C20678. Boase] Wife Sarah Reynolds, and clerical s. Thomas William Webb. *F.S.A.* (1819).

WEBB, *later* PEPLOE (John Birch) Born Lamberhurst, Kent 9/9/1801, s. Daniel Webb and Anne Birch Peploe. BNC, Oxford 1818, BA1822, MA1825. V. Kings Pyon and Birley, Heref. 1825-69, V. Weobley, Heref. 1826-69, RD, Prebend of Preston Wynne in Hereford Cathedral 1844. Lived at Garnstone Castle, Weobley, Heref., and died there 26/1/1869, leaving £60,000 [Not yet in CCEd. F. as Peploe] Married Ludlow, Shropshire 3/1/1828 Annie Molyneux (w), with issue. Name changed 1866.

WEBB (John Robert Hill) Bapt. Southampton 11/3/1757. Clare, Cambridge 1774, dn81 (C&L for York), p81 (York), LLB1786. R. Thornton (le) Dale, Pickering, Yorks. 1781 to death 21/7/1837 aged 81 [C20679. YCO] Married (2) York 7/4/1801 Mrs Ann (Johnson) Maynard. 'The benevolent Rector.'

WEBB (William) Born Sutton Coldfield Feb. 1775, s. William Webb (schoolmaster). Clare, Cambridge 1793, BA1797, Fellow 1799, MA 1800, dn00 (Peterb.), p01 (Peterb.), BD1807, DD1816, tutor, Master of Clare College, Cambridge 1815-56, Vice Chancellor 1817-18 and 1832-3. R. Fornham All Saints, Suffolk 1815-16, V. Littlington, Cambs. 1816 to death 4/1/1856 [C109542. Boase] Married Truro, Cornwall 20/8/1816 Anne Gould (a clergy dau.). *F.L.S.* 1815.

WEBB (William) Born Castle Church, Staffs. 1/10/1806, s. Henry Webb and Elizabeth Heath. Trinity, Cambridge 1824, BA1828, dn29 (C&L), p31 (C&L), MA1834. R. Tixall, Staffs. 1831 to death 27/3/1883 aged 76, leaving £7,101-10s-6d. [C20683] Married 1831 Maria Morgan, with clerical sons Arthur Henry, and Henry James Webb.

WEBBER (Charles, sen.) Bapt. Chichester 17/5/1762, s. Rev. William Webber and Anne Smith. Christ Church, Oxford 1778, Student [Fellow], BA1782, dn85 (Ox.), MA1785. V. Boxgrove, Sussex 1795, Sequestrator of Westhampnett, Sussex 1795-1805, V. Eartham, Sussex 1797-1822, R. Tangmere, Sussex 1798-1828 (res.), Prebend of Bishopshurst and Canon Residentiary in Chichester Cathedral 1803-48, Archdeacon of Chichester 1808-40, V. Amport, Hants. 1808-28, R. Felpham, Sussex 1815-25 (res.). Dom. Chap. to 3rd Duke of Richmond and Lennox 1787; to 5th Duke 1828. Died 15/6/1848 [C38432] Married St George's Hanover Square, London 18/11/1789 Mary Peirson, with clerical sons Charles, and George Henry, below.

WEBBER (Charles, jun.) Bapt. Boxgrove, Sussex 30/8/1794, s. Ven. Charles Webber, sen., Archdeacon of Chichester (above) and Mary Peirson. Christ Church, Oxford 1813, Student [Fellow] 1813-18, BA1816, dn17 (Ox.), p18 (Ox.), MA1820. Highleigh Prebend in Chichester Cathedral (w. Master of the Prebendal School) 1824-40, (succ. his father as) V. Amport, Hants. 1828, Canon Residentiary

Chichester Cathedral 1829-50 (w. Somerleigh Prebend 1840), R. Felpham, Sussex 1830-2 (res.), R. Staunton on Wye, Heref. 1837 to death 6/3/1850 [C21915] Married St George's Hanover Square, London 18/11/1829 Caroline Mason. Brother George Henry, below.

WEBBER (Edward) Born Bathealton, Som., s. Rev. Alexander Webber. Pembroke, Oxford 1783 (aged 18), dn87 (Ox. for B&W), SCL, p88 (Bristol). R. (and patron) of Bathealton 1788-1842, R. Raddington, Som. 1791, PC. Thorne St Margaret, Som. 1806 and R. Runnington, Som. 1809 to death there 11/2/1842 [C38433] Married Bathealton 21/5/1799 Elizabeth Pearse (w), w. issue.

WEBBER (Frederic) Born Otterton, Devon, s. William Webber. Pembroke, Oxford 1819 (aged 18), dn24 (Ex.), BA1824, p25 (Ex.), MA 1865, Chaplain *H.E.I.C.* Bombay 1827-32; PC. Merther, Cornwall 1834-53, R. St Michael Penkevil, Cornwall 1842 to death. Dom. Chap. to Viscount Falmouth, his patron. Died 6/11/1879 aged 78, leaving £10,000 [C123866] Married York 7/5/1835, and issue.

WEBBER (George Henry) Born Boxgrove, Sussex 14/2/1801, s. Ven. Charles Webber, sen. (Archdeacon of Chichester, above) and Mary Peirson. Christ Church, Oxford 1820, Student [Fellow] 1820-7, BA1824, dn24 (Ox.), MA1826, p26 (Ox.). V. Great Budworth, Cheshire 1826-58, Somerleigh Prebend in Chichester Cathedral 1827-40 (res.), V. West Hampnett, Sussex 1827, 3rd Prebend of Ripon Collegiate Church 1829 (then Canon of Ripon Cathedral 1836) to death (Great Budworth, Cheshire) 4/3/1858 aged 56, leaving £4,000 [C21916] Married Hovingham, Yorks. 18/5/1835 Frances Worsley (w) (a clergy dau.), with issue. Brother Charles, jun., above.

WEBBER (James) Born Chichester, Sussex 4/5/1772, s. Rev. William Webber. Christ Church, Oxford 1789, BA1793, dn95 (Ox.), MA 1796, p96 (London), BD1807, DD1829. Chap. to Lord Robert Fitzgerald's Embassy to Copenhagen 1795; PC. Drayton, Oxon. 1798, V. St Mary Magdalen, Oxford 1803-8, V. Sutton in the Forest, Yorks. 1811-12, Prebend of Strensall in York Minster 1812-28, Chaplain of the House of Commons 1812-15, R. Kirkham, Lancs. 1813-47, Canon of Collegiate Church of Ripon 1814, Prebend and Sub-Dean of Westminster Abbey 1816-47, R. St Margaret, Westminster 1827-35, Dean of Ripon Collegiate Church (then Cathedral) 1828 (and Warden of St Mary Magdalen Hospital [almshouses] and of St John the Baptist Hospital [almshouses] 1828) to death 3/9/1847 aged 75 [C21917] Married Cromwell, Notts. 13/9/1813 Caroline Frances Fynes-Clinton (a clergy dau.), w. clerical s. William Charles Fynes Webber. 'Very short in stature'.

WEBBER (Simon) Bapt. St. Stephen by Launceston, Cornwall 20/6/1782, s. Rev. Simon, sen. and Martha Webber. Wadham, Oxford 1800, BA1805, MA1825. R. Fonthill Bishop, Wilts. 1817 and R. Tisbury, Wilts. 1826 to death. Dom. Chap. to 2nd Baron Nugent 1826. Died 24/1/1858, leaving £3,000 [C89472] Married Holborn, London 1/8/1816 Elizabeth Sinkins (w), with issue.

WEBSTER (George Edis) Born Deene, Northants. 15/3/1787, s. Daniel Webster and Elisabeth Edis. Trinity, Cambridge 1804, BA 1808, Fellow 1810-32, dn11 (Bristol), MA1811, p12 (Bristol), etc. R. Grundisburgh, Suffolk 1832 to death 25/11/1869, leaving £4,000 [C54134] Married Bildeston, Suffolk 1/3/1832 Elizabeth Growse.

WEBSTER (George Horatio) Bapt. Surlingham, Norfolk 10/12/1798, s. Stephen Webster and Lucy Phillips. Queens', Cambridge 1819, BA1823, dn23 (Nor.), p24 (Nor.), MA1828. R. Norwich All Saints w. St Julian 1825-52. Died Great Yarmouth, Norfolk (a bachelor) 12/1/1871, leaving under £100 [C116036]

WEBSTER (George Mountjoy) Born Reading, Berks., s. Rev. William Theophilus Mountjoy Webster. St John's, Oxford 1792 (aged 17), BA 1796, dn98 (Ox.), p99 (Chester for Ox.), MA 1802, BD1808, Fellow to 1817, DD1845. PC. Bourton Chapel, Gillingham, Dorset 1813, R. Codford St Mary, Wilts. 1816 to death (a widower) 8/1/1861 aged 86, leaving £1,000 [C38438] Married Gillingham 23/9/1817 Ann Newton.

WEBSTER (James) Born St Michael on Wyre, Lancs., s. Joseph Webster (glazier). St John's, Cambridge 1766 (aged 19), BA1770, dn70 (Chester), p71 (Win.), MA1773, Fellow 1774-93, BD1780. V. Wootton, Hants. 1771-91, R. Meppershall, Beds. 1791 to death 14/5/1833 [C79552] Married Marlborough, Wilts. 1793 Dorothy Savery Gillard (of Yarde, Devon) (w). J.P. Beds.

WEBSTER (John) Born Morland, Westmorland 23/5/1781, s. John and Hannah Webster. Literate: dn04 (Car.), p06 (Car.). S/M Barton G/S, Westmorland 1801; PC. Thrimby, Morland 1806 to death 1845 (3rd q.) [C6428. Platt] Married Barton 12/11/1806 Rachel Nicholson.

WEBSTER (Stephen) Born Loddon, Norfolk, s. Rev. Thomas Webster. Magdalene, Cambridge 1777 (aged 17), BA1782, dn84 (Nor.), p85 (Nor.), Fellow 1786, MA1789. V. Claxton, Norfolk 1791-1837, R. Norwich All Saints and St Julian 1800-25. Died 5/8/1837 aged 78 [C116038] Had issue.

WEBSTER (Thomas) Bapt. Boston, Lincs. 13/1/1780, s. Thomas Webster and Susanna Scott. Queens', Cambridge 1800, BA1805, dn05 (Win. for York), p05 (York), Fellow 1807-9, MA 1808. BD1833. V. Oakington, Cambs. 1809-40, Min. Tavistock Proprietary Chapel, Drury Lane, London 1821-[9], R. Cambridge St Botolph 1834 to death. Editor of the *Christian Guardian* from 1801. Died Oct. 1840 [C100484. YCO. DEB] Married St James, Westminster, London 1809 Mary Ann Butcher, with clerical sons William, and Samuel King Webster.

WEBSTER (William) Bapt. Beverley, Yorks. 7/4/1757. St John's, Cambridge 1775, dn79 (Peterb. for York), BA1780, p87 (Cant.). R. Dymchurch, Kent 1787 and R. Blackmanstone, Kent 1810 to death 28/4/1835 (CCEd thus) [C111478. YCO]

WEBSTER (William) From Derbyshire, s. William Webster. Trinity, Cambridge 1814, then Trinity Hall, returned to Trinity, then Jesus 1819 [adm. Inner Temple 1820], dn25 (Heref.), LLB 1827, p27 (Heref.). PC. Church Preen, Shropshire 1827-32, R. Easthope, Shropshire 1832 to death 19/1/1843 aged 46 [C174402] Married Louisa Port (of Ham, Middx.).

WEDDALL (William Langstaff) Born Selby, Yorks. 222/3/1807, s. Charles Latham Weddall and Susanna Maria Fisher. St John's, Cambridge 1824, then St Catharine's 1826, BA1829, dn30 (Lin.), p31 (Nor.), MA1833. R. Chillesford, Suffolk 1832-8, V. Darsham, Suffolk 1832 and PC. Dunwich, Suffolk 1843 to death (Tuxford, Notts.) 16/2/1851 [C79555] Married 27/9/1836 Louisa Mary Smear (a clergy dau.), with issue.

WEDDELL (John Grenside) Bapt. Yarm, Yorks. 4/6/1777, s. William Weddell and Elizabeth Grenside. Literate: dn15 (Chester for York), p16 (York). PC. Battersea St George's Chapel, Surrey 1828 to death (Wandsworth, London) 23/7/1852 [C109075. YCO] Married Orpington, Kent 24/9/1807 Caroline Foyster.

WEDGE (Charles) Born Gazeley, Suffolk 9/9/1780, s. Charles Wedge (a farmer from Westley, Cambs.) and Elizabeth Fletcher. Christ's, Cambridge 1800, BA1804, dn05 (Ely), p05 (Ely), MA1807. R. Borough (Burrough) Green, Cambs. 1805 to death 28/3/1875 aged 94, leaving £4,000 [C100485] Married Bury St Edmunds 15/1/1816 Mary Anne Harwood (Mill Hill, Newmarket), with issue.

WEDGWOOD (John Allen) Born Etruria, Staffs. 20/6/1796, s. John Wedgwood (of the pottery family, and Cote House, Westbury, Bristol) and Louisa Jane Allen. Literate: dn21 (Chester), p22 (Chester), then Downing, Cambridge 1824 (a Ten Year Man). PC. Maer, Staffs. 1825-63. Died unmarried (Stanton Court, Glos.) 19/7/1882, leaving £5,797-15s-3d. [C20688]

WEGUELIN (William Andrew) Born Hornsea, Middx. 7/9/1807, s. William Andrew Weguelin and Charlotte Willmott. St John's, Cambridge 1827, then Emmanuel 1828, BA 1831, dn31 (Chich.), p32 (Chich.), MA1835. R. South Stoke, Sussex 1832-56. Became a Roman Catholic and moved to Italy. Died (West Hoathley, Sussex, as 'Esquire') 8/6/1892 aged 84, leaving £1,333-11s-4d. [C71462] Married (1) Marylebone, London 8/9/1831 Emma Hankey, 1 dau. She [Emma] was 'expelled from the rectory' for adultery. 'Petition for divorce by private Act of Parliament in the House of Lords 30/4/1839 in order to remarry' (She also remarried) (2) Westminster, London 23/7/1840 Harriet Penny (an Essex clergy dau.). His son John Reinhard Weguelin was a known painter. Port. in NPG and online.

WELBY (John Earle) Bapt. West Allington, Lincs. 17/9/1786, s. Sir William Earle Welby, 1st Bart. (Denton House, Grantham, Lincs.) and Mrs Elizabeth (Cope) Williamson. Lincoln's Inn 1805. Emmanuel, Cambridge 1806, BA1811, dn11 (Lin.), p12 (Lin.), MA1814. V. Keddington, Lincs. 1812-16, R. Haceby and Sapperton, Lincs. 1813-16, R. West Allington, Lincs. 1814, R. Stroxton, Lincs. 1816, R. Harston, Leics. 1816 to death there. Dom. Chap. to Sarah Elizabetha, Lady Monson 1812. Died 9/7/1867, leaving £50,000 [C79561] Married St James,

Westminster, London 20/5/1819 Felicia Elizabetha Hole (a clergy dau., of Chumleigh, Devon), with issue. Brother below. *J.P.* Grantham.

WELBY (Montague Earle) Bapt. West Allington, Lincs. 27/9/1780, s. Sir William Earle Welby, 1st Bart. (Denton House, Grantham, Lincs.) and Elizabeth Cope. Emmanuel, Cambridge 1797, BA1801, dn01 (Lin.), p02 (Lin.). R. Newton, Lincs. 1802, V. Long Bennington, Lincs. 1808-49. Lived at Allington Manor, Grantham, Lincs. to death 12/10/1871 aged 93, leaving £35,000 [C79562] Brother above.

WELCH (Thomas Coleman) Born Adderston, Northumberland 24/2/1795, s. Rev. Thomas Welch and Elizabeth Gascoigne. Wadham, Oxford 1814, then Lincoln 1816-20, BA1819, dn20 (Peterb. for Lin.), p20 (Lin.). V. (and patron) of Pattishall (2nd Moiety) [blank in ERC] 1820 and R. (and patron) of Slapton, Northants. [blank in ERC] 1820 to death 8/11/1872, leaving £4,000 [C79567] Married Bywell St Andrew, Northumberland 27/7/1821 Jane Bacon, with issue.

WELFITT, WELLFITT (William) Bapt. Hull 4/4/1745, s. William Welfitt. University, Oxford 1764, BA1768, p69 (York), MA1772, BD and DD1785. R. Blyborough w. Bland, Leics. 1770-95, R. Rand w. Fulnetby, Lincs. 1773-80, V. Welton, Yorks. 1779-95 (res.), Canonry of the 3rd Prebend in Canterbury Cathedral 1785-1833, R. St Benet Gracechurch Street, City of London 1791, R. Hastingleigh, Kent 1795-1833, V. Elmsted, Kent 1795 and R. Ticehurst, Sussex 1795 to death. Dom. Chap. to 3rd Duke of Roxburgh 1773; to Frances, Viscountess Irwin 1779. Died 3/2/1833 (CCEd says 16/2/1833) [C71465. YCO] Married Hull 22/6/1772 Elizabeth Barry, w. issue. Freemason.

WELLAND (Robert Palk) Bapt. Topsham, Devon 8/11/1758, s. Richard and Grace Welland. Exeter, Oxford 1777, Fellow 1780-7, dn81 (Ox.), p83 (Ex.), BA1784, MA1785. Naval Chaplain HMS *Egmont;* R. Shottesbrooke and White Waltham, Berks. 1786, R. (and patron) of Talaton, Devon 1787-1835 and R. Dunchideock w. Shillingford St George, Devon 1793 to death 24/6/1841 [C38443] Married Exeter 20/5/1789 Susanna Kennaway, w. issue.

WELLESLEY, *born* **WESLEY (Gerald Valerian, Hon.)** Born Wesley at Dangan Castle, Co. Meath 7/12/1770, s. 1st Earl of Mornington (and thus brother to the 1st Duke of Wellington) and Hon. Ann Hill (dau. 1st Viscount Dungannon). St John's, Cambridge 1788, MA 1792, dn93 (Ely), p94 (Lin.), DD (Lambeth) 1810. Chaplain at Hampton Court 1793-1848, R. Beachampton, Bucks. 1794-8, R. Hampton, Middx. 1798-1803, R. Staines, Middx. 1799-1809, Prebend of Westminster Abbey 1802-9, V. Chaddleworth, Berks. 1803-5, (first) R. St Luke, Chelsea, London 1805-32, V. West Ham, Essex 1809 (res.), Canon and Prebend of Neasden in St Paul's Cathedral 1809-27, R. Therfield, Herts. 1822-32, R. Bishopwearmouth 1827 [net income £2,899], Prebend of 5th Canon in Durham Cathedral 1827 to death there. Chap. to George III 1799, 1803, 1805. Died 21/10/1848 aged 77 [C43781] Married St George's Hanover Square, London 2/6/1802 Lady Emily Maud, dau. 1st Earl of Cadogan (from whom he was separated), with military issue. A fine port. in: D. Cross, *Joseph Bouet's Durham* (Durham, 2005)

WELLESLEY (Henry) Born 1794, natural s. of 1st Marquess Wellesley (and his French mistress - later wife - Hyacinthe Gabrielle Roland, an 'opera dancer'). Christ Church, Oxford 1811, Student [Fellow] 1811-28, BA 1816 [Student of Lincoln's Inn 1816] MA1818, BD and DD 1847. Vice-Principal New Inn Hall, Oxford 1842-7, Principal 1847-66. V. Flitton, Beds. 1827, R. Woodmancote, Glos. 1838, R. Hurstmonceux, Sussex 1855 to death 11/1/1866, leaving £14,000 [C21919. ODNB. Boase] Married Hascombe, Surrey 12/6/1835 Charlotte Anne Mackenzie Van Dyke, and had issue. Curator in the Bodleian Library; collector of old master drawings, and of topographical and historical prints, coins and manuscripts.

WELLINGS (Thomas) From Worcester, s. Edward Wellings. Worcester, Oxford 1776 (aged 18), BA1780, dn81 (Ox.), p82 (Ox.), MA 1783. R. Church Lench, Worcs. 1786 and V. Bromfield, Shropshire 1822 to death. Dom. Chap. to 1st Baron Delamere 1822. Died 5/7/1841 [C38447] Was married. 'Classical scholar, lover of the fine arts, and antiquary,' and numismatist.

WELLINGTON (William) Bapt. Upton Helions, Devon 13/1/1806, s. Rev. William Wellington. Pembroke, Oxford 1823, BA1828, dn29 (Ex.), p30 (Ex.). R. Upton Helions 1831 to death 22/11/1869 aged 63. Will not traced

[C146615] Married Bockley, Som. 14/6/1844 Florence Smyth Pigott.

WELLS (George, sen.) Born Manningford, Wilts. 16/8/1767, s. Rev. George Wells, sen. and Frances Ballard. New, Oxford 1787, dn90 (Ox.), p91 (Ox.), BCL1794. R. Albourne, Sussex 1795-1839, V. Billingshurst, Sussex 1795-1823, R. Wiston, Sussex 1796, Exceit Prebend in Chichester Cathedral 1822 to death 24/5/1839 [C38449] Married Chawton, Wilts. 13/10/1796 Elizabeth Hinton, w. clerical sons Charles, Edward, George (below), and Francis Ballard Wells. Brother John Wells, below.

WELLS (George, jun.) Born Wiston, Sussex, s. Rev. George Wells, sen. (above) and Elizabeth Hinton. Exeter, Oxford 1821 (aged 18), then Magdalen 1823-9, BA1825, MA1828, Fellow 1829-35, etc. Curate Stourbridge, Old Swinford, Worcs. 1833-51-, R. Boxford, Berks. 1841 to death 11/6/1872. Will not traced [C21921] Married Bromham, Wilts. 4/8/1835 Augusta Starky, w. issue.

WELLS (John) Born Manningford, Wilts. 5/7/1770, s. Rev. George Wells and Frances Ballard. New, Oxford 1789, BA1793, dn93 (Salis.), p94 (Salis.), MA1797. V. Colerne, Wilts. 1799-1814, R. (and patron) of Boxford, Wilts. 1805-42, V. Uffington, Berks. 1814-16, R. Manningford Bruce, Wilts. 1816 to death. Dom. Chap. to 7th Earl of Westmeath 1805; to 11th Earl of Kinnoull 1815. Died (unm.) 20/7/1842 [C89748] Brother George, above.

WELLS (Samuel) Bapt. East Allingham, Devon 2/2/1759, s. Rev. Nathaniel Wells and Catherine Bury. Wadham, Oxford 1777, BA 1781, dn81 (Ex.), p83 (Ex.). R. East Portlemouth, Devon 1791 to death 26/2/1839 [C146617] Married South Pool, Devon 3/1/1785 Elizabeth Lake, w. clerical s. Thomas Bury Wells. Brother, below.

WELLS (William) Bapt. East Allingham, Devon 19/5/1756, s. Rev. Nathaniel Wells and Catherine Bury. Oriel, Oxford 1774, SCL, dn79 (Ex.), p80 (Ex.). R. East Allington 1780 to death 29/8/1839 [C146618] Married Elizabeth Pearce. Brother, above.

WELLS (William) Born Petersfield, Sussex, s. Henry Wells. Magdalen Hall, Oxford 1799 (aged 21), no degree, p02 (Win.). PC. Liss, Hants.

1806, R. Harting, Sussex 1822 to death 12/3/1863, leaving £5,000 [C71471]

WESLEY (Gerald Valerian, Hon.) see under **WELLESLEY**, above

WEST (Edward Walter) Bapt. Bradford Abbas, Dorset 3/4/1786, s. Rev. Edward Matthew West and Anne Cotes. St John's, Oxford 1802, BA1806, dn07 (Bristol), p08 (Salis.), MA1826. V. Haydon, Dorset 1812-35, V. North Wootten, Dorset 1818-35, R. Goathill, Som. 1833, R. Milborne Port, Som. 1835 to death 9/10/1864, leaving £2,000 [C20693] Married Melcombe Regis, Dorset 16/7/1846 Elizabeth Whitley.

WEST (Harry) From London, s. of a wine merchant. St John's, Cambridge 1783, BA1788, dn88 (Chich.), p89 (Chich.), MA1792. V. Wartling, Sussex 1795-7, R. Berwick, Sussex 1797 and V. Laughton, Sussex 1801 to death. Dom. Chap. to Jane Elizabeth, 12th Countess of Rothes 1801. Died (Lewes, Sussex) 21/2/1846 [C71477] Married (1) West Retford, Notts. 11/1/1814 Louisa Elizabeth Verelst (d.1821) (2) St Pancras, London 7/2/1823 Louisa (dau. Sir Robert Barker, Bart.).

WEST (James John) Born Tonbridge Castle, Tonbridge, Kent, s. James Eldridge West and Alicia Ashburnham. Jesus, Cambridge 1825 (aged 19), BA1829, dn29 (Chich.), p30 (Chich.), MA1832. R. Winchelsea St Thomas the Apostle, Sussex 1831 to death 7/8/1872, leaving £1,500 [C71480] Married (1) Ludlow, Shropshire 27/4/1829 Margaret Molyneux (d.1831), 1 dau. (2) 24/6/1833 Charlotte Margaret Blair (Walton Grove, Surrey), w. further issue.

WEST (John) From Farnham, Surrey, s. George West. St Edmund Hall, Oxford 1801 (aged 21), BA1804, dn04 (London), p06 (Win.), MA 1809. PC. Aldershot, Hants. 1818-20, R. Chettle, Dorset 1820 and R. Farnham 1835 to death. Dom. Chap. to 4th Earl of Bessborough 1835. Died 31/12/1845 [C54141]

WEST (John) Born Kingston, Jamaica 13/11/1794, s. Rev. John West (a Church of Scotland minister there, *q.v.* Smart) and Anne Kelly. Exeter, Oxford 1813, BA1816, MA1819 [barrister Lincoln's Inn 1819], dn24 (Chester), p25 (B&W). V. Evercreech w. Chesterblade, Som. 1825, R. Clipsham, Rutland 1846 to death

15/12/1857 [*not* 1858] aged 63, leaving £6,000 [C40815. LBSO] Widow Mary. *J.P.* Rutland.

WEST (John) Born Holborn, London, s. John West and Anna Maria Jones. Worcester, Oxford 1822 (aged 19), BA 1826, MA1829. R. (and patron) of Aisholt, Som. 1832 to death 29/4/1888, leaving £18,536-0s-6d. [C40816] Married (1) Clifton, Bristol 27/10/1840 Elizabeth Cape Seager,, 1 ch (2) Charlton Kings, Glos. 22/6/1852 Charltte Willimott.

WESTCOMBE (Thomas) Born Winchester, s. Rev. Nicholas Westcombe and Sarah Kingsman. Trinity, Oxford 1803 (aged 19), BA1807, dn07 (Win.), p08 (Win.), MA1810. Minor Canon of Winchester Cathedral, R. Winchester St Peter Cheshill 1818-32, V. Piddletrenthide, Dorset 1820-6, PC. Winchester St John 1821-6, V. Preston Candover w. Nutley, Hants. 1826 and V. Letcombe Regis, Berks. 1827 to death. Dom. Chap. to 2nd Earl of Enniskillen 1827. Died 25/7/1852 [C54142] Married Winchester 20/1/1824 Lucy Deverell.

WESTCOTT (Thomas) Born Kenn, Devon 27/11/1777, s. Thomas Westcott. Balliol, Oxford 1796, BA1800, dn00 (Ex.), p01 (Ex.). V. St Nicholas, Devon 1810 and R. Stokeinteignhead, Devon 1810 to death 6/8/1834 [C146620]

WESTERMAN (James) Born Leeds 17/5/1768, s. Thomas Westerman. Magdalene, Cambridge 1786, BA1791, dn91 (Glos. for York), Fellow 1794, p93 (B&W), MA1795. V. Finchingfield, Essex 1810 to death 31/8/1841 aged 72 [C50054. YCO] Wife Elizabeth, and issue.

WESTERN (Charles) Born Great Abington, Cambs. 22/3/1760, s. Thomas Western and Jane Calvert. Hertford, Oxford 1778, SCL, dn84 (B&W), p84 (Ox.). R. Kingham, Oxon. 1785 to death 1/10/1835 [C38453] Married St James's Palace, London 7/7/1784 Mary Pensiton Goostrey, and had issue. 'Reputed to have been the richest man in England' [*sic*].

WESTHORP (Sterling Moseley) Born Yoxford, Suffolk 14/1/1795, s. Richard Moseley (a Lambeth merchant) and Ann Westhorp. Caius, Cambridge 1814, BA1818, dn18 (Nor.), p19 (Nor.). V. Sibton, Suffolk 1821 to death 28/4/1871 aged 76, leaving £800 [C116045] Married Cringleford, Norfolk 4/2/1829 Martha Bellamy Browne, with clerical sons Sterling Browne, and Richard Alexander Westhorp.

WESTMORLAND (Thomas) Bapt. Culgaith, Westmorland 31/3/1774, s. Joseph Westmorland [*pleb.*] and Elizabeth Lancaster. Queen's, Oxford 1794, BA1798, dn00 (Car.), p00 (Car.), MA1801. S/M Allenhead in Allendale, Northumberland 1807-9, S/M Barnsley, Yorks. 1816-18; PC. Buttermere, Cumberland 1802-45; V. Sandal Magna (Great Sandal), Yorks. 1818 to death 25/3/1845 aged 71 [C6431] Married 1801 Anne Williamson, with clerical son.

WESTON (Charles Fleetwood) Born Therfield, Herts. 11/4/1778, s. Rev. Charles Weston and Arabella Delabere. Clare, Cambridge 1796, BA1801, dn01 (Ely), p02 (Ely). PC. Melton Ross, Lincs. 1811-46, R. Ruckland w. Farforth and Maidenwell, Lincs. 1814 and R. Somerby, Lincs. 1816 to death (Somerby Hall) 1853 aged 75 [C79788]

WESTON (Charles Henry Samuel) Bapt. West Horsley, Surrey 5/9/1780, s. Henry Perkins Weston and Marianne Bergier de Rovereaz (of Lausanne). Trinity, Cambridge 1799, BA1803, dn03 (Win.), p04 (Win.), MA 1814. R. Culbone, Som. 1809-21 (res.), R. West Horsley, Surrey 1816-41, R. Ockham, Surrey 1821-43. Dom. Chap. to 7th Earl of Aylesford 1817. Died (unm.) Nice 20/4/1849 [C50060] Succ. his brother to the West Horsley estates 1835.

WETHERALL (John) [NiVoF] R. New Fishbourne, Sussex 1799-1833, V. Patcham, Sussex 1804 and V. Streatley, Berks. 1808 to death 4/11/1833 (CCEd thus) [C71487]

WETHERALL (John [White]) Born Rushton, Northants., s. Rev. John Laycock Wetherall (below) and Sarah Wetherall. BNC, Oxford 1818 (aged 18), BA1821, dn22 (Peterb.), p23 (Peterb.), MA1824. R. East Carlton, Northants. 1829, R. Rushton, Northants. 1838-51-, R. Glendon, Northants. 1848-51-, Hon. Canon of Peterborough Cathedral at death. Dom. Chap. to Lord Sondes. Died 14/8/1856 [C111467] Married Cransley, Northants. 1/10/1827 Louisa Rose, with issue.

WETHERALL (John Laycock) From Lincoln, s. William Wetherall and Sarah Laycock. Trinity Hall, Cambridge 1775 (aged 24), dn91 (Lin.), p93 (Lin.), LLB1794. R.

Rushton, Northants. 1798 to death 1/12/1837 aged 74 [C79795] Married Sarah Wetherall, w. clerical son John [White] Wetherall, above. *J.P.* Northants.

WETHERELL (Charles) Born London 4/9/1784, s. Thomas Wetherell and Mary Desborough. St Edmund Hall, Oxford 1807 (aged 23), BA1811, dn11 (Lin.), p13 (Lin.), MA1814. R. Byfield, Northants. 1819 [income £1,503] to death 20/10/1867, leaving £300 [C79796. Boase] Married City of London 31/12/12 Charlotte Wilson. Charged by his son-in-law with incest with his own daughter; the case went against him and he was fined £3,000 [*n.b.* incest not then a criminal offence]: https://books.google.co.uk/books?isbn=075249676X

WETHERELL (Henry) Born Oxford 8/3/1775, s. Very Rev. Nathan Wetherell (Dean of Hereford, and Master of University College, Oxford) and Richarda Croke. Magdalen, Oxford 1791, BA1795, dn97 (Salis.), MA1798, p99 (London for Salis.), then University, Fellow 1802, BD1817. R. Thruxton, Heref. 1799-1857, R. Kingstone, Heref. 1799, R. Kentchurch, Heref. 1817-57, Archdeacon of Hereford 1825-52 (res.), Canon of Gloucester Cathedral 1825 to death there 23/12/1857, leaving £30,000 [C89764. Boase] Married Marylebone, London 9/6/1825 Harriet Maria Clive. Clerical brothers James, Richard, and Robert, here.

WETHERELL (James) Born Cowley, Oxford 12/7/1786, s. Very Rev. Nathan Wetherell (Dean of Hereford, and Master of University College, Oxford) and Richarda Croke. New, Oxford 1805, dn10 (Ox.), dn10 (Glos.), BCL 1813, Fellow to 1816. PC. Upton St Leonard, Glos. 1815, V. Lyonshall, Glos. 1816, Prebend of Hunderton in Hereford Cathedral 1821 to death 16/7/1857 [C21927] Married 3/10/1815 Lucy Huntingford. Clerical brothers Henry, Richard, and Robert Wetherell, here.

WETHERELL (Richard) Bapt. Oxford 3/12/1773, s. Very Rev. Nathan Wetherell (Dean of Hereford, and Master of UIniversity College, Oxford) and Richarda Croke. University, Oxford 1791, BA1795, dn96 (Salis.), p97 (Salis.), MA1798. R. Westbury-on-Severn, Glos. 1798, R. Wick Rissington, Glos. 1809, R. Notgrove, Glos. 1810 to death. Dom. Chap. to 3rd Earl Bathurst 1809. Lived at Pashley House, Ticehurst, Sussex. Died (Almond's Hotel, Bond Street, London) 22/1/1858, leaving £9,000 [C89765] Married (1) Ticehurst 23/11/1796 Caroline May (d.1833), 8s, 6 dau. (2) Walcot, Bath 12/7/1836 Mrs Sarah Maria (Gray) Duff. Clerical brothers Henry, James, and Robert, here. *J.P.* Gloucestershire.

WETHERELL (Robert) Born Oxford 20/9/1768, s. Very Rev. Nathan Wetherell (Dean of Hereford, and Master of University College, Oxford) and Richarda Croke. New, Oxford 1784, BCL1791, dn91 (Nor.), Fellow to 1814. V. Stanford-in-the-Vale w. Goosey, Berks. 1792-1835, Prebend of Church Withington in Hereford Cathedral 1796, R. Newton Longueville, Bucks. 1813 to death 20/8/1842 [C79797] Married 1814 Ann Merewether. Clerical brothers Henry, James, and Richard, here.

WETHERELL see also **WETHERALL**

WETHERHERD (Thomas) Bapt. Leeds 3/4/1775, s. Theophilus Wetherherd. Trinity, Cambridge 1793, then Peterhouse 1797, BA 1798, dn98 (York), p99 (York), MA1804. Chaplain *H.E.I.C.* 1810-29; PC. Loversall, Doncaster, Yorks. 1805. Died London. 9/10/1839 aged 70 [C130571. YCO]

WHALEY (Joseph Gibson) Born Whitley Bay, Northumberland 16/4/1781, s. Alexander Whaley and Jane Gibson. Emmanuel, Cambridge 1800, re-adm. Peterhouse 1800, BA1804, dn04 (Ely), p05 (Ely), Fellow 1805-24, MA 1807, etc. V. Cambridge Little St Mary 1810 and 1814-22, R. Witnesham, Suffolk 1822 to death 11/1/1836 [C100487]

WHALLEY (John) Born London, s. Daniel Whalley. Exeter, Oxford 1780 (aged 19), dn83 (Lin.), BA1784, p85 (Lin.), MA1788. V. Worlaby, Lincs. 1799-1806 (res.), R. Rushall, Staffs. 1807 to death 12/7/1839 [C20697]

WHALLEY, WHALEY (John) Bapt. Aysgarth, Yorks. 31/8/1777, s. Francis Whaley and Ann Routh. Literate: dn01 (York). PC. Hawes, Yorks. 1812 to death 8/11/1845 [C103013. YCO] Married Hawes, Yorks. 2/1/1806 Alice Routh, w. clerical s. William.

WHALLEY (John Christopher) Bapt. Marylebone, London 31/12/1806, s. Rev. Thomas Palmer Whalley and Catherine Maria Packe. BNC, Oxford 1824, BA1828, dn30 (Peterb.), p30 (Lin. for Peterb.). R. (and patron) of Ecton,

Northants. 1830-49. Died Tonbridge, Kent 15/3/1895 aged 88. No will traced [C79803] Married Tonbridge 11/4/1833 Theodosia Barbara Meade, and had issue.

WHALLEY (John Master, *but born* James) Born Roche Court, Fareham, Hants., s. Sir James Whalley-Smythe-Gardiner, 2nd Bart. and Jane Master (a clergy dau.). Balliol, Oxford 1812 (aged 19), BCL1813, dn17 (Chester, no degree noted), p18 (Chester). PC. Whitewell, Whalley, Lancs. 1818-35-, R. Slaidburn, Yorks. 1838 (living at the enormous Clerk Hill House, Whalley) to death 27/10/1861, leaving £8,000 [C170855] Married Whitewell 5/12/1829 Hannah Nightingale, with issue.

WHALLEY (William Morgan) Bapt. Kington, Radnor 30/12/1772, s. William Whalley and Katherine Elizabeth Price. Queen's, Oxford 1790, MA1795, Fellow, p97 (Cant. for Glos.). Chap. of the Donative of Waltham Holy Cross (*now* Waltham Abbey), Herts. 1795. Died Cheltenham 16/4/1846 aged 73 [C148414, Foster as William] Married Upper Slaughter, Glos. 25/2/1796 Mrs Martha (Travell) Buxton, w. issue.

WHARTON (Henry James) Born Rickinghall, Suffolk 31/10/1798, s. Thomas Wharton and Jane Perriman. Emmanuel, Cambridge 1816, BA1820, MA1823, dn23 (Nor.), p23 (Ely for Nor.). V. Babraham, Cambs. 1831-3 (res.), V. Mitcham, Surrey 1846 to death there 15/5/1859, leaving £5,000 [C588] Married (1) Lewisham, Kent 8/7/1826 Caroline Wynell Mayow (d.1842, 4th q.?) (2) Beckenham, Kent before 1844 Mary Courtenay (w), with issue.

WHARTON (Thomas) Bapt. Bampton, Westmorland 31/3/1785, s. Thomas and Mary Wharton. Literate: dn08 (York), p09 (York), MA1827 Lambeth. H/M St Edmund School, Canterbury 1817-37, Min. St John's Wood Chapel, Marylebone, London 1825-[55] (and Master of the Clergy Orphan School there 1817-37). Died 31/8/1854; buried Shap [C103014. YCO] Married (1) Marylebone, London 8/8/1822 Charlotte Maria Rose, 1 ch. (2) Marylebone 12/12/1829 Mary Soilleux.

WHARTON, *born* HALL (William) Born Skelton Castle, Yorks. 17/9/1769, s. Joseph William Wharton and Ann Hall. Trinity, Cambridge 1787, BA1791, dn94 (York), p95 (York), MA1795. PC. Yarm, Yorks. 1797-1837, V. Gilling, Yorks. 1801-43 [net income £1,021], V. Kirk Leatham, Yorks. 1801-2, V. Stanwick, Yorks. 1807. Died 26/5/1843 aged 74 [C86795. Venn. YCO all under Hall] Married 19/4/1808 Charlotte Dundas [after whom the world's first steamboat was named], dau. 1st Baron Dundas, with clerical s. who succeeded him. 'Not distinguished for pulpit ability or piety, but a pleasant and kind-hearted man'.

WHATELY (Thomas) Born Ware, Herts. 7/1/1773, s. Joseph Whately and Jane Plumer. Christ's, Cambridge 1791, BA1795, dn95 (Nor.), p97 (London for Salis.), MA1800. V. Cookham, Berks. 1797-1837, R. Chetwynd, Shropshire 1837 to death (Sunninghill, Berks.) 10/5/1864 aged 91, leaving £20,000 [C89766] Married Marylebone, London 12/1/1813 Isabella Sophia (dau. Sir William Pepys, 1st Bart.), with clerical son Charles Whateley.

WHATLEY (Charles) Bapt. Cirencester, Glos. 20/12/1757, s. George Whatley and Hannah Clifford. Pembroke, Cambridge 1773, BA1777, MA1779, dn79 (Heref.), p84 (Wor.). R. Aston Ingham, Heref. 1785, PC. Lea Chapel (in Linton, Heref. and not Glos.) 1794 and V. Lower Guiting (Guiting Inferior), Glos. 1797 to death (Aston Ingham) 11/2/1835 [C167284] Married Stroud, Glos. 13/2/1776 Margaretta Anne Elizabeth Lawson, with issue.

WHEELDON (John) From Wheathampstead, Hunts., s. Rev. John Wheeldon, sen. Corpus Christi. Cambridge 1792, BA1796, dn06 (Lin.), p97 (Lin.), MA1799. PC. Market Street (o/w Caddington St John Markyate Chapel), Herts. 1808 to death. Dom. Chap. to 1st Earl of Ducie 1809. Died 4/4/1844 aged 70 [C79813] Married Wheathampstead 14/6/1796 Martha Pickford (dau. of the 'eminent waggon-master'). 'Guileless and single-minded'.

WHEELER (Allen) Born Kidderminster, Worcs. 20/11/1775, s. Allen Wheeler (Great Whitley, Worcs.) and Decima Green. Wadham, Oxford 1792, BA1798, dn98 (Heref.), MA1800, p00 (Wor.), BD1810. Minor Canon of Worcester Cathedral 1799-1851 (Precentor and Sacrist 1820-51). H/M Worcester College School to 1832; R. Bredicot, Worcs. 1801-21, R. Broadwas, Worcs. 1821-37, R. Worcester St Martin 1837-51, V. Old Sodbury, Glos. 1851 to death (Bath) 25/12/1855 [C122296. Boase] Married Burford, Shropshire 18/6/1801 Sarah

Harwood (*or* Harvard), with clerical son Thomas Littleton Wheeler.

WHEELER (Charles) Born Bridgnorth, Shropshire 26/1/1797 (bapt. 24/1/1803), s. Cornelius [*pleb.*] and Ann Wheeler. Christ Church, Oxford 1815, servitor 1815-19, BA 1819, dn20 (Ox.), Chap. 1820-21, p21 (Ox.), MA1823, then Merton, Chaplain 1824-35. PC. Stratton Audley, Oxon. 1831 to death 30/8/1835 [C29134]

WHEELER (William) Born Hungerford, Berks., s. William and Mary Wheeler. Lincoln, Oxford 1792, BA1796, dn97 (Salis.), then Magdalen, MA1799, BD1824, DD1828. R. Saltfleetby All Saints, Lincs. 1807 to death 29/10/1841 [C79817]

WHEELWRIGHT (Charles Apthorp) Born Stoke Newington, Middx. 24/6/1787, s. Charles Wright Wheelwright and Catherine Apthorp. Trinity, Cambridge 1805, BA1809, dn10 (London), p11 (Lin.), MA1811. V. Castle Wytham w. Little Bytham >< Lincs. 1811-58 (non-res.), Prebend of Carlton Kyme in Lincoln Cathedral 1811 and R. Tansor, Northants. 1811 to death. Dom. Chap. to Eleanor, Dowager Countess Lilford 1811. Died Tansor (a widower) 20/11/1858, leaving under £200 (unadministered) [C79818. Boase. Bennett2] Married (1) Bury St Edmunds 5/6/1811 Ann Hubbard (d.1858), with clerical s. George (2) Tottenham, London 27/3/1859 Mrs Mary Burbridge.

WHELER (Henry Trevor) Bapt. Leamington Hastings, Warwicks. 8/9/1804, s. Charles John Wheler and Isabella Close. Jesus, Oxford 1828, dn31 (C&L), BA1832, MA1836. V. Pillerton Hersey w. Pillerton Priors, Worcs. 1831, R. Berkeley, Som. 1834 to death 28/4/1860, leaving £1,500 [C20706] Married Polebrooke, Northants. 11/12/1834 Charlotte Isham (w), with issue. Relation below?

WHELER (William) Bapt. Leamington Hastings, Warwicks. 1/11/1770, s. Rev. Charles Wheler and Lucy Strange. Trinity, Oxford 1788, BA1792, dn93 (C&L), p95 (C&L), MA1796. R. Ladock w. Roche, Cornwall 1796-1811, R. Sutton on Derwent, Yorks. 1814 to death. Dom. Chap. to Elizabeth, Dowager Baroness Amherst 1813. Died 30/5/1834 (CCEd says 5/12/1834) [C20710] Married Alveston, Warwicks. 3/3/1807 Charlotte Sophia Harding, w. issue. Relation above?

WHICHCOTE (Christopher) Born Aswarby, Lincs. 6/2/1806, s. Sir Thomas Whichcote, 5th Bart. and Diana Turnor. St John's, Cambridge 1824, BA1828, dn29 (Lin.), p30 (Lin.), MA 1834. V. Swarby, Lincs. 1830, V. Deeping St James, Lincs. 1830-4 (res.), R. Milton Ernest, Beds. 1832-4 (res.), R. Panton, Lincs. 1834-7, R. East Torrington w. Wragby, Lincs. 1834, R. Aswarby 1850 (and RD) to death. Dom. Chap. to Louisa Maria, Viscountess Downe 1834. Died 4/1/1885, leaving £14,659-16s-11d. [C79821] Married Bulwick, Northants. 26/6/1832 Harriet Tryon, *s.p.* Brother below.

WHICHCOTE (Francis) Born Aswarby, Lincs. 3/6/1793, s. Sir Thomas Whichcote, 5th Bart. and Diana Turnor. Christ's, Cambridge 1812, BA1816, dn16 (Lin.), p17 (Lin.), MA 1819. R. Aswarby 1818-50, V. (sequestrator) Swarby, Lincs. 1818-22 (res.), V. Deeping St James, Lincs. 1818-23, R. Timberland, Lincs. 1822-41. Dom. Chap. to 6th Earl of Harborough 1819. Died 7/12/1878. Will not traced [C79822. Kaye] Married St George's Hanover Square, London 4/11/1826 Eliza Bree, *s.p.* Brother above.

WHICHER (John) From Petersfield, Hants., s. John Whicher. Corpus Christi, Oxford 1776 (aged 15), BA1779, MA1783, dn83 (Ox). R. Babcary, Som. 1787. Died 26/5/1845 aged 84. [C38526]

WHICHER (John Cobb) Bapt. Petworth, Sussex 22/12/1771, s. Joseph Whicher and Mary Cobb. Queen's, Oxford 1788. Naval Chaplain, (present at Battle of Trafalgar), R. Stopham, Sussex 1796-1841, V. [sequestrator] Bury, Sussex 1818. Died 12/3/1841 aged 69 [C71667. Foster as John]

WHIDBORNE (Thomas Vining) Born Newton Abbott, Devon 20/12/1772, s. George Ferris Whidborne and Tryphena Vining. Balliol, Oxford 1791, BA1795, dn95 (B&W for Ex), p97 (Ex.). R. East Ogwell, Devon 1797 to death 1845 (3rd q.) [C50092. Foster as Thomas only] Married Clifton, Bristol 4/9/1797 Sarah Elderton, with issue.

WHIELDON (Edward) Born Stoke-on-Trent, Staffs. 19/7/1787, s. Thomas Whieldon (Hales Hall, Cheadle, Staffs.) and Sarah Turner. Clare, Cambridge 1806, BA1810, dn10 (C&L), p11 (C&L), MA1813. R. Burslem, Staffs. 1811, PC. Bradley-le-Moors, Staffs. 1825 to death (Hales Hall) 22/7/1859, leaving £25,000 [C20712]

Married Alton, Staffs. 22/5/1823 Mary Bill (Farley Hall, Staffs.), with clerical son Edward Whieldon. According to Josiah Bateman, his curate at Burslem, he was 'a most excellent man - handsome, pious, amiable, and evangelical - but had not the nerve to meet the turmoil of such a parish'; lived in [a] neighbouring charming country house and took duty in a small parish, only visiting Burslem occasionally: (Senex [Josiah Bateman], *Clerical Reminiscences* (1880).

WHINEREY (Thomas) Bapt. Broughton in Furness, Lancs. 25/9/1796. Literate: dn23 (Chester), p24 (Chester). PC. Silverdale, Warton, Lancs. 1828-37. Died 20/8/1850 [C20713]

WHINFIELD (Henry Wrey) Born Lacock, Wilts. 11/7/1793, s. Rev. Edward Henry Whinfield and Ellen Wrey. Peterhouse, Cambridge 1808, BA1815, dn15 (Lin.), p16 (Lin.), MA 1818. (succ. his father as) R. Battlesden w. Pottesgrove, Beds. 1821 and R. Tyringham w. Filgrove, Bucks. 1822 to death. Dom. Chap. to 1st Viscount Keith 1815. Died 23/12/1848 [C80005] Married Tyringham 17/1/1822 Sarah Arabella Praed, with issue.

WHINFIELD (Richard) Born Orton, Westmorland 39/3/1786, s. John Whinfield and Isabell Capstick. [NiVoF] Literate: dn10 (Chester), p11 (Chester). V. Heanor, Derbys. 1821 to death 25/5/1866 aged 80. No will traced [C20717] Married Coniscliffe, Co. Durham 6/12/1819 Mary Ann Richardson, w. issue.

WHIPHAM (Thomas) Born London 3/12/1773, s. Thomas Whipham and Rebecca Tillyer. Oriel, Oxford 1791, BA1795, dn96 (London), p97 (London), MA1798, BD and DD1836. PC. New Brentford, Middx. 1803-5, R. Kingsteignton, Devon 1813, R. Ideford, Devon 1835 to death 1/7/1844 [C124041] Married Wickham, Hants. 9/5/1805 Frances Atkins, and had issue.

WHISH (Martin Richard) Born Northwold, Norfolk 1781, s. Rev. Richard Whish (V. West Walton, Norfolk) and Philippa Sandys. Caius, Cambridge 1799, BA1794, dn04 (Nor.), p05 (Nor.), MA1807. V. Bedminster St Paul, Bristol (and Prebend of Bedminster and Redclyffe in Salisbury Cathedral) 1806-52, R. St Mary Redcliffe w. Beaminster St John the Baptist, Bristol 1806, PC. Bishopsworth, Bristol 1806, R. Bristol St Thomas 1806 and V. Abbot's Leigh 1806 to death 7/4/1852 aged 71 [C50099. Boase] Married Alderley, Glos. 30/10/1812 Elizabeth Blagdon Hale, with clerical sons Martin Henry Whish, and John Matthew Hale Whish. 'Though Mr Whish was somewhat eccentric, he was a pious and conscientious pastor, and very charitable to the poor, strongly attached to the evangelical doctrines of the Church of England' (Boase).

WHISH (Richard Peter) Born Marylebone, London 2/5/1788, s. Martin Whish (Commissioner of Excise) and Harriet Tyssen. Emmanuel, Cambridge 1807, BA1811, dn11 (London), p12 (London), MA1814. V. Broxted, Essex 1812-32, R. Meesden, Herts. 1812-19, R. Downham, Essex 1821-7, R. Wickford, Essex 1823-7, Prebend of Ashill in Wells Cathedral 1819-66 (res.), V. Monkton, Kent 1832 and R. Birchington, Kent 1832 to death. Dom. Chap. to 4th Duke of Newcastle 1812. Died (Northumberland House Asylum, Stoke Newington, Middx., adm. 1870) 10/1/1871, leaving £18,000 [C50101] Married Chiddingstone, Kent 13/11/1822 Sophia Catherine Streatfield, with clerical son Henry Fulham Whish.

WHITAKER (George Ayton) Born Syleham, Suffolk *c.*1806, possibly s. Thomas Whitaker, below. Emmanuel, Cambridge 1826, BA1830, dn30 (Nor.), p31 (Nor.), MA1842. V. Mendham, Suffolk 1833-50, R. (and patron) of Knoddishall w. Buxlow, Suffolk 1835 (and RD of Dunwich) to death 5/5/1877, leaving £3,000 [C116051] Married Beccles, Suffolk 24/8/1830 Anne Maria Farr (w), with issue. *J.P.* Suffolk. Brother of Thomas Wright Whitaker, below?

WHITAKER (John) Bapt. Doncaster, Yorks. 19/10/1769, s. John Whitaker. St Catharine's, Cambridge 1785, LLB1792, dn92 (Car. for York), p93 (York). V. (and patron) of Garforth, Yorks. 1797 to death July 1833 [C6437. YCO] Was married with clerical son.

WHITAKER (Robert Nowell) Born Leeds 4/12/1800/1, s. Rev. Thomas Dunham Whitaker (V. Whalley, Lancs.) and Lucy Thoresby. St John's, Cambridge 1821, BA1826, dn27 (London), p27 (London), MA 1831. PC. Langho, Whalley, Lancs. 1828-40 and PC. Holme (in Cliviger), Whalley 1830-40, (succ. his father as) V. Whalley 1840 to death 9/8/1881 aged 80, leaving £7,248-18s-8d. [C124042. Boase] Married Llanbebig, Carnarvon 7/7/1830

Anne Jones (a clergy dau., from Llangeinwen, Anglesey), with issue.

WHITAKER (Thomas) Born Norfolk 14/8/1763, s. Rev. Thomas Whitaker, sen. Emmanuel, Cambridge 1781, BA1786, dn86 (Nor.), p88 (Nor.), MA1793. V. Mendham, Suffolk 1788-1833, PC. Wingfield, Suffolk 1789-1803 (res.), V. Syleham, Suffolk 1797-1833, V. Weybread, Suffolk 1814-29 (res.), R. Stanford Dingley, Berks. 1819-25 (res.). Died 29/12/1832 aged 69 (CCEd says 9/1/1833) [C145691] Married Weybread, Suffolk Jane Ayton, w. clerical son George Ayton (above), and brother Thomas Wright Whitaker (below).

WHITAKER (Thomas Wright) Born Syleham, Suffolk, s. Rev. Thomas Whitaker (above) and Jane Ayton. Emmanuel, Cambridge 1818, BA1822, dn22 (Nor.), p23 (Nor.), MA 1825. R. Stanton by Bridge, Derbys. 1830-68 (and RD), Prebend of Bobenhall in Lichfield Cathedral 1852, R. Swarkstone, Derbys. 1830 to death 24/9/1868, leaving £7,000 [C20723] Married Hackney, London 21/6/1825 Anna Patteson (a clergy dau., Drinkstone, Suffolk), with clerical son John Ayton Whitaker. Brother George Ayton Whitaker, above.

WHITAKER see also WHITTAKER

WHITBY (Edward) Born Stafford 28/12/1775, s. Rev. Thomas Whitby (Creswell Hall, Staffs.) and Mabella Turton. Trinity, Cambridge 1792, BA1797, dn99 (Win. for Salis.), p00 (Salis.), MA1807. V. Sleighford, Staffs. 1800-20, (Sinecure R. Creswell) 1806 to death. Sometime Chap. at Nice. Died (Creswell Hall) 23/3/1852 [C20725. Boase. ERC as Wright] Married Marylebone, London 7/8/1810 Mary Anne Way (of Denham Place, Bucks.).

WHITCOMBE (Charles) Born Wotton House, Gloucester 13/2/1797, s. Sir Samuel Whitcombe and Mary Aubrey. [Student Lincoln's Inn 1814]. Oriel, Oxford 1814, BA 1819, dn25 (Glos.), p25 (Glos.), MA1834. V. Sherston Magna (Great Sherston) w. Sherston Parva (Little Sherston), Wilts. 1830 to death 14/3/1884, leaving £196-7s-10d. [C89814]

WHITE (Charles) [MA but NiVoF] V. Mickleton, Glos. 1797-1818 (res.), V. Tewkesbury, Glos. 1818-45, V. Hexton, Herts. 1820 [C124043: ERC links], PC. Deerhurst, Glos. 1823 to death. Dom. Chap. to Dowager Countess of Rosslyn. Died 1845 (4th q.). [C167723] Had issue. Important in the civic life of Tewkesbury.

WHITE (Charles Henry) Born Fyfield, Hants. 4/10/1766, s. Rev. Henry White and Elizabeth Cooper. St Alban Hall, Oxford 1787, BA1793, MA1797. R. Shalden, Hants. 1797 (and V. 1829) to death (Wokingham, Berks.) 25/10/1859, leaving £18,000 [C109084] Married Monxton, Hants. 3/6/1802 Christian St Barbe, with issue.

WHITE (Edmund) Born London, s. Benjamin White. Oriel, Oxford 1782 (aged 22), dn85 (Glos. for Win.), p85 (Win.), BA1786, MA1789. V. (and patron) of Newton Valence, Hants. 1785-1838, R. Greatham, Hants. 1785-1813 (res.). Dom. Chap. to 1st Marquess of Downshire 1816. Died 18/4/1838 [C109085]

WHITE (Henry) Bapt. Lichfield Cathedral 19/5/1761, s. Rev. Thomas White (Sacristan of Lichfield Cathedral) and Lucy Hunter. Christ's, Cambridge 1779, BA1783, dn83 (C&L), p85 (C&L), MA1786. Priest Vicar and Prebend of Flixton and Offley 1784-5 (and Sacristan) of Lichfield Cathedral 1785-1836, V. Chebsey, Staffs. 1785-1836, PC. Pipe Ridware, Staffs. 1786, PC. Lichfield St Chad 1805 and V. Dilhorne, Staffs. 1809 to death 8/4/1836 aged 75 [C20731] Samuel Johnson called him 'the rising strength of Lichfield'. Had an important library.

WHITE (Henry) Born Holborn, London, s. Richard White. Christ's, Cambridge 1811, p13 (Chester), BA1816, MA1819. R. Claughton, Lancs. 1813-44. Died 20/4/1854 aged 51 [C170866] Married Kew, Surrey 28/7/1821 Elizabeth Stackhouse (and lived there).

WHITE (James) Born Nottingham 1788, s. John (a butcher) and Mary Neville. Pembroke, Cambridge 1811, BA1815, dn16 (C&L), p17 (C&L), MA1818. PC. Manchester St George Oldham Road 1826-42, R. Stalham, Norfolk 1842-52, R. (and patron and Lord of the Manor) of Sloley Scottow, Norfolk 1852 (and living at Sloley Hall) to death 9/3/1885 (unmarried) aged 97, leaving £43,686-8s-7d. [C20732. Boase] Brother of the poet Henry Kirke White, and of John Neville White, here.

WHITE (James) Born Midlothian March 1803, s. John White and Elizabeth Logan. Glasgow University, then Pembroke, Oxford

1823 (aged 20), BA1827, dn27 (B&W), p27 (B&W). PC. Stoke Lane, Som. 1827-30 (res.), V. Loxley, Warwicks. 1833-7 (res.). Retired to Bonchurch, IoW; died there 26/3/1862, leaving £4,000 [C40826. ODNB as prolific historical and miscellaneous writer. Boase] Married April 1829 Rosa Hill (w), 2s, 3 dau.

WHITE (John) Born Romsey, Hants., s. John White. Christ Church, Oxford 1773 (aged 18), then New, Fellow, dn78 (Ox.), p79 (Ox.), BCL 1781 [barrister Inner Temple 1785?]. Prebend of Yetminster Prima in Salisbury Cathedral 1804-33, R. Hardwick, Bucks. (and Preacher throughout the Diocese of Lincoln) 1807-33, R. Landford, Wilts. 1800-33 (res.). Died 18/7/1833 [C141799]

WHITE (John) Born Torr Farm, Woodland, Devon 11/2/1757, s. John White [*pleb.*] and Mary Hamlyn. Queen's, Oxford 1776, BA1780, dn80 (Ex.), p81 (Ex.). H/M Ashburton Free G/S, Devon 1788; PC. Buckland in the Moor, Woodland 1788 to death 9/12/1841 aged 84 [C146624] Married 17/2/1791 Mary Hele, with issue.

WHITE (John) Bapt. St James's, Westminster London 13/11/1761, s. William White. Oriel, Oxford 1780, BA1784, dn84 (Ex.), p86 (Ox. for B&W), MA1794. V. Exminster, Devon 1803 to death 2/9/1841 aged 80 [C38914]

WHITE (John) Bapt. Chevington, Suffolk 8/11/1785, s. Rev. John White (sen.). Caius, Cambridge 1804, BA1808, dn08 (Nor.), Fellow 1808, p10 (Salis. for Ely), MA1811, etc. S/M The Perse School, Cambridge 1810-19, R. (and patron) of Chevington, Norfolk 1819 and R. Hargrave, Norfolk 1819 to death 9/7/1851 [C89920] Married Whepstead, Suffolk 12/9/1826 Mary Image (a clergy dau.), w. issue.

WHITE (John) From Dublin. Queen's, Cambridge 1823, dn27 (Lin.), p27 (Lin.), BA 1828, MA 1831. V. Saxilby w. Ingleby, Lincs. 1831-2, V. Marton, Lincs. 1832-[39]. Died? [C80062]

WHITE (John) From Canterbury, s. John White. Queen's, Oxford 1825 (aged 18), BA 1829, dn30 (Cant.), p31 (London for Cant.), MA1832. PC. Fairfield, Kent 1832, PC. Thanington, Kent 1833, R. Canterbury St Andrew w. St Mary Bredman to 1847, V. Hackington (o/w St Stephen), Canterbury, Kent 1840 to death 5/2/1879, leaving £160,000 [C124561] Had issue.

WHITE (John Calcutta) Born Colchester 20/12/1790, s. Thomas (schoolmaster) and Ann White. Pembroke, Cambridge 1808, BA1813, Fellow 1814, dn16 (Ely), MA1816, p18 (Nor.). R. Rawreth, Essex 1821 to death 30/9/1872, leaving £7,000 [C54146] Married (1) Sarah Pyne (d.1848), with issue (2) Rochester, Kent 22/5/1849 Lucy Peché (d.1860), with further issue (3) Rochford, Essex 1861 (2nd q.) Frances Ellen Smith.

WHITE (John Neville) Bapt. Laneham, Notts. 16/1/1782, s. John White (butcher) and Mary Neville. Peterhouse, Cambridge 1819 (a Ten Year Man?), dn19 (Nor.), p20 (Nor.), BD1829. PC. Great Plumstead, Norfolk 1822, V. Ruishall, Norfolk 1828 and R. Tivetshall St Margaret w. Tivestshall St Mary, Norfolk 1832 to death 2/12/1845 [C1130 has no details] Married Norwich 12/6/1820 Charlotte Sewell, with clerical sons Herbert Southey White, and Joseph Neville White, jun. Brother of the poet Henry Kirke White (*qv.* ODNB), and James, here. Port. online.

WHITE (Richard) From Essex. Emmanuel, Cambridge 1778, BA1783, dn83 (Lin. for London), p85 (Cant.), MA1787. V. Shalford, Essex 1810 and R. Alkerton, Oxon. 1821 to death 9/9/1835 (CCEd thus) [C21938] Had issue.

WHITE (Richard Walton) Bapt. Whippingham, IoW 20/6/1783, s. John White and Grace March. Merton, Oxford 1802, BA1806, MA 1809. R. Wotton, IoW 1808-55, R. Marksbury, Som. 1816, R. Upcerne, Dorset 1828 [ERC as Walter] to death 2/12/1855 [C40827. Boase] Married Binstead, IoW 1812 Mary Popham, w. issue. *J.P.* Hants. and Chairman Petty Sessions IoW. *F.S.A.* (1819).

WHITE (Samson Henry) Bapt. Maidford, Northants. 27/2/1802, s. Rev. Samson and Hannah White, Merton, Oxford 1820, BA1823, dn25 (Peterb.), p26 (Peterb.). R. Maidford 1826 to death (unm.) 22/10/1871, leaving £600 [C111433]

WHITE (Samuel) Bapt. Whitechapel, London 8/7/1765, s. William and Sarah White. St Mary Hall, Oxford 1788, BA1792, dn92 (London), p93 (London), MA1801, BD and DD1811. R.

Brightwell Baldwin >< Oxon. 1801 and PC. Hampstead, London 1807 to death. Dom. Chap. to 1st Viscount Combermere 1817. Died 10/1/1841 [C38534]

WHITE (Thomas) Born Marylebone, London, s. John White. Oriel, Oxford 1794 (aged 17), BA 1797, then Queen's, MA1800, p00 (Lin.). PC. St James Chapel, Marylebone, London 1802, R. Epperstone, Notts. 1819 to death 18/4/1849 aged 72 [C135827] Was married.

WHITE (William) From Beds. St John's, Cambridge 1788, BA1792, dn92 (Chester), p93 (Lin.), MA1795. V. Lidlington, Beds. 1797-1835. Died? [C80092]

WHITE, *born* TUCKER (William) Born Wedmore, Som. 3/2/1793, s. John Tucker and Abigail White. [MA but NiVoF] (first) PC. Teale, Som. 1828-35 (resigned on inheriting Sand House, Wedmore). Died 3/6/1867 aged 74. Will not traced. Married Wedmore 3/2/1825 Jane Tyley [C40829. *The life of the Rev. William White, for some time incumbent of Teale Chapel, Wedmore, Somerset.* Written by himself (1860)]

WHITE (William) Born Blanford, Dorset, s. Henry White (a vintner). Pembroke, Cambridge 1813 (aged 18), BA1818, dn18 (Salis.), then Jesus, p19 (Ely for Bristol), Fellow 1819, MA 1821. V. Stradbroke, Suffolk 1823. Died? [C89923]

WHITEFOORD (George) Born Marylebone, London 29/9/1799, s. Sir John Rousselet Whitefoord and Deborah Ann Middleton. St John's, Cambridge 1817, dn22 (Ely for Bristol), BA1823, p23 (Nor.), then Jesus, Fellow 1824-6. R. Westerfield, Suffolk 1824-35, V. Dilham w. Honing, Norfolk 1826-28, R. Burgate, Suffolk 1828-34, PC. St Benet Fink, City of London 1834-5, R. Whitton cum Thurleston, Suffolk 1834-5, R. Newton in the Isle, Cambs. 1835 to death 26/3/1851 [C54149] Married 17/9/1827 Arabella Wyndham, of Cromer.

WHITEHEAD (George) Bapt. Harthill, Yorks. 17/10/1773, s. Rev. George Whitehead, sen. (a schoolmaster). Sidney, Cambridge 1793, BA1798, dn98 (York), p99 (York), MA1801. PC. Firbeck cum Letwell, Yorks. 1811-35 [in ERC twice]. Dead by 1838 [C111023. YCO. Kaye]

WHITEHEAD (George Davenport) Bapt. Tunbridge, Kent 17/8/1791, s. Rev. Robert and Jane Whitehead. Queen's, Oxford 1809, BA 1814, dn14 (York for Car.), p16 (York for Chester), MA1816. PC. Hensingham Chapel, St Bees, Cumberland 1817-31, V. Saxilby w. Ingleby, Lincs.1823-31, Senior Vicar in Lincoln Cathedral 1831-3 (and Prebend of Gretton in Lincoln Cathedral 1845), V. Hainton, Lincs. 1831 to death (Lincoln) 29/12/1864, leaving £2,000 [C8026. YCO] Married (1) Streatham, Surrey 18/12/1823 Inger Maria Wolff (d.1854), with issue (2) St James, Westminster, London 2/9/1862 Marian Russell Wilford (w).

WHITEHEAD (Gervas) Bapt. Ash by Wrotham, Kent 25/11/1763, s. Rev. Charles Whitehead and Ann Dunstan. Jesus, Cambridge 1781, BA1785, dn86 (Roch.), p87 (Cant.), MA 1788, Fellow 1790, BD. V. Cambridge All Saints 1809, V. Kemsing, Kent 1816 to death 23/7/1838 aged 75 [C593]

WHITEHEAD (Robert) From London, s. William Whitehead. Queen's, Oxford 1785 (aged 18), BA1789, dn89 (Roch.), MA1792, p96 (Car.). R. Great Musgrave, Westmorland 1807-11, R. Ormside, Westmorland 1811-51 (non-res.), Chap. *R.N.* Chatham Dockyards in 1820 (and of Bermuda Dockyards in 1828), PC. Hensingham, Cumberland 1831 to death (Rochester, Kent) 31/5/1851 aged 88 [C2557. Platt] Married Brighton 9/2/1790 Jane de Passow, with clerical son. Was in debt 1818.

WHITEHEAD (William Baily) Born Deane, Lancs. 16/4/1786, s. Rev. Christopher Whitehead and Mary Baily. Worcester, Oxford 1803, BA1807, MA1809, dn09 (Ox.), p12 (B&W), Fellow 1812-13. R. Pudleston w. Whyle, Heref. 1814, V. Twerton on Avon, Som. 1815-25, Preacher throughout the Diocese of Bath and Wells 1825, V. Timberscombe, Som. 1826 and V. Chard, Som. 1826 (and Prebend of Ilton in Wells Cathedral 1830) to death (Chard) 22/8/1853 aged 68 [C21950. Boase] Married Northover, Som. 23/11/1812 Marianne Tuson, w. clerical s. William. *J.P.* Somerset. Temperance worker.

WHITELOCK (John) Bapt. Skelton, Cumberland 30/1/1771. Literate: dn99 (Car.), p00 (Car.). V. Dearham, Cumberland 1814 to death 22/3/1834 [C6444. Platt]

WHITELOCK (Richard) Born Farthingoe, Northants, 20/1/1803, s. Richard Hutchins Whitelock and Frances Storer. Lincoln, Oxford

1822, BA1826, dn26 (Lin.), p27 (Lin.), MA1828. PC. Rochdale, Lancs. 1828, PC. Saddleworth, Yorks. 1831 to death 22/8/1879 (CCEd thus), leaving £2,000 [C80236] Married Rochdale, Lancs. 22/6/1830 Mary Elliott. Surrogate.

WHITELOCK (Richard Hutchins) Bapt. London 28/5/1772, s. Peter Whitelock [*pleb.*] and Frances Ann Hutchins. Lincoln, Oxford 1789, BA1792, dn95 (Peterb.), MA1796, p02 (Peterb.). V. Skillington, Lincs. 1805-34, PC. Chorlton cum Hardy St Clement, Manchester 1816 to death there 14/8/1833 aged 61 [C80237. Bennett2] Married Purley, Berks. 19/9/1800 Frances Storer (Purley Park, Reading and Jamaica), 12 ch. (some clerical).

WHITELOCK (William) Bapt. Kendal, Westmorland 19/2/1769, s. Joseph [*pleb.*] and Margaret Whitelock. Queen's, Oxford 1789, BA1793, MA1797, Fellow to 1823. R. Sulhampstead Abbotts w. Sulhampstead Bannister, Berks. 1822 to death 11/7/1836 [C20751]

WHITELOCKE (William Spencer) From Marylebone, London, s. John Whitelocke and Mary Lewis. Balliol, Oxford 1813 (aged 18), BA 1818, dn18 (London), p19 (Bristol), MA 1820. V. Gedney, Lincs. (and Preacher throughout the Diocese of Lincoln) 1822 and V. Foston, Yorks. 1835 to death 23/7/1855 [C40831] Married Clifton, Bristol 29/11/1831 Mrs Caroline (Sewell) Fornnereau.

WHITER (Charles Walter) Born Somers Town, London. Clare, Cambridge 1819, BA 1824, dn25 (Nor.), p26 (Nor.), MA1827. R. Little Bittering (o/w Bittering Parva), Norfolk 1833, R. Clowne, Derbys. 1834 to death (Carlton in Lindrick, Notts.) 4/2/1870, leaving £3,000 [C20752]

WHITFIELD (Thomas) Born Southwark, London, s. George Whitfield. St John, Oxford 1783 (aged 18), Fellow 1783-1838, BA1787, dn88 (Ox.), p89 (Chester), MA1791, BD1797, Chap. 1831, etc. R. Winterbourne, Glos. 1827 [net income £1,187] to death 16/2/1834 aged 68 (CCEd says 19/4/1834) [C38543]

WHITFIELD (William Brett) Born Lewes, Sussex 11/9/1769, s. Francis Whitfield (banker) and Elizabeth Brett. St John's, Cambridge 1787, BA1791, p93 (Chich.), MA1794, Fellow 1795-1824, BD1801, etc. R. Lawford, Essex 1822 to death 26/9/1847 [C71681]

WHITLEY (William) Bapt. Chester 29/2/1796, s. George and Ann Whitley. BNC, Oxford 1815, BA1818, dn19 (Chester), p21 (Chester). V. Whitegate, Cheshire 1825 to death (unmarried) Winsford, Cheshire 14/5/1876 aged 60, leaving £30,000 [C170871]

WHITMORE (Charles Blaney Cavendish) Born Stockton, Shropshire 9/3/1787, s. Thomas Whitmore and Mary Foley. Christ Church, Oxford 1805, BA1809, dn10 (C&L), p11 (C&L), MA1811. R. Stockton 1811 [blank in ERC] to death there 30/10/1856 aged 69 [C20753] Married Brewood, Staffs. 1829 Anne Giffard, 3 dau.

WHITMORE (John) Bapt. Wiston, Suffolk 10/12/1765. Jesus, Cambridge 1783, BA1788, dn88 (Lin. for Ely), p89 (Nor.), MA1792. R. Polstead, Suffolk 1795 to death 5/9/1840 aged 74 [C80296]

WHITNEY (George) Born Norton Canon, Heref. 18/11/1768, s. James and Elinor Whitney. Jesus, Oxford 1790, no degree, dn92 (Heref.), p00 (Heref.). R. Stretford, Heref. 1807 to death 27/1/1836 [C174478] Married Shrewsbury 18/2/1794 Catherine Davies, w. issue.

WHITTAKER (John William) Born Manchester 13/1/1791, s. of William Whittaker (a bankrupt Bradford cotton trader who fled to America) and Sarah Buck. St John's, Cambridge 1810, BA1814, Fellow 1814-26, MA1817, dn20 (Ely), p20 (Ely), BD1824, DD1830. V. Blackburn St Mary, Lancs. 1822 (and Hon. Canon Manchester Cathedral 1852) to death 3/8/1854 aged 63 (living also at Pwllheli, Carnarvon). Examining Chap. to Archbishop of Canterbury [C109549. ODNB. Boase. An extensive and unflattering coverage of him in B. Lewis, *Middlemost and the milltowns* (Stanford, 2001), Chapter 6, *passim*] Married 20/6/1825 Mary Haughton Feilden (dau. Sir William Feilden, 1st Bart., Feniscowles Hall, Lancs., a cotton manufacturer and *M.P.*), 9 ch. (1 clerical). *J.P.;* a founder of the Royal Astronomical Society 1820.

WHITTAKER see also **WHITAKER**

WHITTINGHAM (Paul) From Oxford, s. John Whittingham [*pleb.*]. Oriel, Oxford 1771 (aged 17), BA1774, dn76 (Ox.), Chap. Magdalen 1777-9, MA1778, p78 (Ox.). Minor Canon of Norwich Cathedral 1779-82, V. Westhall,

Suffolk 1781-87-, V. Martham, Norfolk 1792-1834, V. Sedgeford, Norfolk 1808-31 (res.), R. Badingham, Suffolk 1831 to death 14/6/1834 [C1131 - where the Career Model Record shows the extraordinary complexity of the parochial movements of this man] Possibly married Norwich 20/12/1781 Mary Millard.

WHITTINGHAM (Richard) Born Cheshire 22/5/1759, s. Samuel Whittingham and Hannah Nixon. Literate: dn82 (Lin.), p83 (Lin.). R. Potton, Beds. 1806 to death there 12/6/1845 aged 87 [C80301] Married St Pancras, London 10/4/1780 Mary Gaussen.

WHITTINGTON (John) Born Waterhouse, Wilts. 1771, s. Thomas Whittington and Ann Fisher. Queen's, Oxford 1790 (aged 18), BA1794, dn94 (Glos.), p95 (Glos.), MA1809. R. Cold Aston, Glos. 1795 until death 27/5/1842 [C167770] Married (1) Pucklechurch, Glos. 1/5/1797 Rachel Croome (d.1807), w. issue (2) Pucklechurch 24/7/1810 Elizabeth Gandy Kates (w).

WHORWOOD (Thomas Henry) Born Holton, Oxon. 29/4/1778, s. Henry and Mary Whorwood. Worcester, Oxford 1795, BA1799, dn01 (Ox.), MA1802, p04 (Ox.). V. (and patron) of Headington, Oxon. 1804 and V. Marston, Oxon. 1805 to death 21/7/1835 (CCEd thus); probate 17/5/1836 [C21955] Married by 1812 Mary Grape, with s. of same name.

WHEELER (Charles) Born Bridgnorth, Shropshire 26/1/1797 (bapt. 24/1/1803), s. Cornelius [*pleb.*] and Ann Wheeler. Christ Church, Oxford 1815, servitor 1815-19, BA 1819, dn20 (Ox.), Chap. 1820-21, p21 (Ox.), MA1823, then Merton, Chaplain 1824-35. PC. Stratton Audley, Oxon. 1831 to death 30/8/1835 [C29134]

WHYLEY (Gregory Edward) Born Birmingham 27/10/1798, s. Gregory Southworth Whyley and Elizabeth Bower. Trinity, Cambridge 1817, BA1821, dn22 (Cant.), p22 (London for Cantab.), MA1824. V. Eaton Bray, Beds. 1825-71, RD1839, V. Stanbridge, Beds. 1844 to death 6/1/1871, leaving £3,000 [C80308] Married Broadwater, Sussex 30/11/1825 Jane Morrah, with clerical son Edward Bowyer Whyley.

WICKENS (John) From Mapperton, Dorset, s. John Wickens. Wadham, Oxford 1793 (aged 18), then Merton 1797, dn97 (Bristol), p99 (Bristol), MA1802. R. Lytchett Maltravers, Dorset 1808-10 (res.), R. Swyre Dorset 1817, R. Manston, Dorset 1817-20, R. Wootton Glanville, Dorset 1835 to death. Dom. Chap. to 4th Viscount St John 1817. Died 5/8/1856 [C54154] Wife Sarah, and son.

WICKHAM (Thomas Whalley) Born Frome, Som., s. James Wickham (attorney) and Mary Whalley (dau. of the clerical Master of Peterhouse). Jesus, Cambridge 1792, BA1796, dn96 (B&W), p98 (B&W). R. Horsington, Som. 1798 to death 1855 (4th q. as Whaley) [C50178] Married 1799 Mary Bennett (dau. of the previous rector).

WIGGETT (James) Bapt. Norwich 15/12/1754, s. James Wiggett. Clare, Cambridge 1773 [adm. Lincoln's Inn 1774] BA1778, dn79 (Peterb. for Nor.), p79 (Peterb. for Nor.), MA 1781. R. Crudwell, Wilts. 1782, V. Hankerton, Wilts. 1785. Dom. Chap. to 4th Earl de la Warr 1783. Probably died 1840 (2nd q.) [C89930 ordinations corrected] Married (1) Ayot St Lawrence, Herts. 27/10/1791 Rachel Lyde (d.1802), with clerical son James Samuel, below (2) Walcot, Bath 6/6/1811 Elizabeth Humphreys, with 1s.

WIGGETT (James Samuel) Born Crudwell, Wilts. 12/7/1797, s. Rev. James Wiggett (above) and Rachel Lyde. Exeter, Oxford 1816, BA 1820, dn27 (Nor.), p27 (B&W), MA1828. V. Moulton St Michael (Great Moulton), Norwich 1827; living at Allanbay Park, Binfield, Berks. Died 8/4/1873 aged 75, leaving £20,000 [C40840] Married 23/1/1834 Mary Ann Thompson, with issue.

WIGGLESWORTH (Henry) Bapt. Settle, Yorks. 3/4/1758, s. James Wigglesworth and Barbara Simpson. Sidney, Cambridge 1776, BA1781, dn82 (Chester for York), p82 (Chester for York), MA1784. R. Slaidburn, Yorks. 1782 to death. Dm. Chap. to 3rd Baron Ducie 1786. Died 14/4/1838 aged 80 [C137086. YCO] Married (1) Burnsall, Yorks. 26/1/1795 Elizabeth Batty (d.1820) (2) Linton in Craven, Yorks. 6/11/1821 Mary Brown. Owner of the large Townhead estate in the parish and kept a pack of hounds, being known as the 'Bold Rector of Slaidburn'. 'A famous rider, his exploits in the hunting field are celebrated in several songs'.

WIGHTMAN (John) Born Scotland. 1779, s. John Wightman. Edinburgh University, MA, dn12 (Salis), p12 (Salis). R. Saltford, Som. 1812, R. Shrewsbury St Alkmund 1818-[41], PC. Kingsthorpe, Northants. 1850-53-. Chap. to HRH Duke of Kent 1818. Died 30/5/1854 aged 75 [C20768] Married 1815 Eliza (companion of Princess Charlotte, and illegitimate dau. of Prince Gagarin, a Russian prince, and calling herself Mrs Eliza Gagarin Wightman), w. 3 ch. (inc. clerical son Charles Edward Leopold, bapt. with 3 royal sponsors, and who succ. his father at St Alkmund's).

WIGHTWICK (Henry) From Bruton, Som., s. Rev. Walter Wightwick. Pembroke, Oxford 1786 (aged 17), BA1789, Fellow, dn92 (Salis.), MA 1792, p93 (Ex. for Salis.). R. Little Somerford, Wilts. 1794 to death 11/10/1846 [C89934] Clerical son of same name.

WILBERFORCE (Robert Isaac) Born Clapham, London 19/12/1802, s. William Wilberforce, *M.P.* (and abolitioner of slavery), and Barbara Ann Spooner. Oriel, Oxford 1820, BA1824, Fellow 1826-33, MA1827, dn28 (C&L), p28 (Ox.), Tutor 1828-31. V. East Farleigh, Kent 1832 exchanged for V. Burton Agnes, Yorks. 1840-66, Archdeacon of East Riding 1841-56. Became Roman Catholic 1856. Died Albano, Italy 3/2/1857 [C20762. ODNB. D. Newsome, *The parting of friends: the Wilberforces and Henry Manning* (1993) is outstanding] Married (1) Bridlington, Yorks. 16/6/1832 Agnes Everilda Frances Wrangham (d.1834) (2) 29/3/1837 Jane Legard (d.1854); with issue. Brother of Bishop Samuel Wilberforce, below.

WILBERFORCE (Samuel, *later* Bishop of Oxford, *then* of Winchester) Born Clapham, London 7/9/1805, s. William Wilberforce, *M.P.* (the abolitioner of slavery) and Barbara Ann Spooner. Oriel, Oxford 1823, BA1826, MA 1829, BD and DD1845, Hon. Fellow All Souls 1871-73. R. Brightstone, IoW 1830, Archdeacon of Surrey 1839-45 (res.), V. Alverstoke, Hants. 1840, 7th Prebend in Winchester Cathedral 1840-5 (res.), Dean of Westminster 1845 (only). Bishop of Oxford 1845-69, then Bishop of Winchester 1869 to death. Lord High Almoner; Prelate of the Order of the Garter. *Killed* Abinger, Surrey when thrown from his horse) 19/7/1873, leaving £60,000 [entry under Samuel Winchester] [C21960. ODNB. Boase. A.R. Ashwell, *Life of the Rt. Rev. Samuel Wilberforce, DD, Lord Bishop of Oxford and afterwards of Winchester. With selections from his diaries and correspondence* (3 vols. 1880-2). S. Meacham, *Lord Bishop: the life of Samuel Wilberforce, 1805-1873* (Cambridge, Mass., 1970)] Married Woolavington, Sussex 11/6/1828 Emily Sargent (d.1841), with two episcopal sons - the Bishops of Newcastle upon Tyne, and of Chichester; and an Archdeacon of Westminster. Brother Robert Isaac, above.

WILCOCKS, WILCOX (William Wright) From Norwich, s. William Wilcocks. Caius, Cambridge (as Wilcox) 1789, then Trinity 1790 (aged 18), BA1794, dn94 (Nor.), p06 (Nor.), MA1820. V. Barney, Norfolk 1806 and R. Pudding Norton >< Norfolk [blank in ERC] 1807 to death 18/5/1846 [C116173] Married Holborn, London 3/11/1821 Eve Chatten.

WILCOX (John) Probably born Thornburh, Glos. 11/2/1780, s. Thomas (a 'small innkeeper') and Sarah Wilcox. Pembroke, Cambridge 1796, BA1800, dn01 (Glos.), p03 (Glos.), MA 1803. R. Stonham Parva (Little Stonham), Suffolk 1816, Min. of Ely Chapel [St Etheldreda's?], Holborn, London (--), Minister Tavistock Proprietary Chapel, Drury Lane, London 1829 to death. Dom. Chap. to Earl of Kingston 1832. Died 23/12/1835 [C109104]

WILDBORE (Charles) Born Broughton Sulney, Notts. 16/7/1767, s. Rev. Charles Wildbore, sen. and Ann Lee. Sidney, Cambridge 1788, BA1792, dn92 (Car. for York), p93 (Ex. for York). V. Tilton on the Hill, Leics. [blank in ERC] 1796 to death 21/12/1842 aged 76 [C6450. YCO] Married Oakham, Rutland 22/1/1801 Frances Stimson, with issue.

WILDE (Thomas) Bapt. Newport, Shropshire. 3/2/1802, s. Thomas and Martha Wilde. Christ Church, Oxford 1819, BA1823, dn24 (C&L), p26 (C&L), MA1826. R. Worcester St Andrew 1826 to death (Sandyford, Staffs., a bachelor) 15/5/1861, leaving under £20 (unadministered) [C20772]

WILDE (William Taylor) Bapt. Bulwick, Northants. 9/4/1797, s. William and Sarah Wilde. St Bees adm. 1818, dn20 (York), p22 (York). PC. Kirk Levington, Yorks. 1832, V. Westow, Yorks. 1833 to death 16/11/1860. Will not traced [C135810. YCO] Married Steeple Bumpstead, Essex 8/11/1825 Harriet Stuart (a clergy dau.), with issue.

WILDER (Henry Watson) Bapt. Marylebone, London 11/12/1798, s. John Wilder (Purley Hall, Berks.) and Harriet Beaden. Oriel, Oxford 1816, BA1820, MA1822, dn23 (B&W), p23 (Glos.). R. Sulham, Berks. 1823 to death 2/7/1836 (*drowned* with his wife off Yarmouth, IoW) [C40851] Married St George's Hanover Square, London 8/4/1829 Augusta Smith (dau. of an *M.P.*), clerical s. Henry Beaufroy Wilder.

WILDER (William Samuel Parr) Born Westminster, London May 1796 (bapt. 8/2/1799), s. Gen. Sir Francis John Connor Wilder, *M.P.* (Binfield Manor, Berks.) and Frances Ann Phillips. Caius, Cambridge 1815, BA1820, dn21 (Bristol for Nor.), p21 (Nor.), MA1832. V. Thurnham, Kent 1829-33 (res.), R. Thornham w. Allingham, Sussex 1829, R. Carlton cum Willingham, Cambs. 1832 and R. Great Bradley, Suffolk 1835 to death (Bath) 22/8/1863 aged 67, leaving £8,000 [C54185] Married 1829 Augusta Louisa (dau. Lt.-Gen. Sir Henry Augustus Montagu Corby).

WILDIG (George Burgess) Born Lichfield, s. George Wildig (of Betley, Staffs.) and Hannah Pennington. Edinburgh University. 'Entered a mercantile house and became a partner'. Caius, Cambridge 1811 (aged 27), BA1815, dn15 (Chester), p17 (Chester), MA1818. Lecturer in Mathematics at Liverpool Institution from 1817; PC. Liverpool Holy Trinity 1817-21 (res.), R. Norton le Moors, Staffs. 1826 to death (St Helier, Jersey) 9/12/1853 aged 69 [C20774. Boase] Married Liverpool 16/3/1820 Anne Green Park, with issue. *F.R.A.S.*

WILES (Henry) Bapt. Chesterton, Cambs. 20/5/1781, s. William Wiles and Elizabeth Sulman. Trinity, Cambs. 1798, BA1803, Fellow 1805, BA1806, dn06 (Ely), MA1806, p06 (Ely), etc. PC. Cambridge St Michael 1819-21, V. Hitchin, Herts. 1821 to death 1856 (3rd q.) [C80413] Married Wisbech, Cambs. 28/8/1822 Sarah Grounds, w. issue.

WILGRESS (John Thomas) Bapt. Eltham, Kent 13/10/1776, s. Rev. John Wilgress and Elizabeth Kerby. Trinity, Cambridge 1793, BA 1798, dn99 (Ely), Fellow 1800-6, MA1801. S/M Sevenoaks G/S, Kent 1813-31; V. Chalk, Kent 1813-50, V. Gwinnear, Cornwall 1813-33, PC. Riverhead, Sevenoakes, Kent 1833 to death. Dom. Chap. to Bishop of Bristol 1802. Died Riverhead 1850 (2nd q.) [C2562. LBSO] Married (1) Tonbridge, Kent 3/9/1806 Mary Ann Scoones (d.1830) (2) Chiddingstone, Kent 22/3/1831 Arabella Streatfield.

WILKINS (Edward) Bapt. Charlcombe, Som. 30/8/1796, s. Rev. Thomas Wilkins and Charlotte Webster. King's, Cambridge 1815, Fellow 1818-33, BA1819, dn19 (Salis.), dn21 (Chester for B&W), MA1823. R. Hempstead w. Lessingham, Norfolk 1832 to death 18/7/1876 aged 80, leaving £1,000 [C40853] Married Weston-super-Mare, Som. 27/7/1833 Mary Leir (Jaggard's House, Wilts.), with clerical son Edward John Paul Wilkins. *J.P.* Norfolk.

WILKINS (George) Born Norwich 22/5/1785, s. William Wilkins (architect, of Newnham, Cambs., and brother of William Wilkins, architect) and Hannah Willett. Caius, Cambridge 1803, BA1807, dn08 (Nor.), p09 (Salis.), MA1810, DD1824. V. Laxton, Notts. 1813-17, V. Lowdham, Notts. 1815, V. Nottingham St Mary 1817-41, PC. Snenton, Yorks. 1818-31, Vicar-General and Prebend of Normanton in Southwell Collegiate Church 1823-65 (and thus the last surviving member of the dissolved Chapter), R. (and patron) of Wing (o/w Wix), Rutland 1827-39, V. Farnsfield, Notts. 1831, Archdeacon of Nottingham 1832-65, R. Hatcliffe, Lincs. 1834, V. Beelsby, Lincs. 1843 (non-res.) to death. Dom. Chap. to 11th Earl of Kinnoull 1813. Died Southwell [total income in CR65 £1,255] 13/8/1865, leaving £9,000 [C80415. ODNB. Boase. Kaye. Austin2, 46-58 and *passim*] Married Cambridge 3/9/1811 (having first eloped with her to Gretna Green) Amelia Auriol, dau. Very Rev. Edward Auriol Hay-Drummond, Hadleigh, Suffolk, with clerical son John Murray Wilkins.

WILKINSON (Christopher William) Bapt. Barwick in Elmet, Yorks. 22/2/1796, s. Edward Wilkinson and Ann Pearse. Sidney, then St John's, Cambridge 1814, BA1818, dn19 (Ex. for York), p20 (York), MA1821. V. Bardsey, Yorks. 1825-49 (living at Ingmanthorpe Hall, Wetherby, Yorks.). Died Bilton, Ainsty of York 9/2/1875, leaving £80,000 [C135826. YCO] Married Loughton, Essex 12/11/1834 Louisa Ann Pearse, with issue.

WILKINSON (Edmund) Born/bapt. Bampton, Westmorland 20/3/1783, s. Edmund and Wilkinson and Jane Thompson. Literate: dn07 (Car.), p08 (Car.). V. Chipping, Lancs. 1816 (and also Parish Constable 'for some years', and schoolmaster of Brabins Endowed

School there 1817-37) to death 23/9/1864 aged 81, leaving £1,000 [C6454. Boase] Married Goosnargh, Lancs. 11/5/1818 Alice Baines, *s.p.*

WILKINSON (George) Born Appleby, Westmorland 31/12/1786, s. Matthew Wilkinson and Margaret Western. Literate: dn13 (Durham), p14 (Car.), then St John's, Cambridge 1822, a Ten Year Man (BD1833). PC. Arlecdon, Cumberland 1829-47, R. Whicham, Cumberland 1847 to death 27/5/1865 aged 78, leaving £200 [C6455. Platt] Married (1) Elizabeth Ralph, with issue (2) Arcledon 21/10/1834 Maria Wright, with issue; some clerical. Surrogate. A noted antiquary, he was commissioned by the Earl of Lonsdale to excavate the Roman fort at Moresby; an 'ardent fan' of Cumberland and Westmorland wrestling.

WILKINSON (Henry Watts) Born Shoreditch, London 7/6/1782, s. Rev. Watts Wilkinson and Elizabeth Marlow. Worcester, Oxford 1800, BA1804, dn05 (Wor.), MA1806, p06 (Ox.). PC. Sudbury St Peter and St Gregory, Suffolk 1816, V. Walton w. Felixtowe, Suffolk 1845 to death 12/5/1851 [C21963. DEB] Married Clifton, Bristol 17/4/1819 Sarah Walker, with issue. Brother Marlow Watts Wilkinson, below.

WILKINSON (John) Born Clerkenwell, London 3/7/1757, s. James and Martha Wilkinson. Literate: dn82 (York for Chester), p86 (York for Chester). PC. Ellerton Priory, Yorks. [the interior is ;"stalled in the vilest maner, and the roof is supported by several poles"] 1814-41 and PC. Cawood, Wistow, Yorks. 1828-41. Died Alne, Yorks. 2/4/1841 aged 83 [C136030. YCO] Wife Esther, and issue.

WILKINSON (John) Born Kirkby Ravensworth, Westmorland 28/1/1780, s. Rev. John Wilkinson, sen. and Esther Elsdon. All Souls, Oxford 1797, BA1801, dn03 (York), p04 (York). V. Gate Helmsley, Yorks. 1810 and V. Bubwith (2nd Mediety), Yorks. 1815 to death 5/11/1846 aged 65 [C111038. YCO] Married York 13 or 29/1/1808 Anna Joanna Newstead.

WILKINSON (John Brewster) Bapt. Halesworth, Suffolk 25/6/1785, s. John William Wilkinson and Sarah Ann Leigh. St John's, Cambridge 1803, BA1807, dn08 (Nor.), Fellow 1809-33, MA1810, p13 (Nor.), BD1817. R. Freston, Suffolk 1832-8, R. (and patron) of Holbrook, Suffolk 1832-58. Died London 20/6/1862 aged 77, leaving £9,000 [C116178] Married Marylebone, London 29/5/1832 Jane Theresa Purcell (w) (dau. of a Kilkenny doctor).

WILKINSON (John Ferdinando) Bapt. South Croxton, Leics. 24/1/1804, s. Rev. William (below) and Lucy Wilkinson. Clare, Cambridge 1822, BA1826, dn27 (Lin.), p28 (Lin.). R. South Croxton 1828 to death 22/3/1868, leaving £1,000 [C80422] Married Gayton-le-Wold, Lincs. 28/11/1827 Harriet Taylor Clough (w).

WILKINSON (Joseph) Born Upleatham, Yorks., s. Rev. Joseph Wilkinson, sen. (a topographical artist) and Ann Harker. St Bees, Cumberland 1826, dn26 (Durham for York), p27 (Durham) (succ. his father as) PC. Upleatham 1827-[55], PC. Redcar, Yorks. 1832-[54] [C136934. ERC links]. Died? [C125529. YCO]

WILKINSON (Marlow Watts) Bapt. Shoreditch, London 10/9/1787, s. Rev. Watts Wilkinson and Elizabeth Marlow. Worcester, Oxford 1806, BA1810, dn10 (Ox.), p12 (Ox.), MA1813, BD1825. R. Uley, Glos. 1823, R. Harescombe w. Pitchcombe, Glos. 1825 to death 28/3/1867, leaving £1,500 [C21964] Married Stony Stratford, Bucks. 10/8/1815 Sarah Roberts. Brother Henry Watts (above).

WILKINSON (Marmaduke) Born Roehampton House, Clapham, London 12/9/1769, s. John Wilkinson (Bury St Edmunds, Suffolk) and Sibella Berdoe. Peterhouse, Cambridge 1787, BA1793, dn97 (Nor.), p98 (Nor.), MA 1802. R. Little Welnetham, Suffolk 1800-32, R. Nowton, Suffolk 1802 and R. Redgrave w. Botesdale, Suffolk 1802 to death 22/1/1844 [C116181] Married (1) Rushbrook, Staffs. 20/12/1792 Elizabeth (natural dau. of Sir Charles Davers, she d.1811), with clerical s. Henry Thomas (2) Stepney, London 31/8/1813 Sarah Shelley Eastfield, with further issue.

WILKINSON (Robert) Bapt. Cockermouth, Cumberland 24/11/1752, s. Thomas Wilkinson and Mary Fisher. Literate: dn76 (York), p77 (York), then Trinity Hall, Cambridge 1780, a Ten Year Man (BD1790). PC. Lightcliffe, Yorks. 1782 and V. Darton, Yorks. 1790 (with H/M Heath Free G/S, Halifax 1789) to death 29/12/1839 aged 87 [C111043. YCO] Married Halifax 15/7/1782 Sarah Robinson, with issue.

WILKINSON (Robert) Born Beetham, Westmorland 25/8/1801, s.William Wilkinson (farmer) and Mary Arabella Dineley. St Bees adm. 1824, p28 (Chester). PC. Killington, Kirkby Lonsdale, Westmorland 1830-74 (and S/M Killington G/S). Died Kendal, Westmorland 30/5/1883 aged 81. Will not traced [C170880] Married Liverpool 15/7/1828 Jane Moore (of Trinidad), with issue.

WILKINSON (Thomas) From London, s. Thomas Wilkinson. Trinity, Cambridge 1789, BA1793, dn93 (Peterb.), p95 (Peterb.), MA 1796, BD1819. V. Kirk Hallam, Derbys. 1801-41, R. Bonnnington, Kent 1803-7, R. Great Houghton, Northants. 1804-5, R. Bulvan, Essex 1805-30, R. Armthorpe, Yorks. 1807-34. Died 1841 'aged 76' [C20779] Married Penrith, Cumberland 26/10/1786 Jane Buchanan, with clerical son.

WILKINSON (Thomas Boston) Bapt. Rudham, Norfolk 10/8/1798, s. William Farley Wilkinson and Eleanora Ann Boston. Corpus Christi, Cambridge 1816, BA1820, dn21 (Nor.), p22 (Nor.), MA1824. R. East Harling, Norfolk 1829-88, RD, R. Saxlingham Nethergate w. Saxlingham Thorpe, Norfolk 1833-5 (res.). Died 15/10/1888 aged 90, leaving £2,178-0s-0d. [C95847] Married East Carleton, Norfolk 10/9/1821 Ann Steward,

WILKINSON (Thomas Chambers) Bapt. Cottingham, Northants. 22/2/1771, s. Thomas and Ann Wilkinson. St John's, Cambridge 1789 BA1793, dn93 (C&L), p97 (Peterb.). R. Stamford All Saints w. St Peter, Lincs. 1802 to death (Amiens, France) 5/12/1836 [C20777] Married Tower of London 28/6/1808 Eliza Porett, w. child.

WILKINSON (William) Born London, s. Thomas Wilkinson. Trinity, Cambridge 1792 (aged 20), dn94 (Lin.), BA1797, p97 (Lin.), MA1801. R. South Croxton, Leics. 1801-28, R. Folksworth, Hants. 1807-20, V. Lowesby, Leics. 1814-20, V. Sproxton cum Saltby, Leics. 1820 and V. Glentham, Leics. 1837 to death. Dom. Chap. to 2nd Baron Rancliffe 1807-20. Died 7/1/1842 [C80456] Wife Lucy, and son John Ferdinando, above.

WILKINSON (William Farley) Born Harwich, Essex, s. William Wilkinson and Mary Whenney. Trinity, Cambridge 1784 (aged 17), BA1789, dn89 (Nor.), p90 (Nor.), MA1792. R. Southwood w. Limpenhoe, Norfolk 1790-1803, R. Reedham, Norfolk 1790-1801, R. Norwich St Lawrence 1803-35, PC. Norwich St Benedict, 1810-35, R. Heigham, Norfolk 1812-13 (res.), V. North Walsham, Norfolk 1818-51, R. East Harling, Norfolk 1818-29, R. Antingham St Margaret, Norfolk 1818-51, R. Saxlingham Nethergate w. Saxlingham Thorpe, Norfolk 1835 to death 22/6/1851 aged 84 [C116175] Married Eleanora Ann Boston by 1792, with clerical son of same name.

WILKINSON (William Hemsworth) Bapt. Grasby, Lincs. 8/11/1785, s. Rev. William and Mary Wilkinson, Trinity, Cambridge 1803, BA 1808, dn11 (York), p11 (York). V. Kirming-ton, Lincs. 1812 and (succ. his father as) V. Grasby 1812 to death 2/5/1835 (CCEd says 27/6/1835) [C80460. YCO. Kaye]

WILKINSON (William John) Bapt. Durham 26/11/1770, s. Thomas Wilkinson. Christ Church, Oxford 1789, BA1793, dn94 (Carlisle for York), p94 (London for York), MA1800. V. Elloughton, Yorks. 1798-1820, R. Kirk Ella, Yorks. 1804-[41], R. Aldbrough, Yorks. 1813. Died York 2/9/1856 aged 85 [C111044. YCO]

WILLAN (Thomas) Bapt. Sedbergh, Yorks. 20/11/1775, s. Miles and Sarah Willan. Literate: dn00 (York), p01 (York). V. Corby, Lincs. 1802 (w. R. Irnham from 1804) to death 3/8/1850 [C80474. YCO. Bennett2] Married Great Carlton, Yorks. 15/12/1802 Esther Walker Burton (a clergy dau.), with clerical son James Henry Willan.

WILLAUME (Charles Dymoke) Born London 26/11/1782, s. John Willliams and Mary Willaume. Oriel, Oxford 1802, dn06 (Win.), BA1806, p06 (Ex. for Win.), MA1809. R. Chilton Candover, Hants. 1807 and R. Brown Candover, Hants. 1809 to death. Dom. Chap. to 3rd Earl Harcourt 1809. Died 27/2/1848 [C109109] Married Nursling, Hants. 22/2/1819 Margaret Anne Lukin.

WILLES (Edward) Bapt. Christian Malford, Som. 31/10/1769, s. Ven. William Willes (Archdeacon of Wells) and Margaret Jeans. Pembroke, Oxford 1786, BA1789, dn95 (B&W), p96 (B&W), MA1801. R. West Camel, Som. 1796-1824, Prebend of Combe V1 in Wells Cathedral 1799-1847, V. Huish Episcopi, Som. 1802-24, R. Morley, Derbys. 1804-7, R. Breane, Som. 1831. Dom. Chap. to 13th Baron Teynham 1802. Died (Bath) 30/10/1847 [C20781] Was never married to Prudence Philips, but his will acknowledged her to be the mother of their six natural children.

WILLES (Edward) Born Cirencester, Glos. 25/1/1803, s. William and Margaretta Willes. BNC, Oxford 1821, BA1825, dn26 (Ox.), p27 (Ox.), MA1827. V. Ampney Crucis, Glos. 1827-9, R. Stratton, Glos. 1827-33, R. Whitnash, Warwicks. 1829-33, R. Hamstall Ridware, Staffs. 1833 and R. Yoxall, Staffs. 1833 to death 13/10/1848 [C20782]

WILLESFORD (Richard Vyvyan) Bapt. Tavistock, Devon 15/4/1770, s. Richard Willesford. Exeter, Oxford 1788, BA1792, dn93 (Ex.), p94 (Ex.), then Peterhouse, Cambridge MA1803. 'Sometime' S/M Tavistock G/S; R. Coryton, Devon 1795 and V. Awliscombe, Devon 1803 to death. Chap. in Ordinary to Prince Regent 1817. Died 30/7/1834 [C146651] Married Bideford, Devon Susannah Bovey, w. issue. *J.P.* Devon.

WILLETT (Wright) Born Hawarden, Flint 31/1/1796, s. Richard Willett (schoolmaster) and Susanna Wright. St Bees College: dn20 (Glos.), p21 (Chester). PC. Rowton, Shropshire 1824. Died Skipton, Yorks. 21/1/1862 aged 66, leaving £300 [C167829] Married Dublin 1/7/1820 Emily Gaynor (w), with clerical son George Thomas Willett.

WILLIAM-POWLETT (Henry, 3rd Baron Boyning) see under **TOWNSEND**

WILLIAMS (Charles) [NiVoF] PC. Buttington, Montgomery [Heref. Diocese] 1792 to death (Welshpool) 15/2/1834 aged 72 (CCEd says 6/11/1834)[C174621]

WILLIAMS (Charles) [MA but NiVoF] R. Barby, Northants. 1815 to death 26/8/1850 [C111425] Married Walthamstow, Essex 1805 Mary Jane Jackson (w), with child. Violently anti-Methodist.

WILLIAMS (Charles) Born Compton, Hants. 29/11/1794, s. Rev. Philip Williams. Corpus Christi, Oxford 1803, then New, Fellow to 1819, BA1808, dn10 (Win.), p11 (Glos.), MA 1812; Fellow Winchester College 1819. R. Cubley, Ashbourne, Derbys. 1819-32, R. Gedling, Notts. [income £1,070] 1832 to death. Died 30/7/1834. Private tutor at Eton and Dom. Chap. to 6th Earl of Chesterfield 1819. Died 30/7/1834 [C20787. Boase. Austin] Married Worplesdon, Surrey 31/5/1821 Charlotte Roberts (dau. of a Provost of Eton), 1 clerical son, 2 dau.

WILLIAMS (David) From Marlborough, Wilts., s. David Williams. Jesus, Oxford 1779 (aged 28). R. Litchfield, Hants 1793. PC. Heytesbury, Wilts. 1795 [C106464], V. Tilshead, Wilts. 1803 [C89943], R. Litton, Som. 1814 to death 13/10/1836 [C50238. ERC links]

WILLIAMS (David) From Barry, Glamorgan, s. John Willliams. Jesus, Oxford 1810 (aged 18), dn14 (B&W), BA1814, p16 (Salis.), MA1820. R. Bleadon, Som. 1820, R. Kingston Seymour, Som. 1820, Prebend of Heytesbury (2nd or Horningham and Tytherington Moiety) in Heytesbury Collegiate Church 1835. Dom. Chap. to 1st Earl Howe 1820. Died 1850. [C40866]

WILLIAMS (David) [NiVoF] V. Romsey (Abbey), Hants. 1829 to death 2/1/1834 (CCEd thus and as Daniel) [C109128]

WILLIAMS (Edward) From Eaton, Shropshire, s. Edward Wiliams. Pembroke, Oxford 1779 (aged 17), BA1783, then All Souls, MA 1787, Fellow to 1818. PC. Battlefield, Shropshire 1786, PC. Uffington, Shropshire 1786, R. Chelsfield, Kent 1817 to death 3/1/1833 [C2567]

WILLIAMS (Ellis) Bapt. Holborn, London 18/9/1791, s. Griffith Williams and Winifred Evans. Literate: dn15 (York), p17 (York). R. Pinxton, Alfreton, Derbys. 1826 to death (Clifton, Bristol) 25/1/1864, leaving £6,000 [C20878. YCO] Married (1) Spondon, Derbys. 30/11/1819 Hannah Coke (d.1833) (2) Islington, London 19/10/1836 Ann Powell, with issue.

WILLIAMS (Erasmus Henry Griffies-, Sir, 2nd Bart.) Bapt. Llwyn y Wormwood, Carmarthen 31/7/1784, s. Rev. Sir George Griffies-Williams, 1st Bart. (born Griffies) and Ann Margaret Evans. St John's, Cambridge 1814, BA1818, dn19 (Glos.), MA1821 p21 (Salis. for B&W). R. Rushall, Wilts. 1829-70, R. Marlborough St Peter and St Paul, Wilts. 1829-58, Chancellor of St David's Cathedral 1858 to death (The Castle Hotel, Llandovery) 30/11/1870, leaving £16,000 [C89944. Boase] Married Walcot, Bath 21/9/1818 his cousin Mrs

Caroline (Griffiths) Hunt-Grubbe, *s.p.* Succ. to title 1843. Fine port. online.

WILLIAMS (Frederick de Veil) Born Surrey 4/7/1798, s. John Williams and Caroline Medkaff. Queens', Cambridge 1818, BA1822, dn11, p22, MA1826, incorporated at Oxford 1834. R. Abdon, Shropshire 1823, R. Wishford Magna (Great Wishford), Wilts. 1823 to death. 19/2/1863, leaving £4,000 [C89947. LBSO]

WILLIAMS (George) Bapt. Hartlebury, Worcs. 19/11/1766, s. William Williams. Wadham, Oxford 1785, BA1789, dn89 (Wor.), p90 (Wor.). R. Martin Hussingtree, Worcs. 1790-1852, R. Sedgeberrow, Worcs. 1825-34 (res.), V. Wichenford, Worcs. 1834. Died 10/12/1852 [C122312]

WILLIAMS (Hamilton John) Born Cerne Abbas, Dorset 27/12/1796, s. Robert Williams and Jane Blair. St John, Cambridge 1826, SCL, dn29 (B&W), p29 (B&W), LLB1833, incorporated at Oxford 1858. V. Buckland Dinham, Som. 1829-46, V. Kempston, Bucks. 1846 to death 13/12/1879, leaving £1,500 [C40869] Married Charminster, Dorset 17/9/1829 Margaret Sophia Taunton, with clerical son.

WILLIAMS (Henry) From Wellsbourne, Warwicks., s. Rev. John Henry Williams. BNC, Oxford 1797 (aged 17), BA1801, then Merton, Fellow 1805-21, MA1805, dn07 (Ox.), p08 (Ox.). V. Diddington, Hunts. 1818, V. Malden, Surrey 1820 to death 1854 [C21972. ERC links]

WILLIAMS (James) From Chepstow, Monmouth, s. James Williams. Jesus, Oxford 1786 (aged 17), BA1790, MA1793. R. Wiverton, Norfolk 1799 to death 31/1/1846 Lived at Motherne, Monmouth [C116193] *J.P.* Monmuth.

WILLIAMS (James Haddy Wilson) Bapt. Maldon, Essex 28/4/1776, s. Rev. William Williams and Ann Elizabeth Wilson. Clare, Cambridge 1792, BA1797, dn98 (London), Fellow, 1799, p01 (Nor.). V. Litlington, Cambs. 1812-15, R. Westley w. Fornham All Saints >< Suffolk 1815 to death 18/3/1842 aged 65 [C109848] Married 1817 Grace Joanna Applebee, with issue. Friend of Charles Lamb, the essayist.

WILLIAMS (John) [MA but NiVoF] R. Ashington, Som. 1785 and V. Marston Magna, Som. 1785, R. Ashby cum Fenby, Lincs. 1810 [C17956. ERC links], Prebend of Buckland Dinham in Wells Cathedral 1798 to death 9/4/1842 [C99176]

WILLIAMS (John) Born Ryadergowy, Radnor, s. David Williams [*pleb.*]. Christ Church, Oxford 1786, BA1790, Chaplain, p92 (Ox.), MA1793. V. North Leverton, Notts. 1795 and V. South Stoke, Oxon. 1795 to death (Rhayader, Radnor) 12/5/1844 aged 77 [C21977] Had clerical son John.

WILLIAMS (John) [NiVoF] R. and V. Kemberton w. Sutton Maddox, Shropshire 1830 to death 10/11/1834 (CCEd thus) [C20883]

WILLIAMS (Richard) Born 11/3/1759, s. Richard and Elizabeth Williams. Christ's, Cambridge 1776, BA1780, dn81 (Lin.), MA 1783, p86 (Peterb.). V. Poddington, Beds. 1801-4, R. Markfield, Leics. 1804-44 and R. Great Houghton, Northants. 1805-44, Prebend of Langford Manor in Lincoln Cathedral 1805 to death. Co-Brother of St John's Hospital [almshouses], Northampton 1805-44. Died 4/7/1844 [C80504] Married (1) Northampton 15/2/1795 Charlotte Atkinson (d.1814), w. issue (2) St Pancras, London 28/6/1819 Bridget Round; with further issue.

WILLIAMS (Theodore) Born Jamaica, s. James Williams and Frances Cecilia Stone. Pembroke, Cambridge 1805 (aged 18), then Trinity 1806, no degree, dn09 (London), p10 (London). V. Hendon, Middx. [net income £1,280] 1812 to death 6/12/1875 aged 90. No will traced [C124076. LBSO] Married Leytonstone, Essex 6/10/1813 Jane Masterman, w. at least 7s, 7 dau..

WILLIAMS (Thomas) Born Frampton, Dorset, s. John Williams. Merton, Oxford 1781 (aged 17), BA1786, dn88 (Car.), MA1792. R. Brympton, Som, 1796, V. Buckland Dinham, Som. 1801-11, R. Cloford, Som. 1801, R. Cameley, Som. 1810, R. Whatley, Som. 1812 and Prebend of Combe 111 in Wells Cathedral 1812 to death 28/7/1852 [C6461]

WILLIAMS (Thomas) From Heytesbury Wilts., s. Rev. David Williams. St John's, Cambridge 1818, BA1824, dn24 (Salis.), p26 (Salis.), MA1827. PC. Imber, Wilts. 1834-41 [blank in ERC], PC. Pitcombe w. Wyke Champflower, Som. 1841 to death (unm.?) 9/1/1846 aged 44

[C90046. Long and worthy obit. in *Gentleman's Magazine*]

WILLIAMS (Thomas Edmunds) From Reading, Berks., s. William Williams. St Mary Hall, Oxford 1809, DD1832 V. Bucklebury, Herts. 1832 to death 30/5/1849 [C7960] Married Reading 16/4/1801 Martha Hawthorne.

WILLIAMS (William) [NiVoF] R. Flyford Flavel, Worcs. 1793-1822, R. ('Reader') Rous Lench, Worcs. 1817. Possibly died 1838 (1st q.) [C122326]

WILLIAMS (William) [NiVoF] R. Little Mongeham, Kent 1803 to death 31/12/1835 (CCEd thus) [C137027]

WILLIAMS (William) [BA by1809 but NiVoF] V. Netheravon, Wilts. 1809-[38]. Died? [C106465]

WILLIAMS (William) [NiVoF] R. Stockleigh English, Devon 1829-45, R. Stokesay, Shropshire 1845-[56]. Died? [Not yet CCEd?]

WILLIAMS (William) From Liskeard, Cornwall, s. Rev. William Williams, sen. All Souls, Oxford 1817 (aged 17), dn22 (Ox.), BA 1823, p23 (Ox.), MA1824. PC. Ascott under Wychwood, Oxon. 1822 and PC. Leafield, Oxon. 1826. Died? [C21991]

WILLIAMS (William Tugwell) Born Avening, Glos., s. Rev. Joseph Williams. Corpus Christi [*not* Christ Church], Oxford 1799 (aged 18), BA1803, MA 1806, dn06 (Ox.), p06 (Ox.), Fellow to 1812 Chap. of the Donative of Freefolk, Hants. 1820, R. Lainston, Hants. 1826. Probate granted 10/1/1851 [C21992]

WILLIAMSON (Edmund) Bapt. Millbrook, Beds. 28/6/1761, s. Rev. Edmund, sen. and Mary Williamson. Trinity, Cambridge 1778, BA1782, dn85 (Lin.), p85 (Ely), MA1786. R. Lolworth, Cambs. 1786-1839, R. Apsley Guise, Beds. 1790-6, R. Campton, Beds. 1790 to death. Dom. Chap. to 8th Earl of Lauderdale 1790. Died 13/1/1839 aged 77 [C80526] Married 4/2/1792 Phoebe Riland (a clergy dau., Sutton Coldfield), with issue.

WILLIAMSON (Robert Hopper) Born Newcastle upon Tyne 9/8/1784, s. Robert Hopper and Anne Williamson (a clergy dau.). St John's, Cambridge 1801, BA1807, dn08 (York for Durham), p09 (Durham), MA1810. R. Hurworth, Durham 1832 to death (Darlington, Co. Durham) 11/3/1865, leaving £70,000 [C125531. YCO] Married Bishopwearmouth, Durham 18/6/1811 Elizabeth Barras, with clerical son of same name.

WILLIAMSON (Thomas Pym) Bapt. Guisborough, Yorks. 24/4/1774, s. Rev. William Leigh Williamson and Judith Place. St Catharine's, Cambridge 1793, BA1797, dn97 (York), p98 (York), MA 1803. V. Guisborough 1798-1835 (res.) and V. (and patron) of Kirkby Stephen, Westmorland 1807 to death (Guisborough, of cholera) 24/5/1836 aged 63 [C6465. YCO] Married Pontefract, Yorks. 10/3/1806 Frances Taylor, with issue.

WILLIAMSON (William) Born Pocklington, Yorks. 12/9/1799, s. Rev. William Williamson, sen. (V. Long Bennington, Lincs.). Sidney, Cambridge 1817, BA1822, dn23 (Lin.), p24 (Lin.), MA1825, Fellow 1826-8. PC. Farnley, Leeds 1827-33, PC. Headlingley, Leeds 1836-63, V. Welton, Lincs. 1849 [where the church was struck by lightning during a service and the man in front of him killed, and he was rendered practically deaf] to death 20/4/1882, leaving £1,356-0s-6d. [C80528] Married (1) Skelton, Cumberland 23/8/1831 Jane Dixon, dau. of a solicitor (2) Kendal, Westmorland 1869 (2nd q.) Sarah Jane Fawcett (a clergy dau., of Leeds).

WILLIAMSON (William) [NiVoF] V. Slipton, Northants. 1826-51-. Died? [C111362]

WILLMOTT (William) Born Scarborough, Yorks. 5/1/1770, s. Samuel and Ann Willmott. Magdalen, Cambridge 1796, BA1800, dn00 (Ex. for York), p01 (York), MA1810. PC. Halifax St Ann in the Grove 1802, PC. Halifax Holy Trinity, Yorks. 1818 to death 22/2/1835 [C130168. YCO] Married Halifax 5/9/1804 Sarah Whitworth (a milliner), with issue.

WILLINS (James) Bapt. Norwich 9/9/1767, s. Rev. James Willins, sen. (V. Catton, Norfolk). Caius, Cambs. 1784, BA1789, dn89 (Nor.), Fellow 1789, p91 (Nor.), MA1792. V. Great Melton (Melton Magna), Norfolk 1804 and V. Norwich St Michael Coslany 1804 to death 16/2/1851 [C116207. LBSO] Married Charlotte Burton, w. issue.

WILLIS (James [Compton]) Bapt. Sopley, Hants. 3/6/1790, s. Rev. James Willis, sen.

Merton, Oxford 1773, BA1777, dn78 (Ox.), p78 (Ox.). V. Sopley 1779-1835, R. Minstead, Hants. 1779-81 (res.). Died 23/4/1835 [C38823]

WILLIS (John) Born Rochester, Kent 5/5/1799, s. Thomas Willis and Catherine Strong. St John's, Cambridge 1817, BA1821, dn22 (Lin. for Roch.), p23 (Win. for Roch.), MA1824. V. Haddenham w. Cuddington, Bucks. 1826 to death 4/5/1855 aged 55 [C2571] Married (1) Catherine Dow, 1s. (2) St Pancras, London 27/10/1843 Sarah Taylor. Very popular and well-liked (his generous Charity survives) in spite of being a delinquent clergyman (suspended 1835; and again in 1845 when he visited a brothel; and was drunk in the pulpit 'and [in] a haystack)'.

WILLIS (Richard Child) Bapt. Petworth, Sussex 3/5/1799, s. Admiral Richard Willis and Ann Child. University, Oxford 1817, dn22 (Chester), BA1822, p23 (Lin. for Chich.), MA 1824, BD1840, DD1841. PC. North Stoke, Sussex 1823, R. Warden, Isle of Sheppey 1845, V. Minster, Isle of Sheppey 1847 to death 27/1/1877, leaving under £100 [C71865] Married Petworth 24/1/1826 Frances Fanny Hale.

WILLIS (William Downes) Born Dublin 9/9/1790, s. William Willis (of Badsworth, Yorks.) and Mary Hamilton Smith. Trinity, Cambridge 1807, then Sidney 1809, BA1813, dn13 (York), p14 (York), MA1819. V. Kirkby in Cleveland, Yorks. 1816-41 [blank in ERC], RD of Bath 1830-40, Prebend of Wanstow in Wells Cathedral 1840 and R. Elsted, Sussex 1842 to death 22/10/1871, leaving £2,000 [C40919. YCO. Boase heavily corrected] Married Startforth, Yorks. 23/3/1822 Dorothy Preston (Warcop Hall, Westmorland, a clergy dau.), with issue.

WILLOUGHBY (Hugh Pollard) Bapt. Marsh Baldon, Oxon. *c*.1802, s. Sir Christopher Willoughby, 1st Bart. and Martha Evans. Exeter, Oxford 1819, BA1826, dn26 (Cashel: the Abp was Prof. of Hebrew at Oxford), p27 (Ox.), MA1829. R. Eastleach Martin, Glos. 1827, R. Burthorpe (o/w Eastleach Martin), Glos. 1827, R. Marsh Baldon 1831. Dom. Chap. to 2nd Earl of Sefton 1831. Died Bethlem Hospital, London 25/12/1857, leaving £387-9s-9d. [C21994] After a trial at the Central Criminal Court in 1854 he was declared insane 'for shooting and feloniously wounding with intent to murder'

Hardinge Stanley Giffard. '*Detained at Her Majesty's Pleasure*': www.oldbaileyonline.org › Breaking Peace › wounding.

WILLS (John) Bapt. Crewkerne, Som. 14/4/1784, s. Rev. Samuel Wills and Mary Seymer. Wadham, Oxford 1801, BA1805, p08 (B&W), MA1810. R. South Perrott w. Masterson, Dorset 1809 to death 26/2/1854 [C50288] Clerical son of same name. Brother William, below.

WILLS (Thomas) Bapt. Helston, Cornwall 29/11/1753, s. Rev. Matthew Wills. University, Oxford 1771, BCL1778, LLB, dn84 (Ex.), p84 (Ex.). V. Wendron w. Helston, Cornwall 1785-1837. Buried 24/2/1837 aged 83 [C146667]

WILLS (William) Born Crewkerne, Som. 28/12/1793, s. Samuel Wills and Mary Seymer. Wadham, Oxford 1812, BA1816, dn17 (Chester for Bristol), p18 (Salis. for Bristol), MA1819. V. Holcombe Rogus, Devon 1824 to death there 8/8/1875, leaving £6,000 [C54179] Married Colyton, Devon 10/12/1824 Judith Wilson. Brother John, above.

WILMOT (Richard Coke) Born Chaddesden, Derbys. 18/5/1802, s. Sir Robert Wilmot, 3rd Bart. and Lucy Grimston. BNC, Oxford 1820, no degree, dn28 (Nor.), p28 (C&L). PC. Stanley, Derbys. 1830, PC. Chaddesden 1830. Died 16/11/1856 aged 54, living at Neswick Hall, Yorks. [C20914] Married Much Marcle, Heref. 3/7/1828 Eleanor Money (a clergy dau.), *s.p.*

WILSON (Christopher) Born Leighton Buzzard, Beds. 23/12/1788, s. Rev. John and Mary Wilson. Pembroke, Cambridge 1807, BA1811, Fellow 1812, dn12 (Lin.), MA1814, p15 (Ely). R. South Collingham, Notts. 1803-13, V. Waresley, Hunts. 1815 to death (Leighton Buzzard) 14/4/1848 [C80598]

WILSON (Daniel) Born Oxford 18/11/1805, s. Rt. Rev. Daniel Wilson, sen. (Bishop of Cacutta, *q.v.* ODNB) and Ann Wilson [*thus*]. Wadham, Oxford 1822, BA1827, dn28 (Ox.), MA1829. R. Over/Upper Worton, Oxon. 1830-3 (res.), V. Islington St Mary, London [net income £1,155] 1832-72, RD. Prebend of St Paul's Cathedral London 1872 to death 16/7/1886, leaving £3,421-7s-0d. [C21996. DEB] Married Over Worton 14/12/1829 Lucy Sarah Atkins, with clerical son Daniel Frederic Wilson.

WILSON (Edward) Bapt. Goathland, Yorks. 9/7/1764, s. Joseph and Betty Wilson. Literate: dn87 (Clonfert for Car.), p89 (York). S/M Leeds 1788; PC. Chapel Allerton, Yorks. 1800 to death (Keswick) 2/7/1835 [C6471. YCO] Married 1796 a Mrs Paley of Leeds, with clerical s.of same name: www.adamscross.co.uk/ewilson.html

WILSON (Edward) Bapt. Crosthwaite, Cumberland 17/12/1781, s. of Joseph (a husbandman) and Sarah Wilson. Literate: dn05 (York), p05 (Car.). PC. St John in the Vale, Crosthwaite 1806-54 (and S/M), PC. Wythburn, Cumberland 1807-12. *Committed suicide* (Keswick, Cumberland) 2/5/1854 aged 73 after the death of his son [C6472. YCO. Platt] Married Crosthwaite 6/5/1817 Anne Wilkinson, with issue (and perhaps a second marriage?)

WILSON (Edward) Born Ditchingham, Norfolk 2/7/1799, s. Rev. George Wilson (Kirby Cane Hall, Norfolk) and Anna Maria Millard. Merton, Oxford 1818, BA1822, dn22 (Nor.), p23 (Nor.). R. Topcroft, Norfolk 1824 to death 31/10/1874, leaving £1,500 [C116212] Married 28/5/1827 Lucretia King, with issue. Brother of George, below.

WILSON (Francis) From Isle of St Christopher [*now* St Kitts], West Indies, s. Richard Wilson. St John's, Oxford 1783 (aged 22), dn89 (Lin.), p91 ([Lin.]). V. Alford w. Rigsby w. Ailby, Lincs. 1792-1808, V. Saleby w. Thoresthorpe, Lincs. 1808 to death 10/11/1846 [C80600. Foster mixes up two men]

WILSON (George) Born Kirby Cane, Norfolk. 21/11/1786, s. Rev. George Wilson and Anna Maria Millard. Emmanuel, Cambridge 1787, BA1791, dn91 (Ely), dn92 (Nor.). V. Didlington w. Colveston, Norfolk 1794-1802, 1808-, R. Carleton Forehoe, Norfolk 1795-1800, R. Eccles, Norfolk 1799, R. Frostenden, Suffolk 1802-6. Died? [C100502] Brother of Edward, above.

WILSON (Harry Bristow) Born City of London 23/8/1774, s. William and Jane Wilson. Lincoln, Oxford 1793, BA1796, dn97 (Peterb.), p98 (London), MA1799, BD1810, DD1818. S/M Merchant Taylors' School 1798-1824; R. St Mary Aldermary w. St Thomas the Apostle, City of London 1816 to death 21/11/1853 [C111358. ODNB. Boase. DEB] Married 1/1/1799 Mary Ann Moore, with son Henry Bristow, below.

WILSON (Henry) [BA but NiVoF] R. Great Bedwin, Wilts. 1814-22, R. Collingbourne Ducis, Wilts. 1821 to death. Probate granted 12/6/1855 [C90536]

WILSON (Henry Bristow) Bapt. City of London 8/7/1803, s. Rev. Harry, sen. (above) and Mary Ann Moore. St John, Oxford 1821, BA1825, Fellow 1821-50, dn26 (Cashel for Oxford [the Abp was Professor of Hebrew at Oxford]), p27 (Ox.), MA1829, Tutor 1833-50, BD1834, etc., Rawlinson Professor of Anglo-Saxon, Oxford 1839-44. PC. Northmoor, Oxon. 1832, V. Great Staughton, Hunts 1850 to death (Lee, Kent) 10/8/1888, leaving £861-3s-6d. [C21998. ODNB. Boase] Married Paddington, London 11/12/1850 Jane Morgan (w). Contributed to *Essays and Reviews* (1861).

WILSON (Henry Currer) Born Eshton Hall, Gargrave, Yorks. 8/10/1803, s. Matthew Wilson and Margaret Clive. Lincoln, Oxford 1821, BA 1826, dn27 (York), p28 (London for York), MA1828. R. Marton in Craven, Yorks. 1828-58, V. Tunstall, Lancs. 1828 to death. Dom. Chap. to 2nd Baron Ribblesdale 1828. Died Eshton Hall (unmarried) 1/12/1866 aged 63, leaving £40,000 [C124268] The 'Currer' here was used by the Brontes for their *nom de plume*.

WILSON (Henry William, 10th Baron Berners) Born Didlington, Norfolk 1/10/1762, s. Henry William Wilson and Mary Miller (dau. of a baronet). Emmanuel, Cambridge 1780, BA1785, dn85 (Nor.), p86 (Nor.), MA 1789. R. Alexton, Leics. 1789-1845 [C80603], V. Flixton, Suffolk 1820 [ERC links], R. Kirby Cane, Norfolk 1820 to death 26/1/1851 aged 88 [C80603] Married 1/5/1788 Elizabeth Sumpter (Histon Hall, Cambs.), with clerical son Robert Wilson (below). Succ. to title 1838.

WILSON (Isaac) Born Stainton, Cumberland, s. William Wilson [*pleb.*]. Queen's, Oxford 1763 (aged 19), BA1766, dn67 (Car. for York), p68 (York), MA1769. V. Caistor w. Holton le Moor and Clixby, Lincs. 1777 to death 21/2/1833 (CCEd thus) [C80604. YCO]

WILSON, WILLSON (James) Bapt. Pickering, Yorks. 23/1/1760, s. Gelverton and Elizabeth Wilson. Literate: dn85 (York), p86 (York). PC. Nunkeeling, Yorks. 1806-35 and R.

Atwick, Yorks. 1818 to death before 13/4/1835 [C125303. YCO] Married Hornsea, Lincs. 24/4/1810 Jane Burrell.

WILSON (John) Born Elsing, Norfolk, s. Rev. John Wilson. Caius, Cambridge 1769, BA1773, dn73 (Nor.), p77 (Nor.). V. Scredington, Lincs. 1786, V. Leighton Buzzard, Beds. 1786, V. Welton, Lincs. 1788. Died? [not 1822 as C80627 suggests]

WILSON (John) [NiVoF] V. Mitton, Lancs. 1814 to death 24/8/1841 aged 60 [C136037] Married Chipping, Lancs. 9/2/1812 Catherine Carlisle (a clergy dau.), with issue.

WILSON (John) [NiVoF] PC. Billington, Beds. 1811-[43], PC. Egglington, Beds. 1811-[43]. Died? [C80627. ERC links]

WILSON (John) [NiVoF] V. Surfleet, Lincs. 1815 [C80634], V. Donington, Lincs. 1825-[49]. Died? [C80631. ERC links]

WILSON (John) Literate: dn01 ( ), p02 ( ). V. Alkborough / Auckborough w. Whitton, Lincs. 1818-65-. Died? [C80636]

WILSON (John) [NiVoF]. (first) PC. Goole Chapel, Snaith, Yorks. 1831-7. Died 1837? [Not yet in CCEd] Had issue.

WILSON (Jonathan) Literate: dn16 (Chester for Car.), p18 (Car.), then Peterhouse, Cambridge 1834, a Ten Year Man. PC. Grinsdale, Cumberland 1829 (non-res.; kept a boarding school at Newtown 1829-39) to death 16/2/1848 aged 55 [C6475] Married (1) with issue (2) Stanwix, Cumberland 5/1/1832 Mary Hudson (a clergy dau.).

WILSON (Joseph) Bapt. Whitehaven, Cumberland 6/10/1775, s. John Wilson. Magdalene, Cambridge 1798, BA1802, dn02 (Nor. for York), p02 (York), MA1811. V. North Kelsey, Lincs. 1825 to death 1854 [C79127. YCO]

WILSON (Plumpton) Born Colsterworth, Lincs. 22/11/1799, s. William Wilson and Ann Plumpton. Trinity Hall, Cambridge 1818, SCL, dn24 (Peterb.), p25 (Peterb.), LLB1828. R. Ilchester, Som. 1830, R. Newmarket St Mary w. Wood Ditton, Cambs. 1834-47, PC. Thorpe Arnold, Leics. 1847-52, R. Knaptoft, Leics. 1852 to death (Market Harborough) 26/5/1876, leaving £3,000 [C40925] Married Wellingborough, Northants. 1/7/1825 Mrs Margaretta Margetts, with 14 ch. (inc. Rev. Plumpton Stravenson Wilson).

WILSON (Robert) Born Kirby Cane, Norfolk 1/9/1801, s. Rev. Henry William Wilson, 10th Baron Berners (above) and Elizabeth Sumpter. Emmanuel, Cambridge 1819, BA 1823, dn25 (Nor.), p25 (Nor.), MA1829. R. Ashwellthorpe w. Wreningham, Norfolk 1826 to death 10/12/1850 [C116219] Married (1) Emma Piggott (Doddershall Park, Bucks., a military dau.) (2) 13/4/1832 his cousin Mrs Harriet (Crump) Sheppard (Alexton Hall, Leics.), with issue. His dau. succ. her uncle as Baroness Berners. Note other Kirby Cane connections in Edward and George (above).

WILSON, *or* **CARUS-WILSON (Roger Carus)** Born Casterton Hall, Westmorland 11/10/1792, s. Rev. William Wilson Carus Wilson and Mary Shippard. Trinity, Cambridge 1810, BA 1815, dn15 (York), p16 (York), MA 1818. V. Preston St John, Lancs. 1817 to death. Dom. Chap. to Viscount Galway at Harsworth, Notts. 1815. Died 15/12/1839 [C135821 and YCO under Wilson: Venn under Carus] Married Bath 24/8/1824 Frances Harriet Goodland Parr. Brother William Carus, below. Photo. online.

WILSON (Thomas Fourness) Bapt. Otley, Yorks. 23/8/1769, s. Rev. Henry Wilson and Anne Fourness. Trinity, Cambridge 1788, BA 1793. dn93 (York), p94 (York). PC. Cleckheaton, Yorks. 1805-37, PC. Silsden, Yorks. 1813 (living at Burley Hall, Otley) to death (Doncaster) 17/10/1837 aged 68 [C130210. YCO] Married 1/3/1813 Eleanor, dau. Sir Robert Eden, 4th Bart. (Windlestone House, Rushyford, Co. Durham), with issue. J.P. A sporting parson with a pack of harriers.

WILSON (William) Bapt. Haltwhistle, Northumberland 25/9/1757, s. Rev. Edward Wilson. Lincoln, Oxford 1776, BA1780, dn81 (Durham), p82 (Durham), MA1783. R. Wolsingham, Durham 1786 to death 1/5/1843 aged 85 [C138320] Married Wolsingham 18/1/1792 Elizabeth Wooler, *s.p.* J.P.

WILSON (William) Bapt Kendal, Westmorland 6/7/1783, s. John Wilson and Mary Breeks. Queen's, Oxford 1801, BA1805, dn07 (Roch. for London), dn08 (Win. for London),

MA1808, Fellow 1815-25, BD1820, DD1824, etc. H/M St Bees School, Cumberland; V. Southampton Holy Rood 1824-73, R. Church Oakley, Hants. 1824-32 (res.), RD, Canon of 4th Prebend in Winchester Cathedral 1832 to death 22/8/1873, leaving £16,000 [C2574. Boase. DEB] Married 18/2/1830 Mary Sumner (sister of John Bird Sumner, Archbishop of Canterbury), with clerical son Sumner Wilson.

WILSON (William) Born Bolton Hall, Yorks. Jesus, Cambridge 1801, BA1806, Fellow 1807-22, MA1809, dn14 (Ely), p15 (Ely). V. Elmstead, Essex 1822 to death 25/5/1857 [C109852] Was married. 'His benevolence was commensurate with the ample means with which he was blessed.'

WILSON (William) Born Cheapside, City of London, s. William Wilson and Elizabeth Broke West. Wadham, Oxford 1810 (aged 19), BA 1814, dn14 (Cant.), p15 (Ox.), MA1817, BD 1827, DD1851. V. Walthamstow, Essex 1822-48. Died Over Warton, Oxon. 14/10/1867, leaving £8,000 [C22001. Boase] Married Clapham, Surrey 15/11/1815 (*or* Harrow, Middx. 13/11/1815?) Mary Garratt, with clerical son Alfred William Wilson.

WILSON (William) [NiVoF - but 'doctor [of divinity]' in Bouet]: dn21 (Chester), p22 (Chester). PC. Hartlepool, Co. Durham 1812 to death 17/11/1833 (income rose to £2,000 - coal revenues?) [C170949. Splendid port. in D. Cross, *Joseph Bouet's Durham ...* (Durham, 2005)] Married Egglescliffe. Durham before 1824 Jane Horsley (dau. of a Hartlepool alderman - as was Wilson).

WILSON (William) Born Lower Holker, Cartmel, Cumberland. Literate: dn21 (Chester), p22 (Chester), St John's, Cambridge 1825, a Ten Year Man. PC. Cartmel Fell, Lancs. 1827 (only?), PC. Field Broughton, Cartmel 1829 to death 4/9/1872 aged 76, leaving under £100 [C170949] Left a widow Jane, with issue. Kept a boarding school in 1851

WILSON, *or* CARUS-WILSON (William Carus-) Born 7/7/1791, s. Rev. William Wilson Carus Wilson (of Casterton Hall, Westmorland) and Mary Shippard. Trinity, Cambridge 1810, BA1813, dn14, p16 (Glos), MA1818. R. Tunstall, Lancs. 1816-28, R. Whittington, Lancs. 1825-57 (non-res.), (first) PC. Casterton 1833-56, founded and endowed the Clergy Daughters' School at Cowan Bridge 1824 (then at Casterton 1833) attended by the Bronte sisters; Carus Wilson appearing (to his fury) as Mr Brocklehurst in *Jane Eyre*, 'the black marble clergyman'. Died Russell Square, London 30/12/1859 aged 68, leaving £8,000. Chaplain to Duke of Sussex 1816 [C154849. ODNB. Boase. DEB. Jane M Ewbank, *The life and works of William Carus Wilson, 1791-1859* (Kendal, 1959)] Married St James, Westminster, London 31/1/1815 Anne, dau. Major-Gen. Charles Neville, with clerical son. Succeeded to the Casterton estates 1851.; Brother Roger Carus-Wilson, above.

WILSON (William Corbett) From Bury St Edmunds, Suffolk, s. William Wilson. Trinity, Cambridge 1783 (aged 19), BA1787, dn87 (Cant. for London), p87 (London), MA1795. V. Bozeat w. Strixton, Northants. 1825, V. Priors Hardwick >< Warwicks. 1796 to death. Chap. to the Prince of Wales. Died 17/5/1837 [C20943] Married Stony Stratford, Bucks. 2/4/1794 Catherine Harrison.

WILTON (Paul Henzel) Born Newcastle upon Tyne 1793, s. Rev. Joseph Wilton and Mary Henzel. Trinity, Cambridge 1811, dn17 (London), BA1818, p18 (London). R. Holmpton, Yorks. to 1831, R. Welwick, Yorks. 1832-45, V. Owthorne, Yorks. 1845 to death 28/1/1887 aged 94. Will not traced [C124370] Married Bristol 17/12/1822 Jane King.

WINCHESTER (Bishop of) see under **SUMNER, Charles Richard**

WINDSOR (Andrews, 7th Earl of Plymouth) Born 12/5/1764, s. of Other [*sic*], 4th Earl of Plymouth and Catherine (dau. of 1st Baron Archer). Christ Church, Oxford 1782, then Trinity Hall, Cambridge 1783, MA1786. V. Rhyader, Glamorgan 1789, V. Tardebigge, Worcs. 1791, R. Draycot Cerne, Wilts. 1800-12 (res.), R. Rochford, Essex 1814 to death (unmarried, in London) 19/6/1837 [C90545] Succ. to title 1833.

WINDSOR (James) Bapt. Uffculme, Devon 22/2/1750, s. Rev. John Windsor. Exeter, Oxford 1769, dn73 (Ex.), BA1774, p85 (Ex.). V. Uffculme 1783 to death 21/11/1833 [C106467]

WING (John) Born Thorney Abbey, Cambs. 15/2/1786, s. John Wing and Jane Ansell. Pembroke, Cambridge 1802, MA1807, dn09 (Peterb.), p10 (Peterb.), MA1810. V. Eye,

Northants. 1810-16 (res.), Chap. Thorney Abbey 1821-53, R. Thornhaugh w. Wansford, Northants. 1832-58, R. Chenies, Bucks. 1824-9 (res.), R. Streatham, Surrey 1828-30 (res.). Dom. Chap. to 6th Duke of Bedford 1828. Died 17/5/1858, leaving £20,000 [C80707] Married Holbech, Lincs. 8/9/1812 Charlotte Slater (who, with a dau., was *drowned* by the upsetting of a boat 5/4/1838).

WING (John) Born Bedford 4/1/1802, s. John Wing and Elizabeth Tacy. Clare, Cambridge 1819, BA1823, dn25 (Lin.), p26 (Lin.), MA1841. V. Elstow, Beds. 1832-49, V. Stevington, Beds. 1832-49, V. Leicester St Mary 1849 to death. Confrator of Wyggeston's Hospital [almshouses], Leicester. Died 22/3/1861 aged 59, leaving £800 [C80708] Married Marylebone, London 26/6/1834 Anne Elizabeth Barrow (w), with many ch.

WING (William) Bapt. Cottermole, Rutland 20/8/1755, s. John Wing (land agent, of Glinton, Northants.) and Anne Sisson. St John's, Cambridge 1773, BA1777, dn78 (Peterb. for Nor.), p79 (Lin.), MA1780. R. Stibbington, Hunts. 1780-1831, PC. Sutton St Edmund, Beds. 1814. Died 21/12/1831 (CCEd says 15/3/1832) [C80709] Married 15/9/1785 Elizabeth Rasor (Gosberton, Lincs.), with issue.

WINGFIELD (Edward Oldfield) From Born Tickencote, Rutland 18/3/1795, s. John Wingfield and Mary Anne Muxloe. Clare, Cambridge 1814, BA1818, dn18 (Glos.), p19 (Peterb.), MA1821. R. Tickencote 1830-34, R. Market Overton, Rutland 1834 to death 17/9/1856 [C40941]

WINN (John) Born Nappa Hall, Askrigg, Yorks. 25/2/1798, s. George Winn. St John's, Cambridge 1817, BA1822, dn22 (Chester), p23 (Chester), MA1825. V. Aysgarth, Yorks. 1827 to death (unmarried) 30/3/1873 aged 74, leaving £40,000 [C170954]

WINNING (William Balfour) From Co. Durham, s. Robert Winning. Trinity, Cambridge 1818 (aged 17), BA1823, dn26 (Lin.), MA1827, p27 (Lin.). V. Keysoe, Beds. 1827-36. Lived latterly at Bedford, dying there 16/6/1845 [C80714] Had issue.

WINNINGTON (Charles Fox) Born Stanford Court, Worcs., s. Sir Edward Winnington, 2nd Bart., *M.P.*, and Hon. Anne Foley. Christ Church, Oxford 1812 (aged 19), BA1816, p17 (Heref.).V. Clifton on Teme, Heref. 1817, R. Stanford on Teme, Worcs. 1822. Probate granted 6/11/1841 [C174711] Married Walden, Herts. 10/4/1819 Arabella Eliza Heysham (Stagenhoe Park, Walden) *s.p.* Brothers below.

WINNINGTON (Edward Winnington-) Born Stanford Court, Stanford on Teme, Worcs. 14/6/1785, s. Sir Edward Winnington, 2nd Bart., *M.P.*, and Hon. Anne Foley. Christ Church, Oxford 1803, BA1807, MA1833. R. Stanford on Teme, 1809-22 (res.), V. Clifton on Teme, Worcs. 1809-17 (res.), R. Ribbesford, Worcs. 1815 and Canon of 10th Prebend in Worcester Cathedral 1833 to death 7/5/1851 [C121539. Boase under Winnington] Married Worcester 7/8/1810 Jane Onslow, with issue. Name changed 1817. Brothers above and below.

WINNINGTON (Francis) Born Stanford Court, Worcs., s. Sir Edward Winnington, 2nd Bart., *M.P.*, and Hon. Anne Foley. Trinity, Oxford 1809 (aged 19), BA1812, dn14 (Heref.), p14 (Heref.). V. Wolferlow, Heref. 1814, R. Dowles, Shropshire 1816-18, R. Upper Sapey, Heref. 1816. Died Brighton 31/12/1885, leaving under £100 [C174712] Brothers above.

WINPENNY (Richard Cooke) Born Glos., s. Richard Cooke Winpenny (attorney) and Rachel Terrett. Literate: dn15 (B&W), p16 (B&W). V. Market Weighton, Yorks. 1820 to death Pockington, Yorks. 1844 (4th q.) [C40942] Married Bristol 20/3/1809 Mary Griffith, with clerical son John Winpenny.

WINSCOM (Thomas Cave) Born Brecon 10/10/1787, s. Thomas Winscom and Jane Cave. Trinity Hall, Cambridge 1811, a Ten Year Man (BD1823), dn11 (Llandaff), p14 (Ely for London). V. Warkworth, Northumberland 1820 to death 6/3/1840 [C109160] Married (1) Romsey, Hants. 28/2/1812 Susanna Judith Deschamps (d.1820) (2) Warkworth 1822 Eliza Maria Clutterbuck, with issue.

WINSLOE (Richard) Bapt. Exeter 1/3/1770, s. Thomas Winsloe. Magdalen, Oxford 1789, BCL1796. R. Minster, Cornwall 1800 and R. Forrabury, Cornwall 1800-42, PC. Ruishton, Som. 1800-21-. Died 31/10/1842 [C40943] Had issue.

WINSTANLEY (George) Bapt. Braunston, Leics. 31/3/1789, s. Clement and Jane Winstanley, BNC, Oxford 1807, BA1811, dn12 (Lin.), p13 (Lin.), MA1813. R. Glenfield, Leics. 1813 to death 5/12/1846 [C80718]

WINSTANLEY (John [Robinson]) Born Liverpool 8/5/1785, s. William [*pleb.*] and Isabella Winstanley. St Alban Hall, Oxford 1803, no degree, p13 (Chester), DD. H/M St John Deane's Grammar School, Northwich, Cheshire in 1815; 'Perpetual V'. Bampton, Oxon. (3rd Portion) 1828 to death 26/12/1843 [C22007. Foster as John only] Married Probus, Cornwall 1820 Sarah Stackhouse (w), *s.p.*

WINTER (John) Bapt. Morland, Westmorland 16/11/1781, s. John and Nanny Winter. Literate: dn05 (York), p06 (York). PC. Birdforth, Coxwold, Yorks. 1818 to death 21/7/1873 aged 91, leaving £450 [C136945. YCO] Married Appleby, Westmorland 22/4/1824 Mary Bainbridge, with issue.

WINTER (Thomas) Bapt. Chipping Norton, Oxon. 15/9/1797, s. Thomas and Ann Winter. Lincoln, Oxford 1814, BA1819, dn24 (Chester), MA1819? R. Daylesford, Worcs. 1825 to death 10/1/1872, leaving £30,000 [C122333]

WINTER (William) Literate: dn94 (London), p96 (Chester). PC. Oldham St Peter, Lancs. 1797 (and S/M Oldham G/S 1812-38), PC. Lees (o/w Hey Chapel), Ashton under Lyne, Lancs. 1811 to death. Chap. to Oldham Orange Order; and to the Volunteers. Died 1838 (3rd q.?) [C124373]

WINTLE (Henry) Bapt. Upton-on-Severn, Glos. 3/1/1770, s. Samuel and Ann Wintle. Pembroke, Cambridge 1784, BA1788, Fellow 1788, MA1791, dn92 (Glos.), p94 (Ox.). R. Somerton, Oxon. 1804-31, R. Matson, Glos. 1831 to death 6/5/1850 [C22009] Had issue.

WINTLE (Robert) From Reading, Berks., s. Rev. Thomas Wintle. Christ Church, Oxford 1790 (aged 18), BA1794, dn95 (Salis.), p96 (Salis.), MA1797, BD1805. V. Culham, Oxon. 1797 and R. Compton Beauchamp, Berks. 1803-48, Wilsden Prebend in St Paul's Cathedral, London 1805 to death (Culham) 24/8/1848 [C38836] Brother below?

WINTLE (Thomas) From Wallingford, Berks., s. Rev. Thomas Wintle, sen. St John's, Oxford 1791 (aged 17), Fellow 1791-1841, BA 1795, MA1799, dn02 (Ox.), BD1804, etc. R. Tidmarsh, Yorks. 1814, R. Leckford, Hants. 1840 to death 1/2/1855, leaving £6,000 (unadministered: probate granted 29/7/1864) [C38838] Brother above?

WINTOUR (Fitzgerald) Born Oxford 12/3/1803, s. Prebendary Henry Wintour (of St Paul's Cathedral, London) and Mildred Briggs. Magdalene, Cambridge 1821, BA1825, dn26 (Ely), p27 (Ely), MA1830. R. Little Gransden, Cambs. 1829, R. Barton in Fabis, Notts. 1829-64 (and Prebend of Rampton in Southwell Collegiate Church 1830), V. Rampton, Notts. 1838-56. Died Barton in Fabis 1/12/1864 aged 61, leaving £1,500 [C109855. Boase] Married Shudy Camps, Cambs. 13/9/1826 Jane Elizabeth Dayrell (w), with clerical son. Kept a diary which survives.

WISE (Henry) From Westminster, London, s. Christopher Wise. BNC, Oxford 1791 (aged 17), BA1795, dn96 (C&L), DD? R. Charlwood, Surrey 1797 and V. Offchurch, Warwicks. 1805 to death 23/1/1850 [C20968] Married 1798 Charlotte Mary Porten, 1s, 3 dau.

WISE (Thomas) Jesus, Cambridge 1820 (aged 43, a Ten Year Man). S/M Milton Abbas G/S, Dorset '16 years'; R. Barley, Herts. 1827-9 (res.), R. Hagworthingham, Lincs. 1829 to death (Blandford, Dorset) 22/6/1839 aged 64 [C6480] Had issue.

WISE (William) From Edmonton, Middx., s. Rev. William Wise, sen. St John's, Oxford 1788 (aged 18), Fellow 1788, BA1792, dn92 (C&L for Win.), p93 (Lin. for Win.), MA1797, BD 1801, DD1813. V. Reading St Lawrence, Berks. 1812 and PC. Hurst, Sonning, Berks. 1818 to death 14/10/1833 (CCEd says 25/11/1833) [C20972]

WITHER, *later* **BIGG-WITHER (Harris Jervoise Bigg)** Born Wymering, Hants. 31/10/1796, s. Harris Bigg Wither [who had proposed to Jane Austen] and Anne Howe Frith. Oriel, Oxford 1825, BA1829, dn31 (Win.), MA1831, p32 (Win.). R. Worting, Basingstoke, Hants. 1832 to death (Maidenhead, Berks.) 1/12/1887 aged 81, leaving £5,452-15s-3d. [C109162] Married (1) Basingstoke 7/10/1834 Elizabeth Harriet Appletree (d.1838), 1 dau. (2) Basingstoke 1839 (2nd q.) Elizabeth Maria Blunt, with further issue. Brother below.

WITHER, *later* **BIGG-WITHER (Lovelace Bigg)** Born Wymering, Hants. 17/9/1805, s. Harris Bigg Wither [who had proposed to Jane Austen] and Anne Howe Frith. Oriel, Oxford 1823, BA1826, dn29 (Win.), MA1829, p30 (Win.). V. Herriard, Hants. 1830. Lived at Tangier Park, Wootton St Lawrence, Hants. Died Brighton 6/2/1874, leaving £15,000 [C109161] Married 23/7/1829 Emma Jemima Orde, with about 15 ch. (incl. clerical son Reginald Fitzhugh Bigg-Wither, and dau. Sunda Wither). Brother above.

WITHERSTON (John) Born Bengal, s. John Witherston and 'an Indan lady'. Balliol, Oxford 1809 (aged 18), BA1813, dn13 (B&W), p15 (Glos.), MA1817. Minor Canon in Rochester Cathedral 1825-31, V. Allhallows, Kent 1828-35, R. Kingsdown w. Mappiscombe, Kent 1835. Died Abergavenny, Monmouth 19/7/1875 aged 84, leaving £1,500 [C1508]

WITHY (Henry) Bapt. St Martin in the Fields, London 11/5/1800, s. Robert Withy and Anne Fourdrinier. Merton, Oxford 1818, BA 1822, MA1824, p25 (C&L). PC. Huddersfield Holy Trinity, Yorks. 1830 to death 25/3/1837 [C20973] Married (1) Stoke, Surrey 27/8/1825 Emily Mangles (d.1828), w. child (2) Cheltenham, Glos. 26/3/1829 Christian Dottin (dau. Sir John Gay Alleyne, 1st Bart., of Barbados, *q.v.* LBSO), with issue.

WITT, *otherwise* **DE WITT (Edmund)** Bapt. East Stoke, Dorset 11/8/1785, s. Thomas [de] Witt and Sarah Reynolds. Wadham, Oxford 1804, BA1808, p12 (B&W), MA1832. V. East Lulworth, Dorset 1832 and V. Combe Keynes, Dorset 1832 to death. Dom. Chap. to Earl of Coventry 1832. Died (Stockford, Dorset) 8/1/1835, leaving £3,000 (probate granted 1861) (CCEd says 7/4/1835) [C50317] Married Frome, Som. 12/9/1810 Sarah Taylor Simpson, w. issue.

WITT (Matthew) Born Cambridge 23/8/1777, s. Matthew and Ann Witt. Trinity Hall, Cambridge 1796, BA1800, dn08 (C&L), p11 (C&L). S/M Repton School 1821-67; PC. Ticknall Derbys. 1816 (w. Curate Calke 1816) to death (Repton Priory) 22/12/1837 aged 60 [C20974]

WITTS (Francis Edward) Born Cheltenham 26/2/1782, s. Edward Witts (Swerford Park, Glos.) and Agnes Travell. Wadham, Oxford 1802, BA1805, dn06 (London for B&W), MA 1809. R. Upper Slaughter, Glos. 1808, V. Stanway, Glos. 1814, V. East Lulworth, Dorset 1832. Died Upper Slaughter 18/8/1854 aged 71. Dom. Chap. to 9th Earl of Kellie 1814 [C50319. Alan Sutton (ed.), *The complete diary of a Cotswold parson: the diaries of the Revd Francis Edward Witts 1783-1854* (Stroud, 2008-18. 10 vols.) is the largest clerical diary to be critically edited, and shows the relative *un*importance of clerical duties in his life] Married Walcot, Bath 30/5/1808 (the rather anonymous) Elizabeth Backhouse, with issue. *J.P., D.L.*

WIX (Samuel) Born City of London 9/2/1771, s. Edward Wix and Mary Seagood. Adm. Inner Temple 1793. Christ's, Cambridge 1791, dn95 (Ely), BA1796, p96 (London), MA1799. R. Inworth, Essex 1802 and V. St Bartholomew the Less, City of London 1808 to death. President of Sion College 1830-3; Chap. to HRH Duke of Clarence. Died 4/9/1861, leaving £80,000 [C100497. ODNB. Boase] Married Sible Headingham, Essex 4/5/1801 Frances Walford, with issue. 'A man of singular simplicity of character and of vigorous intellect'. *F.R.S.* (1813), *F.S.A.*

WODEHOUSE (Armine, Hon.) Born 12/3/1776, s. 1st Baron Wodehouse and Sophia Berkeley. Trinity, Cambridge 1793, then St John's 1795, MA1799, dn99 (Nor.), p00 (Nor.), then Clare, Fellow 1800. R. Litcham w. East Lexham >< Norfolk 1800-40, R. Carleton Forehoe, Norfolk 1800-7, R. Barnham Broome (w. Bickserton cum Kimberley), Norfolk 1811-53, R. West Lexham, Norfolk 1820-40. Died 5/4/1853 aged 77 [C116228] Married St George's Hanover Square, London 23/12/1815 Amelia (dau. Sir Thomas Beauchamp Procter, 2nd Bart., Langley Park, Norfolk), *s.p.* Brother William, below.

WODEHOUSE (Charles Nourse) Born 8/9/1790, s. Rev. Philip Wodehouse (Prebend of Norwich Cathedral) and Apollonia Nourse. Trinity, Cambridge 1808, BA1814, dn14 (Nor.), MA1817. R. Morningthorpe, Norwich 1815-50, R. Geldeston, Norfolk 1816-31, Canon of 6th Prebend in Norwich Cathedral 1817 (res. by 1860), R. King's Lynn St Margaret, Lincs. 1850-60. Died Lowestoft, Suffolk 17/3/1870, leaving £6,000 [C1133. Boase] Married Lyndhurst, Hants. 19/12/1821 Lady Dulcibella Jane Hay (dau. of the 17th Earl of Erroll), and had issue. *J.P., D.L.* Norfolk.

WODEHOUSE (Nathaniel) Bapt. Sennowe Park, Great Ryburgh, Norfolk 8/1/1802, s. Thomas Wodehouse and Sarah Campbell. Merton, Oxford 1821, BA1826, dn26 (Nor.), p27 (Nor.), MA 1829. V. Dulverton, Som. 1829 and V. Worle, Som. 1829 to death. Dom. Chap. to 1st Earl Cawdor 1829. Died London 23/10/1870, leaving £4,000 [C41026] Married Watford, Herts. 29/9/1829 Georgina Capell, with issue. Brother below.

WODEHOUSE (Thomas) Born Sennowe Park, Great Ryburgh, Norfolk, s. Thomas Wodehouse and Sarah Campbell. Merton, Oxford 1806 (aged 17), BA1810, dn12 (Nor.), p12 (Nor.), MA1816. R. Norton, Kent 1816, R. Stourmouth, Kent 1816, Prebend of Taunton in Wells Cathedral and Canon Residentiary 1817 to death. Dom. Chap. to Bishop of Rochester 1816. Died 22/3/1840 [C41027] Married Norton 3/6/1817 Ann King, w. clerical sons Walker, and James Wodehouse. Brother above,

WODEHOUSE (William, Hon.) Born Wyndham, Norfolk 4/8/1782, s. John, 1st Baron Wodehouse, *M.P.*, and Sophia Berkeley. Christ Church, Oxford 1801, then All Souls, BA1805, dn06, p07 (Bristol for Nor.), MA1811. R. Carleton Forehoe, Norfolk 1807, V. Itteringham w. Mannington, Norfolk 1807, V. Kimberley, Norfolk 1811, R. Hingham, Norfolk 1811-70 (net income £1,250), R. Crownthorpe, Norfolk 1815, R. Falmouth, Cornwall 1828 to death (Grosvenor Square, London) 3/4/1870 aged 87, leaving £8,000 [C54191] Married Wickmere, Norfolk 11/2/1807 Mary Hussey, and left issue. Brother Armine, above.

WODEHOUSE see also **WOODHOUSE**

WODLEY (William) Bapt. Cublington, Bucks. 28/9/1765, s. Rev. Edmund Wodley and Mary Ashfield. Wadham, Oxford 1782, BA1786, MA 1789, dn97 (Lin.), [89 (Lin.). V. Swanbourne, Bucks. 1792, PC. Soulbury, Bucks. 1808 to death 16/3/1837 [C80841]

WOLFE (Robert Cope) Born in France, s. Rev. Robert Barber Wolfe and Margaret Butler. A prisoner of war 1812-14. Clare, Cambridge 1821, BA1825, dn25 (Bristol for Win.), p28 (Win.). R. Cranleigh, Surrey 1812 [net income £1,195], V. Braithwell, Yorks. 1843 to death 21/5/1851 [C54192] Married Marylebone, London 14/9/1832 Lucy Margaret Russell, with issue.

WOLLASTON (Charles Hyde) Born London 22/11/1772, s. Rev. Francis Wollaston (Precentor of St David's Cathedral and R. of Chislehurst, Kent) and Althea Hyde. Sidney, Cambridge 1789, BA1793, then St Catharine's 1795, dn95 (Ely), MA1796, p96 (Ely). V. East Dereham, Norfolk 1806 to death 24/3/1850 [C100493] Married Cambridge 2/3/1795 Sarah Willett Ottley (St Kitts, West Indies: she left £68,000 at death), with clerical s. William Charles: wwwdepts-live.ucl.ac.uk/lbs/person/view/2146636878

WOLLASTON (Edward) Born Bishop's Castle, Shropshire, s. John Wollaston and Elizabeth Baskerville. Worcester, Oxford 1772 (aged 19), BA1776, p77 (Ox.). Usher Charterhouse School 1804; PC. Bettys y Crwyn, Heref. 1784, PC. Llanfair Waterdine, Heref. 1784, R. Balsham, Cambs. [income £1,104] (and Preacher throughout the Diocese of Ely) 1804 to death 9/3/1838 [C38846] Married Clerkenwell, London 24/5/1784 Elizabeth Ramsden, with son John Ramsden Wollaston, below.

WOLLASTON (Francis Hayles) Born 1/5/1803, s. Ven. Francis John Hyde Wollaston (Archdeacon of Essex) and Frances Hayles. Pembroke, Cambridge 1820, BA1825, dn26 (London), p27 (London), MA1831. (Sinecure R. (and patron) of East Dereham, Norfolk 1827-40), R. Knowlton, Kent 1834-5. Resigned his Orders 1840 (*but how?*). Died 5/11/1849 [C116305] Married 7/6/1825 his cousin Caroline Wollaston, *s.p.* Brother Charles Hyde, above.

WOLLASTON (Henry John) Born Bury St Edmunds 13/8/1770, s. Rev. Frederick Wollaston and Priscilla Ottley (of St Kitts, West Indies). Sidney, Cambridge 1788, BA 1792, dn93 (Lin.), p94 (Lin.), MA1795. R. Paston, Northants. 1800-11, R. Scotter, Lincs. 1803 to death. Royal Chap. 1798; Dom. Chap. to 4th Duke of Grafton 1812. Died 27/10/1833 (CCEd says 14/11/1833) [C80844] Married 5/7/1803 Louisa Symons, with issue.

WOLLASTON (John Ramsden) Born 28/3/1791, s. Rev. Edward Wollaston (Usher at Charterhouse School and V. Balsham, Cambs., above) and Elizabeth Ramsden. Christ's. Cambridge 1808, BA1812, dn14 (Ely), p14 (Ex. for Ely), MA1815. V. Elsenham, Essex 1815-18 (res.), PC. West Wickham, Cambs. 1825-41, Chap. at Albany, Western Australia 1841 (and

Archdeacon of Western Australia 1849) to death there 3/5/1856 [C109857. Boase] Married 11/5/1819 Mary Amelia Gledstanes (a military dau.).

WOLLASTON see also under **WOOLASTON**

WOLLEN (William) Bapt. Bridgwater, Som. 13/6/1759, s. James Wollen and Sarah Bryant. Oriel, Oxford 1779, BA1782, dn82 (Bristol), p83 (B&W), BCL 1788, DCL1815. R. Bridgwater 1786 and V. Kilton, Som. 1815 to death 26/1/1844 [C50321] Married Nether Stowey, Som. 23/3/1786 Anne Poole, w. issue. *J.P.* Somerset

WOLLEY, born BURT (John [Francis Thomas]) Born Wirksworth, Derbys. 26/9/1796, s. Charles Burt, *J.P., D.L.*, and Susannah (dau. Sir Richard Arkwright). St John's, Cambridge 1815, BA1819, dn20 (Peterb.), p21 (York). MA1824, Fellow. R. Beeston, Notts. 1822-53. Died there 16/11/1877 aged 81, leaving £14,000 [C110363 and YCO under Hurt. In *Clergy List* as two separate people] Married Matlock, Derbys. 6/8/1822 Mary Wolley, with clerical son, and changed his name.

WOLLEY see also under **WOOLLEY**

WOLSTON (Christopher) Born London 12/1/1794, s. John Wolston and Catherine Prideaux *or* Hill. St John, Cambridge 1813, BA1817, dn17 (Ex.), p18 (Ex.), MA1821, incorporated at Oxford 1860. R. Torbryan, Devon 1828 to death there (a bachelor) 28/5/1863, leaving £12,000 [C146672]

WOOD (Benjamin) Bapt. Walsall, Staffs. 31/1/1793, s. William Wood. Christ's, Cambridge 1810, BA1814, dn14 (Nor.), p15 (Nor.), MA1817. PC. Haveringland, Norfolk 1823 to death 23/8/1857 aged 66 [C116307] Had issue.

WOOD (Charles Samuel) Born Drayton Beauchamp, Bucks. 9/9/1795, s. Rev. Basil Wood and Sophia Jupp. Queens', Cambridge 1815, dn21 (Lin.), p23 (Glos.). (succ. his father as) R. Drayton Beauchamp 1831 to death 2/6/1838 aged 43 [C80847] Married Mary Lomax (dau. of a London surgeon), with issue.

WOOD (George) Bapt. Dorchester, Dorset 27/8/1783, s. James Wood. Oriel, Oxford 1793, BA1796, dn96 (Bristol), dn98 (London for Bristol), p98 (Bristol), MA1804. V. Winterbourne St Martin (o/w Martinstown), Dorset 1801-6, R. Shaftesbury St Rumbold (o/w Cann), Dorset 1806 and R. Dorchester Holy Trinity 1825 (and Chap. to Dorset County Gaol) to death. Dom. Chap to 6th Earl of Shaftesbury 1826. Died 21/8/1847 [C54195] Wife Betsy.

WOOD (Isaac) Born Davenport Hall, Astbury, Cheshire 11/5/1795, s. Isaac Wood and Annabella Wilson. Trinity, Cambridge 1813, dn18 (Chester), BA1819, p19 (Chester), MA1822. V. (and patron) of Middlewich, Cheshire 1819-64, Archdeacon of Chester 1847 (living at Newton Hall) to death (Moreton Hall, Chirk, Flintshire) 7/6/1865, leaving £3,000 [C90568. Boase. R.W. Dibdin, *Memoir of the Venerable Isaac Wood, MA, Archdeacon of Chester, and forty-five years Vicar of Middlewich ...* (1866 and port.)] Married Brighton 24/5/1824 Mary Nugent, Epsom, Surrey, with issue.

WOOD (James) Born Holcombe, Bury, Lancs. 14/12/1760, s. James Wood (of Tottington, Lancs.). St John's, Cambridge 1778, BA1782 [Senior Wrangler], Fellow 1782-1815, MA 1785, dn85 (Peterb.), p87 (Peterb.), Tutor 1789-1814, BD1793, DD1815, Master of St John's College, Cambridge 1815-39, Vice Chancellor 1815-17. Dean of Ely 1820-39, R. Freshwater, IoW 1823 to death (Cambridge) 23/4/1839, leaving £20,000 [C14227. ODNB]

WOOD (James) From Bicester, Oxon., s. Rev. Zaccheus Wood. Jesus, Oxford 1804 (aged 21), BA1808, MA1811. '25 years curate Blakenham Parva,' Suffolk, PC. Willisham, Suffolk 1830 to death 2/2/1837 [C116308]

WOOD (James) Bapt. Kirk Smeaton, Yorks. 29/8/1795, s. Thomas Wood and Mary Elliiott. [NiVoF] dn20, p21. R. (and patron) of Grimoldby, Lincs. 1832 [C80857], V. Theddlethorpe All Saints, Lincs. 1830 to death 15/9/1871, leaving £12,000 [C80856. Kaye. ERC links them] Wife Elizabeth, and clerical sons William Hardy Wood, and Thomas Wood.

WOOD (John, sen.) Bapt. Milton Abbas, Dorset 16/9/1748, s. Stephen [*pleb.*] and Mary Wood. Oriel, Oxford 1766, then Exeter BA 1770, then Balliol, Fellow, dn71 (B&W), p72 (Ox.), MA1773. V. Duloe, Cornwall 1795 to death 18/9/1833 aged 85 [C38877] Clerical son two below.

WOOD (John) Bapt. Alfreton, Derbys. 25/11/1776, s. Hugh Wood (Swanwick Hall, Derbys.) and Mary Peake. St John's, Cambridge 1794, BA1799, dn99 (C&L), p01 (C&L), MA1802. R. Kingsley, Staffs. 1808-55, V. Pentrich, Staffs. 1818-55 (w. PC. Ripley from 1821). Died 28/10/1858, leaving £10,000 [C20990] Married Uffington, Lincs. 22/9/1803 Emilia Susannah Walford Belairs (Stamford, Lincs.), with clerical son Hugh Wood.

WOOD (John, jun.) Bapt. Milton Abbas, Dorset 24/5/1777, s. Rev. John Wood, sen. (above). Worcester, Oxford 1795, BA1799, p00 (Bristol). V. Milborne St Andrew w. Dewlish, Dorset 1800-34, 'Perpetual V'. Saxthorpe, Norfolk 1825-34, 'Dean' of Collegiate Church of Whitchurch Canonicorum w. Stanton St Gabriel, Dorset 1828. Died 27/1/1834 (CCEd says 10/1/1834) [C54200]

WOOD (John) Bapt. Grinshill, Shropshire 14/5/1801, s. John Wood and Margaret Ravensshaw. Christ Church, Oxford 1818, BA1822, dn24 (C&L), MA1825, p25 (C&L). H/M Shifnall G/S, Shropshire 1825; PC. Dawley Magna (Great Dawley), Shropshire 1832, PC. (and patron of) Grinshill 1850-64, PC. Broughton, Shropshire 1855 to death. Chap. to Earl of Mansfield. Died 18/5/1864, leaving £2,000 [C20991. Boase. V.B. Insley, *A family's history* ... (Nottingham: The author, 2001)] Married Grinshill Elizabeth Pirr, w. cerical son John Ravenshaw Wood.

WOOD (John Ayton) Bapt. Beadnell, Northumberland 10/8/1793, s. John Wood and Ann Craster. St John's, Oxford 1812, BA1815, dn16 (Durham), p18 (Durham), MA1822. PC. Beadnell 1829-31. Died there 30/1/1853 [C131322] Married Cornhill, Northumberland 29/4/1824 his cousin Margaret Compton, with issue.

WOOD (John Mare) Bapt. Whitegate, Cheshire 20/7/1772, s. Richard Wood and Catherine Mare. St Alban Hall, Oxford 1803, dn04 (York as literate), p04 (Roch. for York), BA1807, MA1811. V. Stottesdon, Heref. 1805. Died? [C2579. YCO] Married Over, Cheshire 5/5/1793 Ann Williams, with issue.

WOOD (John Page, Sir, 2nd Bart.) Born 25/8/1796, s. Sir Matthew Wood, 1st Bart. (twice Lord Mayor of London) and Maria Page. Trinity, Cambridge 1814, LLB1821, dn21 (Nor.), p22 (Nor.). R. St Peter Cornhill, City of London (and Preacher throughout the Diocese of London) 1824 and V. Cressing, Essex 1833 to death. Chap. and Private Secretary to Queen Caroline, attending her death ('he closed her eyes') and burial in Brunswick; Chap. to HRH Duke of Sussex 1821-43. Died Romford, Kent 21/2/1866, leaving £6,000 [C116310. ODNB. Boase] Married 16/2/1820 Emma Caroline (dau. of Sampson Michell, *R.N.*, 'Admiral in the Portugese service'), with issue (incl. Field-Marshal Sir Henry Evelyn Wood, *V.C.*). Succ. to title 1843.

WOOD (Nicholas) Bapt. Bradford, Yorks. 1/4/1771, s. Nicholas Wood. Trinity, Cambridge 1789, BA1793, dn95 (Nor. for York), p96 (York), MA1798. Usher Giggleswick G/S., Yorks. 1796; V. Kenton, Suffolk 1819 to death 17/2/1854 [C89017. YCO]

WOOD (Peter) Bapt. Henfield, Sussex 12/8/1768, s. Peter Wood. University, Oxford 1787, dn92 (London), BA1791, MA1794. R. Rusper, Sussex 1793, R. Broadwater, Sussex 1798, Sutton Prebend in Chichester Cathedral 1828 to death. Dom. Chap. to Charlotte, Baroness King 1797. Died 1/4/1853 [C71959]

WOOD (Peter Scrimshire) Born West Horsley, Surrey 26/10/1785, s. Thomas Wood (Littleton, Middx.) and Mary Williams. Oriel, Oxford 1803, BA1807, dn08 (Win.), MA1809, p09 (Win.), BCL and DCL1817. V. (and patron) of Middleton, Norfolk 1810-56, R. Littleton 1813, (last) Dean of Middleham, Yorks. [a Royal Peculiar] 1814 to death 4/2/1856 [C109169. Boase] Married Droitwich, Worcs. 12/7/1810 Frances Penrice, with clerical son Peter Almeric Leheup Wood.

WOOD (Richard) Probably born York 1799. Corpus Christi, Cambridge 1817, BA1822, dn22 (Chester), p23 (Chester), MA1825. PC. Askrigg, Yorks. 1823-68 and V. (and patron) of Wollaston w. Irchester, Northants. 1829 to death (Woodhall Park, Aysgarth, Yorks.) 18/4/1868, aged 68, leaving £5,000 [C170964] Married Wellingborough, Northants. 21/8/1832 Frances Hill, 5 ch. (some clerical, one of the same name).

WOOD (Richard Warner Kendall) Born Leicester 31/10/1807, s. Richard Warner Wood and Mary Kendall. Corpus Christi, Cambridge 1825, then Trinity Hall 1829, BA1831, dn31 (Peterb.), p32 (Peterb.), MA1835. R. Passenham

w. Deanshanger, Northants. 1831. Died 20/3/1851 aged 45 [C111333] Married 29/10/1833 Mary Henrietta Fisher (a clergy dau., of Wendon, Bucks.), 2 ch.

WOOD (Robert) Born Bury, Lancs. 19/6/1770, s. John Wood. St John's, Cambridge 1789, BA 1793, dn93 (York), p94 (York), MA 1796, DD 1808. Usher Nottingham School 1799-1819, then H/M 1819-39; V. Cropwell Bishop, Notts. 1816-39, V. Sneinton, Notts. 1826-[31], V. Wysall, Notts. 1833 to death. Chap. Nottingham Gaol 'upward of 30 years.' Died Mansfield, Notts. 24/12/1839 [C89021. YCO] Married 11/7/1814 a Mrs Weston.

WOOD (Robert) Born Tallentire, Cumberland 18/12/1796, s. of a yeoman farmer. St Bees College, Cumberland adm. 1818, dn20 (Lin. for Durham), p21 (Ox. for Durham). PC. West Ward, Cumberland 1822 (and H/M Westward Church School) to death 15/3/1883 aged 86, leaving £3,073-5s-1d. [C22020. Platt] Married with clerical son. A noted botanist.

WOOD (Theodosius) Bapt. Shrewsbury, Shropshire 15/11/1785, s. Thomas and Mary Wood. Magdalene, Cambridge 1808, BA1813, dn13 (Glos.), p13 (Glos.), MA1834. V. Leysdown, Kent 1828 to death 24/11/1836 [C118805]

WOOD (Thomas) [MA but NiVoF] V. Kingsey, Bucks. 1814-27, V. Ashford, Kent 1826-[47]. Died? [C1509]

WOOD (William) Bapt. Hattton, Shropshire 18/7/1769, s. William and Mary Wood. Christ Church, Oxford 1786, BA1790, MA1792, dn98 (Ox.), p99 (Chester for Ox.), BD1801, Student [Fellow] to 1814, etc. PC. Binsey, Oxon. 1801, V. Cropready, Oxon. 1804-11, Caddington Minor Prebend in St Paul's Cathedral 1810-41, V. Fulham All Saints, London 1811-34 [income £1,135] (and Sinecure R. 1811-41), R. Coulsdon, Surrey 1830, Canon of 9th Prebend in Canterbury Cathedral 1834 to death 11/4/1841 [C22021]

WOOD (William) [NiVoF]. PC. Altham, Lancs. 1823-[48] and PC. Llanfihangel Helygen, Radnor 1823 to death (Altham) 30/6/1848 aged 68 [C133726] Married Prescot, Lancs. 14/1/1806 Elizabeth Hewson, with clerical son. Lived at High Brake Hall, Accrington, where he also had a school. 'A well built man, fully six feet high'.

WOOD (William) Born Martock, Som. 1798, s. William Cole Wood and Sophia Ann Horsey. Exeter, Oxford 1816, BA 1820, dn21 (B&W), p22 (Chester), MA1822. R. Staplegrove, Som. 1826, Incumbent Camp-beltown, Argyll (and Examining Chap. to Bishop of Argyll and the Isles) 1858-73, R. Farnborough, Berks. 1873 to death (Wantage) 27/12/1882, leaving £472-14s-8d. [C41030. Bertie] Married Chelsea, London 1825 Julia Stuckey, w. issue.

WOODCOCK (Elborough) Bapt. Bloomsbury, London 4/2/1801, s. John Woodcock and Amilia Hotham. Oriel, Oxford 1818, BA1822, MA1826, p27 (Llandaff). V. Chardstock, Dorset 1830, R. Winchester St Lawrence 1840-57. Died London 28/10/1877, leaving £70,000 [C90570] Married 14/12/1822 Sophia [Dorothea Frederica Wilhelmina Charlotte] Stuart (dau. of a Scottish baronet), w. issue. See also Henry Woodcock, below.

WOODCOCK (Francis) From Hereford, s. Rev. Francis Woodcock, sen. BNC, Oxford 1800 (aged 17), BA1804, dn06 (Heref.), p06 (Heref.), then Worcester, MA1809. (succ. his father as) R. Moreton on Lugg, Heref. 1807 probably to death 1834. Foster is seriously confused between father and son] [C174748]

WOODCOCK (George) Bapt. Barkby, Leics. 8/11/1789, s. Rev. Henry and Ann Woodcock. Emmanuel, Cambridge 1809, BA1813, MA 1816. (succ. his father as) R. Caythorpe w. Freiston, Lincs. [separate benefices in ERC] 1826 to death 28/3/1844 aged 53 [C80878] Married Leicester 17/7/1817 Anna Elizabeth Walker, with issue.

WOODCOCK (George) Bapt. Coventry, Warwicks. 9/4/1800, s. Rev. John and Anna Woodcock. Trinity, Oxford 1818, BA1822, dn23 (Chester for C&L), p24 (C&L), MA1825. V. Maxstoke, Warwicks. 1824-[48]. Died 24/2/1857 [C20997]

WOODCOCK (Henry) From Mortlake, Surrey, s. Elborough Woodcock. Christ Church, Oxford 1788 (aged 18), BA1792, MA1795, dn95 (Salis.), p95 (Peterb. for Salis.), BD and DD 1817, etc. R. Newdigate, Surrey 1798-1800 (res.), R. Michaelmarsh, Hants. 1800, Stratford Prebend in Salisbury Cathedral 1805-18, then

Chardstock Prebend 1818-40, Canon of 2nd Prebend in Christ Church Cathedral, Oxford 1824 to death 8/8/1840 [C22022] See alsio Henry, above for some relation?

WOODCOCK (John) Bapt. Oxford 23/3/1790, s. William Woodcock and Ann Parsons. Chorister Magdalen, Oxford 1808-16; matr. All Souls 1809, then New, BA1817, dn17 (Ox.), Chap. 1817-23, MA1818, p19 (Ox.). Minor Canon of Canterbury Cathedral 1820, V. Littlebourne, Kent 1824 to death 25/2/1859. No will traced [C22023] Married Oxford 9/9/1813 Sarah Stuart, with issue.

WOODCOCK (Thomas) Born Castleford, Pontefract, Yorks. 21/2/1767, s. of Thomas Woodcock (farmer). Sidney, Cambridge 1787, BA1792. dn92 (York), p93 (York), then St Catherine's, MA1795. R. Swillington, Yorks. 1795 to death. Dom. Chap. to 4th Earl of Cardigan 1781. Died Doncaster 9/5/1837 aged 70 [C129530. YCO] Had clerical son.

WOODFORD(E) (Francis) Born Ansford, Som., s. Thomas Woodford. Pembroke, Oxford 1766 (aged 17), BA1770, dn71 (Ox.), p73 (Ox.). R. Ansford 1773-1832, R. Poynington, Som. 1783-1806, R. Weston Bampfylde, Som. 1825 and R. Hornblotton, Som. 1825 to death. Dom. Chap. to 5th Earl of Cardigan 1781. Died 2/2/1836 aged 89 [C38859. Kaye] Wife Jane Clarke, and clerical son below.

WOODFORD(E) (Thomas) Born Ansford, Som., s. Rev. Francis Woodforde (above) and Jane Clarke. Worcester, Oxford 1797 (aged 17), BA 1800, dn01 (London), p03 (B&W), MA 1805. R. Poynington, Som. 1806 w. PC. South Barrow, Som. 1810, (succ. his father as) R. Ansford 1832 to death. Dom. Chap. to 1st Marquess Wellesley 1820; to 16th Baron Willoughby de Broke 1820. Died 19/2/1836 [C41031] Married Cordelia Cardew (a clergy dau.)by 1818, with issue.

WOODGATE (Stephen) Born Pembury, Kent 21/9/1780, s. William Woodgate and Frances Hooker. Trinity, Oxford 1798, BA1802, dn03 (B&W for Roch.), p04 (Roch.), MA1808. V. (and patron) of Pembury 1804 to death 29/1/1843 [C602] Married St George's Hanover Square, London 11/4/1808 Frances Harding, with issue.

WOODHOUSE (George) Bapt. Leominster, Heref. 24/6/1796, s. Edward Woodhouse and Mary Ann Coleman. Trinity, Oxford 1814, BA 1818, p20 (Glos.), MA1820. V. Leominster, Heref. 1824-46, Chap. of Donative of Hill, Glos. 1830 [C167987]. Died 21/10/1846 [C167988. ERC links] Married 4/2/1828 Anne Sophia Colt.

WOODHOUSE (John Chappell) Born Lichfield, s. Rev. William Woodhouse and Mary Mompesson. Christ Church, Oxford 1767 (aged 17), BA1770, dn72 (Nor. for C&L), MA1773, p73 (C&L), BD and DD1807. PC. Trentham, Staffs. 1773-1805 (res.), R. Donington, Shropshire 1773-1833, R. Ryton, Shropshire 1773-85 (res.), V. Lilleshall, Shropshire 1785-1814 (res.), Canon of 4th Prebend in Rochester Cathedral (and Official of the Royal Peculiar of Tatenhill Regis) 1797-8, 6th Canon Residentiary of Lichfield Cathedral w. Prebend of Freeford and Hansacre 1798-1807, Archdeacon of Salop 1798-1821, Dean of Lichfield 1807-33 (w. R. Tatenhill, Staffs. and Prebend of Brewood both annexed 1807), R. Stoke on Trent, Staffs. 1814-31 (res.). Died 17/11/1833 (CCEd says 11/2/1834) [C1746] Married Stanford-on-Teme, Worcs. 12/4/1779 Mercy Peet/Peate, and had issue.

WOODHOUSE see also WODEHOUSE

WOODINGTON (Henry Thicknesse) Born Bombay 9/12/1794, s. Col. Henry Thicknesse Woodington [on the Town Major's List, *q.v.* Wikipedia] and Catherine Elizabeth Bicknell. Emmanuel, Cambridge 1813, dn24 (Wor.), BA1825, p25 (Wor.). V. Hampton-in-Arden, Warwicks. 1826 to death (Bath) 28/8/1840 [C21001] Married Hatton, Warwicks, 1/2/1821 Martha Kendall, and had issue.

WOODLEY (Charles William) Boirn Bloxworth, Dorset 22/7/1803, s. Charles Woodley ('sometime of the Island of St Kitts, West Indies') and Sophia Ley. Peterhouse, Cambridge 1823, BA1827, dn27 (Ex.), p28 (Ex.), MA1830. V. St Stithians, Cornwall 1829 to death 12/12/1836 aged 33 [C146677]

WOODROOFE (Thomas) Bapt. Ockley, Surrey 23/7/1789, s. Rev. Thomas and Catharine Woodroofe. St John's, Oxford 1806, Fellow 1806-16, BA1810, dn12 (Ox.), p13 (Ox.), MA1814. [Classical Professor at the Royal Military College, Sandhurst 1814-16] Ass. Chap.

C.M.S. 1825-32; PC. Sir George Wheler's Proprietary Chapel, Spitalfields, London 1830-[3], R. Calbourne, IoW 1831-45, R. Winchester St Maurice 1845-54, V. Alton, Hants. 1854-62, R. Peper Harrow, Surrey 1862-73, Residentiary Canon of 10th Prebend in Winchester Cathedral 1845 to death 14/5/1878, leaving £30,000 [C22026. Boase. F. as Woodrooffe] Married Ipsden, Oxon. 26/7/1820 Sophia Brooks, with clerical son Henry Reade Woodrooffe.

WOODROOFFE (Nathaniel George) Bapt. London 5/5/1763, s. Thomas and Martha Woodroofe. St Edmund Hall, Oxford 1786, dn89 (London), BA1790, p90 (London for Cant.), MA1793. PC. Otford, Kent 1791-1812 (res.), R. Hatch Beauchamp, Som. 1798, V. Somerford Keynes, Wilts. 1803 (and RD1812) to death 30/10/1851 [C50354] Married Streatham, Surrey 27/7/1803 Anne Cox (*q.v.* ODNB under Woodrooffe) as an educator, 1 dau.

WOODS (George Henry) Bapt. Fyfield, Hants. 26/11/1802, s. Benjamin Woods and Lucy White. Wadham, Oxford 1820, BA1824, MA 1827. Min. Funtington, Sussex 1829-33 (res.), PC. Sennicot's Chapel, Surrey 1829-31, V. West Dean w. Singleton >< Sussex 1831, Treasurer of Chichester Cathedral 1870 to death 10/4/1879, leaving £25,000. Lived at Shopwycke House, Oving, Sussex [C71999] Married West Dean 5/8/1841 Catherine Bethel.

WOODWARD (George) Bapt. East Hendred, Berks. 28/7/1749, s. Rev. George and Albinia Woodward, Christ Church, Oxford 1766, BA 1766, dn72 (Ox.), p73 (Win.), MA1775. R. Grateley, Hants. 1773-87, V. Ringmer, Sussex 1786-1812 (res.), R. Greatham w. Wiggonholt >< Sussex 1786 [C72002. ERC links], V. Fletching, Sussex 1785-1815, R. Maresfield, Sussex 1812 to death. Dom. Chap. to 2nd Earl of Abergavenny 1786-1812. Died 10/12/1837 [C38880]

WOODWARD (Thomas) Bapt. Akenham, Suffolk 2/1/1784. Clare, Cambridge 1800, BA 1805, dn06 (Lin. for Nor.), p08 (Nor.), MA 1809. R. (and patron) of Strumpshaw w. Bradeston, Norfolk 1812-33 (res.). Lived latterly at Sproughton, Suffolk, dying there 2/8/1861 aged 77, leaving £50,000 [C80897]

WOODWARD (William Peckham) Born Plumpton, Sussex 2/11/1772, s. Rev. William Woodward and Sarah Peckham. Jesus, Cambridge 1790, BA1795, dn95 (Roch.), p96, MA 1803. R. (and patron) of Plumpton 1796-1849, R. West Grinstead, Sussex 1807-49, Sidlesham Prebend in Chichester Cathedral 1819 to death. Dom. Chap. to Jane Elizabeth, 12th Countess of Rothes 1807. Died 1/6/1849 aged 76 [C2052] Married Lewes, Sussex 28/11/1798 Elizabeth Gwynne (a clergy dau.).

WOOLL (John) Bapt. Winchester 18/5/1767, s. John and Elizabeth Wooll. Balliol, Oxford 1785, then New, BA1790, dn90 (Ox.), p91 (Ox.), MA1794, BD and DD1807. S/M Midhurst G/S, Sussex 1799-1806, S/M Rugby School 1807-28; R. Chickerell, Dorset 1793-5, R. Blackford Chapel, Wedmore, Som. 1796. Died (Worthing, Sussex) 23/11/1833 (CCEd says 6/3/1834) [C21004. ODNB as schoolmaster] Married Martyr Worth, Hants. 8/12/1798 Mary Shorland. Thomas Lawrence painted his port.

WOOLLCOMBE (Henry) Born Ashbury, Devon 18/9/1785, s. John North Woolcombe and Harriet Helyar. Oriel, Oxford 1804, BA 1804, dn08 (Ex.), p09 (Ex.), Fellow 1809-12, MA1811. R. Ashbury 1810-61, R. Pillaton, Cornwall 1816 and R. Highampton, Devon 1816 to death. Dom Chap to 9th Earl of Moray 1816. Died Heavitree, Exeter 16/8/1861, leaving £3,000 [C146680] Married Jane Frances Louis [*surname*] (d. 1819), with clerical sons Henry, Louis, and George Woollcombe.

WOOLLCOMBE (John) Bapt. Plymouth 10/4/1767, s. Thomas Woollcombe. Oriel, Oxford 1785, BA1789, Fellow 1791, MA1792, dn93 (Ex.), p93 (Ex.). R. Newton Pinkney, Northants. 1800-10, R. (and patron) of Stowford, Devon 1807, R. Cromhall, Glos. 1809 to death 30/11/1838 [C146681]

WOOLLCOMBE (William) Bapt. East Worlington, Devon 25/9/1786, s. Rev. William Woollcombe, sen. and Ann Walker. Corpus Christi, Oxford 1801, BA1805, MA1808, dn11 (Ex.), Fellow 1812, p12 (Ox.), BD1816. V. Christow, Devon 1831, V. Hennock, Devon 1847 to death there 18/1/1862, leaving £600 [C22028 as Wollcombe] Married Elizabeth Reynolds, with clerical sons Philip, and William Penrose Woollcombe.

WOOLLEY (Charles Birch) Bapt. Birmingham 11/1/1792, s. James Woolley and Mary White. Oriel, Oxford 1808, BA1813, dn14

(Wor.), p15 (C&L), MA1815. V. Thrussington, Leics. 1829 to death 5/11/1834 [C21006] Married Birmingham 13/11/1814 Ann Hawkesford, with issue.

WOOLLEY (Henry Rushworth) Born Northampton 8/12/1796, s. Rev. Thomas and Elizabeth Woolley. Lincoln, Oxford 1794, BA 1798, dn00 (Peterb.), p01 (Lin.), MA1842. R. Shillingstone Okeford >< Dorset 1813, Chap. of Donative of Middleton, Warwicks. 1813, V. Shenstone, Staffs. 1835, R. Handsworth, Staffs. 1841 to death. Dom. Chap. to 2nd Earl of Clonmell 1813. Died (a widower) 7/10/1847, leaving £450 (left unadministered by his dau.) [C21008] Wife Henrietta, and issue.

WORCESTER (Bishop of) see **CARR (Robert James)**

WORDSWORTH (Christopher) Born Cockermouth, Cumberland 9/6/1774, s. John Wordsworth (attorney) and Ann Cookson. Trinity, Cambridge 1791, BA1796, Fellow 1798, MA 1799, dn99 (Nor.), p99 (Nor.), DD1810, Master of Trinity College, Cambridge 1820-41, Vice-Chancellor 1820-1 and 1826-7. R. Ashby w. Oby and Thurne, Norfolk 1804-6, R. Woodchurch, Kent 1806-8, Preacher throughout the Archdiocese of Canterbury 1808, Dean and R. of Bocking [a Peculiar] 1808-16 (w. Monk's Eleigh 1812-16), R. Lambeth, Surrey 1816-20, R. Sundridge, Kent 1816-20, R. Buxted w. Uckfield, Sussex 1820 to death. Dom. Chap. to Archbishop of Canterbury 1805; Chap. to House of Commons 1817. Died 2/2/1846 [C72015. ODNB] Married Birmingham 6/10/1804 Priscilla Lloyd (d.1815, dau. of a banker), 3s. (inc. Christopher, Bishop of Lincoln). 'A strict disciplinarian, and exacted an unquestioning conformity to all College rules'.

WORDSWORTH (John) Born Grasmere, Westmorland 18/6/1803, s. William Wordsworth (the poet laureate) and Margaret Hutchinson. St John's, Cambridge 1821, then New College, Oxford 1823, BA1826, dn27 (Lin.), p28 (Lin.), MA1830. R. Moresby, Cumberland 1829-34, V. Brigham, Cumberland 1832-75 (lived here), R. Workington, Cumberland 1834-40, R. Plumbland, Cumberland 1840 to death. Dom. Chap. to 10th Earl of Westmorland 1834. Died Eaton Square, London 25/7/1875 aged 72, leaving £18,000 [C80976. Boase. Platt] Married (1) 11/10/1830 Isabella Christian Curwen (d. Lucca, Italy 1847), 6 ch. (2) 6/11/1852 Helen Easton Ross (d.1854), 1 dead s. (3) 2/12/1856 Marian Dolan, with further issue (4) 1870 Mary Gamble (w); clerical son John. J.P. Ward, 'Wordsworth's eldest son: John Wordsworth and the Intimations Ode', *Wordsworth Circle*, Vol. 36 (2) Spring 2005. Whilst heavily literary, this article does bring out his plodding, unimagin-ative character; without however mentioning his young Italian mistress in Rome (*q.v.* Kate Summersale, *Mrs Robinson's disgrace* ...' (2012): is she the only person to have noticed this aberration?).

WORKMAN (William) Bapt. Basingstoke, Hants. 4/8/1791, s. Maurice Workman and Ann Ring. St John's, Cambridge 1809, BA1814, dn14 (London), p15 (Heref. for Win.), MA 1817. H/M Basingstoke School from 1816; R. Eastrop, Hants. 1816 to death 19/11/1849 aged 58 [C109183] Married Basingstoke 4/1/1821 Elizabeth Brownjohn.

WORSLEY (Charles) Born Carisbrooke, IoW 11/9/1783, s. Rev. Henry Worsley and Mary Dickonson. St Mary Hall, Oxford 1800, then Wadham, BA1804, dn06 (Win.), MA1807, p07 (Win.). R. Lesnewth, Cornwall 1813 to death 9/8/1854 (living on IoW) [C109185] Married Greenwich, Kent 25/1/1833 Madeline Maria Anne Le Geyt, w. clerical son Edward Worsley.

WORSLEY (Charles Pennyman) Born Wallingwells, Northants. 5/3/1798, s. James Worsley and Lydia White. Christ's, Cambridge 1816, BA1820, dn21 (Lin.), p22 (Lin.), MA 1824. 'Perpetual V'. Hullavington, Wilts. 1826-7, V. Thurlby, Lincs. (and RD) 1827 to death 17/12/1863, leaving £5,000 [C80977. Kaye] Married Rise, Yorks. 10/5/1826 Caroline Acklom, with issue.

WORSLEY (Henry) Born Pidford, IoW, s. Thomas Worsley. St Mary Hall, Oxford 1777 (aged 21), BCL and DCL1791, dn78 (Ox. for Win.), p79 (C&L for Win.). R. Kingston 1779-88, R. Dummer, Hants. 1781, V. Arreton, Hants. 1794, R. Yarmouth, IoW 1794-1801, V. Shalfleet, Hants. 1794-1801, R. Gatcombe, Hants. 1801, R. St Lawrence, IoW 1812, R. Wolverton, Hants. 1804. Died Gatcombe 11/4/1844 [C21013] Note other IoW clerics of this name.

WORSLEY (James) Bapt. Chale, IoW 18/1/1767, s. Rev. Francis Worsley and Anne Roberts. Corpus Christ, Oxford 1785, then

New, Fellow, 1785-94, dn91 (Ox.), p92 (Ox.), BCL 1793. V. Thorley, IoW 1803 to death (Billing-ham, IoW) 16/3/1841 aged 74 [C137023] Married (1) Chale 26/5/1794 Elizabeth Gother (d.1803), with issue (2) Southwark, Surrey 1310/1810 Sophia Pinhor, with clerical son John Henry Worsley. J.P. Hants.

WORSLEY (Pennyman Warton) Born Finchley, London 20/7/1800, s. Rev. Ralph Worsley (Sub-Dean of York Minster, below) and Elizabeth Gildart. BNC, Oxford 1818, then St Alban Hall, BA1821, dn23 (Lin.), p24 (Lin.), MA1824. Prebend and Residentiary Canon of Ripon Collegiate Church (later Cathedral) 1827-79, R. Little Ponton, Lincs. 1829 (and RD) to death 19/5/1885, leaving £51,821-8s-2d. [C80980. Boase] Married (1) Grantham, Lincs. 1829 Charlotte Helena Potchett (d.1854), with clerical son Pennyman Ralph Worsley (2) Bedale, Yorks. 1860 (3rd q.) Caroline Susanna Sargeantson (d.1877). Connections with the man below?

WORSLEY (Ralph) Bapt. Stonegrave, Yorks. 7/7/1765, s. Rev. James Worsley and Dorothy (dau. Sir Ralph Pennyman). Trinity, Cambridge 1784, BA1788, dn88 (York), p89 (York), MA 1792. PC. York St Olave w. St Giles 1790-1848, V. Skipsea, Yorks. 1791, R. Little Ponton, Lincs. 1791-1829, 1st Prebend of Ripon Collegiate Church 1792-1802 (Sub-Dean 1801), R. Finchley, London 1794 to death (Little Ponton) 23/3/1848, aged 82 [C80982. YCO] Married Finchley, London 23/12/1795 Elizabeth Gildart, with son (above). He was charged with extracting money from a spinster lady. Coinnections with the man above?

WORSLEY (Thomas) Born Stonegrave, Yorks. 15/7/1797, s. Rev. George Worsley and Anne (dau. Sir Thomas Cayley, Bart.). Trinity, Cambridge 1815, BA1820, then Downing 1824, dn24 (Ely), MA1824, p25 (Ely), Fellow and Tutor 1824-36, DD1859, Master of Downing College, Cambridge 1836-85 Vice-Chancellor 1837-8, and last Christian Advocate in the University of Cambridge 1844-50. R. Scawton, Helmsley, Yorks. 1826-81. Died Cambridge 16/2/1885 aged 87, leaving £3,313-11s-0d. [C109859. Boase] Married Huddersfield, Yorks. 12/6/1842 Katharine Rawson (w), Wasdale Hall, Cumberland, with issue. Fine port. by Richmond online.

WORSLEY (William) Born Lowton, Lancs., s. James Worsley. BNC, Oxford 1826 (aged 18), then Magdalen Hall, BA1830, dn31 (Chester), p32 (Chester). PC. Norbury, Stockport, Cheshire 1831-74 (res.). Died Torkington, Cheshire 13/5/1887 aged 79, leaving £20,601-19s-6d. [C170973] Married Jane Errington by 1837, with issue.

WORTHAM (Walter) Born Aspenden, Herts. 27/8/1802, s. Hale Young Wortham and Anne Proctor. Magdalene, Cambridge 1820, BA1824, dn24 (Ely for Lin.), p26 (Lin.). V. Weston, Herts. 1832-7, R. Shephall, Herts. 1833 to death 2/1/1877, leaving £5,000 [C80984]

WORTHINGTON (Henry Burdett) Born Bath 11/1/1791, s. Rev. Richard Worthington and Maria Burton. Literate: dn14 (Chester), p15 (Chester). PC. Flixton, Lancs. 1816-22, V. Grinton, Yorks. 1822-[50]. Died York 6/1/1868 aged 76, leaving £2,000 [C170975] Married (1) Richmond, Yorks. 9/8/1826 Mary Wilson, with clerical son (2) Bedford 23/5/1849 Harriet Halfhead [*sic*].

WRANGHAM (Francis) Born Raisthorpe, Malton Yorks. 11/6/1769, s. of George Wrangham (farmer). Magdalene, Cambridge 1785, then Trinity Hall 1787, BA1790, dn93 (York), MA1793, p96 (Glos. for York). V. Hunmanby, Yorks. 1796-1842, PC. Muston, Yorks. 1796-1842, V. Folkton, Yorks. 1796-1820, Archdeacon of Cleveland (w. V. Thorpe Bassett, Yorks.) 1820-28, Prebend of Ample-forth in York Minster 1823-42, Canon of Chester Cathedral (w. R. Doddleston, Cheshire 1827) 1825-42, Canon of Chester Cathedral 1825-42, Archdeacon of the East Riding 1828-41 (res.). Dom. Chap. to 3rd Duke of Montrose 1796-1820; Examining Chap. to Abp of York 1814-54. Died Chester 27/12/1842 aged 73 [C129382. ODNB and port. YCO. DEB] Married (1) Bridlington, Yorks. 7/4/1799 Agnes, dau. Col. Ralph Creyke (Marton, Yorks., she d.1800), 1 child (2) Brompton, Yorks. 14/7/1801 Dorothy Cayley (a clergy dau., of Thormanby, Yorks.), with clerical son (below). F.R.S.; 'an ardent book collector' (15,000 vols. by 1819); classicist; friend of Wordsworth and Sydney Smith; Whig; reformer of every kind; there is an excellent article about this appealing man on the Wrangham Website; portrait online.

WRANGHAM (George Walter) Bapt. Scarborough, Yorks. 30/3/1804, s. Ven. Francis

Wrangham (Archdeacon of East Riding, above) and Dorothy Cayley. BNC, Oxford 1822, then Magdalene, Cambridge 1825, BA1828, dn28 (Llandaff for York), p28 (London for York), MA1829 (Lambeth). R. Thorpe Bassett, Yorks. 1828 and V. Ampleforth, Yorks. 1829 to death. Dom. Chap. to 3rd Duke of Montrose 1829. Died (unmarried) Aston Clinton, Bucks. 24/10/1855 aged 51 [C124405. YCO]

WRAY (George) Bapt. Doncaster, Yorks. 4/12/1781, s. Rev. Henry Wray and Susannah Lloyd. Queen's, Oxford 1799, BA1803, dn04 (Roch. for York), p05 (B&W), MA1806. R. Croscombe, Som. 1805-14, Curate of Dringhouses, Ainsty of York 1827, R. Cowsby, Yorks. 1832, R. (and patron) of Leven, Beverley, Yorks. 1839 [income £1,220] (with RD of South Harthill 1843 and Prebend of Dunnington in York Minster 1848) to death. Dom. Chap. to 3rd Earl of Aberdeen 1811. Died 26/6/1878 aged 96, leaving £50,000 [C2584. YCO] Married Kildwick, Yorks. 30/9/1816 Caroline Wiseman (Skipton, Yorks.), with clerical son.

WRAY (John) Born and bapt. Bardney, Lincs. 22/3/1776, s. John Wray and Ann Woodward. Queens', Cambridge 1801, then St John's 1801, SCL, dn05 (Lin.), p06 (Lin.). V. Bardney 1806 w. R. Manby, Lincs. 1806 to death. Dom. Chap. to 7th Earl of Coventry 1809. Died 5/12/1851 aged 74 [C80992. Kaye, with extensive note] Married (1) Bucknall, Staffs. 30/1/1798 Ann Thistlewood (d.1800), with issue (2) Grantham, Lincs. 23/19/1800 Ann Barton, with further issue.

WRENCH (Jacob George) Bapt. City of London 27/12/1790, s. Jacob George Wrench (merchant) and Mary Buxton. Balliol, Oxford 1811, migrated to Magdalene, Cambridge 1811, then Trinity Hall 1813, dn13 (Lin. for Chich.), p14 (London), LLB1817, LLD1825, incorporated at Oxford 1842. R. Stowting, Kent 1814-35, V. Blakeney, Glos. 1826-34, V. Salehurst, Sussex 1827 to death. Chap. to HRH Duke of Sussex 1815-17; to British Embassay at Constantinople 1817-22. Died 7/7/1860 aged 69, leaving £10,000 [C72020. Boase] Married Awre, Glos. 3/11/1830 Eliza Brant (w), w. clerical son of the same name. *F.S.A.*

WRENCH (Thomas Robert) Born London 22/7/1784, s. Jacob Wrench and Elizabeth Mary Padden. Queen's, Oxford 1784, BA1788, MA 1792. V. Shipton Bellinger, Hants. 1789-93 (res.), R. St Michael Cornhill, City of London 1793 to death. Chap. to the Drapers' Company. Died 29/9/1836 aged 72 [C1209189] Married 1793 Sarah Clarke, w. issue. 'No-one reads the psalms so well as Rev. Wrench' (George 111)

WREY (Bourchier William) Born Tavistock, Devon (CCEd thus) 6/5/1761, s. Sir Bourchier Wrey, 6th Bart. and Ellen Thresher. All Souls, Oxford 1778, BA1784, dn84 (Ox.), p85 (Ex.). R. Combe in Teignhead, Devon (and Preacher throughout the Diocese of Exeter) 1785-1838, R. Tawstock 1801-39, (where he rebuilt Corffe House), Chap. of the Donative of Temple, Cornwall 1789. Dom. Chap. to Mary, Countess of Darnley 1801. Died 19/8/1839 aged 78 [C38887. Not in Foster] Married Bradford on Avon, Som. 26/11/1789 Sarah Bethell, with clerical son John Wrey.

WRIGGLESWORTH (John Dawson) Bapt. Ledsham, Yorks, 6/6/1770, natural s. Anne Wrigglesworth. St Catharine's, Cambridge 1789, BA1793, dn93 (Lin.), p94 (Lin.). V. Loddon, Norfolk 1833 to death (Chesterton, Cambs.) 5/12/1848 aged 80 [C80995] Married Cambridge 25/7/1783 Elizabeth Apppleyard, with child.

WRIGHT (Edward Collins) Bapt. Bradley, Staffs. 7/12/1776, s. Rev. Samson Wright and Elizabeth Collins. Worcester, Oxford 1796, BA1800, dn00 (Ox.), p01 (C&L), MA1805. PC. Bradley 1801 and of R. Pitsford, Northants. 1824 to death 17/8/1842 [C21030] Married (1) Pitsford, Northants. 26/12/1808 Mary White (w. slave money, she d.1821), w. issue (2) Camden, London 9/8/1821 Frances Ellen Pemberton, w. clerical s. Robert Blayney Wright.

WRIGHT (George) Bapt. Stepney, London 28/5/1786, s. Samuel and Kitty Wright. S/M London. Literate: dn11 (York), p12 (York). PC. Nun Monkton, Yorks. 1815-37. Died? [C135650. YCO] Was married with issue.

WRIGHT (Henry) Born Market Bosworth, Leics. 25/10/1791, s. Rev. Thomas Wright (below, of Maxstoke Castle) and Mary Dilke. Emmanuel. Cambridge 1809, BA1815, dn14 (Lin.), p15 (Lin.). PC. Stockport St Peter, Cheshire 1816, PC. Maisemore, Glos. 1823-9, V. Winkleigh, Devon, 1829 to death (Teignmouth, Devon, and not at Mottram Hall, Leics. which he inherited 1842) 12/4/1856 aged 69 [C81001] Married 1817 Croft, Leics. Mary Catherine Adnutt (a clergy dau.), with issue.

WRIGHT (James Camper) Bapt. Woodham Mortimer, Essex 26/6/1774, s. James Wright and Sally Camper. [Sometime Capt. in The Royals]. King's, Cambridge 1792 [adm. Lincoln's Inn 1794] Fellow 1795-1817, BA 1797, MA 1802, dn15 (B&W), p15 (B&W). Fellow of Eton College. R. Walkern, Herts. 1817 to death (London) 13/10/1838 [C41036] Married 4/6/1821 Maria Sarah Wallace-Ogle (Causey Park, Castle Morpeth, Northumberland), with issue.

WRIGHT (John) Bapt. Farnworth, Prescot, Lancs. 20/9/1761, s. Thomas and Jane Wright. BNC, Oxford 1781, BA1785, MA1787, dn88 (Chester), p89 (Chester), BD and DD1820. R. Great Billing (Billing Magna), Northants. 1801 to death 2/3/1843 [C38888]

WRIGHT (John) [NiVoF] PC. Newcastle under Lyme St George, Staffs. 1831-[40]. Died? [Not yet in CCEd]

WRIGHT (John Marsden) Bapt. Hornby, Lancs. 9/9/1798, s. George Wright and Margaret ?Marsden. BNC, Oxford 1817, BA 1820, dn22 (Chester), p23 (Chester), MA1823. R. Tatham, Lancs. 1823 to death 8/7/1873 aged 74, leaving £4,000 [C170980] Married Everton, Liverpool 29/7/1829 Mary Lea Salisbury, with issue.

WRIGHT (Peter) Born Knutsford, Cheshire 22/11/1759, s. Samuel Wright (attorney). BNC, Oxford 1779, BA1782, dn84 (Nor.), then Balliol, Fellow 1785, etc., p85 (Ox.), MA1785. PC. Over Peover, Cheshire 1790, R. Baddeley, Cheshire 1796-1839, R. Marks Tey, Colchester, Essex 1802-39, R. Colchester St Nicholas 1807-30, R. Colchester Holy Trinity 1830 to death (Marks Tey) 8/7/1873 [C38889] Married Eccles, Lancs. 3/6/1803 Elizabeth Frodsham, (Worsley, Lancs.), with issue.

WRIGHT (Robert [Henry]) From Shipston, Worcs., s. John Wright. Trinity, Oxford 1788 (aged 16), BA1793, MA1809. R. Itchen Abbas, Hants. 1803-50, V. Steeple Barton, Oxon. 1808 and R. Ovington, Hants. 1817 to death 26/3/1850 [C22032] He was alleged to have visited the parish only once - to read himself in (Wilberforce).

WRIGHT (Thomas) Born Mobberley, Cheshire 1/11/1756, s. Rev. Henry Offley Wright (V. Derby St Peter). S/M Audley Free G/S, Staffs. 1782; St John's, Cambridge 1775, BA1779, then Emmanuel 1779, dn80 (Ely), Fellow 1780-9, dn81 (Chester), MA1782. R. Curdworth, Warwicks. 1782-9, V. Derby St Peter 1786-8, R. Market Bosworth w. Shenton, Leics. 1788 to death 29/11/1840 [C21041] Married 24/8/1789 Mary Dilke (Maxstoke Castle, Warwicks.), with son Henry, above.

WRIGHT (Thomas) Born London, s. Thomas Wright (merchant). Pembroke, Cambridge 1794, BA1798, dn98 (London), p98 (London), MA 1801. R. Foxearth, Essex 1798-1810 (res.), R. Otton Belchamp >< Essex 1798-1820, R. Little Henny, Essex 1811-21 (res.), R. Middle Claydon 1820 and V. Steeple Claydon w. East Claydon, Bucks. [separate in ERC] 1820 to death. Dom. Chap. to Mary, Baroness Fermanagh 1807; to 16th Lord Somerville 1821. Died 11/4/1841 [C81031] Had issue.

WRIGHT (Thomas Bailey) Born Wrangle, Lincs. 7/7/1790, s. Rev. Richard Wright and Susanna Hill. Sidney, Cambridge 1808, then Peterhouse 1811, BA1813, dn13 (Lin.), p14 (Lin.). V. Wrangle 1826 to death 25/5/1858, leaving £800 [C81032] Married West Keal, Lincs. 5/8/1817 Henrietta Weeks Franklin (w) (of Spilsby, Lincs., a sister of the lost arctic explorer), and had issue.

WRIGHT (Thomas Preston) Born City of London 10/7/1803, s. Thomas Wright and Jane Ann Preston. St Catharine's, Cambridge 1822, BA 1826, dn28 (C&L), p29 (C&L), MA1830. V. Roydon, Essex. 1830, living in Hackney, London without cure 1841-3, PC. Dalston St Philip, London 1844-60. Died Wray Park, Reigate, Surrey 4/11/1868, leaving £30,000 [C21042] Married South Hackney 16/8/1840 Elizabeth Phillippa Williams (w), and issue.

WRIGHTE (Thomas William) Born Bridgnorth, Shropshire 1759, s. Rev. William Wrighte. 'Removed from Winchester College for rioting in the streets and for assault 1778.' Queens', Cambridge 1778, BA1782, dn82 (Peterb. for London), p83 (Lin. for London), Fellow 1783-6, MA1785. V. Rochester St Nicholas 1795-1803, R. Wychling, Kent 1795 and V. Broughton under Blean, Kent 1803 to death. Secretary to the Society of Antiquaries 1790-1813. Chap. to Bishop of Rochester. Died Bearsted, Kent 5/9/1854 [C2559. Boase] Married Westminster, London 20/12/1786 Elizabeth Moss, and had issue. *F.S.A.* (1789).

WRIGHTSON (Arthur Bland) Born Cusworth, Yorks. 12/2/1793, s. William Wrightson, *M.P.*, and Henrietta Heber. Trinity, Cambridge 1812, BA1816, dn16 (York), p17 (Chester for York), MA1820. PC. Campsall, Yorks. 1817-45, R. Edlington, Yorks. 1818-43, R. Hemsworth, Yorks. 1840 (and RD of Pontefract 1841 and Prebend of Botevant in York Minster 1843) to death. Dom. Chap. to Baron Beresford 1818. Died 7/12/1878 aged 85, leaving £25,000 [C135653. YCO]

WROTH (William Bruton) Bapt. Kingsbridge, Devon 18/7/1785, s. William Wroth and Mary Lory. St John's, Cambridge 1803, BA 1808, dn08 (Lin.), p09 (Salis.), MA1811. V. Edlesborough, Bucks. [blank in ERC] 1815 and V. Totternhoe, Beds. 1819 to death. Dom. Chap. to 2nd Viscount Lake 1818. Died 7/5/1863, aged 78, leaving £9,000 [C81040] Married Bath 15/6/1818 Anne Marie Barker (d.1859), with clerical s. Edward Barker Wroth.

WROTTESLEY (Charles) Born Wrottesley Hall, Tettenhall, Staffs. 8/7/1783, s. Maj.-Gen. Sir John Wrottesley, Bart., *M.P.*, and Hon. Frances Courtenay (dau. of Viscount Courtenay). Christ Church, Oxford 1801, BA 1805, dn07 (Ox.), p07 (Ox.), then All Souls, Fellow 1808-21, MA1808, BD 1817, etc. PC. Tettenhall Regis 1807-25, V. New Romney, Kent 1817-21, R. East Knoyle, Wilts. 1820 to death. Dom. Chap. to Charlotte, Countess of Rosslyn 1811; to 1st Earl of Bradford 1815. Died 17/2/1848 [C21049] Brother below.

WROTTESLEY (Robert) Born Wrottesley Hall, Tettenhall, Staffs. 2/6/1801, s. Maj.-Gen. Sir John Wrottesley, Bart., *M.P.*, and Hon. Frances Courtenay (dau. of Viscount Courtenay). Christ Church, Oxford 1818, BA 1822, dn24 (C&L), MA1825, p25 (C&L). R. Tettenhall Regis 1825 and R. Himley, Staffs. 1830 to death 20/1/1838 aged 36 [C21050] Married 8/1828 Georgiana (dau. of Gen. Sir George Pigot, 3rd Bart.), *s.p.* Brother above.

WULFF (James Gee) Probably Irish. Born Quebec, s. Capt. George Wulff, *Royal Artillery*, and Mary Chanden. TCD 1815 (aged 19), BA 1819, dn20 (Ex.), p21 (Ex.). PC. St Day, Cornwall 1829, V. Gwinnear, Cornwall 1833-35-, R. Illogan, Cornwall 1851 to death there 1884 aged 88, leaving £10,601-4s-10d. [C146688. Al.Dub. as John George Wulffe] Married 24/11/1840 Mary Ann Molesworth (w).

WYATT (Charles Francis) Born Banbury, Oxon. 29/3/1795, s. Charles Wyatt and Ann Walford. Oriel, Oxford 1813, then Jesus, Cambridge 1815, BA1818, dn18 (Ox.), p19 (Ox.), MA1821. R. (and patron) of Broughton, Oxon. 1819-70. Died 27/3/1877, leaving £30,000 [C22035] Married (1) Broughton 12/10/1819 Susan Heydon (d.1834), with clerical son of same name (2) Banbury 1847 (2nd q.) Maria Frederica Walford, w. clerical s. of same name. 'Not very devout' (Wilberforce). Brother Thomas, below.

WYATT (George) Bapt. Tattenhall, Cheshire 9/9/1782 (but of Trent, Staffs.), s. Charles and Jane Wyatt. St John's, Cambridge 1812, dn17 (Nor.), p18 (Bangor), LLB1819. R. Burghwallis, Yorks. 1823 to death 1/4/1856 aged 74 [C81042. Boase] Married 1810 Llandogai, Carnarvon Eliza Ann Wyatt [*sic*], with issue. Probably some relation to James Wyatt, the architect, and may have had architectural training himself.

WYATT (Thomas) Bapt. Banbury, Oxon. 30/9/1796, s. Charles Wyatt and Ann Walford. Trinity, Oxford 1815, BA1819, dn19 (Ox.), p20 (Ox.), MA1821. V. Wroxton w. Balscot, Oxon. 1825 to death 14/3/1853 [C22036] Married Goudhurst, Kent 21/8/1824 Elizabeth Newington, with issue. Brother Charles Francis, above.

WYATT (William Hindes) Born Framlinham, Suffolk 20/8/1797, s. Rev. William Wyatt and Ann Hindes Groom. Pembroke, Cambridge 1814, BA1819, dn21 Chester), p21 (Nor.), MA 1822. PC. Sneinton, Notts. 1831-68, RD, V. Melton Ross, Lincs. (and Prebend of Sexaginta Solidorum in Lincoln Cathedral) 1868 to death (Hope under Dinmore, Heref.) 27/6/1875 aged 77, leaving £1,500 [C116340] Married Brantham, Suffolk 18/11/1840 Anne Newson, with clerical son. Surrogate.

WYBERGH (Christopher Hilton) Born Wetherby, Yorks. 30/12/1799, s. Thomas Wybergh (Isel Old Hall, Cockermouth, Cumberland) and Isabella Hartley. Pembroke, Cambridge 1818, BA1822, dn23 (Car.), p25 (Car.), MA1825. V. Isel 1825 and V. Bromfield, Cumberland 1826 to death. Dom. Chap. to Bishop of Carlisle 1826. Died Isel 9/7/1876 aged 76, leaving £25,000 [C6489. Platt] Married Westminster, London 22/4/1826 Anna Maria

Minshull (a clergy dau.), with clerical son Christopher.

WYLD (George) Bapt. Holborn, London 21/10/1762, s. Thomas Wyld and Diana Moor. Pembroke, Oxford 1780, BA1784, dn86 (Salis.), p87 (Salis.), MA1787. V. Chieveley w. Winterbourne and Oare, Berks. [net income £1,174] 1789-1836, R. Hampstead Marshall, Berks. 1806-9, R. Blunsden St Andrew, Wilts. 1809-14, RD of Newbury 1812, R. Woodborough, Wilts. 1814-35. Dom. Chap. to Anne, Baroness Rodney 1806-14. Died Speen, Berks. 31/12/1836 aged 75 [C90579] Married Scampston, Yorks. 26/11/1796 Mary Dionisia Calcraft, with clerical son below.

WYLD (Thomas John) Born Speen, Berks. 11/11/1801, s. Rev. George Wyld (above) and Mary Dionisia Calcraft. Christ Church, Oxford 1820, BA1823, dn24 (Salis.), p25 (Salis.), MA 1826. R. (and patron) of North Wraxall, Wilts. 1830-64-. Died Paris 17/9/1866, leaving under £200 [C90581] Married Southampton 27/4/1836 Maria Neeld, with clerical son Calcraft Neeld Wyld.

WYLDE (Robert) Born Glazely, Shropshire 25/3/1774, s. Rev. Edmund Wylde and Mary Fewtrell. Christ Church, Oxford, 1789, BA 1794, MA1796, dn97 (C&L), p98 (C&L). R. Alveley, Shropshire 1801, PC. Stafford St Chad 1822-5 (res.), R. Claverdon w. Norton Lindsey, Warwicks. 1828 to death 31/10/1833 [C21057] Married (1) Shrewsbury, Shropshire 5/5/1803 Emma Pritchard (d.1808), with issue (2) Wedmore, Som. 20/11/1817 Caroline Georgiana Andrews.

WYLIE (George) Bapt. Whitehaven, Cumberland 22/07/1804, s. Mark Wylie and Janet Bishop. Queen's, Oxford 1821, BA1826, Fellow 1826-45, dn27, MA1829, p30 (Chester). PC. Warton, Kirkham, Lancs. 1830, R. Newnham w. Maplederwell, Hants. 1844-79. Died Bath 8/4/1884 aged 79, leaving £6,200-8s-8d. [C171000] Married Whitehaven 2/3/1847 Helen Craik Hunter (Kirkcudbrightshire).

WYMER (Edward) Bapt. Reepham, Norfolk 6/5/1804, s. George Wymer and Elizabeth Varlo. St John's, Cambridge 1823, BA1827, dn27 (Nor.), p28 (Nor.). R. Westwick, Norfolk 1828 and PC. Ingham, Norfolk 1832 to death (Lowestoft, Suffolk) 21/2/1873, leaving £600 [C116341] Married (1) Ingham 7/2/1831 Elizabeth Whaites (d.1841), with issue (2) 9/1844 Elizabeth Stephenson Toll (his governess), with further issue.

WYNCH (Henry) Born Madras 5/10/1792, s. George Wynch (Cowbridge, Glamorgan) and Mary (Secker) Smith. Sidney, Cambridge 1811, BA1815, MA1818, dn18 (Salis.), p18 (Salis.). R. Pett, Sussex 1823-52, R. South Heigton, Sussex 1831-61. Died Tunbridge Wells, Kent 17/11/1868, leaving £6,000 [C54204] Married Stratford St Mary, Suffolk 6/9/1826 Mary Goldin, with issue.

WYNDHAM (Henry Penruddock) Born Salisbury, Wilts. 25/12/1775, s. Henry Penruddock Wyndham and Caroline Hearst. New, Oxford 1795, BA1800, dn04 (Chester for Salis.), p04 (Win. for Salis.), MA1805, Fellow to 1823. V. Compton Chamberlayne, Wilts. 1806-22, R. Little Sampford, Essex 1822 to death 4/2/1838 [C22037] Married Salisbury 31/7/1823 Catharine Mary Tatum.

WYNDHAM (John Heathcote) Born Dinton, Wilts., s. William Wyndham and Elizabeth Heathcote. Wadham, Oxford 1794 (aged 17), BA1798, dn00 (Ox.), MA1801, p01 (Ox.), Fellow 1800-13. R. Corton Denham, Som. 1813 and R. Sock Dennis, Som. 1819 to death 5/1/1852 [C38903. Boase] Married 1813 Jane Dorothy Eveleigh, with issue. Brother below.

WYNDHAM (Thomas) Born Dinton, Wilts., s. William Wyndham and Elizabeth Heathcote. Wadham, Oxford 1788 (aged 16), BCL1794, dn95 (Salis.), p95 (Salis.), DCL1809. V. Haslebury Plucknett, Som. 1797-1833, V. Compton Chamberlayne, Som. 1801-6, PC. Hinton Admiral, Wilts. 1806, R. Pimperne, Dorset 1806 and R. Melcombe Regis, Dorset 1809 to death (Hinton Admiral) 25/5/1862, aged 91, leaving £8,000 [C41053] Married Stratford on Avon, Warwicks 18/3/1809 Anne Stubbs, with issue. Brother above.

WYNN, *born* NANNEY, *otherwise* WYNN-NANNEY (Simon Hart) Born Vepery, Madras 18/11/1798 (bapt. 28/9/1800), s. Capt. Robert Nanney (Madras Native Infantry - but of Bala, Merioneth) and Elizabeth Hart. St John's, Cambridge 1819, then Magdalene 1822, dn23 (Win.), BA1824, p25 (Lin.). V. Burgh on Bain, Lincs. 1825-65, R. West Barkwith, Lincs. 1840-60. Died 15/11/1865, leaving £4,000 [C81049] Married (1) Sophia Sarah Beaumont (d.1862, 3rd q.) (2) Milton, Kent 18/11/1862 Mary Louisa Hannam (a clergy dau., of Borden, Kent), *s.p.* Online photo.

WYNNE (John Welchman) From Denbighshire. St John's, Cambridge 1785, BA1790, dn90 (Bangor for St Asaph), p91 (London). PC. Plaxtol, Kent 1821 to death 3/9/1841 aged 76 [C90585] Married (1) 4/10/1792 Ann Bones (Grays Thurrock, Essex) (2) Elizabeth.

WYNNE (Maurice) Born Wrexham, Denbigh, s. Owen Wynne. Jesus, Oxford 1783 (aged 22), dn86 (Ox.), p87 (Ox.), BCL 1790, DCL1798. PC. Bourton, Salop 1793-1833, V. Much Wenlock, Shropshire 1793 and R. Bangor Monachorum w. Overton, Flint [net income £1,200] (and Preacher within Chester Diocese) 1798 (living at Nerquis Hall, Flint) to death 27/5/1835 (not 9/6/1835) aged 75 (unmarried, 'the last male descendant of the [Royal] House of Gwydir') [C38906]. Fine monument illustrated online.

WYNNE (Thomas) From Hereford, s. Thomas Wynne. St John's, Cambridge 1796 (aged 18), BA1801, dn01 (Ox.), p03 (Ox.), MA1821, BD 1824. R. Hereford St Nicholas 1820 and R. Colwall, Heref. 1831 to death 18/7/1839. 'He had been insolvent, allowing the rectory house to become derelict even though he received money for dilapidation' [C22038] Was married.

WYNNIATT (Reginald) Born Stanton Court, Stanton, Glos., s. Rev. Reginald Wynniatt, sen. and Frances Phillips. Queen's, Oxford 1804 (aged 18), BA1808, dn09 (Glos.), p10 (Glos.), MA1811. R. Stanton 1819, R. Oaksey, Wilts. 1857 to death 7/10/1860, leaving £450 [C167948] Married Walcot, Bath 8/12/1811 Catherine Brydges (w), with issue.

WYNTER (James Cecil) Born Aldeburgh, Suffolk, s. Philip Wynter and Anne Hamilton. St John's, Oxford 1823 (aged 16), BA1827, dn31 (Lin.), p31 (Lin.), MA1834. R. Donnington on Bain, Lincs. 1831-3, R. Gatton, Surrey 1833-77, RD Ewell (Southwest Division), Hon. Canon of the Cathedral of the Isles, Cumbrae 1862 and Hon. Canon of Winchester Cathedral 1872 to death 26/10/1877, leaving £4,000 [C81052. Bertie. Kaye] Married (1) Marylebone, London 30/6/1837 Elizabeth Broadwood (d.1840) (2) Marylebone, London 13/7/1843 Margaret Lyall (d.1852), with issue (3) Chipstead, Surrey 18/4/1855 Mary Cattley. Brother below.

WYNTER (Philip) Born Aldeburgh, Suffolk 2/2/1793, s. Philip Wynter and Anne Hamilton. St John's, Oxford 1811, Fellow 1814-28, BA1815, dn16 (Chester), p17 (Ox.), MA1819, Tutor 1822-8, BD1824, President St John's College, Oxford 1828-71, DD1828, Vice Chancellor 1840-4. R. Hanborough, Oxon. 1828, R. South Warnborough, Hants. 1854, Canon Residentiary Worcester Cathedral (with Master of St Oswald's Hospital [almshouses]) 1869 to death 4/11/1871 aged 78, leaving £14,000 [C22040. Boase] Married (1) Hastings, Sussex 1828 Harriette Anne Deane (2) Wem, Shropshire 1838 (2nd q.) Diana Ann Taylor, with issue. Port. online. Brother above.

WYNYARD (Montagu John) Born Hayes, Middx. 24/3/1781, s. Lt.-Gen. William Wynyard (3rd Guards, and Equerry to George 111) and Sarah Lilly. Capt. Coldstream Guards 1809-11. Literate: dn15 (Nor.), p16 (Nor.), then Downing, Cambridge 1817, a Ten Year Man (BD1827). V. Brafferton, Yorks. 1818-22, R. York St Martin, Micklegate 1822 and R. West Rounton, Yorks. 1822 to death. Chap. in Ordinary 1834-57; Dom. Chap. to 4th Earl of Rosebery 1818. Died 14/12/1857 aged 77, leaving £3,000 [C116344. Boase] Married Burghclere, Hants. 21/2/1802 Jane (w), dau. Lt.-Gen. Francis Lascelles, 10 ch. (1 clerical).

WYTHE (Thomas) Bapt. Eye, Suffolk 5/10/1749, s. Thomas (a grazier) and Susan Wythe. Caius, Cambridge 1767, BA1771, dn72 (Peterb. for Nor.), MA1774, Fellow 1774-85. V. Eye 1783-1835, V. Great Bradley, Suffolk 1786-1835, Prebend of Tachbrook in Lichfield Cathedral 1797 to death 21/9/1835 aged 85 [C21059]

WYVILL (Edward) Bapt. Fingall, Yorks. 5/10/1794, s. Rev. Christopher Wyvill and Sarah Codling. BNC, Oxford 1811, BA1816, dn16 (Chester), p18 (Chester), MA 1819. R. Fingall 1820-69, RD of Fingall 1820, R. Spennithorne, Yorks. 1829 to death. Dom. Chap. to Archbishop of Armagh 1829. Died 15/9/1869 aged 76, leaving £3,000 [C137032] Married Bedale, Yorks. 13/19/1824 Frances Anne Pulleyne Mosley (widow of Rev. Frederick Dodsworth), with clerical son of same name. Brother below?

WYVILL (William) Born 11/5/1796, s. Rev. Christopher Wyvill. Trinity, Cambridge 1814, BA1818, dn19 (Chester), p20 (Chester), MA 1823. R. Spennithorne, Yorks. 1821-9 (res.), R. Black Notley, Essex 1829 to death 4/3/1834 (CCEd says 22/8/1834) [C124482] Brother above?

YARKER (Luke) Born Leyburn Hall, Leyburn, Yorks. 6/7/1786, s. Rev. Luke Yarker, sen. and Elizabeth Robinson. Trinity, Cambridge 1804, BA1809, MA1812 [Called to the Bar, Middle Temple 1813] dn15 (Heref. for Win.), p16 (Salis. for Win.). V. Mitford, Northumberland 1829-33 (and Chap. to Morpeth Gaol and House of Correction 1829), V. Chillingham, Northumberland 1833 to death. Died Berwick upon Tweed 21/7/1849 aged 63 [C90588] Married Fawley, Southampton 14/1/1818 Mary Beata South (a clergy dau.), Much Dewchurch, Hereford, 4s. (including clerical), 5 dau. J.P. Durham, Northumberland and North Riding of Yorks.

YARKER (Robert) Born Ulverston, Lancs. 13/3/1798, s. John Yarker and Elizabeth Kendal. Queen's, Oxford 1818, BA1821, dn21 (Win.), p22 (Win.), MA 1824. Minor Canon of Chester Cathedral 1827- 36, R. Chester St Olave 1827 and R. Neston, Cheshire 1847 to death 10/5/1853 [C109192. Boase] Married Chester 30/12/1847 Frances Humberston (w), *s.p.*

YATE (George Lavington) Born Madeley Court, Madeley, Shropshire 25/5/1795, s. Timothy Yate and Anne Gilbert. Queens', Cambridge 1813, BA1817, dn18 (Heref.), p19 (Heref.), MA1820. V. Wrockwardine, Heref. 1828 (w. Wrockwardine Wood, Heref. to 1846) and RD 1837, to death 27/10/1873 aged 78, leaving £4,000 [C21062. Boase] Married Grappenhall, Cheshire 15/8/1820 Margaret Elizabeth Allix, with clerical son Charles Allix Yate. Surrogate 1842.

YATES (Richard) Born Bury St Edmunds, Suffolk 20/7/1769, s. Richard Yates (custodian of the Abbey ruins). S/M Chelmsford G/S 1789-92; S/M Hammersmith, London 1792. Jesus, Cambridge 1793 (a Ten Year Man), dn96 (Salis. for Win.), p97, BD1805, DD1818. Chap. of Chelsea Hospital 1798-1804, R. Ashen, Essex 1804 to death (Penshurst, Kent) 24/8/1834, but 'lived chiefly in London, where he was in great request as a preacher at the fashionable chapels' [C90590. ODNB] Married 1810 Ann Telfer, and had issue. Edited his father's extensive collection of drawings and notes on the history of Bury St Edmunds Abbey.

YATES (William) Born Bury, Lancs. 8/9/1776, s. William Yates. BNC, Oxford 1795, BA1799, dn00 (Chester), p01 (Chester), MA 1805. R. (and patron) of Eccleston, Chorley, Lancs. 1812 to death 23/1/1854 [C17104. Boase] Widow Frances, with issue. Another contemporary of this name.

YEADON (William) Bapt. Guisley, Yorks. 30/6/1776, s. John Yeadon and Betty Clayton. Lincoln, Oxford 1790, then Magdalen 1791-3, BA1794, MA 1797, Fellow 1797-1823, p99 (Chester for Ox.), BD1806. R. Waddington, Lincs. 1822 to death 12/2/1848 [C38909]

YEATMAN (Harry Farr) Bapt. Weymouth, Dorset 15/2/1786, s. Prebendary Harry Farr Yeatman, sen. and Louisa Shuttleworth. Balliol, Oxford 1804, Fellow, dn09 (B&W), p10 (B&W), BCL1812. R. Stock Gaylard, Dorset 1819 to death 22/4/1861 (living at Stock Gaylard House), leaving £14,000 [C50356. Boase] Married (1) Lyme Regis, Dorset 25/11/1810 Sarah Wolcott ('an heiress'), with issue (2) Warminster, Wilts. 1837 (3rd q.) Emma Biggs. J.P. and Chairman of Dorset Quarter Sessions. Master of the Vale of Blackmoor Harriers, and writer on hunting subjects.

YEOMANS (William Bohun) From Worcester, s. William Yeomans. New, Oxford 1800 (aged 19), BA1804, dn04 (Wor.), p06 (C&L), MA1808, BD and DD1823, Fellow to 1823. R. Bucknell, Oxon. 1822 [blank in ERC], and R. Warndon, Worcs. 1823 to death 2/6/1833 aged 55 (CCEd says 14/8/1833) [C21068]

YERBURGH (Richard) Bapt. Frampton, Lincs. 7/12/1774, s. Richard Yerburgh and Bridget Arnall. Pembroke, Cambridge 1793, BA1797, dn99 (Lin.), MA1800, p03 (Lin.), DD 1815. V. New Sleaford, Lincs. 1809 and R. Tothill, Lincs. 1810 to death 21/2/1851 aged 76 [C81064. Kaye] Married Little Stanmore, Middx. 9/10/1811 Elizabeth Eardley Norton, with issue.

YONGE (Duke, sen.) Born Puslinch, Devon 3/12/1750 (bapt. 26/11/1751), s. Rev. John Yonge (R. Newton Ferrers, Devon) and Elizabeth Duke. Studied medicine. University, Oxford 1771, dn74 (Ex.), BA1775, p76 (Ex.), then Sidney, Cambridge 1782, MA1782. V. Otterton, Devon 1782-95, R. West w. East Putford, Devon 1783, V. Cornwood, Devon 1793-1823, R. Newton Ferrers, Devon 1798-1808, V. Morwenstow, Cornwall 1807, V. Sheviock, Cornwall 1808-23. Died 3/12/1833? Married Flaxley, Glos. 12/3/1777 Catherine

Crawley-Boevey, with clerical son (below) [C137600]

YONGE (Duke, jun.) Born Yealmpton, Devon 13/10/1779, s. Rev. Duke Yonge, sen. (above) and Catherine Crawley-Boevey. King's, Cambridge 1799, Fellow 1802-6, BA1803, dn04 (Lin.), p05 (Lin.), MA1808. R. Willoughton, Lincs 1805-36, V. Antony, Cornwall 1806-36, R. Newton Ferrers, Devon 1808-12. Died Plymouth 29/7/1836 [C81065] Married Barkway, Herts. 14/5/1806 Cordelia Anne Colborne, with clerical son. Uncle of Charlotte Mary Yonge, the religious novelist.

YONGE (Frederick Langford William) Born Great Torrington, Devon 6/1/1805, s. Rev. Denys and Charlotte Yonge. Jesus, Cambridge 1824, BA1828, dn28 (Ex.), p29 (Ex.). PC. Frithelstock, Cornwall 1828 to death 7/6/1841 aged 36 [C146583] Married 24/6/1830 Isabel Foulkes, with clerical son.

YONGE (John) Bapt. Newton Ferrers, Devon 5/12/1788, s. Rev. James Yonge and Ann Granger. University, Oxford 1807, BA1811, dn12 (Ex.), p13 (Ex.). R. (and patron) of Newton Ferrers, 1812 to death (Puslinch, Devon) 23/8/1877 aged 88, leaving £45,000 [Not yet in CCEd] Married Chelsea, London 25/3/1813 Alethea Henrietta Bargus.

YONGE (William) Born Great Torrington, Devon 1/3/1753, s. Rev. Henry Yonge and Sarah Wolley. Jesus, Cambridge 1770, BA1774, dn75 (Nor.), p77 (Nor.), MA1777. PC. Hoveton St John w. Hoveton St Peter, Norfolk 1777-80, V. Felmingham, Norfolk 1778-9, V. Threxton, Norfolk 1779, V. Swaffham w. Threxton, Norfolk 1779-1845, Archdeacon of Norwich and Chancellor of Norwich Cathedral 1782-1814, R. Hilborough, Norfolk 1806-37, R. Necton, Norfolk 1838 to death (Swaffham) 2/12/1845 aged 92 [C1136] Married 1784 Frances Johnson, with clerical son (below)

YONGE (William Johnson) Born Great Torrington, Devon 15/10/1785, s. Rev. William Yonge (above) and Frances Johnson. King's, Cambridge 1804, Fellow 1807-24, dn08 (Nor.), BA1809, p10 (Nor.), MA1815. Chap. of the Donative of Rockbourne, Hants. 1824 to death 2/5/1875, leaving £4,000 [C109196] Married Halsdon, Devon Elizabeth Furse (a clergy dau.), with clerical son William Wellington Yonge.

YORK (Archbishop of) see under **VENABLES-VERNON, *later* HARCOURT (Edward, Hon.)**

YORKE (Charles Isaac) Born Great Horkesley, Essex 7/10/1801, s. Rev. Philip Yorke and Hon. Anna Maria Cocks (dau. of 1st Earl Somers). Trinity, Cambridge 1818, BA 1823, dn25 (St Asaph), p26 (Salis.), MA1827. V. Latton w. Essey, Wilts. 1826-9, R. Shenfield, Essex 1829 to death 25/7/1863, leaving £12,000 [C90587. Boase] Married 17/12/1840 Ellen Leigh (of Sandhills), with issue.

YORKE (Henry Reginald, Hon.) Born Bursledon, Hants. 30/10/1803, s. Vice-Adm. Sir Joseph Sydney Yorke, *M.P.*, and Elizabeth Weake Rattray. St John's, Cambridge 1820, BA 1826, dn26 (Lin.), p27 (Lin.), MA1829. R. Aspenden, Herts. 1830-59, R. Wimpole, Cambs. 1831-71, Archdeacon of Huntingdon 1856-9, Canon of Ely Cathedral 1859 to death 26/9/1871 aged 68, leaving £4,000 [C81068. Boase] Married St George's Hanover Square, London 19/11/1833 Flora Elizabeth (dau. Gen. Sir Alexander Campbell, 1st Bart.) and granted precedence of an earl's son on his brother Charles's accession to the peerage as 4th Earl of Hardwicke in 1836. Had issue. *J.P.* Cambs.

YORKE (Philip Wynne) From Dyffryd Aled, Denbigh, s. Philip Wynne and Mrs Diana (Wynne) Meyrick. St John's, Cambridge 1806, BA1811, dn11 (Chester), p12 (London), MA 1820. R. South Shoebury, Essex 1812-58, R. Rayleigh, Essex 1838-43, R. Hawkwell, Essex 1848 to death (unmarried) 21/3/1858 aged 70, leaving £7,000 [C124492]

YORKE (Thomas Henry) Born Long Preston, Yorks. 25/1/1785, s. of Thomas Yorke (barrister). University, Oxford 1804, BA1808, dn09 (Ox.), p09 (Ox.), MA1810. V. Bishop Middleham, Durham 1813 and R. York St Cuthbert w. St Helen on the Walls and All Saints, Peasholm 1818-[58]. Died (Bishop Middleham) 16/2/1868 aged 83, leaving £14,000. Dom. Chap. to Countess de Grey in 1818 [C22044] Married Edinburgh 29/6/1823 Maria, dau. Major-Gen. Hon. Mark Napier, *s.p.*?

YOULL (Abraham) Bapt. Hatfield, Yorks. 5/10/1759, s. Thomas Youll. St John's, Cambridge 1780, BA1784, dn84 (York), p84 (York), MA1787. R. West Retford, Notts. 1787 and R. Grove, Notts. 1798 to death. Dom. Chap. to 4th

Duke of Newcastle 1798. Died 27/11/1836 aged 76 [C109827. YCO] Married West Retford 14/9/1789 Mary White, with clerical son. *J.P.* for the Liberty of Southwell and Scrooby; *aka* Daddy Youll.

YOUNG (Edward Newton) Born Thorpe Malsor, Northants. 21/11/1795, s. John Young and Mary Wood. Christ Church, Oxford 1814, BA1818, dn19 (London), p20 (London). S/M Charterhouse School; R. Quainton, Bucks. (and Preacher throughout the Diocese of Lincoln) 1822 [64]. Dom. Chap. to Duke of Buckingham and Chandos. Died (Herne Bay, Kent) 26/7/1885, leaving £637-12s-5d. [C81074. Boase] Married Scarborough 1829 Ann Catherine Travis, w. clerical son William Edward Allen Young.

YOUNG (James) Bapt. Reading, Berks. 4/3/1785, s. Joseph and Ruth Young. Pembroke, Oxford 1802, BA1806, MA1808. V. Heathfield, Sussex 1822 to death 26/3/1858, leaving £1,000 [C72201] Married Reading 3/8/1826 Mary Elizabeth Deane (w), with clerical son.

YOUNG (John) Born Orlingbury, Northants. 18/4/1760, s. Allen Young and Mary Boddam. New, Oxford 1778, BCL1787. R. Akeley, Bucks. 1789 and R. Thorpe Malsor, Northants. 1793 to death 14/1/1841 [C111012] Married Great Amwell, Herts. 17/12/1790 Mary Wood, with son Richard, below.

YOUNG (Richard) Born Thorpe Malsor, Northants. 10/3/1798, s. Rev. John Thorpe (above) and Mary Wood. Exeter, Oxford 1818, then New, Fellow 1818-34, BA1822, MA1826, etc. V. Riseley, Beds. 1832-71, V. Melchbourne, Beds. 1841-64, R. Yalden, Beds. 1871 to death (Bedford) 5/6/1888, leaving £327-6s-8d. [C22046] Married Clapham, Surrey 1/8/1833 Caroline Ellen Wood, with issue.

YOUNG (Thomas) Bapt. Dalston, Cumberland 29/12/1772, s. of Thomas (a husbandman). Trinity, Cambridge 1789, BA1794, Fellow 1795, MA1797, dn01 (Lin.), Tutor 1801-13, p02 (Lin.), etc. R. Gilling (West), Yorks. 1813 to death 11/11/1835 aged 63 [C81079] Married 15/8/1814 Mary Simpson Blamire, with clerical son William Blamire Young

YOUNG (Thomas) Born Swaffham, Norfolk, s. Rev. William Young (R. & V. Necton, Norfolk) and Anne Pigge. Caius, Cambridge 1784 (aged 17), BA1789, dn89 (Nor.), MA1792. p92 (Nor.). V. Necton w. Holme Hale [net income £1,122] 1794-1838, R. Cranwich 1800-1804. Died 1838? [C116350]

YOUNG (William) Born Dalston, Cumberland 6/3/1783, s. Thomas Young. Emmanuel, Cambridge 1801, BA1806, MA1809, dn07 (Durham), Fellow 1808, BD1816. R. Aller, Som. 1829 to death ('at Denston railway station, Suffolk, from the rupture of a blood vessel') 30/11/1857 [C41058] Married East Gilling, Yorks 1830 Sarah Susannah Blamire, Cumberland, with issue.

YOUNG (William) Born Claypole, Lincs. 20/8/1775, s. Edward Young (a farmer). Sidney, Cambridge 1794, BA1799, dn99 (London), p00 (London), MA1803. V. Layston, Herts. 1800-44. Died *c.*1844 [C124497] Married Newport Pagnell, Bucks. 28/5/1807 Harriet Eliza Malpas.

YOUNGE (John Cole) From Calne, Wilts., s. John Younge. St Edmund Hall, Oxford 1803 (aged 17), BA by 1809, dn09 (Cant.), p10 (Cant.). R. Biscathorpe, Lincs. 1814-35, V. Stainton le Vale, Lincs. 1835 and R. Walesby, Lincs. 1835 to death 18/11/1852, leaving under £100 (probate granted 1858) [C52482. Kaye] Married Walcot, Bath 4/8/1806 Abigail Burroughes, w. clerical s. John Parkinson Bayly Younge..

YOUNGER (Ralph) Born Workington, Cumberland 15/12/1779 (bapt. into a Presbyterian congregation), s. Ralph and Martha Younger. H/M Goat House School, Rishworth, Yorks. Literate: dn05 (Win. for York), p06 (York). PC. Scammonden, Huddersfield 1807 to death 26/11/1856 aged 76 [C109200. YCO] Married Workington 17/3/1808 Mary Robertson, with issue.

ZILLWOOD (John Old) Born Dorchester, Dorset, s. William Zillwood and Christian Old. Wadham, Oxford 1808 (aged 23), then Magdalen Hall, dn12 (B&W), p12 (Salis.), BA1814, MA1815. R. Compton, Hants. 1831 to death 11/9/1871, leaving £600 [C52473. Boase] Married Walcot, Bath 13/7/1814 Elizabeth Mason.

www.ingramcontent.com/pod-product-compliance
Lightning Source LLC
Chambersburg PA
CBHW050717090526
44588CB00014B/2316